BURT FRANKLIN: BIBLIOGRAPHY & REFERENCE SERIES 396
Essays in Literature and Criticism 142

DICTIONARY OF WRITERS OF THIRTEENTH CENTURY ENGLAND

DICTIONARY OF WRITERS OF THIRTEENTH CENTURY ENGLAND

BY

JOSIAH COX RUSSELL

BURT FRANKLIN
NEW YORK

Published by LENOX HILL Pub. & Dist. Co. (Burt Franklin)
235 East 44th St., New York, N.Y. 10017
Originally Published: 1936
Reprinted: 1971
Printed in the U.S.A.

S.B.N.: 8337-43643
Library of Congress Card Catalog No.: 77-153022
Burt Franklin: Bibliography and Reference Series 396
Essays in Literature and Criticism 142

Reprinted from the original edition in the Ohio State University Library.

To

CHARLES HOMER HASKINS

PREFACE

BIBLIOGRAPHY is an ancient subject of study among scholars interested in the middle ages and must of necessity be fundamental for a proper understanding of that period. So much attention has been devoted to it that it has become a complicated subject, full of pitfalls for the unwary and none too easy for the more experienced. The conjectures of Bale are often not easy to distinguish from the wisdom of Tanner. And even the great occasionally fall into error. To the bibliographical tradition which is usually the first resource of scholars there has been opened up, especially in recent years, a vast body of previously inaccessible sources, much of which has appeared in print. This body of material has encouraged the production of monographs and studies scattered widely in a variety of publications.

The purpose of this volume is to present a large body of available information about one group of mediaeval authors, the writers of thirteenth century England. If this work has any pioneer aspect it is the attempt to search systematically a body of sources for the writers of the period of both Latin and the vernacular languages. As a research project it has proved satisfactory. The evidence is not too great for effective examination, and the search for evidence of this group of about 350 writers turns up items in sufficient quantity to keep interest on a high level and to give the feeling that the results justify the effort expended upon the study.

Despite the comprehensive nature of the project completeness cannot be claimed. Information about previously unknown writers continues to appear, and one can hardly afford the time to re-examine all the material already explored. Then, mediaeval nomenclature is often to blame for lack of finality. After looking for Master Alexander Neckam, canon and abbot of Cirencester, one discovers that he was also called Alexander of St. Albans. In such circumstances the excuse offered for publication is that this work marks an advance in our knowledge of most of the writers of the thirteenth century.

The plan of the volume is simple. The authors are listed by the only real mediaeval name, the Christian name. Under each article an effort is made to define the claims of the man as an author if there is any doubt in the matter, or to point out where such information is available. No effort is made to duplicate large bodies of easily accessible and well arranged material, especially about the authors' works. In general, the episcopal periods of authors' lives have not been described : this is usually well done in the Dictionary of National Biography. Likewise the common law writers are mentioned without biographies, as Professor Woodbine of Yale and his co-workers are doing this work well. References are given to persons whose scholastic exercises and sermons are discussed by Dr. Little and Father Pelster in 'Oxford Theology and Theologians.' I have not stressed instances in which I have differed from previous writers, since I have tried to avoid an air of controversy. I have also tried to give proper recognition to my sources of information. I have given references to Tanner, the Dictionary of National Biography, and to the real sources of information. Much of the usual bibliography consists of references to authorities who merely repeat others. Finally, I have not carried conjectures very far. It is too easy for bibliographical tradition to convert guesses into statements which develop after repetition an unjustified semblance of worth.

This comprehensive study has naturally brought me into pleasant contact with many scholars in the field. I am glad to mention my gratitude to them in general and to certain ones in particular. Professors F. M. Powicke and F. M. Stenton have looked at the work in its early stages and Dr. A. G. Little in its final form: to them I owe many corrections and suggestions. For assistance and advice I am indebted to three scholars who are no longer with us: Professor T. Atkinson Jenkins, Monsignor George Lacombe, and Professor James Field Willard. Canon A. J. Carlisle of Worcester, Professor Allan H. Gilbert of Duke University, Professor C. C. Mierow of Carlton College, and Dean Elbert Russell have been of assistance to me in various ways.

This study of the writers of thirteenth century England has been made possible by a fellowship from the John Simon Guggenheim Memorial Foundation in 1930–1 and by grants from the American Council of Learned Societies supplemented by the Smith Fund of the University of North Carolina in the summers of 1933 and 1934. The editors of the 'Annals of Medical History,' 'Harvard Theological Review,' 'Modern Philology,' and 'English Historical Review' have given permission to reprint material from my articles in their periodicals.

To Professor Charles Homer Haskins my obligation is very great and requires no explanation. The long list of books dedicated to him is but one indication of the appreciation of his students: to that list it is a pleasure to add this study.

ABBREVIATIONS

A.F.H. = *Archivum Franciscanum Historicum.*

Ann. Monast. = *Annales Monastici* (Rolls Series). Ed. H. R. Luard. 5 vols.

B.M. = British Museum.

B.N. = Bibliothèque Nationale.

B.S.F.S. = British Society of Franciscan Studies.

Bale, *Index* = *Index Britanniae Scriptorum quos ex variis bibliothecis non parvo labore collegit Ioannes Baleus, cum aliis.* Ed. R. L. Poole and Mary Bateson. Oxford, 1902.

Blomefield = Blomefield, F.: *An Essay towards a Topographical history of the county of Norfolk.* 1805–10. 11 vols.

C.Ch.R. = *Calendar of Charter Rolls.*

C.Cl.R. = *Close Rolls,* 1227–64; *Calendar of Close Rolls* from 1272.

C.E.P.R. = *Calendar of Entries in the Papal Registers relating to Great Britain and Ireland.* Ed. W. H. Bliss, J. A. Twemlow, and C. Johnson.

C.F.R. = *Calendar of Fine Rolls.*

C.L.R. = *Calendar of Liberate Rolls.*

C.P.R. = *Calendar of Patent Rolls.*

C.Y.S. = Canterbury and York Society.

Cal. Gen. = *Calendarium Genealogicum. Henry III and Edward I* (Rolls Series). Ed. C. Roberts. 2 vols.

Ch., Chs. = charter, charters.

Chr. Maj. = *Matthaei Parisiensis Chronica Majora* (Rolls Series). Ed. H. R. Luard. 7 vols.

D.N.B. = *Dictionary of National Biography.* 1908–9.

Dugdale, *Monasticon* = Dugdale, William: *Monasticon Anglicanum.* 1817–30. 6 vols. in 8.

Eccleston = *Tractatus Fr. Thomae de Eccleston De adventu fratrum minorum in Angliam.* Ed. A. G. Little. 1909.

E.E.T.S. = Early English Text Society.

E.H.R. = *English Historical Review.*

Ep. Grosseteste = *Roberti Grosseteste episcopi quondam Lincolniensis Epistolae* (Rolls Series). Ed. H. R. Luard.

Expl. = *Explicit.*

Foedera = *Foedera.* Ed. T. Rymer. Record Comm. 1816–30. 3 vols. in 6.

Glorieux = Glorieux, P.: *Répertoire des maîtres en théologie de Paris au xiii*[e] *siècle.* Paris, 1932–4. 3 vols.

H.M.C. = Historical Manuscripts Commission.

Inc. = *Incipit.*

Index = *An Index of British and Irish Latin Writers* A.D. 400–1520. (*Bulletin du Cange,* vii.) Compiled J. H. Baxter, C. Johnson, and J. F. Willard. Paris, 1932.

James, *A.L.C.D.* = James, M.R.: *Ancient Libraries of Canterbury and Dover.* Cambridge, 1903.

James, *Peterborough* = James, M.R.: *Lists of Manuscripts formerly in the Peterborough Abbey Library.* 1926.

Leland, *Collect.* = *Joannis Lelandi Antiquarii de Rebus Britannicis Collectanea.* Ed. T. Hearne. Oxford, 1715. 5 vols. in 6.

Little, *F.S.O.* = Little, A. G.: 'Franciscan School at Oxford in the Thirteenth Century,' *Archivum Franciscanum Historicum,* xix (1926). 803–74.

Little, *G.F.* = Little, A. G.: *Grey Friars in Oxford* (Oxford Historical Society). Oxford, 1892.

Little-Pelster = Little, A. G., and Pelster, F.: *Oxford Theology and Theologians c. A.D. 1282–1302* (Oxford Historical Society). Oxford, 1934.

M.G.H.SS. = *Monumenta Germaniae Historica Scriptorum.*

Mon. Fr. = *Monumenta Franciscana* (Rolls Series). Ed. J. S. Brewer and R. Howlett. 2 vols.

N.E.MSS. = *Notices et extraits des manuscrits de la Bibliothèque du Roi.* Paris, 1787, etc.

O.C. = Ordo Carmelitarum.

O.F.M. = Ordo Fratrum Minorum.

O.P. = Ordo Praedicatorum.

P.R.O. = Public Record Office.

Powicke = Powicke, F. M.: *Mediaeval Books of Merton College.* Oxford, 1931.

Pressutti = *Regesta Honorii Papae* III. Ed. P. Pressutti. Rome, 1888, 1895. 2 vols.

Quétif-Echard = Quétif, J., and Echard, J.: *Scriptores Ordinis Praedicatorum recensiti.* Paris, 1719, 1721. 2 vols.

R.S. = Rolls Series.

Reg. Peckham = *Registrum epistolarum Johannis Peckham archiepiscopi Cantuariensis* (Rolls Series). Ed. C. T. Martin. 3 vols.

Reg. Walter Giffard = *Register of Walter Giffard, archbishop of York* 1266–79 (Surtees Society). Ed. W. Brown.

Reg. Winchelsey = *Registrum Roberti Winchelsey archiepiscopi Cantuariensis* (Canterbury and York Society). Ed. Rose Graham.

Rot. H. de Welles = *Rotuli Hugonis de Welles episcopi Lincolniensis* (Canterbury and York Society). Ed. W. P. W. Phillimore. 3 vols.

Rot. R. Gravesend = *Rotuli Ricardi Gravesend diocesis Lincolniensis* (Canterbury and York Society). Ed. F. N. Davis.

Rot. R. Grosseteste = *Rotuli Roberti Grosseteste episcopi Lincolniensis* (Canterbury and York Society). Ed. F. N. Davis.

S.P.C.K. = Society for Promoting Christian Knowledge.

Sarum Chs. and Docs. = *Charters and Documents illustrating the history of Salisbury* (Rolls Series). Ed. W. R. Jones and W. D. Macray.

T. = Tanner, Thomas: *Bibliotheca Britannico-Hibernica*. Ed. D. Wilkins. 1748.

Vising = Vising, Per Johan: *Anglo-Norman Language and Literature*. 1923.

WRITERS OF THIRTEENTH CENTURY ENGLAND

Adam of Barking,[1] monk of Sherbourne,[2] was a religious poet. In writing of the books which he saw at 'Shireburne,' Leland says:

Adam Berchingensis, monachus Sireburnensis, de divina et humana natura carmine, sed rithmico.

Idem super quatuor evangelia ad Joannem, canonicum Sarisbiriensem.

Idem de serie sex aetatum carmine rithmico, quod si indoctum incidisset seculum magnus in utroque scribendi genere evasisset (*Collect.* iv. 150).

Bibliographical tradition has identified the last with the incomplete poem beginning 'Scribere decrevi decursum labilis evi' in MS. 277 (H. ix) of the library of Corpus Christi College, Cambridge. Of this there seems no evidence in the MS., nor are the other additions in Tanner convincing. The MS. is of the 12th to 13th centuries.

Tradition also assigns the early part of the 13th century as the time of this monk's life. Beyond Leland's information that Adam of Barking was a monk of Sherbourne it does not seem safe to go.[3]

Adam of Bechesoueres,[4] O.F.M., was possibly the author of commentaries upon three Aristotelian treatises:—

'De Anima': (a) Venice, St. Mark's, class X, MS. 61, fos. 130–61, with a colophon 'Expliciunt notule libri de anima edite a magistro Adam Bouchermefort'; (b) Rome, Vatican Lib. Cod. Urbin. lat. 206, fos. 258–99.

'Libri Phisicorum': (a) Venice (MS. as above), fos. 45–130; (b) Madrid, Bibl. nac. MS. 1580, fos. 1–115*b*, with a colophon 'Explicit viii libri physicarum scientiarum magistri Ade et per consequens omnes alii libri.'

'De Causis' (pseudo-Aristotelian): Venice (MS. as above), fos. 1–44*b*. Though anonymous, this resembles the two treatises in the same MS. described above.

The name 'Bouchermefort' is enough like 'Bechesoueres' to suggest that the commentator was the franciscan physician who was the friend of Adam Marsh and Robert Grosseteste. The name may represent Barksore, Kent.[1] In an early 'exemplum' Friar Adam de Bethegore, while in Greenwich, and not yet licensed as a confessor, brought sanity to a demented person by hearing his confession and absolving him.[2] Greenwich is not far from Barksore. Buxtehude, Germany, has also been suggested as the place from which he derived his name.[3] Nearly all the information about him comes from Adam Marsh's letters; only one of these relating to Bechesoueres is dated, 1250.[4] Marsh thought so highly of the physician that he recommended him to Grosseteste,[5] whom he seems to have attended. Marsh

[1] T. p. 6; *D.N.B.* under Adam.

[2] Dorset.

[3] A chaplain, Adam de Berkinges, was presented by the abbess and nuns of Barking to the church of 'Slaptone' in 1223 (*Rot. H. de Welles*, ii. 65).

[4] M. Grabmann, 'Mittelalterliche lateinische Aristotelesübersetzungen und Aristoteleskommentare in Handschriften spanischer Bibliotheken,' in *Sitzungsberichte der Bayerischen Akademie der Wissenschaften, Phil.-phil. und hist. Klasse*, 1928, pp. 46–51. Possibly he is Adam of Buckfield [q.v.].

[1] Cf. *Pipe Roll*, 10 *Ric. I* (Pipe Roll Soc.), ed. D. M. Stenton, p. 198.

[2] B.M. Add. MS. 33956, fo. 83*b*; (J. A. Herbert, *Catalogue of Romances*, iii. 634).

[3] *Collectanea Franciscana* (B.S.F.S.), ii. 35 *n.*

[4] Little, *G.F.* p. 139, *n.*; *Mon. Fr.* i. 320. Little gives a biography based upon the *Mon. Fr.* (*op. cit.* p. 187).

[5] *Mon. Fr.* i. 137.

directed to Bechesoueres two letters which evidently were intended for the bishop: in one, Walter of Merton is said to desire ordination as a subdeacon [1] and in the other some help, probably for preferment, is mentioned for a brother of a friar of Stamford.[2] Bechesoueres was not at Oxford. Marsh wanted him to attend John of Reading at Oxford,[3] and at another time requested permission of the custodian at Oxford for a sick scholar there to visit the physician who had helped him previously.[4] On one occasion Bechesoueres had gone with Robert de Santa Cruce (de Cruce? [q.v.]) to the minister general in France.[5]

Adam of Buckfield, canon of Lincoln, was a commentator upon several translations of Aristotelian and pseudo-Aristotelian works [6]:—

'De Sensu et Sensato': *inc.* 'Cum intentio physici.' Oxford, Balliol Coll. MS. 313, fos. 130–42*b* (early 14th cent.), colophon, 'Expliciunt notule de sensu et sensato a magistro A. de Bocfelde.' The expression 'ut in libro de iuventute et senectute, de inspiratione et expiratione que nondum pervenerunt ad nos' shows that Adam wrote before the only translation of these works was made by William of Moerbeke about 1260.[7]

'De Sompno et Vigilia': *inc.* 'Quoniam scientia tradita de sensu et sensato.' This follows 'De Sensu et Sensato' on fos. 143–57*b*, and has a similar prologue.

Metaphysics: *inc.* 'Consideratio autem . . . Supposito ut vult Avicenna.' (a) Same MS. fos. 241–79*b*, bearing on ancient flyleaf, 'Liber domus de Balliolo in Oxon in quo cont expositio Bucfeld super libros me$^{te.}$'; (b) Oxford, Balliol Coll. MS. 241, fos. 2–80.

Meteorology: *inc.* 'Postquam precessit . . . Intentio est in libro de corpore mobili.' (a) Formerly at Assisi, Bibl. Segreta MS. 249, Alessandri, 89, 'Summa magistri Adam Befeld super libros Meteororum extabat in Bibliotheca secreta sac. conventus S. Fran. Assisi in VI solario versus orientem, ex inventario illius bibliothecæ an. 1381, confecto cuius finis erat: et sic determinatur sententia totius libri methaurorum' (J. Sbaralea, *Scriptores*, p. 1); (b) Florence, Bibl. Laurent. Bibl. S. Crucis, Plut. XIII, sin. cod. 7, fos. 167–82*b*, heading 'Incipit sententia magistri A de Bocfeld super librum metheororum. . . . Finitur sententia quarti libri metheororum de magistro A de Bocfeld'; (c) Rome, Vatican Lib. MS. Urbin. lat. 206, fos. 210–56*b*. The information about these two manuscripts comes from M. Grabmann ('Mittelalterliche lateinische Aristotelesübersetzungen und Aristoteleskommentare in Handschriften spanischer Bibliotheken,' in *Sitzungsberichte der Bayer. Akad. Phil.-phil. und hist. Klasse*, 1928, pp. 46–51).

'De Caelo et Mundo': (a) Florence, Bibl. Laurent. Bibl. S. Crucis, Plut. XIII, sin. cod. 7; (b) Rome, San Isidoro MS. I–IV, fos. 99–111*b*, entitled 'Glosule incipiunt libri celi et mundi a magistro A de Bocfeld.' Also below, 'Super librum celi et mundi secundum Adam de Bocfeld'; (c) Rome, Vatican Lib. MS. Urbin. lat. 206, fos. 104–183. (See Grabmann, *loc. cit.*, for these MSS.)

'De Vegetalibus': Rome, Vatican Lib. MS. Urbin. lat. 206 (Grabmann, *loc. cit.*).

The author of the commentaries is to be identified very probably with a canon of Lincoln about whom considerable information exists. His father, Robert of Granteleye or Graunteleye, was alive about 1206–1210.[1] Since his name was different from

[1] *Mon. Fr.* i. 405.

[2] Roger of Kirkby, brother of Friar Richard of Kirkby (*ibid.* p. 404).

[3] *Ibid.* p. 320.

[4] *Ibid.* p. 388.

[5] *Ibid.* p. 333.

[6] T. p. 137; *D.N.B.* under Adam and Bocfeld.

[7] I am indebted to Mgr. G. Lacombe for this information.

[1] *Three Early Assize Rolls for Northumberland* (Surtees Soc.), ed. William Page, pp. 178, 265; *Northumberland Pleas from the Curia Regis and Assize Rolls*, 1198–1272 (Newcastle-upon-Tyne Record Series), ed. A. H. Thompson, pp. 37, 314; *Feet of Fines, Northumberland and Durham* (Newcastle-upon-Tyne Record Series), p. 13.

that of his son and heir,[1] it is probable that the latter was born at Buckfield, Northumberland. At that place Robert held a free tenement and common of pasture.[2] Over the pasture rights litigation lasted at least until near the end of Adam's life: it was still going on in 7 Edw. I.[3] Adam usually appeared by attorney. Adam was at Oxford during the serious disturbances of 1238 and was among those mainprised before the king.[4] He is designated as a clerk. As Master Adam 'de Bokefeld' he was presented by the prior and convent of Durham to the church of Rountain (Rungeton) on 20 July 1243.[5] At Oxford he was a friend of Adam Marsh [q.v.], who gave him a letter of recommendation to Bishop Grosseteste for the living of Iver.[6] He is lauded as a man of commendable excellence of manners, of divine eloquence, and skill in human letters: he was presumably a master of theology by this time. He was presented to Iver in 1249–50,[7] being at the time a subdeacon. In 1259 and later he with Eustace de Balliol owed twenty shillings for having a royal writ.[8] As canon of Lincoln, Buckfield admitted Gonnora, nun of Marlow, as abbess of the same house by commission from the bishop, on 19 Mar. 1264 or 1265.[9] By an order of 15 Jan. 1267 the pope appointed him and the archdeacon of Lincoln to collect the papal tenth in the diocese of Lincoln.[10] Within the next three years he acted as an executor of the will of Richard de Munfichet, one of the last of the Magna Carta

[1] *Three Early Assize Rolls*, pp. 178, 265.

[2] *Ibid.* pp. 178, 218, 265; *Northumberland Pleas*, p. 314.

[3] *Three Early Assize Rolls*, pp. 265, 356; other references pp. 103, 173, 220.

[4] *C.P.R.*, 1232–47, p. 219.

[5] *Register of Walter Gray* (Surtees Soc.), p. 92 *n*.

[6] *Mon. Fr.* i. 165.

[7] *Rot. R. Grosseteste*, p. 379.

[8] *Magnus Rotulus Pipe for Northumberland*, ed. J. Hodgson, pp. 250, 257, 262, 271, 280, 289, 296.

[9] *Rot. R. Gravesend*, pp. 239, 340.

[10] P.R.O., papal bulls 43 (5), not in *C.E.P.R.*; he is described as 'Adam de Bokingfeud,' a canon of Lincoln.

rebels.[1] From the 'Rotuli Hundredorum' it appears that Adam, the precentor, and the subdean of Lincoln, had placed their houses upon the wall of Lincoln 11 or 12 years before, that is, about 1263–4.[2] The position of the houses is given as 'in latitud. xx ped. inter portam domini episcopi versus orientem et portam ballii versus occidentem.' Buckfield was not in residence as a canon in 1278.[3] However, he seems to have held his living of Iver into the time of Archbishop Peckam (1279–92) when his will was proved.[4] He had apparently resigned Rountain [5] before his death and the canonry of Lincoln before 1278.[6]

Adam of Domerham, monk, cellarer, and sacristan of Glastonbury, continued for 1126–1291 a continuation of William of Malmesbury's 'De Antiquitate Glastonie' [7]:—'Historia de Rebus Gestis Glastoniensibus': *inc.* 'Quoniam universos ecclesie sue historiam.' Cambridge, Trinity Coll. MS. 724, fos. 21–73*b*, probably autograph. This was edited by T. Hearne in 'Adam de Domerham, Historia de rebus gestis Glastoniensibus' (Oxford, 1727), pp. 303–596, and is discussed by J. Parker in Somersetshire Archaeological and Natural History Society, 'Proceedings,' xxv (1880). 70–3.

Adam probably entered Glastonbury abbey in the time of Abbot Michael, 1235–52.[8] By 18 Feb. 1255 he was important enough to be chosen by the prior and convent one of the five who were to choose an abbot to

[1] P.R.O., Exchequer of pleas, plea roll, 53–4 Hen. III, E. 13/1e, C. 24, a mandate to the bishop of Lincoln to distrain their ecclesiastical benefices if they (Adam and Robert Galle) did not appear.

[2] i. 311, 325, 397.

[3] *Statutes of Lincoln Cathedral*, ed. H. Bradshaw and C. Wordsworth, ii. p. ccviii.

[4] Lambeth Palace MS. 1294, fo. 34 (Reg. Winchelsey).

[5] In 1276 it was in another's possession (*Reg. Walter Giffard*, p. 289).

[6] Iver was probably not a Lincoln canonry (*Rot. R. Grosseteste*, p. 379).

[7] T. pp. 230–1; *D.N.B.* under Adam; Domerham, Wiltshire.

[8] *Adam de Domerham, Historia*, ed. Hearne, i. p. ix.

succeed Roger de Ford [q.v.], just deposed by the bishop of Bath and Wells.[1] Nine years later he was one of the monks representing his house in the wardrobe.[2] In 1272 a dispute arose as to whether Glastonbury held directly of the king or indirectly through the bishop of Bath and Wells. For a time, according to Adam, the episcopal officers seemed to be winning, but he spoke for his house and apparently brought the case to a satisfactory conclusion.[3] In the three previous instances his name appears as that of a monk without office. He seems to have become cellarer by 1274 and sacristan by 1276.[4] He witnessed the visit of Edward I to his abbey in April 1278 and the translation of the bodies of the alleged King Arthur group at that time.[5] Possibly he died on 4 Nov. 1291.[6] The chronicle, which is carried into 1291, is the record of the interests of an active monk for four decades. It contains bulls, charters, and other documents, as well as narrative. Naturally the writer favours his house and follows, as a propagandist, in the tradition of his predecessor, William of Malmesbury.

Adam, Abbot of Dore, theologian and poet,[7] was the subject of the following note by Bale:

Adamus, abbas Dorensis, Ade abbati succedens, ad philosophie sue grandis ostentationem, carmina quedam scripsit contra speculum ecclesie Giraldi Cambrensis, cui idem Giraldus atque Simon de Fraxino epigrammatibus respondebant. *Ex speculo ecclesie eiusdem Giraldi.*

Adamus Dorensis abbas, Cisterciensis ordinis prope Herefordiam, amaritudinem animi contra Giraldum Cambrensem ostendens, Carmina scripsit in eundem. Idem composuit Rudimenta musices, sub titulo Gammaud, are, li. i. *Ex speculo Giraldi* (*Index*, p. 4).

[1] *Adam de Domerham, Historia*, ed. Hearne, p. 255; H.M.C., *Dean and Chapter of Wells MSS.* i. 310.

[2] Feast of St. Edward the Martyr (18 March), 1264; *Rentalia et Customaria of Michael of Ambresbury* (Somerset Record Soc.), p. 234.

[3] *Adam de Domerham, Historia*, p. 537.

[4] *Ibid.* p. xii, quoting a register of Mr. Cox Macro.

[5] *Ibid.* pp. 587, 589.

[6] 'Obiit Adam, monachus Glastonie' (John Dart, *Hist. and Antiquities of the Cathedral Church of Canterbury*, p. xxxix).

[7] T. p. 7.

The surviving portions of the 'Speculum Ecclesie' do not mention Adam's writings (*Giraldi Cambrensis Opera*, R.S., ed. J. F. Dimock, iv.).

To Adam may also be ascribed other verse.

Bible in verse, Bodl. Lib. MS. Rawlinson, C. 67, fos. 22–85*b*, prologue (in prose) *inc.* 'Dolens in sanctuario dei': text *inc.* 'Dicit deus serpente de muliere.' In a modern hand on the flyleaf someone has written titles for three pieces by Alexander Neckam which appear again upon the first page of each piece. The fourth title reads 'Versus Ade Dorensis,' but this heading does not appear on fo. 22 as the writing has been clipped off in binding.

Sermons. B.M. MS. Reg. 8 A v, fos. 110–32, ancient title, 'Sermones abbatis de Dora.' The catalogue suggests as author one Abbot John. However, since these sermons end in verse it seems easier to attribute them to Abbot Adam, who mixed prose and poetry in the piece above.

Information about Adam's life, like that about his bibliography, is unsatisfactory. Gerald of Wales had much to say about the two abbots of cistercian Dore, who were both called Adam, but it is very difficult, if not impossible, to distinguish them.[1] Probably the first was the prelate who roused the ire of Gerald and Walter Map by his greed and questionable stratagems,[2] and was apparently abbot in 1198.[3] The second abbot was the writer, who was still alive when Gerald was writing, *c.* 1217. Adam had passed from the Cluniac order to the Cistercian after first being a clerk. Gerald suggested that Adam should make a final jump to a 'Carthusian prison.'[4]

[1] *Giraldi Cambrensis Opera*, i. 104; iv. 203, 206, 220.

[2] For summaries of Gerald's stories of this abbot see A. T. Bannister's *History of Ewias Harold*, p. 46.

[3] *Giraldi Cambr. Op.* i. 104; this Adam witnessed a charter of William de Vere, bishop of Hereford, 1186–99 (B.M. Add. MS. 33354, fo. 94*b*).

[4] The one definite statement about the second Adam occurs in the *Opera*, iv. 194.

WRITERS OF THIRTEENTH CENTURY ENGLAND

Adam of Elingham, disputant at Cambridge *c.* 1282 (Little-Pelster, p. 79), *c.* 1275, see App. A.

Adam of Eynsham, monk and abbot of Eynsham, was chaplain to St. Hugh of Lincoln, and author of two important religious works :—

'Vision of the Monk of Eynsham' : *inc.* 'Usu notissimum habetur quod.' The many MSS. and three recensions of this work are described by H. E. Salter in the preface of his edition in 'The Cartulary of the Abbey of Eynsham' (Oxford Hist. Soc.), ii. 276–83. Other editions are in 'Analecta Bollandiana,' xxii (1903). 226 *et seq.*, by Father H. Thurston, S.J., and in 'Romanische Forschungen,' xvi (1904). 641–733, by Michael Huber, O.S.B. Father Thurston in an article in the 'Dublin Review' (Oct. 1904) has shown that Dante was among those influenced by this vision. Ralph of Coggeshall [q.v.], writing of the vision of Thurkill, mentions that of the monk of Eynsham and says of the author of the account :

> Non credo tantum virum, tam religiosum ac tam litteratum nisi comperta et probabili auctoritate subnixa uoluisse scripto mandare, maxime cum tunc temporis extiterit capellanus domni Hugonis Lincolniensis episcopi sanctissimi uiri (B.M. MS. Reg. 13 D V, fo. 45 ; *Cartulary of Eynsham,* ii. 258 ; British Archaeol. Assoc. *Journal,* xxxi, 1875. 441).

'Life of St. Hugh, bishop of Lincoln' : *inc.* 'Silentium mihi, patres dulcissimi.' (a) B.N. MS. latin 5575, fos. 130–69 (15th cent.) ; (b) Bodl. Lib. MS. Digby 165 (13th cent.). The life has been edited by J. F. Dimock in 'Magna Vita S. Hugonis episcopi Lincolniensis' (R.S.). From Leland (*Itinerary,* viii. fo. 48*b*) and John Molanus (*Usuardi Martyrologium,* p. 195, *n.* 4) Dimock has reconstructed the original salutation as 'Dominis, et amicis in Christo carissimis, R. Priori, et qui cum eo sunt Withamiensibus monachis, minimus frater Adam——' (*op. cit.* p. 1).

The life of Adam has been discussed before, but the material is as yet somewhat scattered.[1] If we may believe the opening rubric of a Digby MS. of the vision, Adam was prior of Eynsham when he wrote, a brother of the monk Edmund who saw the vision, and his father 'in professione.' [2] His home would be Oxford and his father a pilgrim to the holy land, where he met his death.[3] There seems no other evidence that Edmund and Adam were brothers, although, had it been the case, it would have been an obvious thing to mention. It seems doubtful whether Adam was prior. Ralph of Coggeshall, quoted above, states that Adam was sub-prior and chaplain of St. Hugh and Thomas of Binham was prior.[4] In 1208 and again in 1217 the name of the prior began with an N.[5] Even though it can be shown that Adam probably was called 'de Oxonia' the Digby rubric seems dangerous to follow.

Adam had a brother William of Oxford who held two small properties in the parish of St. Peter in the East, and was described as 'faber.' [6] Adam was thus probably from Oxford also. This brother had a son and heir named Adam.[7] Presumably Adam entered Eynsham abbey after securing an education which Salter has commented upon favourably ; [8] while there Adam heard from Edmund's own lips the story of the strange vision of the sick monk.[9] He probably

[1] T. p. 7 ; *Magna Vita S. Hugonis,* pp. xxxiv–xliv ; *Cartulary of Eynsham,* i. pp. xviii–xxi ; ii. 257–276 *passim.*

[2] 'Incipit prefatio domini Adam prioris de Aineshamma super uisione quam uidit Eadmundus monachus, bone indolis adolescens, frater ipsius, scilicet prioris, & in professione filius, anno ab incarnatione domini M°C°XCVI°' (*Cartulary of Eynsham,* ii. 285).

[3] *Ibid.* pp. 263–8, 269, citing *Magna Vita S. Hugonis,* p. 238.

[4] 'Interrogatus autem a nobis domnus Thomas, prior de Binham, qui illis diebus extitit prior de Einesham' (*Cartulary of Eynsham,* ii. 258).

[5] *Ibid.* i. pp. xix, xxi ; *Collections for a Hist. of Staffordshire* (Salt Archæol. Soc.), xvii. 248.

[6] 'Willelmus de Oxonia frater Ade quondam abbatis de Egnesham' (*Cartulary of Eynsham,* i. 305, see also i. 159, 160, 162, 179, 245 ; ii. 271).

[7] *Ibid.* i. 245.

[8] *Ibid.* ii. 274.

[9] *Ibid.* p. 258.

wrote the first version of the vision while still at Eynsham during the important law-suit between the bishop of Lincoln, as patron of his house, and Richard I.[1] Perhaps this writing caused Bishop Hugh to secure him as a chaplain from 12 Nov. 1197 to his death on 16 Nov. 1200.[2] There is evidence that the bishop caused this work to be published: he may have been responsible for its later editions.[3]

Adam says that, save perhaps for one night, he was in constant attendance upon Bishop Hugh[4] and heard the bishop's dying confession.[5] He was Hugh's monk and priest, and seems to have been in charge of the bishop's jewels and relics.[6] He says that he was closer to the bishop than others.[7] At the death of his patron he would naturally return to his monastery. From chance remarks in the 'Life of St. Hugh' it is clear that the interdict caused Adam to go to France. While there he stayed three months at Paris with a relative of Bishop Hugh, Raymond, archdeacon of Leicester,[8] and visited the cistercian abbey of Clermaretz near St. Omer.[9] Another remark shows him back in England in 1211 or 1212 at Cheshunt in company with Abbot Richard of Waltham.[10] He was engaged upon the prologue to the fifth book of the 'Life' in July 1212.[11] Some years had probably passed after St. Hugh's death before Adam began his work, since in the interval several lives had been written.[12]

The abbey of Eynsham had no abbot as late as June 1213 and in July it was surrendered into the hands of the bishop of

1 *Cartulary of Eynsham*, ii. 282.

2 For date of his association with the bishop see *Magna Vita S. Hugonis*, p. 47.

3 *Cartulary of Eynsham*, ii. 259–60.

4 *Magna Vita S. Hugonis*, pp. xxxvi, 47.

5 *Ibid.* p. 333.

6 *Ibid.* pp. 315, 318, 339.

7 *Ibid.* pp. xxxvii, 361, 372.

8 *Ibid.* pp. 303, 304.

9 *Ibid.* p. 326.

10 *Ibid.* p. 274.

11 *Ibid.* p. 221; cf. also p. 282, which indicates that he was writing during the interdict.

12 *Ibid.* pp. 47–8.

Lincoln.[1] Adam appears as abbot in June 1214.[2] That he was St. Hugh's chaplain and author of his biography is clear from a comparison of his testimony before the delegates investigating the sanctity of St. Hugh in 1219 and a passage in the 'Life.'[3] As abbot he appears in documents of 1215, 1219, 1220–2, 1222, 1224, 1225, and 1228.[4] In this last year he was deposed.[5] Apparently he was not a capable administrator. He contracted debts with the bishop of Lincoln and the Jews, and was alleged to have wasted the abbey's woods. On 8 Sept. 1227 he was restricted in action by the requirement that nothing should be sealed until it had been read in chapter.[6] For his support he appears to have received the manor of Little Rollright. He was exempted from doing suit in person for it on 20 May 1233,[7] and had been granted, a few weeks earlier, protection without term.[8]

Adam of Hoveden, O.F.M., preached a number of sermons at Oxford about 1290. For these and his life see Little (*F.S.O.* p. 862), Little and Pelster (p. 266), and also App. A.

Adam of Lincoln, O.F.M., was also among the preachers at Oxford about 1290. See Little (*F.S.O.* p. 860), and Little and Pelster (p. 92).

Adam Marsh, O.F.M., theologian and man of affairs,[9] can claim the following writings identified by Little (*F.S.O.* p. 836):—

1 *Cartulary of Eynsham*, i. pp. xix–xx.

2 *Ibid.* i. 171.

3 'Abbas de Eynsham qui capellanus fuit Hugonis episcopi, juratus dicit . . .' (*Magna Vita S. Hugonis*, p. xxxix).

4 *Cartulary of Eynsham*, i. 60, 135, 144, 145, 147, 151, 237, 323; ii. 163, 166; less easily dated documents appear in i. 138, 147, 149, 153, 155, 161, 162, 163, 165, 179, 239, 240, 305; ii. 164, 167, 172; Bannister, *History of Ewias Harold*, p. 57; B.M. Harley charter 44, D. 43.

5 *Ann. Monast.* i. 70; *Cartulary of Eynsham*, i. p. xx; ii. p. v.

6 *Ibid.* i. p. xx, citing Bodl. Lib. MS. Bodl. 435.

7 *C.P.R.* 1232–47, p. 16.

8 *Ibid.* p. 14.

9 T. p. 8; *D.N.B.* under Adam. The best account of his life is in Little (*F.S.O.* pp. 831–7).

Letters, edited by J. S. Brewer as 'Adæ de Marisco Epistolæ' in 'Monumenta Franciscana' (R.S.), are largely for the years 1250–5.

'Pastorale Excerptum,' Vienna, Bibl. Palat. MS. 4923 (Theol 547), fos. 40*b*–2*b* (15th cent.) (see 'Tabulae codicum manuscriptorum' in *Bibl. Palatina. Vindobonensi Asservatorum*, iii. 421). Possibly, as Little suggests, this is an extract from his letters or from the 'Summa de Penitentia' mentioned below (*F.S.O.* p. 836).

Sermon : *inc.* 'Simon onie (?) filius . . . Symon interpretatur.' Cambridge, Corpus Christi Coll. MS. 459, fo. 133. In the margin is 'Fr Adam de Ma . . .' He wrote also an 'Additio' to a topical concordance of Robert Grosseteste. Lyons MS. 414, fos. 17–9, entitled 'Incipit tabula Magistri Roberti lincolniensis episcopi cum addicione Magistri Ade de Marisco' (*Speculum* ix, 1934. 140).

Ancient catalogues mention the following :—

'Summa de Penitentia.' Christchurch, Canterbury, no. 618, 'Summa de Penitentia secundum fratrem Adam de Marisco' (James, *A.L.C.D.* p. 71).

'Quedam Leccio.' Peterborough, MS. B. vi, 'Quedam leccio Mag. Ade de Marisco fratris minoris' (James, *Peterborough*, p. 46).

Commentaries upon Holy Scripture. There is reference to these in the 'Catalogus de eruditis Franciscanis' seen by Leland (*Commentarii de Scriptoribus Britannicis*, p. 268). A commentary upon Genesis is mentioned by Salimbene (*Cronica*, ed. Holder-Egger, *M.G.H.SS.*, xxxii. 296).

Adam mentions some 'Expositiones super angelicam hierarchiam' which may be his own (*Mon. Fr.* p. 206).

Adam Marsh was born in the diocese of Bath,[1] apparently of a wealthy family. As early as 1226 he had a clerk, Lawrence,[2] and Master Adam Rufus [q.v.] seems to have served him in like capacity.[1] He was a nephew of Richard Marsh, bishop of Durham (1217–26) and influential courtier of King John, from whom he received a 'bibliotheca,' *i.e.* bible or library.[2] A Robert Marsh appears in Adam's letters as the object of his solicitude [3] ; and Brewer calls him Adam's brother.[4] One Thomas Marsh is called a relative.[5] Adam also wrote in favour of other relatives, Juliana of Horningdene [6] and William, bailiff of Bugden.[7]

The two chief sources for Adam's life are his letters, mostly of the years 1250–5, and official records which refer also in large part to his later years. The information for his early life is meagre.[8] He had doubtless studied at Oxford with Grosseteste [q.v.], as he states that Grosseteste has had an interest in him from his youth.[9] Grosseteste may have presided at Adam's vesperies.[10] By 1226 Adam was a master.[11] For a 'triennium' during the episcopate of his uncle, Richard Marsh, at Durham (1217–26) he is supposed to have been parson of Wearmouth.[12] In the 'Liber Vitæ' of Durham there appear together in the same handwriting 'Magister Robertus Archidiaconus Leycestr.' and 'Magister Adam de Marisco persona de Weremuth.' [13] If, as seems probable, the

[1] *Nicholai Triveti Annales* (Eng. Hist. Soc.), ed. Thomas Hog, p. 243 ; Bale, *Index*, p. 6.

[2] Little, *F.S.O.* p. 832 ; *Rot. Litt. Claus.* ii. 136.

[1] Little, *F.S.O.* p. 832 ; *Eccleston*, p. 22.

[2] Little, *F.S.O.*, p. 832 ; *Rot. Litt. Claus.* ii. 136 ; *Chronicon de Lanercost* (Bannatyne Club), ed. J. Stevenson, p. 24.

[3] *Mon. Fr.* i. 99, 135, 137.

[4] *Ibid.* p. lxxvii.

[5] *Ibid.* pp. 223, 243, 399.

[6] *Ibid.* p. 239.

[7] *Ibid.* p. 252.

[8] 'Oxoniæ legit primus frater Adam de Marisco anno Domini MCCCVIII,' an obvious mistake. Possibly it should be emended to MCCXVIII and refer to his original teaching at Oxford, or to MCCXLVIII (*E.H.R.* xlix, 1934. 301).

[9] *Mon. Fr.* i. 145.

[10] 'In vesperijs Ade,' but it might possibly be Adam Rufus (Bale, *Index*, p. 376).

[11] The date of his inheritance from Richard Marsh ; see above.

[12] Little, *F.S.O.* p. 832 ; 'Ricardus de Marisco . . . qui cognatum sibi magistrum Adam de eodem induxit in patriam illam' (*Chronicon de Lanercost*, pp. 24, 58).

[13] *Liber Vitæ Ecclesiæ Dunelmensis* (Surtees Soc.), fo. 25.

two entries were written at the same time Adam must have been parson when Robert Grosseteste was archdeacon of Leicester (1229–32). One suspects that Robert and Adam accepted these preferments at about the same time and relinquished them also in the same way. Adam became a franciscan shortly after Adam Rufus [q.v.] entered the order: the latter was a franciscan by the autumn of 1232.[1] Marsh entered before John of Reading, abbot of Oseney, 4 Oct. 1235.[2]

For several years after Adam entered the order he can only be traced with difficulty. He was asked to come to Liddington by Grosseteste in September 1235 or 1236 to talk over matters of importance and to see that some friars minor were attached to the bishop's household.[3] In 1241 Adam was one of the friars selected to consider and report upon doubtful points in the franciscan rule.[4] He accompanied Grosseteste to the great church council at Lyons, leaving England on 18 Nov. 1244 and arriving at Lyons on 7 Jan. 1245.[5] Between this date and the following June he asked his prior provincial to send him several books.[6] On his return he remained at Mantes with his sick companion, John of Stanford, which caused Grosseteste to fear that Adam might be asked to fill the professorship at Paris caused by the death of Alexander of Hales [q.v.][7] and to request that others should care for John in order that Adam might return to England. Adam went abroad again in July 1247 with the dominican provincial, for which journey they were given 40 marks.[8] On 18 October, probably two

[1] Little, *F.S.O.* p. 832.
[2] *Ibid.* p. 833; *Ann. Monast.* iv. 82.
[3] Little, *F.S.O.* p. 834.
[4] *Eccleston*, p. 88; *Mon. Fr.* p. 48.
[5] *Chr. Maj.* iv. 390–1; *Mon. Fr.* i. 376.
[6] *Ibid.* p. 378.
[7] *Ep. Grosseteste*, pp. 334–5.
[8] Little, *F.S.O.* p. 835; *C.L.R.* 1245–1251, p. 132.

or three years later, he incurred the king's displeasure by a sermon.[1]

In July 1247 Thomas Wallensis was elected bishop of St. David's. Adam Marsh succeeded him as lector of the Oxford franciscans, probably retaining this post until 1250.[2] A letter from the custodian of the friars minor of Paris, dated 1251, is addressed to Adam.[3] He was re-appointed lector at Oxford in 1252.[4] In February 1253, asked to approve a statute requiring candidates in theology to rule in arts first, he stated that he was almost a stranger to the university.[5] In this same year Grosseteste died and left his library to the Oxford franciscans on account of his affection for Marsh.[6]

The last years of Marsh's life were probably busy ones. In the summer of 1252 his 'nuntius' received a gift from the king.[7] After the death of Bishop Grosseteste, Archbishop Boniface acknowledged that he was following the advice of the dean of Lincoln and of Adam Marsh concerning the exercise of episcopal jurisdiction during the vacancy.[8] In 1256 the pope named him as a member of the commission to examine the life and miracles of Richard of Wych [q.v.], who was to be considered for canonization.[9] The king and archbishop are said to have urged his election as bishop of Ely in 1257.[10] He apparently went abroad, by way of Dover, as a royal messenger in the same year.[11] In

[1] *Mon. Fr.* i. 275; probably 1248, since 18 October (St. Luke's day) fell on Sunday in that year.
[2] Little, *F.S.O.* p. 835.
[3] *Ann. Monast.* i. 290.
[4] Little, *F.S.O.* p. 835.
[5] *Ibid.* pp. 823–4.
[6] *Triveti Annales*, p. 243.
[7] 'Simon nuntio fratris A. de Marisco vi d de dono' (P.R.O., various accounts, nuncii, E. 101/308/1).
[8] H.M.C., Wells MSS. App. i. 135; *Chr. Maj.* vi. 266, 267.
[9] Mandate of 22 June (*C.E.P.R.* i. 332); C. Bourel, *Registres d'Alexandre IV*, i. 427; *C.P.R.*, 1247–58, p. 522.
[10] *Chr. Maj.* v. 619, 635.
[11] *C.Cl.R.*, 1256–9, pp. 133, 197; *C.P.R.*, 1247–1258, p. 594.

a will, dated 1 Jan. 1259, Simon de Montfort advised his wife to follow the advice of the bishop of Lincoln and of Adam.[1] Adam died on 18 November of the same year [2] and masses were said for his soul at the general council of Narbonne in the following year.[3]

The letters of Adam Marsh tell us that Adam's advice was very highly regarded, even by persons of widely different outlook. They have been arranged, perhaps by Adam, in an order based approximately upon the social rank of the recipients.[4] By far the largest number was sent to Bishop Grosseteste, as we should expect, while many went to his friend and minister provincial, William of Nottingham, and to Simon de Montfort.

Adam of Nutzard,[5] grammarian, poet, and possibly abbot of St. Benet Holme, was certainly author of :—

'Neutrale' : *inc.* 'Aspirans precibus vestris persepe rogatus.' (a) Bodl. Lib. MS. Digby 100, fo. 33, anonymous ; (b) formerly MS. Syon A 4, entitled 'Neutrale magistri Ade de Nydthard Oxoniensis' (Mary Bateson, *Catalogue of the Library of Syon Monastery*, pp. xxi, 72) ; (c) 'Ex domo Ricardi Grafton' ? 'Adamus de Nydzarde, poeta, magister Oxon., scripsit carmine, Neutrale' (Bale, *Index*, p. 6). Bale adds two pieces which probably followed the 'Neutrale' but which are probably not by Adam, 'De speciebus lapidum, li. 1,' *inc.* 'Euax rex Arabum legitur scripsisse,' and 'Verborum significata, li. i,' *inc.* 'Quoniam saxea distinguere sophist.'

'De Verbis Deponentibus' : *inc.* 'Vobis ignota ne deponencia uerba.' Cambridge, Gonville and Caius Coll. MS. 136, fos. 125–31, anonymous, but stated by M. R. James in the library catalogue to be by Adam de Nutzarde.

This Oxford master may possibly be the Adam de Neteshirde or Neteshurde, abbot of St. Benet Holme, who is described by a chronicler of his house as 'vir omnino predecessoribus suis laude dignior.' The place is probably Neatishead, Norfolk. His predecessor died on 21 Apr. 1256,[1] and Adam must have been elected very soon after as his election received the royal assent on 8 May.[2] The chronicler tells of Adam's building operations and additions to the property of the monastery. Evidence of his activity appears in the copies of his many charters in the cartulary of St. Benet Holme.[3] He died on 19 Aug. 1268 [4] to the great regret of the brothers. 'Erat enim vultu hilaris et amabilis, et sermone jocundus ac rationabilis, necnon et omni morum honestate compositus.' [5]

Adam of Ross was author of an Anglo-Norman poem :—

'The Vision of Saint Paul,' of which the MSS. are listed by Vising (*Anglo-Norman Language and Literature*, p. 43). The poem is edited by L. E. Kastner in *Zeitschrift für französische Sprache und Litteratur*, xxix (1906). 274–90. The poet gives his name in the closing lines of one manuscript :

> Jeo sui serf Deu Adam de Ros
> Isci fai jo mien repos,
> Kar plus ne dit ici li livre
> Ne jo ne voil nient plus escrivre.

Adam, to judge from the writing, lived near the beginning of the 13th century. He possibly came from the town of Ross in Herefordshire, since one manuscript containing his poem seems to have had some

1 Ch. Bémont, *Simon de Montfort*, p. 328.

2 *Itineraria Symonis Simeonis et Willelmi de Worcestre*, ed. Nasmith, p. 81.

3 *A.F.H.* iii. 504.

4 Except that letters to members of his order have been separated.

5 T. p. 547.

1 *Chronica Johannis de Oxenedes* (R.S.), ed. Henry Ellis, p. 298.

2 *C.P.R.*, 1247–58, p. 472.

3 *Chronica Johannis de Oxenedes*, pp. 298–9 ; B.M. MS. Cotton, Galba E ii, fos. 128–40.

4 *Chronica Johannis de Oxenedes*, p. 299 ; H. R. Luard gives the year 1269 (*Flores Historiarum*, R.S., iii. 19).

5 *Chronica Johannis de Oxenedes*, p. 298.

connexion with that county.[1] The 'serf Deu' may mean that Adam was a monk, possibly of Dunbrothy in Ireland.[2]

Adam Rufus of Exeter or Oxford,[3] **O.F.M.,** was possibly the author of an Anglo-Norman piece upon the Lord's Prayer, Cambridge, Pembroke Coll. MS. 112, fos. 71–92, entitled 'Le expositiun meistre adam de eccestre sur la pater nostre.'

The author is possibly the Master Adam Rufus of Exeter or Oxford who influenced Adam Marsh [q.v.] to join him in the franciscan order.[4] Critically the 'Exeter' is to be preferred, since Adam's association with the university makes the corruption of 'Exonia' to 'Oxonia' more probable than the reverse. The presence of a prominent Adam Rufus as well as others bearing the name Rufus at Oxford[5] would give more probability to the 'of Oxford' if the name Rufus were not so common in England.

A few hints exist that he was a relatively young man although Grosseteste addressed a long epistle upon an important theological question to him[6] and Eccleston [q.v.] spoke of him as 'toto famosus orbe.'[7] We know first that he was companion and probably valet to Adam Marsh,[8] secondly that he had not yet studied theology,[9] and thirdly that he entered an arduous missionary career.

[1] Kastner, *op. cit.* p. 275.

[2] He represents his abbot 'coram rege,' 1279 (*Cal. of Docs. relating to Ireland*, 1252–84, p. 305).

[3] Little, *G.F.* p. 179 ; *F.S.O.* p. 832.

[4] *Eccleston*, p. 22.

[5] Little, *F.S.O.* p. 832 ; *Cartulary of the Hospital of St. John the Baptist* (Oxford Hist. Soc.), *passim* ; in a charter mentioning the land of William Rufus at Toternho a Master Adam is a witness (P.R.O. cartæ misc. 41, p. 55) ; a Master Adam Rufus, rector of St. Peter's church, witnesses a charter in the time of Roger abbot of Pershore (*c.* 1234) and Bishop Walter of Worcester (1236–65) (P.R.O. ancient deeds, D. 3082).

[6] *Ep. Grosseteste*, p. 1 ; the date of the letter is before Grosseteste became archdeacon of Leicester, probably in 1229.

[7] *Eccleston*, p. 21.

[8] 'Fuit autem tunc socius magistri Adæ de Marisco et ad robas suas' (*ibid.* p. 22).

[9] *Ibid.* p. 21.

Adam had vowed that whatever was asked of him in the Virgin's name, he would grant. He told this vow to a recluse, and she repeated it to a cistercian monk, a friar preacher and a monk of Reading. Adam dreamed that he saw men who were trying to enmesh him, but that he escaped. Later he met William de Colevile, senior, who asked him for the love of the Mother of God to enter the franciscan order. This he did with William of York[1] upon 25 January of an undesignated year while Grosseteste was archdeacon (1229–32),[2] probably in 1231 or 1232.[3] Shortly after this he journeyed to the papal curia and started eastward to preach to the Saracens. He died at Barletta in Apulia, and miracles were reported at his tomb.[4]

Adam of Whitby was a commentator upon Aristotelian treatises 'Meteorology,' 'De Memoria,' and 'De Sensu et Sensato,' B.N. MS. fonds lat. 16149, fos. 51, 60, and 62. Their rubrics are 'Super libros meteororum,' 'de memoria,' and 'de sensu auctore Ad. de Wyteby' (L. Delisle, *Inventaire des MSS. de la Sorbonne conservés à la B.N. sous les nos.* 15176–16718 *du fonds latin*, p. 41).

Possibly this commentator was of the family of Adam de 'Withebi,' sheriff of London in 1210.

Alan, monk of Meaux, wrote a treatise upon St. Susanna, *inc.* 'Cum mea mens loquitur,' B.M. MS. Harley 2851, fos. 2–9*b* (*c.* 1300). The colophon is 'Explicit tractatus fratris Alani, monachi de Melsa, magistri quondam de Beverlaco.'

Alan of Wakerfeld, O.F.M. and theologian,[5] wrote two academic exercises which

[1] *Eccleston*, p. 22.

[2] *Ep. Grosseteste*, pp. 17–21.

[3] Little, *F.S.O.* p. 833 ; the time designated by Eccleston by 'non multo post' until Adam Marsh entered is very uncertain.

[4] Little identifies Adam Rufus with Adam of Exeter (*F.S.O.* p. 832).

[5] Little, *F.S.O.* p. 857.

remain in Assisi, MS. 158, qu. 76: 'Respondit Orfort. Waker' and near the end, 'Waker dis. R[espondit] Penn[ard].' Little gives two other instances of an Alan, possibly Wakerfeld (*F.S.O.* p. 857; Little-Pelster, p. 102). He may also be the author of the 'Impugnacio fratrum minorum per fratres predicatores apud Oxoniam,' MS. Phillips 3119, fos. 86–8 (13th–14th cent.), published by Little (*G.F.* pp. 320–35). Little says 'It is the work of an Oxford Minorite who was an eyewitness of, and probably a participator in, the events which he records.'

Alan of Wakerfeld is said to have been rector of Branxton, 1234–52, and to have been headmaster of the Durham school.[1] He gave a volume of biblical books to the priory of Durham.[2] In 1269 he took a prominent part in the controversy with the dominicans.[3] One speech of his when he was alone with the dominicans must have come from him or have been written by him.[4] He was regent master of the franciscans probably in 1284–86.[5]

Alard, O.P., was the author of a sermon which remains in an early collection of dominican homilies, B.M. MS. Egerton 655, fo. 144, *inc.* 'Cum venit spiritus veritatis. Gratia super se veniente' with a note, 'Dom iii post Octab. Pasch, et fratris Alard.'

Probably this was the prior provincial of

[1] *Fasti Dunelmenses* (Surtees Soc.), p. 133; ancient sources not given.

[2] Proverbs, Ecclesiastes, Song of Solomon, Ecclesiasticus, and 'Sapientia'; 'V. libri Salomonis dono Magri Alani de Wakerfeld, extra commune armariolum nulli accommodand' (Little-Pelster, p. 102).

[3] Little, *G.F.* pp. 320, 321, 335.

[4] In both lists of friars Alan's name appears last, although he took an important part. Such a work would normally be entrusted to a clerk, who would usually place his name last. For this custom see Russell ('The Significance of Charter Witness Lists in Thirteenth Century England,' in New Mexico Normal Univ. *Bulletin*, Aug. 1930, supplement).

[5] See App. A.

English dominicans in 1235[1] and 1236[2] who is said to have been chancellor of Oxford in 1215.[3]

Alberic of London was the author of two works upon classical mythology,[4] 'De imaginibus Deorum' and 'Poetarium,' both of which are discussed by M. Esposito (*E.H.R.* xxx, 1915. 467). The 'Poetarium' appears in two forms, the shorter of which is attributed to Alexander Neckam [q.v.] in several MSS. The share of each needs to be worked out carefully. If Alberic added an introduction and commentary to a work of Alexander, then he might have lived at the time suggested for him by bibliographical tradition, the reigns of John and Henry III. The two 'explicits' of the Worcester MS. favour this.[5] However, the name Alberic and the material suggest the 12th century. There we find an Alberic, canon of St. Paul's, London, in the time of the dean, Hugh,[6] although most of the charters in which his name appears are of the time of Ralph de Diceto (1180–1202).[7] He left three service books to St. Paul's.[8] If Neckam (1157–1217) wrote the 'Poetarium' early in life, Alberic, if he were canon, might have been the author of the commentary and expanded version, but this is, at best, conjecture.

Alderman of London is said by Pits[9] to have written poetry incorporated in the 'Speculum Ecclesie' of Gerald of Wales.[10] This chapter, entitled 'De capella Lammete,'

[1] *Ep. Grosseteste*, pp. 59, 61.

[2] *C.Cl.R.*, 1234–7, p. 358.

[3] *E.H.R.* xxxiii (1918). 244.

[4] T. p. 19.

[5] 'Explicit Mithologia Alexandri. Explicit Albricius in Poetario' (MS. F 154, fo. 16).

[6] St. Paul's, MS. W.D. 4, fo. 30*b*; a Master Albericus was official of W. de Rupibus, archdeacon of Winchester in 1241 (*C.P.R.*, 1232–47, p. 249).

[7] H.M.C., 9th Rep. App. i. 32, 68; B.M. MS. Cotton, Faust. B. ii. fo. 55; St. Paul's MS. W.D. 4, fos. 24, 28, 34.

[8] St. Paul's MS. W.D. 4, fos. 133, 132*b*, 133*b*.

[9] John Pits, *Relationum Historicarum*, p. 822.

[10] Book ii, chap. 20.

is lost (*Giraldi Cambrensis Opera*, R.S. ed. J. S. Brewer, iv. 63). The Lambeth chapel was a great source of conflict between Archbishop Hubert and the monks of Canterbury at the turn of the century.

Alexander, prior of Ashby, was the author of several pieces of religious content[1] :—

'De artificioso modo predicandi' ('Upon the art of preaching'): *inc.* prologue, 'Venerabili abbati salutem et dilectionem in Christo,' *inc.* text, 'Non in scriptura et sermone'. (a) Cambridge Univ. Lib. MS. Dd. vi. 27, fos. 6–9, fragments; (b) *ibid.* MS. Ii. i. 24, fos. 332*b*–46*b* (13th cent.) with heading, 'Incipit prologus (prioris de essebi above line) de artificioso modo predicandi'; (c) MS. formerly in Cambridge Univ. Lib. MS. Ee. vi. 39, in which the ancient table of contents mentions an 'Alexandri de arte predicandi' with four other pieces now gone from it; (d) MS. formerly at Peterborough, MS. X. vii, entitled 'Tractatus prioris de esseby de arte predicandi' (James, *Peterborough*, p. 52); (e) MS. formerly at Sion Abbey, entitled 'Alexander prior de eseby de arte predicandi' (M. Bateson, *Catalogue of the Library of Syon Monastery, Isleworth*, p. 203).

Sermons: In Cambridge Univ. Lib. MS. Ii. i. 24, fos. 347–63, a series of sermons follows the treatise on preaching with the title, 'Sermones prioris de essebi.' The sermons begin respectively, 'Vigili cura mente' (fo. 347); 'Beati misericordes' (fo. 349); 'Tota religiosorum' (fo. 349); 'Lavamini mundi estote' (fo. 351); 'Vias tuas due' (fo. 353); 'Pria in nobis' (fo. 356*b*); 'Custodiens paruulos' (fo. 357); 'Germinauit radix Jesse' (fo. 358*b*); and 'Feram sibi fecit rex' (fo. 361).

'Festivalis:' *inc.* first prologue, 'Duo preclara divine pietatis,' *inc.* second prologue, 'Omnia cum nequeam sanctorum scribere gesta.' This is probably the book mentioned in Alexander's treatise on preaching: 'Forte adhuc tibi transmittam libellum de miraculis sanctorum quem iam ex magna parte metrice composui infra presenti anni' (Cambridge Univ. Lib. MS. II. i. 24, fo. 332*b*).

(a) Bodl. Lib. MS. Bodley 40, fos. 1–38 (13th cent.), in which a 16th or 17th century hand gives 'Alexander Essebiensis'; (b) MS. Bodley 527, fos. 85–129, anonymous; (c) Eton Coll. MS. 20, fos. 166–76 (12th cent.), entitled 'Alexandri prioris de Essebie liber festiualis'; (d) a MS. from the collections of Nicholas Brigan (Bale, *Index*, p. 21). The various saints' lives attributed to him, probably not his, are possibly the result of a confusion with this piece.

'Argumenta Bibliorum' or History: *inc.* prologue, 'Laborem in ludum vertit fructus consyderatio,' *inc.* text, 'Ante dies omnes mundi, fuit omnis:' (a) York Cathedral, MS. xvi. Q. 14, fos. 55*b*–8*b* (13th cent.); (b) MS. 'Ex museo Roberti Talboti' (Bale, *Index*, p. 22).

This is the book referred to as Alexander's history and its relationship to the following MSS. needs to be considered :—

B.M. Add. MS. 6924, fos. 112*b*–8; MS. Cotton, Claud. B. vii, fos. 214–5; Lambeth Palace MS. Y. 13; and Cambridge, Corpus Christi Coll. MS. E. ii.

'Instructio ad novitios:' formerly at Peterborough, MS. Z. iv, 'Instruccio prioris de Esseby ad Novicios cum distinctionibus virtutum et viciorum et philosophia' (James, *Peterborough*, p. 43).

Meditations: *inc.* prologue, 'Qui in subsequentium,' *inc.* text, 'Confitebor tibi domine': (a) B.M. MS. Reg. 7, D. xvii, fos. 241–2*b* (13th cent.), entitled 'Alexander prior de Esebi'; (b) Bale speaks of one from Exeter Coll., Oxford (*Index*, p. 21). He mentions another meditation from the same library, *inc.* 'Due sunt vite que in sacra scriptura plurimum commendantur.'

This writer is probably the prior of the house of Austin canons, at Canons

[1] T. p. 29; *D.N.B.* under Alexander. I am indebted to Mr. R. W. Hunt, who is making a study of this writer with other contemporaries, for several corrections and additions to this biography.

Ashby, Northamptonshire, at the beginning of the 13th century. His name appears in many charters, few of which, however, are dated.[1] One contains the name of Roger of Rolveston, not designated as dean, therefore probably before he attained that office in 1195; another bears the name of Abbot Robert of Eynsham (1197–1205), and a third the year 1201. The prior was appointed a judge delegate in Oxford in the period 1197–1200.[2] A successor, Hugh, was apparently in office by 1215.[3]

Alexander of Hales, O.F.M., author of theological treatises,[4] enjoyed a great reputation as the first franciscan doctor of theology at Paris which has caused various works by others to be attributed to him. Even his 'Summa theologica,' edited by Bernardine Klumper (*Doctoris Irrefragabilis Alexandri de Hales Summa Theologica*) has been questioned by M. Gorce ('La Somme Théologique d'Alexandre de Hales, est-elle authentique?' in *The New Scholasticism*, v, 1931. 1–72). His literary output is in need of definition. Of writings upon his books may be noted J. A. Endres's 'Des Alexander von Hales Leben und psychologische Lehre,' D. O. Lottin's 'Alexander de Hales et la "Summa de anima" de Jean de la Rochelle' in *Recherches de théologie ancienne et mediévale*, ii (1930). V. E. Keogh's 'The Notion of Fate in Boethius, Thomas Aquinas, and Alexander of Hales,' J. Goergen's 'Untersuchungen . . . zu den Quästionen de fato, de divinatione, de sortibus des Magister Alexander,' in *Franziskanische Studien*, xix (1932). 13–39, Johann Fuchs's 'Die Proprietäten des Seins bei Alexander von Hales,' and F. Pelster's articles upon Hales's 'questions' (*Scholastik*, v, 1931. 66–78, vi. 321–53; *Gregorianum*, xiv, 1933. 401–22, 501–20).

The chief account of Hales's life has come down to us in the pages of Roger Bacon, who did not think highly of him:

> qui mortuus est fuit bonus homo, et dives, et archidiaconus magnus, et magister in theologia sui temporis . . . tamen non legit naturalia nec metaphysica nec audivit ea, quia non fuerunt libri principales harum scientiarum nec commentarii translati quando rexit in artibus. Et diu postea fuerunt excommunicati et suspensi Parisius, ubi ipse studuit. Unde citius ordinem intravit antequam fuerunt hi libri semel perlecti. Istud notum est per ejus ingressum in ordinem, et per dispersionem universitatis Parisiensis [parum]; nam usque ad eum fuerunt libri prohibiti, et usque quo rediit Universitas, post quem reditum ipse intravit religionem, jam senex et magister in theologia.[1]

From this description we learn that Alexander of Hales studied and ruled in arts at Paris, and was already an old man when he entered the franciscan order, at the latest, about 1238. Old probably meant fifty or more. He was doubtless studying and ruling in arts in his twenties, that is, in 1218 and earlier. If Bacon means that Hales was studying the arts before the prohibitions upon the works of Aristotle then he was there before 1210, which is probable. Before he left Paris at the dispersion of 1229 he was probably doctor of theology and may have held the prebend of Holborn.[2]

While Ralph of Maidstone [q.v.] was still archdeacon of Chester (1231 and earlier)

[1] B.M. MS. Reg. 11, B. ix, fos. 33, 33*b*, 34, 34*b*, 131*b*; MS. Cotton, Vesp. E. xvii, fos. 36*b*, 37, 35; MS. Cotton, Tib. E. v, fo. 52*b*; Cott. Ch. v. 34; Add. Ch. 22380; MS. Harley, 4714, fos. 22, 22*b*; Harley Ch. 85, B. 18; Westminster Abbey muniments, nos. 2471, 2479; Thomas Madox, *Formulare Anglicanum*, p. 250; Dugdale, *Monasticon*, v. 193; *The Cartulary of St. Frideswide, Oxford* (ed. S. R. Wigram), ii. 19. The more important witnesses are Walkelin, abbot of St. James (nos. 5, 7, 8, 18, 19; W., prior of St. Andrew's (2, 11); Walter (1, 3, 8, 19); Adam, abbot of Sulby [Saleby] (2, 3, 6, 11); Geoffrey, abbot of Bruern (20); Richard of Kent, archdeacon of Northampton (7, 8, 19).

[2] *Oseney Cart.* (Oxford Hist. Soc.), ed. H. E. Salter, iv. 62.

[3] Dugdale, *Monasticon*, vi. 442; evidence not given.

[4] T. p. 370; *D.N.B.* under Alexander.

[1] *Fr. Rogeri Bacon Opera Inedita* (R.S.), ed. J. S. Brewer, pp. 325–6.

[2] G. Hennessey, *Novum Repertorium Ecclesiasticum Parochiale Londoniense*, p. 29; he is supposed to have held this prebend after Peter de Colle Medio, said to have possessed it in 1222, and before William de Wellborn, in 1239.

a Master Alexander of Hales appears as a canon of Lichfield.[1] Since Ralph had returned from Paris in 1229, where he had been a famous teacher, and the bishop was another famous teacher, Alexander of Stavensby [q.v.], there is little reason to doubt that this Hales was the professor. In 1231 when Richard de Glovernia was promoted to the treasurership of Lichfield, succeeding Richard de Stavensby [q.v.], Hales became archdeacon of Coventry.[2] The dated documents in which his name appears with this title are of 1231 and 1232.[3] He was appointed royal envoy to the king of France in 1235.[4] A successor in the archdeaconry had appeared by 1240.[5] Both his epitaph and Roger Bacon mention that he had been an archdeacon. Probably he returned to Paris to teach about 1233.

The register of the franciscans at London [6] has the following statement about Hales :

> Fr. Alex. Hales, natione Anglicus, doctor, cancellarius et archidiaconus Parisiensis, relicta pompa secularis conversationis, habitum fratrum Minorum anno Domini MCCXXVIII assumpsit, in quo virgo et doctor irrefragabilis xvii annos supervixit, et anno MCCXLV Parisiis obiit circa festum Assumptionis ; in cujus sepultura Odo legatus domini papæ missam celebravit cum assistentia multorum venerabilium prælatorum venientium de concilio domini papæ.

Alexander of Hales may well have served as chancellor of the university of Paris, but that he was archdeacon of Paris is more doubtful. This statement may be a scribal inversion of 'archidiaconus et cancellarius Parisiensis.' Possibly also the MCCXXVIII is a mistake for MCCXXXVIII with the xvii corrected from vii to make the calculation correct. He was one of the doctors chosen in 1239 to aid in explaining the franciscan rule.[1] He died on 21 Aug. 1245 and was buried in the franciscan church in Paris.[2] His epitaph reads : 'Gloria doctorum decus et flos philosophorum, auctor scriptorum vir Alexander uariorum, norma modernorum fons ueri, lux aliorum, inclitus Anglorum fuit archilevita, sed horum spretor cunctorum frater collega minorum factus egenorum fit primus doctor eorum.' [3] His picture is supposed to be known.[4]

Alexander Neckam of St. Albans, professor at Oxford, canon and abbot of Cirencester, was the author of numerous writings [5] of which no adequate bibliography is as yet in print. M. Esposito has a tentative list (*E.H.R.* xxx, 1915. 461–71) to which there are additions (*E.H.R.* xlvii, 1932. 266–8). A list of printed works is given in the 'Index' (p. 50). These lists show that England has possessed the majority of the MSS. of Neckam's works since the 13th century. The number of MSS. extant indicate that Neckam had a very great influence upon English thought both in arts and theology. For influence upon a late writer see F. F. Covington Jr.'s 'Spenser and Alexander Neckam' in *Studies in Philology*, xxii (1925). 222–5.

Neckam, according to one story, was born at St. Albans on 13 Sept. 1157 and had as foster-brother for a time the young Prince Richard.[6] His mother may have been the

[1] B.M. MS. Harley 3868, fo. 19*b* ; P.R.O. ancient deed, D. L. 273 ; *Great Register of Lichfield Cathedral* (Salt Archaeol. Soc.), ed. H. E. Savage, p. 205.

[2] B.M. MS. Cotton, Vesp. E. xxiv, fo. 26*b*.

[3] *Ibid.* ; B.M. MS. Cotton, Vesp. E. xx, fo. 42, according to Le Neve, ii. 391 ; B.M. MS. Cotton, Calig. A. xiii ; B.M. Harley Ch. 83, A. 43 ; *Great Register*, pp. 178, 343 ; Bodl. Lib. MS. Ashmole 1527, fo. 40.

[4] *C.P.R.*, 1232–47, p. 116.

[5] *Great Register*, p. 261 ; Felder, *Storia degli studi scientifici dell' ordine francescano dalla sua fondazione*, pp. 229–30.

[6] T. p. 371, *n.* ; C. L. Kingsford, *Grey Friars of London*, pp. 199–200.

[1] M. M. Davy, *Sermons universitaires parisiens de* 1230–31, p. 142 ; *Collectanea Franciscana*, i. 21.

[2] Klumper, *op. cit.* p. xiv ; for the opinion that his death was on 15 August see *Chronicon de Lanercost* (Bannatyne Club), ed. J. Stevenson, p. 53.

[3] Klumper, *op. cit.* pp. xiv, xviii.

[4] J. R. Green, *Short History of the English People*, illustrated ed. (New York, 1893), p. 287.

[5] T. pp. 29, 538 ; *D.N.B.* under Neckam. This article is largely revised from *E.H.R.* xlvii (1932). 260–8.

[6] T. p. 539, *n.* citing 'Jamesius, *Coll.* vii. 34 ex MS. quodam penes comit. Arundel.'

nurse, Odierna, to whom Richard I later gave a pension.[1] From the short autobiographical account at the end of his poem, 'Laus sapientie divine,' it is clear that he spent his boyhood and received his early schooling at St. Albans.[2] In some MSS. of his writings his name is given as Master Alexander of St. Albans.[3] There was a contemporary of the same name, a clerk of Bishop John of Norwich and of King John, Alexander 'dictus Cementarius,'[4] with whom Neckam has been confused.

The autobiographical account of Neckam's life carries us only through some years of study at Paris, where he had as one master William de Monte,[5] and then breaks off abruptly. The bibliographical tradition, based apparently upon this accident, that he spent much of his teaching career at Paris does not seem to be accurate. For a time he taught at Dunstable and while there he was summoned to teach at St. Albans by Abbot Warin, 1183–95. His successor at St. Albans was another Warin, nephew of both the abbot and prior, and is stated to have been like a brother to his uncles and to have exercised power with them as a triumvirate. He was probably master of the schools of St. Albans during a considerable portion of his uncle's term as abbot. Neckam's incumbency doubtless belongs to the early years of the abbot.[1] Neckam would still probably be in his twenties. Normally the arts were studied and taught before theology. It is probable that the dedication of the treatise 'De Motu Cordis' by Alfredus Anglicus [q.v.] belongs to this period of his early teaching, perhaps about 1180–95.

References which Tanner culled directly or indirectly from a sermon preached at the council of Basel and from William of Worcester indicate that Neckam was associated with Oxford,[2] and his writings confirm this. In his treatise 'Super Cantica Canticorum' Neckam says that at Oxford while reading in theology he held a class regularly upon the feast of the Conception of the Virgin Mary, but was afflicted with illness upon that day several years running.[3] By the advice of wise men he gave up holding lectures on that day and, as his illness ceased, he was converted to a belief in that holiday's importance. This experience became an 'exemplum' of the time.[4] His connexion with Oxford may also be deduced from the MSS. of a sermon appearing in one great collection of his sermons[5] and in another with the colophon 'Alexandri in primo adventus scolaribus Oxonie.'[6] The sermon reads very much like an elementary textbook on theology usually ascribed to Alan de l'Isle.[7]

Neckam had intended to join the Benedictines of St. Albans and wrote to the abbot 'Si vis veniam, sin autem, tu autem.' To this the abbot is alleged to have answered 'Si bonus es, venias. Si nequam, nequaquam.'[8] At which Neckam was so indignant that he joined the Austin canons

1 'Wiltescir'. Et Odierne nutrici R. vii li bl. in Cheppeham dum vixerit' (*Great Roll of the Pipe*, 10 *Ric.* I, Pipe Roll Soc., ed. D. M. Stenton, p. 65); *Chronica Rogeri de Honedene* (R.S.), ed. W. Stubbs, iii. p. xviii.

2 *De Naturis Rerum* (R.S.), ed. T. Wright, p. 503.

3 De Naturis Rerum, B.M. MS. Reg. 12, F. xiv, flyleaf; MS. Harley 3737, fo. 2; MS. Reg. 12, G. xi, fo. 4; 'Symbolum Athanasii,' MS. Harley 3133, fo. 100; 'Questiones,' Lambeth Palace MS. 421, fo. 124.

4 For the curious history of this man's reputation see F. M. Powicke, 'Alexander of St. Albans: a Literary Muddle,' in *Essays presented to Reginald Lane Poole*, pp. 246–60. Additional information about him appears in *E.H.R.* xlvii. 264–5. The 'dictus Cementarius' probably means that Mason was a surname, therefore the clerk was probably not the mason at Worcester (*ibid.* p. 265).

5 *De Naturis Rerum*, pp. 503, 460

1 *Gesta Abbatum Monasterii Sancti Albani* (R.S.), ed. H. T. Riley, i. 195–6.

2 T. pp. 538–9.

3 Passage published in *E.H.R.* xlvii. 261.

4 *Ibid.*

5 Bodl. Lib. MS. Wood empt. 13, fo. 3*b*.

6 Merton Coll. MS. 180, fo. 161.

7 Cf. excerpt in *E.H.R.* xlvii. 262 with Migne, *Pat. Lat.* ccx. cols. 617–84; this treatise is attributed to Neckam by a late hand in Cambridge Univ. Lib. MS. Gg. i. 5, as Esposito notices (*op. cit.* p. 465).

8 T. p. 539, from Boston of Bury, but see also *Gesta Abbatum Monasterii Sancti Albani*, i. 196.

at Cirencester. Peter of Blois wrote to Master Alexander of St. Albans, apparently after 1189, congratulating him upon entering a religious order.[1] His entrance was before 8 May 1203, the date of a papal letter of delegation in a dispute which was settled by a composition in Aug. 1205.[2] Twice in 1212 there are royal payments to messengers going to Master Alexander Nequam at Cirencester,[3] and on 30 Aug. 1213 he was sent with two others to inquire into the royal rights in the priory of Kenilworth.[4] He was evidently in the favour of both pope and king and was made abbot by the end of this year,[5] having the house's temporalities restored to him by a letter close of 19 May 1214.[6]

Of Neckam's career as abbot some evidence remains. He shared in a decision involving Kirkham priory[7] and apparently refused a request from King John, according to an *exemplum*.[8] In 1215 a series of documents shows him on his way to the fourth Lateran council. He was at court on 8, 9, and 15 July, receiving a patent to leave for the council on the last named day.[9] On 19 August the king ordered a boat for him,[10] on which he probably sailed soon after attesting a charter at Dover on 13 September.[11] Since the bishop of Worcester, Walter Gray, attests the same charter the tradition seems

[1] Migne, *Pat. Lat.* ccvii. cols. 404–8 ; not in the original collection of 1189 (*E.H.R.* xli, 1927. 51) ; verses on wine by these two men appear in Cambridge Univ. Lib. MS. Gg. vi. 42, fos. 223, 225*b*, 228 by Neckam, fo. 223 by Peter.

[2] Madox, *Formulare Anglicanum*, p. 25 ; the delegates were Robert, abbot of Malmesbury, Walter, prior of Lanthony, and Master Alexander of St. Albans, canon of Cirencester.

[3] Henry Cole, *Documents illustrative of English History*, pp. 242, 266.

[4] *Rot. Litt. Pat.* p. 103*b*.

[5] *Ann. Monast.* i. 63 ; ii. 289 ; iii. 40 ; iv. 409.

[6] *Rot. Litt. Claus.* i. 204*b*.

[7] Bodl. Lib. MS. Fairfax 7, fo. 97.

[8] B.M. MS. Harley 2851, fo. 184*b*.

[9] *Rot. Litt. Pat.* p. 149 ; *Rot. Chart.* p. 212*b* ; *Rot. Litt. Claus.* p. 220 ; *Rot. Litt. Pat.* p. 149.

[10] *Rot. Litt. Claus.* p. 227.

[11] *Rot. Chart.* p. 218*b*.

correct which would have him accompany Neckam to this council.[1] Neckam was apparently on good terms with this bishop's successor, since he died at Kempsey, an episcopal manor, and was buried in the cathedral of Worcester.[2] Neckam died 18 Feb. 1217[3] and by 27 April the king had approved his successor.[4] Money was left for the celebration of Neckam's anniversary.[5]

The mutilated effigy of Neckam is still in the north cloister of Worcester cathedral.[6] It has been described as :

> A cumbent statue of a priest, with a large tonsure, vested for the altar ; his beard was bushy, a thing not usual in these latter days. In his right hand is a staff of authority and in his left a book.[7]

The inscription upon his tomb read :

> Eclipsim patitur sapientia, sol sepelitur.
> Cui si par vnus, minus esset flebile funus.
> Vir bene discretus, et in omni more facetus.
> Dictus erat Nequam, vitam duxit tamen equam.[8]

Many stories circulated about this facetious man whose name was so easily punned upon. The stories of his refusal to enter St. Albans, of his rejection of a request by King John, and of his conversion to belief in the immaculate conception have been mentioned. The other Master Alexander of St. Albans is nicknamed by a chronicler Alexander Nequior.[9] The abbot exchanged couplets with Philip [prior ?] of Repingdon [q.v.].

[1] *D.N.B.* under Neckam.

[2] *Ann. Monast.* i. 63 ; ii. 289 ; iv. 409. William of Worcester has a note to the effect that the bishop of Worcester did not wish Neckam to be buried at Cirencester, so excommunicated him upon his return from Rome (J. Nasmith, *Itineraria Symonis Simeonis et Willelmi de Worcestre*, p. 279).

[3] J. K. Floyer, *Cat. of MSS., Worcester*, p. 92.

[4] *Rot. Litt. Claus.* p. 307*b*.

[5] *Register of Worcester Priory* (Camden Soc.), p. 107.

[6] J. K. Floyer, 'On a mutilated effigy in the cloisters of Worcester Cathedral,' in Assoc. Archit. Soc. *Reports*, xxiv (1898). 188–96.

[7] V. Green, *Hist. and Antiquities of Worcester*, i. 166.

[8] Bale, *Index*, p. 24.

[9] *Rogeri de Wendoveri Flores Historiarum* (R.S.), ed. H. G. Hewlett, ii. 53.

There are also stories about his testing of the humility of an abbess [1] and a monk by accusing them of pride or hypocrisy. In each case the accused puns upon Neckam's name for making such an unwarranted accusation and in each the accuser feels justified in the results.

Alexander, abbot of St. Augustine's, Canterbury.[2] For the history of the unjustified attribution of writings to this abbot see F. M. Powicke, 'Alexander of St. Albans: a Literary Muddle,' in *Essays presented to Reginald Lane Poole*, pp. 246–60.

Alexander of Stavensby was professor of theology at Toulouse and Bologna and bishop of Coventry and Lichfield.[3] Of his writings but one has survived apparently and should probably be classed as an official act rather than as literature :—

Advice to archdeacons : *inc.* 'Et sic vigilias noctis super.' This is in the form of a letter with the salutation, 'Universis archidiaconis per Coventrensem diœcesim constitutis, Alexander, permissione divina ejusdem minister ecclesæ humilis, salutem,' and has been published by Wilkins (*Concilia*, i. 640). The following may be a part of it :—

About vices, MS. N. xiv. 'Diuisiones vij Capitalium vitiorum cum speciebus et ramis et circumstanciis eorum sec. Mag. Alexandrum Episcopum Cestrie' (James, *Peterborough*, p. 76).

The other items mentioned by bibliographers, 'Commentarii super Psalterium,' 'Sermo ad Populum,' and 'Diversarum in Scholis Lecturarum,' seem to have as their source the following item :

> Hoc magister Alexander, vir honestus et verax super versu illo psalmi, 'Misericordia et veritas obviaverunt sibi,' in scola [scolis] dixit, et in suis postillis notavit. Hic fuit multo tempore doctor Bononie in theologia et post factus est episcopus in Anglia unde erat oriundus.

See B. M. Reichert's 'Fratris Gerardi de Fracheto Vite Fratrum' (p. 20) ; Balme and Lelardler's 'Cartulaire ou histoire diplomatique de Saint Dominique' (i. 511).

The quotation above which gives information about his postils also gives a 'résumé' of his life which can be checked in several particulars. The designation Alexander of Wendock is, however, not proved.[1] He was apparently generous to his family after he became bishop. His brother, Richard [q.v.], was first his clerk and then treasurer of Lichfield. A Master William of Stavensby, possibly a brother,[2] and a Gilbert described as his brother appear in his charters,[3] while a Ralph of Stavensby was canon of Lichfield in 1259.[4] An Anglo-Norman poem by an unidentified William dedicated to him probably shows that his generosity was not limited to his relatives.[5]

Master Alexander of Stavensby was teaching in the cathedral school of St. Stephen in Toulouse about 1215. To him St. Dominic went with several of his followers,[6] and doubtless was inspired with much of that interest in theological education which distinguished his order. From Toulouse he passed to Bologna, where, we have been told, he taught theology many years. The dominicans again came into touch with him, apparently in 1219.[7] He is probably the Master Alexander, doctor of theology, to whom a case was sub-delegated

1 Abbess-elect (J. T. Welter, *Thesaurus Exemplorum*, v. 86) ; B.M. Add. MS. 33956, fo. 83*b*. ; MS. Reg. D. vii, fo. 122*b*.

2 T. p. 29.

3 *Ibid*. pp. 690–1.

1 Balme and Lelardler, *op. cit.* i. 512.

2 B.M. Add. MS. 36869, p. 39 ; *Coucher Book of Whalley Abbey* (Chetham Soc.), ed. W. A. Hulton, pp. 143–4 ; H.M.C., *Rutland MSS.* iv. 167.

3 Bodl. Lib. MS. Ashmole 1527, fo. 93*b*.

4 *Great Register of Lichfield Cathedral*, ed. H. E. Savage (Salt Archaeol. Soc.), pp. 206, 319.

5 *Zeitschrift für Romanische Philologie*, iii (1879). 225 (see App. B). He may have endowed a hospital at Tarvin and the house of the grey friars at Lichfield (Tanner, *Notitia Monastica*, pp. 63, 501). But see *Ep. Grosseteste*, pp. 120–22, for evidence of his antipathy to the franciscans.

6 Quetif-Echard, i. 11.

7 Balme and Lelardler, *op. cit.* i. 511.

by the bishop of Padua and a doctor of canon law as delegates of the pope.[1] The document tells us that the case was heard in the home of Guidolino Marchesii 'in porta S. Petri' at Bologna on the last day of March 1223. Alexander was apparently living there at the time.[2] When he was chosen bishop the following year, and possibly for some time before this, he was 'clericus de camera domini Papæ.'[3] At the instance of the pope, Alexander was made bishop of Coventry to end the dispute occasioned by the irregular election of Geoffrey, prior of Coventry [q.v.]. He was ordained a priest and consecrated bishop shortly afterwards, on 14 Apr. 1224.[4] In England he led an apparently successful life as bishop, dying on 26 Dec. 1238.[5]

Alexander of Swereford, legal writer, see T. p. 30 and *D.N.B.* under Swereford.

Alfred Presbyter or Anglicus wrote a treatise, 'Practica artis musice,' *inc.* 'Licet mihi, ipsi in omni scientia': (a) Bamberg, MS. Ed. iv. 6, fos. 65–80 (13th–14th cent.), attributed to 'Amerus presbyter Anglicus'; (b) Trier, Seminar, MS. 44 (15th cent.), headed 'De practica artis musice magistri Amieri presbiteri'; (c) Bodl. Lib. MS. Bodley 77, fo. 138 (14th–15th cent.). The prologue says 'Ego Aluredus presbiter Anglicus in domo et familia venerabilis patris domini Octoboni sancti Adriani diaconi cardinalis, anno gracie 1271 mense Augusti compilavi.' This has been edited by M. P. Aubrey (*Cent motets du XIIIe siècle*). This information is from D. P. Blanchard ('Alfred le Musicien et Alfred le Philosophe,' in *Rassegna Gregoriana*, viii. 419–31); (d) MS. mentioned by Bale (*Index*, p. 28) is probably the same as (c); (e) Boston of Bury had seen another complete copy (Blanchard, *op. cit.* p. 426).

See also Lehmann (*Hist. Vierteljahrschrift*, xxvi, 1931. p. 608).[1]

Thus Alfred, an English priest, or more probably Alfred Presbiter (a name), an Englishman, wrote a compilation upon music in August 1271 while a member of the household of Cardinal Ottobon.

Alfredus Anglicus de Shareshull, canon of Lichfield, wrote on scientific subjects.[2] His most original work is 'De motu cordis,' which has been edited by C. Baeumker ('Des Alfred von Sareshel Schrift de motu cordis' in *Beitraege zur Gesch. der Phil. des Mittelalters*, xxiii. 1, 2). Baeumker also comments upon this work ('Die Stellung des Alfred von Sareshel . . .' in *Sitzungsberichte der Bayerischen Akademie der Wissenschaften, Phil.-phil. und hist. Klasse*, 1913, 9 abh.). One title is 'Liber magistri Alvredi de Sareshel ad magistrum magnum Alexandrum Nequam de motu cordis.'

Alfred translated at least two works from the Arabic:—

'De vegetalibus': (a) Barcelona, University Lib. MS. 7–2–6, with heading, 'Incipit liber de plantis quem Alveredus de arabico transtulit in latinum mittens ipsum magistro Rogero de Herfodia' (C. H. Haskins, *Studies in the History of Mediaeval Science*, p. 128); (b) Oxford, Balliol Coll. MS. 112, fos. 173*b*–4*b* (early 14th cent.), entitled 'Albredus super librum de plantis.'

'Liber de congelatis' of Avicenna, attached to the translation of Aristotle's 'Meteorology.' Grabmann[3] gives the following colophons of the piece: (a) Madrid, *Bibl. Nac.* MS. 1726, fo. 171, headed 'tria

[1] M. Sarti et M. Fattorini, *De Claris Archigymnasii Bononiensis Professoribus*, i. 626.

[2] 'In domo . . . in qua moratur infrascriptus magister Alexander.'

[3] 'Magister Alexander de Stanebi, clericus de camera domini Papæ' (*Ann. Monast.* ii. 299).

[4] H. Wharton, *Anglia Sacra*, i. 437–8, probably from B.M. MS. Cotton, Cleop. D. ix, fo. 73*b*; *Ann. Monast.* ii. 299.

[5] His seal is attached to a charter, P.R.O. ancient deed, B.S. 195.

[1] This item by courtesy of Miss Eleanor Rathbone.

[2] T. p. 37; *D.N.B.* under Alfred; cf. also *A.F.H.* xii (1919). 44–67.

[3] 'Mittelalterliche lateinische Aristotelesübersetzungen' in *Sitzungsberichte der Bayerischen Akademie* (1928), pp. 46–51.

ultima capitula transtulit Alfredus Anglicus de arabico in latinum' ; (b) MS. 9726, headed 'Tria ultima capitula transtulit Alvredus Anglicus Sarvalacensis'; (c) Nuremburg, Cod. Cent. v. 59, fo. 214 as above with name 'Aluredus Anglicus Sehrelensis.'

Alfred also wrote commentaries ; one upon the 'De vegetalibus' usually accompanies the translation, and is to be found alone in Vienna, Cod. lat. 2302, fos. 126*b*–128 (M. Grabmann, *op. cit.* under Simon of Faversham, p. 35). There is evidence of others :—

Meteorology : thought by A. Pelzer to be 'Une source inconnue de Roger Bacon' (*A.F.H.*, xii. 44–67). It is mentioned in glosses in MSS. (a) Escorial, MS. f. ii. 4, fos. 255–314*b* (Nuremberg, Cod. Cent. v. 59, fo. 201 ; Grabmann, *op. cit.* p. 50).

'Parva naturalia' (see Haskins, *op. cit.* p. 128). 'The library of Beauvais cathedral possessed in the seventeenth century "Alfredus Anglicus in Aristotelem de mundo et celo, de generatione et corruptione, de anima, de somno et vigilantia, de morte et vita, de colore celi"' (Omont, 'Recherches sur la bibliothèque de l'église cathédrale de Beauvais,' in *Mémoires de l'Academie des Inscriptions*, xl. 48).

Alfredus Anglicus was included by Roger Bacon among the outstanding, if ignorant, translators of the sciences [1] : like most of them he had visited Spain. He dedicated books to both Roger (Infans) of Hereford [q.v.] and to Alexander Neckam. His dedication to the latter probably fell within the period 1185–95.[2] We may suppose that he was a younger contemporary of these men.

A curious document gives a clue to the life of this rather important although obscure character. In 1252 in a dispute between Lenton priory and Lichfield a document of about 1220 was called in question because the chapter of Lichfield stated that various of its members had not been present at the earlier date and named among them 'magister Alueredus de Sarutehill [or Sarntehill] canonicus Lich.' [1] This is probably the translator. The place is apparently Shareshull near Lichfield, a village held by the Purcell family of the barony of Stafford in the forest of Cannock.[2] In view of the rarity of the name Alfred at this time and of the translator's connexion with Roger of Hereford it is possible to conjecture that he was the Master Alfred who was at Hereford in the second half of the 12th century.[3] However, this was probably an older man.[4]

[1] Haskins, *op. cit.* p. 129 ; *Fr. Rogeri Bacon Opera Inedita* (R.S.), ed. J. S. Brewer, p. 471.

[2] *Isis*, xviii (1932). 18–9.

Angier, canon of St. Frideswide, Oxford, was author of two translations into Anglo-Norman from Latin, which both appear in one MS., probably autograph, in which the author gives valuable data about himself :—

Dialogues of St. Gregory : B.N. fonds fr. MS. 24766, fos. 2–151 :

> Explicit opus manuum mearum quod compleui ego frater A subdiaconus sancte Frideswide servientium minimus, anno uerbi incarnati M CC XII mense XI ebdomada IIII feria VIa in uigilia Sancti Andree apostoli, anno conuersionis mee VII, generalis interdicti per Angliam (V).

This has been edited by T. Cloran (*The Dialogues of Gregory the Great translated into Anglo-Norman French by Angier*).

Life of St. Gregory the Great, by Johannes Diaconus : same MS., fos. 152–74, bearing a note 'Istud compleui conversionis mee anno IX sacerdotii II in vigilia Apostolorum Philippi et Jacobi' (*Dialogues*, p. 2). Upon this piece see P. Meyer, 'La vie de Saint Grégoire le Grand,' in *Romania*, xii (1883). 145–208.

Upon the philology of these pieces see Mildred K. Pope's 'Etude sur la langue de frère Angier.'

[1] B.M. MS. Harley 4799, fo. 62*b* ; certainly in the time of Ralph Neville, dean, 1214–22.

[2] *Collections for a Hist. of Staffordshire* (Salt Archaeol. Soc.), iv. 34, 107, 223, ; v. 178.

[3] *Isis*, xviii (1932). 19.

[4] There may have been more than one Master Alfred there.

From the data given by Angier certain events in his life may be dated with some accuracy. The one definite date is 29 Nov. 1212, upon which he finished his translation in the 'Dialogues.' This was in the seventh year of his conversion, that is, since his entrance into St. Frideswide. He completed the 'Life of St. Gregory' on 30 April of the ninth year of his conversion, that is, in either 1214 or 1215.[1] He was a subdeacon in 1212; he would normally be deacon for two years before entering the priesthood. Thus he probably finished the 'Life' on 30 Apr. 1215. The holy orders of deacon were probably conferred between December 1212 and April 1213 and of priest between December 1214 and April 1215. Sometime between 30 Apr. 1205 and 29 Nov. 1206 he entered St. Frideswide.

Arnald Fitzthedmar, London alderman and chronicler,[2] wrote 'Cronica maiorum et vicecomitum Londoniarum,' London, City Records, in MS. 'Liber de Antiquis Legibus.' This has been edited by T. Stapleton (Camden Soc.) and translated by H. Riley (*Chronicles of the Mayors and Sheriffs of London*). Extracts were edited by Pauli and Liebermann (*M.G.H.SS.* xxviii 527–47). Biographical data about Fitzthedmar and his family in the text as well as the facts that he was in charge of the 'scrinium' of London in 1270 and that he died shortly after the chronicle ceases suggest him as the author.

This biographical information [3] tells how his maternal grandparents, Arnald Grevingge and his wife Oda, had come to Canterbury from their home in Cologne to pray for children at the shrine of St. Thomas Becket. They stayed temporarily at London until two children, Thomas and Juliana, were born, and then at the death of Oda's mother decided to make London their permanent home, and became citizens. Thomas died on the third crusade. Juliana married Thedmar of Bremen and had six daughters and five sons. Four daughters married well in London. The four oldest sons had died by the time Arnald was twenty-four. He survived the whole family by some years. Before Arnald was born his mother dreamed that the baby would be heir to the family property. His birth occurred at the ninth hour on the vigil of St. Lawrence (9 August), 1201.

Arnald Fitzthedmar was an important man in the city by 1246, when he witnessed a charter, his name being ninth in a list of fifteen.[1] In 1257, 1259, and 1267 or 1268 he also witnessed charters which are extant.[2] In 1267–8 he appointed an attorney to represent him in a suit.[3] While, as these items show, he ranked among the great men of London, he retained his interest in the German merchants in the city. He appears on 1 Aug. 1251 as alderman of the Germans in a treaty with Lübeck.[4] Again between 6 Nov. 1259 and Michaelmas 1260 he bought, on behalf of the German merchants, of William son of William Reyner, the yearly rent of two shillings from a piece of land situated to the east of the Germans' guildhall.[5] In 1253 he was a chirographer of the exchequer of the Jews at London, and, with Roger Aliz and Master Moses, was asked by the justices how it happened that a certain transaction concerning a minor, named Peter, was permitted.[6] On 3 Apr.

[1] 1214 is the date usually given (*Dialogues*). The references suggested by Cloran to persons named Angericus do not seem very promising. A Master Angerius appears as a witness of several Durham documents of the time of Bertram, prior 1189–1212 (*Foederium Prioratus Dunelmensis*, Surtees Soc., ed. W. Greenwell, pp. 16, 22, 23, 132, 142, 199).

[2] T. p. 48; *D.N.B.* under Fitzthedmar.

[3] *De Antiquis Leg. Liber*, p. 238; MS. fo. 157.

[1] London, St. Paul's, A, box 1, no. 727.

[2] *Ibid.* A, box 15A, no. 286; box 9, no. 250; B.M. MS. Harley 4015, f. 94.

[3] P.R.O., Exchequer of pleas, plea roll 52 Hen. III (E. 13. 1*d*).

[4] Lappenberg, *Urkundliche Geschichte des Hansischen Stahlhofes zu London*, pp. 11, 12.

[5] *Ibid.* p. 13; he is called 'aldermannus mercatorum Alemannie in Angliam venientium' and may be a different Arnald Fitzthedmar.

[6] *Cal. of the Plea Rolls of the Exchequer of the Jews*, ed. J. M. Rigg, i. 128.

1266 he was appointed a guardian of the Jews for two years.[1]

An important business man, he also shared in the city's political transactions. In 1257, 1265, and 1273 he is named in royal documents among the city's representatives.[2] He was alderman for a considerable period (probably after 1249, since his name does not appear in a list of twenty aldermen of that year).[3] Besides being alderman of the Germans, he was also alderman of the ward in which lay the parish of St. George's, Eastcheap, in 1260–4.[4] He was allowed to retain his ward, name not mentioned, in 1257,[5] and was still alderman in 1272.[6] This brought heavy responsibilities especially in time of civic disturbance. In 1258 he was among several prominent London citizens restrained by royal writ from selling their holdings in London,[7] but he was fully restored to his rights in the following year.[8] He was relieved of part of heavy financial penalties inflicted on the citizens after the barons' wars.[9]

In 1270 he drew up a list of documents in the archives of London which were at that time in his custody.[10] He probably held this office until his death and made use of it to write his exceptional chronicle. His will was proved in the hustings' court in February 1275.[11] He was listed among the founders of the new church of the franciscans of London :

Dominus Arnaldus de Tedemar, ciuis Londonie, legauit in subsidium ecclesie predicte cli. sterlingorum, de quodam domo vendita in *Tamesestrete*, pro edificiis construendis, areis emendis et ampliandis, ac redditibus redimendis, qui eam tali modo vendendam legauit, ut certis porcionibus solutis, prout in testamento continetur, residuum cederet in usum fratrum minorum Londonie.[1]

[1] *C.P.R.*, 1258–66, p. 577.

[2] *De Antiquis Leg. Liber*, pp. 34, 165 ; *C.P.R.*, 1258–66, p. 457.

[3] *Cat. Ancient Deeds*, v. 55 ; Beaven, *Aldermen*, i. 373.

[4] *Ibid.* i. 205, Thomas fitz Richard (*sic*, probably Thomas), mayor.

[5] *De Antiquis Leg. Liber*, p. 37.

[6] B.M. Harley Ch. 56, D. 32, name of ward effaced.

[7] *C.Cl.R.*, 1256–59, p. 298.

[8] *De Antiquis Leg. Liber*, p. 43.

[9] *Ibid.* pp. 239–42.

[10] *Ibid.* p. 253.

[11] *Cal. Wills, Court of Husting*, ed. Sharpe, i. 22.

Baldred Bissait was the author of two known pieces,[2] 'Lamentatio pro morte regis [? Sancti] Davidis' : *inc.* 'Adeo secundum naturam virtus est' (*Johannis de Fordun Chronica gentis Scotorum*, Historians of Scotland, ed. Skene, i. pp. xxxv, 332) and 'Processus Baldredi Bisset contra figmenta malefici regis Angliae' (*ibid.* ii. 325, 394).

If the 'Lamentatio' was addressed to Henry III Bissait must have written it by 1272.[3] By 1284 he was official of the bishop of St. Andrews and a canon.[4] In the years 1289–92 he was a student, probably of canon law,[5] at Bologna. In 1300–1 he was a member of a commission to represent Scotland before Pope Boniface VIII, concerning the independence of the Scotch Church from England. At this time he wrote his 'Processus' in which he apparently created some legends of his own as well as refuted those of the English king.[6] He was rector of Kinghorn and in 1305 vicar general of the bishop of Bologna and was given jurisdiction over a dispute between the scholars and the canons regular of St. Saviour.[7]

Bartholomew Anglicus de Glanville, O.F.M., was the author of a famous work on science and possibly of some sermons.[8]

Sermons : A book of sermons entitled 'Sermonum Liber' (Strasburg, 1491) is attributed to him (*Index*, p. 42).

[1] C. L. Kingsford, *Grey Friars of London*, p. 164.

[2] T. p. 102 ; *D.N.B.* under Bissait.

[3] T. p. 102.

[4] *Historie Dunelmenses Tres* (Surtees Soc.), ed. J. Raine, pp. 68, xciii.

[5] M. Sarti et M. Fattorini, *De Claris Archigymnasii Bononiensis Professoribus*, i. 327, 328, 330 ('Baldredus,' 'Bixer,' 'Biseh,' 'Bixet,' 'Bistr scotus' ; called 'Mr.' in 1290).

[6] Skene, *Coronation Stone*, pp. 19–21.

[7] A. Allaria in *Dublin Review*, cxii (1893). 76.

[8] T. p. 326 ; *D.N.B.* under Glanville.

'De proprietatibus rerum' appears in very many MSS. and has been printed in early editions. The MSS. call the author 'Bartholomeus Anglicus de ordine fratrum minorum.' There is one unusual colophon, in the same hand as that of the text, of the early 14th century in MS. 67, fo. 203, Peterhouse, Cambridge :

> Expliciunt xix libri de proprietatibus siue de naturis rerum quos compilauit fr Bartholomeus de Glaunvile anglicus de ordine fratrum minorum in honore trinitatis indiuidue quos signis diligenter . . .

This note was read by Leland and from him passed into use by other bibliographers (*Collect.* iv. 24). Extracts from this treatise have been published (R. Steele, *Medieval Lore*). Other work upon him appears in A. E. Schoenbach's 'Des Bartholomaeus Anglicus Beschreibung Deutschlands gegen 1240' (*Mitteilungen des Instituts für österr. Geschichtsforschung*, xxvii, 1907. 64), Thomas Plassmann's 'Bartholomaeus Anglicus' (*A.F.H.* xii. 68–109), A. Schneider's 'Metaphysische Begriffe des Bartholomaeus Anglicus' (*Beiträge zur Gesch. der Phil. des Mittelalters.* Sup. i, 1913. 139–79), and G. E. Se Bajar's 'Bartholomaeus Anglicus and his Encyclopaedia,' (*Journal of English and Germanic Philology*, xix, 1920. 168–89).

The somewhat unusual Christian name, Bartholomew, was used in the Glanville family of Norfolk whose most prominent member was Ranulf de Glanville. A person of this name made a grant to Bromholme abbey in the mid-12th century.[1] From 1221 to 1233 there are references which might well be to the father of the friar. He and his wife, Isabel, were party to a fine in 1221.[2] In 1223 and 1229 he served as justiciar at Bury St. Edmunds [3] and again at Ipswich in 1229, 1230, and 1231.[4] His name occurs as a witness in several undated charters.[1] A Geoffrey son of Bartholomew Glanville appears in a fine of 1239–40.[2] If the friar came from this family he was born to great wealth. Of the friar himself little is known. Salimbene, writing about 1283, said that Bartholomew was a great clerk who read through the whole Bible 'cursorie' at Paris.[3] He was probably the Bartholomew Anglicus sent by the franciscans as teacher of theology from Paris to the province of Germany in 1231.[4] From these two statements it would seem that Bartholomew was a mature man in 1230. There are references to a house of Bartholomew the Englishman at Paris by December 1212 : [5] in view of the wealth of the Glanville family, of his age, and of his connexion with Paris it is possible that it was his house before he became a franciscan. His own work was probably completed or a revision edited about 1250.[6] One of the books of his library may remain.[7]

1 Bodl. Lib. MS. Eng. Hist. a. 2, fo. ix ; A. S. Napier and W. H. Stevenson, *Crawford collection of early charters*, pp. 32–3.

2 Walter Rye, *Short Calendar of the Feet of Fines for Norfolk*, p. 37.

3 *C.P.R.*, 1216–25, p. 480 ; *ibid.*, 1225–32, p. 298.

4 *Ibid.* 1225–32, pp. 306, 356, 444.

Bartholomew Cotton, monk of Norwich priory and chronicler,[8] wrote a History : (a) B.M. MS. Reg. 14, C. 1, fos. 80–137 ; (b) MS. Cotton, Nero C. v, fos. 160–280 ; and (c) Lambeth Palace MS. 188, fos. 175 *et seq.* (14th–15th cent.). The colophon of (a) (fo. 278) reads :

> Explicit tractatus de archiepiscopis, et episcopis Anglie, compilatus a fratre Bartholomeo de Cottun, monacho Norwycensi, anno gratie MCCXCII cum

1 B.M. MS. Harley 2110, fo. 68*b* ; MS. Cotton, Galba E. ii, fos. 58, 59*b*, 61 ; Dugdale, *Monasticon*, v. 63.

2 Rye, *op. cit.* p. 61.

3 *D.N.B.* ; *M.G.H.SS.* xxxii. 94.

4 *D.N.B.*, citing Wadding, *Annales Minorum*, ed. 1733, ii. 248 ; *Chronica Fratris Jordani*, ed. H. Boehmer, pp. 50, 54.

5 *Cartulaire de l'Eglise Notre-Dame de Paris*, ed. M. Guerard (Coll. de Docs. Inédits), i. 120 ; iii. 229.

6 He cites John of St. Giles and Richard Rufus as authorities (Plassmann, *op. cit.* p. 94) ; 1240 would probably be as suitable for the careers of these men.

7 Plassmann, *op. cit.* p. 87. Presented to the dominicans of Chartres by 'fratre Bartholomeo qui fuit Anglicus.' However, one would expect such a donor to have been also a dominican.

8 T. p. 202 ; *D.N.B.* under Cotton.

ii precedentibus libris scilicet primo de regibus Britonum, et secundo de regibus Anglie, Dacis, et Normannis; cuius anime propicietur Deus. Amen.

(c) continued to 1298, was published by H. Wharton (*Anglia Sacra*, i. 397–402). From (a), (b), and Wharton's print H. E. Luard published the better edition (*Bartholomæi de Cotton Historia Anglicana*, R.S.). Excerpts have been published in *M.G.H.SS.* xxviii. 604–21.

Compilation from Geoffrey of Monmouth: Cambridge, Corpus Christi Coll. MS. 460, fos. 86–151:

Incipiunt optime compilaciones de libro Britonis secundum ordinem alphabeti per Bartholomeum de Cottune anno domini M ducentesimo nonogesimo primo.

In 1283 Bartholomew drew up the camera roll for the prior of Norwich[1] and from this has been suspected of being 'master of the cellar.'[2] He began and probably completed his compilation of Geoffrey de Monmouth in 1291. In the following year he finished his first recension of his history which later he carried on to 1298. Probably he died on 8 October or 1 December.[3]

Beatrice of Kent, abbess of Lacock, was authoress of works now apparently lost. In an ancient catalogue of the Cottonian library an almost illegible item gives Beatrice as the author of a piece about Ela, countess of Salisbury, as well as of 'Epitaphia et versus ridiculi' (B.M. MS. Harley, 6018, fo. 9 and the last part of MS. Cotton Tiberius B. xiii). In T. Smith's Catalogue of 1696 an item reads:

Epistola Beatricis, S. Marie, et S. Benedicti de Lacoc, ministræ continens elogium foeminæ nobilissimæ et venerabilis matris Elæ quondam Abbatissæ et Comitissae de Warwike.[4]

The works of Beatrice are not mentioned in the Cottonian catalogue of 1706 (B.M. MS. Harley 694, fo. 15*b*). They may have already disappeared or have been burned in the fire of 1731. Tanner probably saw only Smith's catalogue and converted the two Elas into one, 'Elogium foeminae nobilissimae Elae comitissae de Warwick.'[1]

Ela, countess of Salisbury, founded Lacock and was its first abbess. She resigned apparently on 31 Dec. 1256[2] and died on 24 Aug. 1261. Beatrice of Kent succeeded her probably on 5 Apr. 1257[3] and was still abbess in May 1269.[4] The date of her death is not known, but probably it was after 1280.[5] By 1283 Alice was abbess.[6] Ela Longespee, countess of Warwick, the daughter of Ela, countess of Salisbury, made donations to Lacock in 1260,[7] 1283–4,[8] and doubtless at other times.

Beroul was the author of the Anglo-Norman poem upon St. Patrick's purgatory. For MSS. see Vising (*Anglo-Norman Language and Literature*, p. 53). The poem has been edited by Marianne Moerner (cf. also *N.E.MSS.* xxxiv. pt. 1, pp. 241–6). The earlier MS. (Cheltenham 4156) belongs to the second half of the 13th century and the language of the poem does not seem to be much earlier. Possibly Beroul is a corruption of Brykhulle.

Brykhulle was the author of the Anglo-Norman version of 'La geste de Blancheflour e de Florence,' Cheltenham MS. 25970 (cf. *Romania*, xxxvii. 224–34). William Banastre [q.v.] wrote an English version of the poem. Possibly the con-

1 W. Hudson, 'The Camera Roll, compiled by Bartholomew de Cotton,' in Norfolk and Norwich Archaeol. Soc. *Original Papers*, xix (1917). 268–313.
2 *Ibid.* p. 271.
3 Bodl. Lib. MS. Gough, Norfolk 24, fos. 6*b*, 7*b*.
4 P. 24.

1 *Bibliotheca*, p. 82.
2 Dugdale, *Monasticon*, vi. 502.
3 *Ibid.*; B.M. MS. Cotton, Vitell. A. viii. fo. 127*b*.
4 *Cat. Ancient Deeds*, iv. 418; *ibid.* iv. 419.
5 Not recorded in the ancient chronicle in the years before 1281; the folio containing the events of the years following this is badly burned.
6 *Cat. Ancient Deeds*, iv. 405; B.M. Add. ch. 28662.
7 *C.Ch.R.*, 1257–1300, p. 29.
8 P.R.O., Chancery inq. ad quod damnum, 11 Edw. I, C. 143, file 6, no. 21; *C.P.R.*, 1281–1292, p. 120.

junction of the names, Brykhulle and Banastre, may offer a clue.[1]

Cadogan, or Martin, bishop of Bangor,[2] is said by Leland to be the author of a 'Speculum Christianorum,' a collection of sermons, *inc.* 'Dominus in evangelio dixit, qui ex Deo.'

Cadogan was abbot of Alba Landa probably after 1203.[3] In the royal license to the canons of Bangor to elect a bishop is a hint that 'Caducan,' abbot of Alba Landa, would be a suitable person.[4] He is alleged to have been a brother of a prince of Galway.[5] This license of 13 Mar. 1215 was apparently acceded to within a month,[6] and Cadogan was consecrated on 16 June.[7] In 1235 he resigned as bishop [8] and joined the monks of Dore.[9] He died on 11 Apr. 1241.[10]

Chardry, Anglo-Norman poet, was author of three poems, 'Barlaam and Josaphat,' 'Seven Sleepers,' and 'Petit Plet.' All three are in B.M. MSS. Cotton, Caligula A. ix, and Oxford, Jesus Coll., 29, fos. 207*b*–57, while the third is also in Vatican, Reg. 1659 (14th cent.). They have been edited by J. Koch in 'Chardry's Josaphaz, Set Dormanz und Petit Plet' (Altfranz. Bibl. 1879). (For literature see Vising, pp. 44, 48.) Chardry probably lived about 1200, to judge from philologists' estimates.

Clement, O.P., was author of a sermon which remains in an early dominican collection, B.M. MS. Egerton 655, fo. 142*b*, *inc.* 'Alleluya, bonum est audire verbum' with a note above 'Sermo Fratris Clementis.'

Clement, almoner of Barnwell, was probably the author of the 'Liber Memorandorum Ecclesie de Bernewelle,' edited by J. W. Clark under that title. In telling of the house's struggle against Master Ralph de Cropper, the writer, after mentioning the presence of several persons of obviously inferior social status to an almoner, ends, 'Clemente elemosinario et aliis.' This is precisely the way that a clerk writing a document would include his own name. Moreover, the author knows the exact hour of the transaction (*ibid.* pp. 142–4). Again, in speaking of the almoner's activities, he does not give his name although the author is usually very careful to write both first and last names, and adds that :

> Elemosinarius vero intellexit quod daret pro inrotulacione dimidiam marcam, et ideo non multum curavit de recognicione (*ibid.* p. 170).

Finally, in speaking of the income of the almoner, 'infirmarer,' and 'refectorius,' he speaks in the first person (*ibid.* p. 290). Clark[1] says that the author was 'at least a canon of the house, and probably one who held some high office, for in no other way could he have had access to the documents and private matters with which he deals.'

The author was writing in 1295 and probably finished soon after 1 Aug. 1296.[2] He was a man bound up in the activities of his priory. His knowledge of canon law was very wide.[3] His personal information would seem to go back to 1266. With these he combined an ability to relate his story in an interesting fashion and a sense of

[1] Cf. *Modern Philology*, xxviii (1931). 259, for one conjecture ; a 'Mr. Elias de Brichulle' was probably a canon of Hereford in the latter half of the 13th century (Bodl. Lib. MS. Rawlinson B. 329, fo. 136*b*).

[2] T. p. 145. The best biography is by Browne Willis (*Survey of the Cathedral Church of Bangor*). Willis says Caducan is Welsh for Martin.

[3] Gerald of Wales calls the abbot of that date Peter (Davies, *De Invectionibus*, p. 177).

[4] Willis, *op. cit.* p. 186.

[5] 'Ut Cambrie Annales testantur' (C. de Visch, *Bibliotheca Scriptorum Sacri Ordinis Cisterciensis*, p. 54).

[6] Willis, *loc. cit.* ; *Rot. Litt. Pat.* p. 132*b*.

[7] 'Martinus abbas Blanch-Landiae consecratur in episcopum Bangorum xvi. die Junii' (*Ann. Monast.* iv. 404).

[8] Willis, *loc. cit.*

[9] *Ibid.* ; Madox, *Formulare Anglicanum*, p. 302 ; P.R.O., ancient deeds, B. 11297, 12582.

[10] *Ann. Monast.* i. 122.

[1] *Liber Memorandorum*, p. xiv.

[2] *Ibid.* pp. x, 282.

[3] Cf. Maitland's introduction.

humour.[1] The time of the incident related about the almoner is unknown. The episode about Ralph de Cropper probably occurred about 1280 or later.[2] By 1291 the almoner was John of Gretton.[3] Clement, if the author, had either resigned or been promoted.

Copland, disputant at Oxford *c.* 1282–90 (Little-Pelster, p. 77).

Daniel of Merlai,[4] parson of Flitcham, was the author of a well-known treatise, 'Philosophia.' For a bibliography of this writer, who properly belongs to the 12th century, see C. H. Haskins's 'Studies in the History of Mediaeval Science' (p. 126, *n.* 39). Some facts have been added to his life by Russell.[5] It should be noted that Northampton is given in one MS. as the place to which Daniel had intended to go, instead of Hereford as suggested in 'Isis' (*Archiv für die Geschichte der Naturwissenschaften*, ix, 1920. 47).

Edmund of Abingdon, theologian, was archbishop of Canterbury.[6] His most famous work was the 'Speculum Ecclesie' or 'Merure de Seinte Eglise.' This has been studied by H. W. Robbins (*Le Merure de Seinte Eglise by Saint Edmund of Pontigny*) who gives a list of MSS. of this work on pp. vi–xi and printed editions on p. xi. He believes that the French version was the original. An Anglo-Norman variant by Edmund on the 'Hours' is edited by M. Dominica Legge (*Modern Language Review*, xxix, 1934. 72–74), who has also described a hitherto unknown MS. of the 'Merure' (*ibid.* xxiii, 1928. 475).

Edmund's devotional literature also includes a considerable body of scattered pieces not always easily identified. The English Confession is to be found in B.M. MS. Reg. 18 A. x, fos. 60–1. 'Prayers' exist at Dublin, Trinity Coll. MS. 432 ; B.M. MS. Harley 206, fo. 14, and 211, fo. 146 ; Oxford, All Souls Coll. MS. 12, and MS. 22 ; and Bodl. Lib. MS. Bodley 57, fo. 6. The prayer, 'O. Intemerata' is older than Edmund (A. Wilmart, *Auteurs Spirituels et Textes Devotes du Moyen Age*, pp. 482–6). The sermons are to be found in B.M. MS. Cotton, Julius D. vi, fos. 127–56, 60, and MS. Harley 325, fos. 162*b*–163*b*.

Some letters of his are in the Bodleian Library (MS. Rawlinson B. 254, fo. 86 *et seq.*). The 'Summa Abendonensis' (B.M. MS. Reg. 9 E. xiv, fos. 83–117) is attributed to him by G. Lacombe (*Melanges Mandonnet, Bibliothèque Thomiste*, xiv. 163–81). He also wrote the 'Moralitates in Psalmos,' *inc.* 'Beatus vir. . . . Huiusmodi vir esse non patierit' (Worcester Cathedral, MS. Q. 67, fos. 128–37*b*), entitled 'Moralitates in Psalmos S. Edmundi archiepiscopi.' He is also said to have written a 'Commentaria in duodecim prophetas minores' (*Hist. Litt. de la France*, xviii. 269).

The best work upon the life of St. Edmund is in A. B. Emden's 'An Oxford Hall in Medieval Times.' Other recent works are M. R. Newbolt's 'Edmund Rich, Archbishop and Saint' (S.P.C.K.), Bernard Ward's 'St. Edmund, Archbishop of Canterbury,' Frances de Paravicini's 'Life of St. Edmund of Abingdon, Archbishop of Canterbury,' and Wilfrid Wallace's 'St. Edmund of Canterbury.' The chief sources for his life are the depositions prepared as a part of the process of canonization and contemporary biographies, based largely upon them. The relations of the several accounts are complicated and require careful study. Some depositions are edited by Martene and Durand (*Thesaurus Novus*, iii. 1775 *et seq.*), the originals being preserved in the treasury of Sens Cathedral.

[1] Cf. Maitland's introduction, pp. xiv–xv.

[2] Ralph became rector of Hyston between October 1257 and May 1258 (*C.E.P.R.* i. 51, 56), and kept up the struggle for more than twenty years.

[3] *Liber Memorandorum*, p. 209.

[4] T. p. 532 ; *D.N.B.* under Merlai.

[5] *Isis*, xviii. 22–3.

[6] T. p. 630 ; *D.N.B.* under Edmund. For advice about this biography I am indebted to Mr. A. B. Emden, principal of St. Edmund's Hall, Oxford.

The authorship of the biographies is still a problem. A. T. Baker has edited an Anglo-Norman life by Matthew Paris [q.v.] (*Romania*, lv, 1929. 332–81), and has identified the Latin biography by the same Matthew (in B.M. MS. Cotton, Julius D. v, fos. 123–57), confirming the identification proposed by F. de Paravicini. It is edited by Wallace (*op. cit.* pp. 543–88). H. W. C. Davis, in ' An Unpublished Life of Edmund Rich ' (*E.H.R.* xxii, 1907. 84–92), has compared the biography, written *c.* 1246–50, in Cambridge Univ. Lib. MS. Mm. iv. 6, Lambeth Palace MS. 135, and Oxford, Balliol Coll. MS. 226, fo. 48 *et seq.*, with the biography printed by Martene and Durand (*op. cit.*) and has suggested that both came from an archetype probably by Bertrand. A version appearing in an Auxerre MS. and B.M. Add. MS. 15264 is attributed by F. de Paravicini to Robert of Abingdon [q.v.]. The cistercian connexion (the MS. belonged to Mons Regalis) and the tradition of a ' Robert ' as author may mean that its author was Robert, austin canon, and later cistercian monk. He, with the monk, Eustace, Stephen the subdeacon, and Richard of Dunstable, wrote depositions, now forming a ' Quadrilogus ' (Oxford, Corpus Christi Coll. MS. 154). Other biographies are in Cambridge, St. John's Coll. MS. C. 12. 9, edited by Wallace (*op. cit.* pp. 589–612) ; Oxford, Corpus Christi Coll. MS. 375, and Bodl. Lib. MS. Fell 2 ; and B.M. MS. Faustina B. i, edited by Wallace (*op. cit.* pp. 613–24).

Edmund of Abingdon, the son of Reginald or Edward[1] and Mabel Rich, was born at Abingdon.[2] His parents were of moderate means.[3] The other children, all younger, were Robert [q.v.], Margaret, Alice, and possibly Nicholas.[4] Reginald entered Eynsham monastery and died shortly afterwards, apparently when the children were young. Mabel brought them up in the strictest religious practices. Edmund and Robert were sent off to Oxford at an early age and by the age of about twelve Edmund had devoted himself to the Blessed Virgin Mary.[1] Other stories of the time of his study at Oxford are given in the various biographies.[2] Mabel then sent the boys on to Paris,[3] where Edmund studied and ruled in arts many years.[4] His study was interrupted by the illness of his mother, whose bedside he reached in time to be with her at death.[5] After this he placed his sisters in the nunnery at Catesby,[6] Margaret becoming prioress and dying in 1257.[7] Alice is said to have died in 1270.[8]

Edmund was regent in arts (at Oxford ?) for six years.[9] During this time he seems to have founded the lady chapel, probably in St. Peter's in the East.[10] He turned to the study of theology after a dream in which his mother requested him to do so[11] and apparently went to Paris.[12] Returning to England he spent a year at Merton priory[13] before acceding to the general request to teach theology at Oxford.[14] After a number of years he ceased[15] because ' it seemed to him that the subtleties of disputation could not be pursued without a certain vainglory.'[16]

[1] Ward, *op. cit.* pp. 246–7.
[2] Wallace, *op. cit.* p. 543.
[3] *Ibid.* p. 595.
[4] *Ibid.* pp. 246–7 ; notice also a William, son of Reginald of Abingdon (*Cat. Ancient Deeds*, i. 217).

[1] *Chronicon de Lanercost* (Bannatyne Club), ed. J. Stevenson), p. 36.
[2] Emden, *op. cit.* chap. v.
[3] Wallace, *op. cit.* p. 593.
[4] *Ibid.* p. 603.
[5] *Ibid.* p. 594.
[6] *Ibid.* pp. 595–6 ; he gave a house to Catesby (*Cat. Ancient Deeds*, i. 217).
[7] *Chr. Maj.* v. 621, 642 ; *Ann. Monast.* iii. 156.
[8] Wallace, *op. cit.* p. 39.
[9] Emden, *op. cit.* p. 268 ; Bacon says that he first read the ' Liber Elenchorum ' at Oxford (*Fratris Rogeri Bacon Compendium studii theologiae*, B.S.F.S., ed. H. Rashdall, p. 34).
[10] Emden, *op. cit.* pp. 90–2.
[11] *Ibid.* p. 268.
[12] Wallace, *op. cit.* pp. 548, 600.
[13] *Ibid.* p. 88.
[14] *Ibid.* p. 552.
[15] *Ibid.* p. 553.
[16] Emden's translation (*op. cit.* p. 95).

He was apparently a rector in the time of a king who threatened him.[1] This, if accurate, must have been John. According to another story he was still lecturing on theology at Paris while treasurer of Salisbury.[2] Matthew Paris follows the story of Edmund's relinquishing his teaching by a statement about the crusading activities of the saint, probably in 1227.[3] He was at Oxford in 1221,[4] but became treasurer of Salisbury between 17 January[5] and 16 Aug. 1222. Documents showing him at Salisbury are dated 7 May 1223, 1225, 1226,[6] 3 Oct. 1227,[7] 7 July 1228,[8] 3 May 1231,[9] and 19 Oct. 1233.[10] He was elected archbishop of Canterbury on 4 Apr. 1234 and died on 16 Nov. 1240.

Thus the chronology of Edmund's life before 1221 is very uncertain. Wallace conjectures the following sequence: birth *c.* 1180; Paris 1195–1202; regent in arts, Oxford, 1202–8; Paris, as a student of theology, 1208–13; Merton 1213–14; regent in theology at Oxford 1214–22. This would make him sixty at death. Yet a contemporary says that he was not old at death.[11] Moreover, he performed a severe penance[12] for thirty-six years and for such a vow fourteen would seem a more fitting age than twenty-four. Possibly he was born later than 1180. He was about five feet, eleven and a half inches in height. 'His features were well proportioned: and there was about him a subtle and winning grace: his complexion was ruddy, much more so than is usual with men of serious temperament.'[1] He had a beard and an unsightly tooth.[2]

1 Wallace, *op. cit.* p. 103; Martene et Durand, *op. cit.* col. 1822.
2 See below under **Richard de Wicio.**
3 Wallace, *op. cit.* p. 553.
4 *Rot. Hugonis de Welles*, ii. 5.
5 *Sarum Chs. and Docs.* p. 121.
6 *Register of St. Osmund*, i. 330, 339; ii. 37, 60.
7 *Sarum Chs. and Docs.* p. 189.
8 *Ibid.* p. 200; *Reg. of St. Osmund* (R.S.), ii. 108.
9 *Ibid.* p. 24.
10 *Sarum Chs. and Docs.* p. 229; *C.Cl.R.*, 1227–31, pp. 490, 535; B.M. MS. Stowe 925, fo. 143*b*.
11 Wallace, *op. cit.* pp. 42, 611.
12 *Ibid.* p. 78.

Edmund of Hadenham,[3] if author of the chronicle attributed to him, was a monk of Rochester.

History to 1307: (a) B.M. MS. Cotton, Nero D. ii, fos. 1–199, anonymous; (b) MS. Cotton, Vesp. A. v, fos. 53–7, late extracts, which have been published by H. Wharton (*Anglia Sacra*, i. 341–55) and by H. R. Luard (*Flores Historiarum*, R.S.). The chronicle is that of Matthew of Westminster interspersed with notices relating to the history of Rochester. Wharton gives this about the chronicle's authorship:

> Pars secunda de rebus ecclesie Roffensis omnino habet. Chronicon istud, saltem additamenta Roffensis, Edmundo de Hadenham deberi ex Willelmi Lambardi collectaneis didici. In his enim multa ex chronico Roffensi Edmundi de Hadenham ad annum 1307, deducto proferuntur que cum nostris verbatim conveniunt (*op. cit.* i. p. xxxi).

Lambard gives a list of Kentish writers, which he says he got chiefly from Bale's catalogue, but Bale does not include Edmund of Hadenham (*Perambulation of Kent*, pp. 58–9). Edmund is not included in the 1826 edition of the 'Perambulation.'

See **John de Renham** below.

Elias of Dereham, canon of Salisbury, sculptor and architect, was also the author of a few lines of poetry (*Chr. Maj.* vi. 465). For accounts of his life see 'Speculum,' v (1930). 378–87 and literature given in the 'E.H.R.' xlviii (1933). 542–4. Mr. H. L. Honeyman has written on one detail of his architecture in 'Archeologia Aeliana,' 4th series, viii (1931). 119–48. Mr. Honeyman and Mr. J. C. Russell plan to continue their study of his life and work.

Elias of Trikingham[4] was a donor of books to whom a 13th century chronicle of Ramsey has been attributed (*Annales Eliæ de*

1 Wallace, *op. cit.* p. 94.
2 Ward, *op. cit.* p. 50; Wallace, *op. cit.* p. 94.
3 T. p. 368; *D.N.B.* under Hadenham.
4 T. p. 722.

Trickingham, ed. S. Pegge). In his Catalogue of the Lambeth library, M. R. James has disproved his authorship. For Elias see *C.E.P.R.* ii. 327 and B.M. Add. ch. 21756.

Eustace, monk of Christchurch, Canterbury, was the author of a deposition which formed a part of a 'Quadrilogus de vita Sancti Edmundi,' Oxford, Corpus Christi Coll. MS. 154, fos. 375–86, which bears a note :

Quadrilogus de vita et moribus S. Edmundi de Pounteney, archiepiscopi Cantuariensis per clericos suos cubiculariosque scriptus, videlicet, Ricardum de Dunstapel, ord. Praed., Stephanum, subdiaconum secretarium, Robertum, canon. regular S. August. postea ord. Cisterciensis et Eustachium monachum.

Canterbury retained a tradition of his disloyalty to his house and loyalty to Edmund in the struggle between the two.[1]

Everard of Gately was monk of Bury St. Edmunds, and Anglo-Norman writer [2] of the 'Miracles de la vierge' : (a) Bodl. Lib. MS. Rawlinson, poetry 241, fos. 77*b*–96*b* (early 14th cent.) ; (b) Cambridge Univ. Lib. MS. Ee. vi. 30, flyleaf (13th cent.). For these see Paul Meyer, 'Notice du MS. Rawlinson Poetry 241' (*Romania*, xxix, 1900. 27–47), and 'Les manuscrits français de Cambridge, II' (*ibid.* xv, 1886. 272–3).

The author, who translates a Latin original, gives his name in the introduction :

Everard de Gatelé ay noun ;
Moyne su de seint Eadmon.[3]

Paul Meyer conjectures that the monk lived in the second half of the 13th century and took his name from the parish of Gately near Fakenham in Norfolk.[4] Everard was a rather uncommon name : a man of this name appears as the first witness of a Bury charter.[5] A Master Everard attested a charter of Nicholas Fitzroger of Waltham.[1] On 13 May 1241 was issued an order to pay a Master Everard thirty shillings 'when he went to procure the seals of the abbots and priors.'[2] More evidence is needed before the monk can be identified as one of these.

Geoffrey of Aspal, pluralist, and commentator upon Aristotelian writings,[3] wrote :—

'Libri physicorum,' *inc.* 'Quoniam autem oportet : Queritur de unitate scientie naturalis.' (a) Oxford, Merton Coll. MS. 272, fos. 88–113, entitled 'Questiones in quatuor libros physicorum, secundum magistrum Galfridum de Haspyl' ; (b) Oxford, New Coll. MS. 285, fos. 111–58.

'De coelo et mundo,' of which the first folio is missing, *expl.* 'idem est sensibile et sensale,' Bodl. Lib. MS. Digby 55, fos. 1–21, colophon, 'Explicit liber quartus de coelo et mundo secundum ma. Gal. Haspalle.'

'De generatione et corruptione,' *inc.* 'Queritur an de generatione' : (a) Oxford, New Coll. MS. 285, fo. 36, with a note 'G. de Chaspal' ; (b) Durham Coll., seen by Leland (T. p. 53).

'Summa,' formerly at Ramsey abbey : 'Summa magistri Galfridi de Haspal in uno volumine' (T. Gottlieb, *Über Mittelalterliche Bibliotheken*, p. 172).

Possibly other treatises of the same character in these MSS. may be by Geoffrey. Merton 272 was probably once in the library of Thomas Markaunt (Cambridge Antiquarian Soc., *Proceedings*, octavo series, xxxiii, 1899. 79).

The biographical information about Geoffrey de Aspal increases rapidly toward the end of his life but is scarce for his early years. Yet he must have been an outstanding scholar to have written the works attributed to him. He was a fellow student of John Peckam,[4] probably at Oxford or Paris, but the locality of his teaching career is un-

1 Wallace, *Life of St. Edmund*, p. 292 ; 'Polistoire MS. del Eglise,' B.M. MS. Harley 636, fo. 207.

2 Vising, p. 53.

3 *Romania*, xxix. 37.

4 *Ibid.*

5 Cambridge Univ. Lib. MS. Ff. ii. 33, fo. 101*b* ; since the second witness, Master Peter of Lynn, was probably a clerk, we might expect that Everard was also.

1 H.M.C., *Various Collections*, vii. 238.

2 *C.L.R.*, 1240–5, p. 50.

3 T. p. 53.

4 *Reg. Peckham*, p. 937.

known. If he had letters from Innocent IV (1245–54) and Alexander IV licensing him to hold several benefices, he must have been already a pluralist by 1254. Possibly he was Geoffrey 'de Aosfetes,' vicar of Hunstanton, who received a dispensation in 1248.[1] The first evidence of him in England is at London on 7 May 1262 when he witnessed the charter of Richard de Clare granting Walter of Merton permission to vest the manors of Malden and Farleigh in the priory of Merton to support scholars at Oxford.[2] Another naturalist, John of Seckvill [q.v.], also attested this document. Two years later Geoffrey witnessed a charter of Gilbert de Clare to Merton,[3] being at the time a clerk in the Clare household.[4] In 1264 he was given the church of Tonge by the king and in 1265 the church of Staunton.[5] In 1265, 1266, and 1268 the king granted him further favours.[6] On 20 Sept. 1272 he was granted free warren on three demesne lands.[7]

Information about him increases suddenly in 1275: synchronizing, as it does, with Edward I's return, it may have been that Geoffrey had been with him abroad. In 1275 he was appointed judge in a case at York on 26 May,[8] given the custody of several manors of Roger le Bigod until their revenues should have paid their owner's debts, on 24 June,[9] and appointed a 'superior' on 24 October for the collection of the fifteenth in the counties of Essex and Hertford.[10] Probably in the same year a messenger was paid to carry letters from the king to Geoffrey at London.[1] On 2 Mar. 1276 he witnessed a document of Thomas of Clare,[2] was present in council at Michaelmas when judgment was given against Gilbert de Clare in his claim of the castle and borough of Bristol,[3] and in November was ordered to restore the Bigod manors. He received an acquittance for £300 in the following June,[4] and on 16 December was appointed an arbitrator between the men of Yarmouth and Bayonne.[5] By 1278 he was queen's chancellor,[6] and grants were made to him for expenses incurred in her name.[7]

In 1278 he witnessed the enrolment of several releases on 29 May,[8] wrote to John de Kirkby on 27 September about the election of the prior of St. Frideswide,[9] and was present at the Michaelmas parliament when King Alexander of Scotland performed his homage before Edward I.[10] In September also he received another and doubtless rich appointment, the archdeaconry of Dublin.[11] During the year he was a party to a fine for the manor of Sodbury, Gloucester.[12] He witnessed another enrolment of release on 6 Jan. 1279, apparently a very busy year for him.[13] He was cited for non-attendance at the visitation of Lichfield, where he was a canon, by Archbishop Peckam on 19 March.[14] He had quittance of common pleas in Surrey on 10 May[15] and five days later received a letter of pro-

[1] *C.E.P.R.* i. 456, 251; *Les Registres de Nicolas III*, ed. M. J. Gay, p. 68.

[2] *Merton Muniments* (Oxford Hist. Soc.), ed. P. S. Allen and H. W. Garrod, p. 8.

[3] J. Heywood, *Foundation Documents of Merton College*, p. 5.

[4] *C.P.R.*, 1258–66, p. 515.

[5] *Ibid.* pp. 345, 468.

[6] *Ibid.* p. 528; *ibid.*, 1266–72, p. 182; Close Rolls, 20 Sept. 1266.

[7] *C.Ch.R.*, 1257–1300, p. 184; P.R.O., Exchequer of pleas, plea roll, 1 Edw. I (E. 13/2) has three items about him: one as executor for Imbertus Pugeys.

[8] *C.P.R.*, 1272–81, p. 120.

[9] *C.F.R.*, 1272–1301, p. 50.

[10] *C.Cl.R.*, 1272–79, p. 250.

[1] P.R.O., Exchequer, K. R., various accounts (nuntii), 5 Edw. I, E. 101/308/3.

[2] *C.F.R.*, 1272–1301, p. 66.

[3] F. Palgrave, *Parliamentary Writs*, i. 6.

[4] *C.P.R.*, 1272–81, pp. 166, 170, 215.

[5] *Ibid.* p. 236.

[6] *C.E.P.R.* i. 417.

[7] P.R.O., Chancery Misc. 6 Edw. I, C. 47/4/1, fos. 8, 12, 38*b*.

[8] *C.Cl.R.*, 1272–9, pp. 497–9.

[9] P.R.O., ancient correspondence, S.C. 1, ix, no. 3.

[10] *C.Cl.R.*, 1272–9, p. 505.

[11] *C.P.R.*, 1272–81, pp. 277, 279.

[12] P.R.O., feet of fines, Gloucestershire, 6 Edw. I, no. 29; Exchequer of pleas, plea roll 8 Edw. I, E. 13/8, *m.* 31*b*.

[13] *C.Cl.R.*, 1272–9, p. 552.

[14] *Reg. Peckham*, p. 1064.

[15] *C.Cl.R.*, 1272–9, p. 564.

tection from the king, with whom he was evidently intending to travel beyond the seas.[1] Since he was nominated attorney by Roger le Bigod on 6 July, he probably did not go.[2] On 18 October he quit-claimed his lands at Denham and Brent Eleigh, Suffolk, to receive in return a yearly payment of £40 for life or for nine years, payable to his executors, in case he died earlier.[3] On 12 November he witnessed a document of Queen Eleanor, and in the spring of 1279 received the manor of 'Helleweford' from Robert Crevequer.[4]

In 1280 evidence of his widespread interests continues. On 12 March a royal order was issued concerning persons who broke into Geoffrey's house at Culing.[5] In a letter of 7 April to the king Archbishop Peckam states that he has excused Geoffrey for not attending his visitation.[6] On 20 July the constable of Windsor castle was ordered to allow Geoffrey six oaks for timber.[7] Three acknowledgments of debt come from the same year, all for considerable sums owed to Geoffrey.[8] On 23 Feb. 1281 there is a reference to an invasion of his property in his prebend of Wolverhampton,[9] an acknowledgment of another debt owed him on 11 May,[10] and on 10 June the grant of the custody of the hospital of St. Leonard, York.[11] On 2 June 1282 the king committed the manor of Hedendon to Geoffrey's care [12] and ordered him to restore it on

[1] *C.P.R.*, 1272–81, p. 316.

[2] *Ibid.* p. 319.

[3] *C.Cl.R.*, 1272–9, p. 576.

[4] *C.P.R.*, 1272–81, p. 333; Westminster abbey docs. nos. 4993, 5001, 5002, and Domesday, fo. 149.

[5] *C.P.R.*, 1272–81, p. 408.

[6] *Reg. Peckham*, i. 111, 392.

[7] *C.Cl.R.*, 1279–88, p. 27.

[8] *Ibid.* pp. 51, 52, 113, 115.

[9] *C.P.R.*, 1272–81, p. 469.

[10] *C.Cl.R.*, 1279–88, p. 124.

[11] *C.P.R.*, 1272–81, p. 443; on 1 July the king requested the bishop of Chichester not to molest his clerk Geoffrey de Aspale, who was on the king's business (*C.Cl.R.*, 1279–88, p. 129), and on 28 October granted the hospital of St. Leonard free warren in their demesne lands (*C.Ch.R.*, 1257–1300, p. 255).

[12] *C.F.R.*, 1279–88, p. 163; *C.P.R.*, 1281–92, p. 34.

30 August of the following year.[1] On 1 July 1282 Walter de la Linde promised that if Geoffrey was impleaded and lost his manor of 'Scaleby,' he would assign Geoffrey other lands worth as much.[2] In 1283 Geoffrey attested a charter of the queen on 2 July,[3] secured an acknowledgment of debt on 1 October,[4] and was appointed, with the bishop of Bath and Wells, custodian of Cumbermere abbey.[5] On 30 March of the same year he was appointed as vicar to the rectory of Tonge,[6] and in the autumn assigned to Bradstoke abbey his holding at North Lydiard, Wiltshire, for which the king requested an inquest to determine his rights.[7] The year 1284 saw him granted four bucks and eight does to stock a park [8] and impleaded in a number of suits over his various holdings.[9] The next year, 1285, he was given 24 bream from the Fosse as a royal gift,[10] shared in several suits as master of the hospital of St. Leonard,[11] and commenced the negotiations for the gift of his manor of 'Halgheford' to Westminster abbey which were completed early the following year.[12]

The gift to Westminster was granted for

[1] *C.Cl.R.*, 1272–1307, p. 189.

[2] *C.Cl.R.*, 1279–88, p. 192.

[3] *C.Ch.R.*, 1257–1300, p. 267.

[4] *C.Cl.R.*, 1279–88, p. 238.

[5] *C.P.R.*, 1281–92, p. 78.

[6] *Reg. Peckham*, iii, 1018.

[7] T. Phillips, *Abbreviation of the Pedes Finium*, p. 22; E. A. Fry, *Abstracts of the Inquisitions post mortem relating to Wiltshire*, p. 150; *Cal. Gen.* p. 336; *C.P.R.*, 1281–92, p. 107.

[8] *C.Cl.R.*, 1279–88, p. 279.

[9] P.R.O., Chancery, Inquis. ad quod damnum, 13 Edw. I, C. 143, file 8, no. 5; Exchequer of pleas, plea roll 13 Edw. I, E. 13/12, A. 15, 19*b*, 25*b*, 29*b*; *Cal. Inq. Post Mortem*, ii. 384; Bodl. Lib. MS. Rawlinson B. 455, fo. 23; P.R.O., Exchequer of pleas, plea roll 11 Edw. I, E. 13/11, *m.* 9*b*.

[10] *C.Cl.R.*, 1279–88, pp. 336, 407.

[11] B.M. MS. Cotton, Nero D. iii, fo. 58*b*.

[12] *C.P.R.*, 1281–92, p. 189; Westminster abbey, Liber Niger, fo. 109*b*; abbey muniments, nos. 5029, 4991; *Cal. Gen.* p. 361; Westminster muniments, nos. 23628, 49868; *Abstracts of charters in a chartulary of the Abbey of St. Peter, Westminster, in the possession of Samuel Bentley*, p. 59.

one clove of garlic yearly and a mass for his soul to be celebrated by two monks and chaplains. It was made just in time, for he lived but a few months longer. Documents show him preparing to cross the seas with the king in February and April 1286,[1] and his departure must have followed soon after. On 25 October he witnessed a royal charter [2] and passed away on the feast of St. Barnabas (11 June 1287).[3] His executors were his brother, John, Ralph de Crepping, Roger de Bikkerwick, and Robert de Bray.[4] His heir was his brother, Richard, then over fifty.[5] He seems to have had another brother, Roger, who had probably died earlier.[6] His will involved valuable property and resulted in litigation.[7] He was one of the outstanding pluralists of the 13th century, holding at his death at least fifteen livings.[8] These, with the additional income from manors and from royal business, probably made him a very wealthy man. Indeed, the archbishop, his former fellow student, John Peckam, reproved him for the scandal which the receipt of so much wealth from the queen was causing.[9]

Geoffrey, monk of Durham, sacrist of Coldingham, hagiographer, and historian,[10] wrote :—

'Vita Bartholomei Farnensis' (*d.* 1193), *inc.* prologue, 'Post transitum venerandi patris,' *inc.* text, 'Igitur Bartholomeus ex provincia Qwyteby': (a) Bodl. Lib. MS. Fairfax 6, fo. 199, which has been edited by T. Arnold (*Symeonis Monachi Opera Omnia*, R.S., i. 295–325); (b) Citeaux, MS. edited in 'Acta Sanctorum,' xxv. 714; (c) B.M. MS. Reg. 5 F. vii, fos. 108–18*b*, of which the salutation reads 'Beatissimis in Christo patribus et dominis Bertramo priori et coenobitis dunelmensibus Galfridus minimus eorum in domino conservis.'

'Vita beati Godrici,' *inc.* prologue, 'Petit a me, immo compellit me,' *inc.* text, 'Venerabilis confessor Domini Godricus': (a) Bodl. Lib. MS. Fairfax 6, fo. 185, edited in 'Acta Sanctorum,' xviii. 70; (b) B.M. MS. Reg. 5 F. vii, fos. 86–107*b* (13th cent.), which begins :

> Dilectis in Christo dominis Thome priori et fratribus in Finchale constitutis G. eorum in domino conservus eternam in Christo salutem . . . caritas vestra venerandi patris nostri Godrici diutinos succinte labores perstringere ut citius in compendio legentium votis occurrere possit quorum desiderio tractatus ille prolixior qui de virtutibus eius a Reginaldo monacho editus est; moram cum tedio fecerit.

Chronicle, 1152–1214: (a) York, dean and chapter, MS. XVI. I. 12, fos. 163*b*–180; (b) B.M. MS. Cotton, Titus A. ii, a part of which has been edited by H. Wharton (*Anglia Sacra*, i. 718–31); (c) Bodl. Lib. MS. Fairfax 6; and (d) Bodl. Lib. MS. Laud. 700, taken from (a), edited by James Raine (*Historie Dunelmensis Scriptores Tres*, Surtees Soc. pp. 3–31). In these MSS. Geoffrey is entitled sacrist of Coldingham.

Of Geoffrey's life but few things are known. He probably wrote the 'Vita Bartholomei Farnensis' shortly after the death of that saint in 1193. Since he addresses it to Bertram and fellow monks of Durham he was probably also a Durham monk. At the instance of Thomas, made prior of Finchale in 1196,[1] he wrote a succinct and abridged biography of St. Godric, using the very long life by Reginald

1 *C.P.R.*, 1281–92, pp. 224, 233, 245.
2 *Reg. Hamonis Hethe* (C.Y.S.), p. 14.
3 *Cal. Gen.* p. 380.
4 *Ibid.*
5 *Ibid.* p. 379.
6 *C.P.R.*, 1272–81, p. 268.
7 P.R.O., Exchequer of pleas, plea roll 15 Edw. I (E. 13/13), *mm.* 27, 28 (3), 35*b*, 41, 49*b*; plea roll 18 Edw. I (E. 13/14), *mm.* 3*b*, 9*b*; plea roll 19 Edw. I (E. 13/15), *m.* 9; plea roll 19 Edw. I (E. 13/16), *mm.* 2, 9*b*, 19; plea roll 20 Edw. I (E. 13/18), *mm.* 26*b*, 55; plea roll 21 Edw. I (E. 13/19), *mm.* 68*b*, 72; and plea roll 24 Edw. I (E. 13/21), *m.* 5*b*.
8 The list is given in Reg. Winchelsey, fo. 34 (Lambeth Palace, now being edited for C.Y.S. by Dr. Rose Graham); B.M. MS. Lansdowne 1040, fo. 506, mentioned by R. K. Richardson (*Archaeologia Aeliana*, ix (1916), 96), and in T. p. 53.
9 *Reg. Peckham*, p. 937.
10 T. p. 188; *D.N.B.* under Coldingham.

1 Raine, *op. cit.* p. 18.

as his source.[1] Doubtless, it was because he had written one saint's life already that Thomas and his monks at Finchale wished him to write this life of their saint while Geoffrey was probably still at Durham. Geoffrey may have carried one recension of his chronicle to 1200,[2] and then have continued it to 1214 later. He was probably the Geoffrey, seventeenth in a list of forty-one, who agreed to the election of Richard in 1215.[3]

Geoffrey, prior of Coventry,[4] was the author of a chronicle now apparently lost. Our information comes from William Dugdale (*Antiquities of Warwickshire*, 1656 ed., pp. 100, 105):

'Chron. MS. Galfr. Pr. de Cov.'

'*And touching its dedication and number of monks take this from an approved writer "Anno domini MXLIII constructum fuit monasterium Coventrense a memorandae recordationis duce* Leurico *et uxore ejus* Godiva; *dedicatumque eodem anno ab Archiepisc. Dorobernensis* Edzio, *quarto Non. Octob. post Pascha, Abbate* Lefwino *cum* XXIIII *monachis in eodem instituto*." '

'Chron. MS. Galfr. Pr. de Coventre.'

Lefwinus anno 1043.
Laurentius, obiit 4 Cal. Feb. Anno 1179 (25 Hen. 2)
Moyes, obiit 17 Cal. Aug. Anno 1198 (10 R. I.)
Joibertus, obiit 18 Cal. Julii, 1216 (18 Joh.)
Galfridus, electus 16 Cal. Aug. 1216.

The chronicle was concerned with the monastery of Coventry and may have been among the historical matters noted by Dugdale in the cartularies of Coventry (*Monasticon*, iii. 185). Excerpts give lists of bishops of Coventry to Alexander de Stavensby. 'Ex prefato codice MS. Miscelli Rob. Gloveri.' Bodl. Lib. MS. Ashmole, 860, fo. 3. 'Episcopi Lich. et Coventria ex registro Galfridi Prioris de Coventria.' Cf. Dugdale, *loc. cit.* note *a*, no. 12. The sworn testimonies, some by Geoffrey, concerning the elections of bishops of Coventry up to the time of Geoffrey remain in a roll (B.M. Cotton Ch., xiii. 26), but do not contain the information given above.

Geoffrey was a monk of Coventry before his promotion to prior in June or July 1216.[1] A charter of his to Dieulacres, a letter to Ralph Neville,[2] an attestation of an indenture of 1221 and an *inspeximus* of 25 Apr. 1223[3] remain as evidence of his activity as prior.[4] On 19 Aug. 1223 William de Cornhill, bishop of Coventry and Lichfield, died. At once a dispute arose between the monks of Coventry and the canons of Lichfield over the right to elect his successor.[5] The monks apparently elected Geoffrey before royal permission had been secured,[6] and the king evaded the issue by giving permission to those who were accustomed to elect. The question was carried before the archbishop, who refused to ratify Geoffrey's election.[7] Geoffrey carried the matter to the papal curia, which confirmed Langton's decision.[8] Honorius III ended the dispute by choosing Alexander of Stavensby [q.v.] on 16 Apr. 1224. Geoffrey apparently acted as bishop for a time, leaving some documents.[9] He witnessed a grant to Bishop Alexander in 1224 or 1225, and on 7 Jan. 1225 was with the delegation of Coventry which met the canons of Lichfield

[1] Arnold suggests that the biography of Godric was a work of Geoffrey's youth, and that he is that Geoffrey who appears near the end of a list of Durham monks about 1170. This does not seem probable (*Symeonis opera*, i. xl).

[2] 'Chronicon Dunolmense, de regibus ac pontificibus Northumbriorum, ab anno domini 634 vsque ad annum 1200. li. i. "Regnante apud Northanymbros Christianissimo rege." *Ex Ioanne Pullano Oxonij*' (Bale, *Index*, p. 490).

[3] *Rot. Chart.* p. 208.

[4] T. p. 304; *D.N.B.* under Geoffrey.

[1] *Anglia Sacra*, i. 464; 17 July according to Geoffrey's own statement above, but the royal assent to the election was given on 8 July; *Rot. Claus.* p. 276.

[2] P.R.O., ancient correspondence, S.C. i. vi, 107.

[3] B.M. Stowe Ch. 142; Jeayes, *Derbyshire Charters*, no. 2573.

[4] B.M. MS. Add. 36869, p. 40; *Great Register of Lichfield Cathedral*, ed. H. E. Savage (Salt Archaeolog. Soc.), p. 145.

[5] *Ann. Monast.* iii. 90.

[6] Langton's letter, dated on the vigil of St. Andrew (30 November) 1223, at Clerkenwell (Bodl. Lib. MS. Ashmole 1527, fo. 80).

[7] *Great Register*, pp. 220–4.

[8] *Ann. Monast.* iii. 90.

[9] B.M. MS. Harley 4799, fo. 39; Add. MS. 30311, fos. 65, 65*b*, 66*b*.

at Coventry and concluded an agreement to settle their dispute.[1]

Evidently the curia still trusted him, for he was named papal delegate on 5 May 1225 to enforce a demand upon St. Mary's of York, should that house not yield voluntarily.[2] A letter of protection of 4 Aug. 1227 stated that the prior had already set out for the curia.[3] Two years later he paid a fine to free himself from furnishing military service over seas.[4] He confirmed a charter of Bishop Alexander in June 1232 when two other writers, Ralph of Maidstone and Alexander of Hales, also were witnesses.[5] In the same year he resisted a visitation by his bishop [6] but lost when he carried his case to Rome. The following year he engaged in a quarrel with the abbot of St. Augustine's, Bristol.[7] In 1233 also he was delegated to hear a dispute between the religious houses of Westminster and Pershore.[8] He apparently died before 19 Sept. 1235 [9] although a chronicler records his death under the year 1236.[10]

Geoffrey of Cumeselz, see **Geoffrey of Eversley.**

Geoffrey of Eversley was the author of an 'Ars scribendi epistolas' to be found in Perugia municipal library, MS. 388 (13th cent.), bearing a MS. note, 'Gaufridus Anglicus hoc fecit opus in laudem domini Alphonsi illustris regis Castelle.' Extracts have been printed by C. V. Langlois ('Formulaires de Lettres du XIIe, du XIIIe, et du XIVe siècle') in *N.E.M.S.* xxxv (2), 427 *et seq.* This MS. gives the author's name as Gaufridus de 'Cumeselz,'

[1] *Great Register*, pp. 179, 199.
[2] *C.E.P.R.* i. 102.
[3] *C.P.R.*, 1225–32, p. 137.
[4] On 4 October (*C.Cl.R.*, 1227–31, p. 215).
[5] P.R.O., ancient deed, D.L. 273.
[6] *Ann. Monast.* i. 89 ; the matter of the visitation was kept up for a long time (*C.E.P.R.* i. 141, 151).
[7] *Ann. Monast.* i. 90.
[8] *C.E.P.R.* i. 134.
[9] The royal assent to the election of his successor was given on that date (*C.P.R.*, 1232–47, p. 118).
[10] *Ann. Monast.* i. 102.

but N. Denholm-Young has shown that this is probably a mistake for Eversley ('The Cursus in England,' in *Oxford Essays presented to H. E. Salter*, pp. 77–9). Among the students at Bologna in 1286 was a 'Mr. Thomaxius Comsal, anglicus' (M. Sarti et M. Fattorini, *De claris archigymnasii Bononiensis Professoribus*, p. 326).

Geoffrey of Eversley appears suddenly in 1276, a man with a married daughter, and in the favour of Edward I. Possibly he was the Geoffrey who shared in the redaction of papal documents in the time of Innocent IV (1244–56).[1] More probably he was the 'Mr. Geoffrey, dictus Legros,' professor of civil law, and rector of the church of 'Werchendune' in the diocese of London, who, at the instance of Prince Edward, was allowed to hold a plurality of benefices in 1262.[2] His name appears also in the 'Liber Vitæ' of Durham.[3]

Geoffrey appears in letters patent of 9 June 1276, as an envoy of the king of Castile, ready to return home.[4] His daughter receives a royal pardon for killing her husband.[5] In November of the same year, as a royal clerk, Geoffrey is going to Gascony on the king's business.[6] In 1277 he appears as the king's marshal.[7] In 1278 he received three ecclesiastical holdings, the most important of which was the rectory of Harrow.[8] He was probably at Rome as envoy for the king of Spain,[9] but was in England at Ascension, 1279.[10] Apparently in 1279 or 1280 he went to Spain with a colleague

[1] E. Berger, *Les Registres d'Innocent IV*, i. p. xv.
[2] J. Guireaud, *Les Registres d'Urbain IV*, iv. 37 ; the letters in the 'Ars' give such impossible initials for many names that little can be derived therefrom, so that Geoffrey's friend the vice-chancellor 'J' may belong to 1257–62 or 1273–74, or neither.
[3] Surtees Soc. fo. 57*b*.
[4] *C.P.R.*, 1272–81, p. 146.
[5] *Ibid.* p. 147.
[6] *Ibid.* p. 169.
[7] *Reg. Thome de Cantilupe* (C.Y.S.), p. 124.
[8] *C.P.R.*, 1272–81, pp. 260, 272, 276 ; *Reg. Peckham*, pp. 1014, 1061.
[9] *Reg. Peckham*, p. 1061.
[10] P.R.O., Exchequer of pleas, plea roll 8 Edw. I (E. 13/8), *mm.* 23, 28.

bearing instructions from Edward I.[1] On 11 Sept. 1280 Geoffrey received a licence for non-residence as he was going to mediate between France and Castile.[2] He also had safe conducts dated 8 July 1281, 23 April and 28 Sept. 1282.[3] He presented a vicar to Harrow in 1282, but died during the next year.[4] He was a notary of the king of Castile, a very important official, but the date is not known.[5]

Geoffrey of Romenal, precentor of Christchurch, Canterbury, may possibly have been the author of a volume of sermons.[6] These were seen by Bale, and described as 'ex officina eiusdem Reineri' (Wolfii) : 'Galfridus de Romenallis, scripsit, Sermones, li. i.' 'Si filius dei es, mitte te deorsum' (*Index*, p. 81 ; cf. also James, *A.L.C.D.* p. 80, no. 744 in Eastry's catalogue). This seems to be one of the books given by Geoffrey to his house, so possibly Bale saw evidence of ownership rather than of authorship.

Geoffrey seems to have entered Christchurch about 1255.[7] In 1270, as an official, he served the monastery well, although violently in the case of the sub-prior of Dover, Guido de Walda [q.v.].[8] He seems even to have made himself an official of the court of Canterbury after the death of Boniface.[9] In 1272 he turned over his task at Dover to Peter of Ickham [q.v.], apparently becoming third prior.[10] By 1275

[1] P.R.O., ancient correspondence, S.C. xiii, 149.

[2] *Reg. Peckham*, p. 1015 ; *Foedera*, i. pt. 2. 586.

[3] *C.P.R.*,1272–81, p. 448 ; *ibid.*,1281–92, pp.16, 36.

[4] *Reg. Peckham*, pp. 1017, 1018, 1059 ; his will is mentioned in P.R.O. Exchequer of pleas, plea roll 11 & 12 Edw. I (E. 13/11) *m.* 9.

[5] *Foedera*, i. pt. 2. 606, 620 ; he is not listed among the notaries of Castile of the time (E. S. Proctor, 'The Castilian Chancery during the reign of Alphonso X,' in *Oxford Essays presented to H. E. Salter*, pp. 115, 120–1).

[6] T. p. 307 ; Romney, Kent.

[7] Cf. App. C, below.

[8] Stubbs, *Chronicles of Gervase of Canterbury* (R.S.), ii. 251, 254, 255, 256.

[9] *Reg. Godfrey Giffard* (Worc. Hist. Soc.), i. 48.

[10] Lambeth Palace MS. 241, fos. 10*b*, 11 ; MS. 242, fo. 12.

he was precentor and the accounts for the next quarter of a century contain records of his travels and expenses.[1] In 1278 he went to Rome and to London in the following year.[2] He was in trouble in 1279 over the collection of papal monies.[3] 1282 saw him at Gloucester and 1283 at London and Northampton.[4] In 1288–9 he had trouble with his leg which required the attention of a surgeon, but he was present at the consecration of the bishop of Ely.[5] In 1292–3 upon the death of Archbishop John Peckham he was chosen one of four who were to elect his successor 'per viam compromissi.'[6] A letter of the prior to the precentor and other officers, written 5 February, remains.[7] Geoffrey and Robert de Saleya soon left for Rome to forward the matter of the election, bearing a letter of introduction from the prior, dated 23 Mar. 1293.[8] They must have remained there for several months, for the prior wrote to Geoffrey and his associates there as late as 26 October.[9] In 1294 he is mentioned in Winchelsea's register.[10] He received expenses in 1300,[11] but probably died in the following year.[12] Besides his books he made other gifts to his house.[13]

Geoffrey de Vinesauf was the author of grammatical and possibly of other pieces, mostly poetry.[14] Edmond Faral has edited the three grammatical treatises in his 'Les

[1] Lambeth MS. 242, fos. 28, 34, 39.

[2] *Ibid.* fos. 49, 53*b*.

[3] *Reg. Peckham*, pp. 58, 60.

[4] Lambeth MS. 242, fos. 76, 87*b*.

[5] *Ibid.* fos. 106, 110*b*, 111.

[6] B.M. Add. MS. 6159, fos. 144, 270 ; Geoffrey had been at the inhumation of the archbishop on 19 Dec. 1292 (*ibid.* fos. 136*b*, 267).

[7] *Ibid.* fo. 139*b*.

[8] *Ibid.* fo. 277.

[9] *Ibid.* fo. 278.

[10] T. p. 307.

[11] Lambeth MS. 242, fo. 216*b*.

[12] Cambridge Antiquarian Soc., *Proceedings*, octavo series, xxxiv. 175.

[13] John Dart, *Hist. and antiquities of the Cathedral Church of Canterbury*, pp. xviii, xix, xxii ; *Literae Cantuarienses*, ed. J. B. Sheppard, ii. 150.

[14] T. p. 736 ; *D.N.B.* under Vinsauf ; Faral, *op. cit.* pp. 15–33.

Arts poétiques de XIIe et du XIIIe Siècle' (pp. 194–327), and has also discussed Geoffrey's works (pp. 18–33). 'Poetria nova': this appears in very many MSS.: the following possess significant or unusual titles. (a) Cambridge, Corpus Christi Coll., MS. 406, fo. 102, 'Incipit liber magistri Galfridi ad Willelmum,' and then the verses beginning, 'Quem pape scripsi,' and entitled 'Item Willermi de Witam poetria nova ad Innocentium Papam tercium' (L. Delisle, *Le Cabinet des Manuscrits de la Bibliothèque Nationale*, ii, 524); (b) Glasgow Univ. Libr., Hunterian museum, MS. 511, has a second dedication to William of Ely: 'Anglice flos Elyense decus rarissime fenix'; (c) Holkham House, MS. 423, *inc.* 'Incipit poetria novella Galfredi Ysmolani,' in 13th-century hand; (d) B.M. Egerton MS. 2261, fo. 224, entitled 'Liber G. de artificio loquendi,' in which the table of contents says, 'artificiosa poesis magistri G. Londoniensis'; (e) Bib. Casanatense, MS. 211, fo. 68, 'Mittit hunc librum domino Guilielmo Remensi Episcopo commendans eum' (A. Wilmart, *Revue Bénédictine*, xli, 1929, 272, 273). For other MSS. see Denholm-Young (*Oxford Essays presented to H. E. Salter*, p. 93). Geoffrey also wrote 'Documentum' or 'Tria sunt circa,' *inc.* 'Tria sunt circa que cuiuslibet,' and 'Summa de Coloribus Rhetoricis,' *inc.* 'Ars semper eadem.'

In the Hunterian Library, MS. 511, Glasgow, is a 'Causa Magistri Gaufredi Vinesauf.' From this Faral secured some biographical information about Geoffrey (*op. cit.* p. 16).

Among the doubtful works Faral lists a treatise on viniculture. Prefixed to it are the following lines:

Palladii librum breviatum per Godefridum,
Accipe cura volens rustica rura colens
Pallidium [*sic*] tantum non hic sequor aut Gallienum
Pingitur et cespis floribus iste meis.
((a) B.M. Add. MS. 18752, fo. 164.)

The author calls himself 'Bononiensis' (fo. 170*b*); (b) Cambridge, Gonville and Caius Coll. MS. 200, fo. 140, of which the 'explicit' is 'Expl. tract. Mag. G. de plantacione arborum et conservacione fructuum.'

Faral also believes that Geoffrey may be the author of a group of poems in B.N. MS. 15157, fos. 35–70 (*op. cit.* pp. 24–7), but see below under **Nicholas of Rivaulx.**

Certain information is derived from the 'Causa.' Geoffrey had studied at Paris, and was teaching at a place called Hampton, probably Northampton.[1] Here he was driven out by one Robert, a former fellow student at Paris. He had been condemned by a Bishop Adam (of St. Asaph, 1175–81)[2] and was appealing to the successor of St. Thomas (Richard, 1175–84). Geoffrey's verses were already in the library of the monastery of Rochester by 1202.[3] He wrote his very famous work, 'Poetria Nova,' after the death of Richard in 1199. If he sent a copy to William, archbishop of Reims, it was written before the prelate's death in 1202.[4] The 'Poetria Nova' is cited by Gervase of Melcheley before 1216.[5] The same dedication is addressed in a MS. to William de Wrotham, identified as one of two important men in King John's navy.[6] A second dedication was written for William of Ely, another important royal official. There is thus something to be said for the tradition that Geoffrey was John's clerk or notary.[7]

The MS. colophons make it clear that the grammarian was called either Anglicus

[1] Faral suggests Wolverhampton, but no school is known to have been there (*op. cit.* p. 17); Hampton for Wolverhampton is unlikely, since the full name is given by Ralph of Coggeshal (*Chronicon*, R.S., ed. J. Stevenson, p. 160); for Northampton see **Daniel of Merlai,** below.

[2] So Faral suggests (*op. cit.* p. 17).

[3] 'Versus M. Ge. Vinisalvi' follows 'Vita Sancte Marie Egiptiace' (*Archæologia Cantiana*, iii. 57).

[4] Wilmart, *op. cit.* p. 272; *Haskins Anniversary Essays*, p. 365.

[5] Before the death of Innocent III.

[6] *Archæologia Cantiana*, xii (1878). 310–4; *E.H.R.* xl (1925). 570–9.

[7] 'Magister Gaufridus notarius regis Anglie' (Erfurt, Amplon. MS. Fol. 50, fo. 1).

or de Vino Salvo. One MS., quoted above, calls him Londoniensis, while another gives him the name 'Ysmolanus,' apparently on good authority, which may stand for Imola in Italy. The treatise or commentary upon Palladius' work on viticulture was written by one called 'Bononiensis,' and Imola is not very far from Bologna. If Geoffrey de Vino Salvo got his name, as bibliographical tradition would have it, from writing this treatise the conjecture that Geoffrey was of an Italian family from the district of Imola or Bologna which had settled in London, like the well-known Bocointe family, is worth consideration.

Gerald du Barri or Gerald of Wales[1] was the archdeacon of Brecknock, many of whose works have been edited under the title 'Giraldi Cambrensis Opera' for the Rolls Series. An edition of the 'De Invectionibus' based upon a Vatican MS. (MS. Reg. 470), by W. S. Davies, is in 'Y Cymmrodor,' xxx (1920). 1–238. Davies has also described the recently found 'Speculum Duorum' (*Archaeologia Cambrensis*, lxxxiii, 1928). 111–34. Ancient MS. catalogues yield a few references: Leicester, St. Mary de Pré, possessed 'Giraldus de instructione principum,' and 'Geraldus in speculo' (John Nichols, *Hist. and Antiquities of Leicestershire*, i. 102, 104); and Winchester, St. Mary's Coll., possessed the 'Itinerarium et Giraldi Cambrensis tractatus de laudabilibus Britannie et Wallie.' In his book, 'Gerald the Welshman,' Henry Owen has given a description of Gerald's books. A very interesting sketch by F. M. Powicke, entitled 'Gerald of Wales,' is in the 'Bulletin' of the John Rylands Library (xii, 1928. 389–410).

Both Owen and Powicke have concentrated upon the 12th-century phases of Gerald's life, before 1203 when he gave up his fight to be consecrated archbishop of St. David's. For the last two decades of his life the chief source is the 'Speculum Duorum.' Gerald resigned his archdeaconry and a prebend of Mathry in favour of his nephew, Gerald Fitz-Philip, who later opposed him.[1] However, Gerald reserved the right to administer them himself. He went to Ireland after this.[2] Shortly after the death of Archbishop Hubert in 1205 he promised never to raise the question of the supremacy of St. David's again.[3] Probably this concession was the price of permission to visit Rome again. This trip was made to satisfy his conscience.[4]

Gerald had returned by 1207. After the council of Oxford in February of that year King John suggested that he should raise the question of St. David's again to embarrass Archbishop Stephen Langton.[5] This Gerald refused to do, but he seems to have remained on good terms with his king for several years. He presented John with a third edition of his 'Conquest of Ireland' after the death of Walter Map [q.v.] probably about 1210.[6] He was in Wales for a time and then returned to Lincoln.[7] He wrote the biographies of the two Lincoln saints, Remi and Hugh, about the time that he was sixty, 1207.[8] About 1208–9 he wrote his 'Speculum Duorum.'[9] He kept his eye upon affairs at St. David's and was displeased when he was passed over in the election of 1215.[10] Possibly this slight caused him to go over to the side of Langton. He dedicated his last edition of the 'Itinerarium Kambriæ' to the archbishop and wrote his 'Dialogus de iure et statu Menevensis Ecclesiæ' for his instruction.[11] He even sided

[1] T. p. 323; *D.N.B.* under Giraldus.

[1] *Opera* (R.S.) ed. J. S. Brewer, i. 398; iii. 352; Davies, *Speculum Duorum*, pp. 113–4.

[2] Davies, *op. cit.* p. 115.

[3] Canterbury MSS. Reg. A, fo. 73*b*, no. 213.

[4] Davies, *op. cit.* p. 117; *Opera*, i. 137, 138, 139; iii. 338.

[5] *Opera*, i. 151.

[6] Owen, *op. cit.* p. 47.

[7] Davies, *op. cit.* p. 119.

[8] *Opera*, iii. 373; the text says 'about seventy,' but sixty is the obvious meaning.

[9] Davies, *op. cit.* p. 119.

[10] *Opera*, iii. 119, 133, 361.

[11] Owen, *op. cit.* pp. 55, 75, 123; *Opera*, iii. 101.

with Prince Louis, writing a poem on his landing [1] and composing his 'De principis institutione' for him, whose father and grandfather were the author's heroes.[2] After he was seventy, in 1217, he wrote his 'Speculum Ecclesie' and a volume 'De Ecclesiasticis Ordinibus.' [3] His letter to Hereford is his latest writing which can be dated.[4] Although he released his archdeaconry of Brecknock, he retained several livings. Bishop Geoffrey of St. David's attempted to eject him from Tenby without success, probably in 1213.[5] The institution of a successor in the church of Chesterton, in the diocese of Lincoln, on account of the death of Gerald de Barri enables us to fix his death in the year 1223.[6]

Gervase, monk and sacristan of Canterbury, was the author of a history, 'Gesta Regum,' 'Actus Pontificum Cantuariensis Ecclesie,' and 'Mappa Mundi.' Since his career was primarily of the 12th century and his works have been well edited with an introduction which includes practically all of the known facts of his life, there seems little need to repeat that account given by William Stubbs (*Chronicle of Gervase of Canterbury*, R.S.). David Knowles has an article upon the last piece entitled, 'The Mappa Mundi of Gervase of Canterbury' (*Downside Review*, xlviii, 1930. 237–47). It should be noted that Gervase is not listed as being among the monks in exile.[7] For continuations of his work see William of Dover and Guido de Walda.

Gervase of Melcheley was a grammarian and poet.[8] His longest work is 'De arte versificatoria et modo dictandi,' *inc.* 'Armata est majorum petitio': (a) Oxford, Balliol Coll., MS. 263, fos. 153–76 (13th cent.), dedicated to 'Discreto suo Johanni Albo non tam socio quam magistro suus Gervasius de Saltu Lacteo hoc opusculum cum salute,' and concluded 'Explicit tractatus Gervasii de Saltu Lacteo de arte versificatoria et modo dictandi'; (b) Oxford, Balliol Coll., MS. 276, fos. 127–53*b* (15th cent.), beginning mutilated, starting at a point reached in the second column of MS. 263, fo. 154; (c) Glasgow Univ. Libr., Hunterian museum, MS. 511, no. 6 (MS. not foliated), fragment beginning, 'In componendis epistolis dubitatur' and ending, 'Hoc tamen ultimum non observavit Bernardus in prosa'; (d) B.M. MS. Arundel 52, fos. 108 *et seq.* (late 13th cent.); (e) MS. A. 18, formerly in Sion monastery library, 'Gervasius anglicus de arte dictandi' (Mary Bateson, *Catalogue of Syon Monastery, Isleworth*, p. xxix).

Life of Stephen Langton. References to this occur in Matthew Paris' life of Langton [q.v.] in rubrics, 'secundum magistrum Gervasium de Melkeleie' and 'Qualiter archiepiscopus Stephanus mundavit in magna parte ab usuris Italiam et Franciam; secundum magistrum Gervasium de Melkeleie' (Liebermann, *Neues Archiv*, xviii, 326, 327, from B.M. MS. Cotton Vesp. B. xiii, fo. 133*b*).

Some poetry by Gervase has survived. Matthew Paris says:

> Unde non sine ratione quidam magister Gervasius de Melckeleia, de eo [William Marshall] versus componens, et quasi ejus personam assumens, ait,
>
> "Sum quem Saturnum sibi sensit Hybernia, solem
> "Anglia, Mercurium Normannia, Gallia Martem."
>
> (*Chr. Maj.* iv. 492–3.)

Following his 'De Arte Versificatoria' in Balliol Coll. MS. 276, fos. 153*b*–4*b* are verses addressed to a Bishop John of Norwich following the death of his predecessor, also named John, *inc.* 'Magnus Alexander bellorum sepe procellas,' entitled 'Sequuntur versus transmissi ad episcopum Norwycensem.' Gervase quotes from this poem in his treatise (fos. 128–9). Another verse to the bishop of Norwich appears in the Glasgow

[1] Davies, *op. cit.* p. 133.
[2] Owen, *op. cit.* p. 134.
[3] *Opera*, i. 415; iii. 373.
[4] Davies, *op. cit.* p. 132.
[5] *Ibid.* p. 121.
[6] *Rot. H. de Welles*, ii. 9.
[7] Cambridge Antiquarian Society, *Proceedings*, octavo series, xxxiv (1902). 172.
[8] T. pp. 313, 314; Faral, *Les arts poétiques*, pp. 34–7.

MS., last item, *inc.* 'Parmenidis rupes Socratis lira, silva Platonis.' The only evidence of authorship lies in the fact that both follow works by Gervase.

Gervase explains in his treatise that his name is in English 'Melclege' or in Latin 'Melcleia,' which can be interpreted 'Lactis saltus' or 'saltus lacteus.'[1] He is thought to have come from the Hertford family of Melcheleys of Standon who held of the earl of Clare.[2] In an example of the address to be employed by a vassal to his lord, he uses the titles of the earl of Clare as an illustration.[3]

If Gervase wrote the verse to John Gray, bishop of Norwich, shortly after the death of John of Oxford, his predecessor, in 1200, he must already have been fairly mature.[4] In view of Gervase's supplying Matthew Paris with information about Langton's career on the continent about 1214, it has been suggested that he was the archbishop's clerk, 'G.,' sent to Rome in that year by Langton.[5] About this time he wrote his long treatise, 'De arte versificatoria,' in which he speaks of 'noster Innocentius tertius' (*d.* 1216) and of the displeasure which the Emperor Otto IV expressed at the treaty of peace between John and Philip Augustus (1214).[6] This work is dedicated to John 'Albus,' possibly John Blund [q.v.], and shows that Gervase was teaching with him at the time, probably at either Paris or Oxford. He had been John's student

[1] Balliol Coll. MS. 263, fo. 165*b*.

[2] F. M. Powicke, *Stephen Langton*, p. 102, citing the *Book of Fees*, i. 123.

[3] 'Dilecto domino suo comite de Clare suus N. Ceptenu' (Balliol Coll. MS. 276, fo. 153).

[4] A Master Gervase appears frequently in witness lists of the first Bishop John, of Norwich (B.M. Cotton, roll. ii. 19 (12); MSS. Cotton, Tib. E. v, fo. 217; Tib. E. vi, fo. 136*b*; Titus C. viii, fo. 11; Harley 3697, fo. 40*b*; *Cartularium Monasterii Sancti Johannis Baptiste de Colecestria*, ed. S. A. Moore, p. 114. In the instances where more than the Christian name is given, the name is 'de Hemeling' or 'Hemelinget' (B.M. MSS. Cotton, Galba E. ii, fos. 51, 67; Harley 2110, fo. 66*b*) or 'filio Nicholai' (MS. Harley 2110, fo. 88*b*).

[5] Powicke, *op. cit.* p. 103.

[6] Balliol Coll. MS. 276, fo. 153.

apparently. In this treatise he quotes many authorities, Geoffrey de Vinsauf being among the most recent, and a Master Roger Devonensis the most intriguing.[1] Probably in 1219 he wrote the epitaph of William of Marshal. He appears on 1 May 1221 as a witness of a convention between William, abbot of St. Albans, and Robert, dean of London, shortly after the consecration of Eustace (Falconberg) as bishop of London.[2] Later he witnessed a grant by Godofridus de Lucy to Geoffrey de Lucy, dean of St. Paul's (1229–41).[3] Matthew Paris tells us that he was 'optimus astrologus.'[4]

Gervase of Tilbury, author of courtier and religious works,[5] wrote a 'Facetiarum Liber' for the young king, Henry III, son of Henry II of England, and also 'De Transitu B. Virginis,' probably in England. He wrote his 'Otia Imperialia' for Otto IV in 1211. However, since there is no evidence that he wrote in England in the 13th century and not much to be added to existing biographies of him, no detailed biography seems necessary. Ralph of Coggeshall [q.v.] has an anecdote about him about the year 1184.[6] A Master Gervase of Tilbury was a witness of a charter of Robert Fitzrobert de Leya to Canons Ashby of uncertain date.[7]

Gilbertus Anglicus, author of a number of medical tracts,[8] like most of the medical

[1] *Ibid.* fos. 127, 129, 136, 140, 149*b*.

[2] Feast of the apostles Philip and James (1 May) (B.M. MS. Cotton, Otho D. iii, fo. 78).

[3] St. Paul's MSS. box A, 17A, 261; MS. W.D. i, fo. xxi; the Master Gervase, chancellor of London, was Gervase of 'Hobregge.' Roger of Wendover, *Flores Hist.* ii. 169; B.M. MSS. Harley 4080, fo. 7*b*; Harley 2110, fos. 119, 120; Cotton, Vitell D. ix, fos. 30*b*, 37*b*, 106*b*; *C.E.P.R.* i. 59.

[4] *Hist. Angl.* ii. 232; *Chr. Maj.* iii. 43.

[5] T. p. 315; *D.N.B.* under Gervase.

[6] *Chronicon Anglicanum* (R.S.), ed. J. Stevenson, p. 122; J. R. Williams, 'William of the White Hands and Men of Letters,' in *Haskins Anniversary Essays*, p. 371.

[7] B.M. MS. Egerton 3033, fo. 2*b*.

[8] T. p. 474; *D.N.B.* under Gilbert. There is a life by Handerson (*Gilbertus Anglicus*) and another

writers of his time, has not been studied with much care. MSS. in fair numbers contain treatises ascribed to him, and his authorship of two of them seems certain, namely 'Compendium medicine,' published under this title at Lyons in 1510, and excerpted in translation by H. E. Handerson and Comment upon the 'De Urinis' of Giles of Corbeil.

Besides these two there are references which may be to parts of these or to separate works, such as the 'Practica' (Vienna, MS. 1634 (Univ. 338), fos. 35*b*–55, *inc.* 'In quibus consistit ars') and the 'Liber Morborum' (Vienna, MS. 2279, fos. 1–239*b*, *inc.* 'Liber morborum tam universalium,' *inc.* 'Morbis universalis propositi'). Possibly he was the author of a treatise upon the diseases of falcons (C. H. Haskins, *Studies in the History of Mediaeval Science*, p. 352).

In spite of the pre-eminence of his works Gilbertus Anglicus is somewhat of a mystery, partly because his writings have not been identified more accurately. In his 'Compendium,' which is frankly a compilation, he usually gives his authorities. These include Averroes, who died in 1198, and translations of whose work in Latin appeared later, and a certain Richard, probably Richard of Salerno of the late 12th century. Giles of Corbeil (*d. c.* 1220) was physician of Philip Augustus of France, so Gilbert's comment upon his 'De Urinis' could hardly have been written before 1200. The 'Compendium' is quoted by Theodoric, bishop of Cervia, about 1266 and by the 'Thesaurus Pauperum' about 1270.[1] It has been suggested that the surgical sections of the 'Compendium' come largely from the 'Rogerina' (written about 1230) of Roger of Parma, professor at Salerno, because of their verbal similarities.[2] Gilbert's failure to acknowledge his indebtedness may be due to the fact that he heard Roger's lectures or both heard the same lectures. In either case it would tend to show that Gilbert published his work before Roger. Probably Gilbert was writing in the first thirty years of the 13th century. He quotes the 'Magistri Salernitani' frequently. Probably he studied and taught there, although Paris has been suggested as the centre of his activity.[1]

John Bale, reading Coggeshall's description of the death of Hubert Walter, identified the archbishop's physician, Gilbert del Egle, with Gilbertus Anglicus.[2] There is much to be said for this as the name Gilbert was not common,[3] and the time, 1205, fits in well with the other information about him. Hubert's physician was no ordinary doctor, apparently outranking another physician, Hendricus de Afaite, who was also attending the dying archbishop. A charter which was probably made just before the prelate's death has as its witnesses Master Gilbertus de Aquila, Master Henry Lafaitie,[4] and Master Jordanus Fisicus.[5] The second and third may be foreign names, of physicians brought in especially to care for Hubert, yet the charter confirms what the chronicler suggests, that Gilbert outranked the others.

by J. F. Payne (*British Medical Journal*, ii, 1904. 1282–4; *Annals of Medical Hist.*, vii, 1935. 334–6.

[1] Payne, *op. cit.* p. 1904.

[2] Handerson, *op. cit.* p. 23.

[1] Payne suggests that a Rue Gilbert Langlois near the medical quarter indicates that Gilbert lived there (*loc. cit.*). The widow of a wealthy Gilbertus Anglicus died in Paris in or before 1263 (*Archives de l'hôtel-dieu de Paris*, ed. L. Brièle, Docs. Ined., no. 714).

[2] *Index*, p. 91; *R. de Coggeshall, Chronicon* (R.S.), ed. J. Stevenson, p. 157.

[3] A 'Mr. Gilbertus' was 'phisicus' of the king and received a gift of cloth and fur at the time of Henry III's sister's wedding in 1235 (P.R.O., chancery miscellanea bundle 3, no. 3); 'Gilbertus medicus' (P.R.O., Exchequer, Chancellor's Roll, 3 John, p. 4); 'Master Gilbert, medicus de Burch' (Cambridge Univ. Lib. MS. Add. 3020, fo. 79); for another Mr. Gilbert and his son Peter see D. M. Stenton's *Earliest Northamptonshire Assize Rolls*, 1202–3, p. 73; *Pipe Roll, 14 Hen. III*, ed. C. Robinson, p. 205. Peter seems to have died in 30 Hen. III (P.R.O., memoranda roll 18, *m.* 1); he held lands in Warwickshire and Leicestershire.

[4] *Cat. Ancient Deeds*, iv. 223; also ii. 25.

[5] Cambridge Univ. Lib. MS. Ll. ii. 15, fo. 7.

This Master Gilbert de Aquila appears in several instances in contemporary records. On 26 Jan. 1205, by a charter witnessed by Archbishop Hubert Walter, he was confirmed in his receipt of 100 shillings from the Earl of Leicester for his homage and service.[1] On 3 Mar. 1207 he was presented by the king to the church of Stithed, from the vacant archbishopric of Canterbury.[2] In the same year Gilbert gave the king 60 marks for holding the manor of 'Cherteham,' Kent, for an annual farm of £40. A group of very prominent men went surety for him, namely Robert de Vipont, Thomas Basset, Master Matthew Medicus, William de Cantilupe, Humphrey, archdeacon of Salisbury,[3] and Richard Marsh.[4] The king ordered that assistance be given to Gilbert on 16 Apr. 1208, in order that he might pay the debt thus incurred.[5] In 1209 a fee was paid to a messenger for carrying a royal letter to him.[6] These items suggest patronage of a rather liberal kind.[7] Gilbert de Aquila was among the clerks sent to Rome in 1214 for officiating during the interdict.[8]

Gilbert of Stratton, disputant at Oxford *c.* 1282–90 (Little-Pelster, p. 100).

Gilbert of Thornton, judge and reputed author of a compendium of Bracton (T. p. 712).

[1] *Rot. Chart.* p. 141.

[2] *Rot. Litt. Pat.* p. 59b; J. Hunter, *Rotuli Selecti,* p. 17.

[3] Tradition has it that Gilbert was of Salisbury (*B.M. Catalogue of Western MSS. in the old royal collections*, ii. 70).

[4] *Rotuli de Oblatis et Finibus,* ed. T. D. Hardy, p. 399.

[5] *Rot. Litt. Claus.* i. 112.

[6] *Rotuli de Liberate ac de Misis et Praestitis,* ed. T. D. Hardy, p. 139.

[7] The name Gilbert ran in two Aquila families. The more prominent one had very extensive feudal holdings. One Gilbert died about 1204 and was succeeded apparently by a son of the same name. The other was a 'parmentarius' of London (Westminster abbey muniments, nos. 13418, 13426; Domesday, fo. 560).

[8] *Ann. Monast.* iii. 40.

Gregory, hagiographer, probably wrote a metrical saint's life,[1] the 'Vita Sancte Katerine Virginis,' *inc.* 'Sepius in sexu fragili constantia mentem,' Bodl. Lib. MS. Laud 515, fos. 109–16*b*. Between this poem and the 'Life of St. Hugh,' by Henry of Avranches, occur these lines:

> Wintoniensis apex, flos cleri, gloria regni
> Inclita, pacato digneris sumere vulto
> Natum Gregorii sterili de pectore carmen
> Tantillum tanto quamvis devotio patri.

The 'Vita Merlini,' *inc.* 'Fatidici uatis rabiem musam que iocosam,' usually attributed to Geoffrey of Monmouth, addressed to a Bishop Robert of Lincoln, has an introduction which bears a distinct resemblance to the opening lines of the 'Vita Sancte Katerine Virginis.' For the 'Vita Merlini' see J. J. Parry in Univ. of Illinois, *Studies in Language and Literature,* x, 1925. no. 3, 1–138.

If the 'Vita Sancte Katerine Virginis,' dedicated to a bishop of Winchester, belongs to the early 13th century, the writer may have been the chaplain, Gregory, who attested several charters of Bishops Godfrey de Lucy and Peter des Roches.[2] If he wrote the 'Vita Merlini,' then he dedicated it to Bishop Robert Grosseteste at the time of his election in 1235.

Gregory, topographer, wrote a description of Rome entitled 'De Mirabilibus Urbis Romae,' Cambridge, St. Catherine's Coll., MS. L v 87, fos. 190–203 (written about 1300), rubric 'Incipit prologus magistri Gregorii de mirabilibus que Rome quondam fuerunt.' This MS. was copied by Ranulph Higden (*Polychronicon*, ed. C. Babington, R.S., i. 206, 212, 236), and has been published by G. M. Rushforth ('Magister Gregorius de Mirabilibus Urbis Romae. A New Description of Rome in the Twelfth Century,' in the *Journal of Roman Studies*, ix, 1919.

[1] Tanner attributes the Life of St. Hugh to Gregory (p. 343); *D.N.B.* under Gregory of Caerwent.

[2] *Chartulary of Winchester Cathedral,* ed. A. W. Goodman, pp. 6, 7, 41, 169, 199, 200.

14–48), and by M. R. James ('Magister Gregorius de Mirabilibus Romae,' in *E.H.R.* xxxii, 1917. 531–54).

The author mentions the Tor de' Conti, constructed in the first few years of the 13th century, was interested in law, had connexions with papal officials, and was contemptuous of pilgrim tales. He was returning to a place which the scribe could not make out, so left a blank space: it could hardly have been England since the scribe was probably English. He was writing at the instance of 'dominus Thomas' and 'magister Martinus' in what was probably a university.[1]

The names of these two masters, Gregory and Martin, a very unusual combination, turn up in the 'Liber Vitæ' of Durham.[2] Papal officials of both names appear in England in the first half of the 13th century. To Master Gregory, chancellor of the papal legate, Otto, the king granted on 8 May 1238

that he shall take by the hands of the guardian of the bishopric of Norwich, so long as the bishopric remains void and in the king's hands, 17 marks yearly, which he used to receive by grant of Th. sometime bishop of Norwich, as he took them in the bishop's time.[3]

A Master Martin, clerk of the papal camera, was apparently in England about 1236–8 [4] and may have been the Master Martin in England in and after 1245 whose activities roused the ire of Matthew Paris. There is one objection to assuming that this is Master Gregory the author with Master Martin of the papal camera and Dominus Thomas, bishop of Norwich, since Gregory, as Otto's chancellor, would doubtless have been in his entourage and Otto does not seem to have been in England while Thomas was bishop (1226–35). Nevertheless, since we are not certain that Gregory was Otto's chancellor before 1238 and the other coincidences point that way, it seems probable that he was the author of the description of Rome.

[1] *Journal of Roman Studies*, ix. 17–8.

[2] Surtees Soc. fo. 23.

[3] *C.P.R.*, 1232–47, p. 219.

[4] *C.Cl.R.*, 1234–7, p. 296; P.R.O., *Lists and Indexes*, xlix. 230; both references concern the church of Wotton in the diocese of Worcester.

Gregory of Caerwent,[1] monk of Gloucester, was the probable author of a chronicle devoted largely to obits and local history:—'Annales sui coenobii,' 682–1290: (a) MS. formerly at King's College, Cambridge, *inc.* 'Anno incarnationis domini 681. Regni Etheldredi regis Mertiorum,' described as 'Ex collegio Regis Cantabrigie' (Bale, *Index*, p. 99); (b) B.M. MS. Cotton, Vesp. A. v, fos. 195 *et seq.*, with the title written apparently in the hand of Robert Cotton, 'Collectanea Laurentii Noelli ex chronica Gregorij Caerguent Monachi Glocestria ab an° 682 ad annum 1290.' At the year 1237 is the sentence:

Gregorius de Kairwent recepit habitum monachalem in e s.p.c. ab H. Foliot abbate 4 kal. novemb'. qui huius libri huc vsque scripsit.

According to this information Gregory of Caerwent, probable author of the above chronicle, entered the monastery of St. Peter, Gloucester, on 29 Oct. 1237. The chronicle continues until 1290 or 1291, but it is doubtful whether the latter part is by him since his name does not appear in the very full list of monks who consented to the election of an abbot in the autumn of 1284.[2] Except for identity of name, there is nothing to connect him with a contemporary of that name who died at the papal curia in 1279,[3] and there is even less reason to connect him with Gregory, hagiographer [q.v.], sometimes called Gregory of Winchester.[4]

Gregory of Huntingdon, prior of Ramsey and donor of books, was possibly also an

[1] T. p. 343; *D.N.B.* under Gregory.

[2] *Historia et cartularium monasterii S. Petri Gloucestriæ*, ed. W. H. Hart (R.S.), iii. 26.

[3] *C.E.P.R.* i. 460; *Register of Bishop Godfrey Giffard*, ed. J. W. Willis Bund (Worcestershire Hist. Soc.), pp. 55, 56, 69, 81, 120; *Eynsham Cartulary*, ed. H. E. Salter, i. 28, 293; *Landboc sive Registrum Monasterii Beate Marie . . . de Winchelcumba*, ed. David Royce, i. 117; *Acta SS.* Oct. i. 545.

[4] As in T. p. 343 or the *D.N.B.*

author.[1] His position in the list of donors and the books chosen show that he belonged to the end of the 13th century. See the better list (T. p. 342) or a shorter list (*Chronicon Abbatiæ Rameseiensis*, R.S., ed. W. D. Macray, p. 365). Bale and Tanner give a list of books supposedly of his authorship together with the first lines : the books are probably comprehended in the list of his gifts (*Index*, p. 99 ; T. pp. 342–3*d*, *e*). The inclusion of the 'Imago mundi,' very widely known and probably much earlier, casts suspicion upon the entire list, which it seems dangerous, at the present stage of our knowledge, to attribute to him. With the exception of the 'Imago' all the books attributed to him by Bale are upon Latin or Greek subjects, while the donations show interest in Hebrew and law as well.

Gryffin, O.P., responsible for sermons at Oxford in 1292 and 1293 (Little-Pelster, p. 186).

Guido de Walda, monk of Canterbury, sub-prior and prior of Dover and chronicler, probably wrote the Continuation of Gervase of Canterbury, 1214–77 (Cambridge, Corpus Christi Coll. MS. 438). The author speaks of being sub-prior of Dover in 1270. He expresses interest in aliens, especially in Archbishop Boniface, and has the habit of calling the king Henry IV. He probably wrote the Annals of St. Martin's, Dover, 1249–70 (B.M. MS. Cotton, Julius D. v, fos. 30*b et seq.* ; the MS. is badly burned). This chronicle is characterized by the same features as the previous work, but has even more biographical details of the author. Certain changes in the two chronicles synchronize with events in Guido's life.

Guido de Walda [2] probably entered Christchurch, Canterbury, about 1218.[3] Two horses were bought for or of him in 1221.[1] He was included among the recalcitrant monks in 1239.[2] He was writing upon the continuation of Gervase of Canterbury before he went to Dover since the Dover items before 1249 are entered in the margin.[3] A note marked for insertion under 1249 tells of the visitation of Dover Priory by Archbishop Boniface 'in vigil. Palmarum' on 21 March when John, the prior, was suspended, and Walter 'de Cant.,' the sub-prior, was absolved from his office, which was then given to Guido 'eiusdem ecclesie monachum qui x annis postea stetit,' (fo. 30*b*). Guido was then sacrist of Canterbury.[4] In 1253 Guido became prior, his letter of profession to the archbishop being dated 16 February (fo. 31). On 9 Apr. 1260 he resigned from office (fo. 33*b*).[5] The reason is not given, but the general pressure on aliens may have been sufficient. Probably he returned to Canterbury and became almoner there (fo. 35*b*). On 31 Mar. 1262 Archbishop Boniface made another visitation at Dover and Guido was raised again to be sub-prior (fo. 35*b*). Probably at this time he was engaged on both chronicles. The MS. of the 'Annals of Dover' was probably in the possession of the priors of Dover (see William of Dover). The 'Annals' change at 1270. Probably Guido left them at Dover. In the Canterbury chronicle the author speaks in 1270 as sub-prior of Dover [6] : then, in the same year, the point of view changes and Robert of Canterbury is given that title.[7] This can be explained by the hypothesis that Guido was absolved again in this year and returned to Canterbury. Certainly he is not listed among the important Dover monks in 1272.[8] He continues the Canterbury chronicle to 1278, ending shortly after an account of the foundation of Dover priory.[9]

[1] T. p. 342–3 ; *D.N.B.* under Gregory.

[2] *Literae Cantuarienses*, ed. J. B. Sheppard (R.S.), iii. 377.

[3] Searle, Camb. Antiq. Soc., *Proceedings*, octavo series, xxxiv (1902). 172–96 ; cf. App. C.

[1] H.M.C., 5th Rep., App. p. 441.

[2] *Historical Works of Gervase of Canterbury* (R.S.), ed. W. Stubbs, ii. 144, 153.

[3] *Ibid.* ii., *passim.*

[4] *Ibid.* p. 204.

[5] *Ibid.* p. 211.

[6] *Ibid.* pp. 255, 256.

[7] *Ibid.* p. 259.

[8] Lambeth Palace MS. 241, fo. 11.

[9] *Hist. Works of Gervase of Canterbury*, ii. 286–9.

Probably he died soon afterwards as he must have been a very old man at the time.

H., prior of Bordesley, was the author of a hagiographical letter 'Miracles of a monk and subdean Adam,' Cambridge, Clare Coll. MS. 30, fo. xiii, headed 'Venerabili patri S. Dei gratia priori Wigorn. et sanctissimo conventui eiusdem ecclesie fr H dictus prior de Bordesle' and dated 1219.

H. de Mordon,[1] ? **O.P.,** was the author of a sermon, Bodl. Lib. MS. Laud Misc. 511, fo. 150, entitled 'Sermo fratris H de Mordon in die pentecostes,' *inc.* 'Repleti sunt omnes spiritu sancto. Quando festum alicuius magnatis debet commendari.' 'This Hugh de Mordon, probably a Dominican, is, so far as I know, quite unknown.' [2]

Haymo of Faversham, O.F.M., minister general of his order, was the author of liturgical literature.[3]

'Rubricae de Caeremoniis missae,' *inc.* 'Indutus planeta sacerdos,' Padua, Bibl. S. Anton. MS. 634, colophon, 'per Aymum Anglicum, qui fuit Minister generalis tertius in ordine atque confirmata in generali capitulo ipso presente A.D. 1239.' Little says 1239 should read 1240 (*F.S.O.* p. 806).

'Ceremoniale ord. min. vetustissimum' *inc.* 'Ad omnes horas canonicas' has been published (*A.F.H.* iii. 64–81). For MSS. and literature see *A.F.H.* iii. 56, 62 ; vii. 715. Haymo apparently had a hand in the revision of the breviary (*A.F.H.* xix. 785–97) :

Frater Haymo de Faversham, Anglicus, fuit V^{us} generalis et ministravit v. annis. Hic ex commissione Domini Innocentii Papæ IV. totum divinum officium cum novis rubricis ordinavit, quod a tota Romana curia et eam sequentibus est assumptum (*Mon. Fr.* i. 533).

The references to his commentary on the sentences and sermons mentioned by the bibliographers have not been checked. The questions on the logical works of Aristotle belong to Simon of Faversham [q.v.].

Haymo of Faversham was one of several famous masters who entered the franciscan order on 12 Apr. 1224,[1] and came over to England soon after.[2] Thus began a career which seems to have covered much territory and which has left for many years only tantalizing traces, chiefly in Eccleston's 'De adventu fratrum minorum.' He served as 'custos' for the house at Paris for a time.[3] In the next few years he seems to have lectured at Tours, Bologna and Padua.[4] In 1230 he served in the franciscan delegation which asked Gregory IX to clear up ambiguities in the rule of St. Francis. He was in England in April 1232 securing a concession from the king.[5] The following year a mission to negotiate for the union of the Latin and Greek churches took him to Constantinople.[6] He shared in the general chapter at Rome which deposed Friar Elias, elected the English provincial minister as his successor, and chose Haymo to be the English provincial. He retained this office only a year. In this capacity he received Ralph of Maidstone [q.v.] into the order at the end of 1238.[7] At the next meeting of the general chapter he was chosen minister general of the order. He seems to have reduced permanently the position of the lay brethren of the franciscans. If, as Eccleston says, Pope Innocent IV visited Haymo on his deathbed at Anagni it must have been between 25 June and October 1243.[8] His epitaph reads :

Hic jacet Anglorum summum decus, Haymo Minorum,
Vivendo frater, hosque regendo pater,
Eximius lector, generalis in ordine rector.

[1] Henry or Hugh ?

[2] Fr. Pelster, 'An Oxford Collection of Sermons of the end of the Thirteenth Century,' in the *Bodleian Quarterly Record*, vi (1930). 169.

[3] T. p. 386 ; *D.N.B.* under Haymo.

[1] Little, *F.S.O.* p. 806, citing *Eccleston*, p. 34 ; Mortier, *Hist. des Maîtres Généraux*, i. 145.

[2] *Eccleston*, pp. 34–6. [3] *Ibid.* p. 35.

[4] *Cronica fratris Salimbene* in *M.G.H.SS.* xxxii. 277 ; *Eccleston*, p. 35.

[5] *C.P.R.*, 1225–32, p. 469.

[6] *Eccleston*, p. 35. [7] *Ibid.* p. 107.

[8] *Ibid.* p. 89.

Henry D'Arci, templar and Anglo-Norman poet whom the philologists have placed in the 13th century, is discussed by Vising (p. 54). There is, however, an exchange between the monks of Kirkstead and the knights of the Temple which ends thus :[1]

Hoc autem factum fuit anno ab Incarn. Dni. 1161 mense Augusti in presentia Walteri abbatis de Kirkested, et Walteri prioris et conventus Kirkested et magistri Ricardi de Hastings et Johannis de Benerivill, et Willelmi Martel et fratris Henr. de Areci et fratris Godefridi et Henrici de Gorham.

The MS. is an early modern copy.

Henry of Avranches, poet,[2] is described by J. P. Heironimus and J. C. Russell (*Shorter Latin Poems of Master Henry of Avranches relating to England*, Mediaeval Academy of America), who give a sketch of his life and a list of poems.

Henry of Brisingham, see **Hugh of Brisingham.**

Henry of Burford, O.F.M. and poet, is described by Thomas of Eccleston [q.v.] :

Venit quoque frater Henricus de Burford, qui cum adhuc novitius esset et cantor fratrum Parisius, contra tentationes, quas sustinuit, versus istos in meditatione composuit :

Qui minor es, noli ridere, tibi quia soli

. . . .

Umbra minoris erit, qui nomen re sine quærit.

(*Eccleston*, pp. 38–9 ; *Mon. Fr.* i. 24–5.)

Henry of Burford entered the franciscan order at Paris early, when there were as yet only thirty brothers there.[3] While still a novice, but already a cantor, he wrote the verse quoted above. He came to England apparently in 1229.[4] Incidents in later career are summed up as follows :

Hic postea pro magna honestate sua quatuor ministrorum generalium et quatuor provincialium in Anglia socius specialis esse meruit. Hic etiam domini patriarchæ Antiocheni in legatione sua in Lombardia primo interpres et prædicator exstitit, et post domini Gregorii papæ noni pœnitentiarius custos que Venetiarum, et custodis Londoniæ quandoque vicarius.[1]

If the meaning of the first expression is that Henry was the special companion of four ministers general in England after 1229, then evidently Albertus, Haymo, and John de Parma are meant, with possibly Crescentius. He would have attended with John the provincial chapter of 1248.[2] If we ask why he should have been the special companion rather than others who possessed 'magna honestas,' the answer may well be the linguistic ability which enabled him to be the 'interpres et predicator' of the patriarch of Antioch in Lombardy in the summer of 1235,[3] and the penitentiary of Gregory IX. If all the expression means is that he was well acquainted with these leaders after 1229 then he must have lived into the time when William of Nottingham [q.v.] was provincial minister. In 1241 he was one of the friars chosen to consider and report upon doubtful points in the Rule.[4] Probably he was 'custos' of the custody of Venice before this and vicar of the custody of London about this time. In any case his life was the eventful one of a man indispensable for unusual, if not great, responsibilities.

Henry de Burgo, poet, was canon of Lanercost. Under the years 1280–90 (and possibly to 1292) there appear in the 'Chronicon de Lanercost'[5] many poems by one H, who appears from two instances cited below to have been Henricus de Burgo.

Epitaph of Queen Eleanor (1290) *inc.* 'Qui legis hoc siste dicendo ; te, rogo, Christe,' 'Unde Henricus de Burgo dicit' (*Chronicon*, p. 138).

[1] B.M. MS. Lansdowne 207 (e), fo. 181 ; for a conjecture about his identity, probably mistaken, see *Modern Philology*, xxviii (1931). 258.
[2] T. pp. 219, 376.
[3] *Eccleston*, p. 59 ; *Mon. Fr.* i. 36.
[4] *Eccleston*, p. 37 ; *Mon. Fr.* i. 24 ; Little, *F.S.O.* p. 806.

[1] *Eccleston*, p. 39 ; *Mon. Fr.* i. 25.
[2] Little, *G.F.* p. 70.
[3] *Registres de Grégoire IX*, ed. L. Auvray, ii. 168–9.
[4] *Eccleston*, p. 88 ; *Mon. Fr.* i. 48.
[5] *Chronicon de Lanercost* (Bannatyne Club), ed. J. Stevenson, pp. 105–147.

Poem addressed to R. Avenel (1282) *inc.* 'Nuncius cum debeat nil habere mali' (*ibid.* p. 110) follows this explanation :

Eodem anno dominus Henricus de Burgo fuit arestatus apud Dunelmum, et in castro per triduum detentus, propter executionem quam fecit pro archiepiscopo Eboracensi ; unde scripsit magistro R. Avenelle sub hac forma.

MS. addressed to the Archbishop of York (1282) *inc.* 'Dudum Dunelmi passus contraria pati' contains the information 'Hugo de Burgo scripsit archiepiscopo (*ibid.* p. 110). ('Hugo' written probably because of poem (below) on Hugh de Hibernia.)

MS. concerning Hugh de Hibernia (1282), *inc.* 'Quid prodest facere saltum et sic resilire,' has the words 'Unde H. dicit' (*ibid.* p. 109).

MS. on the death of David of Wales (1283), *inc.* 'David Walensis, equus, ignis, funis, et ensis,' 'Unde H. dicit versus' (*ibid.* p. 113).

William Grynerig (1287), *inc.* 'Vivere sub veste non queras canonicali' (*ibid.* p. 123) :

Eodem anno stetit inter nos Willelmus Grynerig, qui non comedebat carnes neque pisces ; de quo H. dicit . . .

A Malefactor (1287), *inc.* 'Qui se dant sceleri, claves Petrique vereri,' says 'Item de quodam malifico, H.' (*ibid.* p. 123).

A tithe (1280), *inc.* 'Grex desolatus, pastore diu viduatus,' 'Unde de ista materia dixit H. sic' (*ibid.* p. 105).

A fracture (1280), *inc.* 'Res, cista fracta, surrepta fuit male nacta' contains the explanation 'Tunc temporis fuit fracta quedam cista cuiusdam garcionis, de qua sic H. dixit' (*ibid.* p. 106).

A death (1280), *inc.* 'Garcifer occisus' and written 'Circa idem tempus quidem garcifer occisus, de quo H. dixit' (*ibid.* p. 106).

John of Newcastle (1282) *inc.* 'Mutatis pannis mutetur vita Johannis,' and containing the information 'Hoc anno dominus Johannes de Novo-castro recepit habitum monachalem apud Holm, de quo dixit H. sic' (*ibid.* p. 108).

Epitaph of Dervorvilla de Balliolo (1289), *inc.* 'In Dervorvilla moritur sensata Sibilla,' in which it is said 'Eodem anno obiit domina Dervorvilla de Balliolo, de qua dixit H.' (*ibid.* p. 133).

Possibly he wrote the poems upon the state of Scotland in 1291 and the burning of Carlisle in 1292 (*ibid.* pp. 143, 147).

All of the information about Henry de Burgo comes from a chronicle written by a franciscan, Richard of Durham [q.v.], and added to by canons of Lanercost, possibly from Henry's own notebooks.[1] In his second poem he speaks of being more used to the 'claustrum' than the 'castrum' and we know that he was a canon at Lanercost, dying as prior in 1315 (*ibid.* p. 232). In 1282, while acting for the archbishop of York, he was kept in prison at Durham for three days, whereupon he wrote to Robert de Avenel, chancellor of the bishop of Durham.[2]

Henry de Esseburn, O.P., was the author of biblical commentaries. Leland[3] says that at Cambridge in Queen's college library two books were :

Expositio Magistri Henrici de Esseburn, fratris Prædicatoris, in proverbia Solomonis, secundum quod legit in conventu fratrum suorum apud Cestriam. *Sicut dicit ecclesiasticus.*

Item super Ecclesiasten, qui liber est tanquam 30. cap. adjunctum proverbiis Solomonis. Fuit hic Esseburnus plane bene doctus, ut illa ferebant tempora. Liber autem dono datus erat collegio Regineo 1474.

Bale repeats some of this information but adds that the second book began 'In ecclesiasten, li. i. "Salomon nos inuitans ad."' The book must have disappeared shortly after Leland and Bale saw it as it is

[1] *E.H.R.* xxxi (1916). 272.

[2] W. Hutchinson, *Hist. and Antiquities of the County Palatine of Durham*, p. 227 ; *Foedarium prioratus Dunelmensis* (Surtees Soc.), p. 185 ; H.M.C., 4th Rep., App. p. 448 ; B.M. MS. Cotton, Otho A. ii, fo. 24*b* ; *Register of Thomas of Corbridge*, ed. W. Brown (Surtees Soc.), ii. 132 ; H. E. Salter, *Oxford Deeds of Balliol College* (Oxf. Hist. Soc.), p. 11.

[3] *Collect.* iv. 18.

not in Searle's catalogue (Bale, *Index*, p. 162, *n.* 3 ; T. p. 265).

Bibliographical tradition, beginning from Leland, has placed this man in the reign of Edward I. It seems certain that he was a master, and friar preacher of Chester, who lived before 1474.

Henry de Hanna, O.C., was a letter writer [1] to whom Bale attributes ' Elegantes epistolas,' *inc.* ' Dilectis in Christo filiis,' and ' Ordinationes locorum ' (B.M. MS. Harley 3838, fo. 55). Probably these letters were originally part of his official activity, but the term ' elegantes ' suggests that they may have circulated in the order as literature.

Henry of Hanna was apparently among the early carmelites in England and, like many others, had been at the carmelite house at Burnham.[2] He seems to have been the founder of the carmelite group at Oxford, and their first prior.[3] In the London synod of 1254 he was elected head of the English province,[4] retaining this office until 1272. It was a period of great expansion for the white friars.[5] In 1260 he was called to the headship of the French province. He summoned a meeting at Aylesford and, naming Hervey of Burnham as his vicar, proceeded on a tour of Reims, Liège, Brussels, Ypres, Gand, St. Amand, Rouen, and other towns in that neighbourhood.[6] At the London meeting of 1272 the friars named Roger Crostwyk as president, but he nominated Henry vicar with full authority and apparently retired to a life of contemplation.[1] In 1278, in a meeting at Norwich called by Henry as regent for Peter de Amiliano, William de Hanaberg was elected.[2] According to one account Henry was re-elected prior in 1281 and held office until his death.[3] It is certain that he held this position at the time of a general meeting of the order at Montpellier on 22 July 1287.[4] An undated letter to Edward I remains.[5] Henry apparently visited the house at Burnham in 1283,[6] and died before the Stanford meeting on 28 Nov. 1299.[7] He was buried at Stanford.

Henry of Lexington, bishop of Lincoln,[8] was possibly the author of an ' Expositio super Cantica Canticorum,' Oxford, Balliol Coll. MS. 21, fos. 1–67 (early 15th cent.), entitled ' Henrici episcopi Lincolniensis expositio super Cantica Canticorum,' *inc.* ' Osculetur me. Liber iste, qui est de coniunctione Christi et ecclesie,' *inc.* introduction, ' In funiculis Adam traham.'

[1] T. p. 376.

[2] Bale says he was a Norfolk man (B.M. MS. Harley 3838, fo. 16).

[3] ' Primus prior et fundator conventus Oxoniensis ' (*ibid.* fo. 160*b*). It has been said that the founder of the Oxford ' antiqui loci ' was Dominus Nicholaus Noels, 1260 : he must have given the site for the house or the house itself (B.M. MS. Cotton, Titus D. x, fo. 127).

[4] Bale, *op. cit.* fo. 55.

[5] Cf. the list of houses founded (B.M. MS. Cotton, Titus D. x, fo. 127 *et seq.*).

[6] ' Sequenti anno [1260] in Francorum presidem postulatus Henricus, convocata Generali apud Aylesfordiam Synodo Vicarium sibi substituit Herueum Burnehamiensum . . . et profectus est in Franciam atque Alemanniam, vbi pro multiplicandis edibus plurimum laboratat. Hinc Rhenis. Leodij. Brugis. Ypris, Gandaui, Monstreolis, in Sancto Amando, Valecenis, Rothomagi, et in alijs locis habitari cepit ' (Bale, *op. cit.* fo. 21*b*).

[1] ' In Angliam Sequenti Anno visitationis gratia veniens Londini Synodum convocavit. et unanimi patrum consensu Rogerum Crostwyck Doctorissimum Cantabrigie Bacchalaureum in Tertium Provincie constituit presidem. Henricum vero cum plena Officij potestate per omnia regna Suum fecit Vicarium ' (*ibid.* fo. 22*b*).

[2] *Ibid.* fo. 23*b*.

[3] T. p. 376, citing ' MS. Bal. Sloan. 4to 133 ex catalogo provincialium,' which says that he died in 1300.

[4] ' Fr Henricus de Hanna, prior pro. alis et Diffinitor Prov. Angliæ ' (*Acta Capitulorum Generalium*, ed. G. Wessels, i. 10).

[5] P.R.O., ancient correspondence, S.C. 1, xv. 194.

[6] T. p. 376.

[7] ' Henricus de Hanna iam olim senex omni preconio dignus, post diutinam Ordinis in Anglia, Francia, Germania, Hibernia, et Scotia sub diversis primoribus prefecturam, in Cenobio Stanfordiensi vita finitus est. sepultusque in choro ibidem quarto Kalendas Decembris Anno domini MCCXCIX ' (Bale, *op. cit.* fo. 26*b*).

[8] T. p. 396.

Henry of Renham wrote a volume of Aristotle's 'Parva Naturalia' in Latin with glosses, while a student at Oxford.[1] The volume is B.M. MS. Reg. 12 G. ii, and has this note :

> Quem librum scripsit Henricus de Renham et audivit in scol. Oxonie et emendavit et glosavit audiendo.

The book was given to Rochester priory by one prior John. The work was done after about 1260 when these books first became available in Latin translation. The writer may well have been that Henry of Renham who received holy orders as acolyte in September 1286 and subdeacon in 1288 at the hands of Archbishop Peckham.[2] A Prior John de Renham [q.v.] was elected at Rochester in 1262, resigned in 1283, was re-elected in 1291, and died in 1294.[3] Probably Henry died before 1293, leaving this volume to the prior, who gave it to his priory's library upon his demise.

Henry of Southwark, scientist,[4] was the author of a letter upon 'optical problems,' *inc.* 'Solutionem de topazio' : (a) B.M. MS. Reg. 7 F. vii, fo. 67 ; and (b) MS. seen formerly by Brian Twyne 'penes Tho. Allen' (T. p. 397). The salutation is 'Venerabili domino Const. episcopo Henr. de Suthwerc.' Henry was probably the author of the tract preceding the letter in both MSS., *inc.* 'De speculorum miraculis noster tractatus' : (a) B.M. MS. Reg. 7 F. vii, fo. 64 ; (b) also seen by Twyne. The pieces are also in a MS. with works of Roger Bacon which had belonged to William Herebert who was in school in 1290 (Little, *F.S.O.* p. 873).

[1] T. p. 621 ; the item about Rainhamus (T. p. 615) probably refers to him also.

[2] *Reg. Peckham*, pp. 1040, 1048. Possibly he was a Merton fellow ; a 'Regham' was in the college at this time (*Merton Muniments*, ed. P. S. Allen and H. W. Garrod, p. 11).

[3] *Flores Historiarum*, ed. H. R. Luard (R.S.), ii. 477 ; iii. 59, 74, 92.

[4] T. p. 397.

Henry of Sulgrave,[1] probably a monk of St. Martin's, Dover, was a former owner of B.M. MS. Cotton, Cleo. A. xii, and probably author of its contents, described in a note on its flyleaf :

> Liber Henrici de silegrave. Hec continentur In Volumine isto, De primo adventu anglorum in angliam, Quem partita fuit anglia per vij regna, De regibus anglie qui monarchi dicebantur usque ad regem Henricum III. Descriptio Anglie, per comitatus. Et de Domibus religiosis in eis contentis.

The work has been edited by C. Hook, in 'Chronicon Henrici de Silegrave. A Chronicle of English History' (Caxton Soc.). The inscription is in a 13th-century hand. A third hand has added a list of the archbishops of Canterbury as far as John (Peckam, 1279–92),[2] which is not included in the table of contents, which suggests that Henry of Sulgrave was probably dead by 1292 and thus contemporary with the latter part of the chronicle which ends in 1274. The MS. was the property of Dover priory.[3] Since in its lists the first county is Kent, the first monastery Christchurch, Canterbury (mother house of St. Martin's), and the first priory and castle, Dover, it seems probable that Sulgrave was a monk of Dover.[4] The subject matter in the volume is very similar to that of Gervase of Canterbury [q.v.]. A Richard de Sulgrave was almoner of St. Martin's in January 1270.[5]

Henry of Sutton, O.F.M., was the author of sermons preached at Oxford in 1292 and 1293 (Little-Pelster, p. 190).

Henry of Winchester wrote on medical topics.

'Medicinales questiones super Isagogen

[1] T. p. 672.

[2] Fos. 45*b*–46.

[3] Note on flyleaf : 'Liber prioratus de Dover.'

[4] Certainly not the abbot of Ramsey who died in 1268 (Gross, *Sources and Lit. of Eng. Hist.* no. 1841) whose name was Hugh (B.M. Add. chs. 33052, 33053).

[5] Lambeth Palace MS. 241, fos. 62, 63, 113*b*, 124, 127*b*.

Joanitii,' *inc.* 'Presentis negotii est medicinales questiones,' Oxford, New Coll. MS. 171, fos. 1–18 (13th cent.), appears to have no colophon, but Bernard says that it contained 'Medicinales Quæstiones Magistri Henrici de Wynton super Isagogen Joannitii' (*Catalogi Librorum Manuscriptorum*, ii. 35). The colophon may have been clipped off since then, or Bernard may have had other information.

'Liber phlebotomie,' *inc.* 'Propositum est nobis tractare': (a) Oxford, New Coll. MS. 171, fo. 74, entitled 'Incipit flebotomia Henrici' although Bernard has 'Liber phlebotomie Magistri Hen. de Wynton' (*loc. cit.*); (b) Gonville and Caius Coll. MS. 176, fos. 1–11 ? 'And of fleubotomye these thyngs sufisyn aftir Maister Henricus Wyntonyensis.'

Henry may possibly have been responsible for a treatise on urinology, *inc.* 'Albus ut aqua, lacteus ut lac' (Cambridge, Gonville and Caius Coll., MS. 117, fo. 221) with the colophon 'Et hec de urinis iuxta mag. Henricum sufficiant.'

The date of the New College MS. places the writer in or before the 13th century. The combination of the name 'Henry' with the description 'of Winton' appears frequently but not with the title of 'master.'

Henry of Wodstone, O.F.M., was possibly the author of a theological work, 'Summa de Sacrementis'[1] (Bodl. Lib., MS. Laud Misc. 2, fos. 132–67*b*). 'Explicit summa quam composuit frater Henricus lector Oxoniensis fratrum minorum anno domini m.cc.lxi.' The possibility of attribution rests upon Henry of Wodstone's presence at Oxford as a teacher a few years earlier (see **Hugh of Brisingham** below). A short treatise 'Contra Iudeos' remains, *inc.* 'Cum iudei fidei christiane adversantes,' Bodl. Lib., MS. Bodl. 91, fo. 140. This has been edited by A. G. Little, in 'Friar Henry of Wodestone and the Jews' (*Collectanea Franciscana*, B.S.F.S. 1922, ii. 150). There is a reference in Bale to 'Sermones dominicales et festiuales,' by 'Henricus de Oxonio, Minorita,' which began, 'Ecce sponsus venit, exite obuiam ei' (*Index*, p. 166). Bale gives as his source, 'Ex cenobio Minorum Radinge.' Henry was a common name, however.

[1] T. p. 396.

Henry of Wodstone was sent to Oxford by the minorite house at Salisbury and evidently provided with books by friends and benefactors, probably after 1241.[1] An 'exemplum' relating an incident of 25 July 1256 shows that 'he was in 1256 a priest, authorised by the bishop of Lincoln to hear confessions: he was engaged in teaching, and among his pupils there was at least one secular priest.'[2] He attended the provincial chapter at Cambridge in some official capacity and thanked John de Kirkby, treasurer of England, for the royal donation of 100 shillings toward the expenses of the chapter.[3] At this time he was engaged in activity against the English Jews, and, acting for St. Albans, carried a case involving the holding of land by Jews to the royal council.[4] At this time he wrote the 'Contra Iudeos' mentioned above, probably for the use of the council.[5] He was buried in the franciscan convent of London, whose register states that, 'by his efforts all the Jews were finally expelled from England in the time of Edward I.'[6] In this he seems to have had the help of the queen mother, Eleanor,[7] but whether he was her confessor or merely was interested in the same project is unknown.[8] He must thus have lived until 1290, the year of the expulsion. There was

[1] Little, *F.S.O.* pp. 815, 816.

[2] *Ibid.* p. 816.

[3] *Ibid.*; P.R.O., ancient correspondence, S.C. 1, vol. 8, no. 140.

[4] Little, *Collect. Franc.* ii., citing *Gesta Abbatum S. Albani.* i. 400–6; Fitzthedmar, *Liber de Antiques Legibus* (Camden Soc.), p. 234.

[5] Little, *Collect. Franc.* ii. 153.

[6] *Ibid.* p. 150.

[7] *Ann. Monast.* ii. 409.

[8] P.R.O., ancient correspondence, S.C. 1, xiii. 80. Fr. Henry was the queen's confessor and probably not the queen mother's.

a contemporary friar, Henry of Woodstock, whose name might be easily confused with his.[1]

Hiclyng, O.F.M., preached sermons at Oxford in 1292 and 1293 (Little-Pelster, p. 187).

Hotoft, monk of Durham and poet, wrote an epitaph of Richard Marsh : (a) edited by J. Stevenson (*Chronicon de Lanercost*, Bannatyne Club, p. 32) entitled 'Epitaphium Hotoft' ; (b) quoted by Matthew Paris, who says the author is 'quidam monachus Dunelmensis' (*Chr. Maj.* III, 112), but the items stated by Stevenson to be the 'poetical lucubrations of this Hotoft' (*Chronicon*, p. 380) seem rather to belong to Henry de Burgo [q.v.] ; (c) Gonville and Caius Coll., MS. 230, fo. 56, *inc.* 'Culmina qui cupitis laudes pompasque scititis.' Possibly some of the many epitaphs in this MS. also belong to Hotoft (see **William Hotoft,** below).

Hugh, according to Roger Bacon, was the first master at Oxford to read the 'Posterior Analytics' there. Bacon had seen his writing (*verbum*), and the man himself.[2]

Hugh of Brisingham, O.F.M., is the probable author of 'Postils on Exodus,'[3] the beginning of which is destroyed (Worcester, Cathedral Lib., MS. F. 84, fo. 88) attributed in MS. to 'Frater Hugo Birlingham.'

Hugh of Brisingham was eighth franciscan master of theology at Oxford, probably about 1266–8, and thirteenth master at Cambridge

[1] *E.H.R.* xxxiii (1918), 215–8 ; he was also of the convent of London, and 'Wodstok' is not very different from 'Wodston.' He was chancellor of Queen Eleanor in 1277 (*Le Registre de Jean XXI*, ed. E. Cadier, p. 40).

[2] *Fr. Rogeri Bacon Opera Inedita* (R.S.), p. lv *n.* 1 ; *Compendium Studii Theologie*, ed. Rashdall (B.S.F.S.), p. 34.

[3] T. p. 126 ; *E.H.R.* xlix. (1934). 673–6 ; Bressingham, Norfolk.

about 1271.[1] Leland identified him incorrectly with a Henry, franciscan lector at Oxford, in 1261 (see **Henry of Wodstone**).[2] In the spring of 1280 he was a member of the Salisbury friary, probably as guardian or lector. He wrote an interesting letter to the chancellor, Robert Burnell, with certain requests which fell within the scope of the statute of Mortmain. He stated that he had been with the chancellor at Wells and Bristol before Easter of the same year.[3]

Hugh of Croydon, O.P., is alleged to have shared with Richard de Stavensby [q.v.] in the composition of the 'Maxime concordantie,' probably in England. 'Fratres studentes in Anglia concordantias Anglicanas compilaverunt' (Quétif-Echard, p. 209 ; *Archiv für Litteratur- und Kirchengesch. des Mittelalters*, ii. 234).

Hugh of Evesham, cardinal, was the author of medical works,[4] of which only one has left a trace in an ancient library catalogue, the 'Questiones super opere Febrium Isaac,' said to be in Syon monastery, MS. B. 15, 'Questiones super librum febrium ysaak a magistro Hugone de Evesham disputate' (M. Bateson, *Catalogue of the Library of Syon Monastery*, p. 14), *inc.* 'Quoniam de filii bonitate sicut testatur Genesis, creati sumus.' Bale says that the MS. is 'ex domo Ricardi Grafton' (*Index*, p. 170). For the other medical works, 'Medicinales canones' and 'De genealogiis humanis' (if the latter be medical), no source is given in bibliographical tradition.

A sermon remains, *inc.* 'Sic currite, ut comprehendatis' (Bodl. Lib. MS. Bodl. 50, fo. 299*b*).

By 1265 Hugh was already a master and a pluralist,[5] but his first recorded connexion with a university is in 1269, when he acted in a dispute between the franciscans and

[1] App. A. [2] T. p. 126.

[3] P.R.O., ancient correspondence, S.C. 1, xxii. no. 131 ; printed *E.H.R.* xlix. 675–6.

[4] T. p. 418 ; *D.N.B.* under Evesham.

[5] *Reg. R. Gravesend*, pp. 19, 55 ; B.M. MS. Stowe 930, fo. 35.

dominicans at Oxford, and made a speech of which an outline remains.[1]

From 1271 until he went to Rome in 1280 he was the recipient of many royal favours, receiving ten oaks from the forest of 'Galtres' in November 1271, two bucks from 'Fecham' forest in July of the next year,[2] an exemption for a friend at his instance in the same year,[3] an excuse from a debt to Fountains abbey in 1275,[4] and four bucks from the forest of Galtres in 1278.[5] In 1275 he is said to be a royal clerk who has served the king and his mother a long time, probably as medical adviser, but this is not stated.[6] He was presented to the church of Hemingburgh in 1272 by the prior and convent of Durham.[7] At about the same time he resigned the church of Welton to Robert Burnell.[8] He seems to have been archdeacon of Worcester from 1275 to his death, but his chief interests were centred at York at this period. In 1279, as canon of York, he received one vote for archbishop, exchanged his prebend there for Begthorp, and was directed to examine candidates for ordination by a letter of 17 December.[9]

By a letter of 10 Sept. 1280 he was appointed proctor of the archbishop of York at Rome [10] and probably soon proceeded there. At Rome he was made cardinal priest of St. Lawrence on 23 Mar. 1281.[11] At the

1 Little, *G.F.* p. 333.

2 P.R.O. MS. Cal. Close Rolls, ed. H. J. Sharpe.

3 *C.P.R.*, 1266–72, pp. 648, 653.

4 *C.Cl.R.*, 1272–9, p. 158.

5 *Ibid.* p. 478; *Calendar of the Plea Rolls of the Exchequer of the Jews*, ed. J. M. Rigg, p. 135.

6 He resigned the church of Benefeld in 1277, whereupon the queen presented it to William de Hedon [q.v.]. The Hugh, physician to Prince Edward, was probably Hugh de Insula (*C.Cl.R.*, 1253–5, p. 274; *ibid.*, 1254–6, p. 282).

7 *Reg. of Walter Giffard* (Surtees Soc.), ed. W. Brown, pp. 57, 58.

8 *Ibid.*

9 *Reg. of Bishop Godfrey Giffard* (Worc. Hist. Soc.), ed. J. W. W. Bund, p. 58; *Reg. of William Wickwane* (Surtees Soc.), ed. W. Brown, pp. vi. 305, 2, 22; *Les Registres de Nicolas III*, ed. M. J. Gay, p. 231.

10 *Reg. of W. Wickwane*, pp. 183, 184.

11 *Ibid.* p. 194; *Chronica Johannis de Oxenedes* R.S.) ed. H. Ellis, p. 257.

papal curia he apparently looked after the affairs of his English friends. In a letter of congratulation dated 19 June the archbishop of York begged him not to overwork and to beware of poison.[1] Later the archbishop called upon him several times for assistance.[2] He was reckoned among the king's friends at Rome whose help was needed to expedite a matter in 1284.[3] The king, for his part, granted Hugh's nephew, John de Ollinton, freedom from suit in the county of Gloucester for four years and simple protection for two years, his chaplain a similar letter of protection, and at his instance granted a pardon to Robert de Byzel.[4] The queen may have given him the church of Spofford at this time, although it was probably earlier.[5] In 1280–1 Hugh summoned to Rome Richard de Bureyrd, aged sixteen, probably considering him for a career in the church.[6] He was in correspondence with both John Peckham and Edward I.[7]

'A few years afterward, Nicholas III (Giovanni Gaetani Orsini, 1277–1280) and Martin IV (Simon de Brie, 1281–1285) commissioned Hugh of Evesham (Atratus) to find a cure for the "fever" which wrought such havoc in the city. While in Orvieto, Martin IV created this philosopher and student of medicine (his personal physician) cardinal of San Lorenzo in Lucina. Rome owes to Hugh the rebuilding of this church and of other buildings on what is to-day the Corso, but not the liberation from her greatest scourge, the malaria. The learned man himself died of the fever while pursuing his researches.' [8] He was present at the

1 *Reg. of W. Wickwane*, p. 194.

2 *Ibid.* pp. 195, 197, 199, 200, 202, 204, 205.

3 *Calendar of Chancery Warrants*, i. 19.

4 *C.P.R.*, 1281–92, pp. 84, 86, 135, 160.

5 *Ibid.* p. 327.

6 *Cal. of Inquisitions post mortem*, ii. 401.

7 *Reg. Peckham*, i. 219, 228, 281; ii. 573, 711, 749, 761; P.R.O., ancient correspondence, S.C. 1, xv. 161–6.

8 *Speculum*, vii (1932). 106, citing A. v. Reumont, *Archiv. Soc. Roman. Storia Patria*, vii. 549, and A. Potthast, *Reg. Pont. Rom.* nos. 1795, 1824 (undocumented).

funeral of St. Thomas of Cantilupe,[1] but died on 23 Sept. 1287 and was buried in his church of San Lorenzo.[2]

Hugh of Hartlepool, O.F.M., was the author of some scholastic dissertations. For these as well as for the life of Hugh after 1280 see Little (*F.S.O.*, pp. 858–9). A sermon preached at Oxford is edited by Little and Pelster (pp. 192–204). As early as September 1262 a 'Mr. Hugh de Hartlepool' was made attorney by Master Patrick of Hartlepool.[3] In the same year a 'Mr. Patricius,' probably the same, was presented to the vicarage of Berwick by the bishop of St. Andrews. Patricius sealed his letter apparently with the seal of the official of the bishop of Durham as well as with his own.[4] Hugh witnessed a charter from William Fitzbeatrice of Swinton to Coldingham priory at Ayton in 1271.[5] On 5 January of the following year he witnessed an agreement between representatives of Melrose abbey and the same priory.[6]

Hugh of Hoveden appears to have been mistaken for Roger of Hoveden. In the Annals of Burton (*Ann. Monast.* i. 188) a quotation from Roger has the following explanation :

> Quantus etiam fuerit si quis scire voluerit, legat Chronica magistri Hugonis de Hovedene.

Probably a copyist misread 'Hugonis' for 'Rogeri,' creating an error which then misled Robert of Gloucester (*Chronicle*, R.S., ed. W. A. Wright, ii. 872, *n.* 519 [7]; Tanner, p. 414).

[1] *Acta Sanctorum*, October, i. 580, 607.

[2] Leland, *Collect.* ii. 356 ; it has been said, however, that he died of poisoned wine on 27 July (*Ann. Monast.* iv. 494).

[3] B.M. MS. Stowe 930, fo. 21. [4] *Ibid.*

[5] 'In plena curia apud Ayton die sabbati proxima post octab. sancti Martini in hyeme anno gracie M CC lxx primo' (J. Raine, *Hist. and Antiquities of North Durham*, App. p. 78).

[6] *Ibid.* p. 52.

[7] For references to a man of this name see *Register of John de Halton, bishop of Carlisle* (C.Y.S.), ed. W. N. Thompson, ii. 200 ; H.M.C., 9th Rep., App. p. 185.

Hugh, monk of Kirkstall, was the chronicler [1] whose one certain work is 'Narratio de fundatione monasterii de Fontibus,' *inc.* 'Placuit excellentie vestre pater venerabilis' : (a) Cambridge, Trinity Coll., MS. 1104, a 15th-century roll, published by J. R. Walbran (*Memorials of Fountains Abbey*, Surtees Soc., i. 1–128) ; (b) another copy formerly in the library of Sir Henry Langley (Bernard, *Cat. MSS Angliæ*, ii. 216) ; (c) B.M. MS. Lansdowne 404 (late copy) ; (d) B.M. MS. Arundel 51, published in Dugdale (*Monasticon*, v. 292–306) ; and (e) Bodl. Lib., MS. Dodsworth 26. An edition based upon all the MSS. is needed and might explain some curious problems about the time of writing. The salutation is 'Reverendo patri ac domino Johanni abbati de Fontibus frater H monachus de Kirkestall salutem.'

Possibly Hugh may be the author of the 'Historia de fundatione de Kirkestall,' *inc.* 'Factum est post mortem Henrici regis' : (a) Bodl. Lib., MS. Laud Misc. 722 (G. 9), fos. 129*b*–32*b*, printed in Dugdale (*Monas ticon*, v. 530–2) ; (b) a better version, MS unknown, translated from Stevens, 'Continuation of Dugdale,' ii, 37 (*ibid.* v. 527–8 *n.* c).

To him has been attributed the 'Versus de gestibus et laudibus Thurstini Archiepiscopi Eboracensis,' formerly at Syon monastery (T. p. 419).

Hugh, according to his own statement, became a monk about 1183 in the third year of the abbacy of Ralph Haget at Kirkstall (1181–90).[2] There he secured from an aged monk Serlo the account of the early years and history of Fountains. This Serlo had been a monk 69 years, entering the order between 1132 and 1147,[3] which

[1] T. p. 419 ; *D.N.B.* under Kirkstall.

[2] 'Anno tertio creationis ejus in abbatem, ego valedicens seculo, de sacra manu illius hunc nostrum institutionis habitum recepi' (Dugdale, *Monasticon*, v. 305).

[3] Serlo was not a monk of York in 1132, but migrated to Barnoldswick in 1147 (*ibid.* v. 293, 301) ; Walbran says 1207 (*op. cit.* p. xiii).

would place the securing of the information between 1201 and 1216. The 'Narratio de fundatione monasterii de Fontibus' is dedicated to one Abbot John. Since it concludes with the death of John, who died on 14 July 1209,[1] we should expect it to have been presented to his successor, John Pherd. However, there are certain references which, if not interpolations, clearly point to a later date.[2] If the other 'Historia' is by Hugh, he wrote it about the same time, carrying it through the lifetime of Abbot Helias of Kirkstall, who was apparently alive in 1207 but dead before 1217.[3]

Hugh of Manchester, O.P. and theologian, may have been also an author (T. p. 419). His most probable work is a 'Compendium theologie,' *inc.* 'Ad instructionem iuniorum quibus': (a) B.M. MS. Reg. 9 A. xiv, fos. 113–40*b*; (b) Oxford, Balliol Coll. MS. 219, fos. 181–231 (15th cent.), attributed to one Hugh; and (c) Oxford, Merton Coll. MS. 202, fos. 50–88 (13th cent.). Quetif-Echard attribute a work with this title to Hugh of Manchester (p. 498).

One tradition has it that Hugh was a diplomat and dedicated a book about Henry III to Edward I (Thomas Fuller, *Worthies of England*, ii. 150). The 'Historiola de pietate regis Henrici III' is probably not the piece intended (B.M. MS. Cotton, Vitellius D. xiv, now burned; *Archaeological Journal*, xvii, 1860, 317–9). Bibliographical tradition also mentions a 'De fanaticorum deliriis' (T. p. 419). Bale (*Scriptorum Cat.*, Cent. quarta, p. 348) wrote:

Scripsit hic demum, præfati regis iussu, aduersus impudentissimum quendam impostorem, maleficijs ac fraudibus instructum, qui prestigijs eius dementauerat matrem. . . . Finxerat enim se impostor ille diabolicus, caecum & ad Henrici tertij regis tumbam sanatum se iactitabat, ut regis ac matris fauore lucra ei obuenirent.

Hugh of Manchester was born in 1235 or 1236, giving his age as 71 years of age on 14 July 1307.[1] He was a doctor of theology. Since his name is not in the Parisian list he probably secured his degree at Cambridge or Oxford. He became prior provincial of the English dominicans in 1279 and was absolved at the general chapter of Vienna in May 1282.[2] His name is mentioned in a document of 1280[3] and he attended the general chapter at Oxford on 9 June of the same year.[4] At his instance on 15 June 1282 a royal pardon was granted to an outlaw.[5] In 1289–90 he evidently attended the general chapter of his order in Germany.[6] An act of 11 May 1292 was transacted in his presence.[7] He went on an embassy from Edward I to the French King with William of Gainsborough in 1294: his safeconduct is dated 24 August.[8] A chronicler retained a résumé of his speech and a versified account of the journey remains.[9] He probably attended the general chapter of the dominicans at Argentine in 1295.[10] He was summoned to parliament in 1297 and

[1] *Monasticon*, v. 288.

[2] References to Ralph of Newcastle, 'abbas postmodum factus de Kirkestall,' to King John, 'qui tunc regni summam tenebat,' and to Richard Marsh 'de quo multa dicenda sunt tempore suo.' Ralph of Newcastle was abbot in 1216, John died in that year, and Richard Marsh (if he is the bishop of Durham) in 1226.

[3] *Monasticon*, v. 528.

[1] *Acta Sanctorum*, October, i. 590.

[2] *Archaeological Journal*, xxxv (1878). 139; *E.H.R.* xxxiii (1918). 244; *Acta Capitulorum Generalium Ord. Praed.*, ed. B. M. Reichert, i. 220; for references to letters to a prior provincial in 5 and 6 Edw. I from the king, probably to Hugh's predecessor, William of Southampton [q.v.], see P.R.O., Exchequer, K.R., various accounts (nuncii), E. 101/308/3 & 4.

[3] *Reg. Tho. Cantilupe*, p. 232.

[4] *Arch. Journal*, xxxv. 139.

[5] *C.P.R.*, 1281–92, p. 26.

[6] P.R.O., Exchequer, K.R., various accounts (nuncii), E. 101/308/10.

[7] *Reg. of John le Romeyn* (Surtees Soc.), i. 121.

[8] *C.P.R.*, 1292–1301, p. 85; *Willelmi Rishanger chronica* (R.S.), ed. H. R. Riley, p. 142; P.R.O., treaty roll, C. 76/6.

[9] Peter Langtoft, *Chronicle* (R.S.), ii. 206–9; Royal Irish Academy, *Proceedings*, xxvii (1908), C. 46.

[10] *C.Cl.R.*, 1288–96, p. 440.

again in 1305.[1] He testified at the inquest concerning the canonization of St. Thomas of Cantilupe at London on 14 July 1307.

Hugh of Milneburne, medical writer, was the author of a 'Summa super antidotarium parvum,' *inc.* 'Testante Constantino humana corpora.' 'Incipit summa magistri Hugonis de Milneburne super antidotarium paruum' (B.M. Add. MS. 8092, fos. 25*b*–30*b*). Hugh cites Avicenna as an authority (fo. 26*b*).

The time and place of education of this writer are not known; even his identity is uncertain. A 'Mr. H. de Meleburne' was among a group of masters engaged in a controversy in 1220 with the prior and convent of St. Andrews in Scotland.[2] In 1283 and 1286 a 'Mr. Hugh,' a physician from England, was a student in Bologna.[3]

Hugh of Snaith, O.P. and theologian,[4] was the author of an 'Ars predicandi abbreviata,' *inc.* 'Sic dilatandi modus est sermonibus aptus,' Lambeth Palace MS. 357, fos. 35*b*–38 (15th cent.) with a note 'Inc. ars predicandi abbreviata a mag. Hugone de Sneyth de ord. predicatorum.' This MS. is said by Bale to have come 'Ex domo Ricardi Grafton' (*Index*, p. 172). The treatise begins with four lines of verse, but the rest is in prose. Dr. Little has identified this writer with 'Mr. Hugo de Sneyth or Sneyt' who was among the Oxford theologians about 1282–90 (Little-Pelster, pp. 110, 117, 120–3, 127, 130).

Humphrey Necton, O.C. and theologian,[5] is alleged to have written sermons, 'Questiones ordinarie,' 'Lecture scholastice,' and a treatise 'Super articulis theologicis.' Of these the opening words of the sermons only can be suggested ('De debitu dimisi tibi,' B.M. MS. Harley 3838, fos. 55*b*–56). The other three subjects may have been suggested to the bibliographers by his connexion with Cambridge.

[1] F. Palgrave, *Parliamentary Writs*, p. 722; *Rot. Parliamentarum*, i. 267.

[2] *Regesta Honorii Papae III*, ed. P. Pressutti, i. 2604.

[3] M. Sarti et M. Fattorini, *De claris archigymnasii Bononiensis professoribus*, ii. 322, 325.

[4] T. p. 698.

[5] T. p. 542; *D.N.B.* under Necton.

Humphrey Necton joined the carmelite order early and was at its house at Burnham for a time.[1] He studied at Cambridge, taking the degree of doctor of theology about 1292,[2] the first carmelite to attain to this degree.[3] He is said to have preached successfully against heretics in the schools, to have been a favourite with the populace,[4] and to have been the chaplain of William de Luda, bishop of Ely (1290–8).[5] He died at Norwich and was buried in the carmelite church there.[6]

J. de Broy, O.F.M., preached sermons at Oxford in 1292 (Little-Pelster, pp. 184, 364).

J. de Grimsby, scientist, wrote a 'Questio de Compositione oculi,' *inc.* 'Primo videndum est quid sit visus,' Gonville and Caius Coll. MS. 593, fo. 127*b* (13th cent.), bearing the note 'Hic inc. questio de compositione oculi simul et de materia oculi et de natura a mag. J. de Grimesbi.'

Possibly he was the 'Grenesbi' who was disputing in theology at Cambridge contemporaneously with Thomas Bungay *c.* 1275. Grenesbi's questions are given by Little and Pelster (pp. 111–3).

[1] Bale (B.M. MS. Harley 3838), fo. 16.

[2] A canon of Barnwell wrote:

'Et non multo post quidam frater de ordine Carmelitarum nomine Humfridus ad preces domini W(illielmi) de Luda episcopi Elyensis, habuit licentiam incipiendi in theologia, qui postea cito incepit sollempniter, et legit in scolis suis, scilicet in loco novo prenotato in parochia Sancti Johannis. Iste frater Humfridus fuit primus qui gratiam habuit incipiendi de ordine Carmelitarum in universitate' (cf. *Liber Memorandum Ecclesie de Bernewelle*, ed. J. W. Clark, p. 212).

[3] Bale says 1259 (*loc. cit.* fo. 21).

[4] *Ibid.* fo. 56; information here not so reliable as earlier in this MS.

[5] T. p. 542.

[6] Bale, *loc. cit.* fo. 56.

J. de Letheringsett was a disputant at Cambridge, *c.* 1282 (Little-Pelster, p. 92).

J. de Wakefield wrote a commentary upon Aristotle's 'Physics' (Gonville and Caius Coll. MS. 344, fos. 266–79, 13th cent.) entitled 'Questiones primi libri fisicorum date a mag. J. de Wacfeld.' He also wrote a treatise on fevers (Gonville and Caius Coll. MS. 407, fos. *c.* 80–91*b*), with the colophon, 'Expl. tractatus nobilisimus fe(brium) sec. mag. J. Wakfeld.'

This man's exact dates are unknown. His questions are in the same MS. as those of William de Bonkis [q.v.]. A John de Wakerfeld was among the northerners (*boreales*) in the great fight in the university of Oxford in 1285.[1]

James the Cistercian or Jacobus Anglicus[2] is the subject of a bibliographical tradition which apparently goes back through Pits (*Relationum Historicarum*, p. 353).

Pits learned from Sisto da Siena that 'Jacobus Anglicus nomine et natione scripsit in Cantica Canticorum, vixit anno domini 1270 (*Bibliotheca Sancta*, p. 250). His statement that James also wrote 'Conciones in Evangelia' and 'Lecturae scholasticae' looks like conjecture. On the authority of Peter of Vicenza (the origin of whose information cannot be traced) Pits says that James supported St. Thomas Aquinas 'de conceptione beatæ Mariæ Virginis in peccato originali.' Pits describes James as the first doctor of theology in the cistercian studium at Paris set up by Stephen of Lexington.

John was probably author of the English poem, 'Annot and John' (B.M. MS. Harley 2253, fo. 63). His name is given in the verse, which has been edited by Carleton Brown, in 'English Lyrics of the XIII Century,' pp. 136–8.

John of Basingstoke, archdeacon of Leicester,[3] is described by Matthew Paris as follows :

> Memoratus insuper magister J[ohannes] quoddam scriptum transtulit de Græco in Latinum, in quo artificiose et compendiose tota vis grammaticæ continetur ; quod idem magister Donatum Græcorum appelavit.
>
> Item aliud composuit, in quo particulæ sententiarum per distinctiones dilucidantur ; quod sic incipit, 'Templum Domini' ; quod est perutile.
>
> Item aliud scriptum, quod ab Atheniensibus habuit. . . . In illo scripto probatur ordo Evangeliorum (*Chr. Maj.* v. 286).

The 'Donatus Grecorum' is probably lost. The 'Ordo Evangeliorum,' *inc.* 'Omnia tempus habent et suis spatiis,' entitled 'Tractatus magistri Johannis de Basingstoke Evangeliorum, per annum' was formerly at St. Paul's, London (William Dugdale, *History of St. Paul's Cathedral*, App. p. 67). It was seen by Leland (*Collect.* iv. 48) and probably by Bale (*Index*, p. 181). Dugdale's information is from the catalogue of the library made in 1474. 'Templum Dei' is also the title of a work by Grosseteste [q.v.]. John's work may be in B.M. MS. Harley 3244, fos. 138–45 (13th cent.), *inc.* 'Templum Dei sanctum quod estis vos. v. ad Cor. III. Sermo iste quamvis omnis tangat,' 'Incipit tractatus perutilis qui vocatur Templum.' S. A. Hirsch suggests that it was a commentary on the 'Sentences' (*Roger Bacon Essays*, ed. A. G. Little).

Described by Matthew Paris as 'in trivio et quadrivio experientissimus' and learned in Greek and Latin letters, John might well be considered by the chronicler 'ad plenum eruditus.' He had studied and taught at Paris and studied at Athens, probably in that order. At Athens his teacher, the chronicler alleges, was a youthful prodigy, Constantia, 'filia archiepiscopi Atheniensis,' at the time not yet twenty, but already a scholar and a seer. There also he had seen a volume called the 'Testament of the Twelve Prophets' which at his suggestion Robert Grosseteste sent for and had translated.[1] The dates of his education are not known. Indeed the only clue is a charter which he witnessed as

[1] *Snappe's Formulary* (Oxford Hist. Soc.), ed. H. E. Salter, p. 287.

[2] T. p. 426 ; *D.N.B.* under James.

[3] T. p. 430 ; *D.N.B.* under Basing, Basingstoke.

[1] *Chr. Maj.* v. 284–7.

a master between 1223 and 1228.[1] Basingstoke was archdeacon of Leicester by 1 Apr. 1235, a few days after the election of Grosseteste as bishop of Lincoln.[2] He may have been given the office by Grosseteste's predecessor. He remained archdeacon until his death in 1252,[3] a year before that of his bishop.

In 1241 he served with William of Arundel [q.v.] as the bishop's representative in a dispute with John Mansel, a royal favourite. After Arundel's death John wrote to Adam Marsh about a work of his, probably a Hebrew translation.[4] His notification that a dispute between Belvoir priory and William, rector of the church of Muston, had been settled is extant and belongs to the year 1249.[5] He was on intimate terms with Grosseteste,[6] and probably was one of the bishop's assistants in translation from the Greek.[7]

John of Berwick, O.F.M., was described as an author by Leland :

> Collaudat eruditorum Index *Franciscanorum* eius in *Longobardum* elucubrationes. Scripsit insuper libellum de *Formis* (*Commentarii de Scriptoribus Britannicis*, p. 326).

'De formis' : (a) MS. at Venice, library of St. Antonio (J. P. Tomasini, *Bibliothecae Venetae Manuscriptae publicae et privatae*, p. 9) ; (b) MS. formerly at Glastonbury, entitled 'Questiones fratris Joannis de Berwico de formis.' Notes upon his lectures on the 'Sentences' appear in Assisi MS. 158, fos. 88*b*–91 (Little-Pelster, p. 115). There is a notice of William of Nottingham's quotation of John (*ibid.* p. 74), and references in the 'Commentary' of William of Ware (*Franziskanische Studien*, xix, 1932, 102–7).

[1] B.M. MS. Egerton 2104a, fo. 80 ; *Rot. H. Welles*, iii. 42, 44 ; Le Neve, *Fasti*, ii. 49.

[2] *Rot. R. Grosseteste*, p. 391.

[3] *Chr. Maj.* iv. 232–3 ; v. 284–7 ; *Rot. R. Grosseteste*, pp. 209, 223, 385, 388, 434.

[4] See under **William of Arundel.**

[5] H.M.C., *Rutland MSS.* iv. 141.

[6] *Ep. Grosseteste*, p. 63.

[7] See *Harvard Theological Review*, xxvi (1933). 168–9.

The commentary upon the 'Sentences' has not been discovered. The 'Quodlibet Egidii et Berwyk' was formerly in the library of St. Augustine's, Canterbury (M. R. James, *A.L.C.D.*, p. 260). A sermon, preached at Oxford about 1290, remains (Worcester, MS. Q. 46, fo. 247). See also Little (*F.S.O.*, pp. 859–60 ; *G.F.*, p. 159 ; Little-Pelster, p. 74).

There were probably three Johns of Berwick, two of them important men, at the end of the 13th century. One was a royal official who appears in many royal documents. The Master John de Berwick who flourished about 1300–4 is probably another person,[1] and our franciscan yet a third. Probably yet another is the Master John of Berwick, a canon of Glasgow and witness of a charter of John, bishop of Glasgow (1258–68)[2] and student of Bologna, 1280–4.[3] He was rector of Renfrew in 1295.[4] That the canon was a master seems to eliminate the possibility that he was the royal clerk, while Master John of Berwick of 1300–4 hardly seems important enough to have been the canon.

The franciscan was regent master at Oxford about 1289–90,[5] and preached a sermon there on 6 Jan. 1291. He was licensed to hear confessions at Stamford by the Bishop of Lincoln in 1300, was probably the master of the franciscan school there, and died there. The 'Quodlibet Egidii et Berwyk' suggests that he taught at Paris.[6]

John of Beverley, 'doctor Oxoniensis, scripsit, super sententias, li. iiij,' 'Utrum anima separata possit pati,' 'ex collegio regine Oxon' (Bale, *Index*, p. 182). Tradi-

[1] *Register of Thomas of Corbridge* (Surtees Soc.), i. 201, 202, 205, *n*. 1.

[2] *Registrum Episcopatus Glasguensis* (Bannatyne Club), ed. C. Innes, i. 229.

[3] M. Sarti et M. Fattorini, *De claris archigymnasii Bononiensis professoribus*, ii. 319, 321, 322, 323.

[4] *Registres de Boniface VIII*, ed. A. Thomas, i. 234.

[5] Little, *F.S.O.* p. 860 ; cf. App. A.

[6] Little-Pelster, p. 156.

tion has assigned him to the carmelite order and the 13th century, neither of which may be accurate (T. p. 99).[1]

John of Blostmeville, abbot of Abingdon,[2] was responsible for a 'Liber Albus.' An Abingdon compiler of the 14th century wrote:

Hactenus rotularius meus author qui hanc suam chroniculam ex libro monasterii Abendone qui le landbok dicitur, ex martyrologio, ex albo libro quem magister Iohannes Blostmevyle illius monasterii abbas composuit, et ex chronica Thome Mercham compilasse se scripsit (*E.H.R.* xxvi, 1911. 730–1).

He gives as an extract 'Hic terras et tenementa Benedicti de Landario . . .' Evidently it was a register or cartulary, but had it followed the historical tradition of Abingdon it would have mixed the documents with other explanatory and narrative matter.

Blostmeville was a monk of Abingdon[3] who was elected abbot of the house between 3 and 28 Feb.[4] 1241. He presided over the meeting of benedictine abbots at Northampton in March 1246.[5] In 1248 both the pope and king demanded the church of St. Helen's of Abingdon, a very wealthy church, for their candidates.[6] John died on 5 June 1256.[7] As a paralytic, he was in poor health for some time before his death.[8] The house took the precaution of securing for itself the income of the abbey during any vacancy caused by the death or cession of the abbot.[9] A letter of his remains.[10]

[1] Tanner gives a reference to a 'Fr. John of Beverley,' of the order of St. Augustine, who was ordained acolyte 3 Apr. 1294 by Oliver Sutton.

[2] T. p. 327.

[3] Thomas Marcham, mentioned above, was apparently a monk in 1334–5 (*Accounts of the Obedientiars of Abingdon Abbey*, Camden Soc., ed. R. E. G. Kirk, p. 4).

[4] *C.P.R.*, 1232–47, pp. 244, 246, 247.

[5] *Ann. Monast.* i. 136.

[6] *Chr. Maj.* v. 38–40.

[7] *Ann. Monast.* iv. 113.

[8] *Chr. Maj.* v. 567.

[9] *Ibid.*; *C.P.R.*, 1247–58, p. 476.

[10] Addressed to R., prior of Colne (B.M. MS. Harley 209, fo. 10).

John Blund, professor at Paris and Oxford, and chancellor of York,[1] may have been the author of a 'Tractatus de Anima.' (a) Cambridge, St. John's Coll. MS. 120, fo. 123 (13th cent.), *inc.* 'Ut habetur de Aristotele. Omnia scientia est ab anima,' entitled 'Tractatus de anima secundum Joha. Blondum,' writing somewhat uncertain (M. R. James, *Catalogue*, p. 154); (b) a treatise possibly by Johannes Anglicus is in B.N. MS. lat. 16133, fo. 51. Pits suggests him as the author of a 'Summarium sacre facultatis,' *inc.* 'Cupientes aliquid' in Rome, Vatican, MS. 4289 (*Relationum Historicarum de Rebus Anglicis*). This 'incipit' is common, however (A. G. Little, *Initia Operum Latinorum*, p. 63).

Some glosses on the bible given by a Master John Blund to Christchurch, Canterbury, may be the work of this scholar (Cambridge, Trinity Coll. MS. 163), inscribed 'Iste liber est ecclesie Christi Cantuarie de dono Mag. Johannis Blundi [cancellarii Eboracensis].'[2] This includes glosses on Chronicles, Esdras, Nehemiah, Tobias, Judith, and Esther. He also gave a 'Liber Machabeorum' to Christchurch (James, *A.L.C.D.*, p. 113).

Contemporary with the great scholar of Paris and Oxford were at least two other John Blunds. One was a royal messenger, not a master, and therefore not very difficult to distinguish from the professor. But the second was a master who died in 1239,[3] in possession of the church of Bredeburn to which he had been admitted by William, bishop of Coventry, in 1215.[4] Probably he was the Master John Blund who appears very frequently in this bishop's charters as one of his household.[5]

[1] T. p. 107; *D.N.B.* under Blund.

[2] Words in square brackets added above the line.

[3] *Ann. Monast.* iii. 149; G. H. Fowler, *Digest of Charters in the Cartulary of the Priory of Dunstable* (Beds. Hist. Soc.), p. 169.

[4] *Ibid.* pp. 127, 170.

[5] *Collections for a Hist. of Staffordshire* (Salt Archaeolog. Soc.), v. 16, 104; *Chartulary of the Abbey of St. Werburgh* (Chetham Soc.), ed. James

John Blund seems to have been popular with contemporary authors. John of Garland eulogized him as an almsgiver and a revelation of good manners.[1] If we may equate Blundus with Albus he was probably the teacher to whom Gervase of Melcheley dedicated his long treatise.[2] Henry of Avranches addressed a poem to Pope Gregory IX in favour of John Blund when the latter sought papal consecration as archbishop of Canterbury.[3] In this poem we get a glimpse of Blund's early life. Devoting himself to study since his boyhood, he was a pioneer in Aristotelian science, being among the first to read such books both at Paris and at Oxford. Then he turned to theology and spent twelve years in mastering this discipline.[4] He was one of the famous English professors who returned from Paris during the migration from that city in the spring of 1229.[5] Allowing twelve years for theological preparation, the Aristotelian phase of his career must have been before 1217. Even by 1216, the date of the fourth lateran council, he held two benefices with cure of souls.[6] One suspects that he was at Paris during the interdict in England *c.* 1208–13. He may be the John Blund, witness of a charter of William, archdeacon of Huntingdon, 'sede vacante' (1203–9 ?).[7]

From the summer of 1228 until 1238 a Master John Blund acted in important capacities for the king of England. He was summoned to the king in June 1228 and was paid his expenses for going to Rome on 20 September.[1] On 16 May 1229 Master John Blund borrowed £300 for affairs at Rome.[2] On 5 June he received £10 for royal service and in the autumn the same sum again for sitting a half year's term at the exchequer.[3] This was repeated in 1230 and 1233.[4] On 4 Dec. 1231 he was granted a livery of £20 a year for life or until a suitable benefice might be secured for him.[5] On 25 May 1234 he was sent by the king to Peter des Roches, then royal envoy to the king of France.[6] He was one of three who swore a truce with the Welsh upon the king's soul.[7] For such services he received customary rewards: a cask of Gascon wine on 9 June 1231,[8] wood from the royal forests on three occasions,[9] a small grant of land,[10] and, at his instance and that of other masters, several Oxford students were freed from forest penalties.[11] In 1238 he received a gift of cloth from the king.[12]

This English phase began, except for the trip to Rome in 1228, in the spring of 1229, about the time that the famous professor returned to England from Paris. There is little in it (except for the exchequer sessions, and this is uncertain) that a professor might not have done. He was teaching theology at Oxford when he was elected archbishop of Canterbury on 24 or 27 Aug. 1232.[13]

Tait, p. 121; B.M. MS. Harley 3650, fos. 34*b*, 39*b*; P.R.O., ancient deeds, D.L. 271; B.M. Add. MS. 30311, fo. 66; Bodl. Lib. MS. Ashmole 1527, fo. 35; MS. Harley 3650, fo. 35*b*; MS. Cotton, Tiberius E. vi, fo. 137; I. H. Jeayes, *Descriptive Catalogue of Derbyshire Charters*, p. 23; H.M.C., 14th Rep., App. viii, p. 228; B.M. Add. MS. 36869, p. 40 (published in *Coll. for a Hist. of Staffs.*, N.S. ix. 311); B.M. MS. Harley 4799, fo. 6*b*; Add. MS. 30311, fo. 266.

1 *Morale Scolarium of John of Garland*, ed. L. J. Paetow, p. 177.

2 See above under **Gervase of Melcheley**.

3 *Shorter Latin Poems of Henry of Avranches* (Mediaeval Academy of America), ed. J. P. Heironimus and J. C. Russell, pp. 127–36.

4 *Ibid.* lines 77–86.

5 *Chr. Maj.* iii. 168.

6 *Henry of Avranches*, lines 118–22.

7 B.M. MS. Cotton, Tiberius C. ix, fo. 141.

1 *C.Cl.R.*, 1227–31, p. 109; *C.L.R.*, 1226–40, p. 98.

2 *C.L.R.*, 1226–40, p. 130.

3 *Ibid.* pp. 135, 150.

4 *C.Cl.R.*, 1227–31, p. 342; *C.P.R.*, 1225–32, p. 334; *C.Cl.R.*, 1231–4, p. 233.

5 *C.P.R.*, 1225–32, p. 454.

6 *C.Cl.R.*, 1231–4, p. 562.

7 *C.P.R.*, 1232–47, p. 59.

8 *C.Cl.R.*, 1227–31, p. 513.

9 *Ibid.* pp. 278, 514; *ibid.*, 1231–4, p. 226.

10 *C.P.R.*, 1232–47, p. 93.

11 *C.Cl.R.*, 1227–31, p. 520.

12 P.R.O., chancery miscellanea, C. 47/3/43 (3).

13 *Ann. Monast.* iv. 73; Roger of Wendover, *Flores Hist.* (R.S.), iii. 34; B.M. MS. Cotton, Julius D. v, 'Annals of Dover,' fo. 29*b*; *Hist. works of Gervase of Canterbury* (R.S.), ed. W. Stubbs, ii. 129.

On 30 August the king assented to the election and also gave him permission to go to Rome for consecration.[1] He crossed on 2 September.[2] He was, however, the candidate of Peter des Roches and carried with him, according to report, many thousand marks of silver.[3] At Rome Simon Langton [q.v.] opposed his consecration on the technical ground that John held two benefices with cure of souls and the practical one that his consecration would place both the state and church of England in the hands of Peter des Roches. Simon persuaded the pope to this view on 1 June 1233.[4] Nevertheless the pope gave Blund permission on 8 June 1233[5] to hold a bishopric should such a position be offered him. One of his two benefices was a canonry of Chichester which he apparently held until his death,[6] the other was possibly Berton in the diocese of Ely.[7]

John Blund returned from Rome in 1233[8] and, if he is the master mentioned above, remained in the royal service and probably continued teaching at Oxford. He never attained the bishopric which the pope said he might accept, but eventually became chancellor of York. He certainly held this office by 3 Nov. 1244.[9] His activity left many records at York.[10] An official item of 1246 refers to him.[1] At some time Bishop Robert Grosseteste apologized for rejecting one of Blund's relatives on account of illiteracy.[2] He died in the year 1248 and his fame is recorded by Matthew Paris with that of Robert Bacon and Richard Fishacre.[3]

[1] 'Annals of Dover,' fo. 29*b*.

[2] *C.P.R.*, 1225–32, p. 498.

[3] Wendover, *op. cit.* iii. 50.

[4] *Ibid.*; *Ann. Monast.* iii. 132; iv. 73–4; 'Annals of Dover,' *loc. cit.*

[5] *C.E.P.R.* i. 135; *Registres de Grégoire IX*, ed. L. Auvray, no. 777.

[6] *Gervase of Cant.*, ii. 129; *Archaeologia*, xlv (1880). 185; a John Blund was prior of St. Bartholomew's, Smithfield, in 1227 (Norman Moore, *History of St. Bartholomew's Hospital*, p. 394).

[7] Vacant also by his death (*Registres d'Innocent IV*, ed. E. Berger, no. 614).

[8] *Ann. Monast.* iii. 133.

[9] *C.Cl.R.*, 1234–7, pp. 6, 59, 217.

[10] B.M. MS. Cotton, Claudius B. iii, fo. 28*b*; York cathedral, Magnum registrum album, fos. 35, 70; *Reg. Walter Gray* (Surtees Soc.), p. 158, *n.*, citing Domesday MS. at York cathedral, fo. 91; B.M. MS. Cotton, Claudius B. iii, fos. 59*b*, 100; Lambeth Palace MS. 241, fo. 175*b*; *C.Ch.R.*, 1226–57, p. 234.

John of Bologna, notary, wrote a 'Summa' of notarial practice.[4] This has been edited by Ludwig von Rockinger in 'Briefsteller und formelbücher des elften bis vierzehnten jahrhunderts' (Quellen zur bay. u. deut. Gesch.), pp. 603–712 from Munich MSS. The treatise is also in Cambridge, Corpus Christi Coll. MS. 450, and B.M. MS. Cotton, Vespasian A. ii, fos. 123–30*b*.

John of Bologna dedicated his 'Summa' to Archbishop Peckham.[5] This and the prelate's register furnish the information about the notary's life. John gives his name as John Jacobi of Bologna.[6] He had studied the 'ars notaria' for many years both at Bologna and at the Roman curia until he was licensed to practise both by imperial and papal authority.[7] Peckham probably met John at Rome and brought him to England since John was there by 16 Aug. 1279.[8] On this date the archbishop ordered John to show a document to the archbishop-elect of Dublin, John of Darlington [q.v.]. Three documents in the 'Summa' are dated 1281, one at an unnamed place, the others on 20 September and 12 October at London.[9] By the last instrument the archbishop appointed John to act as his proctor at the Roman curia. He was also attorney for John of Lewes, rector of Smarden, while the latter was at Rome at an unspecified time.[10]

[1] York cathedral, Registrum magnum album, iii, fo. 94; *Reg. Walter Gray*, p. 202.

[2] *Ep. Grosseteste*, p. 68.

[3] *Chr. Maj.* v. 41; *Hist. Angl.* iii. 40.

[4] T. p. 112; Rockinger, *op. cit.* pp. 595–602; N. Denholm-Young, 'The Cursus in England,' *Oxford Essays to H. E. Salter*, pp. 68–103.

[5] Rockinger, *op. cit.* p. 603.

[6] 'Johannes quondam Jacobi' (*ibid.* p. 607).

[7] *Ibid.* pp. 604, 607.

[8] *Reg. Peckham*, p. 45.

[9] Rockinger, *op. cit.* pp. 609, 621, 617.

[10] *Ibid.* p. 615.

In 1282 John probably served the archbishop at Rome.[1] The last dateable document in the 'Summa' is for 28 Sept. 1284.[2] A note on the margin of one MS. dated Rieti, May 1289, apparently shows that it was completed before this time.[3] In 1289 John was presented to the church of Llangennith in the diocese of Llandaff, but it is not stated whether he was in England or not.[4] Possibly he is the John of Bologna, notary of Hereford in 1312.[5]

John de Cantia [6] is the probable author of a 'Summa' of canon law: (a) MS. formerly at Ramsey among the 'Libri Johannis precentoris,' entitled 'Summa magistri Johannis de Cantia,' and among books of canon law (*Chronicon Abbatiæ Rameseiensis*, R.S., ed. W. D. Macray, p. 362); (b) MS. formerly at Ramsey among the books of William Forestarius, entitled 'Summa magistri Johannis de Cantia' (*ibid.* p. 364); (c) MS. formerly at Peterborough, MS. I. x, entitled 'Summa magistri J. de Cantia de decretis' (James, *Peterborough*, p. 64); and (d) MS. formerly at Peterborough, MS. H. xii, entitled 'Summa J. de Cantia de penitentia' (James, *Peterborough*, pp. 22, 68; given by Abbot Walter who died in 1246).

A John de Cantia was abbot of Fountains from 1220 to 1247. The most likely person to be identified as the author is a 'Mr. John de Dya,' called 'John de Cantia.' 'Mr. John de Dya' was a royal clerk out of England in 1240.[7] He was being paid an annual pension of £20 in 1241.[8] He joined the franciscans. Bishop Grosseteste told him that his objection to papal provisions was not that they brought non-English speaking people to England but that they brought persons who did not serve.[1] He came to England in 1256 on papal business, a papal chaplain and penitentiary.[2] In 1257 Christchurch, Canterbury, paid a messenger for a journey to him.[3] By 1258 he was papal nuncio in England [4] and served in that capacity again in the years 1263–6.[5] Matthew Paris considered him a 'vir commendabilis.' [6]

John de Cella, abbot of St. Albans and poet, was possibly a chronicler. Some of his lines appear in the 'Gesta Abbatum Monasterii Sancti Albani' (R.S., ed. H. T. Riley, i. 244, 247). He may have compiled a chronicle to 1188, Bodl. Lib. MS. Douce, 207 (mid 13th cent.), which has on one side of text 'Huc usque in lib. cronic. Johannis abbatis,' and on the other 'Usque hoc cronica Johannis abbatis et hic finis.' This is the compilation used by Roger of Wendover [q.v.] and Matthew Paris [q.v.] and is printed in H. R. Luard's edition of the 'Chronica Majora' (R.S.). See Luard's introduction (*ibid.* pp. xi, xvi, xxxi–lxxxiv) and C. Jenkins's 'Monastic Chronicler and the School of St. Albans' (S.P.C.K.).

John de Cella's career before he became abbot of St. Albans in 1195 is thus described in the 'Gesta Abbatum' (i. 217):

> Johannes huic successit, in sæculo sæcularis, dictus 'Magister Johannes de Cella,' non procul a viculo qui 'Stodham' dicitur, ex mediocri prosapia oriundus; vir eximiæ pietatis, amator ordinis, et vigoris disciplinæ claustralis. Hic, in juventute scholarum Parisiensium frequentator assiduus, ad electorum consortium Magistrorum meruit attingere; unde, cum virilis esset ætatis, in Grammatica Priscianus, in Metrico Ovidius, in Physica censeri potuit Galenus.

He was prior of Wallingford before his election as abbot, possibly ceasing his chronicle (in 1189) when he went to that cell. Just before he died, on 17 July 1214,

[1] *Reg. Peckham*, p. 278.
[2] Rockinger, *op. cit.* p. 615.
[3] *Ibid.* p. 597.
[4] *Reg. Peckham*, iii. 1009.
[5] *Reg. Swinfield*, p. 471.
[6] T. p. 432.
[7] *C.Cl.R.*, 1237–42, p. 176; Leland said that he was a canon of Orleans (T. p. 432).
[8] P.R.O., Exchequer of Receipt, enrolments, E. 403/1.

[1] *Mon. Fr.* i. 64.
[2] *C.P.R.*, 1247–58, pp. 470, 498; *Chr. Maj.* v. 568, 590, 681.
[3] Lambeth MS. 242, fo. 2*b*.
[4] *C.P.R.*, 1247–58, p. 631; *Chr. Maj.* v. 722.
[5] *C.E.P.R.* i. 379, 380, 384, 387, 424.
[6] *Chr. Maj.* v. 568, 681.

he gave further evidence of his exceptional medical ability.[1]

John of Cesterlade, O.P., was the author of sermons preached at Oxford, 1292 (Little-Pelster, p. 184).

John of Darlington, O.P., archbishop of Dublin, was reputed to have been one of the authors of the dominican 'Concordantie Magne' or 'Concordantie Anglicane.'[2] The chronicler Rishanger gives the following sketch of his career:

> [1276] Eo tempore Frater Johannes de Derlingtone, Ordinis Prædicatorum, Confessor quondam Regis Henrici, auctoritate Papali in regno Angliæ Collector efficitur decimarum,—salva Papali reverentia, contra sui Ordinis professionem tali officio deputatus. Hujus tamen studio et industria editæ sunt Concordantiæ Magnæ, quæ 'Anglicanæ' vocantur. . . . ex collatione Papali efficitur Archiepiscopus Dublinensis (*Wilhelmi Rishanger Chronica*, R.S., ed. H. T. Riley, pp. 89, 95).

Elsewhere the 'Concordantie' are said to be largely the work of Richard de Stavensby [q.v.] and Hugh de Croydon. It seems that John of Darlington must have been at Oxford about 1250 when this work was completed.

The other works attributed to him by bibliographical tradition, 'Disceptationes scholastice' and 'Sermones ad clerum et populum,' have probably no other basis than his association with the 'Concordantie.'

The second phase of his career is that of his close association with Henry III. He was made a member of the royal council in 1256,[3] which marks the beginning of a long series of pardons procured by the friar. (On 10 Jan. 1256 a pardon was granted to John, a converted Jew, and other pardons followed in 1257 and 1258).[4] In this last year he was included among the eleven or twelve special representatives of the king in the political troubles of that time.[1] For several years there is a lack of information about him. About 1263 he wrote a letter to H., prior of Durham, which still remains.[2] In this year, as prior of the dominicans of London, he was given power with several others to make peace with the barons on behalf of the king.[3] He was thus present at the meeting in which it was agreed to submit the dispute to Louis IX for arbitration.[4] In 1264, 1265, and 1266 many pardons are recorded at his instance.[5] In 1267 the king granted him ten marks for his use,[6] and next year made further grants for his benefit and that of the friars of Winchester.[7]

In November 1272 he was present in the chapel of St. Stephen, Westminster.[8] In 1274 a papal mandate was directed to him[9] and in the same year he seems to have been appointed collector of a papal tenth with Raymond de Nogeriis.[10] Probably he went to Rome on this business some years later, and was in that city in August 1278 with Master Henry of Newark and a Master William. After some argument a satisfactory arrangement was made, and Darlington remained or was again appointed collector.[11] He was apparently back in England in November 1278.[12] On 8 Feb.

[1] *Gesta Abbatum*, i. 246, 249. He was buried in the chapter house (B.M. MS. Harley 3775, fo. 130*b*).
[2] T. p. 225; *D.N.B* under Darlington; MacInerny, *History of the Irish Dominicans*, i. 297.
[3] *Chr. Maj.* v. 549.
[4] *C.P.R.*, 1247–58, pp. 457, 555, 630; *Foedera*, i. 335.

[1] *Ann. Monast.* i. 447; *E.H.R.* xxx (1915). 403.
[2] B.M. MS. Stowe 930, fo. 24.
[3] P.R.O., ancient deed, D.L. 139; *C.P.R.*, 1258–66, pp. 268, 269.
[4] *Foedera*, i. 434; *Royal Letters*, ed. Shirley, ii. 252.
[5] *C.P.R.*, 1258–66, pp. 379, 508, 514, 526, 557, 558, 578, 604, 623, 637, 645.
[6] P.R.O., Chancery liberate roll, C. 62/44, *m.* 3.
[7] P.R.O., Exchequer, L.T.R., pipe roll, 53 Hen. III, E. 372/113; chancery miscellanea, C. 47 bundle 3, no. 7 (11).
[8] *C.Cl.R.*, 1272–9, p. 39.
[9] *Registres de Grégoire X*, ed. J. Guiraud, p. 183.
[10] *Chronicon Petriburgense* (Camden Soc.), ed. J. A. Giles, p. 21; *Register of Walter Giffard*, ed. W. Brown, p. 274; P.R.O., Chancery, liberate roll, C. 62/53, *m.* 6, 9 June 1277.
[11] *Rishanger, Chronica*, p. 89; *Foedera*, i. 560; *Treveti Annales* (R.S.), ed. T. Hog, p. 296.
[12] Nov. 1278: 'Item pro passagio fratris Johannis de Derington [*sic*] et magro H. de Newark . . .' (P.R.O., chancery miscellanea, C. 47/4/i, fo. 41*b*).

1279 he was elevated to the archbishopric of Dublin by the pope.[1] Edward I received his fealty and homage on 27 Apr. 1279 and restored the temporalities on the next day. He was consecrated by Archbishop Peckham on 26 August at Waltham Abbey. His career as a prelate, largely concerned with collections for the papacy, is given elsewhere.[2] He died on 28 Mar. 1284 and was buried in the church of the dominicans in London.[3]

John Duns Scotus, O.F.M. For a statement by Dr. A. G. Little upon the present status of research upon this man see '*E.H.R.*' xlvii (1932). 568–82.

John of Eversden, cellarer of St. Edmunds, was a chronicler [4] for whom Bale gives the following titles: 'Series temporum,' *inc.* 'Fructuosum arbitror, seriem temporum transactorum huic pagine inserere'; 'Concordantie divine historie,' *inc.* 'Barbarismus, corruptus sermo, species Barbarismi'; 'Concordia decretorum,' *inc.* 'Tractaturus Gracianus de iure canonico'; 'Legum medulla carmine,' *inc.* 'Disce quid humanum ius diuinumque vocatur'; and 'De regibus et episcopis anglorum,' *inc.* 'Regna pristina Anglie et eorum episcopatus' (*Index*, p. 200). The MSS. were 'Apud magistrum Bacon prope Carthusianos.'

Of these two have been identified :— 'Series temporum': (a) Cambridge, Corpus Christi Coll. MS. 92, anonymous, which stops at 1295, and has been published by B. Thorpe as a continuation of Florence of Worcester (*Florentii Wigorniensis Chronicon*, Eng. Hist. Soc. ii. 136–279); (b) London, College of Arms, Arundel MS. 30, to 1296 in one hand, then in another to 1301, and a break to 1313; part has been edited under 'Bartholomæi de Cotton, Historia Anglicana' (R.S. ed. H. R. Luard, pp. 159–66).

'De regibus et episcopis anglie' appears in the same MS. according to T. Hardy (*Descriptive Catalogue*, iii. 176).

The 'Hic attonsus fui' under the date 1255 in one MS. of Eversden's work has led bibliographers to believe that John was the person tonsured.[1] The great length of time before the next ascertainable date in his life makes this uncertain. His name appears without title as witness to a charter dated 'Kal. Jun.' but the year is missing.[2] He appears as cellarer in a document of November 1296.[3] Under the year 1300 is a note:

> Dominus Joh. de Everisden, tunc celerarius Sancti Edmundi, validam expeditionem fecit in partibus Norhamptone apud manerium de Werketon de pastura, quæ dicitur Butoneris, sicut in registro Cantoris continentur.[4]

We learn from the 'Registrum Cantoris' that this occurred on 14 Sept. 1300 and that the parson of the local church was fined for his transgression.[5] On 19 Nov. 1301 he made an agreement concerning some land as cellarer.[6] He received a commission from the house to bring the election results to the king on 3 Jan. 1302.[7] He is mentioned in the papal bull of Boniface VIII of 1 June 1302 confirming the election of Thomas Tottington as abbot of his house.[8] In January 1307 he attended parliament at Carlisle as representative of the abbot [9] who

[1] *Les Registres de Nicolas III*, ed. M. J. Gay, pp. 162–4.

[2] See *D.N.B.*

[3] *Ann. Monast.* iii. 313; iv. 297; *Chronica monasterii S. Albani*, p. 108; *Florentii Wigorniensis Chronicon* (Eng. Hist. Soc.), ed. B. Thorpe, ii. 231.

[4] T. p. 271; *D.N.B.* under Everisden.

[1] College of Arms, Arundel MS. fo. 148*b*; see also E. Clarke, *Bury Chroniclers of the Thirteenth Century*, p. 9.

[2] B.M. Add. MS. 14847, fo. 80*b*.

[3] *Ibid.* fo. 68*b*. (See also T. p. 271.)

[4] *Bartholomæi de Cotton Historia*, p. lvii.

[5] 'die exaltationis sancte crucis' (B.M. Add. MS. 14847, fo. 62*b*); this identifies the 'registrum cantoris.'

[6] 'In crastino sancti Edmundi regis et martiris anno r. Edwardi fil. regis Hen. tricesimo' (P.R.O., Duchy of Lancaster, D.L. 42/5, fo. 88*b*).

[7] *Memorials of St. Edmunds Abbey* (R.S.), ed. T. Arnold, ii. 305, 306.

[8] *C.E.P.R.* i. 601; W. Prynne, *Records in the Tower*, iii. 920.

[9] Palgrave, *Parliamentary Writs*, p. 186; *Rot. Parliamentorum*, i. 191.

again appointed him for the forthcoming parliament at Westminster.[1] In 1308 and 1309 he was summoned to the honour court of Clare.[2] He was still cellarer in 1313.[3]

The chronicle was compiled by one hand until the year 1296, and seems to have been written 'at intervals as the events occurred.'[4] It is possible that Eversden ceased writing at the time that he became cellarer. If he was tonsured in 1255 he must have been advanced in years when he became cellarer. Yet it should be noticed that his name is at the head of the list of monks in the one charter in which he appears as a simple monk, which probably means that he was one of the oldest in point of service. It has been suggested that his features are sketched in the College of Arms MS.[5]

John, abbot of Ford, was a theologian[6] to whom bibliographical tradition has attributed a group of writings, based largely upon the theory that only one John at Ford was a writer. The most certain of the attributions is that of a group of sermons on the Song of Solomon: (a) Oxford, Balliol Coll. MS. 24, fos. 24–264 (late 12th cent.), *inc.* 'Adiuro vos filii Ierusalem,' inscription, 'Incipiunt capitula sermonum dompni Johannis abbatis de Forda super extremam partem canticorum'; (b) MS. at Ford, 'Joannis abbatis Fordensis omelie centum et viginti' (Leland, *Collect.* iii. 255). The date of the Balliol MS. seems to identify the author with the first John.

Other sermons attributed to him are: (a) Oxford, Bodl. Lib. MS. Bodley 705, fos. 76–80 (13th cent.), *inc.* 'Hodie dilectissimi suscitavit,' entitled 'Sermo Johannis monachi de Forda in dominica in Ramis Palmarum'; (b) MS. formerly at Oxford, Corpus Christi Coll., colophon, 'Sermones de triplici cruce,' *inc.* 'Vetus homo noster simul crucifixus est' (Bale, *Index*, p. 203).

Leland also saw at Buckfast 'Joannes abbas de Forda De contemptoribus mundi' (*Collect.* iii. 258), and at Ford 'Joannes Fordensis Super Hieremiam' (*ibid.* iii. 255). The latter has been identified with the 'In threnos Hieremie' of one Johannes de Fordeham from the monastery of Norwich (Bale, *Index*, p. 203). So an 'Introductorium eorundem' of the same man has been added. But Ford is not Fordeham, and the similarity of name hardly justified Bale in changing 'Benedictinus' to 'Cisterciensis.'

The Life of St. Ulfric is also attributed to him: (a) Cambridge Univ. Lib. MS. Add. 3037, fo. 81 *et seq.*, *inc.* 'Beatus Uulfricus a mediocri Anglorum gente,' dedicated to 'Reverendo patri et domino B. Dei gratia Exoniensi episcopo fr J. pauper Christi de Forda,' with a second dedication, 'Reverentissimo domino et patri in Christo karissimo B. Dei gratia Cantuariensis archiepiscopo totius Anglie primati fr J. pauper Christi de Forda'; (b) Eton Coll. MS. 109, fos. 81–105, entitled, 'Vita B. Wulurici anachorete Haselbergie per ven. Joh. priorem de Forda ad dom. Barthol. Exoniensem episcopum'; (c) B.M. MS. Cotton, Faustina B. iv. fo. 63; and (d) B.M. MS. Harley 322. This work is abridged by Matthew Paris (*Chr. Mag.* ii. 205–9) and has now been edited by Maurice Bell (*op. cit.*).

John's career as author and friend of King John is doubtless responsible for the undocumented attribution to him of the 'Acta quaedam Joannis regis,' 'Lectiones ordinarias,' and 'Opuscula.'

John was probably called 'Devonius.'[1] Possibly as a monk of Ford about 1180 he began his Life of St. Ulfric.[2] From this

[1] P.R.O., Parl. proxies, S.C. 10, file 1, no. 47, 23 Apr. 2 Edw. II.

[2] *Court Rolls of the Abbey of Ramsey*, ed. W. O. Ault, pp. 76, 94, 95, 97, 101.

[3] *C.E.P.R.* ii. 111.

[4] *Bartholomæi de Cotton Historia*, p. lvii.

[5] Fo. 202; Clarke, *op. cit.* p. 9.

[6] T. p. 433. The most recent life is Maurice Bell's 'Wulfric of Haselbury' (Somerset Record Soc.), pp. x–xiv.

[1] Dugdale, *Monasticon*, v. 376, source not given; items mentioned by Bell, *op. cit.*, are probably conjectures.

[2] Bell, *op. cit.* p. xviii.

period comes also one sermon,[1] whose colophon calls him 'prior of Ford,' though this is possibly a confusion with 'pauper.'[2] If prior, he must have held this office by 1184, the date of the death of the bishop of Exeter to whom one dedication is made. The second dedication is to the archbishop of Canterbury, 1184–7. In 1191 he resigned as abbot of the cistercian house of Bindon [3] to become abbot of Ford.[4] Several instances of his official activity remain.[5] With the prior of Taunton he removed a suspension laid by Savaric, bishop of Bath and Glastonbury (1192–1206).[6] He was among the cistercian abbots writing to the pope about conditions at Canterbury in 1198.[7] He was present at the foundation of Dunkeswell abbey on 15 Aug. 1201.[8] He was a party to several final concords.[9] Abbot John was evidently in the royal party during the years 1204–7, possibly as chaplain, signing writs and ordering wine for church services.[10] When he left the king for a time in 1205 he was permitted to take with him sixty cows and ten bulls.[11] On a visit two years later at the abbot's suggestion the king ordered cloaks for several poor men.[12] The abbot died 21 Apr. 1214.[13] Another John was abbot of Ford during the years 1234–40.[14]

1 'Fr. J. pauper Christi de Forda.'
2 Possibly mistaken in abbreviation.
3 John was probably the first abbot of Bindon (founded in 1171) known to Dugdale (*Monasticon*, v. 656).
4 'Johannes abbas de Bynnadone factus est abbas de Forda' (*Ann. Monast.* i. 21).
5 For other points see Bell, *op. cit.* p. xiii.
6 H.M.C., *Various Collections*, i. 239.
7 *Hist. Works of Gervase of Canterbury* (R.S.), ed. W. Stubbs, i. 569.
8 *Ann. Monast.* i. 26.
9 *Fines sive Pedes Finium*, ed. Joseph Hunter, ii. 76, 98; *Dorset Records*, ed. E. A. and G. S. Fry, v. 15, 37, 68.
10 *Rot. Litt. Claus.* i. 3, 8, 18.
11 *Ibid.* p. 25.
12 *Rot. Chart.* pp. 106, 107, 134, 164; *Rot. Litt. Claus.* pp. 19, 25, 36, 81, 82; T. p. 433.
13 *Ann. Monast.* ii. 281; he was succeeded by the subprior, Roger.
14 *Ibid.* ii. 316, 328.

The author was evidently a man of great authority. He undertook, in his sermons on the Song of Solomon, to finish a work commenced by St. Bernard.[1]

John of Garland,[2] professor at Paris, was the author of a wide variety of works, some of which appear in several editions. The MS. ascriptions are supplemented by valuable glosses and one list of writings by the author himself. The best study of this very complicated problem is to be found in L. J. Paetow's introduction to his edition of the 'Morale Scholarium.' More information has been added by E. Faye Wilson in 'The *Georgica Spiritualia* of John of Garland' (*Speculum*, viii, 1933, 358–77). She has a good list of his printed works, and has in preparation an edition of Garland's 'Epithalamium B. Marie Virginis' (*Index*, p. 47). She has also discussed this piece in her 'Study of the Epithalamium in the Middle Ages' (an unpublished doctoral dissertation for the university of California, 1930).

The old library catalogue of the austin canons of York mentions two rare works: 'Ioh. de Garlandia de mirabilibus mundi,' and 'Stella maris Johannis de Garlandia' (M. R. James, *Fasciculus Ioanni Willis Clark dicatus*, pp. 72, 73, MS. E. 480). A treatise on alchemy is also ascribed to him (H.M.C. 3rd Rep., App. p. 122). The identification of him with the musical authority of the same name is urged by H. E. Wooldridge, *Oxford History of Music*, i. 155 *n.* 1; see also Coussemaker, *Scriptorum de Musica Medii Aevi*, i. pp. viii–x; iii. pp. vii–viii, 23, 424–5). Some 'Versus Proverbiales,' believed to have been his, have been edited by L. K. Born (*Medium Aevum*, iii. 7–12).

The biography of John of Garland has been worked out in a rather sketchy fashion by Paetow from references in Garland's works. He was a native of England, and as a youth had attended the lectures of one

1 Bale, *Index*, p. 202.
2 T. p. 309; *D.N.B.* under Garland.

John of London at Oxford,[1] probably by 1213.[2] At Paris he received his surname because he taught in the 'clos de Garlande.'[3] In the years 1221–3 he published the 'Epithalamium.'[4] Since Garland's list is arranged chronologically he had already finished the 'Dictionarius,' 'Parisiana poetria,' 'Integumenta super Ovidii Metamorphosin,' 'De triumphis ecclesie,' 'Compendium grammatice,' 'Memoriale,'[5] and also the 'Assertationes fidei,' the 'Gesta apostolica,' and 'Georgica spiritualia.'[6] This indicates that he had already studied grammar, rhetoric, and medicine. The 'Epithalamium' may indicate that he was studying theology at this time. At the breakup of the university of Paris in 1229 John of Garland went to Toulouse as a master of grammar.[7] There he apparently wrote a guide for the city, 'Conductum de Tholosa,' argued about the Tholosans' error in computing Easter,[8] and approved of the enthusiasm with which his colleague, Roland of Cremona, O.P., headed a mob which destroyed the house of a heretic, Galvanus, dug up his body, and burned it outside the city.[9] He resigned at Toulouse, alleging irregularity in the payment of his salary, and made his way to Paris in 1232 after a fright described by Paetow as follows:[10]

> Fearing treachery in Toulouse he took to a ship in the Garonne only to fall into the hands of rough sailors who planned to carry him on to Castel-Sarrasin to rob him or to do him still greater harm. Suddenly he observed a cloud in the form of a shield, and pointing to it, cried, 'Behold the sky denounces war and the heavenly avenger of the Church is not far distant.' The superstitious sailors were terrorized by this phenomenon which lasted a full hour. Meanwhile John of Garland made his escape and joined a party of pilgrims near Moissac.[1]

In 1234 he published some of his works at Paris.[2] Before 1241 he returned to England but was appalled by the roughness of the sea and sailors.[3] 'His Morale Scholarium' of 1241 praises very highly both Fulk Basset and John Blund [q.v.].[4] His 'De mysteriis ecclesie' is dedicated to Fulk Basset, then bishop of London (1244–59), and was read before Peter Parvus, chancellor of Paris.[5] His 'Commentarius' upon this work belongs to 1246.[6] Probably he wrote the 'De mysteriis ecclesie' in England, and brought it to France, arriving there before the death of Alexander of Hales [q.v.] in the autumn of 1245.[7] The 'Accentarium' or 'Ars lectoria' followed in the next three years,[8] and the 'Stella Maris' in 1248–9.[9] Apparently he completed another edition of his 'De triumphis ecclesie' in 1252[10] and in 1258 his 'Exempla honeste vite.'[11] A Master John of Garland, royal judge and canon of St. Paul's before 1200, is too early,[12] and a John of Garland, canon of Rouen in 1269–71, probably too late to be identified

[1] *Johannis de Garlandia De triumphis ecclesie* (Roxburgh Club), ed. T. Wright, pp. v, 53–4; *Morale Schol.*, ed. Paetow, p. 83.

[2] A. B. Emden, head of St. Edmund Hall, Oxford, has pointed out to me that Paetow (*op. cit.* p. 83) did not take into consideration the effect of the interdict upon Oxford.

[3] *Morale Schol.*, p. 87.

[4] Wilson, *op. cit.* pp. 361, *n.* 2, 371.

[5] *Ibid.*

[6] *Morale Schol.*, pp. 108, 119.

[7] *Ibid.* p. 90; *De triumphis*, p. 99.

[8] *Morale Schol.*, p. 92; *De triumphis*, p. 99.

[9] *De triumphis*, pp. vii, 101.

[10] *Morale Schol.*, pp. 5–24.

[1] *Morale Schol.*, p. 92.

[2] Paetow, *op. cit.* p. 93; Bruges MS. 546, fo. 76*b*.

[3] Paetow, *op. cit.* p. 95; *Morale Scolarium*, i. 603–613.

[4] L. 631 and 89.

[5] B.M. MS. Harley 4967, fo. 115*b*.

[6] MSS. carry that information.

[7] *Morale Schol.*, p. 112.

[8] *Ibid.* pp. 122–4.

[9] *Ibid.* p. 114.

[10] *De triumphis ecclesie*, p. ix.

[11] Paetow, *op. cit.* p. 95.

[12] Canon of St. Paul's, 1198 (P.R.O., ancient deeds, L. 220); prebend of Newington, London (Le Neve, *Fasti Ecclesie Anglicane*, ii. 417); chaplain of Richard, bishop of London (B.M. MS. Cotton, App. xxi, fo. 57); P.R.O., a typed list by B. F. Davis, 'The Justices from 1166–1215,' *passim*; Archives of Queen's College, Oxford, typed list, Bodl. Lib. p. 108.

with our professor.[1] The professor possessed great crusading ardour, an interest in the classics, and a commendable enthusiasm which promised more than his abilities permitted him to fulfill.[2]

John Godard, abbot of Newenham,[3] wrote two pieces still extant :—

'Apostropha peccatoris in Virginem Gloriosam,' Cambridge Univ. Lib., MS. Mm. vi. 4, fos. 103*b*–19, *inc.* 'Gloriosa virgo, mater Dei, dignare me laudare te,' with a contemporary inscription 'Incipit apostropha peccatoris in virginem gloriosam edita a domino Johanne Godard primo abbate de Newenham.'

Letter of advice to his sister, Margaret, abbess of Tarent, Cambridge Univ. Lib., MS. Mm. vi. 4, fos. 236–56, *inc.* 'Kme sorori sue in Christo deo dicate virgini M. abbatisse de Tharente fr Johannes,' with the contemporary inscription 'Incipit epistola J. Godard quondam abbatis de Neweham ad sororem suam Margaretam abbatissam de Tarente.' He discusses horologues and horoscopes (fo. 238).

Another work is apparently no longer extant, the 'De triplici modo computandi' which Leland saw at Coggeshall (*Collect.* iv. 162) and of which he made the following note : 'Joannes Godard de triplici modo computandi ad R. abbatem de Coggeshawle. *Memini me ad suadelas.*'

An early biography of John Godard reads :

Johannes Godard natus in Cantuaria primus abbas huius monasterii, vir nobilis scientie et mirabilis eloquentie qui octavo idus Januarii die videlicet dominica in festo epiphanie domini domum recepit regendam anno eiusdem millesimo CC XLVI° anno regni regis Henrici filii regis Johannis XXXI qui contulit huic monasterio unam Bibliam, Moralia super Job, Isydorus Ethmiologicarum, Sententias Willelmi Autiodorum' in duobus voluminibus, Luca glos., glos. super totum testimentum, Johannem Belet, Abel, Johannem Damascenum, Boethium de consolatione, Tullium de amicitia et senectute. Et anno domini mille CC XLVIII quarto die mensis Aprilis cessavit et apud Clyva in Somerset per annos plurimos postmodum abbatizavit.[1]

John Godard was born in Canterbury.[2] The lost book dedicated to R., abbot of Coggeshall, was probably to that Ralph [q.v.], abbot 1207–18, who lived until 1228.[3] John became a monk at Beaulieu, a cistercian house like Coggeshall, and as such probably received a present of a tun of ordinary wine from the king on 3 Mar. 1245.[4] He was chosen to lead the group of Beaulieu monks who made up the membership of the new abbey of Newenham in Devonshire. They left their mother house on 2 Jan. 1245[5] and entered their new home on 6 January. On 4 April or 16 Aug. 1248 John retired to Clive in Somerset, living for some years.[6] He left a considerable library to Newenham and a reputation as a 'vir magne auctoritatis.'[7] His letter to Margaret may well have been written during his retirement.

John of Hoveden, poet,[8] was responsible for a series of devotional poems :—

[1] *C.P.R.*, 1266–72, pp. 544, 585 ; *Registrum Johannis de Pontissara* (Cant. and York Soc.), ed. C. Deedes, ii. 629 ; P.R.O., MS. Cal. Close Rolls, ed. H. J. Sharpe, 16 Jan. 55 Hen. III ; see letter from 'Johannes dictus de Garlandia presbyter et canonicus de Castella Tykhillie,' written at Cologne, P.R.O., ancient correspondence, S.C. 1, x, no. 148.

[2] See Paetow, 'The Crusading Ardor of John of Garland,' *Crusades and other Historical Essays presented to Munro*, pp. 207–22.

[3] T. p. 328.

[1] B.M. MS. Arundel 17, fo. 53*b* ; Dugdale, *Monasticon*, v. 690, omits the items about the books.

[2] Probably related to the Godards of Kent, mentioned in *Placitorum in domo capitulari Westmonasteriensi asservatorum Abbreviatio*, pp. 157, 176.

[3] Benedict and Geoffrey followed Ralph, but possibly another R. came before the death of John (Dugdale, *Monasticon*, v. 451). By his retirement John may have imitated the action of Ralph.

[4] *C.L.R.*, 1240–5, p. 293 ; possibly the same as the John Godard who received expenses for service beyond seas in 1227, 1236, and 1237 (*C.L.R.*, 1226–40, pp. 245, 246, 268). He was abbot of 'Funtmoryny' in 1227.

[5] Dugdale states that a description of the journey existed in a register formerly in the possession of William Wavell (*Monasticon*, v. 690).

[6] 4 April as above ; Dugdale, *Monasticon*, v. 690.

[7] B.M. MS. Arundel 17, fo. 45*b*.

[8] T. p. 415 ; *D.N.B.* under Hoveden, contains references to editions of poems of Hoveden. Both confuse him with the astrologer, John of London [q.v.].

'Canticum amoris,' *inc.* 'Princeps pacis proles puerpure': (a) B.M. MS. Cotton, Nero C. ix, fos. 226–8*b*, inscribed 'Canticum amoris quod composuit Johannes de Hoveden'; (b) MS. attributed to John by Boston of Bury (Camb. Univ. Lib. Add. MS. 3470, 101), entitled 'Meditationem de nativitate et passione Christi et vocatur Canticum amoris. Princeps.'

'Cantica quinquagenta,' *inc.* 'In laude nunc omnis exultet,' *expl.* the same: (a) B.M. MS. Cotton, Nero C. ix, fos. 210–8*b*, inscribed 'Hic scribitur meditatio Johannis de Hovedene—et vocatur—meditatio cantica 50 quod in 50 canticis continetur'; (b) MS. mentioned by Boston of Bury, *loc. cit.*

'Cythara,' *inc.* 'Ihesu vena dulcedinis,' *expl.* 'In celebri collegio': (a) Bodl. Lib. MS. Laud Misc. 368, fos. 195*b*–201; (b) B.M. MS. Cotton, Nero C. ix, fos. 218*b*–23*b*, which begins:

In honore domini salvatoris incipit meditatio edita a Johanne de Hovedene clerico Alianore regine Anglie matris regis Edwardi. . . . Hec meditatio vocatur Cythara eo quod verbum amoriferis que quibusdam cordis music' ad delectationem spiritualem legentes invitat.

Fifteen joys of Mary, *inc.* 'Virgo vincens venerantia': (a) Bodl. Lib. MS. Laud Misc. 368, fo. 195; (b) B.M. MS. Cotton, Nero C. ix, fos. 209*b*–10, headed 'Incipiunt XV gaudia virginis gloriose edita a magistro Johanne Hovedene clerico; and (c) MS. mentioned by Boston of Bury, see Bale (*Index*, p. 221).

'Lira,' *inc.* 'O qui fontem gratie,' B.M. MS. Cotton, Nero C. ix, fo. 226, colophon, 'Explicit lira magistri Johannis Hovedene.'

'Philomena,' *inc.* 'Ave verbum ens in principio,' *expl.* 'Qui es verbum ens in principio': (a) Bodl. Lib. MS. Laud Misc. 368, fos. 168–91*b*; (b) Lambeth Palace, MS. 410, fos. 97 *et seq.*; (c) B.M. MS. Harley 985, fos. 1–42*b*; (d) B.M. MS. Cotton, Cleo. A. xii, fos. 67–76*b*; and (e) B.M. MS. Cotton, Nero C. ix, fos. 197–209*b*. Note at beginning of MSS. (b) and (c):

Incipit meditatio Johannis de Hovedene clerici regine Anglie, matris regis Edwardi . . . et voluit editor quod liber meditationis istius Philomena vocaretur.

MSS. were formerly at Norwich in the franciscan house and at Oriel College, Oxford (Bale, *Index*, p. 221).

'Quinquagenta salutationes Beate Virginis,' *inc.* 'Ave stella maris': (a) Bodl. Lib. MS. Laud Misc. 368, fos. 192*b*–4*b*; (b) B.M. MS. Cotton, Nero C. ix, fos. 223*b*–5:

Incipiunt quinquagenta salutationes beate virginis quibus inseritur memoria dominice passiones edita a Johanne de Hovedene ad . . .

(c) MS. formerly at Oxford, Oriel Coll. (Bale, *Index*, p. 221).

'Viola,' *inc.* 'Maria stella maris': (a) Bodl. Lib. MS. Laud Misc. 368, fo. 192; (b) B.M. MS. Cotton, Nero C. ix, fo. 225, 'Incipit laus de beata virgine que viola vocatur edita a Johanne de Hovedene.'

An unidentified work of his was bequeathed to the cathedral of York in 1413:

Librum Jo. Hoveden, Ricardi Heremite, domini Walteri Halton canonici, Willelmi Remyngton, et Hugonis de Institutione Novitiorum in 10 vol. (MS. Harley 6972, fo. 69).

See M. E. Walcott's 'Mediaeval Libraries' (Royal Soc. of Literature, *Transactions*, 2nd series, ix. 75).

Two other works are attributed to him. One is 'Speculum laicorum,' which, however, in type and content would seem to be the work of a mendicant friar (J. T. Welter, *Thesaurus Exemplorum*, p. vii). The earliest known MS. seems to come from a cistercian house in Hainault (A. G. Little, *Studies in English Franciscan History*, p. 38). 'De beneficiis Dei ex Bernardo,' formerly at Oxford, Brasenose Coll. (Bale, *Index*, p. 221), *inc.* 'Iesu Christi celeri, miseratione, et beate virginis, intercessione.' This MS. might easily have been written by the cistercian abbot of Sallay.

The poet is undoubtedly the royal clerk, John of Hoveden, who secured pardons for three men in 1268 and 1269.[1] The notes on his poems state that he was the clerk of Eleanor, mother of Edward I. On 3 Sept. 1275, he was granted a prebend in the collegiate church of Bridgnorth, Salop.[2] On 12 January of the same year he attested a charter.[3] He was apparently holding this prebend in 1284,[4] but not by 1291. The story of his death in 1275 resulted from confusing him with the astrologer of the same name [q.v.]. In the early part of the 14th century there were two Johns of Hoveden, probably, one of which may be our man. One, presented to the church of St. Giles, Winchelsea, on 27 Sept. 1304, probably resigned it by 13 Jan. 1305, and was presented to the church of 'Styveton' on 26 Apr. 1305.[5] The other was a monk of Sallay in 1290,[6] elected abbot, and probably installed in 1303,[7] in difficulties in 1306,[8] absolved from excommunication in 1314, and probably retired or deceased by 1322.[9] We find the first receiving churches by royal benevolence much as the royal clerk had done. The 'De beneficiis Dei ex Bernardo' attributed to a John of Hoveden rather suggests that the poet became a cistercian monk. Sallay was the centre for meditative and contemplative literature such as John of Hoveden wrote. All references suggest that John of Hoveden the poet was not a master.

John of Hyde, monk of Winchester and hagiographer,[10] is described by Bale in these words:

Joannes de Hyda, monachus Wintoniensis, scripsit inter cetera, ad presulem Wintoniensem, Vitam domini Iobi, . . . 'Venerabili patri et amico speciali . . .' *Ex magistro Ioanne Pullano Oxon* (*Index*, p. 222).

He may possibly be the John 'de Haida' upon whose work Bale reports:

Ioannes de Haida, poeta antiquus, versifice scripsit, Vitam Malchi monachi, li. i. 'Sicut in omni artium professione actualium,' etc. Liber incipit 'Prelia gesturus, ludos pius et quasi durus.' Formulam vite honeste, li. i. 'Hei quicunque legit Martini musa quod egit.' De Iona propheta, li. i. 'Vos qui nescitis, nunc dicite de Niniuitis.' Passionem Laurentij, li. i. 'A Decio temptus, gladioque furente peremptus, etc.' *Ex Ioanne Ducket, Lynne* (*Index*, p. 214).

John of Latro was the author of a treatise, 'De natura dictandi': (a) B.M. Add. MS. 17724, fos. 39–53 (not mentioned in the catalogue), *inc.* 'Sumite naturam que,' inscribed 'Incipit documentum magistri Johannis de Latro de natura dictandi secundum stilum Romanum,' in which as an illustration he uses 'Innocentius episcopus servus servorum Dei venerabili in Christo fratri patriarche Ierosolimitano vel archiepiscopo Cantuariensi vel episcopo Londoniensi,' which suggest that he wrote for English patronage; (b) B.M. MS. Reg. 8 A. x, fos. 1–8*b*, in which his name 'John' is given (fo. 5*b*). This MS. of the treatise is not quite the same as (a). Possibly he wrote the 'Varietates salutationum' which follows on fos. 8*b*–10. In it is a letter from H., bishop of Hereford (1216–34), to H. (or probably A.), abbot of Reading, asking him to give 'Mr. J.' the 'regimen' of the schools of Reading (fo. 10). If the abbot is A. (1226–49) this letter belongs to the years 1226–34. Other letters mention Pope Innocent, 1199–1216 or 1243–54 (fo. 41), the emperor Frederick, 1212–50 (fos. 2, 41*b*) and J. cardinal deacon of St. Praxedes, *c.* 1211–44 (fo. 41).

John of Leicester, a poet, wrote some verses upon St. Hugh at the time of his death in 1200, which were described by Adam of Eynsham:

Tunc magister Johannes Leircestrensis, vir litteratus et industrius, huiusmodi distichon ad pedes

[1] *C.P.R.*, 1266–72, pp. 189, 258, 338.
[2] *Ibid.*, 1272–81, p. 103.
[3] *C.Ch.R.*, 1257–1300, p. 189.
[4] R. W. Eyton, *Antiquities of Shropshire*, i. 74.
[5] *C.P.R.*, 1301–7, pp. 259, 309, 337.
[6] P.R.O., Exchequer of pleas, plea roll, E. 13/22, *m.* 44; he served as proctor for his abbot.
[7] Dugdale, *Monasticon*, v. 511.
[8] *C.Cl.R.*, 1302–7, pp. 458, 521; the abbot and some fellow monks were in jail in September.
[9] Dugdale, *loc. cit.*; B.M. MS. Harley 112, fo. 15*b*.
[10] T. p. 435; the additions mentioned by Tanner do not seem plausible.

ejus posuit; in quo multiplices virtutum ejus prærogativas breviter expressit, dicens:

> Pontificum baculus, monachorum norma, scholarum Consultor, regum malleus, Hugo fuit.[1]

He also wrote verses upon the death of Bishop Geoffrey of Winchester (Bodl. Lib. MS. Bodl. 656, fos. 149*b*–50), *inc.* 'Sedes Wintonie, trinus aureus aurea forma,' and on the margin, 'Vs Joh. de Leircestria.' He may have written other verses on fos. 146–56*b*.

There is a Master John of Leicester, who appears in documents of about this time, chaplain to Bishop Roger of St. Andrews.[2] He witnessed charters in 1188 or 1189,[3] on 2 Feb. 1193 at Edinburgh,[4] and in 1199.[5] His patron, Roger, died in 1202. From 23 Jan. 1204 to sometime before 30 Nov. 1205 a Master John of Leicester appears as a prebendary of Morville, of the collegiate church of Bridgnorth.[6]

John of London, prebendary of Hoveden, was an astrologer about whom all information is of the most elusive and deceptive character, so that all statements must be carefully scrutinized.

'Pratica chilindri': (a) B.M. MS. Sloane 1620, fos. 2–4*b*, *inc.* 'Cum volueris scire horas diei,' colophon 'Explicit pratica chilindri Magistri johannis de Hoveden astrologi,' has been published by Edmund Brock in his 'Essays on Chaucer.'

'De astrologia iudicaria,' B.N. MS. lat. 7413, fos. 19*b*–21 (14th cent.), is mentioned by L. Thorndike (*History of Magic and Experimental Science*, ii. 95). A letter addressed by John of London to R. de Guedingue in 1246 or not long afterwards says that he is sending a transcript of tables of the fixed stars which he verified at Paris.

The astrologer's title, master, should prevent confusion with the poet, John of Hoveden. As we shall see, John was probably not called 'of Hoveden' until after his death. Thus we merely call attention to the existence of one and probably more Master Johns of Hoveden in the early part of the 13th century.[1]

In his 'Itinerary' Leland speaks of Hoveden's church[2]:

> The Colligiate Church is auncient and meatly faire. Ther be 5 Prebends by these Names, Hovedene, Thorpe, Saltmarsch, Barneby, and Skelton. In the Quire lyith one John of Hovedene, whom they caul a Sainct, one as they say of the first Prebendaries there.

There are three accounts about him, two apparently more trustworthy than the other:

> Circa istud tempus transiit e seculo quidem ecclesiæ de Howden præbendarius, Johannes nomine, vir honestæ vitæ et private, non pompose, degens, astrologiæ peritus, hospitalitati et misericordiæ intentus. Inchoavit ipse de suis sumptibus chorum ecclesiæ novum, quod superat prædixit post mortem completurum; quod luce clarius intuemur. Nam sepultus solemni mausoleo in medio ipsius chori habetur pro sancto et ex oblationibus frequentantium populorum non tantum chorum sed navem ecclesiæ latam videmus compleri et operosam.[3]

> [1276] Et apud Houden erat frequens concursus populorum ob multa miracula quæ fiebant ibidem ad sepulchrum sancti Johannis, qui nuper obiit habens portionem quandam in ecclesia de Houeden. Theologus etiam fuit oriundus Londoniis, habebaturque despectus in vita sua. Referebatur etiam de eo quoddam mirabile factum per quod innotuit populo. Cum enim corpus ejus jaceret in feretro patenter in ecclesia et cantaretur missa pro eo antequam humaretur, in elevatione Hostiæ ad missam et ipse defunctus manus suas versus corpus Domini elevavit, ut mos

[1] *Magna Vita S. Hugonis* (R.S.), ed. Dimock, p. 377.

[2] Edinburgh, national library MS. 35.3.8. p. 103; *Liber Cartarum Prioratus Sancti Andree in Scotia* (Bannatyne Club), p. 153.

[3] James Raine, *History and Antiquities of North Durham*, p. 85; Roger was still 'elect.'

[4] Edinburgh MS. *cit.* pp. 102, 106; Raine, *op. cit.* p. 86.

[5] Edinburgh MS. *cit.* p. 100.

[6] *Rot. Litt. Pat.* pp. 38, 48; *Archaeological Journal*, lxxxiv (1928). 56.

[1] In time of Bishop Hugh of Durham (1154–95) (Durham cathedral muniments, doc. 3. 1. pont. 3); F. M. Stenton, *Transcripts of Charters of Gilbertine Houses* (Lincoln Record Soc.), p. 61; *C.Ch.R.*, 1226–57, p. 234.

[2] *Itinerary* (3rd ed.), i. 54.

[3] *Chronicon de Lanercost* (Bannatyne Club), ed. J. Stevenson, p. 93.

est, ac, dimissa Hostia, deposuit et ipse manus suas, quo prius fuerunt.[1]

The third account [2] confuses the astrologer with the royal clerk and poet. We have, then, a theologian, coming from London and therefore probably called John of London until his sanctity caused him to be called John of Hoveden. He was a man of very attractive personality, and an astrologer. He had evidently become a doctor of theology in the schools and was doubtless wealthy.

In the year 1267 Roger Bacon stated that Master John of London was one of the only two perfect mathematicians.[3] Writing in 1252, John of Garland seems to infer that a Master John of London who had taught him in his youth, while apparently still a layman (about 1210), was teaching at Oxford.[4] Adam Marsh writes on behalf of 'Mr. John of London,' probably about 1250.[5] The prebendary of Hoveden died before 1276, but the number of years is given only vaguely. If he was the mathematician he must have enjoyed a long life. There was a Master John of London, canon of London, who apparently died in 1209.[6] The John, a youth in care of Roger Bacon in 1267, is certainly not the great mathematician. The name was, of course, very common.[7]

[1] *Chronicles of the Reigns of Stephen, Henry II and Richard I* (R.S.), ed. R. Howlett, ii. 571–2.

[2] 'Ex Alphredo Beuerlacensi' (Bale, *Index*, p. 220).

[3] *Opera Inedita* (R.S.), ed. J. S. Brewer, i. 34–5; possibly the same as Master John of Hendover eulogized by Bacon. One wonders if Hendover could be a corruption of Hoveden (*Opus Tertium*, p. 472).

[4] *Morale Scolarium of John of Garland*, ed. L. J. Paetow, pp. 83, 84, *n.* 17.

[5] *Mon. Fr.* i. 249.

[6] P.R.O., Exchequer, Misc. Books, E. 164/20, fo. 46; B.M. MS. Harley 4080, fos. 1, 13, 14, 12; H.M.C., 9th Rep., App. pp. 9, 17; Cambridge Univ. Lib. MS. Ee. v. 21, fo. 80*b*.

[7] A John of London mediated between factions at Oxford in 1252 (*Med. Archives of Oxford*, ed. H. E. Salter, i. 33); *Pipe Roll of the Bishopric of Winchester*, ed. Hubert Hall, p. 38; B.M. Add. 29436, fo. 32; *Foederium prioratus Dunelmensis*, pp. 109, 251; F. J. Baigent and J. E. Millard, *History of Basingstoke*, p. 652; *Historical Works of Gervase of Canterbury* (R.S.), ed. W. Stubbs, ii. 144, 167.

John of Metingham 'Scripsit *Iudicium Essoniorum*. MS. penes Guibertum Goddard e hospit. Lincoln' (T. p. 525). The treatise of this title, edited by G. E. Woodbine (*Four Thirteenth Century Law Tracts*, pp. 116–42), is tentatively attributed by its editor to Ralph Hengham (*ibid.* pp. 28–36). To him also is attributed a 'Modus componendi brevia' (Woodbine, *op. cit.* pp. 39, 116–62).

John of Monmouth, disputant in theology at Oxford, *c.* 1282–90 (Little-Pelster, p. 97).

John of Morbiry was the author of a treatise upon the 'Compotus' and possibly another upon legal procedure, 'Forma placitandi.' The 'Compotus' *inc.* 'Will's prepositus et R. serviens dicti manerii' Bodl. Lib. MS. Rawlinson C. 775, fos. 117–26*b*), with a note, 'Quis velit scire artem mod' et commod' ad compota in brevianda ordinanda infra margines huius libelli poterit invenire omnia necessaria ordinatim secundum ordinem J. de Morbiria clerici.' A 'Forma placitandi' follows in the MS. (fos. 127–50*b*), *inc.* 'Diversarum curiarum diverse sunt consuetudines et considerationes.' The 'Forma placitandi' is mentioned in the '*E.H.R.*' xlvii (1932). 627. Both treatises are also at Cambridge, Gonville and Caius Coll. MS. 238, fos. 341 and 409.

The 'Compotus' gives a sample of bookkeeping from Michaelmas 42 Hen. III (30 Sept. 1257) to the same day of the next year (fo. 117). The 'Forma placitandi' cites two documents of the year 41 Hen. III (1255–6): one of an essoin concerning a 'Will's Fitz R.' (fo. 136*b*), and the second of an action in the county court of Oxford on the Thursday before St. Barnabas's Day (11 June) when H. was sheriff (fo. 138*b*). Possibly the author taught at Oxford. One sentence reads: 'Qualiter autem hec omnia fient diligens doctor exponet sufficienter' (fo. 144*b*).

John of Oxford, monk of Luffield, was the author of a conveyancer, Cambridge

Univ. Lib. MS. Ee. i. 1, fos. 225 *et seq.*, colophon, 'Explicit modus et ars componendi cartas, cyrografa, etc. secundum Johannem de Oxonia.' This has been discussed in 'A conveyancer of the thirteenth century' (*Law Quarterly Review*, vii, 1891. 36–69), by F. W. Maitland, who also published a part of it in 'The Court Baron' (Selden Soc.), pp. 68–78.

Possibly John was presented by the king to a church and instituted on 28 Sept. 1268.[1] Of the dateable documents in the conveyancer numbers 17–28 seem to come from Oxford about 1272–4. They include a quit-claim supposed to have been made by J. de Oxford, and his will in which he is described as John of Oxford, clerk, dated 1274.[2] One document relating to Luffield is included which may suggest that he was in touch with Luffield even at that date. Another mentions Oliver, bishop of Lincoln (1280–1300). By another, Prior Adam and his convent appoint their fellow monk, John of Oxford, to be their proctor before the bishop of Lincoln [3] in 1273. Since the only known Prior Adam held office from 1279 to 1284 and John was still a clerk in 1274 this date should probably be emended to 1283.[4] A letter patent of 21 Dec. 1284 announced that John of Oxford, monk of Luffield, had letters of licence for the election of a prior since Prior Adam was now dead.[5]

John of Oxnead was probably a monk of St. Benet Holme and author of two historical works [6] :—

'Chronica,' *inc.* 'A principio mundi usque ad diluuium,' *expl.* 'et canonicus sancti Pauli Londonie' : (a) B.M. MS. Cotton, Nero D. ii, fos. 1–39, entitled 'Chronica Johannis de Oxenedes, monachi Sancti Benedicti de Hulmo' (mid. 17th cent.)'; (b) MS. in the duke of Newcastle's library. The chronicle was published from (a) by Henry Ellis (*Chronica Johannis de Oxenedes*, R.S., pp. 1–287), MS. (b) was then discovered and the variant readings added on pp. 403–11.

A history of St. Benet Holme, *inc.* 'Postquam locus Holmensis, Wifrico,' *expl.* 'Nicholaus de Swthwalesham de priore in abbatem electus,' B.M. MS. Cotton, Nero D. ii, with flyleaf. This has also been published by Ellis (*op. cit.* pp. 291–300).

The author of the two chronicles was obviously a monk of St. Benet Holme, so great is his interest in that house. That his name was John of Oxnead rests now upon a late ascription upon the Cotton MS., repeated probably from this source by T. Smith and Wharton.[1] The chronicler was probably the best historian from this house and is one of the better authorities for the 13th century.[2] It is continued to 1293.

John Peckam, O.F.M., theologian, was archbishop of Canterbury.[3] For the bibliography of his works see A. G. Little's preface to his edition of Peckam's 'Tractatus Tres de Paupertate' (B.S.F.S.) and his additions in *F.S.O.*, pp. 53, *n.* 3–8, 54.

'John de Pecham derived his name from the village of Patcham near Lewes in Sussex.' [4] He grew up in the neighbourhood of Lewes and retained kindly memories of the monks there.[5] A Master John de Pageham attested a charter in the time of Walter, bishop of Rochester, and William, prior of Canterbury.[6] The writer had a

[1] *Rot. R. Gravesend*, p. 221.
[2] No. 26.
[3] Nos. 22, 42, and 36.
[4] That is, mcclxxxiii for mcclxxiii ; Maitland noticed the difficulty but suggested no solution (*Law Quarterly Review*, vii. 36 ; *Court Baron*, pp. 11–3).
[5] *C.P.R.*, 1281–92, p. 146.
[6] T. p. 567 ; *D.N.B.* under Oxenedes, Oxnead.

[1] Quoted by Ellis in his preface *Chronicon*, p. iii.
[2] See Reginald de Cressy, below, for another. Minor chronicles of St. Benet Holme are edited by Ellis (*ibid.* pp. 300–15, 412–39).
[3] T. p. 584 ; *D.N.B.* under Peckham. The best account of his pre-episcopal life is in Little, *F.S.O.* p. 852.
[4] *Tractatus*, ed. Little, preface ; Bartholomew Cotton says that Peckham came from Kent (*Historia Anglicana*, R.S., ed. H. R. Luard, p. 371).
[5] *Reg. Peckham*, iii. 902 ; Annals of Lewes, B.M. MS. Tiberius A. x, fo. 172.
[6] B.M. MS. Stowe 924, fo. 164.

brother, Richard, whose son, Walter, received preferment from him.[1] A Simon of Peckham may also have been his relative. He was a schoolmate of Geoffrey de Aspal [q.v.] at an unstated time.[2]

His education was secured at Oxford and Paris, but the exact dates of his residence at each are uncertain. At Paris he enjoyed the favour of Queen Margaret and had Thomas de Canteloupe as a student.[3] He studied under Bonaventura (thus before 1257)[4] and shared in the defence of the mendicant orders against the attacks of William de St. Amour.[5] He ruled in theology at Paris, once as regent master during the second regency of St. Thomas Aquinas about 1269–71.[6] His position in the dispute about the substantial unity of man is open to doubt.[7] How early he studied at Oxford is also uncertain: he speaks of early training there.[8] He was tutor to a nephew of a 'Master H. de Anjou'[9] and entered the franciscan order apparently about 1250. He seems to have resumed teaching at Oxford about 1272–4, after ruling in theology at Paris.[10] Possibly at this time he wrote his treatise against Kilwardby.[11] A chronicler says that he was the first to introduce the practice of disputing 'de quolibet' at Oxford.[12]

At Oxford he succeeded Thomas of Bungay [q.v.] as eleventh master of the franciscans. Probably it was in this capacity that he was named by the king with the prior of the Oxford dominicans to decide a suit in 1275.[1] On 21 Dec. 1276 the king paid ten shillings to Friar John Peckam for going to Oxford.[2] Little thinks that he was already minister provincial.[3] If he was, he received letters from the king sent to the 'minister fratris minorum' by a messenger, Roger,[4] who was paid only a shilling for expenses (23 June 1277) which would suggest that John was still in England. However, on 13 June 1277 the king gave Friar Ralph Buzun forty shillings for expenses in carrying letters to Friar John Peckam at the roman curia.[5] This tends to cast doubt upon the statement that John Peckam held a teaching post at the curia for two years before he was chosen archbishop of Canterbury on 25 Jan. 1279.[6] He died on 8 Dec. 1292, leaving his vestments to Christchurch,[7] but apparently some of his books went to St. Augustine's.[8] He retained his provincialate while at Rome.[9]

John of Pershore, O.F.M. and scientist,[10] wrote a 'Canon kalendarii': (a) B.M. Add. MS. 17368, fos. 36–51*b*, *inc.* 'Veritas et medula totius astrologie,' colophon, 'Explic. canon. kalendarii fratris Johannis de Persorio, magistri in theologia, de ordine fratrum minorum'; (b) at St. Mary's, Leicester, among the authors of 'Astronomica' is listed 'Johannes Perchorie' (J. Nichols, *Hist. and Antiquities of Leicestershire*, i. 105).

1 *Reg. Peckham*, iii. 1010, 1048–50.
2 *Ibid.* p. 937.
3 *Reg. Peckham*, i. 315; iii. 827.
4 Little, *F.S.O.* p. 853.
5 *Reg. Peckham*, i. lvii.
6 Little, *F.S.O.* p. 853; *Triveti Annales* (Eng. Hist. Soc.), ed. T. Hog, p. 299; at this time he wrote his 'Tractatus Pauperis' (Little, *F.S.O.* p. 853).
7 See Little (*loc. cit. n.* 4).
8 *Reg. Peckham*, iii. 977–8.
9 *Mon. Franc.* i. 256.
10 *Triveti Annales*, p. 299; see App. A; 'doctor Parisius et resumpsit Oxonie' (*Mon. Fr.* i. 537).
11 Little, *F.S.O.* p. 853, *n.* 7.
12 *Chronicon de Lanercost*, ed. J. Stevenson, pp. 100–101.

1 *C.Cl.R.*, 1272–9, p. 232.
2 Little, *F.S.O.* p. 854; P.R.O. Exchequer K.R., various accounts, wardrobe and household, 5 and 6 Edw. I., 350 (23).
3 *Loc. cit.*
4 P.R.O., Exchequer, K.R., various accounts, nuncii, E. 101/308/3.
5 *Ibid.* E. 101/308/4, and Chancery miscellanea, C. 47/4/1, fo. 23.
6 *D.N.B.*
7 John Dart, *Hist. and Antiquities of the Cathedral Church of Canterbury*, p. ix.
8 James, *A.L.C.D.* pp. 33, 313, 481, 521, 628, 835.
9 Little, *F.S.O.* p. 854.
10 An account is given in Little, *F.S.O.* p. 859; Little-Pelster, p. 99.

John also shared in academic exercises reported in MSS. at Assisi and Todi (Little, *F.S.O.*, p. 859).

The calendar is said to cover the time, 1256–1332, four cycles of nineteen years. To have been of use it must have been written in the first cycle, 1256–74. John seems to have followed the scientific tradition of the Oxford franciscans. He was twenty-first reader in theology for the franciscans at Oxford, about 1289–90.[1] Hugh of Hartlepool [q.v.] presided at his vesperies, and he responded at the vesperies probably of Walter de Knolle and at a disputation of Master Richard de Clif.[2] His relatives may have been the Pershores with interests near Oxford.[3]

John of Renham, prior of Rochester, was probably author of part of the 'Annales Roffenses,' usually attributed to Edmund of Hadenham [q.v.], edited by Wharton (*Anglia Sacra*, ii. 351–4) and by H. R. Luard (*Flores Historiarum*, R.S., ii, iii). The chronicle is a very erratic performance, some years being fully chronicled and others neglected. The activities of the prior are prominent (*cf. Angl. Sacra*, ii. 353). The author in telling of the change in attitude of the former monk, John, who was promoted to be bishop, says, 'Promotus autem in episcopum, de claustralibus nihil curabit, de priore parum . . . cogitabit' (*ibid.* ii. 352), which would seem to be a personal complaint. The chronicle jumps from John's death in 1294 to 1301. Merton college and its founder are mentioned prominently (*ibid.* ii. 352): the prior was probably related to Henry of Renham [q.v.], who was at Merton then. The author gives the name, John of Renham, usually without the title 'frater' by which he usually designates the other religious.

John of Renham became prior of Rochester first in 1272 (*Flores Hist.*, ii. 477–8) when 'Mr. N.' was official and 'Fr. R.' de Lewis scrutinized the votes of the monks. Just before Christmas 1283 he resigned (*Angl. Sacra*, ii. 353). The chronicle then skips the following years until 1291, when 'in crastino Epiphanie' John became prior again (*ibid.* ii. 354), which office he retained until his death three years later.

John Russell, O.F.M. and theologian,[1] wrote, or others reported, a 'Postilla in cantica canticorum,' *inc.* 'Cogitanti mihi canticum,' Lambeth Palace, MS. 180, fo. 1 (15th cent.).

'Lectura super apocalypsim,' *inc.* 'Statuit septem pyramides unam,' Oxford, Merton Coll., MS. 172, fos. 106 *et seq.* (in the hand of William of Nottingham, 14th cent.), entitled 'Lecture fr. Johannis Russel, ordinis minorum, super Apocalysin.'

'Memorialia de Sacra Cruce,' *inc.* 'Mich. absit . . . Antequam locuor de cruce.' A MS. offered by Messrs. Hodgson (Sale Catalogue, 21 June 1934, no. 488) contains 'Fratrem Joh'e Russel memorialis huius signi scriptorem' and the title 'Memorialia de sacra cruce que viris literatis proferunt predicari' (fo. 1) and 'Pro fratre J. Russel' (fo. 8).

The other piece ascribed to him, 'De potestate imperatoris et pape' (Bale, *Index*, p. 244 and *n.*), is probably too late.

John Russell was twenty-second master of the franciscans at Cambridge, probably about 1289.[2] About 1293 as private chaplain of Edmund, earl of Cornwall, he carried certain presents from the minister general of the order, Raymond, to the earl, who expressed his thanks in a letter dated 29 August, at his manor near Oxford.[3] About the

[1] Little, *F.S.O.*, p. 859.

[2] *Ibid.*; cf. App. A.

[3] A grant from a John of Pershore, citizen of Gloucester, belongs to 1278–9 and one by his widow to 1301 (P.R.O., Exchequer, K.R., misc. books, E. 164/20, fo. 48; *Oxford Deeds of Balliol College*, Oxford Hist. Soc., ed. H. E. Salter, p. 254).

[1] T. p. 647; Little, *G.F.* p. 218. Dr. Little very kindly gave me several of the new items below 'for the name's sake.'

[2] App. A.

[3] Little, *G.F.* p. 218; Bodl. Lib. MS. Digby 154, fo. 38. The manor's initial letter was B, for which Little suggests Beckley.

same time he wrote to Roger de Merlawe that he had come to the chapter of his order at Oxford in 1294,[1] but, on account of illness, would not be able to visit him as he had intended.[2] He was licensed by the bishop of Lincoln on 21 Sept. 1305 to hear confessions. He was at Leicester at the time.[3]

John de Sacro Bosco,[4] mathematician, is occasionally called an Englishman,[5] but is also described as a Frenchman,[6] a Catalonian,[7] and a baptised Jew,[8] who translated works from Hebrew. He is also said to have translated works from the Arabic [9] or Greek.[10] Obviously he is as yet a man of mystery but of such great importance that he deserves careful study. This involves an examination of a multitude of MSS. scattered about Europe. The name 'sacer boscus,' it should be noticed, is very rare in England.

John of St. Albans was a physician and theologian. While none of his writings has been identified, he was important both for his connexion with the Paris dominicans and for the men with whom he has been confused.

This 'Mr. John of St. Albans' came from the town of St. Albans [11] and probably studied at Oxford.[12] He was physician to a

[1] P.R.O., Exchequer T.R., misc. Books, E. 36/202, fo. 37.

[2] Bodl. Lib. MS. Digby 154, fo. 37*b*.

[3] Lincoln Diocesan Record Office, Reg. Dalderby, fo. 87*b* ; one John Russell was witness to a charter of Robert Walerand in 52 Hen. III (P.R.O., Chancery misc., evidences, C. 47/9/2).

[4] T. pp. 371–2 ; *D.N.B.* under Holywood.

[5] Munich, Cod. Lat. Mon. 26812, fo. 293.

[6] Bodl. Lib. MS. Add. A. 2.

[7] Cambridge, Trinity Coll. MS. 567, fo. 15.

[8] *Die Handschriften-Verzeichnisse der K. Bibliothek zu Berlin*, ed. V. Rose, ii. no. 957.

[9] *Ibid.* ii. no. 960.

[10] Munich, Cod. Lat. Mon. 11067, fo. 142.

[11] *M. Paris Hist. Angl.* (R.S.) ed. F. Madden ii. 66 ; *Chr. Maj.* iii. 312.

[12] He witnessed a charter of Godstow (P.R.O., Exchequer, Misc. Books, E. 164/20, fo. 189) ; see also Cambridge Univ. Lib. MS. Add. 3020, fo. 79.

king of France,[1] probably Philip Augustus, and was probably made dean of St. Quentin on his nomination about 1218.[2] He gave the friars preachers of Paris his house before 1222,[3] whence they got the title 'Jacobites' since it was called the 'Domus Sancti Jacobi.'[4] Litigation over the gift arose because the canons of St. Quentin insisted later that the dean could not alienate the house.[5] In 1234 he resigned this deanship and succeeded Edmund of Abingdon as treasurer of Salisbury.[6] The Pope selected him as one of the preachers for the crusade in 1235.[7] He appears in documents of 1237 and 1238, as Master John of St. Quintin.[8] Possibly his successor was in office by 1239.[9] He has been confused with John de Barastre [10] and with John of St. Giles.[11] He was a 'magister theologie' and apparently the first master of the dominicans at Paris.[12] Stephen of Bourbon mentions a story of his about the purgatory of St. Patrick.[13]

John of St. Giles, O.P.M.D., was a theologian [14] of whose work little remains, in spite of his fame as first dominican doctor of theology at Paris. Medical recipes remain in at least two MSS. : (a) Bodl. Lib. MS.

[1] *Hist. Angl.* ii. 66 ; *Annales Monasterii Sancti Albani* (R.S.), ed. R. T. Riley, ii. 306.

[2] Denifle-Chatelain, *Cart. Univ. Paris.* i. 100–2, 114, 117, 420.

[3] *Hist. Angl.* ii. 66 ; *M.G.H.SS.* xxviii. 396 ; *Annales Monasterii Sancti Albani*, ii. 306.

[4] *Ibid.*

[5] Denifle-Chatelain, *loc. cit.*

[6] *Registres de Grégoire IX*, ed. L. Auvray, p. 989 ; *C.E.P.R.* i. 139.

[7] *Chr. Maj.* iii. 312 ; *Ann. Monast.* i. 95.

[8] *Charters and Documents of Salisbury* (R.S.), ed. Jones and Macray, pp. 241, 246.

[9] Le Neve, *Fasti*, ii. 645.

[10] C. Hemeraeus, *De scholis publicis sancti Quintini*, p. 50 ; hence much later error.

[11] *D.N.B.*

[12] Denifle-Chatelain, *op. cit.* i. 101 ; *N.E.MSS.* xxi. 2, 182.

[13] *Ibid.*

[14] T. p. 10 ; *D.N.B.* under John. The most recent work is by P. Glorieux, *Répertoire des maîtres en théologie de Paris au XIIIe siècle*, iii. 51–2). Cf. *Annals of Medical History*, N.S. vii (1935). 329–30.

Bodley 786, fos. 170–1*b*, *inc.* 'Sirupus contra febrem,' with a note 'Experimenta magistri Johannis de Sancto Egidio'; and (b) Cambridge, Peterhouse, MS. 222, about fo. 10 (James, *Catalogue*, p. 274). A sermon is mentioned by Haureau (*Notices et extraits de quelques manuscrits*, ii. 83; B.N. MS. 12418) and extracts from other sermons also remain (Haureau, *op. cit.* iv. 230–5). The other works assigned to him by bibliographers were probably merely suggested by the name Giles or because they were appropriate to his career. Of his writings a dominican chronicler wrote, probably fifty years after his death:

> Suavissimus quippe moralizator erat, ut satis considerare poterit, qui libros ejus inspexerit manu propria emendatos. Fuit nihilominus in arte medicinæ expertissimus, utpote qui tam Parisius quam in Montepessulano rexerat in eadem; de cujus curis et pronosticationibus referentur plurima admiranda (*Triveti Annales*, Eng. Hist. Soc., ed. T. Hog, p. 212).

The career of John of St. Giles has been confused with that of an archdeacon of Oxford of the same name [1] and with that of Master John of St. Albans [q.v.].

A Master John of St. Giles attested a charter of Stephen Langton, archbishop of Canterbury, probably in the years 1216–22.[2] He had probably studied medicine at Paris and at Montpellier before he took up theology. Since Roland of Cremona took his theological degree under him and went to Toulouse about 1229, John had doubtless finished his degree in theology by 1228 and probably earlier.[3] In 1230 he was teaching at Paris and made his sensational entry into the dominican order on 22 September, after preaching a sermon which is probably

[1] As in the *D.N.B.* The archdeacon was probably not a master, being called that only once in the many documents which I have seen that carry his name (B.M. MS. Harley 3688, fo. 137*b*).

[2] Lambeth Palace MS. 241, fos. 184, 225. The witness list includes William de Beauton and Giles de Bristol (*E.H.R.* xlviii, 1933, 532).

[3] *Triveti Annales*, p. 211; Quétif-Echard, p. 100, quoting list of masters by Salanhaco; cf. *Archiv für Litteratur und Kirchengeschichte des Mittelalters* ii. (1886), 171.

extant in abstract.[1] While preaching upon the virtues of poverty he interrupted his sermon to accept a dominican habit and then, returning to the pulpit, finished his sermon.[2] Abstracts remain of other sermons preached by him on 17 Nov. and 30 Dec. 1230, and on 12 Jan. and 15 June 1231.[3] In 1233 he went to Toulouse to succeed Roland of Cremona as lecturer.[4] From this he retired in 1235 and in the summer of that year was in attendance upon the Empress Isabella at Mayence.[5] In the autumn he returned to England with information concerning the pregnancy of the empress for her brother, Henry III.[6] Bishop Grosseteste asked permission for John to be with him, expecting him about Michaelmas.[7] He may have served with the bishop this year, 1235–6, but in the years 1237–40 he was high in the royal favour. On 7 Sept. 1237 the sheriff of Cambridgeshire was requested to find good horses for Friar John in order that he might come to the king at York.[8] He was an executor of the will of the king's sister, Joan, in the next year.[9] In 1239 he was called a royal councillor [10] and, probably at his request, the king granted a favour in 1240.[11] After this the information about his

[1] M. M. Davy, *Sermons Universitaires Parisiens de* 1230–1231, pp. 9, 271.

[2] *Triveti Annales*, pp. 211–2; 'Intravit etiam frater Johannes de Sancto Egidio, Anglicus natione, magister in theologia, facto sermone prius' (B. M. Reichert, *Fratris Gerardi de Fracheto Vite Fratrum*, p. 327).

[3] Davy, *op. cit.* pp. 43, 84, 98, 207, 271–98.

[4] 'In illis diebus magister Rolandus recessit Tolosa et ivit ad terram suam et in loco eius legit theologiam magister Johannes de Sancto Egidio vir bonus et sanctus et facies eius et vita eius gratiosa qui magister fuerat in theologia Parisius cathedralis' (Quétif-Echard, p. 100, quoting Pelhisso Tolosanus, under 1233).

[5] 'Mag. Johannes de Sancto Egidio iam recessit de domo cum sociis suis' (*ibid.* under 1235).

[6] *Chr. Maj.* iii. 324.

[7] *Ep. Grosseteste*, pp. 60, 61, 62, 132.

[8] *C.L.R.*, 1226–40, p. 291.

[9] *Ibid.* p. 318.

[10] *Chr. Maj.* iii. 627.

[11] *C.Cl.R.*, 1237–42, p. 215.

life grows scarce. In 1242 he heard the confession of a famous pirate, William Marsh. He was a papal delegate, with the bishop of London and Adam Marsh, to hear a case between the bishop of St. David's (Menevensi) and the king.[1] Shortly before his death in 1253, Bishop Grosseteste summoned him to his bedside and had a famous talk upon the shortcomings of the mendicant orders.[2] John had apparently cured the bishop at an earlier date of an attack supposedly due to poison. In 1258 he cured the earl of Gloucester of a similar complaint.[3] His death is not mentioned by Matthew Paris, but had occurred in time to be included in the 'Vite Fratrum' under the year 1259.

John of St. Omer, poet, was the author of a defence of Norfolk, B.M. MS. Titus A. xx, fos. 168*b*–70*b*, which has been edited by T. Wright in 'Early Mysteries and Other Latin Poems,' and translated by Richard Hewlett in the 'Norfolk Antiquarian Miscellany,' ii. 373–82. The author gives his name in the concluding lines:

> Constare facio de meo nomine
> Sum dei gratia dictus cognomine
> de sancto nuncupor Omero, crimine
> me mundes deprecor tu tutem, Domine.
> (*Early Mysteries*, p. 106.)

This John of St. Omer wrote his defence of Norfolk in answer to a poem by a Peterborough monk, entitled the 'Descriptio Norfolkiensium,' which appears in the same B.M. MS. (fos. 167*b*–8) and is also edited by Wright.[4] Beyond the fact that he is a native of Norfolk he tells little. In the 13th century there was a royal painter of the name,[1] and also a royal physician,[2] but the author was probably, like his antagonist, a monk.

John de Sampis was the author of 'Questiones de generatione et corruptione,' *inc.* 'Quia generatio et corruptio sint actus,' Oxford, Balliol Coll., MS. 313, fos. 163*b*–4 (13th cent.), colophon, 'Auctore Johanne de Sampis, magistro.' 'Sampis' is possibly a corruption of 'Samp',' the abbreviation for 'Sampson' or 'Sampford.'

John of Schipton, prior of Newburgh, owes his reputation as an historian[3] to the following statement of Matthew Paris:

> Ipso namque tempore, missus erat pro arduis domini regis Angliæ negotiis ab ejus latere dominus J[ohannes] prior de Neuburgo, specialis ejusdem regis consiliarius et nuntius in partes illas, qui super his casibus per magnates certificatus hæc scripturæ commendabat (*Chr. Maj.* v. 437).

He is also alleged to have written 'Vaticiniorum' and 'Poematum' (Pits, *Relationum Historicarum*, p. 324; T. p. 150).

John of Schipton, once chaplain of John of Lexington, appears as royal chaplain on 25 May 1250, receiving a deer as a gift from the king.[4] On 12 November of the same year the king ordered a casula worth 10 marks to be made for John's use.[5] Some time before 12 Jan. 1251 he was made prior of the canons of Newburgh, probably at the instance of the king. On that day he was exempted from suits in the king's counties, wapentakes, and hundreds.[6] Ten days later is dated a letter of protection to John until his return as envoy of the king beyond the sea.[7] On 20 June 1251 he was granted custody of houses in London during the minority of the heir.[8] On 29 June the king

[1] *Chr. Maj.* iv. 196; *Mon. Fr.* i. 342.
[2] *Ibid.* v. 400–11.
[3] *Ibid.* v. 705.
[4] Other MSS. are: (a) a MS. probably formerly at Peterborough, F. xiii, 'Descriptio Northfolchie,' and K. xiii, 'Descriptio terre Northfolchie' (James, *Peterborough*, pp. 71, 72); (b) Cambridge, Trinity Coll. MS. 1149, fos. 340–2; and (c) *ibid.* MS. 1450, fos. 59–62; and (d) Bodl. Lib. MS. Bodley 487.

[1] *C.Cl.R.*, 1247–51, p. 203; W. H. Blaauw, *The Baron's Wars*, p. 225.
[2] *C.Cl.R.*, 1272–9, p. 395; *C.P.R.*, 1272–81, p. 96.
[3] T. p. 150; Hardy thus says that he wrote 'Historia de bello inter Flandros et Gallos sub Comitissa Margareta' (*Descriptive Catalogue*, iii. 146).
[4] *Chr. Maj.* v. 610; *C.Cl.R.*, 1247–50, p. 285.
[5] *Ibid.* pp. 377, 423.
[6] *C.P.R.*, 1247–58, p. 84.
[7] *Ibid.* p. 85.
[8] *Ibid.* p. 99.

gave him six good oaks for a 'maeremium'[1] and on 20 March 1255 a 'maeremium' in the forest of Deresley.[2] In August 1251 the king freed him from common summons in the county of York.[3] In 1253 the king sent the prior of Newburgh, J. Canonicus, to secure provisions in England.[4] When the bishop of Carlisle died, the king urged that John should be promoted to fill the place, but the chapter refused.[5] John died in 1256 about All Saints' Day.[6]

John of Shepesheved is described by Tanner: 'historicus Anglicus scripsit, *Historiam de rebus Anglicis*, lib. i. Claruisse fertur A. MCCXLI' (T. p. 666). Pits says that the MS. is 'ex Jo. Stoo' (*Relationum Historicarum*, p. 313). Possibly this is a mistake for William of the same place (*Journal of Brit. Arch. Assoc.* xxi, 1865. 294–315).

John de Siccavilla (Seckville), chancellor of the university of Paris, was a scientist.[7] His main treatise now extant is entitled 'Corde mihi,' *inc.* 'Otium sine litteris mors est': (a) B.M. MS. Reg. 12, E. xxv, fos. 32–59, described as 'Compilationes intitulate "Mihi Corde" colecte per magistrum Johannem de Sicca Villa de principiis nature'; (b) Oxford, Merton Coll., MS. 292, fos. 70–85 (probably the 'De Principiis Nature' of Tanner, p. 233); (c) B.N. MS. lat. 6552, fo. 1; and (d) MS. formerly at Paris, sold for 'vii den, in viiii pecias' in the 13th century (Denifle-Chatelain, *Cart. Univ. Paris*, i. 644).

'Commoditates de relatione,' *inc.* 'De predicamento relationis querunt aliqui,' Oxford, Merton Coll. MS. 292, fos. 87*b*–95 (early 14th cent.), colophon, 'Expliciunt commoditates super relationem tradite a magistro Johanne de Secchevile' (also attributed to Robert Kilwardby [q.v.]). An excerpt from this appears among Cambridge 'questiones' of the time of Thomas Bungay (*c.* 1275) (Little-Pelster, p. 108).

'Tractatus de excellentia philosophie,' *inc.* 'Cum in omni natura,' Oxford, Merton Coll. MS. 292, fos. 85–7.

Three works also attributed to John, entitled 'Contra Seductores Fratres,' 'De Principiis Theologicis,' and 'Conclusiones Scholastice' (T. p. 233), probably represent guesses based upon known incidents in his life.

In 1248, at the request of Richard, earl of Cornwall, the pope granted a dispensation to Master John, learned in physical science, a clerk of Exeter, to hold one benefice with cure of souls besides those which he already held.[1] Since the earl of Cornwall granted Master John de Siccavilla the church of Pilham after 1244–5,[2] this item of 1248 probably refers to our author. The Seckville family is mentioned in connexion with Exeter.[3] By a final concord of 1274 John arranged for a messuage of sixty acres in 'Bradeleg et Nubbeleg.,' Gloucestershire, to pass to Richard de Seckville,[4] but the relationship of the two is not stated.

By 1256 the writer was rector of the university of Paris and so deeply involved in the struggle with the mendicant orders that he went to Rome upon this business.[5] His suit was unsuccessful, which may explain his presence in England a few years later. His 'Corde Mihi' was written in troublous

[1] *C.Cl.R.*, 1247–51, p. 465.

[2] *C.Cl.R.*, 1254–6, p. 55; on 16 July he was allowed to postpone payment on a crusading tithe (*ibid.* p. 209).

[3] *C.Cl.R.*, 1247–51, p. 554.

[4] *Chr. Maj.* v. 409.

[5] *Ibid.* p. 455.

[6] *Ibid.* pp. 588, 610.

[7] T. p. 233 under Driton; Siccavilla is apparently Seckville (J. H. Round in the *Archaeological Journal*, lxiv, 1907. 217–8); see also F. M. Powicke in *Essays in History presented to T. F. Tout*, p. 122.

[1] *C.E.P.R.* i. 241; *Les Registres d'Innocent IV*, ed. E. Berger, no. 3527.

[2] Another person held this in 1244–5 (*Rot. R. Grosseteste*, p. 146); John resigned in 1261–2 (*Rot. R. Gravesend*, p. 89).

[3] As in B.M. MS. Cotton, Vitell. D. ix, fo. 73*b*.

[4] P.R.O., feet of fines, Gloucestershire, 1–4 Edw. I (C.P. 25 (1), 75/30, no. 8).

[5] *Chr. Maj.* v. 599.

times when he seems to have been without active duty:[1]

Nota quod hiis diebus mororis dispersis scolaribus suspensis organis magistrorum terra nostra et gente dispositis igni et gladio, etc.

Probably this was during the barons' wars, in 1258 or later, possibly in 1263, when Oxford was dispersed.[2] He sided with the barons. In 1259 he was presented to the church of Overton, under royal patronage.[3] The treaty rolls record that certain letters about the peace with France were given to Peter de Montfort and Master John 'de Secchevill' at Westminster in 1259 to be taken to the king of France, who would return an answer.[4]

In 1261 John of Seckville resigned Pilham. He was a witness on 7 May 1262 of the charter of Richard de Clare granting Walter of Merton permission to vest the manors of Maldon and Farleigh in the priory of Merton to support scholars in the university of Oxford.[5] He also witnessed a grant by Robert de Ferrers, earl of Derby, to Gilbert de Clare.[6] As rector of Overton and of All Hallows the Great of London he appears in a papal document of 1263,[7] when the alien incumbent of Overton, turned out in 1258, had sued for the church.[8] Curiously enough the matter was placed before the official of Paris, which suggests that John may have returned there to teach. On 6 Dec. 1265 he was in London witnessing a document, probably with the bishop of Exeter.[1] On 24 Jan. 1267, as parson of Lichington, he received simple protection for a year from Henry III.[2] He resigned as canon of Glasney in the diocese of Exeter on 9 Dec. 1271 and was collated on the same day to a prebend worth six marks in the cathedral church of Crediton.[3] On 16 December, a year later, he resigned this prebend to accept another at St. Crantock.[4] About 1275 he was chief executor for the earl of Gloucester and involved in legal proceedings in his official capacity.[5] He acknowledged a debt of £10 15*s.* to Italian merchants in 1279 and seems to have named them as his attorneys.[6] For these debts apparently his revenues from his churches of All Hallows and Badelesmere were held up until released on 23 Nov. 1279.[7] He lived on into the time of Archbishop John Peckham (1279–92), when his executors rendered an account of his holdings. Then he held Bedford in the diocese of Lincoln, All Hallows the Great of London, Lightington in Ely, Malores in St. David's and Wandey in St. Asaph.[8] In addition he held land in Bloomsbury, London,[9] and granted certain rights in London to the Hospital of St. Giles outside London.[10] He had probably sold a capital messuage outside the 'bar of Holborn' to John de Kirkby.[11]

John of Stickborne was author of a series of commentaries[12] in Gonville and Caius Coll. MS. 344 (13th cent.) (James,

1 B.M. MS. Reg. 12, E. xxv, fo. 32.
2 *Ann. Monast.* iv. 449.
3 *C.P.R.*, 1258–66.
4 'In 1259 lendemain de la sainte Margarete et mois de Jul. Omnes predicte littere tangentes pacem Francie tradite fuerunt Petro de Monte Forte et mag. Johi de Secchevill die Mercurii proxima ante festum Sci Petri Vinculi apud West. ad deferend. Regi Franc. et ad recipiendum ab ipso Rege litteras quas idem rex dno reg Angl facere debuit de pace predicta' (P.R.O., treaty rolls, C. 76/2, *m.* 3).
5 *Merton Muniments*, P. S. Allen, H. W. Garrod, p. 8.
6 Derbysh. Archaeolog. and Nat. Hist. Soc., *Journal*, ix. 132; P.R.O., great coucher of Lancaster, ii. fo. 98.
7 *C.E.P.R.* i. 415; *Reg. Peckham*, p. 1020.
8 *Ibid.*

1 *Registers of Walter Bronescombe*, ed. F. C. Hingeston-Randolph, p. 218.
2 *C.P.R.*, 1266–72, p. 29.
3 *Reg. W. Bronescombe*, pp. 142, 129.
4 *Ibid.* pp. 130, 169.
5 P.R.O., Exchequer of pleas, plea rolls, 3–4 Ed. I, E. 13/3, *m.* 9; E. 13/4, *m.* 4*b*.
6 P.R.O., E. 13/8, *m.* 29*b*, 32*b*.
7 *Reg. Peckham* (C.Y.S.), p. 140.
8 T. p. 233; *Reg. Winchelsey*, fo. 36.
9 *Cat. Ancient Deeds*, i. 461.
10 B.M. MS. Harley 4015, fo. 167.
11 *Cal. of Inquisitions post Mortem Edw. I*, ii. 477.
12 T. p. 692.

Catalogue, i. 388): questions on Porphyry's 'Isogogy,' fos. 199*b*–203, entitled 'Questiones libri Porfirii date a domino Johanne de Stycborn'; questions on the 'Libri Predicamentorum,' fos. 203 ff., entitled 'Eiusdem questiones de predicamentorum libris'; questions on the 'Posterior analytics,' fos. 210–18, entitled 'Eiusdem questiones super librum peryermenios.'

His works appear after those of William Bonkis [q.v], who was at Oxford in 1292, and before that of Jo. de Wakerfeld, who was probably there at about the same time.

John of Taxster or Tayster, monk of Bury St. Edmund, was the author of a chronicle, 1173–1265,[1] *inc.* 'Coelum et terra': (a) B.M. MS. Cotton, Julius A. i.; (b) London, College of Arms MS. Arundel 6. This has been edited by H. R. Luard in 'Bartholomaei de Cotton . . . Historia Anglicana' (R.S., pp. 137–40); and excerpts are printed (in *M.G.H.SS.* xxviii. 584–98); and by B. Thorpe in 'Florentii Wigorniensis Chronicon' (Eng. Hist. Soc.), ii.

According to a note in the MSS. containing his work the author, J. de Taxster or Tayster, became a monk of St. Edmundsbury on 20 Nov. 1244.[2] His chronicle ends in 1265.

The last fact recorded by Taxster was a total eclipse on Christmas Eve, 1265, of the moon, which became of a red colour; it lasted three hours at night, the sun being in the head and the moon in the tail of the dragon. It occurred in the year 664 of the Hegira, and on the fifteenth day of the third month according to the Arabian reckoning.[3]

John Trussebot, disputant at Cambridge *c.* 1282 (Little-Pelster, p. 101; App. A).

John Wallensis, canonist, was author of a gloss on 'Compilatio I and II,' and formal apparatus on 'Compilatio III' (*D.N.B.*; Schulte, *Geschichte des Canonischen Rechts*, p. 189)

He seems to have been a professor at Bologna and to have written these works in the years 1212–6.[1] A John Wallensis was monk of Malmesbury and proctor for the abbey in the years 1217–22, and its abbot 1222–46.[2]

John Wallensis, O.F.M., was a moralist[3] of whose writings Little has written:

> He was essentially a moralist. As he himself said, he was 'ignorant of philosophy,' and though he wrote on the lives of the philosophers, he used them simply to draw moral instruction and example. His works enjoyed an enormous and lasting popularity. Extant manuscripts of them—dating from the 13th, 14th and 15th centuries—may be counted by the hundred: it is difficult to name any considerable collection of MS. which does not contain several of them. There are still extant four distinct Italian translations of one of his treatises, made in the fourteenth and fifteenth centuries. Between 1470 and 1520 twelve printed editions of one or several of his works were issued (*F.S.O.* p. 846).

His treatises have been catalogued by Little (*Studies in English Franciscan History*, pp. 174–92, and *G.F.* pp. 144–51). The confusion of the names John Gualensis and John de Garlandia has led Tanner (p. 434) to attribute to Wallensis Garland's 'Integumenta super Ovidii Metamorphosin' (L. J. Paetow, *Morale Scolarium of John of Garland*, p. 117). The works of John Wallensis were given such titles as 'Breviloquium,' 'Communiloquium,' 'Floriloquium,' and 'Legiloquium.'

The name, John Wallensis, is of uncertain meaning. He came from the franciscan custody of Worcester which included north Wales,[4] and may have been a Welshman. Yet it is possible that he was actually of

[1] *D.N.B.* under Taxster.

[2] 'Hoc anno [1244] scriptor præsentis voluminis habitum suscepit monachicum, dictus J. de Taxster die Sancti Edmundi' (*B. de Cotton Hist. Anglicana*, R.S., ed. H. R. Luard, p. liii). Arundel MS. gives 'Tayster.'

[3] E. Clarke, *Bury Chroniclers of the Thirteenth Century*, p. 8.

[1] *D.N.B.*; Sarti, Fattorini, *De Bononiensis Professoribus*, i. 384–5.

[2] *Registrum Malmesburiense* (R.S.), ed. J. S. Brewer, i. 392, 394, 402–5; Dugdale, *Monasticon*, i. 255.

[3] T. p. 434; *D.N.B.* under Wallensis. The best biography is by Little (*F.S.O.* p. 845).

[4] Little, *F.S.O.* p. 845, citing Cambridge, Jesus Coll. MS. 67.

Worcester and that Wallensis is a surname denoting that his father or forefathers had been Welsh.[1] He was regent master at Oxford about 1262–4,[2] and was thus probably already a man of considerable experience. Possibly he was the Johannes Walensis presented to Cowley by the abbot and convent of Osney in 1231.[3] He bore letters from the archdeacon of Gloucester and from a 'Mr. W. de Welleburn': presumably he was young then, possibly a student. Little has given the rest of the known facts of his life as follows: [4]

In October 1282 he was employed by Archbishop Pecham (who no doubt had been one of his pupils) in negotiations with Llewelyn, prince of North Wales. In 1283 he was in Paris where he took part in examining the doctrines of Petrus Johannis Olivi, he preached sermons there on 19 April and 1 May, and is described as regent. Friar John of Wales died at Paris, perhaps on 3 April 1285.

He is the subject of an early exemplum.[5]

John of Wallingford, monk and infirmarer of St. Albans and historian,[6] was the compiler of B.M. MS. Cotton, Julius D. vii, which is obviously inspired by the work of his fellow monk, Matthew Paris (MS. Nero D. i). The most important work is a chronicle, edited by T. Gale, in 'Rerum Anglicanum scriptores veterum,' i. Excerpts have also been printed (*M.G.H.SS.* xxviii. 505–21). John also included a picture of himself, possibly by Matthew Paris (Green, *Short History of the English People*, p. 283), and of the famous elephant, as well as a list of monks who had died since his entrance into monastic life. There is also some astronomical material (on fos. 1–7) and 'Versus de mensibus anni.'

John of Wallingford entered St. Albans on the feast of Saints Dionisius, Eustachius and Eleutherius (9 October), 1231.[1] Infirmarer of his abbey probably before 1250 and again in 1252, he represented it as proctor in a suit at Northampton and elsewhere in 1252 and 1253.[2] He became a priest and died on 14 August possibly of 1258, at Wymundham.[3]

John of Westerfeld, O.P., author of sermons at Oxford, 1292–3 (Little-Pelster, p. 190).

Joscelin, O.P., has a sermon reported in a group of early dominican sermons, B.M. MS. Egerton 655, fo. 146*b*, *inc.* 'Vovete et reddite. Iste pertinet ad religiosos qui viverunt,' with the marginal note 'Ad claustrales et sermo fratris Jocel.' He appears with Alard [q.v.] and thus probably belongs to the early 13th century. A Jocius was prior of the Oxford dominicans in 1233.[4]

Joscelin of Brakelonde, monk and almoner of Bury St. Edmunds, was an historian[5] whose chronicle of the years 1173 to 1202 gives an elaborate account of the history of his house and especially of the abbot, Sampson of Tottington. This account appears in B.M. MS. Harley 1005, fos. 121–63*b* (13th cent.). It seems that it was formerly also in B.M. MS. Cotton, Vitellius

[1] 'Summa de regimine huius vite Jo. Waleys, minorite Wigornie' (Royal Soc. of Literature, *Transactions*, 2nd series, ix. 78); 'Ioannes Gualensis, seu Walleys, iunior (vt fertur) doctor Parisiensis, Minorita Wigorniensis scripsit . . .' (Bale, *Index*, p. 211).

[2] Little, *F.S.O.* p. 845; see below, App. A.

[3] *Rot. H. de Welles*, ii. 32.

[4] Little, *F.S.O.* pp. 845–6.

[5] J. T. Welter, *L'exemplum dans la littérature religieuse et didactique du moyen âge*, p. 248 (from B.N. MS. lat. 3555, fo. 208).

[6] Tanner has mixed him up with John de Cella (T. p. 750); *D.N.B.* under Wallingford.

[1] B.M. MS. Cotton, Julius D. vii, fo. 112*b*.

[2] *Chr. Maj.* vi. 202; B.M. MS. Cotton, Nero. D. i, fos. 123*b et seq.*; *Gesta Abbatum Monasterii Sancti Albani* (R.S.), ed. H. T. Riley, i. 330, 334, 336, 337; 'Responsio partis abbatis Sci Albani et conventus per dominum Johannem de Walingeford tunc infirmarium in hoc negotio procuratorem' (B.M. MS. Cotton, Claud. E. iv, fo. 146*b*).

[3] In another hand than that of John, 'xix kal Septembr' apud Wymund o[bit] Johannes de Walingford sacerdos et scriptor huius libri' (B.M. MS. Cotton, Julius D. vii, fo. 113*b*).

[4] *Cartulary of Oseney Abbey* (Oxford Hist. Soc.), ed. H. E. Salter, i. 364, 365.

[5] T. p. 121; *D.N.B.* under Jocelin.

D. xv, now lost (T. p. 121). This chronicle has been edited by J. G. Rokewode as 'Chronica Jocelini de Brakelonda' (Camden Soc.) and by T. Arnold in 'Memorials of St. Edmund's Abbey' (R.S.), i. 209–336. It is translated by T. E. Tomlins in 'Monastic and Social Life in the Twelfth Century,' and has influenced Carlyle's picture of the abbot in 'Past and Present' (pp. 51–156). The chronicler also wrote an account of the 'Miracles of St. Robert,' a boy alleged to have been murdered by the Jews of St. Edmundsbury on 10 June 1181. Joscelin says:

Eodem tempore fuit sanctus puer Robertus martirizatus, et in ecclesia nostra sepultus, et fiebant prodigia et signa multa in plebe, sicut alibi scripsimus (*Chronica*, ed. Rokewode, p. 12).

This writing is not known to be extant.

Joscelin probably came from the town of Bury St. Edmunds of which two streets had the name Brakelonde in the middle ages.[1] He entered the monastery in 1175 and passed his novitiate under the direction of the future abbot, Master Sampson of Tottington,[2] a man of considerable learning who said that he preferred the life of a librarian to that of abbot.[3] Probably he received his schooling here, since he speaks of himself as being still very young in 1181.[4] In that year, in the course of a discussion of the qualities desirable in the next abbot, Joscelin recalls that he said that he would not consent to a candidate who knew no dialectic and could not distinguish right from wrong.[5] At the time of the election of Abbot Sampson in 1182 Joscelin was a chaplain of the prior.[6] Within four months, as he tells us, or about June-July of the same year, he was made chaplain to the abbot,[1] and remained with him continuously for six years,[2] appearing in this capacity in one charter.[3] He speaks of accompanying the abbot to Clarendon in 1187 [4] and at another time presented him with a schedule of livings in the abbot's gift with their values.[5]

[1] *Chronica*, ed. Rokewode, p. v, citing B.M. MS. Harley 27, fos. 5, 10*b*, 14, 15.

[2] *Ibid.* p. 3.

[3] *Ibid.* p. 27.

[4] 'Et ego quidem, tunc temporis juvenis, sapiebam ut juvenis, loquebar ut juvenis, et dixi quod non consentirem alicui ut fieret abbas, nisi sciret aliquid de dialectica, et sciret discernere verum a falso' (*Chronica*, p. 10).

[5] *Ibid.*

[6] *Ibid.* p. 19.

For the nine years from 1188 to 1197 he remained at Bury St. Edmunds, probably as an 'officialis' rather than a 'claustralis,' and doubtless in charge of some of the abbot's duties. He may be the monk, Joscelin, whose name appears in a charter of Bury, but this may be the contemporary cellarer of the same name.[6] In 1197 Abbot Sampson made radical changes in the housekeeping department of his monastery, especially in the cellar,[7] where the cellarer and 'hospitiarius' were at odds. In 1198 [8] and again in 1200 [9] Joscelin appears as 'hospitiarius' and was thus probably appointed to that office during the reorganization of 1197. This title is probably the same as almoner by which a contemporary monk calls him,[10] and by which he appears in at least two charters.[11]

In the struggle over the election of a successor to Abbot Sampson in 1214 Joscelin was in the party favouring accession to the

[1] 'Quando hec fiebant, eram capellanus prioris, et infra quatuor menses capellanus abbatis factus, plurima notans et memorie commendans' (*ibid.*).

[2] *Ibid.* p. 27.

[3] P.R.O., Duchy of Lancaster, D.L. 42/5, fo. 46.

[4] *Chronica*, p. 47.

[5] *Ibid.* p. 46.

[6] P.R.O., Duchy of Lancaster, D.L. 42/5, fo. 108; *Chronica*, pp. 84, 90, 91; Joscelin calls the cellarer Jocellus, but in the time of Sampson there was a cellarer, Jocelinus (Cambridge Univ. Lib. MS. Ff. ii. 33, fo. 80; MS. Gg. iv. 4, fo. 411); MS. Add. 4220, fos. 81*b*, 96; *Pinchbeck Register*, ed. Francis Hervey, ii. 22; B.M. MS. Lansdowne 416, fos. 47*b*–48*b*.

[7] *Chronica*, p. 64.

[8] 'Quod non sine gaudio scribo, qui curam hospitum habeo' (*ibid.* p. 71).

[9] 'Facto capitulo, sedebam ego hospiciarius in porticu aule hospitum' (*ibid.* p. 95).

[10] *Ibid.* p. 50.

[11] *Archaeologia Aeliana*, vii. 90.

king's wishes.[1] The author of the account of the election, who was of the opposing party, describes him as 'vir duplex animo et varius.[2] A monk more favourably inclined toward him calls him 'vir religionis eximie, potens in sermone et opere.' [3]

Lawrence Anglicus was a theologian (Glorieux, p. 350). A number of his sermons have survived in B.M. MS. lat. 16482.

This Lawrence was apparently a regent master of theology at Paris in 1256. In the next year, with others, he represented the university at Rome. Possibly he was a representative again in 1263, but appears to have died by 1264.[4]

Lawrence of Somercote, papal subdeacon and canon of Lichfield, was the author of a treatise upon canonical election,[5] *inc.* 'Licet circa diversas formas.' The treatise, which appears in numerous MSS., gives examples from about two hundred documents, largely from Gloucester and Hereford. For discussion about it see Henry Bradshaw and Charles Wordsworth's 'Statutes of Lincoln Cathedral,' ii. p. cxxiv. It has been edited by A. von Wretschko (*Der Traktat des Laurentius de Somercote*).

The 'Abbreviata Quedam,' attributed to Lawrence by Tanner, is the same treatise or, at least, has an incipit, 'Omnibus S. Matris ecclesie,' of a part of this treatise. Tanner also gives 'Super articulis fidei' (*inc.* 'Jesu gloriose suavitatum omnium'), apparently upon the authority of Bale, who says also of Lawrence, 'Idem Gallice composuit, modum mensurandi narrationes, *Ex collegio regine, Oxon*' (*Index*, p. 281). This MS. is not mentioned in any of that library's catalogues.

[1] *Memorials of St. Edmund's*, ii. 35, 44, 50, 52, 64, 75, 84, 115.

[2] *Ibid.* ii. 64.

[3] *Chronica*, p. 50.

[4] Denifle-Chatelain, *Cart. Univ. Paris.* i. 330, 425–9.

[5] T. p. 681 ; *D.N.B.* under Somercote ; Von Wretschko, *Der Traktat*, pp. 9–12.

Lawrence may have belonged to one of several Somercote families of Lincolnshire.[1] In view of the fact that he was a papal subdeacon [2] it seems probable that he was a relative of the English cardinal, Robert of Somercote, who died in 1241 at Rome.[3] If Lawrence wrote certain glosses on his work he had been for some time at the papal curia.[4] Of his education nothing is known, unless he is that student who wrote notes left in an early MS., about whom M. R. James has written : [5]

> The student is hearing the Digest : mentions Joh. de Ludham : commends Adam de Nortoft : has written a tract de electionibus prelatorum.

Master Lawrence of Somercote belonged to the household of Walter, bishop of Norwich, almost from the beginning of his episcopate, attesting a charter at Gaywood on 8 May of his first year (1244).[6] At Thorp on 12 May 1245 and in 1246 he attested other charters of the same bishop.[7] Bishop Walter is thought to have given him the vicarage of Woolpit,[8] but it seems doubtful whether he possessed that right.[9] By 20 July 1247 Lawrence was canon of Chichester, attending a meeting of the chapter,[10] and was already an official of Bishop Richard de Wych of Chichester. He acted again in such a capacity in 1251.[11] He was one of the delegates of the dean and

[1] Bodl. Lib. MS. Laud 642, fos. 81*b*, 82 ; Associated Architectural Societies, *Reports*, xxvi. 352, 363.

[2] *C.P.R.*, 1247–58, p. 372.

[3] *M. Paris Hist. Angl.* (R.S.), ed. F. Madden, ii. 457.

[4] Von Wretschko, *op. cit.* pp. 10, 52, 56.

[5] Cambridge, Corpus Christi Coll. MS. 63, fo. 195*b* ; James, *Catalogue*, i. 135.

[6] B.M. MS. Harley 2110, fo. 131*b*.

[7] Cambridge Univ. Lib. MS. Mm. iv. 19, fo. 144 ; B.M. MS. Claudius A. xii, fo. 84*b* (Lawrence de Somerton [*sic*]) ; B.M. MS. Lansdowne 416, fo. 85.

[8] *D.N.B.*

[9] Bury St. Edmunds contested this right (B.M. MS. Claudius A. xii, fos. 84–96 ; *Memorials of St. Edmunds* (R.S.), ed. T. Arnold, iii. 82).

[10] *Archaeologia*, xlv. 185.

[11] *Chartulary of the Priory of St. Peter at Sele*, ed. L. F. Salzmann, p. 32.

chapter of Chichester to secure permission to elect a bishop, receiving the answer desired on 14 Apr. 1253.[1] He occupied a central position in the electoral procedure, being chosen to announce the decision of the three canons selected to make a choice 'per viam compromissi.'[2] Within the next year he completed his great treatise on canonical election, apparently finishing it in the summer,[3] and based largely upon his experience in the election.

Then began Somercote's connexion with Ireland. With Luke, archbishop of Dublin, and John de Frissinon, he was to act in place of Walter, bishop of Norwich, John, bishop of Chichester, and R., abbot of Westminster, to collect the crusading tithe in that island. According to the document of 22 July 1254, Somercote was in charge of the money and was to take out of the receipts £100 a year for the expenses of himself and of his retinue.[4] The announcement of his appointment to the clergy of Ireland is dated 4 August,[5] and the king mentions the appointment in a letter of 5 August.[6] By a letter of 19 March in the following year he restrained Somercote from collecting from the Templars.[7] On 13 Feb. 1256 the king ordered Somercote to hold 4000 marks to pay Bishop Peter of Hereford who had advanced that sum to the pope.[8] Another modification of his orders was made on 4 Aug. 1256.[9] He attested a charter of which Alan de la Zouche, justiciar of Ireland (1255–9), was the first witness.[10] Lawrence was not happy in Ireland, writing to the king that he would not stay there for

[1] *C.P.R.*, 1247–58, p. 187.

[2] Von Wretschko, *op. cit.* pp. 38, 40.

[3] 'Perfecta fuit hec summa a Laur. Somercot. mense Iulio, A.D. 1254' (Bradshaw and Wordsworth, *op. cit.* ii. p. cxxiv).

[4] *C.Cl.R.*, 1253–4, pp. 92, 145 ; *Calendar of Documents relating to Ireland*, p. 59.

[5] *C.P.R.*, 1247–58, p. 372.

[6] *C.Cl.R.*, 1253–4, p. 92.

[7] *C.Cl.R.*, 1254–6, p. 9 ; *Cal. of Docs.* p. 70.

[8] *Ibid.* p. 80 ; *C.Cl.R.*, 1254–6, pp. 393–4.

[9] *C.P.R.*, 1247–58, p. 524.

[10] *Register of the Abbey of St. Thomas, Dublin* (R.S.), ed. J. T. Gilbert, p. 191.

double his salary.[1] Apparently the king complied with his request for recall of 20 May 1256. By 14 Nov. 1257, another seems to be in his place,[2] and on 26 November of the next year his substitute is definitely named.[3] With a notice of a royal grant of clothing, Somercote apparently drops from the records in 1257.[4]

Layamon Fitz-Leoveneth, English poet,[5] was the author of an epic, 'Brut' : (a) B.M. MS. Cotton, Caligula A. ix (early 13th cent.) ; (b) B.M. MS. Cotton, Otho. C. xiii (late 13th cent.). For literature about this work see Wells (*Manual of Early English Writings*, Chronicles (3)). The epic has been edited by Sir Frederic Madden, as 'Layamons Brut' (Soc. of Antiquaries).

In his prologue Layamon states that he is a priest, the son of Leoveneth, and resident at the church of Ernleigh near Redstone. (This was apparently Areley Kings in north Worcestershire.) There are some references to a man or men named Leveneth,[6] but little to identify him beyond doubt. Layamon probably lived in the early years of the 13th century.

Leulyn, O.P., was the author of sermons at Oxford, 1292, and disputant at Oxford, 1300–2 (Little-Pelster, pp. 188, 269).

Lucas of Ely, disputant at Oxford *c.* 1282–90 (Little-Pelster, p. 92).

Martin, theologian, was the author of a 'Summa,' Cambridge, St. John's Coll., MS. 57, fos. 9 *et seq.* (13th cent.), with the inscription 'Summa magistri Martini et questiones theologie a Cantuar. disputate.'

Martin was not a common name. Henry III confirmed a grant by 'Mr. Martin of Wynton' to St. Augustine's,

[1] *Royal Letters of Henry III* (R.S.), ed. W. W. Shirley, ii. 103, 117.

[2] *C.P.R.*, 1247–58, p. 606.

[3] *C.Cl.R.*, 1256–9, p. 465 ; *Cal. of Docs.* p. 99.

[4] *C.Cl.R.*, 1256–9, p. 170.

[5] T. p. 462 ; *D.N.B.* under Layamon.

[6] Palgrave, *Rot. Curiæ Regis*, i. 181, 300 ; *Rot. Chart.* pp. 76, 205.

Oxford,[1] who may have been the author. Possibly he was connected with Archbishop Stephen Langton.[2]

Martin, monk of Bury St. Edmunds, was probably author of an Anglo-Norman prayer to the Virgin Mary, B.M. MS. Royal 11 B. iii, fos. 360*b*–1 (13th–14th cent.), with the inscription 'Frater Martinus me scripsit cui Christus prospicius. Amen.' This has been edited by J. Priebsch ('Zwei altfranzoesische Mariengebete,' in the *Modern Language Review*, iv, 1909. 70–80).

The MS. was certainly written at Bury St. Edmunds, and seems to have been in continuous possession of that house. Probably Friar Martin was a monk there.

Matthew Paris was a monk of St. Albans and author of historical and hagiographical works.[3] His historical works included parts of four chronicles at least :—

'Chronica Majora' (to 1259). (a) B.M. MS. Reg. 14 C vii (1254–1259); (b) Cambridge, Corpus Christi Coll. MS. 26 to 1189 (13th cent.); (c) *Ibid.* MS. 16, 1189–1253 (13th cent.); and (d) B.M. MS. Cotton, Nero D v, to 1250. This chronicle is edited by H. R. Luard) R.S.), and excerpts have also been published (*M.G.H.SS.* xxviii. 107–389).

'Historia Anglorum,' 1067–1253. B.M. MS. Reg. 14 C vii, fos. 9*b*–156*b*. At the year 1235 is the note 'Dns Rog. de Wendoure, prior aliquando de Belvero hucusque Chronica sua digessit. Incipit frater Math. Parisiensis.' A 16th century transcript is in Cambridge, Corpus Christi Coll. MS. 56. It is edited by F. Madden in *Matthæi Parisiensis Historia Anglorum* (R.S.). Excerpts are edited (*M.G.H.SS.* xxviii. 390–434).

'Gesta Abbatum Sancti Albani': *inc.* 'Hic prenotantur nomina abbatum ecclesie S. Albani.' B.M. MS. Cotton, Nero D i, fos. 30–68*b*. Paris' share of the compilation by Thomas of Walsingham of a book of this name in B.M. MS. Cotton, Claudius E iv, fos. 98 *et seq.*, is discussed by H. T. Riley (*Gesta Abbatum Sancti Albani*, R.S., x–xix). Excerpts are edited (*M.G.H.SS.* xxviii. 434–40).

'Abbreviatio Chronicorum,' B.M. MS. Cotton, Claudius D vi. Excerpts from this are edited (*M.G.H.SS.* xxviii. 443–55).

The hagiographical works are several. Three are ascribed to him by Thomas of Walsingham (B.M. MS. Cotton, Claudius E iv, fo. 322*b*), 'Vitas SS. Albani, Thome, et Edmundi archiepiscoporum Cantuarie conscripsit et depinxit elegantissime.' The 'Life of St. Edmund,' in Anglo-Norman, remains at Welbeck Abbey Lib. (fos. 85*b*–100), and is edited by A. T. Baker ('Vie de Saint Edmond, archevêque de Cantorbéry,' in *Romania*, lv, 1929. 339). The author gives his name as 'Maheu' in line 1692 and claims, in line 1976, that he has written the life of St. Edmund in two languages. Baker identifies the Latin 'Life' in B.M. MS. Cotton, Julius D v, fos. 123–157 (*ibid.*, pp. 336–8). This has been edited by Wilfred Wallace (*St. Edmund of Canterbury*, 543–88). The 'Life of St. Alban,' possibly also in the same Trinity MS., is edited by Robert Atkinson (*Vie de Saint Aubin*) and by M. R. James. The 'Life of St. Thomas' is probably in B.M. MS. Cotton, Vespasian B xiii, fos. 133*b*. *et seq.*

In addition to these Paris wrote a 'Life of Stephen Langton,' fragments only of which remain in B.M. MS. Cotton, Vespasian B xiii, about fo. 130, which has been published (*M.G.H.SS.* xxviii. 441–3). His 'Vite Regum Offarum' also remains, in B.M. MS. Cotton, Nero D i: *inc.* 'Inter occidentalium Anglorum reges.' In the same MS. is an unusual book, a description of some of the treasures of St. Albans, the 'Libellus de Anulis et Gemmis et Pallis.'

The precedents of Matthew Paris, artist and writer, are important but conjectural. He may have learned his art at St. Albans,

[1] P.R.O., chancery miscellanea, C. 47/9/52 (570).
[2] F. M. Powicke, *Stephen Langton*, p. 52.
[3] T. p. 572; *D.N.B.* under Paris.

a notable art centre,[1] or he may have been a member of an artistic family,[2] or both.[3] Such is his knowledge of the city of Leicester that Madden has suggested it as his home.[4] He mentions certain items told him by King John.[5] On 21 Jan. 1217 he took the monastic habit at St. Albans.[6] His chronicle indicates that he was probably an eyewitness of important events, such as the translation of St. Thomas in 1220,[7] and the marriage of Henry III and Alienor of Provence in 1236.[8] Upon the death of Roger of Wendover [q.v.] in 1236 Matthew apparently became the historian of his house, compiling and writing industriously until his death.

In 1245 or 1246 Matthew Paris, acting for the abbey of Holm in Norway, freed it from the claims of money lenders in London.[9] Probably at the request of the monastery, the pope directed the abbot of St. Albans to reform the house at Holm, by a letter of 27 Nov. 1247.[10] This started Paris upon what was probably the great adventure of his life. He landed at Bergen in the summer of 1248 at the time of a terrible conflagration which was followed by a fearful storm upon the next day.[11] From the time of his return he seems to have remained in England; possibly this commission made his reputation. Even before his journey, in October 1247, while attending the celebration of the Feast

[1] For this art centre see W. Page, 'The St. Albans School of Painting, Mural and Miniature,' pt. I, Mural Painting, *Archaeologia*, lviii (1902). 275–92.

[2] A Master Richard Paris was paid 100*s*. in 37 Hen. III for working marble, a large sum suggesting that he was a very skilled worker (Lethaby, *Westminster Abbey and King's Craftsmen*, p. 151).

[3] Others bearing the name of Paris are numerous: see Madden (*op. cit*. iii. p. viii); also a Dom. Wm. Paris, knight (P.R.O., Exchequer, K.R., Misc. books, E. 164/20, fos. 77*b*, 78, 80*b*; *Cat. Ancient Deeds*, iv. *passim*).

[4] *Op. cit*. p. ix.

[5] *M.G.H.SS.* xxviii. 117.

[6] B.M. MS. Cotton, Nero D. i, fo. 165*b*.

[7] *Hist. Angl.* ii. 242.

[8] *Chr. Maj.* iii. 338.

[9] *Ibid.* v. 43.

[10] *Hist. Angl.* iii. 40.

[11] *Chr. Maj.* v. 36.

of St. Edward the Confessor he was recognized by King Henry III and invited to sit near him so that he might be able to write a better account of the occasion.[1] With the king he seems to have remonstrated about a St. Albans privilege at Easter, 1251.[2] The chronicler was at Winchester in July of the same year,[3] and at the dedication of the church of Hayles in Gloucestershire in November.[4] Shortly thereafter at Christmas he apparently attended the marriage of the king's daughter.[5] Possibly at this time he had a conversation with Aaron, a Jew of York.[6] In 1257 the king was at St. Albans, where the chronicler apparently enjoyed association with him.[7] Before his death in the late spring or early summer of 1259[8] the chronicler caused many of his severe strictures against the king in his chronicles to be removed. Portraits of him remain, one probably by his own hand.[9] He left several books to his house.[10]

Maurice, O.F.M., was author of the very popular 'Distinctiones Mauritii,'[11] *inc*. 'Circa abieccionem nota qualiter in scriptura.' Salimbene says that a Franciscan Maurice, who came from Provins, said to him:

> Sed adiuva me in scribendo, quia ego volo facere bonum opus distinctionum, quod valde utile erit ad predicandum (*M.G.H.SS.* xxxii. 237).

That Maurice's plan materialized is indicated by Salimbene's rubric, 'De fratre Mauricio qui fecit Distinctiones ad predicandum.' The incident was probably of about 1248.

[1] *Chr. Maj.* iv. 644.

[2] *Hist. Angl.* iii. 62.

[3] *Ibid.* p. 112.

[4] *Chr. Maj.* v. 262.

[5] *Ibid.*

[6] *Ibid.* p. 136.

[7] *Ibid.* pp. 617–8.

[8] B.M. MS. Reg. 14, C. vii, fo. 218*b*.

[9] B.M. MS. Reg. 14, C. vii, fo. 218*b*; MS. Cotton, Nero D. i. This MS. was imitated by John of Wallingford [q.v.]. Some of his pictures are reproduced in Green's *Short History of the English People* (1893), pp. 236, 256, 269, 271–7, 279, 280–1, 283, 284.

[10] Madden, *op. cit*. p. xxvi, note 1.

[11] T. p. 519.

The author, Maurice, has been variously designated as English, Irish, dominican, and franciscan : it is obvious that the identity of this rather obscure friar was not well known even in his own day. If he had been a dominican he would probably have been included in the list of dominican writers. That he was called English or Irish probably indicates that his work was attributed to a well-known Parisian master, Maurice of Ireland, who appears as proctor of the English nation at Paris in 1275.[1]

Maurice (of Glamorgan) was probably the literate knight, used to completing verses as a game, to whom a vision occurred at night, described by Gerald of Wales (*Giraldi Cambrensis Opera*, viii. 310). He was probably Master Maurice of Glamorgan who had a vision about Gerald before the bishopric of St. David's was vacant[2] (*ibid.* i. 170).

Michael of Cornwall was a Latin poet.[3] The longest of his poems is his 'Versus contra Henricum Abrincensem' : *inc.* 'Archipoeta vide.' (a) Camb. Univ. Lib. MS. Ff. vi. 13, fos. 1–8*b* ; (b) B.M. MS. Cotton, Titus A. xx, fos. 52–65 (14th cent.) ; (c) Bodl. Lib. MS. Bodley 851, fos. 81*b*–9 (S.C. no. 4031) (14th cent.) ; (d) B.M. MS. Reg. 14 C. xiii, fos. 269*b*–75*b* (late 13th cent.) ; (e) Cambridge, Trinity Coll. MS. 982, fos. 44*b*–5 (late 13th cent.), containing only verses 627–922. It is edited from these MSS. by Alfons Hilka ('Eine mittellateinische Dichterfehde : Versus Michaelis Cornubiensis contra Henricum Abrincensem,' *Festgabe H. Degering*, pp. 124–54). The inscriptions commence, 'Versus magistri Michaelis Cornubiensis contra . . .' Possibly this was the 'Laus Cornubie edita a M. Michaele de eadem,' formerly at Christchurch, Canterbury (James, *A.L.C.D.* p. 67).

'De Crure J. Mansel' : *inc.* 'Cum sis Romanus, Cincy, tuus est michi vanus.' Camb. Univ. Lib. MS. Dd. xi 78, fo. 188. The MS. bears an entry in ancient index on flyleaf, 'De crure I. Mansel Mich.' The 'Mich' would seem to denote the name of the author. For evidence of his authorship and an edition of the text see Heironimus and Russell (*op. cit.* pp. 9, 137, 157).

'Cur Homo Delinquis' : *inc.* 'Cur homo delinquis.' Bodl. Lib. MS. Bodley 233, fo. 107 (S.C. 2188), with the heading 'Versus magistri Michaelis le Poter de Corn.' The work is written in a curious form of verse used by Michael of Cornwall in the last part of his 'Versus contra Henricum Abrincensem.' Possibly Michael wrote the 'Lament upon the Death of Montfort.' B.M. MS. Cotton, Otho D viii, fo. 219, edited by J. O. Halliwell, 'The Chronicle of William de Rishanger' (Camden Soc.), pp. 139–46. It is anonymous in MS., but remarkable similarities exist between this piece and the first poem above (see Heironimus and Russell, *op. cit.* p. 150).

Michael of Cornwall was probably also called Michael le Poter.[1] The name Blaunpayn is not confirmed by the manuscripts and was possibly a nickname.[2] If he wrote the 'De crure J. Mansel' he was probably with Henry III at the siege of Verines in France in the summer of 1243, when the

[1] Denifle-Chatelain, *Cart. Univ. Paris.* i. 530.

[2] See references to several Maurices (*Cartae et Alia Munimenta de Glamorganica*, i. 214, 215 ; ii. 235, 238, 246, 276, 376). The knight's brother was Clement, abbot of Neath. Possibly the charter with Mr. Maurice and Clement his son as witnesses of 1203 refers to him (*ibid.* ii. 276).

[3] T. p. 432 ; *D.N.B.* under Michael. Best account in Heironimus and Russell, *Shorter Latin Poems of Master Henry of Avranches relating to England* (Medieval Academy of America), pp. 149–55.

[1] See heading of 'Cur homo delinquis.' 'Corn' might be lengthened to Cornhill : a Walter le Poter was alderman of St. Michael, Cornhill, near this time (*Cat. Ancient Deeds*, ii. 24, A. 1992).

[2] A loaf of white bread seems to have been called a 'mich.' 'Une corrodie, ceste a dire, apprendre chescun jour un blank payn, que home apele Mich, un galon de cervayse conventuel, et un mees de potage, etc.' (*Cartularium Prioratus de Gyseburne*, Surtees Soc., ed. W. Brown, p. xvii).

accident occurred. The controversy with Henry of Avranches took place during the years 1250–4. From Michael's poem some data about him are secured, but more about Henry: unfortunately Henry's share in this controversy seems lost. Michael speaks of his loss of the savings of thirty years, yet in comparison with Henry he is a boy. He had probably studied rhetoric under his adversary. The controversy was conducted in the presence of important persons upon several occasions. Of the first the judges were the abbot of Westminster and the dean of St. Paul's; of the second, the bishop of Ely and the chancellor and university of Cambridge; and of the third, Hugh de Mortimer, official of the archbishop of Canterbury.[1] If he was the author of the 'Lament' he lived on until after the death of Montfort in 1265.

Michael of Dover was owner of a MS. and possibly an author. Glasgow, Hunterian Museum, MS. 467 has as a note, 'In isto volumine Michael' monachi Dovor' continetur . . .' The MS. opens with a treatise by Helperic on Compotus and also contains, among other mathematical matter, the work of Ralph of Lenham (1256). It is possible that the arithmetical treatise on fo. 45 may be by the same Michael. The writing is apparently of the thirteenth century.

Michael Malebuche was the author of verses upon the death of Geoffrey, Archbishop of York: *inc.* 'Spurie quid iactas attavis te regibus ortum.' B.M. MS. Cotton, Cleopatra B ii, fo. 39*b*, with the heading 'Versus magistri Michaelis Malebuche de Galfrido archiepiscopo Eboracensi qui filius Henrici regis genitus de quedam meretici.'

Michael Scot[2] was an astrologer and translator, for whose writings and career see C. H. Haskins (*Studies in the History of Mediaeval Science*, pp. 272–98) and note corrections at beginning. It is possible that Scot was a family name rather than a designation of nationality. Thus he may have come from Spain or Italy. The mother of Innocent III, for instance, was of a family of that name. A Master Michael Scot appears in the 'Liber Vitæ' of Durham.[1]

Nicholas (called **Anglicus**), **O.F.M.**, was the author of a life of Innocent IV.[2] He was actually an Italian from Calvi. (Cf. J. Pagnotti, 'Niccolo da Calvi e la sua Vita di Innocenzio IV,' *Archivio della R. Societa Romana di Storia Patria*, xxi, 1898. pp. 7–120).

Nicholas Bozon, O.F.M., was the author of many religious poems in Anglo-Norman. For these see Vising (pp. 52–73, nos. 86, 96, 121, 134, 152, 177, 184, 211, 265, 282, 287, 291, 355, 356, 359, 361–6, 368). The name Bozon is not common. A Nicholas Bozun was instituted rector of the church of Minister in the diocese of Exeter on 16 Mar. 1259, and this he probably held until 1265.[3] The church was in the patronage of the Bozon family.[4] The author was a friar minor, apparently of one of the northern houses: he mentions the Trent and Derwent and speaks of ships coming from Scotland.[5] He speaks of John Dalderby, bishop of Lincoln (1300–20), possibly referring to him as dead.[6] For such a prolific and influential writer certainly very little is known of him.

Nicholas of Breckendale[7] was a grammarian, and probably an instructor at

[1] See Heironimus and Russell, *op. cit.*, pp. 151–2.
[2] T. p. 525; *D.N.B.* under Scot.

[1] *Liber Vitæ Ecclesiæ Dunelmensis* (Surtees Soc.), fo. 57*b*.
[2] T. p. 545.
[3] *Registers of Walter Bronescombe and Peter Quivil*, ed. F. C. Hingeston-Randolph, pp. 35, 152.
[4] *Contes Moralisées de Nicole Bozon* (Société des Anciens Textes Français), ed. L. T. Smith et P. Meyer, p. ii.
[5] *Registers of Walter Bronescombe*, p. 152.
[6] *Contes Moralisées*, p. ii, in nos. 19, 78.
[7] T. p. 123.

Cambridge. His chief work was apparently a 'Deponentale': *inc.* 'Sinderesis rogitata refer quo pandere tractu,' *expl.*

> Scriptoris nomen et honoris, si placet omen
> sic est eiusdem quem Brakyndalia fovit,
> eiusdem studio quem Cantabrigia novit
> Ore patenter ay liber hic finit Nicholai.

(a) Dublin, Trinity Coll. MS. 270; (b) Bodl. Lib. MS. Digby 100, fos. 115–27*b*; (c) B.M. MS. Harley 4967, fos. 104–13 (13th cent.); (d) *Ibid.*, fo. 149*b*, fragment of beginning; (e) MS. formerly at Syon monastery entitled 'Deponentale magistri Nicholai de Birkendalia' (M. Bateson, *Catalogue of the Library of Syon Monastery*, p. 2; Bale, *Index*, p. 299).

'Commentary in Exoticon': *inc.* 'O probaton mithos phoros ymas ton que.' (a) Bodl. Lib. MS. Digby 92, fos. 96–8; and (b) *Ibid.* MS. Digby 100, fos. 129–37. Lines added at end of (b):

> Pro precibus Nicholaus habet quod quisque precetur
> ut sibi sana fides, bona mens et gracia detur.
> 'Editus est liber iste et perlectus in studio Cantebrigie sub venerabili cancellario magistro Stephano de Wylton anno ab incarnatione domini Mo CCo sexagesimo primo XV kal. Decembris libro perlecto Nicholao de Brachedel, exeunte lectore.'
> Hoc ydioma legens, qui pro lectore precetur
> ut rex cuncta regens, anime dicte memoretur.

This may be the same as the 'De verborum significationibus,' as suggested by Tanner (p. 123).

'De Grammatica': *inc.* 'Ad lucem subsequentum diversis acceptionibus.' Douai, MS. 454, with a colophon, 'Tractatus mag. Nicholai de grammatica et omni genere constructionum.' For this item I am indebted to Miss Eleanor Rathbone.

'Sermones de Sanctis.' MS. formerly in the library at Syon (M. Bateson, *op. cit.*) appears in the index under Brekendale, probably in MS. R. 19.

'Sermones Dominicales super Evangelia.' MS. formerly in library of Syon. As above, probably in MSS. P. 41 and P. 42.

Nicholas of Breckendale was a lector in grammar at Cambridge, finishing his treatise on the Exoticon on 17 Nov. 1261. He wrote his 'Deponentale' at the instance of Master Richard de Ecton, according to a MS. and its gloss.[1]

Nicholas of Dale, O.P., wrote sermons at Oxford in 1292 and 1293 (Little-Pelster, p. 185).

Nicholas of Derleigh was probably author of a medical recipe. Cambridge, Peterhouse, MS. 222, part VI, fo. 1, with the title 'Coll[? irium] magistri Nich. de Derleg.'

Possibly he was the Nicholas of Derley of *c.* 1308,[2] but more probably the Master Nicholas 'de Derl.' who appears a century earlier, attesting several charters.[3]

Nicholas of Farnham was bishop of Durham.[4] Bale gives a list of medical books alleged to have been written by Nicholas, but it may consist of conjectures (*Scriptorum Illustrium Catalogus*, p. 293). Until the authorship of the very popular 'Antidotarium Nicholai' has been determined there remains the possibility of Farnham's authorship, especially since the English form 'of Hotresham' is associated with it in bibliographical tradition. This begins 'Ego Nicholaus rogatus a quibusdam in practica medicine studere volentibus.' However, the few local allusions in that treatise are to Sicily (B.M. MS. Sloan 2527, fo. 9*b*), and some MSS. seem too early for Farnham.

Nicholas of Farnham told Matthew Paris that he had seen Master Simon of Tournai being taught by his son:[5] this

[1] B.M. MS. Harley 4967, fo. 104*b*.

[2] *Register of John of Halton* (C.Y.S.), ed. W. N. Thompson, i. 328.

[3] Charters of Geoffrey, bishop of Coventry, 1198–1208 (B.M. MS. Harley 3764, fos. 15*b*, 16). Probably Derleya is Darley. See B.M. MS. Harley 3739, fo. 91*b*, for a charter of Eustace, bishop of Ely; and MS. Add. 5844, fo. 192*b*, for a charter of B., abbot of Peterborough (? Benedict, who died in 1193 or 1194).

[4] T. p. 277; *D.N.B.* under Nicholas.

[5] *M.G.H.SS.* xxviii. 116, 397.

must have been before Simon's death in 1202. Matthew also says that Nicholas taught in the arts course at Paris for many years and then in medicine at Bologna.[1] He had apparently held the chair in arts in Paris for some years prior to 1218.[2] He is first mentioned as a physician in 1228.[3] His years at Bologna probably just preceded this.

About 1216 he appears as the recipient of favours from Westminster and its cell, Malvern, witnessing also some of their charters.[4] He was presented to Audenham in 1219.[5] In 1221–3 he is designated as 'our clerk' by the king, and receives various gifts,[6] among them the church of Essenden.[7] One item, for spices, of 1223 might show that he was already a physician.[8] He witnessed a royal charter of 19 July 1223, and then disappears from the documents for a time.[9]

In 1227 Nicholas appears in the royal documents again, apparently securing a safe conduct for the abbot of Waverley on 9 January and receiving a tun of wine by an order of 19 May.[10] By the will of Richard de Elmham, canon of St. Martin's, London, of 1228 he was to receive a 'portehors,' a small portable breviary.[11] In this document he is called the king's physician. He is listed by Matthew Paris among the outstanding professors who left Paris in the spring of 1229, returning to

1 *Chr. Maj.* iv. 86.

2 Master Nicholas was apparently of the diocese of Worcester, to which Great Malvern belonged (*C.E.P.R.* i. 55).

3 Westminster muniments, no. 13262; *Archaeological Journal*, xxiv. (1867). 340.

4 Westminster Domesday, fos. 306, 336, 447, 575*b*; muniments, nos. 1846, 2017, 32628, 16739, 22493 respectively.

5 *Rot. H. de Welles*, i. 137; iii. 44.

6 *Rot. Litt. Claus.* i. 468*b*, 532; *C.P.R.*, 1216–25, p. 328.

7 *Ibid.* p. 328.

8 *Rot. Litt. Claus.* i. 532.

9 *C.P.R.*, 1216–25, p. 379.

10 *C.P.R.*, 1225–32, p. 106; *C.L.R.*, 1226–40, p. 33.

11 Westminster muniments, no. 13262; *Archæological Journal*, xxiv (1867). 340.

England.[1] By a letter close of 18 November of the same year he was to have four oaks, but he had not received them by 6 April of the next year.[2] Other gifts of wood followed in 1232 and 1234,[3] while a pardon was granted at his instance in 1235. In the same year came a royal gift of grain.[4] When the legate, Otto, came to England he advised the king and queen to have Nicholas as both physician and confessor.[5]

From 1237 until his election as bishop of Durham in 1241 Nicholas enjoyed many favours from the king and queen whom he served as physician.[6] He apparently had a residence at Greenford near Windsor at the time.[7] From the king he received gifts of wood,[8] game,[9] and wine.[10] He witnessed a royal charter,[11] procured pardons for others,[12] and secured an exemption from a papal contribution.[13] The king gave him a fair sum 'for the use of the damsel whom the king proposes to make a nun at Tarent.'[14] Was she the damsel to whom Nicholas was accused of having been married before he became bishop?[15] Nicholas refused the bishopric of Chichester,[16] but after considerable persuasion accepted election as bishop of Durham in 1241.[17] The king assented on 12 Feb. 1241.[18]

Nicholas was bishop of Durham until 1248,[19] when he resigned and was granted

1 *Chr. Maj.* iii. 168.

2 *C.Cl.R.*, 1227–31, pp. 265, 287, 316.

3 *Ibid.*, 1231–4, pp. 72, 411.

4 *Ibid.*, 1234–7, pp. 56, 145.

5 *Chr. Maj.* iv. 86.

6 *C.P.R.*, 1232–47, pp. 196, 204, 220, 233.

7 *Cal. to the Feet of Fines for London and Middlesex*, ed. Hardy and Page, p. 24; *C.Cl.R.*, 1237–42, p. 81.

8 *Ibid.* pp. 81, 205; *C.L.R.*, 1226–40, p. 481.

9 *C.Cl.R.*, 1234–7, p. 496; *ibid.*, 1237–42, pp. 5, 84.

10 *Ibid.* pp. 109, 205; *C.L.R.*, 1226–40, p. 481.

11 *C.Ch.R.*, 1226–57, p. 243.

12 *C.Cl.R.*, 1234–7, p. 507.

13 *Ibid.*, 1237–42, p. 347.

14 *C.L.R.*, 1226–40, p. 374.

15 *Chronicon de Lanercost*, p. 54.

16 *Chr. Maj.* iv. 87.

17 *Scriptores Dunelmenses Tres*, ed. J. Raine, p. 40.

18 *C.Cl.R.*, 1237–42, p. 272.

19 *Chr. Maj.* v. 53.

three manors for his support.[1] He lived on until 1258 [2] and was thought to be on his way to heaven on account of his good life.[3]

Nicholas Grecus was a canon of Lincoln and translator.[4] He assisted Robert Grosseteste in his translation of the 'Testament of the Twelve Patriarchs' from the Greek. 'Assistente eidem clerico Nicholao ab ecclesia beati Albani beneficiato nacione et educatione greco.' B.M. MS. Reg. 4 D. vii, fo. 246*b*, dated 1242 (see also *Chr. Maj.* iv. 233). He is cited as an authority in an anonymous lexicon also, possibly referring to oral rather than written information (M. R. James, 'A Graeco-Latin Lexicon of the Thirteenth Century,' *Mélanges Chatelain*, pp. 399–401).

As noted above, this Nicholas was by birth and education a Greek and a clerk of the abbot of St. Albans. He is to be distinguished from a contemporary Master Nicholas of St. Albans.[5] One would like to think him that son of Master Aristotle who appears as witness to a charter with his father.[6] He was more probably one of the Greek teachers invited to England by Grosseteste,[7] mentioned by Roger Bacon. Upon his first appearance, 6 Apr. 1236, he was already a master.[8] He appears frequently as a clerk of the bishop for a decade.[9]

[1] *C.Ch.R.*, 1226–57, p. 338.

[2] *C.Cl.R.*, 1254–6, pp. 131, 242, 325, 449.

[3] *Chronicon de Lanercost* (Bannatyne Club) ed. J. Stevenson, p. 66.

[4] T. p. 545. Best life by Russell (*Harvard Theological Review*, xxvi, 1933, 169).

[5] *Chr. Maj.* v. 261 ; *Rot. R. Grosseteste*, pp. 68, 212, 297. He seems to have died in 1252 (B.M. MS. Cotton, Julius D. iii, fo. 4).

[6] B.M. MS. Cotton, Claudius D. xi, fo. 223*b*. Miss E. Rathbone tells me that this Mr. Aristotle was not a Greek.

[7] *Opera Inedita* (R.S.) ed. J. S. Brewer, p. 434 ; *Compendium Studii*, cap. VI. Another was probably Master Robertus Grecus, who seems to have been connected with Northampton (*Rot. R. Grosseteste*, p. 300 ; B.M. MS. Cotton, Tiberius E. v, fo. 13 ; Bodl. Lib. MS. Top. Northants C. 5, p. 286*b*).

[8] *Rot. R. Grosseteste*, p. 395.

[9] *Ibid.* pp. 16, 23, 24, 57, 166, 172, 173, 186, 216, 237, 254, 257, 310, 351, 395, 400, 401, 407, 425, 452, 460, 461, 487.

He was presented to the church of Dachet by the abbot and convent of St. Albans in 1239–40.[1] Sometime before 14 Sept. 1246 he had become a canon of Lincoln,[2] and as such witnessed charters in 1249 and 1259.[3] In his work as translator and as clerk of Grosseteste he was doubtless in close touch with the bishop. Thus it is not surprising that he was sent to Rome to aid in procuring the canonization of Grosseteste in the papacy of Alexander IV (1254–61).[4] About 1267 he sued to recover a loan in the king's court.[5] He was still serving regularly as a canon of Lincoln in 1278,[6] but died on 4 Dec. 1279.[7] At the time of his admission to Dachet he was a subdeacon.

Nicholas of Norton was a monk and sacristan of Worcester and probable author of part (1280–1303) of the 'Annals of Worcester.' B.M. MS. Caligula A. x, edited by H. R. Luard (*Annales Monastici*, R.S., iv, 479–560). He may possibly be the author of the whole compilation which is written in one hand of the early fourteenth century to 1303 (*ibid.* p. xxxv). Luard suggests Norton as the author (*ibid.* p. xlii). Certainly the work mentions Norton frequently and is probably the continuation of one sacristan's work, that of 'W. de Bradewas' [q.v.] and possibly that of another, William de Cirencestria.

In 1272 William of Cirencester became prior and possibly Nicholas succeeded him as sacristan.[8] However, he first appears in

[1] *Rot. R. Grosseteste*, p. 354.

[2] *Ibid.* p. 92 ; see also pp. 93, 104, 112, 113, 118, 237, 332, 336, 428, 435.

[3] T. p. 545.

[4] R. E. G. Cole, 'Proceedings relative to the Canonization of Robert Grosseteste, Bishop of Lincoln,' *Associated Architectural Societies Reports*, xxiii (1915–16). 6.

[5] P.R.O., Exchequer of pleas, plea roll 51–2 Hen. III, E./13/1*b*.

[6] *Statutes of Lincoln Cathedral*, ed. Bradshaw and Wordsworth, ii. p. ccviii.

[7] He still possessed Dachet (*Gesta Abbatum S. Albani*, R.S., i. 440).

[8] *Ann. Monast.* iv. 462.

this capacity in 1280 (*Annales*, p. 480), the year in which apparently an enlargement of the chronicle begins. In 1280 he resigned, but he was in again before long.[1] As sacristan he took gifts for consecration in 1282 (p. 484) and in 1283 (p. 489). He mentions the entrance of John Harley in 1277 (p. 473; cf. pp. 480, 498), and John Wikes, who became prior in 1300 (p. 550). Possibly these were early monastic friends. He resigned again in 1288 and was reappointed in 1290.[2] He was one of the central figures in the struggle with the franciscans over the body of H. Poer in 1289 (p. 500) and 1290 (p. 504). As sacristan he placed new pictures in the church in 1292 (p. 510). Possibly he took holy orders in 1294 and 1295.[3] He mentions hearing or seeing things in 1294 and 1298 (pp. 518, 537). As sacrist he presented a priest to a vicarage in 1300.[4] In the same year he was one of a commission to visit the prior and chapter of Worcester (p. 546),[5] but shortly after this he was deposed and required to remain in the house for a year (p. 549). Possibly this enforced retirement may have been the occasion for writing his history. He ceased to write in 1303. A rather unusual amount of poetry appears in the later years (1287–1300) of his work, possibly by Thomas Wikes.

Nicholas of Ocham, O.F.M.,[6] the MSS. and editions of whose 'Commentary on the Sentences' and 'Questions' are given by Little (*F.S.O.*, pp. 857–8; Little-Pelster, pp. 89, 124–5, 126), may have been the author of other works. Leland has ascribed to him a work 'De Verbo' from the 'Catalogus eruditorum Franciscanorum'

[1] *Reg. of Godfrey Giffard* (Worc. Hist. Soc.), ed. J. W. W. Bund, ii. 123. Thomas Hyndelep succeeded, but was in 1286 a simple monk again (*ibid.* pp. 124, 304).

[2] *Ibid.* pp. 320, 366.

[3] *Ibid.* pp. 452, 458, 466.

[4] *Ibid.* pp. 368, 524.

[5] *Ibid.* pp. 528, 530.

[6] T. p. 556; Little-Pelster, p. 89; Little, *F.S.O.* p. 857.

(*Comment. de Script. Brit.* p. 325), and also a 'Libellum de Latitudine Oppositionum' which Little thinks is doubtful (*loc. cit.*). However, this falls in line with the interests of the Oxford franciscans.

On 20 Feb. 1267 or 1268 the custody of the church of Bransby and of William de Bayose, clerk, deficient in knowledge and age, was granted to Master Nicholas of Hocham.[1] On 30 Aug. 1268 he was to receive fourteen marks of the gift of the archbishop of York, Walter Giffard.[2] He made his commentary upon the 'Sentences' apparently about 1280.[3] He incepted at Oxford in 1286 and was 18th lector of the Oxford franciscans.[4] An exemplum about a friar Nicholas Anglicus may be about this little-known man.[5] He preached a sermon at Oxford on 28 Oct. (1290?), of which a report remains.[6]

Nicholas, monk of Rivaulx, was a poet. About this person C. Visch wrote:

> Nicholas Rievallensis cenobii Anglia monachus, vir fuit in omnibus tam sacris, tam prophanis scientiis insigniter eruditus, poesi tamen precipue addictus; unde *Versibus elegantibus, plurimorum sanctorum ordinis nostri pietatem sacraque facinora descripsit.* Inter alia referuntur *Panegyrica Guilelmi, Aelredi et Sylvani Abbatum Rhievallensium* (*Bibliotheca Scriptorum Sacri Ordinis Cisterciensis* (Douai, 1649), p. 205).

He also states that Henriques said that these poems were to be found in the Victorine library at Paris. Probably they are the collection in B.N. MS. lat. 15157, fos. 35–70*b*. Rotographs of these folios will be deposited in the library of the university of North Carolina. His works are being edited by J. P. Heironimus and J. C. Russell.

Their principal contents are:—'De incarnatione Domini': *inc.* 'Virginei partus mysteria scribere cogit,' fo. 35. 'The

[1] *Register of Walter Giffard* (Surtees Soc.), ed. Wm. Brown, p. 44.

[2] *Ibid.* p. 128.

[3] Little, *op. cit.* p. 857; Little-Pelster, p. 89.

[4] Little, *F.S.O.* p. 858.

[5] B.N. MS. lat. 3555, fo. 187*b*.

[6] Little-Pelster, p. 162.

Trinity': *inc.* 'Pagina nostra brevi lusit tenuique susurro,' fo. 36. 'De Sancta Maria': *inc.* 'Cur Manichee notas Christum fantasma vel undam,' fo. 36*b*. 'De disciplina prelati circa subiectos': *inc.* 'Sobrietatis ebur pastor pie pacis amator,' fos. 37–8. 'De mistico templo Salomonis': *inc.* 'Concha repletur aquis typice per opus Gedeonis,' fo. 38*b*. 'Quod pacis custodia maxime competit bono pastori': *inc.* 'Forma lucerna gregis pastor pater columpna,' fo. 39. 'Vera amicitia': *inc.* 'Dulcis amor Ihesu nos ( ) tempus prisco,' fo. 40. 'Quod nulla virtus sufficit sine temperantia': *inc.* 'Qui legis ystoriam Samsonis viribus amplum,' fo. 40. Miscellaneous poems, fos. 40*b*–2*b*. 'De sancto Bernardo': *inc.* 'Religionis apex et nostri gloria seculi,' fo. 43. 'De Willelmo primo abbate Rievall': *inc.* 'O ( ) dilecte Deo primus patriarcha,' fo. 43*b*. 'De Aeldredo abbate': *inc.* 'Inclitus Aelredus conditus aromate morum,' fo. 44. 'De Silvano abbate': *inc.* 'Silvanus mea prima salus hic paupere vita,' fo. 44*b*. 'De tribus Mariis': *inc.* 'Qui legis ista vide quod pingitur illud inepte,' fo. 45. 'De disciplina psallendi': *inc.* 'Ierarchia poli superum chorus atque cherubin,' fos. 45*b*–6. 'De interdicto Anglie, De tributo Anglie, Johannes, De discordia Anglorum': *inc.* 'Papa stupor mundi sed Christi miles,' fos. 46*b*–9*b*. 'De venerabili Stephano, Cant. arch': *inc.* 'Rex regum domine fons et bonitate origo,' fos. 49–50*b*. Miscellanea, fos. 50*b*–1. 'De doctoribus sancte ecclesie': *inc.* 'Aspice Ieronimi compendia cerne Johannis,' fo. 51. 'De liberalibus artibus': *inc.* 'Gramatica pueros sapiens prius imbuit heros,' fos. 51*b*–2. 'De magistro Willelmo de Montibus': *inc.* 'Filius in matris utero merito sepelitur,' fo. 52. 'De quodam nobili auctore' (another hand writes 'Petro Riga') : *inc.* 'Inclitus Ysidorus vir nobilis auctor Hyberus,' fos. 52*b*–3. 'De ambitione': *inc.* 'Est Agar inferior Sara sed et Anna fenene,' fos. 53–5. 'Willelmus Bastard': *inc.* 'Nobilis ille nothus quem dudum fata tulere,' fo. 55. Hymns to several saints on fos. 55*b*–8. 'De sermone Magistri Johannis Otuy in die apostolorum,' fos. 58*b*–9. Miscellaneous poems on fos. 59–62. 'De Johanne rege': *inc.* 'Unica nostra salus Jhesu salvare Johannem,' fos. 62–3. Miscellaneous poems on fos. 63–70.

From the poems about the abbot of Rivaulx it is clear that the author was probably a member of that house. Indeed the line 'Silvanus mea prima salus' would seem to show that the poet entered in his abbacy (1167–88). However, he was writing after the abbot's burial at Byland (fo. 43*b*). He wrote a long poem or series of poems upon the events of 1212–5. At some time he was apparently precentor of his house (fo. 63*b*). He was interested in scholarship, writing upon the liberal arts (fo. 51*b*), a work of Peter of Riga (fo. 52*b*), the funeral monument of William de Montibus (fo. 52), and at some length upon a sermon of Master John Otuy (fo. 58*b*). He mentions also a Simon of Lestingham (fos. 66*b*, 67*b*), and other unnamed friends, especially the prior of the neighbouring house of Byland (fo. 65).

Nicholas of Wadingham [1] was chancellor of Lincoln and author of some sermons. (a) Cambridge, Corpus Christi Coll. MS. 459, fo. 81, *inc.* 'Ecce elongavi fugiens,' with the inscription 'Sermo magistri Nich' de Wadingham, cancell' Lincoln.' (b) MS. formerly at Peterborough, MS. X x, entitled 'Sermones Mag. Nicholai Cancellarii Lincoln' (James, *Peterborough*, p. 62).

Master Nicholas of Wadingham appears as a witness of a charter of Bishop Robert Bingham [q.v.] of 17 Feb. 1236.[2] He probably appears as chancellor in a document of 21 Aug. 1240.[3] A predecessor with the initial W was in the office on 1 Apr.

[1] T. pp. 546, 744.

[2] *Sarum Chs. and Docs.*, p. 237. The designation 'master' is given in the inspeximus of the following day.

[3] *Rot. R. Gravesend*, p. 163.

1235.[1] In an undated charter his full name is given with his title.[2] Nicholas shared in the controversy between Bishop Grosseteste and his chapter, even writing out the chapter's side of the argument, probably in 1246.[3] In 1247 he was delegated to assist in a case between the bishop of Durham and the abbot of St. Albans in regard to the patronage of the parish church of Tynemouth.[4] He was a papal delegate again in 1251 in a dispute settled by a cirograph of that year.[5] He seems to have been still in office in 1259,[6] but his successor had appeared by 1268.[7] His name is in the 'Liber Vite' of Durham as a member of the fraternity of that house.[8] There are several citations of a Nicholas of Wadingham, possibly a relative, about 1202.[9] In 1241–2 a Nicholas of Wadingham, subdeacon, was presented to Kirkby,[10] and probably died just before 18 Sept. 1277, called a master.[11] This Nicholas was not the chancellor, but may well have been his nephew or other relative.

Odo of Cheriton was the author of a series of religious pieces [12] :—

'Summa de Penitentia' : *inc.* 'Penitentiam agite appropinquabit,' *expl.* 'est secunda mors de qua liberare nos. Dignetur, etc.' (a) Leipsic, MS. 543, fos. 255–85 (15th cent.), entitled 'Tractatus de penitentia magistri Odonis' ; (b) *ibid.* 77, fos. 142–4 (13th cent.) ; (c) Munich, MS. 7801 ; (d) *ibid.* 14491 ; (e) B.N. MS. lat. 12387, 'Odonis de Cicestre summa de penitentia' ; (f) *ibid.* 12418 ; (g) *ibid.* 16506, fos. 7–19 ; (h) Oxford, New Coll. MS. 125, fos. 173–88 (13th cent.), with colophon, 'Explicit summa magistri Odonis de Celython' ; (i) Prague, MS. 780 (14th cent.), entitled 'Odonis tractatus de penitentia' ; (j) *ibid.* 814, fo. 179 (14th–15th cent.) ; (k) *ibid.* 820, fos. 26*b*–37 ; (l) *ibid.* 929, fos. 210*b*–32 ; (m) *ibid.* 2492, fos. 44*b*–59*b* (14th cent.).

'Parables' : *inc.* 'Aperiam in parabolis os meum.' This appears in very many MSS. and has been published by L. Hervieux in 'Les Fabulistes latins.'

'Narrationes' : *inc.* 'Quomodo arbores elegerunt sibi regem.' 'Iverunt ligna ut ungerent super se' (T. p. 560).

'In Cantica Canticorum' : *inc.* 'Osculetur me osculo oris sui.' Burgo de Osma, MS. 176, fos. 12–214 (14th cent.). *Expl.*

de malo veniam deposco. Completum est hoc opus anno gracie MCCXXVI in vigilia epifanie a magistro O. ad laudem illius qui est alpha et O.

Burgo de Osma also possessed a copy of his sermons.

Possibly he was also the author of the 'Super Psalterium' of Oxford, Balliol Coll. MS. 37, entitled 'Odonis super Psalterium expositio' : *inc.* 'Beatus vir, sciendum quod intentio.' Perhaps also the 'Expositio Passionis' at Balliol Coll., MS. 38, fos. 94–122, and the sermons which follow (fos. 122–217), both of which end 'ad laudem istius qui est alpha et ω,' may be attributed to him.

Odo also wrote two sets, probably more, of sermons. The following is a far from complete list :—

'Sermones de Tempore' : *inc.* 'Cum appropinquasset, etc. Presens evangelium bis in anno legitur.' (a) Burgo de Osma,

[1] *Rot. R. Grosseteste*, pp. 163, 391.

[2] P.R.O., Duchy of Lancaster, Misc. books, D.L. 42/5, fo. 446*b*. W. de Beningworth was subdean at that time.

[3] Bodl. Lib. MS. Bodley 760, fos. 175*b*–8. Appended is a papal letter of 25 Aug. 3 Innocent IV, Lyons.

[4] *Chr. Maj.* iv. 615.

[5] B.M. Harley Ch. 53, A. 23.

[6] Le Neve, *Fasti*, ii. 91, citing 'Reg. Linc.' pars I, p. 52.

[7] *Ibid.* ii. 91, citing 'Reg. Ebor.'

[8] *Liber Vitæ Ecclesiæ Dunelmensis* (Surtees Soc.), pp. 110–1, fo. 66*b*.

[9] *The Earliest Lincolnshire Assize Rolls* (Lincoln Record Soc.), ed. D. M. Stenton, *passim*.

[10] *Rot. R. Grosseteste*, p. 64, where he is not called a master.

[11] *Ibid.* p. 77.

[12] T. pp. 559–60 ; *D.N.B.* under Odo.

MS. 136, fos. 1–159, with the heading 'O de Critonia doctor ecclesie minimus evangelia dominicalia et que in precipuis solemnitatibus in ecclesia recitantur ad laudem dei'; (b) Leipsic, MS. 77, fos. 1–142 (13th cent.); (c) Lincoln, MS. 52 (15th cent.); (d) *ibid.* 11, fos. 115 *et seq.* (14th cent.), entitled 'Epistole dominicales secundum magistrum Odonem'; (e) Oxford, Balliol Coll. MS. 38, fos. 83–94; (f) *ibid.* Bodl. Lib. MS. Bodl. 420.

'Sermones de Sanctis': *inc.* 'Ambulans Jesus iuxta mare.' (a) B.N. MS. lat. 698, fo. 104, with a colophon, 'anno incarnationis M CC XIX hoc opus completum est a magistro Odone, etc.'; (b) *ibid.* 16506, fo. 218; (c) B.M. MS. Egerton 2850, fo. 168*b*; (d) *ibid.* MS. Arundel 31.

He also seems to have preached a series 'in unum compacte super evangelia per totum annum' with John de Abbatisvilla and Roger of Salisbury [q.v.].

Unlike most contemporary writers Odo came of a family of such feudal importance that it can be traced with some definiteness.[1] He states in one charter, and the evidence is confirmed elsewhere, that his father was William de Cheriton, who had an uncle William Fitz Helton.[2] The latter indeed had three sisters, Alice, Sybil, and Emma, each with one son, at least, Anfrid de Cancy, William of Cheriton, and Robert de Septem Vannis, respectively.[1] The Hugh de Cheriton, also a nephew of William Fitz Helton, was probably a brother of William of Cheriton.[2] Walerand was the heir of Odo,[3] but previously provision had been made for their sister Lucy, who had married William de Insula.[4] It seems probable that William de Cheriton was the son of an earlier Odo de Cheriton, described as 'nepos archiepiscopi,' which, to judge from the date 1166 assigned to the document, means Thomas Becket.[5] The inquisition post mortem of 1247 reveals that Odo had possessed the manor of Delce of the king 'in capite' by service of one knight's fee and ward at Rochester Castle as much as belonged to one knight's fee.[6] The manor was worth sixteen pounds (probably in yearly income). William of Cheriton was a prominent man whose name appears in many charters of Kent.[7]

In the year 1211–2 William of Cheriton gave the king a 'good hautein falcon' as a fine for securing the custody of the church of Cheriton for his son, Master Odo.[8] 'That he studied at Paris seems a reasonable inference from his allusions to that city.'[9] A MS. at St. Mary's College, Winchester, calls him Odo Parisiensis,[10] and he preached sermons with Roger of Salisbury and John de Abbatisvilla, who was probably of Paris. Probably between 1215 and 1220 he wrote

1

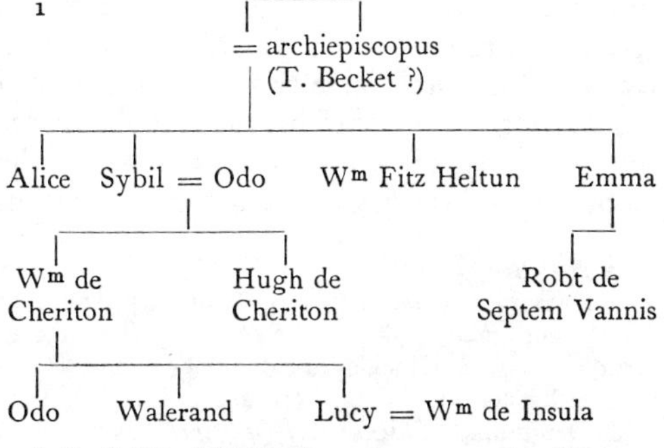

2 Bodl. Lib. MS. Dodsworth 102, p. 98; Norman Moore, *History of St. Bartholomew's Hospital*, p. 181.

1 *Abbreviatio Placitorum*, pp. 56–7.

2 William and Hugh witness a charter of 1184 (Norman Moore, *op. cit.* pp. 181–2).

3 *Archaeologia Cantiana*, ii. 296.

4 *Excerpta e rotulis finium*, ii. 26 (12 June 1248).

5 'Odo de Ceritone, nepos Archiepiscopi tenuit a tempore Regis Henrici feodam i militis et Willelmus filius suus, hoc ipsum tenet' (*Red Book of the Exchequer*, p. 303). 1166 is probably the wrong date, however.

6 *Archaeologia Cantiana*, ii. 296.

7 Bodl. Lib. MS. Rawlinson B. 336, fos. 39, 40*b*, 41, 59, 110*b*, 113, 140*b*, 141, 143, 169; MS. B. 335, fo. 92*b* (with William de Insula), 93*b*.

8 T. Madox, *History of the Exchequer*, i. 428, 508.

9 Hervieux, *Les Fabulistes Latins*, iv. 24.

10 'Odo Parisiensis super Evangelia de dominicis et sanctis' (W. H. Gunner, in the *Archaeological Journal*, xv. 59).

his 'summa.'[1] In the year 1219 he finished one recension of his 'Parables,' and probably of his Sermons 'de sanctis.'[2] In 1226 he completed his commentary 'In Cantica Canticorum.' On 18 Apr. 1233 Odo paid a relief of twenty-five pounds for his father's lands, one knight's fee in Delce and another in Feringham. He also held land of the archbishop of Canterbury and a fee of two and a half knights of William of Avranches. From this time on he shouldered the responsibilities of a feudal lord, and probably spent more time in England. His name is in two undated charters.[3] On 6 Aug. 1233 the king granted him exemption from crossing over to Ireland with him.[4] By 13 Nov. 1234 he had given the mill at Estdelc to his sister Lucy in pursuance of his father's wish.[5] Twice in 1235 he named men as his attorneys in a suit.[6] In 1235–6 he quitclaimed to Andrew son of Andrew Bukerel, a famous citizen of London, the rent of a shop 'in foro London.'[7] He was evidently associated, at least occasionally, with Archbishop Edmund. A story is told about them.[8] On 16 May 1241 he secured a letter of protection until Christmas.[9] The combination of the story possibly coming from Paris and the existence of the letter of protection suggests that he may still have been teaching in that city. He died in 1247.[10] His seal is extant.[11]

[1] It mentions the Fourth Lateran Council of 1215 (New Coll. MS. 125, fo. 183*b*) and calls Hugh of Avalon 'beatus'; he was 'sanctus' only in 1220.

[2] See above under titles.

[3] Bodl. Lib. MS. Rawlinson B. 335, fo. 49*b*; P.R.O., Exchequer K.R., misc. books E. 164/29 (Langdon cartulary), fo. 110. Confirmed by his brother Walerand in 1246 (fo. 111).

[4] *Cal. of Documents for Ireland*, p. 305.

[5] *C.Ch.R.*, 1226–57, p. 119; probably William had given this previous to his death.

[6] *C.Cl.R.*, 1234–7, pp. 160, 176.

[7] B.M. Harley charter 49, B. 45. In the parish of St. Mary-le-Bow.

[8] See below under Robert of Abingdon.

[9] *C.P.R.*, 1232–47, p. 251.

[10] *Archaeologia Cantiana*, ii. 296.

[11] Attached to Harley charter 49, B. 45.

Orm was an Austin monk and author of a series of English sermons which he called the 'Ormulum.'[1] Bodl. Lib. MS. Junius i (*c.* 1200) is probably his autograph copy. This has been edited by R. M. White (Oxford, 1854) and by Robert Holt (Oxford, 1878). The bibliography of writings about this work may be followed in J. E. Wells' 'Manual of the Writings in Middle English' (under ch. V (14)).

Orm states in his work that he is an Austin monk and dedicates his work to Walter, who is his brother in flesh, baptism, and profession. Two conjectures about Orm have been made, but both contribute nothing to our knowledge of the man since they are possible but hardly probable.[2]

Paulin Piper is the probable author of a poem upon the patron saint of the English, St. George, now lost (Camb. Univ. Lib. MS. Dd. ii. 78). The flyleaf gives in the additions to the table of contents, 'Quedam rithmice composita de Sancto Georgio per Paulinum Piper.' For this MS., which contains poems of Henry of Avranches, see J. P. Heironimus and J. C. Russell (*Shorter Latin Poems of Master Henry of Avranches relating to England* (Mediaeval Academy of America), pp. 10, 138–9).

The writer is probably to be identified with a Paulinus Peyvre, described by Matthew Paris as a 'miles literatus sive clericus militaris,' who died on 5 June 1251.[3] At the court he rose from poverty to wealth through the favour of the king, who made him a steward and his special counsellor. He apparently appeared at court in positions of some importance in the summer of 1238.[4] A charter attestation

[1] *D.N.B.*

[2] H. Bradley (*Athenaeum*, 1906, pt. 1, p. 609) and J. Wilson (*ibid.*, 1906, pt. 2, p. 43). The recent article by H. B. Hinckley would tend to place Orm in the first half of the 12th century ('The Riddle of the Ormulum,' *Philological Quarterly*, xiv. 1935, 193–216).

[3] Several epitaphs are given (*Chr. Maj.* v. 242).

[4] *C.P.R.*, 1232–47, p. 224; *C.Cl.R.*, 1237–42, p. 62.

shows that he ranked well among the barons.[1] He was married and a crusader:[2] even the design of his shield remains.[3]

Peter d'Abernon of Peckham[4] was an Anglo-Norman author or translator. The best known work is his 'Lumiere as Lais.' A rubric at end runs:

> Les quatre livres de cest romaunz furent fetz a Novel Lyu en Surie e les deus dreyn a Oxneford. Si fu comence a la Pasche al Novel Lyu, termine a la Chaundelure apres a Oxenford. Le an nostre seygnur mil e deus cenz, e seisaunte setyme.

The MSS., as well as citations in ancient catalogues, are given in M. Dominica Legge's 'Pierre de Peckham and his Lumiere as Lais' (*Modern Language Review*, xxiv (1929), 43). She also discusses this work as a part of the article.

'Vie de St. Richard.' The MS. at Welbeck has been edited by A. T. Baker ('Vie de Saint Richard, Evêque de Chichester,' in *Revue de langue romanes*, liii (1910), 244–396). The author gives his name in two lines (*ibid.* p. 245):

> Pieres de Pecham a nun ay
> ke cest romanz tut translatay.

This was translated at the request of Isabel, countess of Arundel.

'Le Secret des Secrets.' B.N. MS. fr. 25407, fos. 173–96. In this he gives his name as Peter d'Abernon and states that he has written the 'Lumiere as Lais' (l. 2367). This is edited in 'Opera hactenus inedita Rogeri Bacon,' v. 286–313. Lines 2376–9 run:

> Mes ore priez, pur Deu amur
> En ceste fin pur le translatur
> De cest livre, ke Piere ad nun
> K'estreit est de ces de Abernun.

This Peter of Peckham finished his 'Lumiere as Lais' at Oxford in 1268 after commencing it at Newark in Surrey. The 'Vie de Saint Richard' was written after the 'Lumiere,' whose fame, indeed, led a canon of Chichester to send Peter a copy of Ralph of Bocking's prose life of St. Richard[1] apparently at the request of Countess Isabel of Arundel, who died in 1272. Probably later he wrote his translation of the 'Secret of Secrets.' This Peter was a master and a clerk, called d'Abernon, doubtless a family name, and of Peckham or, after one MS., of Fetcham. Since many of the d'Abernons were from Fetcham this would be a natural name, but no Peter of Fetcham appears in documents. 'Fetcham' may have resulted from a scribe's writing an F for a P or his assuming that Fetcham was correct because of the d'Abernon connexion. The history of the family of this name has been given in some detail.[2] There is additional information in a collection of charters now in the British museum.[3] A Master Peter of Peckham turns up in several documents of the time, but his connexion with the family is not defined.

This Master Peter of Peckham was illegitimate.[4] About 1279 an inquest of pleas 'de quo warranto' determined that a village in Kent, Weteringhery, was usually represented in the hundred court of Twyford by three men, among whom was Master Peter of Peckham. After the battle of Lewes, 1264, they had withdrawn their suit and attended the court of Warin de Munchanesi.[5] For some such act, described as 'pro placitibus transgressionibus,' Peter was apparently fined 100 marks, a

[1] His name follows that of John de Plesseto and precedes that of Robert de Muscegros (B.M. MS. Harley 3868, fo. 26).

[2] *Chr. Maj.* v. 101, 242.

[3] Cambridge, Corpus Christi Coll. MS. 16, fo. 250.

[4] Probably Peckham, in Surrey.

[1] Baker, *op. cit.* p. 247.

[2] *Surrey Archæological Collections*, v (1871).

[3] Add. chs. 5539–83. At least two Peters were parsons of Fecham in the 13th century (Add. chs. 5540, 5541, 5542, 5549). In 1295 a Robert d'Abernon was parson there (Add. ch. 5552). Nearly all of these charters concern the d'Abernons.

[4] *C.P.R.*, 1307–13, p. 265; *Placitorum in Domo Capitulari Westmonasteriensi asservatorum Abbreviatio* (Record Comm.), Rich. I–Ed. II, p. 310.

[5] *Placita de Quo Warranto temporibus Edw. I, II, III* (Record Comm.), i. 346.

large sum.[1] His legal activity is evident elsewhere. In 1282 Lewes priory retained him as legal counsel for all cases in London and agreed to pay him ten marks annually. He was designated as a professor of law.[2] There remain two copies of a letter of Christchurch, Canterbury, granting him 100 shillings annually as a pension and retainer's fee to represent the monastery in all legal matters.[3] This was in 1286. The first copy is voided and slightly different from the second. The latter has deleted the words given in italic below :

> . . . has et auxilium prestabit contra omnes personas cuiuscumque condicionis quotiens super hoc per nos fuerit requisitus *exceptis abbate de Lesnes et priore de Beremundeseye.*

Evidently Peter had served or expected to serve them also. The letters call Peter a clerk and suggest the possibility of a benefice for him. He had apparently been in touch with Christchurch as early as 1283.[4]

On 10 Sept. 1285 he secured letters patent granting him a safe conduct, as he was going abroad.[5] He had probably been abroad during the previous biennium, as later litigation indicates. About three years later, 15 Mar. 1288, five men holding land in Surrey acknowledged that they owed him six marks.[6] In 1291 Thomas de Meredon acknowledged a debt of nineteen pounds ' to be levied in default of payments of his lands and chattels in county Kent.' [7] In 1290 as Master Peter of Peckham, clerk of William de March, treasurer of the king, he sued Lewes priory for 20 marks owed

[1] F. Palgrave, *Antient Kalendars and Inventories of his Majesty's Exchequer*, p. 136.

[2] P.R.O., Exchequer of pleas, plea roll E. 13/16, *m.* 9.

[3] Dated ' die Martis proxima ante festum sci. Michaelis, 1286 ' (Camb. Univ. Lib. MS. Ee. V. 31, fos. 24*b*, 25).

[4] A payment, ' Valetto magistri P. de P'ham vi d ' (Lambeth Palace MS. 242, fo. 82).

[5] *C.P.R.*, 1281–92, p. 192.

[6] *C.Cl.R.*, 1279–88, p. 532.

[7] *Ibid.*, 1288–96, p. 192.

him on account of his pension.[1] The prior replied that Peter had been out of England for two years and had not earned his pension. He compromised for twelve half marks in the autumn of 1292.[2] Peter died on 21 Aug. 1293.[3] He seems to have died intestate as well as illegitimate, so that his possessions fell into the hands of the king. The latter gave to his clerk, 'Iterius de Ingolisma ' some of his books.[4] Possibly others found their way into Merton College library.[5] Some years later the king also recovered a messuage in London which Peter had held.[6]

The identification of this Peter de Peckham with the author is probable in view of the marked coincidences in the time of their lives, their status as clerks and masters, and their connexion with Surrey.

Peter of Blois was archdeacon of Bath and a widely read author.[7] His works have not been subjected to comprehensive study, but an excellent beginning has been made. E. S. Cohn has examined the letters of Peter in his study, ' The manuscript evidence of the letters of Peter of Blois ' (*E.H.R.*, xli, 1926. 43). For another treatise, ' De Amicitia,' see the edition by M. M. Davy (*Un traité de l'amour du XIIe Siècle*). The works attributed to Peter were edited a century ago by J. A. Giles (*Omnia Opera Petri Blesensis*), and from this were reprinted by Migne (*Patrologia Latina*, vol. ccvii).

The most recent life of Peter of Blois is given by Davy (*op. cit.* pp. 7–20), and is based largely upon Peter's letters. He has not utilized the large body of documentary

[1] P.R.O., Exchequer of pleas, plea roll E. 13/16, *m.* 1*b*, 9 (Sussex).

[2] P.R.O., E. 13/18, *mm.* 64*b*, 74*b*.

[3] *Historical Works of Gervase of Canterbury* (R.S.), ed. Wm. Stubbs, ii. 301.

[4] *C.Cl.R.*, 1288–96, p. 433.

[5] Powicke, p. 116. Certain books given by P. Pecham probably in the 14th century.

[6] *Cf.* references above concerning illegitimacy.

[7] T. pp. 105, 595 ; *D.N.B.* under Peter.

material available. The early part of Peter's life belongs rather to the intellectual history of the twelfth century than to the thirteenth and has received better biographical treatment. We shall limit our study to his life after 1190 except for pointing out references hitherto unused. They include a reference to an incident of 1162,[1] many attestations of charters of Archbishop Richard of Canterbury and of his time,[2] similar items of the time of Archbishop Baldwin,[3] and other miscellaneous items probably before 1190.[4]

Peter of Blois seems to have been in high favour with William Longchamp, bishop of Ely and chancellor of England, and his brother, Henry, abbot of Croyland. The former apparently made Peter vice-chancellor and protonotary, a long title by which he appears in a letter from Henry.[5] The latter requested him to write a life of St. Guthlac, which Peter agreed to and seems to have done. The exchange of letters on this subject had a later and curious history.

[1] *E.H.R.* xxi (1906). 92–3.

[2] *Archæologia Cantiana*, v. 201–2 ; vi. 193 ; Cambridge, Gonville and Caius Coll. MS. 238, fo. 147 ; Camb. Univ. Lib. MS. Ll. ii. 15, fo. 14*b* ; Canterbury, Dean and Chapter MS. Reg. 1, fo. 87*b* ; *Eynsham Cartulary*, ed. H. E. Salter, i. 58, 59 ; H.M.C., Wells MSS. i. 20, 21, 22 ; B.M. MS. Cotton, Claudius A. vi, fo. 60 ; *ibid*. D. xii, fo. 166 ; *ibid*. MS. Galba E. ii, fo. 44*b* ; *ibid*. MS. Otho D. iii, fos. 109, 117*b* ; *ibid*. MS. Vespasian F. xv, fos. 27, 135*b*, 165*b* ; *ibid*. MS. Harley 3688, fo. 59 ; *ibid*. 3697, fo. 42*b* ; *ibid*. MS. Reg. 11, B. ix, fo. 29*b* ; London, Lambeth Palace MS. 1131, p. 24 ; *ibid*. MS. 1212, fos. 98*b*, 99, 132*b*, 206 ; P.R.O., Exchequer K.R., misc. books, E. 164/20 (Godstowe Cartulary), fo. 153 ; E. 164/27, fos. 59, 147 ; Exchequer, Cartæ Misc. E. 315/31/1, no. 45 ; London, Society of Antiquaries MS. 194, fos. 6, 7*b* ; Westminster abbey Domesday, fo. 502 ; Rymer, *Syllabus*, i. 6.

[3] B.M. Add. MS. 32098, fos. 1*b*, 2 ; MS. Cotton, Claudius A. vi, fo. 61 ; MS. Domitian A. x, fo. 185 ; Lambeth Palace MS. 1212, fo. 107.

[4] *Charters of Hereford Cathedral*, ed. W. W. Capes, pp. 28, 29 ; H.M.C., 8th Rep. pp. 1, 328 ; B.M. MS. Burney 303, fo. 70 ; Bodl. Lib. Ch. Glouc. a. 1, no. 22.

[5] For a more extended treatment of this problem see Heironimus and Russell (*Shorter Latin Poems of Master Henry of Avranches relating to England* (Med. Acad. of America), pp. 106–8).

A fourteenth century forger at Croyland added to both letters. He had the abbot ask and the author agree to a continuation by Peter of the pseudo-Ingulph forgery, and then wrote the chronicle in Peter's name. In 1193 Peter was in the 'familia' of Eleanor of Aquitaine, during the captivity of her son, Richard.[1]

William Longchamp's fall from power in 1192 doubtless caused a decline in Peter's fortune. Possibly after it he was with Archbishop Geoffrey of York,[2] for whom he wrote a 'Life of St. Wilfrid.'[3] To him he probably owed his canonry at Ripon.[4] In any case his life during the succeeding years is obscure. Possibly for a part of this period he was with Bishop Gilbert of Rochester.[5] By 22 Oct. 1198 Peter was in France, witnessing a charter along with the next archbishop, Hubert Walter.[6] He was witnessing this prelate's charters apparently as a member of his household within the year,[7] and was with him at Canterbury in the first year of the reign of John.[8] Gerald of Wales tells of an incident following a sermon by Peter on the Feast of the Holy Trinity (25 May), probably of 1200, in which the archbishop committed a terrible theological howler.[9] In 1203, still as

[1] See a charter of Eleanor's. 'Apud Barchamst. post reditum nostrum de Sicilia, scilicet Natale anni quarti regni regis Ricardi' (B.M. MS. Harley 391, fo. 51*b*). At London, in time of the captivity of Richard (Add. MS. 29347, fo. 40).

[2] London, College of Arms MS. 60, fo. 36*b*. Geoffrey was in the north of England at the time.

[3] Leland, *Collect*. iv. 110.

[4] *Memorials of Ripon* (Surtees Soc.), i. 10, *n*. 4, 255.

[5] London, Lambeth Palace MS. 1212, fos. 135, 220, both in the time of Bishop Richard of London.

[6] B.M. MS. Cotton, Tiberius E. vi, fo. 93 : 'Apud Rupem Dandely.'

[7] B.M. Add. ch. 33596, a charter confirmed previously by Bishop Hugh of Lincoln (*d*. 1200) ; *Cart. Mon. de Rameseia* (R.S.), ii. 173 ; Harley Ch. 43, G. 25, an inspeximus of Bishop John of Norwich (*d*. 1200).

[8] 'Acta apud Cant. anno primo regni Johannis' (B.M. MS. Cotton, Domitian A. xx, fo. 207*b*).

[9] W. S. Davies, 'Giraldus Cambrensis de Invectionibus,' in *Y Cymmrodor*, xxx (1920). 101.

archdeacon of Bath, he was commissioned by Innocent to act in a case with the abbot of St. Albans and the dean of Lincoln.[1] In spite of his self-confessed poverty he was a notable pluralist. He held his archdeaconry at Bath as late as 1206,[2] his canonry at Ripon still in 1208,[3] and he was parson of Sorham in the early years of the century.[4]

Probably upon the death of Ralph de Diceto, Alard was promoted from archdeacon of London to dean of St. Paul's, leaving a vacancy which Peter of Blois filled. The date is uncertain: unless he held it concurrently with the archdeaconry of Bath it must be as late as 1206. Peter's name appears in a number of documents with this title.[5] In his old age,[6] probably while he was archdeacon of London,[7] he wrote his treatise 'De Amicitia.' A London agreement is dated 'in Lent after the death of Master Peter of Blois, archdeacon of London.'[8] Since letters close to his executors are dated 20 May 1212[9] it seems that Peter probably died in the months preceding Lent of 1212. He left several gifts to St. Paul's.[10]

[1] *C.E.P.R.* i. 3, 13; *cf.* letters 51 and 151.

[2] A subscription to the election of Jocelin of Wells as bishop by P., archdeacon of Bath (*Archæologia*, li (1888), 304).

[3] *Rot. Litt. Claus.* p. 108*b*.

[4] H.M.C., various collections, i. 240.

[5] H.M.C., 5th Rep. p. 481; 9th Rep. i. 9*a*; B.M. MS. Cotton, Vesp. F. xv, fos. 185*b*, 186; MS. Harley 4080, fos. 11, 13 (2); N. Moore, *History of St. Bartholomew's Hospital*, p. 207; London, Dean and Chapter of St. Paul's MS. W.D. 1, fos. 7, 12*b*, 12, 13*b*, 13; P.R.O., Exchequer K.R., misc. books, E. 164/20, fo. 46.

[6] 'Subsannabit aliquis et arguet quod senex amatoria ludam, qui iam delibor, et in membris meis responsum mortis accepi' (Davy, *op. cit.* p. 106).

[7] The better of the MSS. calls Peter archdeacon of London (Berlin MS. lat. 1720, fo. 23). Davy is under the impression that Peter died *c.* 1199 and thus suggests 1185–95 as the date of writing (*op. cit.* p. 21).

[8] H.M.C., 9th Rep. i. 30*a*.

[9] *Rot. Litt. Claus.* p. 117*b*.

[10] *Archæologia*, l (1887). 481, 483, 488, inventory of 1245.

Peter of Cornwall was a canon and prior of Holy Trinity, Aldgate.[1] His longest treatise was a theological treatise called 'Pantheologus': *inc.* 'Deus in scriptura sacra tribus.' Parts appear in the following MSS. (a) B.M. MSS. Reg. 7 E. iv and 7 E. viii; (b) MSS. Reg. 7 C. xiii and xiv; (c) Oxford, Balliol Coll. MS. 82; (d) St. John Baptist, MS. 31; (e) Lincoln Coll. MS. 83; and (f) Merton Coll. MSS. 191, 192. There remains a short list of his treatises in the cartulary of Holy Trinity, Aldgate:

> Diversos libros composuit, acetiam, pantheologon, de reparatione lapsus, de duabus corrigiis predestinationis et reprobationis et plures alios perutiles penes nos et alios habitos in diversis locis (City of London Guildhall transcript, p. 22).

Besides the 'Acetia' and the 'De Duabus Corrigiis Predestinationis et Reprobationis,' which have not been identified, he wrote a book 'De Visionibus': *inc.* 'Licet fere omnes hominum.'

(a) London, Lambeth Palace MS. 51, fos. 2–464, written about 1200; (b) *ibid.* MS. 477, extracts (13th cent.).

Parts of the 'De Visionibus' are translated by G. G. Coulton in 'Social Life in Britain,' pp. 218 *et seq.*

'De Adventu Messiah': *inc.* 'Aures sanctitatis vestre, in crucis,' dedicated to Simon (Langton ?) (Bale, *Index*, p. 321). Probably this is the same as the 'De reparatione lapsus' (Leland in T. p. 594).

'Summa': *inc.* 'Tantum unum est.' Worcester Cathedral MS. 114 (Q. 13), fos. 24*b et seq.*, entitled 'Summa magistri Petri Cornubiensis super sophestriam et logicam.' It may be by a later writer, possibly the proctor of the English nation at Paris in 1267 (*Cartularium Univ. Paris*, ed. Denifle-Chatelain, i. 468).

In his 'De Visionibus' Peter gives a description of several members of his family.[2]

[1] T. p. 594.

[2] See M. R. James' catalogue of the Lambeth library MSS. p. 74.

His grandfather, Ailsi (Aethelsige),[1] who lived in the time of Henry I near Launceston in Cornwall, was Anglo-Saxon. His children were Bernard, a confessor of Henry I, Nicholas, a canon of Merton, Jordanus de Trecarl, Peter's father, Paganus, and a daughter. Peter was about sixty near the year 1200, and therefore was born about 1140. By 1190 he had written a part of his 'Pantheologus' for Ralph, archdeacon of Colchester, who died in that year. He was probably a master and a canon of Holy Trinity by this time. There is a possibility that he may have been Peter, archdeacon of London [q.v.], under Bishop Richard (*c.* 1190–7). His biography in the Holy Trinity cartulary tells little about his life before he was prior. Even his famous dispute with a Jew which lasted three years, to end in the latter's conversion, may have been later.[2] He was elected prior on 2 May 1197 and remained in that office until his death on 5 July 1221.[3] He was buried in the middle of the chapel of the Virgin which he had built.[4] His name appears in many documents of his house.[5] He may have been the patron of Richard, canon of Holy Trinity [q.v.], but this was more probably his predecessor.

Peter of Henham was a chronicler. Leland [6] states that in the library of the monastery of Walden he saw a chronicle of England 'qui a tempore Hengisti Saxonis, usque ad annum MCCXLIV res Anglicas scripsit tam bona fide, quam qui unquam optima.' He suspected that Peter was a monk of Walden. This seems quite possible, since history was being written there even earlier than the date given for Peter,[1] and the monastery had contacts with Henham.[2]

Peter of Ickham was a monk of Canterbury and probably a chronicler.[3] Tradition has it that he is the author of a series of chronicles commencing 'Non solum audiendis scripture.' An edition of these chronicles is being prepared by me.

'Le Livere de Reis de Britannie, e le Livere de Reis de Engleterre.' Glover in his edition of this work [4] suggests Ickham as the author upon the basis of a statement of Bale:

> Petrus de Ykham, Anglus scripsit Gallice Geneologiam regum Anglie et Britannie, li i. Durat usque Edwardum Primum. Cantuarie morabatur. Ex bibliotheca Johannis Lelandi (*Index*, p. 323).

It may possibly be one of the books mentioned below from Ickham's library which bore evidence of his ownership which has been mistaken for evidence of authorship.

'Casus Decretalium,' formerly at Dover priory, entitled 'Casus decretalium petri de ykham de dono Walteri Caustoni priori. "potius quam diminuatur"' (James, *A.L.C.D.* p. 425).

Tradition says that Peter studied at Paris and was a friend there of Philip de Greve, chancellor.[5] Possibly he entered Christchurch about 1262.[6] In 1264 he was paid expenses for going to Clive [7] with another.

[1] Professor F. M. Stenton suggested the Anglo-Saxon form to me.

[2] City of London Guildhall transcript, p. 22; T. p. 594.

[3] The transcript says of his death 'et obiit vi July mccxxi.' Tanner gives 'nones' (p. 594); possibly it read 'vi kal. Jul.' (26 June).

[4] 'Et sepultus est in medio capelle beate Marie Virginis quam ipse edificavit' (*ibid.* p. 22).

[5] *Ibid., passim*; P.R.O., ancient deeds, A. 14312, A. 14323, A.S. 449, A.S. 453, A. 15692; B.M. MS. Cotton ch. xiii. 18 (21, 22).

[6] Leland in T. p. 392; Leland, *Collect.* iv. 163.

[1] A history of the early years of the 13th century is in B.M. MS. Arundel 29. Another going into the 15th century remains in B.M. MS. Cotton, Titus D. xx, fos. 66–92*b*. For the years before 1241, however, there are few entries and there is a break to 1250.

[2] See B.M. MS. Harley 3697, fo. 195, for Walden's lands in Henham. Various persons named 'de Henham' gave lands or witnessed the abbey's charters (*ibid.* fos. 76*b*, 83, 90*b*, 128).

[3] T. p. 787; *D.N.B.* under Ickham; *cf. Modern Philology*, xxviii (1931). 267–9. I am indebted to Mr. Schofield of the British Museum for several items.

[4] R.S., p. ix.

[5] T. p. 787.

[6] *Cf.* App. C below. Four names before 'Will. de Clynstede.'

[7] Lambeth Palace MS. 242, fo. 8*b*.

He was one of seven monks of Christchurch chosen by the chapter on 7 Sept. 1270 to have authority to elect a prior.[1] He was given charge of the Dover priory question by Geoffrey de Romsey [q.v.] in 1272.[2] His obit is given in a Lambeth MS. as of 5 May.[3] The year is said to have been 1289.[4] There were probably two other contemporary Peters of Ickham.[5] He left some vessels to his church,[6] as well as a long list of books which have value in showing his interests [7]:

Libri Petri de Ikham. 1538 Decretales. 1539 Casus decretalium Bernardi. 1540 Item casus decretalium I. de Deo. 1541 Casus decretorum W. Brixensis. 1542 Parabole Magistri Odonis. *In hoc uol. cont.*: Expositiones biblie, uersifice. Anselmus de monte humilitatis. Hugo de abusionibus claustri. Gesta Saluatoris. Epistola Dionisii ad Thymotheum, de morte Pauli. Bernardus de moribus et uita honesta. Iohannes Crisostomus de reparacione lapsi. Libellus qui dicitur grece suda. Ambrosius ad Susannam Monacham, [col. 3] de reparacione lapsi. Ambrosius de moribus et uita honesta. Dispensaciones Magistri I. de Deo. Tractatus de penitentia. Tractatus de uiciis principalibus. Tractatus de uirtutibus cardinalibus. Libellus de Summa Trinitate. 1543 Digestum uetus. 1544 Codex. 1545 Instituta Iustiniani. 1546 Brutus Latine et Gallice. 1547 Tractatus de creacione mundi gallice.

Peter de Insula was a canon of York, archdeacon of Carlisle, and probably the writer (or speaker) of some academic treatises, now in Cambridge, Gonville and Caius Coll. MS. 512 (late 13th cent.), 'Questiones super Libros Posteriorum' on fo. 81 and 'Expositio super Libros de Generatione et Corruptione Mag. Petri de Insula' on fos. 171–175. There were at least two masters of this name at the end of the thirteenth century.

The first was collated to the rectory of St. Allen in 1284,[1] but resigned it for Farendon in 1286.[2] He was archdeacon of Exeter in the years 1289–94 [3] and archdeacon of Wells 1295–1302.[4] He was also a canon of St. Crantock by 1286.[5] He was an executor of the will of Bishop Quivil.[6] Possibly he became dean of Wells.[7] The other was admitted to South Killington in 1294,[8] became a canon of York in 1301,[9] archdeacon of Carlisle in 1302,[10] possibly subdean of York,[11] and died in 1311.[12] He is supposed to have been the fellow of Merton of about 1285 of that name and the donor of eighteen silver dishes and saltcellars to the college.[13] He was certainly a professor of canon law.[14]

Peter of Ireland shared in a disputation before King Manfred. His reported share has been edited by C. Baeumker (*Phil-phil-et hist. Kl., Sitz. der Bay. Akad. der Wissensch.*

[1] *Historical Works of Gervase of Canterbury* (R.S.), ed. Wm. Stubbs, ii. 253.

[2] Lambeth Palace MS. 241, fo. 11.

[3] Petrus de Ykham (MS. 20, fo. 185); also in B.M. MS. Arundel 68, fo. 26*b*.

[4] Tanner (p. 787) quotes Thomas Cowston (*Hist. de Mon. Cant.*) in support of this year. Lambeth MS. Wharton F. iii, however, gives 1295, Searle, Camb. Antiquarian Soc., Octavo Series, xxx (1902). 175.

[5] One commissioned for certain duties by Christchurch in 1294 (Camb. Univ. Lib. MS. Ee. v. 31, fo. 64*b*); another died before an inquisition of 3 Edw. I (*Rotuli Hundredorum*, i. 284).

[6] John Dart, *History and Antiquities of the Cathedral Church of Canterbury*, App. pp. xix, xxi, xxiii.

[7] James, *A.L.C.D.* pp. 128–9.

[1] *Reg. of Walter Bronescombe and Peter Quivil*, ed. Hingeston-Randolph, p. 352 (8 July).

[2] Brodrick, *Memorials of Merton College*, p. xiii; *Reg. of Walter Bronescombe*, p. 352. Resigned St. Allen on 31 March (*Reg. Pontissara*, pp. 22, 25).

[3] *C.Cl.R.*, 1288–96, p. 116; *C.P.R.*, 1281–92, pp. 447, 513; *Cal. of Inq. post mortem*, iii. 34; *C.P.R.*, 1292–1301, p. 91 (28 Sept. 1294).

[4] *C.P.R.*, 1292–1301, p. 213 (11 Dec. 1295); *C.Cl.R.*, 1296–1303, pp. 424, 479; Brodrick, *op. cit.* p. 179; death mentioned in P.R.O., Exchequer of pleas, plea rolls 31–5 Edw. I, E. 13/26; E. 13/27 *m.* 64; E. 13/28 and E. 13/29.

[5] *Reg. of Walter Bronescombe*, p. 353.

[6] *Reg. Pontissara*, p. 731; P.R.O., E. 13/18, *mm.* 6*d*, 18.

[7] *Cf.* Le Neve, *Fasti*, i. 150.

[8] *Register of John le Romeyn* (Surtees Soc.), i. 181.

[9] *Register of Thomas Corbridge* (Surtees Soc.), ed. Wm. Brown, ii. 11.

[10] *Register of John de Halton* (C.Y.S.), ed. W. N. Thompson, i. 176, 177, 208, 215, 228; ii. 41, 72.

[11] Brodrick, *op. cit.* p. 179.

[12] *Ibid.*; *Reg. Halton*, ii. 72.

[13] Brodrick, *op. cit.* p. 179.

[14] *Reg. Corbridge*, ii. 11; *Reg. Halton*, i. 176. One Mr. Peter of Insula had died by 1308 (*Reg. of Walter Reynolds*, Dugdale Soc., ed. R. A. Wilson, pp. 161, 163, 173, 176).

(1920), heft 8), *inc.* ' Sic determinavit magister Petrus de Hibernia gemma magistrorum et laurea morum ' (Erfurt, Cod. Amplon. F. 335, fos. 117*b*–20).

Master Peter of Ireland was apparently a teacher of St. Thomas Aquinas ' in naturalibus ' about the years 1240–3.[1] The disputation mentioned above probably occurred in the years 1258–66. Peter also undertook to answer a question of King Manfred ' Utrum membra essent facta propter operaciones vel operaciones essent facte propter membra ? '[2]

Peter Langtoft was a canon of Bridlington and Anglo-Norman writer.[3] His most extensive work was a ' Chronicle ' to 1307. This has been edited by T. Wright (R.S.) and excerpts have also been printed (*M.G.H.SS.* xxviii. 647–62). For lists of MSS. of the chronicle see Wright (*op. cit.* pp. xxii–xxvi) and M. Dominica Legge (*Medium Aevum*, iv, 1935. 20–4). Studies of it appear in Behrenroth's ' Das Verhältnis des 1 Teiles der Reimchr. Pierre de Langtoft zu seinen Quellen ' and in W. Tischbein's ' Über Verfasser und Quellen des 2 Teiles der alrfr. Reimchronik Peter Langtofts.'

Peter also translated an official letter of Pope Boniface VIII to Edward I with other matter. (a) B.M. MS. Reg. 20, A. xi ; (b) MS. Cheltenham 25970 (14th cent.), with the heading ' Ci comence la letre qe l'apostoille Boneface manda al bon rois Edwarde por le realme d'Escoce translatez en franceoise par Sire Pieres de Langtoft, chanoigne de Bridelingtone,' which is edited by Wright (*op. cit.* App. I). In B.M. MS. Cotton, Julius A. v, are ' Un Conte ' and a ' Priere à la Vierge ' on fo. 172 by him, also edited by Wright (*op. cit.* App. II).

Peter Langtoft represented Prior Geoffrey of Bridlington and the house in a series of negotiations from 1271 to 1286. He was a party to fines in May 1271 at Westminster,[1] on 10 Feb. 1275 at Bamberg,[2] after Easter 1282 at Lincoln,[3] in January 1285 at Warwick,[4] and near Easter 1286 at Westminster.[5] He was also mediator in a dispute at Bridlington in November 1282.[6] His chronicle is strong in the years 1275, 1280, 1282, 1283, 1286, and 1289, several of which were years in which the records show that he made trips to the royal court. In 1291 with other members of his house he was accused by Margaret, daughter of Simon le Clerke, of burning goods and chattels at Fleming Burton to the value of twenty marks.[7] Two years later Archbishop John le Romeyn of York complained to the prior of Bridlington that Peter Langtoft had gone south alleging that he had his permission, which was not true.[8] He demanded that the prior recall Peter and punish him for his act. Peter carried his chronicle through the reign of Edward I and wrote it for an unidentified patron or friend named Scaffeld.

P[eter ?], monk of Lewes, was probably the author of part of the chronicle known as the ' Annals of Lewes,' B.M. MS. Tiberius A. x, fos. 145–75*b*, headed ' Liber iste tractat de imperatoribus Romanis . . . ad tempus presens ' (1309). Extracts of this are edited and translated by W. H. Blauuw (*Sussex Archaeological Collections*, ii, 1849. 23–37). In its present form the chronicle was obviously composed at Farleigh, Wiltshire, a cell of Lewes, but much of the material came from the parent house. Under 1245 is the statement ' In hoc anno successit P. ordinem sacerdocii ' (*Sussex Archaeol.*

1 Baeumker, *op. cit.* p. 6.
2 *Ibid.* pp. 9–10.
3 T. p. 466 ; *D.N.B.* under Langtoft.

1 *Feet of Fines, Yorkshire*, 1242–72, ed. J. Parker, p. 178 ; *Chartulary of Bridlington Priory*, ed. W. T. Lancaster, p. 169.
2 *Chart. of Bridlington*, p. 354.
3 *Ibid.* pp. 351, 360.
4 *Ibid.* p. 55.
5 *Ibid.* p. 13.
6 *Ibid.* p. 420.
7 *Notes on the Religious and Secular Houses of Yorkshire* (Yorks. Archæol. Soc.), i. 20.
8 *Register of John le Romeyn* (Surtees Soc.), i. 229 ; *Historical Papers and Letters from Northern Registers* (R.S.), ed. J. Raine, p. 101 ; *cf. Modern Philology*, xxviii (1931). 266.

Collections, ii. 25), and under 1255 'Item hoc anno factus est monachus P. v nonis Octobris' (*ibid.* p. 26). These, the editor believes, probably correctly, are indications of authorship. The part to be attributed to him would seem to be fos. 168*b*–75*b* (*c.* 1240–89).

We should naturally expect that 'P' would be a priest associated in some way with Lewes. There are several who might fall within this class, but none whose identification would be more than conjectural.[1] P. became a priest in 1245 and a monk of Lewes in 1255. Possibly he is the subprior Peter who was one of the vice-regents of Lewes in 1281.[2] His descriptions of the battle of Lewes in 1264 and of the visit of Archbishop John Peckham to Lewes in 1282 [3] are so detailed that they would seem to be those of an eyewitness. Until 1283 the scene of the chronicle is Lewes, then it shifts abruptly to the cell of Monte Acute: 'Isto anno v id. Jan. venit prior Petrus apud Montem Acutum'; and in 1284 there is a statement that Bishop Quivil visited the same place.[4] Had the author been made prior of Monte Acute? In 1285 the chronicle concerns Lewes again,[5] but soon shifts back to Farleigh. On 22 Mar. 1289 the prior of Farleigh left for the general chapter of the Cluniac order.[6] On 21 Feb. 1290 is recorded the obit of Peter, prior of Farleigh.[7] It is probable that this Peter was the author and took his chronicle with him to Farleigh from Lewes.

[1] All references in the Lewes cartulary (B.M. MS. Cotton, Vespasian F. xv): Master Peter, parson of Clayton, fos. 111 (1230), 117; Master Peter Heldham, rector of Torringes, fos. 103 (1236), 103*b* (1234); Master Peter Medicus, fos. 23*b*, 131*b*, 238; Peter, rector of Sudfield, fo. 238; Philip, chaplain and vicar of Rettingeden, fo. 100.

[2] *Ibid.* fos. 161*b*, 165*b*; *C.P.R.*, 1272–81, p. 437 (May 26).

[3] B.M. MS. Cotton, Tiberius A. x, fo. 172 (*Sussex Archaeol. Collections*, ii. 33).

[4] Fos. 172*b*, 173.

[5] Fo. 173 (*Sussex Archaeol. Collections*, ii. 35).

[6] Fo. 173*b*.

[7] Fo. 174.

Peter, archdeacon of London, was the author of a religious treatise on sins and virtues, 'Remediarum Conversorum'[1]: *inc.* 'De beata mentis solitudine.' (a) Cambridge, Trinity Coll. MS. 44, fos. 1 *et seq.*, preface *inc.* 'Viri venerabili et domino ecclesie Londoniensis episcopo R. tertio suus Petrus archidiaconus eiusdem ecclesie'; (b) Hereford, Cathedral Library MS. P. 3, xii; (c) Bodl. Lib. MS. Bodl. 809, fos. 1–107 (15th cent.); (d) *ibid.* MS. Laud Misc. 6 (15th cent.); (e) Oxford, Merton Coll. MS. 48, fos. 17 *et seq.* (15th cent.).

Since the treatise is dedicated to Bishop Richard III of London, its author cannot be Peter of Blois [q.v.], who did not become archdeacon of London until after the death of the bishop. The author appears in charters dated 1193 and 5 Ric. I (1193–4).[2] He appears as a witness in many charters of Bishop Richard.[3] His surname is uncertain.[4] A Master P. de Watham occurs as sole witness of two charters of the bishop [5] and may possibly be the archdeacon.[6] Tanner makes a curious statement which suggests confusion or identification with Peter of Cornwall [q.v.] that does not seem probable.[7]

Peter Quesnel, O.F.M., was the author of a treatise upon canon law,[8] 'Directoria iuris': *inc.* 'Si quis ignorat ignorabiliter.' Two

[1] T. p. 106.

[2] B.M. Add. ch. 28336 and *Cat. Ancient Deeds*, ii. 83 (A. 2462).

[3] H.M.C., various collections, vii. 29; B.M. Add. MS. 5860, fo. 132*b*; MS. Cotton, app. xxi, fo. 53*b*; MS. Cotton, Nero C. iii, fo. 201; MS. Lansdowne 417, fo. 85; *Registrum Malmesburiense* (R.S.), ed. J. S. Brewer and C. T. Martin, ii. 13; Norman Moore, *History of St. Bartholomew's Hospital*, p. 207; St. Paul's, Dean and Chapter Lib. MS. W.D. 4, fos. 56*b*, 57*b*; MS. W.D. 16, fo. 38; MS. W.D. 1, fo. 12; Westminster abbey Domesday, fos. 603*b*, 617*b*.

[4] Tanner suggests Peter Canonicus? (p. 106).

[5] St. Paul's MS. W.D. 1, fos. 6, 16*b*.

[6] A John de Watham appears also as a witness of the archdeacon (MS. Cotton, Nero C. iii, fo. 201).

[7] 'Petrus a fano Servatoris sive S. Trinitatis, SS. theologiae doctor et archidiaconus Londonensis' (T. p. 594).

[8] T. p. 609; *D.N.B.* under Quesnel.

MSS. are in England, Oxford, Bodl. Lib. MS. Canon. Misc. 463, and Merton Coll. MS. 223, with the heading :

> Incipit summa que vocatur directoria iuris in foro conscientie et iudiciali composita a fratre Petro Quesnel de ordine fratrum minorum ex viribus et doctorum sentenciis diversorum.

For the Continental MSS. see F. von Schulte (*Die Geschichte der Quellen und Literatur des kanonischen Rechts*, ii. 262).

The statement that Peter Quesnel was franciscan warden of Norwich has probably no firmer basis than the early known fact of the existence of his book in the library of that house.[1] He may not have been in England at all, for most of his MSS. are Continental. Professor Powicke has shown that probably this work was not written until after 1314.[2] A Peter Quesnel represented the abbot of Montebourg at Westminster in 1288.[3]

Peter of Ramsey, bishop of Aberdeen, is said to have written ' Varias Ecclesiae Sanctiones ' and ' Decreta ad Sacerdotes,'[4] although these attributions may have been merely deduced from his career. He was probably the second secular master of the franciscans at Oxford, following Grosseteste in 1235.[5] Several references occur to him in Scotland [6] before he became bishop in 1247. He died in 1254.

Peter of Swanington, O.C., was an author about whose writings much uncertainty exists.[7] His ' Quodlibeta ' with the *incipit* ' Utrum aliquis spiritus malus,' mentioned by Bale (B.M. MS. Harley 3838, fo. 56*b*) are probably the ' quodlibeta magistri Petri Carmelite ' with the same *incipit* in Worcester MS. Q. 99, fo. 49, with the statement ' Incipit quaternus de disputationibus Carmelitarum anno gracie M CC(C) ' (B.M. Xiberta, *De Scriptoribus Scholasticis saeculi XIV ex ordine Carmelitarum*, p. 14 ; Little-Pelster, p. 304).

The ' Commentarii Sententiarum ' are said to have begun ' Super sententias xxxviii questiones ' (T. p. 701). Much question remains about his account of a ' Miracle of St. Simon Stock.' This was published by a certain Chéron in 1642, but the MS. has never been known otherwise. For the controversy over it see L. Saltet's ' Un faussaire bordelais du 1642 : le prétendu Pierre Swanington, secretaire de saint Simon Stock ' (*Bulletin de Littérature Ecclésiastique*, Jan.–Feb. 1911) and Fr. Derksen's ' M. Saltet, a-t-il prouvé que le fragment de Pierre Swanington publié par le P. Chéron est un faux ? ' (*Etudes Carmélitaines*, i (1911). 300–305), where the controversial document is published. The chief difficulty with this document is that the incident is dated 1251, fifty-two years before the only certain dates in Peter's life.

If we accept the account of the miracle as authentic Peter was a secretary of St. Simon Stock in 1251.[1] Sometime after 1292 he was the first carmelite to take the D.D. at Oxford.[2] He was apparently disputing at Oxford about 1300.[3] He had originally come from the famous Carmelite house at

[1] Bale, *Index*, p. 323.

[2] Powicke, p. 142 *n.*

[3] *C.P.R.*, 1281–92, p. 294.

[4] T. p. 616.

[5] Little, *F.S.O.* pp. 8, 10 ; *Eccleston*, p. 61.

[6] *Liber Cartarum Sancte Crucis* (Bannatyne Club), ed. C. Innes, p. 47 ; *Liber Cartarum Prioratus Sancti Andree in Scotia* (Bannatyne Club), ed. T. Thomson, several citations ; possibly *Cat. Ancient Deeds*, i. 58 (A. 492).

[7] T. p. 701.

[1] In this account a Peter, provost of the church of St. Helen of Lintonia, was so impressed by the miracle of the conversion of his nephew, Walter, that he told it to St. Simon, who had it published. According to B.M. MS. Titus D. x, fo. 127*b*, the ' Wintonie fundator, dominus Petrus de Wintonia, prepositus ecclesie St. Helene eiusdem urbis qui propter quoddam Marie miraculum fratres ibidem fundavit 1278.' Simon Stock is alleged to have retired to Mt. Carmel in 1258 and to have died in 1265. For Petrus de Wintonia see also the Derbyshire Archaeological Soc.'s *Journal*, xiii. 72, 73, 80, 82, 88.

[2] After the statement about Humphrey Necton [q.v.]. ' Quod et Oxonie postmodum fecit Petrus Swanyngtonus vir scientia ac religione preditus qui et Nordovolgus erat ' (B.M. MS. Harley 3838, fo. 21).

[3] See ' quodlibeta ' above (Little-Pelster, p. 304).

Burnham.[1] In 1303 he was among the 'rarissime eruditionis theologi' who objected to the division of England into two provinces at the general chapter of the carmelites at Narbonne in 1303.[2] After the provincial chapter at London in 1305 he was sent to Bordeaux to expound the 'Sentences.'[3] This was the punishment meted out to him as a result of his conduct at Narbonne.[4]

Philip of Bridlington, O.F.M., was the author of a 'Commentary upon the Sentences.'[5] This is quoted by William of Ware [q.v.], I Sent. d. 26, q. 1; Little, *F.S.O.* 863. He also responded at Oxford about 1290 to Master Richard de Heddrington or Herington upon the question, 'An omnes beati equaliter participant beatitudine?' (Little, *F.S.O.* p. 862).

He was at Oxford about 1290 and after attaining his S.T.D. he was 29th lector at Oxford, about 1300. In this year also he was licensed by the bishop of Lincoln to hear confessions.

Philip Ingelberd of Beverly[6] is the supposed author of logical works formerly in the library at Glastonbury. Bale says 'Philippus Beverley scripsit questiones in periermenias et in sex principia' (*Index*, p. 514).

Probably the Philip Ingelberd of Beverley presented to the church of Kangham in Yorkshire in 1305 and 1306.[7] In 1319 he gave a grant of land to support his associates at the university of Oxford.[8] There are

[1] B.M. MS. Harley 3838, fo. 16.

[2] *Ibid.* fo. 27. [3] *Ibid.* fo. 27*b*.

[4] Bale curiously gives the impression that this assignment was a favour (*ibid.* fo. 56).

[5] Little, *G.F.* p. 163; *F.S.O.* p. 862–3; Little-Pelster, p. 255.

[6] T. p. 99; *D.N.B.* under Beverley.

[7] T. p. 99 under 14 kal. Jan. 1306. He was nominated on 13 Jan. 1303 (*C.P.R.*, 1301–7, p. 106); an order for admission is dated 24 May 1306 (*ibid.* p. 433).

[8] T. p. 99.

some charter references to the Ingelberd family.[1]

Philip of Repingdon Priory[2] was probably a poet.

Versus Nechami Cirencestris ad Philippum Repingdunum Leircestr. Abbatem.

Phi nota foetoris, lippus malus omnibus horis:
Phi foetor, lippus, totus malus ergo Philippus.
Philippi responsio.
Es niger et nequam dictus cognomine Necham:
Nigrior esse potes, nequior esse nequis.
(Leland, *Itin.* vi. 51.)

Philip of Repton was abbot of Leicester 1393–1404 and therefore could not be the contemporary of Neckam. The 'Leircestr. Abbatem' is probably a later addition, possibly by Leland.[3] 'Repingdunum' is clearly parallel to 'Cirencestris,' the house of which Neckam was canon and later abbot. Probably, then, this Philip was a canon or prior of the austin priory of Repindon of the same order as that of Cirencester.[4]

Philip of Winchester was the author of several medical recipes in B.M. MS. Reg. 12, B. xii, fo. 115: *inc.* 'Contra colericam discursiam sirupus,' *expl.* 'secundum mag. Ph. ad E[cclesiam] Wint[onie]'; fo. 112, *expl.* 'ad bene incorporandum, secundum M.Ph.'; fo. 124*b*, 'Ph. probavit'; fo. 126*b*, 'Dianthos magri Phi mirabil' efficacie et optim. delicatis'; and fo. 170*b* on margin, 'secundum ph.' The author is as yet unidentified.[5]

[1] B.M. Lansdowne chs. 207–9, 211, 215, 230. There was a franciscan friar of York in 1298 (*Notes on the Religious and Secular Houses of Yorkshire*, Yorkshire Archæol. Soc., i. 244).

[2] T. p. 622.

[3] The contemporary abbot of Leicester was apparently named Paul (*Cat. Ancient Deeds*, i. 313, B. 1035; Robert White, *Dukery Records*, p. 239).

[4] B.M. Stowe charters 132–66 contain many references to priors of Repton of about 1190–1230, but no mention of a prior Philip occurs. A Philip 'de Riptone' gave books to Ramsey abbey (*Chronicon Abbatiæ Rameseiensis*, R.S., ed. W. D. Macray, pp. lxxxix, 359).

[5] For several conjectures about this physician see Russell in *Annals of Medical History*, N.S. vii (1935). 328–9. Possibly the Master Philip of Eton whose 'De Etatibus hominis' appears in Camb., Corpus Christi Coll. MS. 177, fo. 246*b* (16th cent.).

R. de Leicestria was the author of 'Distinctiones,' from which excerpts remain in Cambridge, Pembroke Coll. MS. 87, fos. 1–16 : entitled 'Inc. encheridion penitentiale ex summa Reymundi et ex distinctionibus W. autisodor. et R. lincoln. et R. de leycestria et cuiusdam doctoris Parisie excerptus.' A second MS. was formerly at Ramsey, with a treatise on the 'Poene Infernales,' 'De eisdam secundum magistrum R. de Leycestre,' and a 'De Mercede Iustorum' (*Chronicon Abbatiæ Rameseiensis*, R.S., ed. W. D. Macray, p. lxxxviii).

Since these Ramsey notices are of the books of Robert Dodford [q.v.], R. de Leicester must be at least as early as the middle of the 13th century. R. stands for so many names that with the present data identification is difficult.[1]

R. de Lincoln was probably an author. For 'Distinctiones,' see under R. de Leicestria. Short accounts of parts of sermons by an R. de Lincoln, a monk of Ramsey, appear in MS. Reg. 5, F. xv, fos. 34, 125*b*. There was formerly at Peterborough 'Super duodecim prophetas, collecta inter prælectiones magistri Stephani Langeton per R. de Lincolnia' (Leland, *Collect.* iv. 31). G. Lacombe suggests that this may be Robert Grosseteste or possibly R. de Lincoln is the donor ('Studies on the Commentaries of Cardinal Stephen Langton,' in *Archives d'Histoire doctrinale et littéraire du Moyen Age*, p. 63). There were other works at Peterborough, 'Tract. Mag. Rob. de Lincoln de confessione,' 'Qui cogitato' (James, *Peterborough*, p. 63) ; 'Liber penitentialis sec. R. lincoln' (*ibid.* p. 70) ; and 'Predicatio Rob. Lincoln viris religiosis' (*ibid.* p. 71). Formerly at York, Austin canons, was a MS. 'Ricardus de Lincoln' super sententias' (M. R. James, in *Fasciculus Ioanni Willis Clark dicatus*, p. 39).

[1] A Master Richard de Leicester witnessed a charter of William de Mandeville, thus before 1189 (B.M. MS. Harley 3697, fo. 21). A Ralph of Leicester was to be vicar of Houghton (*Rot. H. de Welles*, i. 7, undated).

Some of these are probably by Robert Grosseteste, but others may be by other authors from Lincoln.

Ralph of Baldock was a historian, dean of St. Paul's and bishop of London.[1] Leland wrote about his book :

> Historiam igitur Anglicam ab origine inchoavit, quam postea, ut erat in hac parte instructissimus, magna cum felicitate absolvit. Nuper enim cum studiose legerem Joannis, abbatis Burgensis, *Annales de rebus Anglicis*, et pervenirem ad annum D. MCCXCII, incidi in locum, ubi honestam mentionem fecit *Historiæ* Radulphi Baldochii. Hinc ego, justam nactus occasionem, quaesivi librum non contemnendum, et tandem Londini in fano Pauli inveni et perlegi (T. p. 66).

He also gives another description as follows :

> In tabulis, sive Chronicis Radulphi de Baldoc est abbreviatio historiæ Galfredi Monemutensis. Tum præterea Epitome historiæ regum Saxonicorum. Postremo etiam a tempore Gul : Conquestoris ad sua tempora (*Collect.* ii. 357).

Ralph also drew up statutes and other documents which seem to be in MS. W.D. 20 at St. Paul's now. Possibly they are the same as the work described by Leland.

There remains a demise by William, son of William 'de Baudak' and Agnes 'de Bray,' his wife, of the manor which descended to the said Agnes by the death of Hugh de Bray, her father, in the vill of Landbech in co. Cambridge, to Ralph in 1291.[2] This evidence would lead us to suspect that Ralph was related to both of them and thus was probably their son, but the document mentions no relationship. A Master Robert of Baldock who followed Ralph in the archdeaconry of Middlesex and was one of his executors [3] was probably a relative. In 1271 the dean of St. Paul's named a Master Richard of 'Baudak' as his attorney.[4] This would show that either Ralph (if Richard is a mistake for Ralph) or probably another relative was already in

[1] T. p. 66 ; *D.N.B.* under Baldock.
[2] H.M.C., 9th Rep., App. p. 38*b*.
[3] *Ibid.* p. 51*b*.
[4] *C.P.R.*, 1266–72, p. 599.

contact with St. Paul's. He apparently succeeded Robert Burnell in the prebend of Holborn in 1271,[1] and became archdeacon of Middlesex in 1276.

In 1275 he was presented by Combwell Priory to Little Wolsiston, co. Bucks.[2] Outside London he held, in 1294 and probably earlier, the church of Westhanyngfeld.[3] Either he or his valet had been before 1275 a clerk of the exchequer.[4] If he were the former exchequer clerk it explains perhaps why Combwell presented him to a church and also why the prioress of St. John de Haliwell mentions his counsel and advice in 1283 in arrangements for obituary services.[5] He was evidently a man of great ability. On 2 Oct. 1276 he witnessed a composition between Bishop Walter of Exeter and Abbot William of Ford.[6] He was one of the canons of St. Paul's to bring news of the death of the bishop of London and to receive permission to elect a successor in 1280.[7] As archdeacon of Middlesex he witnessed some undated documents,[8] as well as others of the year 1282.[9] In 1284–5 he sued his bailiff in regard to his accounting.[10] The prior of Tunbridge had become indebted to him and upon the prior's death his executors were sued for the debt.[11] In 1291 he acted as a judge in a dispute between the franciscans and the abbey of Westminster over a franciscan who had left the order and become a monk of Westminster.[12] On 21 Mar. 1292

[1] Le Neve, *Fasti*, ii. 326, 391.
[2] T. p. 66 ; *Rot. R. Gravesend*, p. 253.
[3] *C.P.R.*, 1291–1301, p. 121.
[4] 'Barth. de London vallettus magri Radi de Baudac quondam clerici de Scaccario etc.' (P.R.O., Exchequer of pleas, plea roll E. 13/4).
[5] H.M.C., 9th Rep., App. p. 19*a*.
[6] *Registers of Walter Bronescombe*, ed. F. C. Hingeston-Randolph, p. 89.
[7] *C.P.R.*, 1272–81, p. 368.
[8] St. Paul's MS. W.D. 1, fos. 71, 73*b* ; H.M.C., 9th Rep., App. p. 12*b*.
[9] St. Paul's MS. W.D. 1, fos. 67, 68*b*.
[10] P.R.O., Exchequer of pleas, plea roll 15 and 16 Edw. I, E. 13/13, *mm*. 40, 50.
[11] *C.Cl.R.*, 1279–88, p. 550 ; *ibid.*, 1288–96, p. 30.
[12] *Mon. Fr.* ii. 38–57.

he secured a safe-conduct to go to Rome on the affairs of the Holy Land.[1]

Although on 18 Oct. 1294 he was still archdeacon, by 25 Aug. 1295 he had become dean of St. Paul's.[2] At the end of 1296 he was preparing to cross the seas in the king's service.[3] He witnessed a charter of 1298.[4] He was elected bishop of London on 23 Feb. 1304.[5] The king approved his election on 22 March and restored the temporalities on 1 June.[6] The election was contested so that, after securing letters of protection and nominating attorneys,[7] he sailed for Rome about the time of the feast of the assumption of the Virgin Mary.[8] The pope confirmed his election and consecrated him, but he was not enthroned until 1306. He had a magnificent career as bishop, being lord chancellor in 1307 and a lord ordainer in 1310. His portrait is said to have been in old St. Paul's.[9] A book of his remains.[10]

Ralph of Bocking, O.P., was the author of a 'Life of St. Richard de Wicio' (Droitwich)[11] : *inc.* prologue, 'Nobilis generositatis,' etc., *inc.* text, 'Sicut dicit Cassiodorus in principio.' This has been printed (*Acta Sanctorum*, April, i. 282–318). The name of the author is not given in MSS. used by the Bollandists. Bale says : 'Radulphus Bockynge, dominicanus, inter alia composuit, ad Isabellam Arundelie comitissam. Vitam Ricardi Cicestrensis, li. i. "Sicut dicit Cassiodorus in principio." . . . *Guilhelmus Botoner in antiquitatibus*, 58' (*Index*, p. 327).

[1] *C.P.R.*, 1281–92, p. 480.
[2] *Ibid.*, 1292–1301, p. 121 ; *C.Cl.R.*, 1288–96, p. 423.
[3] *C.P.R.*, 1292–1301, pp. 177, 178.
[4] St. Paul's MS. W.D. 1, fo. 71*b*.
[5] *Chronicles of the reigns of Edw. I and Edw. II* (R.S.), ed. Wm. Stubbs, i. 132 ('die Lune in vigilia Sancti Matthiae ap.').
[6] *C.P.R.*, 1301–7, pp. 216, 227.
[7] *Ibid.* pp. 244, 258.
[8] *Chronicles of Edw. I*, i. 133, 148.
[9] *D.N.B.*
[10] Oxford, Oriel Coll. MS. 30. A part of the 'Summa' attributed to Alexander of Hales.
[11] T. p. 109 ; *D.N.B.* under Bocking.

He may also be the author of a 'Historia de Antichristo,' Cambridge, Pembroke Coll. MS. 93, fo. 142*b*, 'Historia de Antichristo secundum Bockyng a diversis auctoribus compilata.' A Thomas Bocking, probably a monk of Canterbury, lived in the next century and might be the author.

Ralph, probably of Bocking, and certainly a dominican, gives a few items about himself in his 'Life of St. Richard.' He shows also that he had a good education and was fond of quoting classical and patristic writers. He was a priest to whom Richard had related most of his life some years before he died in 1253.[1] He was probably the saint's confessor. In 1259 on his way to the dominican chapter general at Valenciennes he stopped at the monastery of St. Amand.[2] He wrote the biography at the request of the countess of Arundel (1247–72) and of his prior provincial, Robert Kilwardby (1261–71).[3] A canon of Chichester seems to have heard of the fame of the 'Lumiere as Lais' written by Peter d'Abernon [q.v.] in 1268 and sent Peter a copy of his 'Life,' which Peter then translated into Anglo-Norman.[4]

Ralph of Bristol was bishop of Kildare and said to have been the author of a 'Life of St. Lawrence O'Toole'[5] (W. Harris, *Whole Works of Sir James Ware* (Dublin, 1739), i. 385). On the question of authorship see J. O'Hanlon's 'Life of St. Lawrence O'Toole,' pp. 2–6. Possibly the attribution is occasioned by the fact that Ralph was one of the group which presented the evidence of Lawrence's sanctity. But in this case it is difficult to explain why biographies were not attributed to other members of the group also.

Of Ralph's life in England there seems to remain no evidence.[1] He was probably a clerk of William de Pyro, bishop of Glendaloch (*d.* 1212[2]), who gave him a moiety of the church of Salmon Leap.[3] This bishopric was apparently consolidated with the archbishopric of Dublin. He witnessed a charter of Henry, archbishop of Dublin.[4] About his holding of the treasurership of Dublin the following is written :

> 1219. Ralph de Bristol was nominated by the founder. He was Prebendary of Clonkene ; which church, together with that of St. Audoen's, Dublin, and the rectory of St. Mary's, near the Castle of Dublin, was assigned as the prebend or corps of his dignity. Archbishop Luke substituted Ballymore for Clonkeen [Mason] ; and Archbishop Tregury gave half the prebend of Luske instead of St. Audoen's. In 1223 he was raised to the bishopric of Kildare.[5]

He was a witness of a charter of Henry III, as appears from an inspeximus of 1268.[6] On 12 Mar. 1223 as Master Ralph of Bristol he was approved as one of several candidates for vacancies in Ireland.[7] He was given, as noted above, the bishopric of Kildare, which he held until his death in 1232.[8]

Ralph, abbot of Coggeshall,[9] was the author of a chronicle and visions :—

'Chronicon Anglicanum' : (a) B.M. MS.

[1] *Acta Sanctorum*, i. 285*a*.

[2] *Ibid.* p. 300*b*.

[3] *Ibid.* preface of *Life*.

[4] A. T. Baker, 'Vie de Saint-Richard, Evêque de Chichester,' *Revue de langues romanes*, liii (1910). 247.

[5] T. p. 127 ; *D.N.B.* under Ralph.

[1] A Master Ralph 'de Britollio' witnesses two charters, one of Northampton (B.M. MS. Reg. 11, B. ix, fo. 35*b* ; 'H. archd. Leic.' also a witness, thus probably before 1189) and one of Archbishop Roger of York (1154–81) (P.R.O., Carte Misc. i. 74). He was thus probably too early.

[2] Reg. Alan. ii. 182.

[3] *Register of the Abbey of St. Thomas, Dublin* (R.S.), ed. J. T. Gilbert, p. 329. A Master Ralph also witnessed a deed of another bishop, Simon ('Midensi episcopi') of about 1210 (Lawlor, 'Calendar of the Liber Niger and Liber Albus of Christ Church, Dublin,' in *Proceedings of the Irish Academy*, xxvii (1908), c. 19).

[4] J. H. Bernard, 'Calendar of Documents in the Chartulary commonly called "Dignitas Decani" of St. Patrick's Cathedral,' Royal Irish Academy *Proceedings*, xxv. 486 ; Gilbert, *op. cit.* p. 306 ; P.R.O., Dublin, D.K. Rep., Ireland, xx. App. vii, p. 41.

[5] H. Cotton, *Fasti Ecclesiæ Hibernicæ*, ii. 121.

[6] *C.Ch.R.*, 1257–1300, p. 93.

[7] *C.P.R.*, 1216–25, p. 368.

[8] *Cf.* also *C.E.P.R.* i. 103 in regard to St. Lawrence.

[9] T. p. 187 ; *D.N.B.* under Coggeshall, Coggeshal, cistercian monastery in Essex.

Cotton, Vesp. D. x, fos. 43–128*b*, autograph; (b) Paris, St. Victor MS. 476 (13th cent.); (c) London, Lambeth palace MS. 371, fos. 53, 59, extracts. The chronicle is edited by Joseph Stevenson, 'Radulphi de Coggeshall Chronicon Anglicanum' (R.S.). Excerpts are edited (*M.G.H.SS.* xxviii. 344–358; *cf. E.H.R.* xxi (1906). 286). An interpolation at the year 1207 reads:

> Cui successit domnus Radulfus, monachus ejusdem loci, qui hanc chronicam a captione Sanctæ Crucis usque ad annum undecimum Henrici regis III., filii regis Johannis, descripsit, ac quasdam visiones quas a venerabilibus viris audivit, fideliter annotare ob multorum aedificationem curavit (*Chronicon*, R.S., pp. 162–3).

'Vision of Thurkill': (a) B.M. MS. Reg. 13, D. v, fos. 45–50*b*; (b) B.M. MS. Cotton, Julius D. v, fos. 168–76, rearranged. The vision of Thurkill took place in 1206 at Stisted, four miles from Coggeshall, described by the author as 'in partibus nostris' (MS. (a), fo. 45*b*). The interpolation quoted above gives Ralph as the author of 'quasdam visiones' (see H. L. D. Ward, *Cat. of Romances in the British Museum*, ii. 506; edited by him in *Journal of the Archaeol. Assoc.* xxxi, 1875. 440). For a probably unjustified attribution of a 'Distinctiones Monasticæ' to him see 'Revue Bénédictine' xlvii (1935). 348–55.

Ralph, we learn from the interpolation above, a monk of Coggeshall, became abbot in 1207 and carried his chronicle on to the year 1228. Another interpolation says that in 1218 he resigned his office against the wish of the convent because of ill health.[1] He had been abbot from April 1207 to about 24 June 1218. He wrote the 'Vision of Thurkill' before Adam of Eynsham [q.v.] became abbot of that house, since he calls him sub-prior. He witnessed a charter of the abbot of Colchester.[2]

John Godard [q.v.] dedicated a mathematical treatise to an abbot R. of Coggeshole, possibly Ralph.

[1] *Chronicon* (R.S.), p. 187.

[2] *Cartularium Monasterii Sancti Johannis Baptiste de Colecestria* (Roxburgh Club), ed. S. A. Moore, p. 557.

Ralph of Fresburn, O.C.,[1] is said to have written 'Epistole ad diversos': *inc.* 'Quoniam sedulus est' (given by Tanner as 'Quoniam sedulis ac frequentibus'), B.M. MS. Harley 3838, fo. 54, and 'Pia Monita.'

Ralph of Fresburn was a carmelite living at Mount Carmel. He was one of several who introduced the order into England about 1239 under the protection of two barons, Vescy and Gray.[2] He founded the house at Alnwick,[3] and ruled over the order in England from 1240 to 1254, when he was succeeded by Henry of Hanna [q.v.].[4] On 2 Aug. 1276 Ralph de Fryston, prior-general of the carmelites, received a safe-conduct overseas.[5] He died at Holm in 1277 and a year later a miracle occurred at his sepulchre.[6]

Ralph of Hengham was a justice and author (*cf.* W. D. Dunham, *Radulphi de Hengham Summae*).

Ralph of Lenham was the author of an Anglo-Norman 'Calendar' (for 1256): (a) Camb. Univ. Lib. MS. Gg. I. i, fos. 8–16*b*, with the colophon 'Explicit de compotu secundum Radulphum de Lynham'; (b) Glasgow, Hunterian Museum MS. 467, no. 5 (12th–14th cent.); (c) B.M. MS. Cotton, Vitellius D. iii (burned); (d) Bodl. Lib. MS. Bodley 399, fo. 95*b*, with the inscription 'Rau de Linham.'

Probably this was the Ralph of Lenham who witnessed an agreement between Robert de Beauchamp and John de Vautort in 1261.[7] He may possibly be the Ralph of Lenham whose name appears twice in the pipe roll of 14 Hen. III, 1229–30.[8] The 'Mr. R. of

[1] T. p. 298.

[2] B.M. MS. Harley 3838, fos. 13*b*, 54*b*.

[3] *Ibid.* fo. 54*b*.

[4] *Ibid.* fos. 16, 55.

[5] *C.P.R.*, 1272–81, p. 158.

[6] 'Anno domini MCCLXXVII migraverat illic etiam sanctissimus senex Radulphus Fresborne. Anno domini MCCLXXIIII [*sic*] ferunt quoque luminaria sepius in nocte super illorum mausolea (Ralph and Roger of Croswell) visa' (M.S. Harley 3838, fo. 23).

[7] *Two Beauchamp Registers* (Somerset Record Soc.), ed. H. C. Maxwell-Lyte, p. 105.

[8] *Great Roll of the Pipe*, 14 *Hen. III* (P.R.S.), ed. C. Robinson, pp. 346, 347.

Lenham ' who appears about the same time seems to have been named Roger.[1]

Ralph of London was the author of a religious book entitled ' De Lapsu et Reparatione seu Redemptione Hominis quod Vocavit Electuarium' [2] : *inc.* ' Consideranti diligentius quid sit homo ' : (a) Cambridge, Corpus Christi Coll. MS. 63, fos. 57*b*–81, a volume which was apparently the property of Thomas Stoye, monk of Christchurch, Canterbury, admitted 1299 and died 1333 (Searle, Camb. Antiq. Soc., Octavo Publications, xxxiv. 178) ; (b) London, Lambeth palace MS. 142, fos. 124–44*b*, with the heading ' Auctor huius fr Rad. de Lond. Fo. 124r.' (13th or 14th cent.).

In view of the connexion of both of the surviving MSS. with Canterbury it seems probable that the author of the ' Electuarium' was the Christchurch monk, Ralph of London, who entered about 1227.[3] There was a monk of Bury St. Edmunds of the same name,[4] which was fairly common.[5]

Ralph of Maidstone [6] was a professor at Paris and Oxford, an archdeacon, a bishop, and O.F.M. A fragment of his ' Commentary on the Sentences ' remains in London, Gray's Inn MS. 14, fos. 28–32 (13th cent.) : *inc.* ' Ad hoc quod baptismus fiat ista exiguntur,' *expl.* ' Propter opera bona que fecit existens malus,' with the colophon ' secundum mag. R. de Maidinstan archidiaconum Cestrensem super Sententias.'

The glossed New Testament which he gave to the friars minor of Canterbury remains to-day in the British Museum (MS. Reg. 3, C. xi).[1] He also gave some service books to Hereford cathedral [2] :

ii antiphonaria cum psalteriis et i legendum in ii voluminibus et i gradale cum tropario.

Until he appears in the chapter of Lichfield holding important offices in the episcopate of William of Cornhill, the career of Ralph of Maidstone is unknown. It seems probable that he was archdeacon of Salop before he was treasurer, although it is not certain. As such he attested several charters,[3] probably before 23 Apr. 1219, when one H., canon of Hereford, was archdeacon.[4] He witnessed a charter as treasurer on 21 September of the same year,[5] one or two probably in 1220 [6] and several which are undated.[7]

A number of documents show that Ralph was made archdeacon of Chester before the death of Bishop William in 1223.[8] One R., archdeacon of Chester, was present at the consecration of Eustace Falconberg as bishop of London on 26 Apr. 1221.[9] On 12 November of the same year a final concord between him as canon of Lichfield and a William Fitzhugh and Mabel, his wife, was made in regard to Ralph's prebendal lands.[10] After Bishop William's death he does not seem to have been active in the Lichfield

1 Dugdale, *Monasticon*, iv. 382 ; *C.Ch.R.*, 1341–1417, pp. 198–99.

2 T. p. 614.

3 *Camb. Ant. Soc. Publ.* xxxiv (1902). 173 ; *cf.* App. C, thirteen names after Jeremias.

4 *Memorials of St. Edmunds*, ed. T. Arnold, ii. 76.

5 See a witness of Bishop Robert of London, 1147–1167 (B.M. Add. MS. 5844, fo. 218*b*) ; a witness of Bishop Robert Grosseteste, 1235–53 (B.M. MS. Reg. 11, B. ix, fo. 27) ; B.M. MS. Faustina C. i, fo. 18 ; and a rector of Southe, in 1221–2 (*Rot. H. de Welles*, iii. 38).

6 *D.N.B.* under Maidstone ; Little, *G.F.* p. 182.

1 ' Ex dono fratris Radulphi de Maydenestane, quondam episcopi Herefordensis.'

2 Royal Soc. of Lit. of the U.K. *Transactions*, 2nd series, ix (1870), 74.

3 H.M.C., 14th Rep., App. viii. 228 ; *Chartulary of the Abbey of St. Werburgh, Chester* (Chetham Soc.), ed. James Tait, p. 133 ; B.M. MS. Harley 4799, fos. 31 (without title), 39*b*, 62*b* ; Dugdale, *Monasticon*, iii. 234 ; *Great Register of Lichfield Cathedral* (1924, Salt Archaeol. Soc.), ed. H. E. Savage, p. 213.

4 *C.P.R.*, 1216–25, p. 191.

5 *Great Register*, p. 178.

6 Le Neve, *Fasti*, i. 581 ; B.M. MS. Cotton, Tiberius F. vi, fo. 125 ; Bodl. Lib. MS. Top. Salop d. 2, p. 19.

7 B.M. Add. MS. 30311, fos. 67, 266 ; Bodl. Lib. MS. Top. Salop d. 2, p. 44.

8 B.M. MS. Harley 2064, fo. 308 (68) ; P.R.O., Exchequer, ecclesiastical docs. E. 135/43, no. 129 ; *Great Register*, pp. 15, 124.

9 B.M. Add. ch. 36449.

10 *Great Register*, p. 150.

chapter, but he appears in a few documents until 1229.[1] During this period he was probably teaching at Paris, as in 1229 he was one of the famous Parisian masters who returned to England.[2] He may well have written his ' Commentary on the Sentences ' at this time, or at least while he was archdeacon of Chester.[3] He was apparently a doctor of theology.[4] He appears as a witness in documents of 1231 [5] at Lichfield and was also chancellor of the university of Oxford.[6] He retained his prebend at Lichfield [7] even after his election as dean of Hereford.

After becoming dean on 22 Sept. 1231 [8] he received royal gifts of deer on 28 July 1232 and 21 Aug. 1234.[9] Late in 1232 the king took under his protection Ralph's men and possessions at Lideneie.[10] Of his official activity there is little evidence.[11] Before his election as bishop and possibly even before his connexion with Hereford Ralph had made a vow to become a friar.[12] He was elected bishop of Hereford in 1234, the royal assent being dated 30 September.[13] He was consecrated on 12 November.[14] He

[1] B.M. MS. Harley 3868, fo. 19*b* ; *Coucher Book of Whalley Abbey* (Chetham Soc.), pp. 143–4 ; *Chartulary of Sallay* (Yorks. Archæol. Soc.), ed. J. McNulty, p. 153 ; B.M. MS. Harley 112, fo. 69, probably of this date ; I. H. Jeayes, *Descriptive Cat. of Derbyshire Charters*, no. 182.

[2] *Chr. Maj.* iii. 168.

[3] See above.

[4] *Ann. Monast.* iv. 80.

[5] P.R.O., ancient deed, D.L., 273 ; *Great Register*, p. 205.

[6] *C.Cl.R.*, 1227–31, p. 520. He was placed in charge of students violating forest laws.

[7] *Great Register*, pp. 178, 343.

[8] *Ann. Monast.* i. 80 (Tewkesbury).

[9] *Cl.R.*, 1231–4, pp. 91, 504.

[10] *C.C.P.R.*, 1232–47, p. 5.

[11] An undated charter, Bodl. Lib. MS. Ashmole 1527, fo. 30.

[12] *Hist. Angl.* ii. 374 (Paris says dominican) ; *Ann. Monast.* ii. 320 ; Little, *G.F.* p. 182 ; there is an account of the vision in Barth. of Pisa, Lib. Conform. fos. 82, 101*b*.

[13] *C.P.R.*, 1232–47, p. 72 ; *C.Cl.R.*, 1231–4, p. 529 ; *Ann. Monast.* iv. 80.

[14] *Ann. Monast.* i. 94 ; ii. 316 ; B.M. Tib. A. x, fo. 168.

was apparently an able bishop, well liked by the king. He was allowed to collect an aid from his knights and free tenants in 1235.[1] Later in the year he was abroad in the king's service.[2] He served as a judge in a divorce case in 1236,[3] was one of the escort for Henry III's bride, and went to Wales as royal envoy to Llewellyn.

In 1238 Ralph of Maidstone experienced a very bad fall, according to the Dunstable chronicler, which injured his hand so severely that he could not celebrate mass for a time.[4] Probably after this, since the chronicler mentions it later [5] and since the event comes so near the end of the year, Ralph resigned the bishopric and became a friar minor on 17 December at Oxford.[6] His example was apparently followed by other prelates who did not have the same excuse of a previous vow, much to the disgust of Matthew Paris.[7] He is supposed to have lived on for about five years, mostly at Gloucester, where he was buried.[8] A Hereford obituary gives the date of his death as vi kal. Jan.[9] probably 27 Dec. 1243.

Ralph of Necton was a physician and probable author of an epitaph of Paulin Piper [q.v.] (*Chr. Maj.* v. 243). He may have been the author of a medical recipe in Peterhouse, Cambridge, MS. 222, item 5 (see M. R. James' catalogue of the library, p. 274). It is not certain that he was an author.

Necton's career is known to have extended from 1236 to 1259.[10] For part of this time he was physician of Henry III and the recipient of many favours, mentioned in the rolls.

[1] *C.P.R.*, 1232–47, p. 89.

[2] *Ibid.* p. 122.

[3] *Ibid.* p. 154.

[4] *Ann. Monast.* iii. 148, 156.

[5] Little thinks the succession of events is doubtful (*G.F.* p. 182).

[6] *Flores Historiarum*, ii. 232 ; *cf.* also *Ann. Monast.* i. 113 ; ii. 320 ; iv. 430.

[7] *Chr. Maj.* iv. 163.

[8] *Mon. Fr.* i. 59 ; *cf.* Little, *G.F.* p. 182.

[9] Royal Soc. of Lit. of the U.K. *Proceedings*, 2nd series, ix. 74.

[10] *C.P.R.*, 1232–47, p. 167 ; H.M.C., 9th Rep., App. p. 36*b*.

Ralph of Walpole, archdeacon of Ely, was a disputant at Cambridge *c.* 1282 (Little-Pelster, p. 78) or *c.* 1275 (see App. A).

Reginald of Wroxham, probably Reginald of Cressy, was parson of Wroxham, and author of a 'Chronicle.' Extracts from his chronicle appear in a version of the 'Flores Historiarum' (formerly attributed to Matthew of Westminster), which was apparently written at the abbey of St. Benet Hulme. They are printed by H. R. Luard (*Flores Historiarum* R.S., i. pp. liii–lvii). The headings of the extracts read:

1213. (fo. 184*b*) 'In cronicis Reginaldus de Wroxham sic ait.'

1215. (fo. 187) 'Cronica Reginaldi de Wroxham revera sic dicunt in postscriptione.'

1216. (fo. 188*b*) 'In cronicis R. de Wroxham inventa est hec narratio, scilicet sequens de electione Lodowici.'

1216. (fo. 189) 'Hec sequens narratio inventa est in cronicis R. de Wroxham' (B.M. MS. Reg. 14, C. vi).

Matthew Paris seems to have included information drawn from him also (*Flores Historiarum*, i. pp. xxii–xxiii).

The St. Benet Hulme 'Flores Historiarum' has the following item under the year 1235: 'Hoc etiam anno obiit Reginaldus de Cresi persona de Wroxham.'[1] He is probably the chronicler, and since he was in touch with St. Benet he is probably the priest Reginald who witnessed a charter of Stephen, sacristan of that house.[2] There was a Master Reginald in Norfolk during the period 1194–9.[3]

Ricardus Anglicus, see **Richard of Wendover.**

Richard, possibly author of the English poem, 'I Repent of Blaming Women,' in B.M. MS. Harley 2253, fo. 66, which is edited by Carleton Brown (*English Lyrics of the Thirteenth Century*, pp. 141–3).

[1] *Flores Historiarum*, ii. 217; MS. Reg. 14, C. vi, fo. 201*b*.

[2] Other witnesses were Wm. de Neteshirde, Hugo, Reginaldus, presbyteri (B.M. MS. Cotton, Galba E. ii, fo. 73).

[3] *Rotuli Curiæ Regis*, ed. F. Palgrave, pp. 224, 297.

Richard de Mores Anglicus,[1] prior of Dunstable, was a chronicler and jurist who wrote several treatises upon canon law:—

'Summa de Ordine Iudiciario': *inc.*

Ne quis insufficientem huic opponat, sciat me singula argumenta per ordinem decretorum usque ad ultimum capitulum compilasse et generalium solutiones in commento Decretalium addidisse et tam utilem quam necessariam summam de ordine iudiciario fuisse.

(a) Brussels MS. 131; (b) Douai MS. 580; (c) probably B.N. MS. lat. 18240; (d) formerly at Lanthony were three copies of the tract known as 'Olim' which is attributed to Ricardus Anglicus (Bristol and Glouc. Archaeol. Soc. *Transactions*, xxi, 1908. 141). It was edited by Ludwig Wahrmund in 'Die Summa de Ordine Judiciario des Ricardus Anglicus' (*Quellen zur Gesch. des Romänisch-Kanonischen Processes im Mittelalter*) and by C. Witte in 'Magistri Ricardi Anglici Ordo Judiciarius ex codice Duacensi.' Witte gives the incipit as 'Incipit ordo iudiciarius magistri Ricardi de eden do R Olimedebatur.' The last few words should probably be emended to 'Ricardi de edendo R[. . .]. Olim edebatur.' They might be emended to 'Ricardi de Eden d[omin]o R,' or to 'de Eden Deo R[?].' That the treatise began with 'Olim' may be deduced from item (d).

'Distinctiones per Ordinem Decretorum': *inc.* 'Patres nostri omnes sub nube fuerunt.' (a) Apparently in Douai MS. 580 (Wahrmund, *op. cit.* p. xvi); (b) probably at Dublin, Trinity Coll. MS. 275, entitled 'Ric. de Mores Summa de decreta Gratiani,' according to the library catalogue.

'Gloss on the *Summa* of Bernard of Pavia,' mentioned above, in Munich MS. S. Nicol. 83 (Wahrmund, *op. cit.* p. xvi).

He wrote 'Annals of Dunstable' to his death in 1241. (a) B.M. MS. Cotton, Tiberius A. x, fos. 5–89*b*, probably autograph; (b) B.M. MS. Harley 4886, good

[1] *D.N.B.* under Morins; *cf.* Luard, *op. cit.* Introd.

transcript by Humphrey Wauley, of value since the Cotton MS. was injured in the fire of 1731. From the transcript it was published by T. Hearne in 'Chronicon sive Annales Prioratus de Dunstable' and from both MSS. by H. R. Luard in 'Annales Monastici' (R.S.), iii. 3–158. The authorship is given at the beginning 'Et exinde usque ad octavum annum nostrum MCCX.'

The name of the historian appears in three places, as 'Morins' (or Morius ?),[1] 'de Mora,' [2] and 'de Mores' (or Mores).[3] The name is thus identical with that of the Trinity Coll. rubric. A note in the 'Gesta Abbatum Sancti Albani' speaks of him and a Thomas de Tinemouth, canon of Merton, in the following terms :

> Magistris solemnibus, qui et Bononiæ et alibi, præcognita ad plenum Logica, in Jure et Canonum rexerant Sanctionibus.[4]

This period probably preceded his life as canon of Merton, his status when he became prior of Dunstable in 1202.[5] Even from the beginning of his priorate he was entrusted with affairs of great importance in canon law. His literary efforts are indicative of a bent along that line. He was thus identical with Richard Anglicus, canonist, who was writing in or about 1193 and 1196.[6]

The jurist has been identified with other well-known men. The story which might seem to identify him with Richard Poore [q.v.] is probably derived from a late and poor account of the life of Richard de Wicio [q.v.],[7] who is certainly too late for such an identification. There was a Richard Anglicus, a theologian of 1218,[8] and a Master Richard Anglicus whose death is recorded as of 15 August in the obituary of the canons of St. Saviour at Bologna.[1] The position of Richard Anglicus in regard to the development of canon law is given by a successor as follows :

> Desideriis vestris satisfacere rem mihi arduam sed vobis et posteris fructuosam, aggrediar, quam primo Richardus Anglicus, ad instar cuiusdam compilationis, leges et canones sub paragraphis inducendo, et pro utraque parte in singulis articulis allegando tractavit, postmodum Pileus Medicinensis, legum doctor egregius, civile ordine, paucos tamen canones inducendo, ad modum summe scribendo perfecit, quem pro sui sapientia et doctrina in pluribus imitari dispono.[2]

Most of the information about Richard comes from his chronicle. As yet a deacon when elected prior, he became (probably soon afterward) a priest on 21 Sept. 1202 and celebrated his first mass on the 29th of the same month.[3] In the following February King John sent him to Rome to obtain papal aid in making peace with France.[4] He returned in July, bringing with him as papal legate a cardinal, John, of St. Mary in Via Lata.[5] The cardinal made him visitor of the religious houses in the diocese of Lincoln in 1206.[6] Richard witnessed a document in 1210 ;[7] in 1212 he was engaged in the inquest of the losses of the church on account of the interdict and assisted the preachers of the crusade in the counties of Huntingdon, Bedford, and Hertford.[8] In 1214–5 he was a member of the commission appointed to consider the election of Hugh de Northwold, abbot of St. Edmunds.[9] He attended the Lateran Council in the autumn of 1215 and broke his return journey to spend a year at Paris studying theology.[10] Honorius III

[1] In the continuation of the Dunstable chronicle (*Ann. Monast.* iii. 158).

[2] 'Magistro R. de Mora, priore de Dunstable' (H.M.C., Rutland MSS., App. iv. 33–4).

[3] *Gesta Abbatum Mon. Sancti Albani* (R.S), i. 307.

[4] *Ibid.*

[5] *Ann. Monast.* iii. 28.

[6] Wahrmund, *op. cit.* p. xx.

[7] Witte, *op. cit.* p. v, citing Pancirol, lib. III, c. iv.

[8] *C.E.P.R.* i. 60.

[1] A. Allaria, 'English scholars at Bologna during the Middle Ages,' *Dublin Review*, cxii (1893). 81.

[2] Witte, *op. cit.*, citing *Tancred*, ed. Bergmann (Göttingen, 1842), p. 89.

[3] *Ann. Monast.* iii. 28.

[4] *Rot. Litt. Pat.* p. 26.

[5] *Ann. Monast.* iii. 28.

[6] *Rot. Litt. Pat.* p. 124*b* ; *Ann. Monast.* iii. 29.

[7] H.M.C., Rutland MSS. iv. 33–4.

[8] *Rot. Litt. Pat.* pp. 140, 140*b* ; *Ann. Monast.* iii. 39, 40.

[9] *Memorials of St. Edmund's Abbey*, ed. T. Arnold, ii. 119.

[10] *Ann. Monast.* iii. 44.

named him a member of two commissions in 1217.[1] In 1222 he was a judge in a dispute involving the bishop of London and the abbot of Westminster.[2] In the following year he was a visitor for his order in the province of York and again in 1228, for Lichfield and Lincoln.[3] About this time he served as papal delegate with the prior of Newenham and the dean of Newport.[4] In 1234 he served again as a papal delegate, with the abbot of St. Albans and the archdeacon of Northampton.[5] The next year he was one of the learned men invited to St. Albans to give counsel to the monks upon the death of their abbot.[6] He was involved in the question of the archbishop of Canterbury's right to visit houses in the dioceses of his suffragans in 1239,[7] and in 1241 he was among those to whom letters of absolution for the Canterbury monks were directed.[8]

Richard's chronicle reflects not only a wide interest in general affairs, but still more a particular interest in the financial [9] and judicial affairs [10] of his own house. He even mentions two suits which he lost.[11] The more religious side of the story, such as the dedication of altars, comes in for a certain amount of attention,[12] and he had visions of his own.[13] He records the promotion of his own men and occasionally of the canons of Merton.[14] His deepest interest was apparently in law: he tells with obvious pride of holding his own court before the royal justices at Dunstable [1] and of winning over the townspeople of Dunstable in a matter which they took so seriously that they said that rather than yield they would go to hell.[2]

1 5 May (B.M. MS. Cotton, Faustina A. iii, fo. 271); *C.E.P.R.* i. 49.
2 *Chr. Maj.* iii. 75.
3 *Ann. Monast.* iii. 80, 112.
4 B.M. MS. Reg. 11, B. ix, fo. 39*b*.
5 *C.E.P.R.* i. 143.
6 *Gesta Abbatum Sancti Albani*, i. 307.
7 *Ann. Monast.* iii. 151.
8 *Chr. Maj.* iv. 103.
9 *Ann. Monast.* iii. 29, 32, 54, 60, and *passim*.
10 *Ibid.* in nearly every year.
11 *Ibid.* pp. 80, 108.
12 *Ibid.* pp. 29, 42, 56, and *passim*.
13 *Ibid.* pp. 33, 39.
14 *Ibid.* p. 39 and *passim*. He mentions the defection of two of his canons to the franciscans (*ibid.* p. 134).

Richard of Devizes was a monk of Winchester and author of 'De Gestis Ricardi Primi' and 'Annales Wintonienses' to 1202. (For these see *Chronicles of the Reigns of Stephen, Henry II and Richard I*, R.S., ed. R. Howlett, iii, and *Ann. Monast.* ii.)

Richard of Dunstable, O.P., was part author of a 'Life of St. Edmund of Abingdon.' (See **Eustace, monk of Christchurch, Canterbury.**)

Richard of Durham, O.F.M., was a chronicler [3] whose chronicle was formerly in the franciscan house at London. Excerpts of it are extant:

> *Nomina illorum qui fuerunt Fratres Minores, quondam Reg[es] terreni in seculo habitu sunt . . .*
> Frater Johannes, quondam Rex Armenie; frater Henricus, quondam Rex Ciprie; frater Antonius, quondam Rex Castellie; de quibus habetur in chronicis fratris Ricardi de Dunelmo, lib. viij. c. 9.
> Frater Johannes, Rex Jherosolimorum. De quo in chronicis predictis, lib. vii. c. 4.
> Frater   Rex saxonie. Frater Alphurnus, Rex Arragonie. Frater Alphonsus, rex Beluarie. De quibus in eisdem chronicis (C. L. Kingsford, *Grey Friars of London*, p. 196).

Dr. A. G. Little identified some of these passages in the Lanercost Chronicle (*Chronicon de Lanercost*, Bannatyne Club, ed. Joseph Stevenson), translated by H. Maxwell (*E.H.R.* xxxi. 269–79). He has presented proof that Richard of Durham was the author of much of the material, now rearranged and abridged, of the chronicle as far as 1297. Possibly it was also in B.M. MS. Cotton, Vitellius D. v (*cf. Memoriale Fratris Walteri de Coventria* R.S., ed. W. Stubbs, i. pp. xxvii–xxx).

1 *Ann. Monast.* iii. 54, 55, 108.
2 *Ibid.* pp. 65, 105, 119–24.
3 Dr. A. G. Little has given most of the biographical information about Richard in *E.H.R.* xxxi (1916). 269–79; xxxii (1917). 48–9.

From the autobiographical information in the chronicle the life of Richard of Durham until 1297 falls into three periods: youth in the north of England, in which it is not certain that he was a franciscan, a period of study at Oxford about 1280–5, and a period of residence as a franciscan in northern England to 1297 at least. As Dr. Little has pointed out, Richard of Durham may be Richard of Sleckburn [*e.v.*]. The name 'de Dunelmo' turns up only once and might refer to the custody of Durham.

The author was alive during the famine of 1257 (*Chronicon de Lanercost*, p. 65), was in Newcastle-on-Tyne in 1265, buried Nicholas Moffet, bishop-elect of Glasgow, in 1270 'in ecclesia sua de Tinigham' (p. 53), and was well acquainted with the countess of Dunbar, Euphemia, and her son, Patrick (*d.* 1289) (pp. 54, 82–3). He was at Oxford (p. 36), where he apparently learned of many incidents recorded in his chronicle.[1] He seems to have had accurate knowledge of the foundation of Balliol college (p. 69). Of his later years he mentions that he was at Newcastle in 1285 (p. 119), at Carlisle in 1292 (pp. 144–5), and resident in the franciscan friary at Berwick in 1296 (p. 172). He seems to have been well acquainted with the houses of his order in the custody of Newcastle, but not those in the south.[2]

Richard Fishacre, O.P., was a theologian[3] of whom Trivet wrote:

> Hic Ricardus super Sententias scriptum temporibus suis perutile composuit, et super Psalterium usque ad psalmum septuagesimum postillas edidit pulcherrimas, moralitatibus suavissimis intermixtas (*Annales*, Eng. Hist. Soc., ed. T. Hog, p. 230).

His 'Commentary on the Sentences' existed in many MSS.: *inc.* 'O altitudo.' (a) Bologna Univ. Lib. MS. 1546 (13th cent.), with the colophon 'Expliciunt postille secundum fratrem Richardum Anglicum de ordine fratrum predicatorum super tres primos libros sententiarum Magistri Petri Lumbardi'; (b) Cambridge, Corpus Christi Coll. MS. 156, fos. 13–5 (fragment); (c) Cambridge, Gonville and Caius Coll. MS. 329 (13th cent.); (d) B.M. MS. Reg. 10, B. vii (13th cent.); (e) Oxford, Balliol Coll. MS. 57 (13th cent.); (f) Oxford, New Coll. MS. 112 (13th cent.); (g) Oxford, Oriel Coll. MS. 43 (13th cent.); (h) B.N. MS. fonds lat. 15754 (13th cent.); (i) B.N. fonds lat. 16389 (13th cent.); (j) Rome, Vatican, Ottobon MS. 294 (O) (13th cent.); (k) Vienna MS. 1514 (13th cent.). This book is mentioned in many old catalogues of libraries: (1) Cambridge, Dominican Lib. (Leland, *Collect.* iv. 15); (2) Canterbury, St. Augustine's, entitled 'Summa Ricardi de Fissacre super IIIIor libros Sentenciarum John de Sellyng' (James, *A.L.C.D.* p. 260); (3) Colchester, St. John's (Boston of Bury in Camb. Univ. Lib. Add. MS. 3470, p. 128); (4) Guildford (Leland, *Collect.* iv. 148); (5) Holm, Cumberland (MS. Harley 3897, fo. 53*b*); (6) Hulme, St. Benedict (Boston of Bury, *loc. cit.*); (7) London, Friars Minor (Leland, *ibid.* p. 51); (8) London, Dominicans (Bale, *Index*, p. 513); (9) Peterborough (James, *Peterborough*, p. 23); (10) Ramsey (Boston of Bury, *loc. cit.*). A 'Tabula,' an index of this work, is in Oriel Coll. MS. 31, fos. 306–15.

The 'Super Primum Nocturnum Psalterii' is apparently not discovered. It was formerly at (a) Norwich, Dominican lib., entitled 'Fyzaker super primum nocturnum Psalterii usque ad "Deus, deus meus respice." "Iste liber docet"' (Leland, *Collect.* iv. 28); (b) London, Dominican lib. (*ibid.* iv. 51; Bale, *Index*, pp. 347, 513); (c) site unknown (Boston of Bury, *loc. cit.*).

[1] *Chronicon*, pp. 118, 130, 136, etc.

[2] *E.H.R.* xxxi. 275.

[3] T. pp. 282, 597; *D.N.B.* under Fishacre. An excellent study of his life and writings is by F. Pelster ('Das Leben und die Schriften des Oxforder Dominikanerlehrers Richard Fishacre,' in *Zeitschrift für katholische Theologie*, liv, 1930. 517–53); see also *Zeitschrift*, liv. 162 *et seq.*, for an account which adds but little to Pelster's information. For his teachings see D. E. Sharp's 'The Philosophy of Richard Fishacre,' in *The New Scholasticism*, vii (1933). 281–97.

Besides these two there are references to other works :—' In Parabolas Salomonis ' : *inc.* ' Multiplici ratione audiendum.' Plumpton, ' Ricardus Fizaker super parabolas Salomonis ' (Leland, *Collect.* iv. 152). ' De Poenitentia ' : ' Quia ut habet St. Augustinus,' at Hulme, St. Benedict (Boston of Bury, *loc. cit.*). ' Quodlibeta ' : ' Quodlibeta Fizaker,' at Cambridge, King's Coll. (Leland, *Collect.* iv. 18). ' Super Deus illuminatio,' formerly at Rivaulx (*ibid.* iv. 38).

A number of his ' Sermons ' remain. (a) Cambridge, Trinity Coll. MS. 373, fo. 24 : *inc.* ' Ego autem sicut oliva. Tria hic videamus,' with a note ' Fratris R. de Fisaker,' which may cover sermons to fo. 30, including those upon the texts ' Replebimur in bonis ' (fo. 24*b*), ' Holocausta medulatio ' (fo. 25), ' Visitasti terram ' (fo. 25*b*), ' Terra dedit fructum suum ' (fo. 26), and ' Ave Maria gratia ' (fo. 26*b*) ; (b) *ibid.* fos. 87 *et seq.*, *inc.* ' Plus amat deus minorem mundum,' with a marginal note ' R. Phisaker ' ; (c) Cambridge, Gonville and Caius Coll. MS. 408, fo. 204, with MS. note ' Secundum fr Ricardum de Fissaker ' ; (d) Ipswich Museum MS. 6, entitled ' Destructiones de vii peccatis mortalibus,' with a note ' Sermo fratris Ric. de Fishakel ' (Cambridge Antiq. Soc., *Publications*, octavo series, xxviii, 1895. 59) ; (e) Bodl. Lib. MS. Laud. Misc. 511, fo. 96*b*, *inc.* ' Non enim heres erit filius ancille cum filio libere,' with a note ' De libro rubeo maiori. Sermo fratris R. de Fisacre.' An unidentified sermon is mentioned by an anonymous compiler of exempla (*Liber Exemplorum ad usum praedicantium*, B.S.F.S., ed. A. G. Little, p. 19). An unidentified tract is mentioned at the end of Magdalen Coll. Oxford MS. 60 : ' patet satis clare in tractatu quod frater Ricardus Fisacre composuit.'

Richard Fishacre came from the diocese of Exeter,[1] where members of the Fishacre family were prominent.[2] He is said to have been the first dominican to incept under Robert Bacon [q.v.], probably sometime after 1227, and to have been the first of his order in England to have written a ' Commentary on the Sentences.'[1] This he apparently wrote before *c.* 1240, the date of Grosseteste's translation of the ' Ethics,'[2] which Fishacre apparently did not use.[3] Fishacre lectured to the Oxford dominicans with Robert Bacon in the school of St. Edward,[4] where they acquired reputations as great preachers as well as great theologians.[5] In 1248, not long before his death, Fishacre served as an executor of a very important baron, Herbert Fitzpeter, according to a document dated at Reading on the Sunday before the ascension.[6] The death-bed vision described under Richard of Stavensby may possibly refer to Fishacre, assuming that the date in the anecdote is wrong. Fishacre died in 1248 and was buried next to the east wall of the dominican church in Oxford.[7] He is mentioned in a contemporary treatise and in an exemplum.[8] Despite his prominence very little is known of him.

Richard Grant was chancellor of Lincoln and archbishop of Canterbury.[9] To him may be attributed a sermon : B.M. MS. Reg. 8, C. v, fo. 5, with a note ' Mag. Ricardus Magnus.'

[1] Exoniensis to be preferred to Oxoniensis (*Triveti Annales*, p. 229).

[2] Robert Fishacre, 1250 (Dugdale, *Monasticon*, vi. 211) ; Dominus William de Fissacre (P.R.O., Exchequer, Misc. Books, E. 164/19, Torre abbey, fos. 99, 103) ; B.M. MS. Harley 3660, fo. 68*b* ; Martin de Fissacre (E. 164/19, fo. 93).

[1] Assuming that Robert entered the order in that year. (See Oxford, Oriel Coll. MS. 43, flyleaf, note : ' qui fuit primus qui scripsit super sententias de ordine suo in Anglia et iacet Oxonie inter fratres predicatores.')

[2] F. M. Powicke in British Academy *Proceedings*, xvi (1930) ; *cf. Speculum*, ix (1934). 143.

[3] Pelster, *op. cit.* p. 531.

[4] *Triveti Annales*, *loc. cit.*

[5] *Chr. Maj.* v. 16.

[6] B.M. MS. Harley 1708, fo. 114*b* ; MS. Cotton, Vespasian E. xxv, fo. 61*b*.

[7] *Chr. Maj.* v. 16 ; Leland, *Collect.* iv. 59.

[8] James, *Cat. of Lambeth Lib.* p. 86 ; Little, *op. cit.* pp. 75–8.

[9] T. pp. 626, 759 ; *D.N.B.* under Grant.

Unless the tradition is correct which identifies this man with Richard of Wetheringsett [1] [q.v.] little is known about him until he became chancellor of Lincoln. Probably he came from Nasinges.[2] The group of sermons among which his appears may represent the work of a university group, probably of Paris. This supposition is strengthened by the papal statement that members of the curia had known him in the schools.[3] As chancellor Richard succeeded Roger of Insula, who became dean of York, succeeding a Dean Hamo, who apparently died on Leap Day (25 February) 1220.[4] Richard's first appearance as chancellor is as a witness of a document of 16 Dec. 1220.[5] He attested other documents of 12 Apr. 1221,[6] 15 Aug. 1222,[7] 25 Nov. 1222,[8] 12 Mar. 1223,[9] 20 Mar. 1226,[10] and 8 Sept. 1227.[11] He is described by Matthew Paris as 'stature elegantissime facundie admirabilis, scientia et moribus incomparabilis.'[12] Possibly his name of 'Magnus' [13] or 'le Grant' [14] came from his height. The story of his choice by Gregory IX and his consecration and episcopate is known.[15] His handwriting may remain.[16]

[1] An identification not proved.

[2] His brother and sister are called 'de Nasinges' (*C.Cl.R.*, 1227–31, p. 570).

[3] *Flores Historiarum* (R.S.), ed. H. G. Hewlett, ii. 363 ; M. Gibbs and J. Lang, *Bishops and Reform*, p. 32.

[4] On Dean Hamo's death see Heironimus and Russell, *Shorter Latin Poems of Master Henry of Avranches* (Mediaeval Acad. of America), pp. 60–3.

[5] *Liber Antiquus Hugonis de Welles*, p. 103.

[6] *Rot. H. de Welles*, ii. 191.

[7] B.M. MS. Harley 2110, fo. 122*b*.

[8] *Rot. H. de Welles*, ii. 198 ; B.M. MS. Reg. 11, B. ix, fo. 37.

[9] B.M. MS. Cotton, Nero D. iii, fo. 17.

[10] *Rot. H. de Welles*, ii. 213.

[11] B.M. Add. Ch. 21999.

[12] *Chr. Maj.* iii. 205.

[13] The usual name (*Ann. Monast.* i. 245 ; 'Annals of Dover,' B.M. MS. Cotton, Julius D. v, fo. 28).

[14] *Hist. Works of Gervase of Canterbury* (R.S.), ed. W. Stubbs, ii. 127.

[15] See *D.N.B.* under Grant.

[16] 'Magister R. Linc. eclle. Cancellarius R decan de Chomonbly salutem et dilectionem.' The volume, a 13th century glossed Isaiah, was probably loaned to the dean of Cholmondeley (Lincoln Cathedral MS. 172, fo. 146).

Richard de Hetherington was a disputant at Oxford *c.* 1282–90 (Little-Pelster, p. 87).

Richard of Insula was abbot of Bury St. Edmunds and probable author of some 'Sermons' in Cambridge, Pembroke Coll. MS. 87, fos. 217*b*–20*b*. After the sermons is the note 'Frater Ricardus permissione divina Abbas de S Eadmundo dilectis.'

Rather unusual information about this abbot remains :

> Richard's body was no doubt embalmed at Pontigny and brought back to Bury, where he was buried, as we learn from the Douai MS. of 1435, 'at the feet of Abbot Henry,' i.e. as no. 3 from the east of the row of six abbots buried in the chapter house. Skeleton no. 3 exhumed on 1st January, 1903, had the skull split longitudinally by saw and chisel and the sternum sawn through (evidently for purposes of preservation of the body), so that it was obviously that of Richard de Insula.
>
> From the careful measurements of the bones of this skeleton that were made at my request in January 1903 (before they were reinterred) by Professor Macalister, M.D., F.S.A., F.R.S., Professor of Anatomy at the University of Cambridge, Richard of Insula must have been a fine tall man nearly 5 feet 10 inches high. His bones were long, straight, and healthy : he was, in fact, the tallest and largest of the six abbots whose bones were examined by Professor Macalister. The indications of the bones showed him to be a man of probably between 55 and 65 years of age.[1]

Since Richard died in 1234 he was probably born within the decade 1170–80. A Ricardus de Insula, possibly a clerk,[2] was a witness of a charter of Robert de 'Wauci,' the first witness being Alexander, prior of Ashby [q.v.]. Richard is said to have been a monk of St. Edmund's.[3] He does not figure in the long list of monks who shared in the election of Abbot Hugh in 1214–5 unless he was the precentor Richard. This

[1] Ernest Clarke, *Bury Chroniclers of the Thirteenth Century*, pp. 5–6.

[2] He appears after a parson (B.M. MS. Harley 4714, fo. 22).

[3] *Chronicon Abbatiæ Rameseiensis* (R.S.), ed. W. D. Macray, p. 342.

official took a prominent part in the action, but a part which the narrator disliked so much that he called the precentor a Pontius Pilate.[1] Richard came of a distinguished family and was a relative of Richard de Argentin.[2]

Richard de Insula succeeded Robert, abbot of Thorney, as sacristan of St. Edmunds, probably in 1216.[3] A letter of advice from Robert to his successor remains.[4] Richard was promoted to be prior, probably in 1220[5]: a letter to him as prior is extant.[6] He was chosen as abbot of Burton in June 1222.[7] As such he figures in a number of ordinary monastic documents.[8] On 5 June 1229 he was elected abbot of his old house and was installed on St. Edmund's Day, 9 June.[9] He went to Rome on business in 1232.[10] His abbacy lasted slightly more than five years and his death occurred on 26 Aug. 1234.[11] As gifts to his abbey he left: 'tabulam argenteam et deauratam pro magno altari.'[12] He also gave a hanging to St. Albans.[13]

Richard of Knapwell, O.P., was a theologian[14] whose writings are listed as follows:

> Frater Ricardus Clapoel Anglicus magister in theologia scripsit super quatuor libros sententiarum. Item contra corruptorium St. Thome. Item de unitate formarum. Item de mediata visione divine essentie (Martène and Durand, *Veterum Scriptorum*, vi. 370).

(See Denifle in *Archiv für Litteratur- und Kirchengesch. des Mittelalters*, ii. 227). The 'De Immediata Visione Divine Essentie' has not been identified.[1] 'Commentary on the Sentences': *inc.* 'Ut uerbo abbreuiato libro Sent.' (a) Cambridge, Peterhouse MS. 128, fos. 106–13; (b) Oxford, Magdalen Coll. MS. 56, fos. 185–91, entitled 'Notabilia super primum Sententiarum usque ad distinctionem xix secundum magistrum Ricardum de Clapperwelle.' The rest seems lost. The 'Correctorium Corruptorii quare detraxisti' is edited by P. Glorieux in 'Les premières polémiques Thomistes.' Glorieux identifies the author as a dominican and an Englishman (*ibid.* pp. xliv–lv). For other work about Richard see F. Pelster's 'Richard von Klapwell, O.P. Seine Questiones disputatae und sein Quodlibet' (*Zeitsch. f. Kath. Theol.* lii, 1928. 473–91); see also Little-Pelster (*passim*). He was not the compiler of the questions in MS. Assisi 158 (Little-Pelster, p. 18).

Richard of Clapwell seems to have responded at a disputation of Roger of Marston [q.v.] at Oxford, incepting there in 1284.[2] From 1284 to 1288 a controversy raged over his teachings.[3] In 1284 he was accused by Archbishop Peckham of promulgating unorthodox interpretations of the Thomist doctrine of the unity of substantial form.[4] At a council held at the church of

[1] *Memorials of St. Edmunds* (R.S.), ed. T. Arnold, ii. 76; also pp. 35, 36, 41, 55, 56, 70, 86, 99, 125.

[2] *Ibid.* i. 376; *Chr. Maj.* iii. 239.

[3] *Memorials of St. Edmunds*, ii. 293.

[4] *Ibid.* p. 133.

[5] *Ibid.* pp. xxvi–xxvii; Herbert died 4 Sept. 1220 (*ibid.* iii. 26).

[6] *Ibid.* i. 376.

[7] *Ann. Monast.* i. 225.

[8] I. H. Jeayes, *Descriptive Cat. of Derbysh. Charters*, p. 211, nos. 1697, 1698; p. 325, no. 2575; B.M. Stowe, chs. 61, 82.

[9] Dugdale, *Monasticon*, iii. 105; B.M. MS. Harley 3977, fo. 52*b*; *Ann. Monast.* i. 245. A memorandum of his election is in Bodl. Lib., Suffolk ch. 37.

[10] *Chr. Maj.* iii. 239.

[11] Dugdale, *Monasticon*, iii. 105; *Chr. Maj.* iii. 239.

[12] Cambridge Antiq. Soc. *Proceedings*, xxviii (1895). 181.

[13] *Chr. Maj.* vi. 390.

[14] T. p. 180. His name is given as either Cnapwell or Clapwell. A 'Dominus William de Cnapwell, tunc seneschal' attests a charter of Margaret, countess of Winchester (P.R.O., Aug. Off., Misc. Books, Cartæ, E. 135/44, no. 267). There remain charters in transcript of William, son of Richard de Glapwell, and of Thomas, his son (B.M. MS. Titus C. ix, fos. 116*b*, 117, 118*b*, 120, 124; *cf.* Little-Pelster, pp. 89-91, and literature cited there).

[1] Unless it is the 'questio' on this topic in Bologna Univ. Lib. MS. 1539, fos. 51–4*b* (Pelster, *op. cit.* p. 491).

[2] Little, *F.S.O.* p. 856.

[3] *Cf.* Pelster, *op. cit.* pp. 474–6, 471, *nn.* 1 and 2.

[4] *Reg. Peckham* (R.S.), ed. C. T. Martin, pp. 840–843, 896–902; *Reg. Johannis de Pontissara* (C.Y.S.), ed. C. Deedes, p. 306.

St. Mary le Bow in London 20 Apr. 1286 eight heresies were condemned.[1] Although the official documents do not name Richard, chroniclers state that the accusations were directed against him.[2] The dominican prior provincial, William of Hothum [q.v.], then refused to admit that the archbishop had jurisdiction over the friars preachers and appealed to Rome. Richard is said to have gone to Rome and then, losing his appeal, to have withdrawn to Bologna. There he seems to have taught the unorthodox doctrines until he came to a miserable end.[3]

Richard de Mediavilla, O.F.M., was the author of a well-known ' Commentary on the Sentences.'[4] For the MSS. of this work see E. Hocedez's ' Richard de Middleton ' (p. 14 *et seq.*) and Josef Lechner's ' Die Sakramentenlehre des Richard von Mediavilla ' (*Studien zur hist. theol.*, p. 7 *et seq.*). For his ' Quodlibeta ' and ' Questiones ' see Lechner (p. 12) and Hocedez (pp. 14–27). ' Frater Ricardus de Mediavilla magister fuit. Scripsit super sententias multum utiliter, et postillas cum aliis pluribus fecit ' (P. Glorieux, *Bibliothèque thomiste*, v, 1925. 267–73). On a sermon written about 1281–3 attributed to him see Hocedez (pp. 56–60).

Father Pelster has shown that Mediavilla is probably Meynell rather than Middleton,[5] but Richard's family has not been identified. In 1283, still a bachelor, he was engaged in examining the orthodoxy of the works of Petrus Johannes Olivi.[6] He preached sermons during the years 1281–3 which are extant.[7] He seems to have finished his commentary during this period.[8] He was

[1] Wilkins, *Concilia Magnae Britanniae*, ii. 123, 127 ; Labbe, *Concilia*, xi. 261 ; Spelman, *Concilia*, ii. 347.

[2] *Ann. Monast.* iv. 306–7 (Oseney) ; *ibid.* iii. 323–5, 341 (Dunstable).

[3] *Ibid.* iii. 341.

[4] T. p. 526 ; *D.N.B.* under Middleton.

[5] Little-Pelster, p. 96 and citations there.

[6] *Analecta Francescana*, iii. 347 (from *Chron. XXIV Gen.*).

[7] Hocedez, *op. cit.* pp. 27–38.

[8] Lechner, *op. cit.* p. 13 ; but *cf.* Hocedez (*op. cit.* pp. 49–55), who thinks that that part was composed in 1294–98.

at Paris disputing scholastically during the years 1284–7[1] and became a doctor of theology, probably by 1286.[2] He served as one of the preceptors of the sons of Charles of Anjou, king of Naples, in Spain and Italy from this time until about 1295.[3] The activity of his later years is uncertain. He died after Walter of Poitiers (1307) and before John Duns Scotus (1308).[4]

Richard Morins, see **Richard de Mores Anglicus.**

Richard Poore was a prelate and theologian.[5] He was formerly believed to be the author of the ' Ancren Riwle,' but that does not seem probable now, nor can he be identified with the canonist, Richard Anglicus [q.v.]. He has been credited with a large share of the authorship of the Salisbury consuetudinary (J. M. J. Fletcher, *Tarrant Crawford, and the Founder of Salisbury Cathedral*, Dorset Nat. Hist. and Antiq. Field Club, p. 6). Possibly he was the author of the ' Littere ad Instruendum Clericum,' Oxford, New Coll. MS. 210, entitled ' Ricardi episcopi Sarum littere ad instruendum clericum in minoribus existentem et infra legitimam etatem, et de custodia ipsius clerici ac ecclesie.'

Richard was the brother of Herbert Poore, bishop of Salisbury (1194–1217),[6] and probably son of Richard of Ilminster, bishop of Winchester (1173–88).[7] He secured a dispensation for illegitimacy from the Curia.[8] His academic career, as far as can be ascertained, was associated with Paris, where he was a fellow student of Thomas of Marl-

[1] Hocedez, *op. cit.* pp. 27–30.

[2] *Ibid.* p. 29 ; *Archiv für Litt.- und Kirchengesch.*, ii. 295 ; iii. 430.

[3] *Analecta Bollandiana*, ix. 294 ; *Acta Sanctorum*, Aug., iii. 810.

[4] Wetzer und Welles, *Kirchenlexikon*, i. 1523.

[5] T. p. 605 ; *D.N.B.* under Poor.

[6] For his career see *D.N.B.* under Poor.

[7] *Chronica Rogeri de Houedene* (R.S.), ed. W. Stubbs, iv. p. xci. *n.* 4.

[8] *C.E.P.R.* i. 24.

borough under Stephen Langton [1] and in 1213 was teaching theology.[2] His brother probably secured his election as dean of Salisbury on 8 Mar. 1198.[3] He served as papal judge-delegate in at least three cases during the next twenty years.[4] In 1202 a divided election at Winchester sent both Peter des Roches and him to Rome as bishops-elect, but he lost.[5] A few years later the pope demanded that Richard should not be persecuted for his share in the Winchester proceedings.[6] He was elected bishop of Durham in 1213, but this election was likewise quashed.[7] However, he was confirmed in his choice as bishop of Chichester in 1215,[8] and was then translated to Salisbury in 1217 and to Durham in 1228. He died on 15 Apr. 1237 and was buried in the church of Tarrant Crawford.[9] Besides being a great churchman he spent much time at court. He was doubtless responsible for the advancement of Edmund of Abingdon and probably also for that of other outstanding men connected with Salisbury and Durham, such as Thomas Chobham, Robert of Bingham, Elias of Derham, Adam Marsh, and William of Durham.

Richard Porland, O.F.M.,[10] was probably author of some ' Sermons.' Bale is the only known source of information about him :

[1] *Chronicon de Evesham* (R.S.), ed. W. D. Macray, p. 232. In 1213 Richard was with Archbishop Stephen Langton at Croydon.

[2] Glorieux, under Thomas of Chabham.

[3] *Ann. Monast.* ii. 65.

[4] *Rot. Litt. Pat.* pp. 129*b*, 132 ; *C.E.P.R.* i. 49 ; *Memorials of St. Edmunds* (R.S.), ed. T. Arnold, ii. 69, 71.

[5] *Ann. Monast.* iv. 51.

[6] *C.E.P.R.* i. 25.

[7] *Rot. Chart.* p. 208 ; *Hist. Dunelm. Script. Tres.* (Surtees Soc.), ed. J. Raine, pp. 29, 30.

[8] For ' viii^vo kalendas Februarii ' as the date of consecration see *Historical Works of Gervase of Canterbury* (R.S.), ed. W. Stubbs, ii. 108–9, and for ' viii kal. Martii ' see *Flores Historiarum* (R.S.), ed. H. R. Luard, ii. 156.

[9] Fletcher, *op. cit.* pp. 10–9 ; *Chronica de Mailros* (Bannatyne Club), p. 148 ; *Chr. Maj.* iii. 391.

[10] T. p. 605.

Ricardus Porlonde, Minorita . . . scripsit, Sermones per annum, li i. ' Christus passus est pro nobis.' Apparently 'ex Bibliotheca Nordovicensi' (*Index.* p. 357).

Bibliographical tradition has erected a large and shaky structure upon these simple details. Perhaps the most elaborate account is given by Blomefield (iv. 112).

Richard Rufus of Cornwall, O.F.M., was a theologian.[1] According to Adam Marsh (*Mon. Fr.* i. 349) and Roger Bacon (*Fratris Rogeri Bacon. Compendium Studii Theologiae*, R.S., ed. Rashdall, p. 52 ; see also T. p. 627 ; Little, *F.S.O.* p. 842), Richard was the author of commentaries upon the ' Sentences.' Copies of some of them seem to have once existed at Assisi : MS. 346, *inc.* ' Quia secundem Hugonem de S. Victore in libro de sacrementis ' ; MS. 339, with the same *incipit* ; MS. 346, with the title ' Primus et secundus fratris magistri Ricardi de Cornubia anglici ordinis minorum ' ; MS. 375, ' Compilatio quatuor librorum sententiarum secundum fratrem magistrum Riccardum Ruphi de Anglia ordinis minorum facta Parisiis,' *inc.* ' Cupientes. Totali libro premittit mihi prologum.' Another copy of this is possibly at Todi, MS. 33, *inc.* ' Cupientes. Premittit hic magister totali libro prologum.' A commentary at Oxford, Balliol Coll. MS. 196, begins ' Toti operi libri Sententiarum premittit magister prologum suum.' The information about the lost books comes from *Inventario dell' antica bibl. de S. Francesco*, pp. 104, 109, and is examined by Little (*F.S.O.* pp. 43–4). Another Balliol MS. (MS. 62) may contain a commentary, according to Fr. Pelster (' Die älteste Sentenzenkommentar aus der Oxforder Franciskanerschule,' in *Zeitschrift Scholastik*, i. 65 ; Little, *loc. cit.*). Apparently there was also a copy at Norwich. ' Ricardus le Ruys, doctor, Minorita, edidit Lecturam Sententiarum : inc. " Materia divinarum Scripturarum." Ex bibliotheca

[1] T. pp. 627, 648. Best life in Little, *F.S.O.* pp. 841–4.

Nordovicensi' (Bale, *Index*, p. 358). See also Pelster in *Scholastik* (1934).

A 'sermo fratris Richardi, de ordine Minorum, in festo beati Nicholai,' 1230, is attributed to Richard Rufus by Davy (*Les Sermons Universitaires de* 1230–1231, p. 361), but is probably too early. There was formerly in the library of St. Augustine's, Canterbury, a 'Sincathegorematica Ricardi Cornubiensis' (James, *A.L.C.D.* p. 354).

The problem of the biography of Richard Rufus, like that of his writings, is complicated: there are references to several men who might be identical with the franciscan whose career is known from 1238 to 1259. A master (or masters) of that name witnessed charters of Giles, bishop of Hereford (1200–16),[1] of Hugh, abbot of Abingdon (1199?–1221),[2] and of Maria, widow of Etard de Crevequer.[3] A Master Ricard of Cornwall, canon of Beverley,[4] canon [5] and chancellor of York,[6] disappears about the time that Richard entered the franciscan order.[7]

[1] B.M. MS. Arundel 19, fos. 31*b*, 37.

[2] P.R.O., Exchequer, Misc. Books, E. 164/20, fo. 7; Robert Bingham [q.v.] was also a witness.

[3] Camb. Univ. Lib. MS. Ll. ii. 15, fo. 31. There was a canon of London, late 12th cent., of the name (*cf.* also *C.Ch.R.*, 1300–26, p. 430).

[4] *Reg. Walter Gray* (Surtees Soc.), pp. 2, 68, 192; B.M. MS. Cotton, Claudius B. iii, fos. 74*b*, 75.

[5] MS. Cotton, fos. 82*b* (1217, possibly of Beverley), 22*b* (1221); *Reg. W. Gray*, pp. 133, 140, 142; *Reg. Corbridge* (Surtees Soc.), ed. W. Brown, i. 49; *Reg. W. Gray*, pp. 143, 144 (1222); London, College of Arms MS. 60, fo. 36; *Reg. W. Gray*, pp. 38 (probably 1216), 64, 128, 132, 133, 141 (time of Hamo, 1214–20), 141*n*, 238*n*, 280, 281; York Cathedral, Magnum registrum album, fos. 34, 74*b*; B.M. MS. Cotton, Claudius B. iii, fos. 14*b*, 25, 87*b*, 91*b*, 92; *ibid.* Nero D. iii, fos. 14*b* (2), 30.

[6] B.M. MS. Cotton, Nero D. iii, fo. 51*b* (1224); Le Neve, *Fasti*, ii. 63 (1225); B.M. MS. Cotton, Claudius B. iii, fo. 44 (1226); *Reg. W. Gray*, pp. 225*n* (1228), 230*n* (1229); Westminster abbey muniments, no. 20619 (1234); *Reg. W. Gray*, pp. 64, 229*n*; B.M. MS. Claudius B. iii, fo. 39.

[7] There is mention of houses and curia belonging to prebend of Risceby which Master Richard Cornubiensis held for life (*Reg. W. Gray*), p. 68. Possibly this is not the same as the canon and chancellor of York. John Blund [q.v.] probably succeeded Richard as chancellor (*Rot. Litt. Pat.* pp. 76, 84*b*).

Another master was at Oxford in 1234.[1] A Master Richard Cornwall was given preferment by Robert Grosseteste about 1240 and appears in other documents later.[2] There are several miscellaneous references to a master or masters of that name.[3]

Richard Rufus entered the franciscan order after 1235 [4] at Paris, returning to England and making his profession there. He spoke in the chapter at Oxford in 1238 and probably had not been in the order long, since he entered while Friar Elias was disturbing the franciscans. Probably he entered at about the same time as Alexander of Hales [q.v.]. He went in 1239 'pro provincia Francie' with Haymo to the general chapter.[5] Although he received permission to go to Paris in 1248,[6] he seems to have remained at Oxford until 1253.[7] He had apparently been lecturing upon the 'Sentences' at Oxford [8] and lectured solemnly upon them at Paris. 'Reprobatus Parisius propter errores quos invenerat,' [9] he was recalled to England in 1256 and became the master of the franciscans at Oxford.[10] The will of Walter le Flemeng of 5 Jan. 1258 was made before Friar Richard of Cornwall, formerly warden of the franciscans of Southampton.[11]

[1] *Cartulary of Oseney Abbey*, ed. H. E. Salter, i. 278.

[2] *Rot. R. Grosseteste*, p. 43; *Ep. Grosseteste*, pp. 138, 140; *Mon. Fr.* i. 134; *Munimenta Academica* (R.S.), ed. H. Anstey, i. 23.

[3] *Landboc de Winchelcumba*, ed. D. Royce, i. 109; *Rot. Litt. Pat.* pp. 76, 84*b*; *Chr. Maj.* vi. 279; *Short Cal. of the Feet of Fines for Norfolk*, ed. W. Rye, p. 47; *Feet of Fines for Yorkshire*, 16–30 Hen. III (Yorks. Archaeol. Soc.), p. 1, *n.* 1.

[4] *Eccleston*, pp. 24, 65.

[5] *Ibid.* pp. 28, 65; Little in *E.H.R.* xlix (1934). 299.

[6] *Mon. Fr.* i. 365–6: a highly laudatory letter about Richard by Adam Marsh.

[7] *Ibid.* p. 330; Little, *F.S.O.* p. 842 for date.

[8] Roger Bacon, *loc. cit.*; *Mon. Fr.* i. 360, 365; Little, *F.S.O.* p. 842.

[9] Bacon, *loc. cit.*

[10] *Eccleston*, p. 65; *Mon. Fr.* i. 39; *cf.* App. A below.

[11] Archives of the Queen's College, Oxford (Sherborn Priory), typescript by Denholm-Young, p. 546. Possibly this refers to a different Richard or shows with next document that he was in the north of England at the time.

Martin of St. Cruce, master of the Hospital of Sherburne, near Durham, by a will dated November 1259, bequeathed him an entire garment and a copy of the 'Canonical Epistles.'[1] He was held in high esteem by some, but by Roger Bacon he was regarded with intellectual contempt.[2]

Richard of Sleckburn, O.F.M., was probably the author of a book of 'exempla' and possibly to be identified with Richard of Durham [q.v.].[3] A 'Speculum Laicorum,' ascribed to John of Hoveden [q.v.], gives an 'exemplum' in honour of St. Benedict which 'refert frater Ricardus de Glickburne de ordine Minorum' (B.M. MS. Add. 11284; Welter, *Thesaurus Exemplorum*, v, 1914. 27–8). This, Dr. Little believes, indicates that he wrote a book containing the story.

Richard was confessor of Devorguila, widow of Sir John de Balliol, and probably more responsible for her establishment of the college than any other person.[4] In a letter of 1284 she encouraged him to aid her with the house of Balliol. He confirmed a grant by Balliol's executors of debts due to Sir John, dated at Coventry 1287. In 1285–6 he advised Devorguila to allow certain grants to the poor scholars. He became confessor to Mabel Giffard, abbess of Shaftesbury, on 10 Sept. 1303.[5]

Richard of Sleckburn resembled Richard of Durham in being a franciscan author with Oxford connexions, apparently acting as confessor to lady patrons, and was probably about the same age. On the other hand, they had different names, and cannot be shown to have been in the same place, even Oxford, at the same time. Furthermore, although Durham has accurate knowledge of the circumstances of the foundation of Balliol (accessible to any franciscan) he fails to define his connexion with the house or with Devorguila. Probably they were not identical.

[1] *Durham Wills* (Surtees Soc.), i. 10–11.

[2] *Mon. Fr.* i. 349, 359, 365; Bacon, *loc. cit.*

[3] The information about Sleckburn comes from A. G. Little in *E.H.R.* xxxii (1917). 48–9.

[4] H.M.C., 4th Rep., App. pp. 442–4.

[5] *Reg. S. de Gandavo* (C.Y.S.), p. 89; Dugdale, *Monasticon*, ii. 473.

R[ichard] de Stanington[1] was the author of commentaries upon Aristotelian translations in Bodl. Lib. MS. Digby 204:—'Libri Physicorum': *inc.* 'Quoniam ut dicit Aristoteles primo physicorum,' with the colophon 'Expliciunt quedam extracta a libro phisicorum per fratrem R. de Staningtona,' fos. 101 *et seq.* In the same manuscript are also these commentaries, possibly by him:—'De Coelo et Mundo': *inc.* 'Summa cognitionis,' fos. 108 *et seq.* 'De Generatione et Corruptione': *inc.* 'De generatione et corruptione in naturali,' fos. 111*b et seq.* 'De Meteorum Libris': *inc.* 'Postquam precessit rememoratio nostra de elementis,' fos. 114 *et seq.* 'De Anima': *inc.* 'Bonorum et honorabilium dicitur esse scientia de anima,' fos. 121 *et seq.* The commentary upon the Meteorology appears also in Bodl. Lib. MS. Laud Misc. 527, fos. 115 *et seq.*

Richard of Stavensby, O.P., was treasurer of Lichfield, joined the dominicans and was the reputed author of a 'Concordance,' according to a letter of Fr. Simon Bertherius to John Bromyard, dated Lyons, 4 July 1500 (Quetif-Echard, p. 209). The statement is:

> Inter quos [sodales Anglos pietate doctrinaque claros] a principio floruit frater Ricardus de Stavenesby nobilis genere, nobillimus autem religionis fervore, qui plantatus circa fluento aquarum scripture sacra impendio composuit Maximas concordantias, que Anglicane dicuntur circa annum 1252: quem aliquantulum iuuit Hugo de Croyndonio etiam Anglicus natione.

Richard of Stavensby had a rather notable career as a pluralist before he entered the dominican order. He had been instituted in the church of Tansor by Roger, dean of Lincoln, before the death of that prelate in

[1] T. p. 689; Little gives Richard as the name (*Initia Operum Latinorum*, p. 17). Stannington, Yorkshire or Northumberland.

1223.[1] In 1226 he received Peakirk and in the next year, upon exhibiting papal letters of dispensation, he added Castle Donnington.[2] All of these were in the bishopric of Lincoln. He was probably the clerk of that name who was assigned to help collect the 'fifteenth' in Stafford and Salop in February 1225.[3] The election of his brother to the bishopric of Coventry opened up new possibilities of preferment for him.

Richard of Stavensby was one of the family of Alexander Stavensby [q.v.], appearing frequently in the charters of his brother in the early years of his pontificate, the first being apparently in his second episcopal year,[4] 1225–6. On 26 Sept. 1226 he wrote a charter in his own hand, being then clearly his brother's clerk.[5] In the fifth year, 1228–1229, he is still without title.[6] He may have been chancellor some time in 1229–1230:[7] by February 1230 he is treasurer of Lichfield.[8] He did not hold this office long. His successor, Richard 'de Glovernia,' was in office by May 1232[9] and probably even in the previous year, since Alexander of Hales [q.v.], who succeeded Richard de Glovernia as archdeacon of Coventry, was in that office in 1231. Richard resigned his Lincoln preferments at the same time. Probably at this time he entered the dominican order, an act not surprising in view of his brother's close connexions with the pioneers of that order. Of his career as a friar little is known; he probably studied in England. He is supposed to have died in 1262,[1] but a story of the death-bed vision of a doctor, Richard, lector in England, may refer to him and thus place his death in 1257.[2]

[1] *Rot. H. de Welles*, ii. 216; vacant in 1232 (*ibid.* p. 165).

[2] *Ibid.* pp. 217, 305; Peakirk filled by another on 14 Oct. 1231 (*ibid.* p. 241); Castle Donnington vacant in 1231 (*ibid.* p. 314).

[3] *C.P.R.*, 1216–25, p. 563.

[4] *Great Register of Lichfield Cathedral* (Wm. Salt Archaeol. Soc.), ed. H. E. Savage, p. 169.

[5] *Ibid.* p. 81.

[6] B.M. Add. MS. 30311, fos. 61, 62, 62*b*, 64*b*; Oxford, Bodl. MS. Top. Salop. d. 2, p. 18; B.M. Stowe Ch. 136; *Great Register*, no. 524; B.M. MS. Harl. 3868, fo. 23; *Coucher Book of Whalley Abbey* (Chetham Soc.), ed. W. A. Hulton, pp. 143–4; B.M. MS. Harl. 4799, fo. 7*b*; P.R.O., ancient deeds, L. 272, 274.

[7] *Great Register*, p. 312.

[8] *Ibid.* p. 312; for other references to him as treasurer see *ibid.* pp. 65, 211, 312.

[9] P.R.O., augmentation office, misc. (E. 315/46), no. 230.

[1] Bede Jarrett, *English Dominicans*, p. 33; a Richard of Stavenesby is a witness of a cyrograph of the abbeys of Barlings and Peterborough in 1260 (London, Soc. Antiquaries MS. 60, fo. 139).

[2] The story is given in two versions: *Fratris Galvagni de la Flamma Cronica Ordinis Praedicatorum* (Mon. Ord. Fr. Pred. ii. 1), ed. B. M. Reichert, p. 97; and *Fratris Gerardi de Fracheto Vite Fratrum*, ed. B. M. Reichert, p. 277, as follows:

1257. Isto anno in festo pentecostes in provincia Anglie frater Riccardus doctor mortuus est. Hic in hora mortis terribilibus oculis fratres circumstantes aspexit, postea ridendo dixit, 'Propter oraciones fratrum saluus factus sum.' Hic in vitis fratrum.

Cum frater Ricardus, lector in Anglia, morti appropinquasset, ait: 'Fratres, orate pro me, quia cito terribiles apparebunt.' Post hoc cepit oculos terribiliter huc et illuc conuertere et admirabilis signa uultu et gestu monstrare. Tandem ad se adiens ait: 'Benedictus Deus, saluatus sum ad instanciam fratrum nostrorum et fratrum minorum quos semper dilexi.' Et glorificans Deum emisit spiritum.

Richard of Thetford was the author of two treatises. 'Treatise on Preaching': *inc.* 'Quoniam emulatores estis spirituum ad edificationem ecclesie.' (a) Cambridge, Corpus Christi Coll. MS. 441, fos. 13–29 (14th cent.), entitled 'Inc. tract. fr. Ricardi de Thetford de modo predicandi'; (b) Lincoln Cathedral MS. H. iv, ascribed to Thomas Lemman, clericus (T. p. 477); (c) B.M. MS. Harley 3244, fos. 186–91 (late 13th cent.), with the rubric 'Inc. ars predicandi secundum frm. Ric. de Theford'; (d) B.M. MS. Reg. 4, B. viii, fos. 263*b*–265*b* (13th cent.); (e) Lambeth Palace MS. 477, fos. 40*b*–53; (f) Bodl. Lib. MS. Bodl. 848, fos. 5*b*–12 (early 14th cent.); (g) Oxford, Merton Coll. MS. 249, fos. 175 *et seq.*, entitled 'Sermo fratris Ricardi de dilatatione sermonum'; (h) Worcester Cathedral MS. F. 84, fos. 1–11 (13th cent.). Possibly he wrote some sermons : *inc.* ' Estote imitatores . . . Nota quid imitari,' entitled ' Sermones fratris Ricardi de Chesard [Thesard ?] ' (Catalogue Worc. MS. Q. 67, fos. 38–48*b*).

' De Angelis tractatus secundum Ricardum de Theford ' : *inc.* ' Septem angeli qui habebant . . . Per septem angelos intelligimus predicatorus universos.' Oxford, Jesus Coll. MS. 9, fos. 123–37*b*. This bears the note ' De angelis tractatus secundum Ricardum de Theford ' at the beginning, and at the end ' angelos Dei ascendendis et descendendis. Non plus fecit frater Ricardus de Theford.' Upon the treatise on homiletics see Thomas Charland, ' Les auteurs d'Artes praedicandi du XIIIe siècle ' (*Etudes d'histoire littéraire et doctrinale du XIII siècle*, i. 41–60).

Richard was thus a monk or friar of the 13th century. Upon the margin of a treatise upon preaching by William Rufus[1] is a note ' de doctrina bone memorie fratris Ricardi de Teford, canonici.' Possibly he was a canon of the order of the Holy Sepulchre, which had a house at Thetford. Richards of Thetford do not seem to be common.[2]

Richard of Wendover was a famous physician, probably identical with Ricardus Anglicus.[3] His medical writings appear in many MSS., notably in Cambridge, Peterhouse MS. 178, and Gonville and Caius Coll. MS. 95. Among them are the following :— ' Anatomia ' : *inc.* ' Galienus in Tegni attestatus,' which has been edited by G. W. Corner in ' Anatomical Texts of the Earlier Middle Ages ' (Carnegie Institution) and by Robert Töply in ' Anatomia Ricardi Anglici.' ' Tractatus Febrium ' : *inc.* ' Ex universalibus in quibus consit.' ' Glosse Tabule Salerni [*sic*] ' : *inc.* ' Omnis practica est theoricus.' ' De Laxativis ' : *inc.* ' Duplice causa me cogente socii.' ' Micrologus ' : *inc.* ' Acutarum alia est.' Of this the ' De Modo Conficiendi et Medendi ' and ' De Signis ' are probably parts. ' De Phlebotomia ' : *inc.* ' Requirendum est nobis breviter.' ' Practica ' : *inc.* ' Adsit principio sancta Maria.' ' De Pulsibus ' : *inc.* ' Quatuor canones et signa.' ' Tractatus Repressivarum ' : *inc.* ' Laxativa solent nimium laxando nocere.' ' Summa ' : *inc.* ' Si quod agam solitum pariter.' ' Tabule ' : *inc.* ' Columna prima. de. emagoga.' ' De Urinis ' : *inc.* ' Qui cupit urinas per compendia scire.'

This Richard wrote his anatomy, according to Corner, after the translation of the ' Abbreviatio Avicenné de animalibus ' by Michael Scot, probably not long before 1232 and the work of Thomas de Cantimpré (*c.* 1225–40). He is called Ricardus Anglicus and in one MS. Richard Vetulus,[1] while he is sometimes called Salernitanus.[2] The ' Summa ' was apparently written at the request of a dean of Beauvais.[3] Probably he was identical with a famous contemporary physician, Richard of Wendover.

Richard of Wendover was a canon of St. Paul's, London, witnessing charters of 1233[4] and 1237.[5] In 1239 St. Paul's gave him a manor.[6] Matthew Paris gives an interesting account of some important events in Wendover's life :

Et sub eodem tempore [1252] obiit magister Ricardus de Wendovre, ecclesiæ Sancti Pauli canonicus, phisicus præelectus. Qui sibi providit et præcavit multo circumspectius quam Robertus [Passelewe] memoratus. Nam ix. sacerdotibus necessaria providit, qui in perpetuum pro anima ipsius et omnium fidelium hostiam Christo cotidie offerent salutarem. De quo in hoc libro specialem duximus

[1] Oxford, Magdalen Coll. MS. 168.

[2] A chaplain of the name was presented to Thetford chapel by Robert and Gilbert de Thetford, knights, in 1247–8 (*Rot. Grosseteste*, p. 96).

[3] T. p. 624 ; *D.N.B.* under Richard.

[1] Possibly Vetulus is a corruption of Wendover (B.M. MS. Add. 28555, fo. 29).

[2] As in Oxford, Merton Coll. MS. 324, fo. 150*b*.

[3] See M. R. James's catalogue of the Peterhouse MSS. under MS. 178.

[4] H.M.C., 9th Rep., App. p. 28*b*, nos. 1059, 1060.

[5] *Cartularium Monasterii Sancti Johannis Baptiste de Colecestria* (Roxburgh Club), ed. S. A. Moore, pp. 97, 98.

[6] H.M.C., 9th Rep., App. p. 39*b*.

facere mentionem, quia ecclesiæ Sancti Albani quandam crucem, legavit et spontanea contulit devotione; in qua plures reliquiæ continentur, prout tituli earum protestantur. Hæc crux, quæ eburnea est, quandoque fuerat papæ Gregorii, et eidem carissima. Et cum memoratus magister R[icardus], ejus phisicus extitisset, papa moriturus carissimum sibi carissimo, scilicet illam crucem, duxerat conferendam.[1]

Presumably Richard spent the time before Gregory's death in 1241 with the pope, Gregory IX. It is then perhaps significant that Richard appears again in England by 8 Nov. 1241 [2] and witnesses charters in 1242, 1243, and 1244.[3] His associations seem to be with St. Paul's and the hospital of St. Bartholomew.[4] In 1246 he received four oaks from Henry III for a cure performed upon Fulk de Castro Novo,[5] and received a respite from a forest fine in the following year.[6]

For a time Richard disappears from the charters: he was probably companion of Bishop Walter Suffield of Norwich (1244–1257) during this period. The bishop gave twenty marks to the poor of his diocese by his will for the soul of his companion, Richard of Wendover.[7] By 1250 Richard began to make the arrangements for the nine altars at which mass was to be said for his soul, an action which was so highly commended by Matthew Paris. A number of the altars can be identified. One was at Lavendon, Bucks; [8] a second at Tremhale.[9] In London he gave thirty marks to

[1] *M. Parisiensis Hist. Angl.* (R.S.), ed. F. Madden, iii. 120; practically the same account appears in *Chr. Maj.* v. 299.

[2] H.M.C., 9th Rep., App. pp. 12*b*, 17*b*.

[3] N. Moore, *History of St. Bartholomew's Hospital*, p. 382 (July 1242); Dean and Chapter of St. Paul's MS. W.D. 1, fo. 49; H.M.C., 9th Rep., App. p. 18*b*; P.R.O., Exchequer L.T.R., memoranda roll no 15, *m.* 10*d* (note an attestation, 28 Hen. III); H.M.C., 9th Rep., App. p. 1*b*.

[4] See under 1242.

[5] *C.Cl.R.*, 1242–7, p. 470.

[6] P.R.O., Exchequer L.T.R., memoranda roll 20, *m.* 3.

[7] Blomefield, iii. 489.

[8] H.M.C., 9th Rep., App. p. 56*b*.

[9] *Ibid.* p. 33*b*.

the priory of Holy Trinity,[1] and to St. Bartholomew's he gave a psalter, a two volume gloss on St. Paul's Epistles, and altar cloths, for which they received him into their fraternity.[2] He was most generous to St. Paul's. He gave nine houses with a return of nine marks a year,[3] from which liberal donatives should be given to the fabric, the clerks of the choir, and to the poor on his anniversary.[4] He made other gifts of ecclesiastical furnishings.[5] His mass was to be said daily at the altar of St. Hippolitus.[6] He died on 5 Mar. 1252.[7]

Richard of Wetheringsett [8] was possibly chancellor of Cambridge and author of a theological treatise called 'Lumina.' It is a copy with additions and slight alterations, or more probably a 'reportatio' of the 'Summa' of William de Monte, chancellor of Lincoln. Both begin 'Qui bene presunt presbyteri duplici honore' (*cf.* the 'Lumina' in B.M. MS. Reg. 9, A. ix, with the 'Summa' in B.M. MS. Harley 3244). The list of MSS. below is probably not complete and may contain MSS. of the 'Summa' of William de Monte. (a) Cambridge, Corpus Christi Coll. MS. 356 (14th cent.), with a rubric 'Inc. tractatus magri R. cancellarii de Cantebruge qui dicitur Numerale [*sic*]'; (b) Cambridge, Gonville and Caius Coll. MS. 211, fo. 91 (13th cent.); (c) Cambridge, Pembroke Coll. MS. 258, fo. 90*b* (13th cent.), with the colophon 'Expl. summa mag.

[1] H.M.C., 9th Rep., App. p. 27*b*; Dean and Chapter of St. Paul's, Ch. A–25–1750.

[2] H.M.C., 9th Rep., App. p. 49*a*.

[3] *Ibid.* p. 96*a*.

[4] Camb. Univ. Lib. MS. Ee. v. 21, fos. 75*b*, 90*b*, 108; *Documents illustrative of St. Paul's Cathedral* (Camden Soc.), ed. W. S. Simpson, pp. 64, 78; Dean and Chapter of St. Paul's MS. W.D. 4, fos. 93, 103*b*.

[5] *Archaeologia*, l (1887). 478.

[6] H.M.C., 9th Rep., App. p. 90*b*. See also *Rot. H. de Welles*, ii. 159, 167, 231 *bis*; Le Neve, *Fasti*, ii. 414, 433; Bodl. Lib. MS. Ashmole 801, fo. 71.

[7] H.M.C., various collect. iv. 161; *Chr. Maj.* v. 299.

[8] T. pp. 624, 759; *D.N.B.* under Wetherset.

Ricardi de Weressete'; (d) Camb. Univ. Lib. Add. MS. 3741; (e) Dublin, Trinity Coll. MS. 318; (f) B.M. MS. Reg. 9, A. xiv, fos. 18, 112*b*, with a colophon 'Explicit lumina Magistri Ricardi de Weresete'; (g) London, Lambeth Palace MS. 144, fos. 35–79, 'Incipit summa mag. Ricardi cancellarii Cantebrig'; (h) Oxford, Bodl. Lib. MS. Bodley 64, entitled 'Summa magistri Ricardi'; (i) *ibid.* MS. Digby 103, ascribed by later hand to 'Tractatus magistri Ric. de Burgo canc. de Cantebrug'; (j) *ibid.* MS. Laud. Misc. 527, fos. 55–95*b*; (k) Oxford, New Coll. MS. 145, fos. 120–4*b* (fragment), with the colophon 'Explicit summa magistri Ric. de Wetheringeseth.'

Leland saw at St. Benet Hulme 'Summa alias speculum sacerdotum Richardi de Leycestria. *Qui bene presunt*' (*Collect.* iii. 29). At Ramsey there was formerly 'Summa magistri Ricardi de Wyrecestre, scilicet, Qui bene presunt' (*Chron. abbatiæ Rameseiensis*, R.S., ed. W. D. Macray, p. 364). Bale says that among the books 'Ex Ioanni Alen pictore' there was a 'Summa magistri R. quondam cancellarij Cantabrigie, li i. "Qui bene presunt presbyteri"' (*Index*, p. 510). He also says: 'Ricardus de Withryngsete, sacerdos, composuit, Summam sacerdotalem, li i." Qui bene presunt presbyteri" . . . *Ex domo Michaelis Hobley.* Prefata summa Ricardi Wetheringsete . . . *Ex officina Hugonis Shyngleton.* Hic Ricardus Wethringseth doctor et cancellarius Cantabrigie fuit. *Ex monasterio Ramesie*' (*ibid.* pp. 363–4). Formerly at Peterborough there was a 'Summa Ricardi cancellarii Cantebrig. *Qui bene presunt*' (James, *Peterborough*, p. 46).

The *D.N.B.* says of this man that he was chancellor of Cambridge about 1350, but since some of the MSS. of his work belong to the 13th century this identification seems to be a mistake. Bibliographical tradition has also confused him with Richard Grant because he was chancellor of Lincoln, as was William de Monte, whose 'Summa' he reported or copied. Indeed Richard is called 'de Montibus' in one MS. In other MSS. his name appears variously as 'Wetheringeseth,' 'Weresete,' 'Wyrecestre,' and 'Leycestria.' The attachment of Leicester to William de Monte's name may be a further result of the confusion of the two.[1]

One would expect him to have been a student of de Monte, thus living in the first half of the 13th century. If the 'Lumina' is a 'reportatio' he must certainly have studied under de Monte at Lincoln or Paris. That he was said to be chancellor of Cambridge may also be a confusion with William de Monte, chancellor of Lincoln, but in this case the Cambridge is hard to explain away. It is probable that he was a chancellor of Cambridge and that this title aided in the confusion with Richard Grant. He is said, probably with little reason, to have been dean of St. Paul's in 1228.[2]

Richard de Wicio (Droitwich) was bishop of Chichester.[3] He wrote an account of the translation of St. Edmund of Abingdon (*Chr. Maj.* vi. 128) and letters concerning the same saint for purposes of canonization (Martène and Durand, *Thesaurus Novus*, col. 1901, 1905). Possibly he is the author of the 'Distinctions on the Psalter' mentioned in his will. Tanner (p. 766) credits him with a 'De Officiis Ecclesie': *inc.* 'Officium ut ex debito fiat,' and 'Statuta Synodalia': *inc.* 'Cum ex injuncto nobis officio,' which more properly belongs to official activity. To him is attributed the following:

> Hoc est documentum mag. Ric. de Wiz bone memorie Cicestr. ep. Benedicto segetis ad dandum porcis infirmis. In primis legatur totum officium natalis domini, etc. Versus de conceptu humano de

[1] Leland, *Collect.* iv. 41. 'Ricardi Cantabrigiensis omeliae. *Qui bene præsunt presbyteri*' at Dunholme. The confusion probably came in some way from Leland's observations.

[2] *Sarum Chs. and Docs.* p. 200; Le Neve gives the date 7 July 1228.

[3] T. p. 766; *D.N.B.* under Richard. The most recent biography is by Caroline Jones (*St. Richard of Chichester*).

VIItem mortalibus peccatis (Cambridge, Corpus Christi Coll. MS. 441, fo. 530).

A prayer of his is supposed to be in existence and has been edited.

Two biographies of St. Richard remain, a contemporary account by Ralph Bocking [q.v.] and a later one by Capgrave. The first seems reliable, the second quite untrustworthy.

Richard's parents were Ralph and Alice, who probably lived in Droitwich, Worcestershire, where Richard was raised.[1] His elder brother, according to Bocking, offered to yield the inheritance to Richard, although the latter was a minor.[2] Evidently his father died while Richard was still young. Possibly his mother re-married since he mentions a 'Master Richard de Bachedene,' his 'frater carnalis' as having charge of the temporal cares of the saint (probably as bishop).[3] A Master John de Wicio attested some of Bishop Richard's charters,[4] and a Master Nicholas de Wicio, his relative, was in his 'familia' and a canon of Chichester, while another brother, Robert Chaundos, is mentioned in his will.[5] His family was evidently wealthy. He himself refused a chance of marriage with a rich heiress, an item which suggests at least some social standing on Richard's part in an age which was wary of disparagement.[6] Even while at school he had to have someone in charge of his property.[7] He was conscientiously opposed to accepting ecclesiastical preferment to aid in education, but probably he did not need it.[8]

[1] *Acta Sanctorum*, April, i. 285, 307.

[2] *Ibid.* p. 285*b*.

[3] The presence of the same name for two brothers is not unknown, but more easily explained by two fathers (*ibid.* p. 291*b*).

[4] Camb. Univ. Lib. MS. Ll. ii. 15, fo. 66*b*.

[5] 'Consanguineus et familiaris' (*Acta SS.*, April, i. 302*b*, 313*a*.

[6] *Ibid.* p. 285; the story of how Richard saved the family fortune is open to question (*ibid.* p. 278).

[7] *Ibid.* p. 295*a*.

[8] *Ibid.* p. 296*a*. Capgrave eliminates the references to relatives which give the distinct impression that Richard aided them and adds a paragraph saying that the saint did not provide for his family. This creates a painful impression of his accuracy.

These clues may be followed up. Richard de Bagingeden was a prominent knight of Gloucestershire [1] and was sheriff of Herefordshire a few years after the death of Richard de Wicio.[2] He was probably the son of a Richard de Bagingeden, whose widow, Alice, was given seisin of his lands and heir in 1216–1217.[3] She had bought this custody from Bartholomew de Wicio or Fil. Ricardi.[4] Ralph, previous husband of Alice, is not so easy to identify. Since the saint had a brother in 1253 named Robert de Chandos, we should expect that Alice's first husband was Ralph de Chandos. There was at least one Ralph de Chandos of the years 1190–1205, who was of importance in Herefordshire,[5] but his widow was apparently named Sarah.[6] Richard de Bagingeden himself held of the Chandos family, whose ramifications are not easy to unravel. There was an Alice, widow of Hugh de Chandos, in 8 Ric. I.[7] In any case, the documents confirm the impression that Richard de Wicio came of a family of means.

From Bocking it appears that Richard's academic life was associated entirely with Oxford. He studied and ruled in arts there [8] and studied canon law.[9] Capgrave states that he studied also in Paris and Bologna.[10]

[1] *Book of Fees*, p. 440 (1235).

[2] *C.P.R.*, 1258–66, *passim*.

[3] *Excerpta e rotulis finium*, ed. C. Roberts, p. 1.

[4] Seisin to Robert Chandos, 'de terra que fuit Barth. de Wich qui cum inimicis meis et mortuus est in Bagingeden' (*Rot. Litt. Claus.* p. 280).

[5] *Chancellor's Roll*, 8 Ric. I (Pipe Roll Soc.), ed. D. M. Stenton, p. 138. The item 'Ricardus de Flet debet C m. ut filia sua dit deliberata de Radulpho de Chandos qui dicebat se eam desponsasse' appears in the pipe rolls from 1190 to 1195.

[6] *Curia Regis Rolls*, iii. 292.

[7] *Chanc. Roll*, p. 91. Can Bocking have mistaken the name of the saint's father?

[8] *Acta SS.*, April, i. 286*a*.

[9] *Ibid.* p. 286*a*.

[10] *Ibid.* p. 278*b*. Capgrave gives a story of Richard's extreme poverty at Paris, where he is said to have shared the barest necessities of life with companions. He also states that Richard studied canon law seven years at Bologna. Certainly he became a kind of patron saint at the place, probably resulting from a confusion with Richard Anglicus [q.v.]. (*Cf. Vita*

While at a banquet at Oxford he escaped death from a falling stone by being summoned outside to see a mysterious person who left before Richard arrived. Of his teachers only Edmund of Abingdon is certain. Richard became chancellor of the university of Oxford,[1] probably before 1237.

By 1237 Richard had become chancellor to Archbishop Edmund.[2] His activities may be traced for the next three years.[3] He went into exile with the archbishop in 1240, remaining with him until that prelate passed away,[4] and possibly received a goblet in his will.[5] He then studied theology in a dominican house in Orleans and entered the priesthood.[6] His ability as an executive was well known. Upon his return to England he apparently became the deputy at the exchequer of Margery de Ripariis, a noble lady, and was sued by her on 8 Feb. 1243 for non-delivery of her money at the royal exchequer.[7] Probably he became rector of Cherringes during this period, since he is so named in the papal letter sanctioning his election.[1] This promotion to the bishopric of Chichester came in the spring of 1244.[2] He died in 1253 and was canonized in 1262.[3] His will remains.[4]

The library disclosed by his will [5] was largely theological. To the mendicant houses he gave glossed biblical books. The franciscans at Chichester were to have his ' Psalter ' ; at Lewes, ' Luke ' and ' John ' ; at Winchelsea, ' Mark ' and ' Matthew ' ; at Canterbury, ' Isaiah ' ; at London, the ' Pauline Epistles ' ; and at Winchester, the ' Minor Prophets.' The dominicans of Arundel were to receive the ' Sentences ' of Peter Lombard ; of Canterbury, ' Hosea ' ; of London, a volume containing ' Job,' the ' Acts,' ' Canonical Epistles,' and the ' Apocalypse ' ; and of Winchester, the ' Summa ' of William of Auxerre. He gave his works of John of Damascus to one friar, Guarinus ; his Anselm, ' Cur Deus Homo,' to another, William of Colchester ; his books on virtues (*scilicet* ' distinctiones super Psalterium ') to Simon de Terringes ; his ' Bible ' to William his chaplain ; his book on vices to William ' de Bremha ' ; and his ' Decreta ' to Master Robert of Hastings.

Richard of Winchester preached sermons at Oxford, 1292 (Little-Pelster, p. 191).

Robert of Abberwick was the author of a ' Commentary upon the De Generatione et Corruptione ' : *inc.* ' Cum de corpore mobili simpliciter,' Oxford, Balliol Coll. MS. 313, fos. 158–63 (early 14th cent.), with the colophon ' Explicit sententia super librum de generatione secundum magistrum R. de Alburwyc.'

This author is probably the fellow of Merton in 1285, mentioned in the bursar's

de S. Ricardo vescovo de Cicestria.) In Camb. Univ. Lib. MS. Mm. vi. 4, fo. 120, is a curious story of how he, a student of Edmund of Abingdon at Paris, sent a wicked woman to Bishop Ralph [*sic*] of Salisbury. This would have been between 1222 and 1233, when Edmund was treasurer of Salisbury, since the tale explicitly says that Edmund was treasurer at the time.

1 *Acta SS.*, April, i. 286*a*.

2 *Ibid.* p. 286*b* ; Capgrave's story that both Grosseteste and Edmund wished to have him as chancellor has no confirmation (*Triveti Annales*, Eng. Hist. Soc., ed. T. Hog, p. 228).

3 In 1237 : P.R.O., Exchequer, Misc. Books, E. 164/27, fo. 93 ; B.M. MS. Claudius D. x, fos. 271*b*–2 ; Lambeth Palace MS. 1212, fos. 134, 265 ; in 1238 : *Hist. Works of Gervase of Canterbury* (R.S.), ed. Wm. Stubbs, ii. 139 ; in 1239 : *ibid.* ii. 155 ; in 1240 : Lambeth MS. 1212, fo. 135 ; B.M. MS. Cotton, Faust A. i, fo. 334*b* ; *ibid.* Claudius D. x, fo. 207 ; Camb. Univ. Lib. MS. Ll. ii. 15, fo. 66*b* (2) ; P.R.O., Exchequer, Ecclesiastical docs. E. 135/45, no. 139 ; Lambeth MS. 1212, fos. 86, 87 ; Dugdale, *Monasticon*, i. 134 ; Bodl. Lib. MS. Tanner 223, fo 50*b* (2).

4 *Acta SS.*, April, i. 287*a*.

5 Jones, *op. cit.* p. 16.

6 *Acta SS.*, April, i. 287*a*.

7 P.R.O., Exchequer L.T.R., memoranda roll 16, *m.* 6.

1 *C.E.P.R.* i. 215.

2 *Registres d'Innocent IV*, ed. E. Berger, no. 1177.

3 *Cf. D.N.B.* for later career.

4 Printed several times ; see *Sussex Archaeological Collections*, i (1848). 164-92.

5 Translated by W. H. Blauuw, *ibid.* pp. 167–92.

roll of 1286,[1] who gave two books, glossed copies of the 'Epistles' of Paul and of the 'Gospels,' to the Merton Library.[2] He served for a time as an official of the bishop of Durham.[3] In 1300, dean of the collegiate church of Auckland and official of Bishop Anthony Bek, he took a prominent part in the struggle between the bishop and the priory of Durham.[4] He was collated to the valuable provostship of Beverly on 3 June 1304.[5] He was a priest at the time. Of his activity as provost little is known ; [6] it has even been suggested that he was never at Beverly at all.[7] He died before 28 Mar. 1306.[8]

Robert of Abingdon, brother of Edmund of Abingdon [q.v.], was possibly his biographer.[9] Leland asserted that the 'Life' was formerly at Thetford (*Collect.* iv. 26). Robert is also credited with an unidentified 'Exegesis in Canonem St. Augustini' (T. p. 630 ; *cf.* the conjectures by F. de Paravicini, *Life of St. Edmund of Abingdon*, pp. xxiii–xxix).

Robert attended school at Paris with his brother, Edmund, but the dates are uncertain. On 1 June 1213 a Robert de Abendon, clerk, received a royal payment.[10] On 25 Apr. 1217 a Robert de Abbendon, clericus, received a letter 'de conductu' valid for an unlimited term.[1] By his fidelity toward the church in the troublous times (of the interdict ?) he gained permission in 1220 to hold additional benefices ; [2] he is called a master. After Edmund became archbishop he gave his brother a rich church, probably Wingham, about 1234.[3] Upon this occasion Odo of Cheriton is alleged to have remarked upon the danger which Edmund's brother incurred from such a gift, but Edmund replied that benefices were for such persons as Robert.[4] In 1237 Robert witnessed one of his brother's documents.[5] He was employed by the archbishop in negotiations with the cardinal legate [6] and Christchurch in 1239.[7] As rector of Wingham he appears in a negotiation with St. Augustine's in 1240.[8] He seems to have accompanied his brother to Pontigny in this same year [9] and was present at his death. The king evidently intended to proceed against him in this year.[10] He received his brother's hair shirt and also a sapphire which later came into the possession of St. Albans.[11]

[1] *Memorials of Merton College* (Oxford Hist. Soc.), p. 186.

[2] Powicke, p. 97.

[3] *Register of Thomas of Corbridge* (Surtees Soc.), ed. Wm. Brown, ii. 159.

[4] *Gesta Dunelmensia* (Camden Soc.), Miscellany, xiii. 2, 7, 8, 21, 30, 42, 51 ; *Memorials of Beverley Minster* (Surtees Soc.), ed. A. F. Leach, ii. 1 ; i. 107 ; his collation of John of Amcoats is dated at Auckland.

[5] *Reg. of Thomas of Corbridge*, ii. 30.

[6] *Memorials of Beverley*, ii. pp. xlix–li ; P.R.O., Exchequer of pleas, plea roll 33 Edw. I, p. 1 (E. 13/28).

[7] *Memorials of Beverley*, ii. p. li.

[8] *Ibid.* i. 116 ; ii. 1 ; *C.P.R.*, 1301–7, p. 421 ; Little suggests that R. de Alburwyc might stand for Roger of Alnwick (*F.S.O.* p. 863, *n.* 6).

[9] T. p. 630.

[10] *Documents illustrative of Eng. Hist.* (Record Comm.), ed. H. Cole, p. 233.

[1] *C.P.R.*, 1216–25, p. 60.

[2] *C.E.P.R.* i. 76 ; Pressutti, i. 442.

[3] The king conferred Wingham on Gilbert Marshall in September 1228 (*C.P.R.*, 1225–32, p. 203). This man was probably the brother of the Earl Marshal (*ibid.* pp. 342–3). Gilbert probably released this church when he became earl in 1234, but possibly he held it until his death in 1239.

[4] 'Fuit enim idem magister Robertus sancte vite, mature etatis et eminentia literature et talibus sunt ecclesiastica beneficia conferenda' (*Thesaurus Exemplorum*, ed. J. T. Welter, v. 12).

[5] B.M. MS. Cotton, Claudius D. x, fos. 271*b*–2*b* ; Lambeth Palace MS. 1212, pp. 134, 264 ; *Registres de Grégoire*, ed. Auvray, ix. 983.

[6] P.R.O., D.K., 7th Rep., App. ii. p. 249, no. 1825 ; P.R.O., ancient correspondence, S.C. xi. 159.

[7] *Hist. Works of Gervase of Canterbury* (R.S.), ed. Wm. Stubbs, ii. 161–5.

[8] Dugdale, *Monasticon*, i. 134 ; Bodl. Lib. MS. Tanner 223, fo. 94*b* ; B.M. MS. Cotton, Claudius D. x, fo. 207 ; Lambeth Palace MS. 1212, p. 315.

[9] *Ann. Monast.* iv. 87–8 (Oseney).

[10] *C.P.R.*, 1232–47, p. 241.

[11] It was given to St. Albans by Nicholas, a goldsmith of St. Albans (*Chr. Maj.* vi. 384).

After his death, before 27 Sept. 1243,[1] miracles were alleged to have occurred at his tomb, so that he was regarded as a saint.[2] A letter of Adam Marsh concerning the execution of Robert's will mentions that Robert was rector of Risberg.[3] There is no evidence that he was called Robert Rich : the documents give only Robert of Abingdon.[4] A book remains which may have belonged to him.[5]

Robertus Anglicus, scientist,[6] wrote a ' Commentary upon the Sphere of John of Sacro Bosco ' : *inc.* ' Una scientia est.' (a) Oxford, Bodl. Lib. MS. Digby 48, fos. 48–88, with the colophon ' Finita est ista compilatio super materiam de spera celesti ad maiorem introductionem scolarium in Monte Pessulane studentium quam compilavit magr Robert Anglicus et finitur anno 1272 sole existente in primo gradu tauri scorpione ascendente in a°, . . .' ; (b) B.N. MS. fonds latin MS. 7392, fo. 1*b*, with the same colophon, with ' 1271 ' for ' 1272 ' (Duhem, *System du Monde*, iii. 292) ; (c) Salzburg, St. Peter MS., cited by P. Tannery (' Le traité du quadrant de Maître Robert Anglès ' in *N.E. MSS.* xxxv. 579). There is another treatise on the ' Sphere.'

[1] The church of Wengham was presented to another (*C.P.R.*, 1232–47, p. 396).

[2] *Chr. Maj.* iv. 378 ; *M. Parisiensis Hist. Angl.* (R.S.), ed. F. Madden, ii. 493.

[3] This disposes of the tradition that he died a monk (*Mon. Fr.* i. 247 ; F. de Paravicini, *Life of St. Edmund of Abingdon*, p. xxvii).

[4] In 1278 the king granted a pardon at the instance of William of Southampton to John, son of Master Robert of Abbinton, for the death of Gilbert le Pestur (*C.P.R.*, 1272–81, p. 269) ; ' Anolinus de Parriaco, facta exomologesi magistro Roberto fratre sancti Edmundi, qui Pontiniacum advenerat, sanatur a morbo sancto Egidii ad sepulchrum sancti Edmundi ' (Martène and Durand, *Thesaurus Novus,* iii. col. 1894).

[5] Oxford, Magdalen Coll. MS. 123, containing ' Numbers ' and ' Deuteronomy,' ' Ex dono magistri Roberti de Abbendonia, postea J. Grene and H. comitis de Rutlandia.' Catalogue says ' sec. XIII exeunte.'

[6] T. p. 636.

Cambridge, Gonville and Caius Coll. MS. 137, fos. 15–24 : *inc.* ' Intentio in hoc tractatu,' with the colophon ' Explicit spera mag. Roberti venerabilis clerici confessoris episcopi Lincolniensis ' (James, *Cat.* p. 150). Robert is apparently the author of a ' Translation of Alkindi's de Iudiciis ' : *inc.* ' Quamquam post Euclidem.' (a) Bodl. Lib. MS. Ashmole 179, part iv (transcript of about 1600), with the title ' Alkindus de Iudiciis ex Arabico Latinus factus per Robertum Anglicum an. dom. 1272,' with colophon ' Finit liber Alkindi translatio Roberti Angligeni de ch . . .' ; (b) *ibid.* MS. Ashmole 209, fos. 211–66, with the colophon ' Finit liber Alkindi translatio Roberti Angligeni de Chebil ' ; (c) *ibid.* MS. 369, fos. 85–101*b* (13th cent.) ; (d) *ibid.* MS. 434, fos. 1–23*b* (16th cent.), with the colophon ' Finit liber Alkindi translatio Roberti Angligeni de c-h-o-e-l-l-e ' ; (e) *ibid.* MS. Digby 91, fo. 86 (16th–17th cent.), with the colophon ' Alkindus de iudiciis ex arabico latinus factus per Robertum Anglicum anno Domini 1272.' Possibly this is the work printed as ' Roberti Anglici viri Astrologia prestantissimi de astrolabio canones ' (Perugia, 1480). Tanner says that Robert was the author of a ' Correctorium Alchymie ' : *inc.* ' Cum omnis rerum emendatio ' (p. 636). He was the author of a ' Treatise on the Quadrant,' written at Montpellier before 1276 : *inc.* ' Geometrie due sunt partes ' (P. Tannery, *op. cit.* pp. 2, 561–640 ; MSS. are given on pp. 570–5 ; to these should be added Bodl. Lib. MS. Canon. Ital. 157, xiv, and B.M. MS. Egerton 844).

About this Robertus Anglicus little is known beyond the fact that he wrote these scientific books at Montpellier *c.* 1270–6. He was probably a teacher there at the time. From a statement in one of his works it is clear that he had travelled widely in England.[1] The place from which he drew his name represented by ' Choelle ' or ' Chebil '

[1] ' Sicut scivi per experimentum quibusdam partibus Anglie ' (Duhem, *op. cit.* iii. 292).

has not been identified.[1] If he was the author of the second work on the sphere he was probably confessor to a bishop of Lincoln: from his interests, probably Robert Grosseteste. A Robertus Anglicus was at Montpellier, probably as a teacher, in 1240.[2] Tannery suggests that his knowledge of the quadrant follows that of William Anglicus [q.v.] so closely that some relationship between them is to be suspected.[3]

Robert Bacon, O.P., was a theologian.[4] The only extant work which is certainly his is the 'Summule Dialectices': *inc.* 'Introductio est brevis et aperta demonstratio.' Tanner gives 'Partium orationis quedam sunt.' Bodl. Lib. MS. Digby 204, fos. 48 *et seq.*, with the colophon 'Expliciunt sumule magistri Roberti Bacun.'

His authorship of the biography of Edmund of Abingdon [q.v.] is uncertain. Bale says that 'plura de illo scripsit, ut quod studuerit Parisiis. Ex Ramesiensi monasterio' (*Index*, p. 366). The editor notes that that monastery had a 'Vita sancti Edmundi' (*Chron. Abbat. Rames.*, R.S., ed. W. D. Macray, p. 362). He wrote a letter concerning Edmund's canonization (Martène and Durand, *Thesaurus Novus*, iii. cols. 1913–4). Matthew Paris states that he got some of his information about Edmund's life from Robert (*Chr. Maj.* v. 369).

He may be the author of the sermons in Bodl. Lib. MS. Bodley 745, fos. 503–799*b*: *inc.* 'Exsurge psalterium et cithara,' 'Deprecamur dominum hodie et cras' (T. p. 62). Same MS. fos. 193–495, with the heading 'Incipit tractatus fratris R. Bacun super Psalterium': *inc.* 'Beatus uir, qui non . . . Hoc exponitur.' This is according to bibliographical tradition. He may have been author of some of the works attributed to Roger Bacon. It has been conjectured that he was the author of the 'Ancren Riwle,' by Vincent McNabb (*Modern Language Review*, xi, 1916. 1–8).

The relationship between Robert and Roger Bacon is a matter of conjecture. Robert had a sister who lived in the forest of Savernake, co. Wilts., to whom the king granted protection at the friar's instance.[1] He was probably a man of some wealth, since Archbishop Edmund owed him a hundred shillings when he died.[2] He had been Edmund's school-fellow.[3] He was already a master when, in 1219, he was presented to a moiety of the church of Lower Heyford, Oxfordshire, by the abbot and convent of Eynsham.[4] He was to reside there and to accept the duties personally. He resigned this living in 1227.[5] Probably he entered the dominican order soon after this: this would be the easiest explanation of his resignation. He took the vows without any novitiate.[6] He was already a regent in theology, apparently continuing his lessons in the school of St. Edward until he died.[7] The first student to incept under him as a dominican was Richard Fishacre, O.P. [q.v.]. In 1233 he preached before the king and insisted that the kingdom would have no peace until Peter des Roches was divested of power; [8] the quip recorded by Roger Bacon concerning 'quidam clericus de curia' certainly does not refer to Robert Bacon.[9] On 23 June 1234 Friar Robert Bacon is ordered, with Robert Grosseteste, to drive the prostitutes from Oxford.[10] A few years later he is probably called to witness by Grosseteste that the bishop would have given

1 Round gives a Choeie (*Feudal England*, p. 39).
2 Tannery, *op. cit.* p. 580.
3 *Ibid.* p. 585.
4 T. p. 62; *D.N.B.* under Bacon.

1 He is called Master Robert Bacon (*C.P.R.*, 1232–1247, p. 488).
2 *C.L.R.*, 1240–5, p. 71.
3 *Triveti Annales* (Eng. Hist. Soc.), ed. T. Hog, p. 229.
4 *Rot. H. de Welles*, i. 170.
5 *Ibid.* ii. 25.
6 *Eccleston*, p. 101; *Mon. Fr.* i. 56.
7 *Annales, loc. cit.*
8 Probably in June (*Chr. Maj.* iii. 244).
9 Robert Bacon was too venerable a person to be so designated.
10 *C.Cl.R.*, 1231–4, p. 568.

a living to a candidate had he been qualified.[1] On 29 Sept. 1235 he was given custody of the lands and heiresses of Warin Doynel.[2]

In 1236 Fr. R. Bacon secured a pardon from the king for Geoffrey of Northampton.[3] During most of his life his interests continued in Oxford [4] and the friar preachers. When on 15 Sept. 1241 the king ordered a subsidy for the annual chapter of the order the 'liberate' named him as the recipient.[5] Apparently the Oxford converts from Judaism were in his charge. In 1242 two of them received royal charity [6] and in 1245 he was ordered to take an apostate Jew and place him in the Oxford gaol.[7] These tasks show him a man of business ability often entrusted with responsibility. Doubtless a more pleasant task was his share in procuring the canonization of his friend, Edmund of Abingdon.[8] He was considered a great theologian and authority in 'aliis scientiis' and one who preached the word of God to the people gloriously.[9] He died in 1248, probably during the first three months,[10] and was buried in the house of his order at Oxford.[11]

[1] The text gives Roger Bacon, which may be accurate (*Ep. Grosseteste*, p. 64).

[2] *C.Cl.R.*, 1234–7, p. 145.

[3] *C.P.R.*, 1232–47, p. 137; Master Robert de Baton' or Bacon', a witness of a charter of Northampton, another witness being Henry of Bath, sheriff of Northampton (B.M. MS. Reg. 11, B. ix, fo. 77*b*); he was appointed sheriff on 23 May 1234 (*C.P.R.*, 1232–47, p. 47); on 2 Jan. 1236 Peter de Malo Lacu was appointed to the same office. Mr. Robert 'de Bacon' or 'Baton' was probably a relative of the sheirff.

[4] For 1238 see *C.P.R.*, 1232–47, p. 218; for 1243 *ibid.* p. 442.

[5] *C.L.R.*, 1240–5, p. 71; P.R.O., exchequer of receipt, issue roll Mich. 26 Hen. III, E. 403/3; *C.Cl.R.*, 1234–7, p. 383.

[6] *C.L.R.*, 1240–5, p. 99.

[7] *C.Cl.R.*, 1242–7, p. 298.

[8] See above under bibliographical evidence.

[9] *Chr. Maj.* v. 16.

[10] *Ibid.* v. 16 (gives 1248); H.M.C., 14th Rep., App. viii, p. 208 (Annals of Chester), gives 1247 (i.e. 1247/8).

[11] T. p. 62.

Robert of Bingham was a canon and bishop of Salisbury. A 'Sermon' of his upon the Resurrection remains in B.M. MS. Harley 325, fo. 84: *inc.* 'Inclinavit se et prospexit in monumentum,' with a marginal note 'Magr R. de Bingh.' He also wrote a letter concerning the canonization of Edmund of Abingdon (Martène and Durand, *Thesaurus Novus*, iii. col. 1900).

Robert of Bingham was already a master when he witnessed a charter of Bishop John Grey of Norwich at Kidderminster, 5 July 1210 (or 1211).[1] His attestation of a charter of Hugh, abbot of Abingdon, to Godstow (*c.* 1199–1221) would lead one to suspect that he was teaching at Oxford.[2] By 1220 he was 'vir summe litteratus et magister a longo tempore in Theologia.'[3] Between 1216 and 1220 he was at Salisbury, acting as arbiter in a dispute between the chapter and R. de Stokes,[4] and witnessing documents,[5] two dated in 1219 [6] and one alleged to be of 25 Mar. 1225.[7] On 25 Sept. 1225 he was present at the first convocation in the new cathedral.[8] He held the prebend of Slape, valued at fifteen marks, upon which he paid a tax of twelve shillings and sixpence in 1226.[9] In the same year he presented letters of excuse and was fined for non-residence.[10] He was elected bishop of Salisbury on 9 Sept. 1228. Upon his journey to Rome for papal confirmation of his election he carried many

[1] B.M. MS. Harley 2110, fos. 128*b*, 130*b*, 'anno XI' of Grey's pontificate.

[2] P.R.O., Exchequer, Misc. Books, E. 164/20, fo. 70; Bingham first in list of masrers. His sermon is also among those of Oxford men.

[3] *Register of St. Osmund* (R.S.), ed. W. H. R. Jones, ii. 16.

[4] *Ibid.* i. 256.

[5] B.M. MS. Lansdowne 417, fo. 56*b*, Wm. de Wanda, precentor.

[6] *Sarum Chs. and Docs.* pp. 91, 92; *Registrum Malmesburiense* (R.S.), ed. Brewer and Martin, i. 398.

[7] R. B. Hoare, *History of Modern Wiltshire*, vi. 728; the document has, however, puzzling features.

[8] *Reg. of St. Osmund*, ii. 38.

[9] *Ibid.* p. 72.

[10] *Ibid.* pp. 61, 76.

complimentary letters ; his chapter related of him :

Elegimus virum providum et discretum, ætate maturum, summè litteratum, in utroque jure peritum, in theologia doctorem optimum, predicatorem egregium.[1]

Robert Carpenter of Haslett [Hareslade] was the author and compiler of legal writings and a chronicle. For his life and writings see N. Denholm-Young's ' Robert Carpenter and the Provisions of Westminster ' (*E.H.R.* l (1935). 22–35).

Robert de Courçon was a cardinal and theologian.[2] His main work was probably a ' Summa ' : *inc.* ' Videndum est primo quid.' (a) A part remains in Cambridge, Gonville and Caius Coll. MS. 331, fos. 1–76*b*, entitled ' Una pars summe magistri Roberti de Cursun ' ; (b) Cambridge, Peterhouse MS. given by Tanner (p. 214, citing Pits) ; (c) MS. formerly at Christchurch, Canterbury (James, *A.L.C.D.* p. 115). For other MSS. see B. Haureau in ' Notices et Extraits,' i. 178. Another treatise was upon Confession, B.N. MS. lat. 12312, fo. 304 (Haureau, *op. cit.* v. 65), ' De Septem Septenis.' (a) Cambridge, Corpus Christi Coll. MS. 459, fos. 99–107, with a rubric ' Inc. prol. mag. Roberti de Cursun ' ; (b) MS. formerly at Peterborough, MS. A. viii, ' Liber Mag. Roberti Cursoun de septem septenis ' : *inc.* ' De difficillimis scripturus tam excellenti ' (James, *Peterborough*, p. 53 ; *cf.* Glorieux, p. 236). Other treatises have apparently not survived. One was ' De Salvatione Origenis,' ' Ex Bostoni Buriensis catalogo ' (Bale, *Index*, p. 370). Possibly the ' Tractatus mag. Roberti ad Stephanum Archiep,' formerly at Peterborough, MS. Q. viii, was also by him.

Robert de Courçon was English by birth,[3] but spent practically his entire life abroad.

[1] *Reg. of St. Osmund*, ii. 115.

[2] T. p. 213 ; *D.N.B.* under Courçon. A work upon this writer by M. Dickson is expected soon ; *cf.* Glorieux, p. 236.

[3] *Chr. Maj.* iii. 40 ; *Hist. Angl.* ii. 229.

He is alleged to have been born near Kedleston, co. Derby,[1] probably about 1155–60.[2] He had a nephew, William Fitz-walter, for whom the king ordered a lay fief provided by the constable of Nottingham in 1216.[3] He was apparently not noted for nepotism.[4] He was regarded as a learned man [5] and of high character, although one chronicler considered some of his actions insolent.[6]

Of his life before he entered academic circles at Paris little is known.[7] There he was a friend and fellow student of the future Innocent III about 1180–6 and was regent master of theology before 1200.[8] He wrote his ' Summa ' about 1202.[9] He was canon of Noyon 1204–9 and of Paris 1210–2.[10] Probably at this time a great preacher,[11] he was engaged in fighting usurers, heretics, and other enemies of the church.[12] He was proposed as patriarch of Constantinople before August 1211 and was named cardinal (St. Stephen of Monte Coelo) between 11 Dec. 1211 and 11 June 1212. The pope sent

[1] T. p. 213, citing Bodl. Lib. MS. Ashmole 816 (*cf. Book of Fees*, ii. 946, 994).

[2] Glorieux, *loc. cit.*

[3] *C.P.R.*, 1216–25, p. 7.

[4] Ralph of Coggeshall mentioning nepotism of the legate Nicholas fails at the same time to accuse Robert of this (*Chronicon Angl.*, R.S., ed. J. Stevenson, p. 170).

[5] *Chronica de Mailros* (Bannatyne Club), ed. J. Stevenson, p. 110.

[6] *Coggeshall, Chronicon, loc. cit.*

[7] There is a suggestion that he attended Oxford (T. p. 213) ; a Robert de Curezon, probably a clerk, attested a late 12th century charter (*Transcripts of charters relating to the Gilbertine Houses*, Lincoln Record Soc., ed. F. M. Stenton, p. 109).

[8] Glorieux, *loc. cit.*

[9] Haureau, *op. cit.* i. 178.

[10] *Ibid.* ; he was commissioned with the bishop of Nevers to examine the orthodoxy of a canon of Langres (Lea, *Hist. of the Inquisition*, p. 307).

[11] Jacques de Vitry, *Hist.* lib. ii. ch. 8.

[12] A ' Usurers' Pater Noster ' calls him ' Master Robert de Cursun ' (Cambridge, Trinity Coll. MS. 1149, fos. 324–6) ; two exempla about him concern usurers and a priest's concubine (B.M. MS. Reg. 7, D. i, fos. 129, 134 ; *cf.* H. L. D. Ward, *Catalogue of Romances*, iii. 500, 501 ; both also in B.M. Add. MS. 33956, fos. 84*b*, 85 ; B. Haureau, *op. cit.* ii. 282 ; *Chr. Maj.* iv. 270).

him to France in the spring of 1213, where he presided over a council of Paris.[1] In the same year he attended a council at Bordeaux in July,[2] a council at Rouen in December,[3] mediated between the kings of France and England,[4] and requested King John to hear the petition of the newly elected abbot of Bury St. Edmunds.[5]

In August 1215 he reorganized the studies of the university of Paris.[6] Later in the year he attended the fourth lateran council.[7] A letter of his to King John remains from this year.[8] From 1215 to 1219 he seems to have been at Rome.[9] In the latter year he went on a crusade to the east, was present at the siege of Damiata, and died in the Holy Land.[10] His interest in the crusades dates from at least 1214, when he shared in a great movement against the Albigenses.[11] In 1220 his servant, Richard de Courtrai, is mentioned in English letters close.[12]

Robert de Cruce, O.F.M.[13] Leland saw references in the 'Catalogue of Illustrious Franciscans' to his 'Commentary on Physics' and 'Commentary on the Sentences' (*Commentarii*, p. 325). If Robert is to be identified with Robert 'Carru' his 'Commentary' was formerly at Oxford, Merton Coll. MSS. T. 125 and T. 133 (Powicke, p. 125), 'ex domo Ricardi Grafton': *inc.* 'Tria sunt mihi difficilia et quartum pe' (Bale, *Index*, p. 382). This Carru was also the author of a 'Commentary upon the Posterior Analytics of Aristotle': *inc.* 'Testante Lincolniensi in primo posteriorum,' 'Ex collegio Achademie, Oxon' (*ibid.* p. 382). He may be the author of a 'Sermon' in Merton Coll. MS. 248, fo. 170, attributed to H. de Cruce, O.F.M. (Little, *G.F.* p. 169).

A 'Fr. Robert de S. Cruce' went to France with Adam de Bechesoveres [q.v.] about 1250, and was probably our man.[1] He was the thirteenth regent master of the Oxford franciscans, about 1276–8.[2] In a letter to the king thanking him for supplying the means to repair the aqueduct which brought water to the Oxford house, he mentioned being in the royal presence at 'Bicleswade,' presumably Biggerswode, co. Bedford.[3] The king was there on 16 Sept. 1279.[4] Robert's letter followed this, probably within a few months. In April 1280 the archbishop, John Peckham, acting upon the accusation of Fr. Robert de Cruce, gave orders concerning an Oxford dominican.[5] Robert was provincial of his order in January 1281; thus probably he had been made minister in 1280.[6] As minister he wrote an interesting letter to the king consoling him upon the death of a nephew.[7] There are records of money given to messengers sent to him, the dates

1 Glorieux, *loc. cit.*
2 *Rot. Litt. Pat.* p. 139*b*.
3 Glorieux, *loc. cit.*
4 *Ibid.*; *Ann. Monast.* iii. 42.
5 *Memorials of St. Edmunds* (R.S.), ed. T. Arnold, ii. 89, 92.
6 Glorieux, *loc. cit.*; *Cartularium Universitatis Parisiensis*, ed. Denifle-Chatelain, i. 78–9; *M.G.H.SS.* xxviii. 335, 442.
7 Glorieux, *loc. cit.*
8 P.R.O., ancient correspondence, S.C. 1, vol. 1, no. 7, written at the instance of the abbot of Mont St. Michel.
9 Glorieux, *loc. cit.*
10 *Flores Historiarum* (R.S.), ed. H. R. Luard, ii. 235; *Chronica de Mailros*, p. 137; *M.G.H.SS.* xxviii. 400.
11 Glorieux, *loc. cit.*
12 *Rot. Litt. Claus.* i. 411.
13 T. p. 154 for Carew, dated there 1325 and he may well be another man. The best biography is by Little, *F.S.O.* p. 855.

1 *Mon. Fr.* i. 333.
2 *Ibid.* i. 552; Little, *loc. cit.*; *cf.* App. A.
3 P.R.O., ancient correspondence, S.C. xvi, no. 90 (edited by A. G. Little in *Studies in English Franciscan History*, pp. 223–4).
4 T. Craib, *Itinerary of Edward I* (P.R.O. typescript, 1898), p. 17.
5 *Reg. Peckham*, i. 117–8.
6 *Reg. John de Pontissara* (C.Y.S.), i. 255; *Reg. Ricardi de Swinfield* (C.Y.S.), p. 23; *E.H.R.* vi (1891). 746.
7 P.R.O., ancient correspondence, S.C. xvi, no. 91, dated 7 kal. March, mentions Wales, but not the name of 'nepotis vestri,' although if 'nepos' is used in the sense of favourite it might refer to his son Alphonso.

of the accounts being 14 and 25 Feb. 1284.[1] In June he secured the privilege of exemption for his order from payment of royal custom at the port of Dover and held a chapter in September.[2] In March 1285 he represented the English province at the general chapter at Milan.[3] A messenger was paid, on 20 Aug. 1285, for going to the provincial minister ; [4] just below this in the accounts is a payment for going to Fr. Robert de Cruce.[5] Possibly he was invited to be lector at Worcester.[6] How much longer he lived is uncertain : he was buried at Bridgwater.[7]

Robert of Dodford was the donor of books to Ramsey abbey, and possibly an author and monk of that house.[8] Bale credits him with being the author of ' Postille in Parabolas Salomonis ' : *inc.* ' Ipse mittet quasi imbres eloquium ' (*Index*, p. 370). Such a title is included among the books bequeathed by him to Ramsey. The entire list follows :

Libri Roberti de Dodeforde. Biblioteca. Secunda pars bibliotecæ Ebrayce. Glosæ super Bibliotecam Ebraice. Derivationes Hugutionis. Liber Ethimologiarum. Rabanus de naturis rerum, cum interpretationibus nominum Hebræorum. Summa Reymundi. Prescianus constructus, cum dupplici et notulis. Psalterium Græcum et Latinum cum aliis. Summa magistri Roberti Grosteste de decem præceptis. Prosæ magistri Henrici versificatoris. Summa extracta de Decretalibus. Minus Mariale. Liber Sententiarum. Quartus liber Sententiarum. [Ricardus] Fishacre super Sententias. Parabolæ Salomonis postillatæ. Exceptiones Crisostomi super Mathæum. Vitæ sanctorum. Breviarium et Psalterium. *Dedit item de novo unum librum qui vocatur* [Alex. de] Hales super tertium librum Sententiarum. Liber Bretonis. Corrogationes Promothei, cum Summa Johannis Belet. Liber partium. Breviarium. Sententiarum (*sic*). Duo Missalia. Duo Antiphonaria, scilicet, Temporalium et Sanctorum. Ysidorus. Liber phisica (*sic*). Item de modo confitendi. Item de sermonibus cum aliis. Item de phisica, cum aliis. Item [Plateraius ?] de simplici medicina (*Chronicon Abbatiae Rameseiensis*, R.S., ed. W. D. Macray, p. 365).

A transcription of Ramsey abbey cartulary (B.M. MS. Vesp. E. ii) to the middle of the reign of Henry III was ' per Robertum de Dodeford clericum.' Was he a monk, as bibliographical tradition suggests ? Not, apparently, when this transcript was made, even though his relations with Ramsey are already clear. His books suggest two things. In the first place he was a student at Oxford as late as 1230 : note the writers, Master Henry [of Avranches], Fishacre [Richard], Alexander Neckam [Corrogationes Promothei], and especially Robert Grosseteste, whose influence appears in the emphasis upon Hebrew and science. Secondly, he was probably a priest, since there are so many books dealing with the service and confession. He may have come of a Buckinghamshire family.[1]

Robert (the Dominican) [2] was an author about whom the source of bibliographical tradition is apparently Sisto de Siena :

Robertus Dominicanus Anglus, ordinis predicatorum, professione scholasticus, postillam fecit IN JOB, IN DANIELEM, IN MATTHAEUM, et IN LUCAM, IN JOHANNEM, que Bononie in Bibliotheca Predicatorum viditur (*Bibliothece Sancte*, Paris, 1610, p. 296).

This man does not appear in the list of early dominican writers and, if a dominican, is thus probably of a later date. However, he may not even have been a dominican. Sisto called William of Milton, O.F.M., a dominican because William's books were in dominican libraries. He may have attributed Robert to his order because of the same accidental circumstance.

Robert of Fletham was a disputant at Oxford *c.* 1282–90 (Little-Pelster, p. 79).

[1] P.R.O., Exchequer, K.R., various accounts, 12–13 Edw. I, E. 101/308/7.

[2] *C.P.R.*, 1281–92, p. 124 ; Little, *G.F.* p. 157. He is called ' Robert de Sancta Cruce ' (*Reg. Peckham*, p. 820).

[3] *C.P.R.*, 1281–92, p. 155 ; Little, *G.F.* p. 157.

[4] P.R.O., Exchequer, various accounts, E. 101/308/7, ' die dom. 20 Aug.,' name not given ; it probably refers to his successor, William of Gainsborough (*cf. Reg. Godfr. Giffard*, Worc. Hist. Soc., ed. J. W. W. Bund, ii. 263).

[5] Before 19 Nov. 1285 (P.R.O., E. 101/308/7).

[6] *Reg. Godfr. Giffard*, ii. 263, ' Robert de Crull.'

[7] *Mon. Fr.* i. 537, 560.

[8] T. p. 230.

[1] B.M. MS. Harley 4714 (Bitlesden), fos. 171*b*, 172, 173, 180, 196, 197, 198.

[2] T. p. 636.

Robert (of Gloucester) was the author of an English chronicle.[1] The MSS. are described and the chronicle published by W. A. Wright in 'The Metrical Chronicle of Robert of Gloucester' (R.S.), and excerpts are given (*M.G.H.SS.* xxviii. 663–9). Possibly he is author of some of the 'Southern Legend Collection' (*cf.* J. E. Wells, *Manual of the Writings in Middle English*, v. 19).

Some facts about the author come from his chronicle, but not enough to identify him. The author of at least a part was named Robert,[2] he was probably at Oxford about 1263,[3] his dialect was of Gloucestershire,[4] and he himself spent much of his life apparently in Gloucester. He was writing about 1300.[5]

Robert of Gretham was the writer of two long Anglo-Norman religious pieces [6] :—

'Miroir or Evangile des Domnes.' (a) Cambridge, Trinity Coll. MS. B. 14/39 (13th cent.); (b) Camb. Univ. Lib. MS. Gi. i. 1 (early 14th cent.); (c) B.M. Add. MS. 26773 (13th cent.); (d) B.N. MS. nouv. acq. 11198 (early 14th cent.); (e) Wollaston Hall (H.M.C., Middleton MSS., pp. 220, 221) (13th cent.); (f) York cathedral MS. 16, K. 14 (13th cent.). The author gives his name in the closing lines :

Ore prie tuz ke les oient e dient
Ke il pur Robert de Gretham prient,
Ki Deu meintenge si sa vie
Ki par li seit en sa baille.
(*Romania*, xv. 305.)

Extracts appear in 'Zeitschrift für romanische Philologie,' i. 543; 'Romania,' xv. 298, xxxii. 29, xlii. 145 (*cf.* also M. Y. H. Aitken, *Étude sur le Miroir ou les Evangiles des Domnées de Robert de Gretham*).

'Corset,' Bodl. Lib. MS. Douce 210 (late 13th cent.).

His name is given again :

A son tres chier seignor Alain
De part Robert son chapelain
Salutz el fitz sainte Marie.
(*Romania*, xv. 296.)

Extracts are given in 'Bulletin de la Société des anciens textes français' (1880), p. 62; 'Romania,' xv. 297.

The author probably lived in the middle of the 13th century, according to philologists.[1] He dedicated his 'Miroir' to a lady Aline [2] and the 'Corset' to Alan, whom he served as chaplain.

Robert Grosseteste was the bishop of Lincoln and one of the foremost scholars in 13th century England.[3] The vast number of treatises attributed to him will be treated comprehensively by S. Harrison Thomson in a forthcoming work.

There are a number of biographies of Grosseteste, but none is very satisfactory for the pre-episcopal period of his life. All reflect a bibliographical tradition which has included a series of mistakes.[4] In spite of the fact that Grosseteste was considered for canonization, no contemporary life has been found. In the later middle ages Richard, a monk of Bardney, produced a verse life of the bishop.[5] The bibliographers have abused it roundly, especially since it disagreed with their tradition. However, curious as some of his statements are, in the main they fit into the outline furnished by the documents. His information would seem to have been too vague for him so that he made it more detailed, and thus included some grotesque statements. In many ways Richard's information is like that furnished by the biographers of Edmund of Abingdon : it lacks chronological signposts. Richard's outline has one point in its favour. It gives

1 T. p. 636; *D.N.B.* under Robert. His biography is also in Wright (*op. cit.* preface).
2 Lines 11746–9.
3 Lines 11186–233.
4 Wright, *op. cit.* p. xii.
5 Line 10943.
6 Vising, pp. 50, 63.

1 Vising, pp. 50, 63.
2 Possibly the feminine of Alan.
3 T. p. 345; *D.N.B.* under Grosseteste.
4 For a criticism of this tradition see my article in the *Harvard Theological Review*, xxvi (1933). 161–72.
5 Published by H. Wharton in *Anglia Sacra*, ii. 325.

the impression, backed by other documents, that Grosseteste wavered in his ambition between administration and scholarship.

Robert Grosseteste was born of an unimportant family in Suffolk,[1] possibly at Stowe,[2] probably by 1170. He had a sister who was alive in 1232,[3] and the Grossetestes who received preferment at Lincoln during his episcopate were doubtless his relatives.[4] The Master Richard Grosseteste of Salisbury with whom bibliographical tradition confused him may have been of the same family.[5] He witnessed a charter of Bishop Hugh of Lincoln, probably about 1186–9.[6] He was thus a master nearly sixty-five years before his death. However, Roger Bacon said that Grosseteste lived to a great age,[7] and the monk of Bardney states that his first schooling was at Lincoln.[8] Grosseteste's name

[1] *Triveti Annales* (Eng. Hist. Soc.), ed. T. Hog, p. 242; *M. Parisiensis Hist. Angl.* (R.S.), ed. F. Madden, ii. 376.

[2] *Anglia Sacra*, ii. 26.

[3] *Ep. Grosseteste*, p. 43.

[4] *Rot. R. Grosseteste*, *passim*.

[5] *Sarum Chs. and Docs.* pp. 111–3; *Register of St. Osmund* (R.S.), ed. W. H. R. Jones, i. 380; ii. 16, 130, 133; B.M. MS. Cotton, Claudius C. ix, fos. 182, 184. There may have been a contemporary Ralph Grosseteste. He appears in two documents as a papal delegate appointed by Pope Innocent III (Worcester cathedral muniments B. 406, as 'Mr. Ralph Grosseteste'; and *ibid.* MS. A. iv (Reg. 1) as 'Mr. R. Grosseteste').

[6] As 'Mr. Robert Grosteste' (B.M. MS. Reg. 11, B. ix, fo. 25; Dugdale, *Monasticon*, v. 191). There are fifteen names in the list, including two abbots, a prior, and two rural deans, all listed with their titles: the absence of title is thus of some significance. Simon of Sewell was evidently not yet treasurer of Lichfield as he was by 1205 (*Reg. Antiquissimum of the Cathedral Church of Lincoln*, ed. C. W. Foster, i. 254). Moreover, Roger of Rolveston was still canon of Lincoln, not yet archdeacon of Leicester, which he became in 1189, and William de Monte [q.v.] was not yet chancellor. For Roger's succession to Hamo, who became dean in 1189, see B.M. MS. Cotton, Vespasian E. xx, fo. 33*b*. Four of the witnesses appear together in the same order as canons in a charter in which Hamo is described as archdeacon of Leicester, thus before 1189 (B.M. MS. Reg. 11, B. ix, fo. 27*b*).

[7] *Fr. Rogeri Bacon Opera Inedita* (R.S.), ed. J. S. Brewer, i. 472.

[8] *Op. cit.* p. 327.

appears last in the charter after the names of rural deans. He was probably clerk to Bishop Hugh.[1] Possibly the monk of Bardney had some such reference at his disposal, which he changed into a statement that Grosseteste was supported by the mayor of Lincoln.[2]

According to the monk of Bardney, Grosseteste studied next at Oxford and Cambridge and was then associated with a bishop of Salisbury until his death.[3] It is clear that he was one of the clerks of Bishop William de Vere of Hereford before that prelate's demise in 1199.[4] Could Bardney have been again confused, substituting an exact name for an anonymous bishop? In any case, Hereford was at the time a centre of scientific learning.[5] Grosseteste's treatise on comets has been described as an early work by one who should know.[6] A great comet which appeared in the winter of 1197 possibly is the one mentioned by our writer.[7] If the monk of Bardney is correct about the bishop of Salisbury, then Grosseteste must have been with Bishop Herbert at his death in 1217. This has attractive possibilities: it would probably mean that Grosseteste had gone from Oxford to Cambridge when the former was closed in 1208. Cambridge might claim him as one of her founders. Moreover, the monk speaks of a famous visit to

[1] The last name or names were usually those of the clerks who were of the household of the bishop and who wrote out the charters.

[2] *Opera*, p. 328.

[3] *Op. cit.* pp. 330 *et seq.*

[4] A letter from Gerald of Wales to the bishop says that Grosseteste was already proficient in liberal arts, law, and medicine (*Giraldi Cambrensis. Opera*, R.S., ed. J. S. Brewer, i. 249). Grosseteste appears as a witness among the clerks (Oxford, Balliol Coll. MS. 271, fos. 56*b*, 88*b*); his status undesignated (fos. 6*b*, 79*b*). His surname is given as 'Grossecapitis.' He may be the Master Robert of a Tintern abbey charter (B.M. MS. Arundel 19, fo. 31).

[5] *Cf. Isis*, xviii (1932). 14–25.

[6] *Ibid.* xix (1933). 25. Thomson thinks that Halley's comet is indicated: it should have appeared in 1229.

[7] 'Cometa apparuit tota hyeme fere' (*Ann. Monast.* i. 55; iv. 389).

Rome before the bishop's death : this would be probably to the fourth Lateran council of 1215. Grosseteste was evidently in France during the interdict.[1] However, we need here a few certain dates.

Grosseteste, according to Bishop Oliver Sutton, had not been allowed the title of chancellor of Oxford university, but only the older title of 'Magister Scholarum' by Bishop Hugh of Welles (1209–35).[2] This incident probably occurred when Oxford reopened in 1214 : it was the bishop's first opportunity to take up the question. Certainly by 1221 the new title was established.[3] The monk of Bardney states that Grosseteste returned to Oxford after the death of the bishop of Salisbury and made a famous orologium.[4] Then Lincoln gave him his first prebend, Clistona,[5] possibly a mistake for Leicester, a Lincoln prebend which he is known to have held.[6] On 25 Apr. 1225 he was presented to the church of Abbotsley by the bishop of Lincoln.[7] In 1227 another presentment took place, but the item is so badly mutilated that little can be made of it.[8]

The monk of Bardney states that Grosseteste became a doctor of theology before his appointment as 'custos sigilli' to an aging king.[9] This is inexplicable unless it refers to the archdeaconry of Leicester, which he held from 1229 to the fall of 1232 :[10] this was a position assisting an aging bishop. However, it is probable that he was regent in

[1] He heard Jacques de Vitry, Stephen Langton in exile, and Robert Courçon (*Chr. Maj.* v. 404).

[2] *Snappe's Formulary and Other Records*, ed. H. E. Salter, p. 52.

[3] *Mediaeval Archives of the University of Oxford*, ed. H. E. Salter, i. 10.

[4] *Op. cit.* p. 332.

[5] *Op. cit.* p. 333.

[6] St. Margaret of Leicester (*Ep. Grosseteste*, p. 43 ; *Rot. R. Grosseteste*, p. 391 ; *Rot. H. de Welles*, ii. 238).

[7] *Ibid.* iii. 48 : Grosseteste was still a deacon.

[8] *Ibid.* iii. 54.

[9] *Op. cit.* p. 334. Note that probably before the monk confused the bishop of Lincoln with a lay official, the mayor of Lincoln.

[10] *Rot. H. de Welles*, ii. 308–21.

theology before he became archdeacon.[1] He presided at the vesperies of an Adam [Marsh or Rufus, or some other].[2] Adam Marsh was certainly a very close friend of Grosseteste : their letters reveal this friendship, and Grosseteste left his library to the Oxford franciscans on account of their friendship.[3] Their names appear in the 'Liber Vite' of Durham together,[4] and they accepted and resigned their preferments as archdeacon of Leicester and parson of Wearmouth at about the same time.[5] Possibly Grosseteste still taught at Oxford while an archdeacon.[6]

Grosseteste resigned his preferments, except for his prebend at Lincoln, in the autumn of 1232, after an illness.[7] Probably he became master of the franciscan school soon after this,[8] where he established a famous tradition.[9] Of his activity during the next two years and a half, besides teaching, one curious item remains. Letters close commanded Robert Bacon and Grosseteste to drive the prostitutes out of Oxford.[10] He

[1] His 'Topical Concordance of the Bible and the Fathers,' which Thomson dates 1235–43 (*Speculum*, ix. 143), is probably of the years 1220–9. It mentions Aristotle's 'De Animalibus' translated by Michael Scot about 1220. The colophon reads 'Incipit tabula magistri Roberti Lincolniensis episcopi cum addicione Magistri Ade de Marisco.' Probably the episcopal title is a later insertion in the original. Thomson thinks that the MS. is an original written under the direction of Grosseteste. If so and if Grosseteste were bishop the clerk would almost certainly have written 'venerabilis patris' or 'domini' for Grosseteste and 'fratris' for Adam Marsh. It seems probable, then, that the treatise was written before Adam became a friar in 1232 and even before Grosseteste became an archdeacon in 1229.

[2] Bale, *Index*, p. 376 ; Little, *F.S.O.* p. 828.

[3] *Triveti Annales*, p. 243.

[4] *Liber Vitae Ecclesiae Dunelmensis* (Surtees Soc.), p. 21.

[5] Grosseteste also witnessed a Hereford charter during the period 1219–34 of Bishop Hugh Foliot (W. A. Leighton in Shropshire Archaeol. and Nat. Hist. Soc. *Transactions*, N.S., i, 1878. 182).

[6] *C.Cl.R.*, 1227–31, p. 52.

[7] *Ep. Grosseteste*, p. 43.

[8] *Mon. Fr.* i. 37 ; *Eccleston*, p. 35.

[9] Little, *F.S.O.* pp. 807–11.

[10] *C.Cl.R.*, 1231–4, p. 568.

was elected on 27 Mar. 1235 as bishop of Lincoln against considerable opposition.[1] He apparently dated his episcopal year from the death of his predecessor.[2]

Robert of Haudlo was the author of a 'Treatise on Music.'[3] (a) B.M. MS. Cotton, Tiberius B. ix, burned in the Cottonian fire, but previously described by T. Smith in the Cotton catalogue of 1696:

Regule, cum maximis, magistri Franconis cum additionibus aliorum musicorum, compilate a Roberto de Haudle.

(b) B.M. MS. 4909, modern transcript, with the colophon

Finito libro reddatur gloria Christo. Expliciunt regule cum additionibus finite die Veneris proximo ante Pentecost anno Domini millesimo tricentesimo vicesimo sexto etc. Amen. Fo. 11.

The date above may be the date of Robert's composition[4] or possibly that of a scribe. The authors quoted include Peter de Cruce (contrasted with the moderns),[5] Peter le Viser,[6] James de Hokoti, and John 'de Garlandia.'[7] If the latter is the grammarian [q.v.] the treatise must belong to the 13th[8] or 14th century.

Robert Kilwardby, O.P., was archbishop of Canterbury and a theologian.[9] An early list of his writings gives:

Fr Rupertus natione anglicus, magister in theologia archiepiscopus Cantuariensis scripsit (1) super Porphyrium et (2) predicamenta, (3) peryermenias, (4) sex principia divisionum, (5) topica, Boetii, (6) super lib. priorum et (7) posteriorum, (8) topicorum Aristotelis, (9) super librum elenchorum, (10) super Priscianum minorem. Item (11) librum de natura relationis. Item (12) sophisticam grammaticalem et sophisticam logicalem. Item (13) librum de ortu scientiarum. (14) De rebus predicamentalibus, (15) de unitate formarum, (16) super librum physicorum, (17) super metheorum, (18) super de anima, (19) super de celo et mundo, (20) de generatione et corruptione, (21) super metaphysicorum, et (22) omnes alios libros naturales. Item (23) super omnes libros sententiarum (*Archiv für Litteratur- und Kirchengeschichte des Mittelalters*, ii. 236):

Trivet also refers to his writings:

Post ordinis vero ingressum studiosus in divinis scripturis, originalibus, sanctorum patrumque lirbos Augustini fere omnes, aliorumque doctorum plurium, per parva distinxit capitula, sententiam singulorum sub brevibus annotando. Exstant tractatus ejus de Tempore, de Universali, de Relatione, et de Ortu scientiarum curiosus utilisque libellus (*Annales*, Eng. Hist. Soc., ed. T. Hog, p. 278).

His works appear in many MSS. A careful bibliography of them is much needed.

Kilwardby's early career is the subject of a few vague remarks by Trivet:

Qui non tantummodo religiosæ vitæ sanctitate, sed scientia atque doctrina habebatur præclarus. Nempe ante ordinis inrgessum Parisiis rexerat in artibus; cujus in his peritiam, præcipue quoad grammaticam et logicam, redacta in scriptis edocent monumenta.[1]

He ruled (and thus probably studied) in arts at Paris before becoming a dominican. Then after entering the order he took up theology, but he did not become a master of it at Paris.[2] Thus he probably completed his theological study at Oxford and ruled in theology there. Probably also there he had Thomas of Cantilupe as a student: Cantilupe incepted under him after Kilwardby became prior provincial of the order in England.[3] At this time also (or possibly earlier at Paris) Kilwardby was Cantilupe's confessor.[4] In 1261 Kilwardby

[1] *Hist. Angl.* ii. 376; *Ann. Monast.* i. 95; iv. 82.

[2] *Harvard Theological Review*, xxvi. 171.

[3] T. p. 376.

[4] A Robert de Handlo or Haudlo appears in an Essex fine of 1325–6 with John de Handlo and his wife, Maud, concerning a considerable land holding in Stansted Munfichet (*Feet of Fines for Essex*, Essex Archaeol. Soc., ed. R. E. G. Kirk, i. 227, 242).

[5] Fo. 3.

[6] *Ibid.*

[7] Fos. 3*b*, 4, 9*b*.

[8] There remains a confirmation of the institution of Robert de Handlo or Haudlo to Iddesleigh (Exeter) on 22 July 1260 (*Registers of Walter Bronescombe and Peter Quivil*, ed. F. C. Hingeston-Randolph, p. 100).

[9] T. p. 455; *D.N.B.* under Kilwardby.

[1] *Annales*, p. 278, under 1272; for some conjectures see *Revue des sciences philosophiques et théologiques*, ix (1920). 566.

[2] Denifle does not find him in the lists of Parisian masters (*Archiv für Litteratur- und Kirchengesch. des Mittelalters*, ii, 1886. 172, 191, 204–8, 236).

[3] See *D.N.B.*; *Annales*, p. 306; *Willelmi Rishanger, Chronica et Annales* (R.S.), ed. H. T. Riley, p. 102; *Acta Sanctorum*, Oct., i. 600.

[4] Rishanger, *loc. cit.*; *D.N.B.* under Cantilupe.

succeeded Simon of Henton [q.v.] as prior provincial and remained in this office until 1272.[1] Some evidence of his activity in this capacity remains.[2] He apparently induced Ralph of Bocking [q.v.] to write the life of St. Richard Wich.[3] He was elected archbishop of Canterbury in 1272, resigned to become a cardinal in 1278, and died in Rome the year following.[4] He left a gift to Christchurch.[5] Of his family nothing is certain : a Robert of Kilwardby, possibly a relative, held the church of All Hallows of Lombard Street, London, in 1283.[6]

Robert of Leicester, O.F.M., was a computist.[7] This franciscan composed a series of works on the Hebrew calendar and compotus, now in Bodl. Lib. MS. Digby 212 (1) *inc.* 'Operis iniuncti novitatem pater meritis insignissime, magister et domine R dei gratia Herfordensis antistes ecclesie,' with the rubric 'Istud opus composuit fr Robertus de Leycestria fratrum minorum,' fos. 2–7 ; (2) *inc.* 'Prima earum est a creatione mundi,' fos. 7*b*–8*b* (14th cent.) ; (3) *inc.* 'Ad planiorem et pleniorem prescripti tractatus intelligentiam.' One of these is probably in Erfurt, Amplon. MS. Qu. 361, fos. 80–5 (early 14th cent.), headed 'Tractatus Legicester,' *inc.* 'In nomine dni I. Chr. qui est auctor temporum.' 'Ex usu,' *expl.* 'concursu 6 ferie non revellunt. Expl. tract. Leycester.' Leland reported, upon

[1] *E.H.R.* xxxiii (1918). 244 ; *Acta Capitulorum Generalium Ord. Praed.*, ed. B. M. Reichert, i. 156, 165.

[2] P.R.O., ancient correspondence, S.C. 1, ii. 77 ; iii. 146 ; *Cal. of Feet of Fines for Suffolk* (Suffolk Institute of Archaeol.), ed. Walter Rye, p. 66 ; Little and Easterling, *Franciscans and Dominicans of Exeter*, p. 42 ; he was present at the chapter general at Montpellier in 1271, called 'magnus magister in theologia' (Quétif-Echard, p. 374).

[3] *Acta SS.*, April, i. 283.

[4] *Cf. D.N.B.* ; chosen by the pope on 11 Oct. (*Registres de Grégoire*, x. 21).

[5] J. Dart, *History and Antiquities of the Cathedral Church of Canterbury*, App. p. v.

[6] *Reg. Peckham*, p. 1018.

[7] T. p. 636 ; *D.N.B.* under Leicester ; Little, *G.F.* p. 168.

the basis of statements in the catalogue of franciscan writers, that Robert of Leicester wrote a 'Commentary on the Sentences,' 'Quodlibeta,' and 'De Paupertate Christi,' and that Robert was contemporaneous with William Herbert (early 14th cent.) (T. p. 636). In Cambridge, Pembroke Coll. MS. 87, is a compilation, 'Enchiridion Poenitentiale,' 'ex distinctionis . . . R. de Leycester aliorumque.' See under **Richard of Wetheringsett** above and also **R. de Leicestria.**

This writer composed his works on compotus in 1294 and 1295. The problem of his identity is complicated by the fact that Robert of Leicester was a common name and that it is not certain that he was a franciscan at the time that he wrote. His scientific interests are similar to those of Robertus Anglicus [q.v.], who wrote twenty years earlier. A franciscan of the name was 'magister extraneus' of Balliol college in 1325[1] and probably died in 1327–8.[2] If he was writing before he became a minorite he may be identical with a Master Robert of Leicester involved in litigation in 1295,[3] or a chaplain who had simple protection for two years in 1288.[4] And there are other references, some obviously too early.[5]

[1] H.M.C., 4th Rep., App. p. 442 ; Little, *G.F.* p. 168.

[2] *Collectanea* (B.S.F.S.), i. 149.

[3] *Placita coram rege* 1295 (British Record Soc.), ed. W. P. W. Phillimore, p. 159.

[4] *C.P.R.*, 1281–92, p. 290.

[5] Master Robert of Leicester, 'clericus thes' (P.R.O., Exchequer of pleas, plea roll 31 Edw. I, E. 13–26, *m.* 2) ; grant by Master Walter de Cantilupe, rector of Smithfield, to Master Robert de Leicester (ancient deeds, B. 8920) ; witness of a charter of Bishop Gilbert of Aberdeen (*Liber cartarum prioratus sancti Andree in Scotia*, Bannatyne Club, ed. T. Thomson, p. 302) ; a Robert of Leicester had charge of keys of the chirograph chest of the exchequer of the Jews in 1244, his nephew and heir being a certain Robert de Ponte (*Cal. of the Plea Rolls of the Exchequer of the Jews*, ed. J. M. Rigg, i. 69, 99) ; another was archdeacon of Ely about 1241 (Camb. Univ. Lib. Add. MS. 3020, fo. 175*b* ; MS. Dd. x. 28, fo. 111 ; B.M. MS. Harley 230, fo. 37) ; Master Robert of Leicester received remission of certain payments about 1273 (B.M. MS. Harley 2044, fo. 183).

Robert of Milford was the author of a medical treatise in B.M. MS. Reg. 12, B. xii, fo. 176*b*.

Robert of Orford, O.P., was a theologian.[1] An early list gives his writings:

Fr Rubertus nat. anglicus de Erfort, mag. in theol. scripsit contra dicta Henrici de Gande, quibus impugnat Thomam. Item contra primum Egidii ubi impugnat Thomam (*Archiv für Litteratur- und Kirchengesch. des Mittelalters*, ii, 1886. 239).

The first work is probably in Rome, Vatican Lib. (a) MS. lat. 772 (*Mélanges Mandonnet*, i. 397–400); (b) MS. lat. 987. The second is apparently at Oxford. (a) Merton Coll. MS. 276, fos. 22–50 (Powicke, p. 136); (b) Magdalen Coll. MS. 217 (*Revue des sciences philosophiques et théologiques*, 1913, p. 62). He apparently wrote a 'Commentary on the Sentences.' (a) On bk. ii, Klosterneuburg MS. 322; (b) bks. iii and iv, formerly at Oxford, Merton Coll. (Powicke, pp. 97, 125); (c) possibly all in one volume (*ibid.* p. 125).

This Robert of Orford, although his opponents were of Paris, apparently about 1282 became master of theology at Oxford.[2] He had studied probably *c.* 1275 at Cambridge.[3] Robert is alleged to have been one of the stoutest defenders of St. Thomas Aquinas there, some time after 1285.[4]

Eodem tempore Henricus de Gandavo qui doctor solemnis appelatur Parisius, frater Jacobus de Viterbo ordinis Heremitarum et magister Gofridus de Fontibus multa conscripserunt, quibus lucidissimam ac veridicam S. Thome doctrinam impugnare nixi sunt. Contra quos suscitavit Dominus spiritum gloriosorum doctorum ordinis Predicatorum qui doctrinam impugnatam gloriosius defensarent, fundarent et declararent. Quorum primus fuit Robertus Orford Anglicus qui contra Henricum de Gandavo scripsit in his in quibus vult impugnare sanctum Thomam. Item contra primum Egidii ubi adversatur doctrine S. Thome.

He preached a sermon at Oxford on 22 Feb. 1293.[1] He is said to be identical with Robert (William ?) de Torto Collo.[2]

Robert, canon of the order of St. Augustine, was part author of a 'Quadrilogus de Vita Sancti Edmundi' (see under **Eustace,** monk of Christchurch). Robert was later a cistercian monk.

Robert de Pennard was a disputant at Oxford *c.* 1282–90 (Little-Pelster, p. 99).

Robert Ribverius is the subject of the following account by Tanner taken from Pits:

Ribverius [Robertus] sacerdos Anglus, postquam literas humaniores et philosophiam in patriis academiis hauserat, in Galliam trajecit, et Lutetiae metaphysicam publice professus est. Deinde S. Dominici habitum assumpsit, et theologiae tam sedulo invigilavit, ut Parisiis ejusdem facultatis licentiatus factus sit, et tandem sui ordinis praeses provincialis evaserit. Scripsisse fertur *De divisione S. Scripturae*, lib. i. *In epistolam ad Romanos*, lib. i. *In epistolas ad Corinthios*, lib. i. *De differentia spiritus et animae*, lib. i. *Super librum de causis*, lib. i. *De instantibus*, lib. i. Claruit A. MCCL. Pits, p. 323 (T. p. 623).

Pits' account raises certain questions. The lists of writings of the authors belonging to the order do not mention this man.[3] If he really was a prior provincial in England he might have held office in 1272–7 just before William of Southampton [q.v.]. Probably the name 'Ribverius' is a mistake for Kilwardby.

Robert of Swaffham was a monk of Peterborough and chronicler.[4] He wrote a continuation of the history of his abbey from 1175 to 1246 in a MS. now at Peterborough

[1] T. p. 637; *D.N.B.* under Orford; Little-Pelster, p. 98.

[2] *Archiv*, ii. 171, 191, 204–8 (for his absence from the Paris lists); Little-Pelster, pp. 105, 112, 129; Little, *F.S.O.* p. 857; *cf.* Alan de Wakerfield.

[3] Little-Pelster, p. 12.

[4] Martène and Durand, *Veterum Scriptorum*, vi (1729). 370.

[1] Little-Pelster, p. 163.

[2] Powicke, p. 97; Little-Pelster, p. 98; but see William of Torto Collo.

[3] *Archiv für Litteratur- und Kirchengeschichte*, ii. 171, 190–2, 203–40.

[4] T. p. 637; *D.N.B.* under Robert; *cf.* F. Liebermann, *Neues Archiv*, xviii. 231–2. Swaffham, Cambridgeshire.

and called 'Swafham' (see a note in B.M. MS. Eger. 2733, fo. 9*b*, 'Item require in libro R. de Swafham de pisan [pitan ?]'). The history is in the form of a record of the lives of the abbots. It has been published by Joseph Sparke in 'Historiæ Anglicanæ Scriptores Varii,' pp. 97–122. He was probably also responsible for the other contents of the book named after him.

In 1251–2 a Robert de Swafham was presented to the church of Comaneford as perpetual vicar.[1] The chronicler was writing at Peterborough in the time of Abbot John de Calceto (1250–62).[2] He was pittancier in the sixth year of Abbot Robert (1267–8), making a gift of forty shillings at the time.[3] He is said to have been cellarer and to have died about 1273.[4]

Robert of Ware, O.F.M., was the author of 'Twenty-five Discourses on the Virgin Mary,'[5] to be found in London, Gray's Inn MS. 7, fos. 2–138*b* (13th cent.), *inc.* 'Ave rosarium scripturarum per areolas.' A note after title gives 'per fratrem Robertum de Ware.' For an account of the treatise see G. R. Owst's 'Some Franciscan Memorials at Gray's Inn' (*Dublin Review*, clxxvi, 1925. 280–4).

Robert came from Ware near Hertford[6] and entered the franciscan order in the time of the legate, Ottobon (November 1265–July 1268). He entered at Oxford against the wishes of his father, who tried to secure his removal from the order. He was not reconciled with his father until the latter was on his deathbed. Robert was at London when summoned to Ware. He dedicated his book to his younger brother John.[7]

1 *Rot. R. Grosseteste*, p. 300.

2 'Iohannes de Calceto nunc abbas' (Sparks, *op. cit.* p. 119).

3 Sparks, *op. cit.* p. 141 ; B.M. Add. MS. 39758, fo. 94*b*.

4 Swafham MS. fo. 161 (?) ; T. p. 637.

5 Little, *G.F.* pp. 211–2.

6 Little quotes the prologue in translation (*G.F.* p. 212).

7 *Ibid.* ; another Robert of Ware was a membre of the dominican order in 1256 (*C.Cl.R.*, 1256–9, p. 112).

Robert of Winchelsey was an archbishop of Canterbury.[1] Some 'Questiones' of his remain in Oxford in Magdalen Coll. MS. 217, fos. 217 *et seq.* (14th cent.), entitled 'Questiones Roberti de Wynchelse disputate apud London. cum ibi legeret.' In the same MS. fos. 338–64 are 'Roberti questiones quodlibetales numero centum viginti': *inc.* 'Questio est utrum innascibilitas seu ingenitum precedat paternitatem ?' There was formerly in the library of the Grey Friars, London, a treatise entitled 'Winchelsei super Logicam stilo scholastico' (Leland, *Collect.* iv. 50), and formerly at Guisbro. 'Quodlibeta Winchelsey' (*ibid.* iv. 41). There were apparently other Winchelseys to whom this might be attributed. There was also a mass of official publication (T. pp. 779, 780).

According to a 14th century writer, Robert of Winchelsey studied arts at Paris and became master and chancellor there,[2] probably by 7 July 1267.[3] Then returning to England he became a master of theology at Oxford, rector of the university, and then archdeacon of Essex and resident canon at St. Paul's.[4] He attested a charter of Bishop Richard of Lincoln on 15 Apr. 1272 as rector of Wodeaton, a church which he received only that year.[5] By 1278 he was apparently a canon of Lincoln, holding the prebend of Leighton.[6] He probably became archdeacon of Essex and prebendary of Oxgate by 1283,[7] certainly before 1288,

1 T. p. 778 ; *D.N.B.* under Winchelsey. Winchelsea, Sussex.

2 *Stephani Birchingtoni Historia*, quoted in T. p. 779.

3 Denifle et Chatelain, *Cartularium Universitatis Parisiensis*, i. 468.

4 Birchington, in T. p. 779.

5 Camb. Univ. Lib. MS. Dd. x. 28, fo. 111 ; this he held until 1293 (T. p. 779) ; *Rot. R. de Gravesend*, p. 224.

6 *Rot. R. de Gravesend*, p. xxxviii ; his rights there were contested by Almaric de Montfort (*Reg. Peckham*, p. 90 ; Le Neve, *Fasti*, ii. 176).

7 G. Hennessey, *Novum Repertorium Ecclesiasticum Parochiale Londoniense*, p. 41 ; Le Neve, *op. cit.* ii. 333–4.

when he was chancellor of the university of Oxford.[1] He was a regent in theology in this year also.[2] He presided at the vesperies of John of Monmouth.[3] Probably after this he resided at London and wrote the 'questiones' given above: he was apparently conscientious in his pastoral work.[4] As early as 1277 or 1280 he was in touch with the monks of Christchurch, Canterbury,[5] who gave him gifts in 1287 and 1288.[6] Early in 1293 he was elected archbishop of Canterbury,[7] remaining in that office until his death in 1313.[8] To Christchurch he left not only valuable vestments,[9] but also a long list of books, including biblical glosses, the works of Aquinas and the church fathers, sermons, saints' lives, and Aristotle.[10]

Robert de Worsted was a disputant at Cambridge *c.* 1282 (Little-Pelster, p. 103) or *c.* 1275 (according to App. A).

Roger Bacon, O.F.M.[11] A list of his works has been drawn up by Dr. A. G. Little for the 'Compendium Studii Theologie' (B.S.F.S.), ed. Rashdall, pp. 71–118, and revised for the 'Roger Bacon Essays,' pp. 376–426.

Roger Bacon was not an unusual name and was borne by a contemporary master who apparently died in 1237–8.[1] Several autobiographical items enable us to estimate the date of his birth. In a work of 1267 he states that he had been studying for forty years, so, assuming that he commenced his study at about thirteen, the date of his birth would be 1214.[2] In 1267 his mother was still alive,[3] as well as two brothers, one wealthy and one scholarly.[4] In 1233 a Roger Bacon 'quidam clericus de curia' is reputed to have made a witty retort before the king.[5] Our man may well have been its author: he was a royalist.[6] At the instance of a certain Philip the chancellor (probably Philip de Grève, *d.* 1236) he commenced his work 'On the Accidents of Old Age and the Prolongation of Life';[7] by that time he had been 'in partibus Romanis,' but did not yet know Greek. He apparently sent it to Pope Innocent IV (1244–54).[8] By 1247 he had begun to study science[9] and had probably invented gunpowder.[10] He was

[1] *Snappe's Formulary and other Records* (Oxford Hist. Soc.), ed. H. E. Salter, p. 323; *cf. Mon. Acad.* i. 44.

[2] *Reg. Ric. de Swinfield* (C.Y.S.), ed. W. W. Capes, p. 190.

[3] Pelster, *Zeitschrift für kath. Theol.* lii (1928), 480.

[4] Birchington, in Wharton, *Anglia Sacra,* i. 12, giving the impression that Robert was chancellor before he was archdeacon of Essex.

[5] Lambeth Palace MS. 242, fos. 39, 66.

[6] 'Item pro iocalibus archidiacono Essex' datis xxiii s. (*ibid.* fo. 98*b*); 'Pro exenniis missis archid.' Essex vii s. 1d. (fo. 107).

[7] B.M. MS. Add. 6159, fos. 140, 270–1, gives an account of his election, 'date die veneris proximum post diem cinerum, sc. idus Feb.' Owing to a vacancy in the papacy he was not consecrated for more than a year, on 12 September at Aquila, despite franciscan opposition (*Ann. Monast.* iv. 518 (Worcester); Wilkins, *Concilia,* ii. 198).

[8] A good account of his career as archbishop is given by T. F. Tout in *D.N.B.*

[9] John Dart, *History and Antiquities of the Cathedral Church of Canterbury,* pp. ix, xiii.

[10] James, *A.L.C.D.* pp. 135–7; London, Lambeth palace MS. 20, fo. 186, gives a long list of gifts.

[11] T. p. 62; *D.N.B.* under Bacon; *Roger Bacon Essays,* pp. 1–31.

[1] Clerk in 1225–6 and master in 1228 (*C.P.R.,* 1225–32, pp. 3, 38, 232); dead, or resigned (?) in 1238 (*Rot. R. Grosseteste,* p. 32). Another not a master was associated also with Lincoln (P.R.O., Duchy of Lancaster, D.L. 42/2, fo. 253; Exchequer, Misc. Books, E. 164/20, fo. 33; B.M. MS. Harley 3697, fo. 64; MS. Harley 3688, fos. 162*b*, 168*b*; *Rot. H. de Welles,* iii. 112).

[2] *Fr. Rogeri Bacon Opera Inedita* (R.S.), ed. J. S. Brewer, p. 65; J. E. Sandys in *Proceedings of the British Academy,* vi. 371.

[3] *Opera Inedita,* p. 16.

[4] *Ibid.* pp. 16, 13, possibly Thomas Bacon (*Mon. Fr.* i. 349; *C.P.R.,* 1247–58, p. 235).

[5] *Chr. Maj.* iii. 245; a Roger Bacon received a gift of cloth from the king about this time (P.R.O., Chanc. Misc., C. 3/43/3).

[6] *Opera Inedita,* p. 16.

[7] Little in *Proceedings of the British Academy,* xiv. 270.

[8] *R. Bacon Essays,* p. 4; *Opera hactenus inedita Rogeri Bacon,* ed. Little and Withington, ix. pp. xxiv–xxv.

[9] *Opera Inedita* (R.S.), p. 59.

[10] *R. Bacon Essays,* pp. 321–35.

in Paris certainly before 1249[1] and in 1250,[2] and probably in Oxford in the years following.[3] He apparently withdrew from university affairs from 1256 to 1266.[4] He returned to Paris in 1257,[5] but was in England during part of the barons' wars, 1258–1265.[6] In 1263 he was writing upon a 'Compotus Naturalium.'[7] He was engaged upon his 'Opus Majus' in 1267, a work requested by the pope a few years earlier.[8] He completed his 'Compendium Philosophie' in 1271. Probably he was working upon his Greek and Hebrew grammars at this time.[9] In 1278 some of his doctrines were condemned by his ecclesiastical superiors.[10] Possibly he was kept in confinement by his order for a time.[11] His 'Compendium Studii Theologie' was completed in 1292.[12] He was apparently never a doctor in theology.[13]

Roger,[14] monk of Croyland, was the author of a revision of Elias of Evesham's compilation of four lives of St. Thomas Becket, the 'Quadrilogus.' (a) Oxford, Bodl. Lib. MSS. Ashmole 133 and 3512 (E. Mus.); (b) *ibid.* Univ. Coll. MS. 69 (13th cent.); (c) B.N. MS. lat. 5372, with salutation 'Amantissimo domino suo et patri Henrico Dei gratia abboti Croylandie suus Rogerus humilis eiusdem loci monachus'; (d) MS. formerly at Cambridge, Clare Coll. 'Roger prior Fristonie ad Henricum abbatem Croylandie de vita Thome Cantuar' (Leland, *Collect.* iii. 17). The 'Quadrilogus' was published in Migne's 'Patrologia Latina,' cxc. 259 *et seq.* The stages of compilation are given in a note at the end of the introduction:

> Facta est autem prima illa compilatio hortantibus votis pariter et cooperantibus apud Croylandiam, anno regis Ricardi ultimo, et hæc ejusdem compilationis adjectio, itidem apud Croylandiam anno regni regis Joannis quarto decimo, qui fuit annus ab incarnatione Domini juxta Dionysium, millesimus ducentesimus tertius decimus (*ibid.* col. 260).

This compilation was thus made at Croyland in 1213. In 1220 the abbot presented a copy to Archbishop Stephen Langton.[1] To judge from the title in one MS. Roger was prior of the dependant cell of Freston, Lincolnshire.[2]

Roger Ford, abbot of Glastonbury, was credited by the 1803 catalogue of the Cottonian library with the authorship of a 'Speculum Ecclesie': *inc.* 'Ecclesie materialis sive corporalis in qua convenimus.' The end has been burned (MS. Cotton, Tiberius B. xiii, fos. 186–229).

Roger of Ford, a native of Glastonbury,[3] was well educated[4] and of advanced age when he was promoted from chamberlain in the city of Glastonbury[5] to abbot. He was elected over Robert de Pederton on 4 Mar. 1252[6] and consecrated four days later by the bishop of Bath and Wells.[7] He fought the king's claim to collect his aids directly from monastic lands.[8] Probably in 1255, at the

1 He heard William of Auvergne (*Opera Inedita*, p. 74; *Op. Tert.* cap. xxiii).
2 *Opera Inedita*, p. 401.
3 Little, *F.S.O.* p. 842.
4 *R. Bacon Essays*, p. 7.
5 *Opera Inedita*, p. 7.
6 *Liber Exemplorum* (B.S.F.S.), ed. A. G. Little, p. 22.
7 *R. Bacon Essays*, p. 378.
8 *Opera Inedita*, pp. i., xv.
9 *R. Bacon Essays*, p. 20.
10 *Chronicon XXIV Generalium*, ed. Bridges, p. 31.
11 *R. Bacon Essays*, p. 27; an alchemical treatise says that Raymond Gaufridi released him from prison (*loc. cit.*).
12 *Opera Inedita*, p. lv.
13 *R. Bacon Essays*, p. 6.
14 T. p. 640; *D.N.B.* under Roger.

1 *Inqulph's Chronicle of the Abbey of Croyland*, ed. H. T. Riley, p. 317.
2 A Roger, prior of Freston, witnessed a charter of about 1158–89 (B.M. Add. Ch. 20902); Nicholas, prior of Freston, was promoted to be abbot of Eynsham in 1228 (*Ann. Monast.* iii. 109).
3 *Adam de Domerham, Historia de rebus gestis Glastoniensibus*, ed. T. Hearne, p. 523.
4 'Vir etate provectus, literature ingentis' (*ibid.*).
5 *Johannis confratris et monachi Glastoniensis Chronica*, ed. T. Hearne, p. 224, 'camerarius in villa Glaston.'
6 *Ibid.* p. 225.
7 *Ibid.* p. 225.
8 *C.Cl.R.*, 1251–3, pp. 488, 490; *Domerham*, p. 523.

instigation of the 'maior, senior, et sanior' part of the house, the bishop came on visitation and deposed him.[1] His rival was elected.[2] The king reinstated Roger,[3] and both men appealed to Rome.[4] Robert spent five years there, and Roger finally went in person.[5] The pope restored Roger to full possession in 1259.[6] Roger died suddenly at Bromley on 2 Oct. 1261 and was buried in Westminster.[7]

Roger Infans of Hereford was an astronomer.[8] Although it is possible that Roger Infans may have lived into the 13th century, his career really belongs to the 12th. His bibliography is given by C. H. Haskins (*Studies in the History of Mediaeval Science*, pp. 124–6). This may be supplemented by my article in *Isis*, xviii (1932). 14–8. To these may be added the following works:

'Compotus': (a) Madrid, Escorial MS. G. iii. 17, with a rubric 'Istud dicit Rogerus Infans Herfordiae' (S.D.Wingate, *Mediaeval Latin Versions*, p. 98); (b) MS. formerly in the library of John Dee, entitled 'Rogeri Herefordensis compotus' (M. R. James, *Lists of MSS. formerly owned by Dr. John Dee*, p. 30); (c) MS. formerly with the austin canons, York, entitled 'Compotus magistri Rogeri Herford' (M. R. James, 'Cat. of the Lib. of the Augustinian Friars at York' in *Fasciculus Ioanni Willis Clark dicatus*, p. 64).

'Astrology': (a) MS. formerly with the austin friars, York, entitled 'Excerpta introductorii R. Herfordens' (*ibid.* p. 67); (b) MS. from the same library, entitled 'Canones et theorica Rogeri Herfordensis' (*ibid.* p. 57); (c) MS. from the same library, entitled 'Iudicia astronomie magistri Rogeri Herford' (*ibid.* p. 64); (d) MS. formerly at Peterhouse, entitled 'Introductorium magistri R. Herfordensis in artem iudiciariam astrorum' (Leland, *Collect.* iv. 23).

For Roger's life see the *Isis*, xviii. 14–8. He may have been at Bologna.[1]

Roger of Insula was a necromancer and poet. In writing of the death of Simon de Montfort in 1219 Matthew Paris said:

> Erant autem ante obsidionem quidam clerici geomantici, qui mortem comitis praedixerant; quorum unus, natione Anglicus, magister scilicet Rogerus de Insula, hoc de ipso composuit epitaphium.
>
> 'Dantur item fato, casuque cadunt iterato,
> Symone sublato, Mars, Paris, atque Cato.'
>
> (*M. Parisiensis, Hist. Angl.* (R.S.), ed. F. Madden, ii. 240; *Chr. Maj.* iii. 57.)

This would hardly apply to Master Roger de Insula, who was chancellor of Lincoln following William de Monte [q.v.], preceding Richard Grant [q.v.] and who was later dean of York, 1220–35.[2]

Roger of Lacock was a canon of Lincoln and author of a 'Medical Recipe.'[3] B.M. MS. Reg. 12, B. xii, fo. 171, with a marginal note 's m R de Lacoc' [secundum magistrum R. de Lacoc]. The author is probably the Master Roger of Lacock, 'medici,' at whose instance the king of England pardoned a forest transgression in 1224.[4] A canon of Lincoln in 1220, he already outranked several other canons, although only a subdeacon, and therefore of the lowest rank of canons.[5] From 1220 until 1228 he fre-

[1] *Johannis Glaston. Chron.* pp. 228, 229; *Ann. Monast.* i. 156; *Chr. Maj.* v. 534.

[2] *Johannis Glaston, Chron.* p. 230.

[3] *Ibid.* p. 230.

[4] *Ibid.* p. 231.

[5] *Ibid.* p. 232.

[6] *Ibid.* p. 233.

[7] *Domerham*, p. 524.

[8] T. pp. 194, 641, 788; *D.N.B.* under Compotista, Roger Infans and Roger Hereford.

[1] The obituary of St. Saviour's at Bologna has an obit for the parents of 'Mr. R. de Hereford' and another for 'Mr. Roger Anglicus' (*Dublin Review*, cxii, 1893. 79).

[2] *Reg. Walter de Grey, passim*; he appears once as chancellor of Lincoln under dean Hamo (1214–20) (*ibid.* p. 133).

[3] *Annals of Medical History*, N.S. vii (1935). 327–8. Lacock, Wiltshire.

[4] *Rot. Litt. Claus.* i. 580; he must be distinguished from a contemporary Master Ralph of Lacock (*C.P.R.*, 1225–32, p. 356; *ibid.*, 1232–47, pp. 270–8).

[5] *Rot. H. de Welles*, iii. 162; Bodl. Lib. MS. Laud 642, fo. 4*b*. There he has probably been canon for some years before 1220. For arrangement by rank and seniority see *Rot. H. de Welles*, introd.

quently witnessed charters of Bishop Hugh of Welles.[1] In 1227 the bishop granted him the church of Hale.[2] As its parson he ran into difficulty with 46 persons all named in a letter patent of 23 Aug. 1229.[3]

Roger was the recipient of numerous royal favours, probably for his skill as a physician. On 3 Aug. 1223 he was granted eight 'furchias' from a royal forest.[4] On 11 July 1228 the king gave him a prebend in the collegiate church of Bridgnorth, Salop.[5] On 4 Oct. 1229 the king gave him the church of Washingborough,[6] but he was apparently admitted only in 1233.[7] In the summer of 1229 he was to have three oaks in Malkesham 'ad se hospitandum ad Lacoc,' in the next autumn two deer from Sherwood forest, and the same a year later from the forests of Rockingham and Chippenham.[8] On 21 July 1233 the king granted Roger's prebend at Bridgnorth to another,[9] and another presentation to Washingborough is recorded of about the same time.[10] His career was thus probably connected closely with Lincoln from 1220 to 1228 and with the king or Bridgnorth from 1228 to 1233.

Roger of Marston, O.F.M., was the author of some scholastic questions. (See Little-Pelster, pp. 93–5, and App. A.)

Roger Norton, abbot of St. Albans,[11] was the author of two or more works no longer known to be extant. Leland saw at Wymondham:

> Computus Rogeri, abbatis S. Albani, viri in Mathesi peritissimi, cujus opus est Horologium insigne quidam illud in coenobio Albanensi. *Assiduis petitionibus* (*Collect.* iv. 27).

He seems also to have written a 'Liber de Suis Laboribus,' described by H. T. Riley in 'Gesta Abbatum Monasterii Sancti Albani' (R.S.), i. 483:

> Cætera magnifice gesta per Dominum Rogerum Abbatem, nonne hæc scripta sunt in Libro de suis laboribus intitulato? Ibi profecto plene videre lector poterit quantas angarias, quot vexationes, toleraverit pro ecclesiæ sui jure; præter expensas quas fudit ad contuendam ecclesiam suam; quæ quemlibet poterant depressisse, etiam prædivitem, si cuilibet contigissent.

A summary of this volume is probably given in the 'Gesta Abbatum' (p. 480) after a brief mention of a transaction:

> ut habetur plenius in Libro de actibus ejusdem Abbatis specialiter confecto.

Among the books which Roger gave to the St. Albans library was a volume of his sermons written in his own hand.

> Armariolo quoque duo paria Decretalium; Summas etiam Reymundi, Gaufridi, et Bernardi, super Decretales; ac unum librum in quo continentur Seneca et sermones sui, manu propria conscripti, cum multis aliis libris et libellis, contulit devote (*ibid.* p. 483).

Roger of Norton was a monk of St. Albans [1] and probably not very old when he was chosen abbot in 1260.[2] His later career was that of a proud and busy abbot for thirty years. He was probably the recipient of long series of interesting letters from 'R. de A.' (or H.), custodian of Tynemouth, to 'R, abbot of St. Albans.'[3] He visited Tynemouth and Belvoir in 1278.[4] Most of his

1 *Ibid.* ii. 197 (2), 200 (2), 202–6, 210 (2), 213–6, 221, 222, 226; B.M. MS. Reg. 11, B. ix, fo. 30*b*; *Boarstall Cartulary* (Oxford Hist. Soc.), ed. H. E. Salter, p. 7; *Sarum Chs. and Docs.* p. 122; Camb. Univ. Lib. MS. Add. 3020, fos. 72, 73; *Ancient Deeds*, ii. 240 (B. 1877).

2 *Rot. H. de Welles*, iii. 162.

3 *C.P.R.*, 1225–32, p. 303.

4 *Rot. Litt. Claus.* i. 557.

5 *C.Cl.R.*, 1227–31, p. 61.

6 *C.P.R.*, 1225–32, p. 271.

7 *Rot. H. de Welles*, iii. 171.

8 *C.Cl.R.*, 1227–31, pp. 187, 459; *ibid.*, 1231–4, p. 2.

9 *C.P.R.*, 1232–47, p. 21.

10 *Rot. H. de Welles*, iii. 207.

11 T. p. 550.

1 *Gesta Abbatum*, i. 399; P.R.O., papal bulls 33 (1).

2 The writer said of him when he died in 1290, 'Cum autem Abbas memoratus, licet non plenus dierum' (*Gesta Abbatum*, i. 483). His election was confirmed by the pope on 9 Sept. 1263 (*Registres d'Urbain IV*, ii. 191).

3 Bodl. Lib. MS. Digby 20, fos. 105–42*b*.

4 *Gesta Abbatum*, i. 436.

time was probably devoted to legal and financial matters.[1]

Roger of Salisbury was a canon of Salisbury, bishop of Bath and Wells and theologian.[2] He wrote apparently an 'Explicatio Vocum' which accompanied Simon of Tournai's 'Sententiarium Breviarium.' (a) Dublin, Trinity Coll. MS. 275; (b) MS. formerly at Peterborough, MS. U. v, 'Uerborum significationes super librum sententiarum sec. Mag. Rog. Salisburiensem' (M. R. James, *Peterborough*, p. 45). He also wrote a 'Super Psalterium,' which was formerly at Newnham near Bedford (Leland, *Collect.* iv. 12): *inc*. 'Nos debemus esse viri non effeminati.' 'Sermons.' (a) B.M. MS. Arundel 231, fo. 12, with a colophon 'Explicit tabula omeliarum magistri Johannis de Abbatisvilla, magistri Odonis de Cantia et Magistri Rogeri de Sarisbir'; (b) 'Rogerus de Sarisburia, et Odo de Cantia scripserunt morales expositiones super evangelia dominicalia. li. plures. Ex officina Roberti Stoughton' (Bale, *Index*, p. 403); (c) 'Sermones de dominicis diebus': *inc.* 'Dicit Ecclesiasticus verbum dulce' (T. p. 641; saying that the MS. was formerly at Lanthony, then with Henry Parry).

Roger of Salisbury [3] may have been named Roger Parvus.[4] If he heard Simon of Tournai he must have been at Paris before 1201.[5] The association of his sermons with those of Odo of Cheriton and John of Abbeville also show him to have been at Paris, possibly in the years before 1220.[1] On 1 Oct. 1207 a Roger of Salisbury, probably not yet a master, appeared as clerk in a charter of Bishop John of Norwich.[2] He next appears at Salisbury, probably as Master Roger Theologus appointed by the pope on 3 July 1223 to examine the acts of 'S., prior of Worcester.'[3] He attended a chapter meeting at Salisbury in 1224[4] and was present at the first convocation in the new cathedral in 1225.[5] He was a resident canon at the time, reading theology, and holder of the prebend of Netheravon.[6] His predecessor in the precentorship appears in documents of 1224 and 1225,[7] but had been succeeded by Roger by 1228.[8] In 1234 Roger received a royal letter of protection without term.[9] He witnessed charters in 1236 and 1239.[10] In 1244 he was elected bishop of Bath and Wells, but held the office only three years.[11]

Roger of Wendover, monk of St. Albans, was an historian.[12] His work entitled 'Flores Historiarum' is in (a) B.M. MS. Cotton, Otho B. 5 (14th cent.); and (b) Bodl. Lib. MS. Douce 207 (13th cent.), with a colophon at 1235 'Huc usque scripsit cronica dominus Rogerus de Wendovre.' The chronicle was edited by H. G. Hewlett as 'Rogeri de Wendoveri Flores Historiarum' (R.S.).

[1] *Gesta Abbatum*, i. 399–485; he was buried near the altar of the Virgin Mary (B.M. MS. Harley 3775, fo. 130).

[2] T. p. 641.

[3] His name is thus given in *C.P.R.*, 1232–47, p. 56, and *Ann. Monast.* iv. 436 (Worcester).

[4] 'Magister Roger Parvus, canonicus Sarisburiensis' (*Ann. Monast.* iii. 164); a 'Mr. Roger Monoculus,' penitentiary of Salisbury, received the confession of a clerk who had had a vision of Judgment (*Catalogue of Romances*, ed. H. D. W. Ward, ii. 651; *Thesaurus Exemplorum*, ed. J. T. Walter, v. 74).

[5] *M.G.H.SS.* xxviii. 116; Matthew Paris under 1201 (*Chr. Maj.* ii. 476).

[1] See Odo of Cheriton above.

[2] At 'Torp, kal. Octobr. pont. nostr. VIII' (P.R.O., Duchy of Lancaster, D.L. 42/5, fo. 90*b*).

[3] Called a canon of Salisbury (*C.E.P.R.* i. 92; Pressutti, ii. 144).

[4] *Register of St. Osmund* (R.S.), ed. W. H. R. Jones, ii. 22.

[5] *Ibid.* p. 38.

[6] *Ibid.* pp. 41, 72.

[7] *Ibid.* pp. 22, 38.

[8] *Ibid.* ii. 107; R. C. Hoare, *History of Modern Wiltshire*, vi. 728.

[9] *C.P.R.*, 1232–47, p. 56.

[10] Hoare, *op. cit.* p. 731; B.M. MS. Egerton 3031, fo. 111.

[11] On his election, J. A. C. Vincent, *The First Bishop of Bath and Wells*, and on his episcopate, C. M. Church, 'Roger of Salisbury, first bishop of Bath and Wells, 1244–1247' in *Archaeologia*, lii (1890).

[12] T. p. 757; *D.N.B.* under Wendover; C. Jenkins, *Monastic Chronicler* (S.P.C.K.), pp. 42–60.

Excerpts are printed (*M.G.H.SS.* xxviii. 3–73).

Roger of Wendover was possibly precentor of St. Albans [1] and certainly a priest,[2] prior of Belvoir, a cell of St. Albans. His predecessors were Simon and Ralph Simple : the former is said to have died on 4 Feb. 1204 [3] and the latter on 5 Oct. 1217.[4] However, the latter had probably retired before his death, since the obituary does not give him that title. Wendover was visited and deposed by Abbot William of Trumpington, because he dissipated the property of the house ' in prodigalite incircumspecta.' [5] The time of the visitation is given as ' tempore guerre,' which must refer to the war with Prince Louis of France, 1215–8, since this has just been mentioned.[6] He may have been the prior who was a papal delegate in 1217.[7] Wendover must have spent much of the remainder of his life upon his chronicle, for which he was held in great respect.[8] He died on 6 May 1236.[9]

S. Fokes was the author of a sermon in Bodl. Lib. MS. Laud Misc. 511, fos. 133 *et seq.*, with a note on the edge of the MS. ' S. Fokes.'

Since his sermon appears in a volume in which sermons by Richard Fishacre [q.v.] and Simon of Henton [q.v.] occupy prominent positions, he was probably an Oxford dominican of about 1250.[10] He might, of course, be identical with Simon.

[1] Jenkins, *op. cit.* p. 42.

[2] *Chr. Maj.* vi. 274.

[3] Dugdale, *Monasticon*, iii. 287.

[4] ' Radulphys Simple archidiaconus, sacerdos ' (*Chr. Maj.* vi. 270).

[5] *Gesta Abbatum S. Albani* (R.S.), ed. H. T. Riley, i. 270, 274.

[6] Hewlett suggests that this refers to some later war (*Flores Hist.* iii. ix.).

[7] B.M. MS. Harley ch. 45, A. 25.

[8] Especially by a later historian, Walsingham (*Gesta Abbatum*, ii. 303).

[9] *Chr. Maj.* vi. 274.

[10] The Fokes family appears in two cartularies, at least (*Cal. of Charters relating to Selborne*, ed. W. D. Macray, p. 65 ; Holy Trinity, Aldgate, Guild Hall transcript MS. 122, p. 438 (William Fokes).

Samuel Presbyter was an excerpter.[1] His works include ' Collections from William de Montibus ' : Bodl. Lib. MS. Bodley 860, fos. 1–208*b*, with a note ' Hec collecta sunt ex diversis auditis in scola magistri Willelmi de Montibus,' and at the end ' Expliciunt collecta Samuelis presbiteri.' ' Liber monachorum sci Edmundi in quo continentur Postille seu collecta super psalterium in scolis magistri W. de Montibus.' This work is mentioned by G. Lacombe (*New Scholasticism*, v, 1931. 141).

' Collections from Gregory the Great ' : *inc.* ' Illius tractatus ex quo.' Cambridge, Pembroke Coll. MS. 115, all 77 fos., with a rubric ' Collecta Samuelis presbyteri ex speculo b. Gregorii.'

This Samuel Priest (rather than priest) had studied under William de Monte [q.v.] probably at either Paris or Lincoln. The rarity of the name Samuel together with the existence of the MS. at Bury St. Edmunds makes it seem probable that he was the Master Samuel apparently a clerk of John, bishop of Norwich (1200–14),[2] Master Samuel, dean of Reppes,[3] or Master Samuel of Ginningam,[4] all of whom appear in East Anglia about the time that a student of William de Monte should appear, and who may be one, two, or three persons.

Simon, monk of Abingdon, wrote a short ' Chronicle of Abingdon ' : *inc.* ' In principio erat verbum.' B.M. MS. Vitellius A. xiii, fos. 83–7*b* (early 13th cent.), with the heading ' Exceptiones de primis fundamentis Abbendonie, de abbatibus Abbendonie, que vel bona queve mala fecerunt.' The ancient heading now shrunk by fire is almost illegible.

[1] T. p. 651.

[2] Bodl. Lib. MS. ch. Norfolk, a. 6, no. 615, with Master R. de Gloucester, who was a clerk of the second John, bishop of Norwich (*Newington Longeville Charters*, ed. H. E. Salter, p. 93).

[3] Camb. Univ. Lib. MS. Mm. i. 20, fos. 31, 38*b*, 39*b*, 40 ; B.M. MS. Cotton, Galba E. ii, fo. 82. The place is probably Repps, Norfolk.

[4] Camb. Univ. Lib. MS. Mm. i. 20, fo. 52. Probably Gillingham, Norfolk.

It is given as above by T. Smith in the Cotton catalogue of 1696 (p. 83).

The account is continued into the régime of Abbot Hugh (1190 ?–1221). Simon writes of him 'Iste in principio valde modestus et liberalissimus et benignissimus erat.' Part of the account is erased: it is probably not so favourable. The chronicle continues probably in the same hand, but with another pen, about the deeds of Prior William of Colne. Probably this prior is the William who succeeded Hugh as abbot.[1] Simon apparently wrote his account near the end of the incumbency of Hugh.

Simon of Caermarthen was an augustinian friar who wrote two Anglo-Norman pieces,[2] 'Par le Priere de un Men Compagnon' and 'On Penitence,' both in Bodl. Lib. MS. Selden supra 74, fos. 31*b*, 33 (13th cent.), (Madden and Craster, *Summary Cat. of Western MSS.*, ii, pt. 1, p. 643), and both edited by Stengel in 'Zeitschrift für französische Sprache und Literatur,' xiv (1892). 147–51. In the first piece occur the lines:

Frere Simun de Kernerthun
Profés en l'ordre de seint Augstin.

He was thus probably a canon of the austin house of St. John the Baptist of Caermarthen.

Simon of Faversham,[3] chancellor of Oxford, was a theologian and author of a series of commentaries. The most comprehensive study of his works is by M. Grabmann ('Die Aristoteleskommentare des Simon de Faversham' in *Sitzungsberichte der Bay. Akad. der Wiss.*, pt. iii, 1923). He shows that Simon wrote, or there remain, reports of commentaries upon the six books of logic by Aristotle (more than one upon several of them), and upon the 'Summule Logicales' of Petrus Hispanus and Porphirius. He also commented upon the 'Ethics,' 'Physics,' 'Meteorology,' 'Metaphysics,' 'De Anima,' and the 'Parva Naturalia.'

1 Dugdale, *Monasticon*, i. 508.
2 Vising, pp. 56, 58.
3 T. p. 673; *D.N.B.* under Simon.

The life of Simon of Faversham has been the subject of study of two distinguished scholars,[1] but a little may still be added. On 24 Sept. 1289 a Master Simon de Faversham was presented to the church of Preston near Faversham and ordained subdeacon at about the same time.[2] A year later two Simons of Faversham were given holy orders: the first, a rector, the deaconate and the second a subdeaconate.[3] One or the other was certainly our scholar; at the same time Robert de Clothale became a priest. He was author of a report of Simon's commentary upon the 'Physics.'[4] This coincidence is a clue to Simon's age: he was probably Robert's scholastic superior and Robert was a mature man. Simon disputed as a master upon the 'Posterior Analytics' at Paris[5] and is recorded as one of the outstanding Parisian masters of the period.[6]

Simon of Faversham seems to have had difficulty with his chief ecclesiastical preferments, the rectory of Harrow and the archdeaconry of Canterbury. Probably just before his death Archbishop John Peckham conferred Harrow upon Ralph de Cnoville.[7] Then probably Edward I conferred the same church upon Faversham during the vacancy following Peckham's death.[8] There was

1 F. M. Powicke, 'Master Simon of Faversham,' *Mélanges d'histoire du moyen age offerts a M. Ferdinand Lot*, pp. 650–8; Little-Pelster, pp. 262–5.
2 *Reg. Peckham* (C.Y.S.), p. 91; (R.S.), p. 1011.
3 *Reg. Peckham* (R.S.), pp. 1051, 1053.
4 Erfurt, Amplon. MS. Fol. 348, fo. 69; Oxford, Merton Coll. fo. 240, with the colophon 'Expl. questiones disputate a mag. Symone de Faverisham super lib. phis. reportate a Roberto de Clothale.'
5 Vienna, Nat. Lib. MS. lat. 2302, fo. 23, with the colophon 'Expliciunt questiones super libro posteriorum disputate a magistro Symone Anglico Parysius.'
6 B. M Xiberta, *De Scriptoribus Scholasticis Saeculi XIV ex ordine Carmelitarum*, p. 121.
7 Cnoville alleged Peckham's presentation: the date is a conjecture based upon other items (*Reg. Winchelsey*, pp. 294–5).
8 The year books say that the church was in the gift of King Henry, an obvious mistake (*Year Books*,

still a dispute about it in 1298, apparently settled by Cnoville's death.[1] On 22 Sept. 1305 Simon was appointed archdeacon of Canterbury, but was forced to retire before a papal nominee.[2] He had been in contact with the monks of Christchurch, Canterbury, as early as 1299.[3] Simon also held Bishop's Hampton in 1303,[4] Reculver in 1305 or 1307,[5] and Birton at an unknown date.[6] Although he finished an edition of his commentary upon the 'De Anima' as late as 1304,[7] he was studying theology at Oxford after 1300.[8] He served as chancellor of Oxford from about 13 Jan. 1304 to his resignation on 14 Feb. 1306.[9] On 24 May he had permission by letters patent to go to the pope,[10] and by 19 July the latter wrote of Simon's death.[11] He had become a doctor of theology : the date is not certain.[12]

Simon du Fresne, canon of Hereford, was an Anglo-Norman and Latin poet.[13] He wrote two long Anglo-Norman poems, 'Le Roman de Philosophie.' (a) Cheltenham MS. 8336, fos. 107–16 (early 14th cent.) ; (b) B.M. MS. Reg. 20, B. xiv, fos. 68*b*–77*b* (13th–14th cent.) ; (c) Bodl. Lib. MS. Douce 210, fos. 51*b*–9*b* (late 13th cent.). The name 'Simund de Frejne me fist' is given in an acrostic. The poem has been edited by John E. Matzke in 'Œuvres de Simund de Freine' (Soc. des Anciens Textes Français), pp. 1–60. 'La Vie de Saint Georges' in B.N. MS. fr. 902, fos. 108*b*–117*b* (late 13th cent.). Another acrostic reads 'Simund de Freine me fist.' This poem is also edited by Matzke (*op. cit.* pp. 61–117).

Simon also wrote some Latin poems to Gerald of Wales [q.v.]. (1) *Inc.* 'Fons sine fine fluens, flos cleri, gemma sophie.' (a) London, Lambeth Palace MS. 236, fo. 166 ; (b) Cambridge, Corpus Christi Coll. MS. 400, fo. 119 (13th cent.) ; (c) MS. formerly 'ex museo Radulphi Radcliff' (Bale, *Index*, p. 412). The title of (a) is 'Carmen magistri Symonis de Fraxino Herefordensis canonici magistro Giraldo transmissum.' It is edited by Matzke (*op. cit.* pp. vii–viii) and given in 'Giraldus Cambrensis, Opera' (R.S.), i. 382–5. (2) *Inc.* 'Magistrorum omnium flos archilevita.' (a) Lambeth MS. 236, fo. 166*b* ; (b) MS. formerly 'ex speculo ecclesie Geraldi' (Bale, *Index*, p. 412). The Lambeth MS. bears a note :

> Magistri Simonis de Fraxino canonici Herefordensis pro amico leso tam metrica quam ridmica facta conquestio et tanquam candelis cordis accensis promulgata palam excommunicatio.

Bale's notice runs :

> Simon de Fraxino, canonicus Herefordensis, scripsit pro amico Giraldo Cambrensi, convicijs leso, aduersus Adamum abbatem Dorensem, rhithmos quosdam.

It is edited by Matzke (*op. cit.* p. viii) and in 'Giraldus Cambrensis, Opera,' i. 385. (3) *Inc.* 'Nescio quis monachus furtivo ledere morsu.' MS. formerly 'ex speculo Giraldi Cambrensis' (Bale, *Index*, p. 412), edited in 'Giraldus Cambrensis, Opera,' i. 386.

This canon of Hereford was, according

7 *Edw. II*, Selden Soc., ed. W. C. Bolland, p. 65). The important fact in the minds of the crown lawyers was that the king had made a presentation in time of a vacancy in the archbishopric : the name of the king was incidental. Professor Bertha Putnam tells me that such mistakes were common.

[1] Professor Sweet assures me that there were many double presentations of this nature. Cnoville died shortly after this. For another interpretation see Little-Pelster, p. 263.

[2] Le Neve, *Fasti*, i. 39.

[3] 'Datum nuntii [*sic*] ad magistrum Sim. de Fafvesham per sup. vi. d.' (Lambeth Palace MS. 242, fo. 202).

[4] *Reg. Ricardi de Swinfield* (C.Y.S.), ed. W. W. Capes, p. 91, called rector of Harrow.

[5] *Foedera*, i. 975 ; *C.Cl.R.*, 1302–7, p. 434 ; *C.E.P.R.* ii. 336.

[6] Bale, *Index*, p. 411 ; Little thinks that this may be a mistake for Preston (Little-Pelster, p. 262).

[7] Leipsic Univ. Lib. MS. lat. 1359, fo. 77*b*, 'Expliciunt dicta Symonis super librum de anima scripta anno Domini MCCCIIII (Grabmann, *op. cit.*).

[8] Little-Pelster, p. 236.

[9] *E.H.R.* xxvi (1911). 512.

[10] *C.P.R.*, 1301–7, p. 435.

[11] *C.E.P.R.* ii. 22.

[12] *C.Cl.R.*, 1302–7, p. 434.

[13] T. p. 52 ; *D.N.B.* under Simon.

to the poem and to Hereford documents, a resident at that episcopal city at the turn of the century.[1] He appears in a document with Hugh, dean of Hereford, and William, treasurer: thus probably during the years 1183–94.[2] He attests a charter of Bishop William de Vere, 1186–99,[3] a convention between William the treasurer and the chapter, *c.* 1200,[4] and a charter of 'H., abbot of Salop' (1223–44 ?).[5] If the information given by Bale that Gerald's enemy was Adam, abbot of Dore [q.v.], is correct, this exchange was probably of the early years of the 13th century. By the time of Thomas, abbot of Gloucester (1224–8), a document of Bishop Hugh of Hereford informs us that Simon's living of . . . Sutton was in the hands of a certain Bernard.[6]

Simon de Gand was bishop of Salisbury and a professor.[7] Various pieces are attributed to him. He apparently translated the English version of the 'Ancren Riwle' into Latin: *inc.* 'Recti diligunt te.' (a) B.M. MS. Cotton, Nero A. xiv; (b) *ibid.* MS. Vitellius E. vii; (c) Oxford, Magdalen Coll. MS. 67, fos. 1-95 (14th cent.). 'Hic incipit prohemium venerabilis patris magistri Simonis de Gandavo episcopi Sarum in librum de vita solitaria quem scripsit sororibus suis anachoritis apud Tarente.' A 'Sermon' of his as chancellor of Oxford remains. (a) Oxford, New Coll. MS. 92, fo. 94–5*b*; and (b) Worcester cathedral MS. Q. 46, fos. 272–4*b* (edited by Little-Pelster, pp. 205–215). He is also said to have written a 'Meditatio de Statu Prelati': *inc.* 'Solus aliquotiens sedens et.' (a) B.M. MS. Reg. 5, C. iii; (b) Bodl. Lib. MS. Laud Misc. 402, fos. 44*b*–55*b*. As bishop he was responsible for various statutes and letters (Oxford, Balliol Coll. MS. 199, fo. 217*b* (T. p. 307)). For his disputations see Little-Pelster, pp. 104, 117, 120, 121, 128.

Simon was apparently born at London,[1] possibly of a family derived from Ghent. His father, Simon de Gand, the elder, came to the Guildhall, London, on 13 Dec. 1279 and acknowledged himself bound to Simon de Gand, his son, a clerk, in the sum of forty pounds.[2] The latter had been commended to the rectory of Wilford on 13 May 1268 by Archbishop Walter Giffard, but he was not in residence.[3] A master, he received a three years' leave of absence on 5 Aug. 1280.[4] He held Wilford until he became bishop of Salisbury.[5] He was granted a tenement in the bishop's close at Salisbury, while he was called only a clerk.[6] He doubtless attended Oxford. He became archdeacon of Oxford in 1284,[7] and figures in a deed in the succeeding year.[8] He was proposed as an arbiter between the bishops of Hereford and St. Asaph's in a document of 27 Aug. 1288.[9] He heard of and probably testified to a miracle wrought by St. Thomas Cantilupe on 3 Aug. 1290.[10] He was elected chancellor of the university on 17 Dec. 1291 [11] and was

[1] *Cf. Isis*, xviii (1932). 19–20, indicating a school at Hereford.

[2] *Landboc Monasterii de Winchelcumba*, ed. D. Royce, ii. 262.

[3] B.M. MS. Arundel 19, fo. 31.

[4] According to the editor, W. W. Capes (*Charters of Hereford Cathedral*, p. 38).

[5] Oxford, Balliol Coll. MS. 271, fo. 54; this may be a charter of an abbot H. of the 12th century. The list of abbots seems incomplete (Dugdale, *Monasticon*, iii. 514).

[6] Balliol Coll. MS. 271, fo. 70*b*. His obit was 15 July (Gough, *Hist. and Antiquities of Hereford*, p. (17)).

[7] T. p. 307; *D.N.B.* under Ghent; Little-Pelster, pp. 79–81.

[1] T. p. 307, citing *Hist. Roff.*; *Flores Historiarum* (R.S.), ed. Luard, iii. 103.

[2] *Cal. of Letter Books of the City of London*, i. 29.

[3] *Reg. Walter Giffard*, pp. 88, 240.

[4] *Reg. William Wickwane* (Surtees Soc.), p. 69.

[5] *Reg. H. Newark* (Surtees Soc.), pp. 232, 233.

[6] H.M.C., various collections, i. 346.

[7] T. p. 307, citing *Reg. Peckham.*

[8] *Oxford Deeds of Balliol College* (Oxford Hist. Soc.), ed. H. E. Salter, p. 11.

[9] *Reg. Ric. de Swinfield* (C.Y.S.), ed. W. W. Capes, p. 190.

[10] *Acta Sanctorum*, October, i. 673.

[11] B.M. MS. Harley 6951, fo. 28; *Snappe's Formulary* (Oxford Hist. Soc.), ed. H. E. Salter, pp. 47, 50, 324.

confirmed in this position by Bishop Sutton.[1] He apparently held this until 1293.[2] In 1295 he was made a canon of Salisbury, and became successively dean [3] and bishop in 1297. He died in 1315.[4]

Simon of Henton, O.P., was a theologian.[5] Sisto da Siena wrote of him :

> Simon Anglus, ordin. Predicatorum, postillam collegit super Prophetas quatuor, minores et super libros Maccabeorum, in proverbia Salominis, et in prefationes Biblicas D. Hieronymi (*Bibliothece Sancte*, p. 299).

Sisto was an Italian dominican who knew his order's libraries in northern Italy. From him apparently this information entered bibliographical tradition. One of the works can be identified : 'Postille Morales in Prophetas Minores,' in Oxford, New Coll. MS. 45. The *incipits* for the books are as follows :—*Hosea*, 'Fundamentum primum jaspis' (fos. 1–23*b*) ; *Joel*, 'Ebrietas hic interpretari potest' (fos. 23*b*–30*b*) ; *Amos*, 'Tertium Calcedonius sicut' (fos. 30*b*–50*b*) ; *Obadiah*, 'Fundamentum quartum Smaragdus' (fos. 50*b*–54) ; *Jonah*, 'Quintum fundamentum Sardonix' (fos. 54*b*–62) ; *Micah*, 'Sextum fundamentum dicitur Sardius' (fos. 62–83) ; *Nahum*, 'Septimum Crisolitus' (fos. 83–93*b*) ; *Habakkuk*, 'Octavum Berillus' (fos. 93*b*–119) ; *Zephaniah*, 'Nonum Topacius dictum est' (fos. 119–136*b*) ; *Haggai*, 'Decimum Crysopasus Apoc' (fos. 136*b*–150) ; *Zechariah*, 'Un decimum Jacinthus' (fos. 150–211) ; *Malachi*, 'Ametistus duodecimum' (fos. 211–233). Individually several postills are attributed to Simon de Henton, and on fo. 233 is the statement 'Expliciunt postille super parvos prophetas secundum Symonem de Hentona.' Simon probably also wrote the postill on 'Job,' formerly at St. Paul's, London (Leland, *Collect.* iv. 47), 'Usque in tempus sustinebit patiens' (Bale, *Index*, p. 413). He also wrote another series which may possibly have been called collectively his 'Summa,' extracts of which remain in Cambridge, Sidney Sussex Coll. MS. 73, fos. 5*b et seq.* (13th–14th cent.), entitled 'Exceptiones a summa fratris Simonis de Heynton de ordine predicatorum.' Dugdale gives as a group :

> MSS. Tractatus de articulis fidei, de sacrementis, de beatitudinibus, de petitionibus, de virtutibus et viciis. Tractatus fratris Simonis de Henton super eodem (*Hist. of St. Paul's*, App. p. 66).

'De Decem Preceptos' : *inc.* 'Non habebis deos alienos coram me' (Bale, *Index*, p. 412, seen at St. Paul's). 'De Articulis Fidei' : *inc.* 'Primus articulus, quantum ad divinitatem deus' (Bale, *Index*, p. 413). The 'Tractatus de Cruce Christi' was formerly at Peterborough, entitled 'Tractatus Symonis de Henton de cruce Christi' (James, *Peterborough*, p. 65). 'Questiones' : *inc.* 'Cum gentes que legem non habent naturaliter.' (a) B.M. MS. Reg. 9, E. xiv, fos. 117*b*–33 (13th cent.) ; (b) formerly at Ramsey, entitled 'Questiones fratris Symonis de Hentone de peccato originali cum aliis' (*Chron. Abbat. Rameseiensis*, R.S., ed. W. D. Macray, p. 363). The 'Compilationes' were formerly at Christchurch, Canterbury, entitled 'Compilaciones fratris Simon de Hentun' (James, *A.L.C.D.* p. 71).

That Simon of Henton had a number of books is indicated by a note in Bodl. Lib. MS. Laud Misc. 511, fo. 72*b* (13th cent.), 'De libro nigro minori fratris S. de Henton.' This refers to a sermon : *inc.* 'Hec est voluntas Dei sanctificatio vestra.' Possibly the 'Compilationes' mentioned above was another.

Of Simon's career before he entered the dominican order nothing is known unless he is that Simon, rector of Henton, whose activity is recorded in a Godstowe cartulary.[1]

1 T. p. 307, citing *Reg. Sutton* ; P.R.O., Exchequer, ancient deeds, E. 132/18, has a letter of Bishop Sutton about Ela Longespee's gift to Oxford, mentioning Simon as chancellor of 1293 ; T. p. 307, citing *Reg. Winchelsey*, fo. 169.

2 *E.H.R.* xxvi (1911). 501, 505–7, 512.

3 *Sarum Chs. and Docs.* p. 367.

4 *Cf. D.N.B.*

5 T. p. 397 ; Pelster in *Bodleian Quarterly Record*, vi (1930). 171.

1 P.R.O., Exchequer, Misc. Books, E. 164/20, fos. 17, 27, 38, 62, 132*b*. A Simon of Henton and

He is alleged to have probably followed Richard Fishacre as lector for the Oxford house.[1] He probably wrote his 'Questiones' before michaelmas 1239.[2] He seems to have been prior provincial of the English dominicans from 1254 until 1261.[3] In 1255 the king desired him to appoint in the provincial chapter friars to preach the crusade in the several dioceses.[4] On 22 Jan. 1256 the pope appointed him with Fr. Adam Marsh [q.v.] and the bishop of Worcester to inquire into the life of Richard Wich [q.v.].[5] In 1261 he was punished very severely by the general chapter, which absolved him from his position, assigning him to the German province to teach at Cologne or elsewhere, did not allow him to return to England without permission, and imposed a heavy penance.[6] In 1262 he received permission to return to England.[7] His offence was that he violated an ordinance concerning foreign friars at Oxford. A contemporary states that he was a man venerable in religion and eminent in learning.[8]

his wife Isabella appear in an Oxford fine of 3 Feb. 1258 (*Feet of Fines for Oxfordshire*, Oxford Hist. Soc., ed. H. E. Salter, p. 225).

[1] Pelster, *op. cit.*

[2] G. Lacombe notes a document of 23 Hen. III on margin of MS. Reg. 9, E. xiv, fo. 34, about a transaction before michaelmas 23 Hen. III (*Mélanges Mandonnet*, ii. 165).

[3] *Acta Capitulorum Generalium ord. Praed.*, ed. B. M. Reichert, i. 71, 110; Little in *E.H.R.*, viii (1893). 520.

[4] *C.P.R.*, 1247–58, p. 440; *Archaeol. Journal*, xxxv (1878). 136.

[5] *Archaeol. Journal*, xxxv. 136.

[6] 'Absolvimus priorem provincialem Anglie et assignamus eum provincie Theutonie ut legat Colonie vel alibi ubi videbitur priori provinciali expedire nec volumus quod ad provinciam Anglie revocetur sine licentia capituli generalis et iniungimus ei vii dies in pane et aqua et vii disciplinas et vii missas' (*Acta Capitulorum*, p. 110).

[7] *Ibid.* p. 117.

[8] Ralph Bocking in *Acta Sanctorum*, April, i. 300; 'Hoc autem exemplum scripserat in libro suo quidam frater noster qui de fratre Symone de Heynton materiam (?) [math'm, MS] audierat; unde et exemplum habuerat ab aliquo vel ab aliquibus qui de illo certi erant' (*Liber Exemplorum ad usum praedicantium*, B.S.F.S., ed. A. G. Little, pp. 31-2).

Simon of Langton, archdeacon of Canterbury,[1] was a theologian. He wrote a 'Summa de Vitiis et Virtutibus' which was formerly at Peterborough in MS. X. x, entitled 'Summa mag. Simonis Cantuar. de vitiis et virtutibus' (James, *Peterborough*, p. 62). 'De Penitentia Magdalene': *inc.* 'Miserator et misericors dominus Iesus.' (a) Cambridge, Corpus Christi Coll. MS. 226, fos. 112 *et seq.* (13th cent.), attributed to Stephen Langton in the MS.; (b) Dole MS. 99, fo. 106, also attributed to Stephen Langton in the MS.; (c) Oxford, Balliol Coll. MS. 152, with a note on flyleaf 'Summa magistri Simonis Langton.' In the margin is 'Sic voluit dominus Cantuariensis ut vocaretur libellus iste' (fo. 29). G. Lacombe discusses this question of attribution in 'Archives d'histoire doctrinale et littéraire du moyen age,' p. 9. He says of it 'this tiresome treatise full of never-ending considerations which seem foreign enough to Langton's incisive mind, I am not at all convinced that Stephen and not Simon should be regarded as the author.' In view of this difference in mentality and of the ease with which the works of Simon might be confused with those of his greater brother one can hardly say other than that 'it probably belongs to Simon Langton.'

Simon Langton was a brother of Stephen Langton [2] [q.v.]. A person of this name, but not with the title 'master,' attested a charter of Bishop William de Vere of Hereford (1186–99).[3] In view of the close association of the two brothers it is probable that they were at the university of Paris together. Both were canons of Paris: possibly Simon succeeded Stephen either when the latter became cardinal in 1206 or archbishop in 1207.[4] As a canon of Paris he appears as a pledge for certain monies left

[1] T. p. 466; *D.N.B.* under Langton.

[2] *Cf.* H. Loewe, *Starrs and Jewish Charters* (Jewish Hist. Soc.), ii. 144–6.

[3] *Charters of Hereford Cathedral*, ed. W. W. Capes, p. 37.

[4] Stephen secured the archdeaconry of Canterbury for his brother at a later date.

at the Hotel Dieu of Paris.[1] Many years later prayers were said for him and for his brother Stephen at Notre Dame on the nones of July.[2] He had given that church two hundred pounds for distribution. He had also given books, of which a list remains, to poor scholars.[3]

In 1207 certain revelations were reported to Simon, who told them to his brother, the archbishop.[4] He had a safe-conduct for three weeks for a journey to England in March 1208.[5] He seems to have had an interview with King John at Winchester on 12 Mar. 1208. He was in England in the late summer and returned in March 1209. For the next few years he was probably in exile with his brother, returning in 1213.[6] On 13 July of this year the king promised restitution for his losses.[7] He apparently went to York.[8] Early in 1214 he was at Rome defending his brother against allegations of Pandulf.[9] In November of the same year he was in England ready to be installed in the prebend of Strensall, Yorkshire.[10]

In the year 1215 the chapter of York elected Simon archbishop of York,[11] thereby hoping, according to one chronicler,[12] to

[1] Editor says ' End of twelfth century ' (*Cartulaire de l'Hotel Dieu*, Documents inédits, p. 507, no. 902).

[2] *Cartulaire de Notre Dame de Paris*, Documents inédits, iv. 105.

[3] ' Stephen, formerly archdeacon of Canterbury,' changed probably because of the great reputation of Stephen (*ibid.* ii. 495).

[4] *Chronicon de Lanercost* (Bannatyne Club), ed. J. Stevenson, p. 3.

[5] ' Die Mercur. proxima ante mediam Quadrages,' Winchester, 14 March (*Rot. Litt. Pat.* p. 80).

[6] *Ibid.* pp. 79, 82, 85, 89*b*, and 99. Permission to return dated 27 May.

[7] *Ibid.* p. 124 ; *Registrum Antiquissimum of the Cathedral Church of Lincoln*, ed. C. W. Foster, i. 137 ; *Rot. Litt. Claus.* p. 178*b*.

[8] *Rot. Litt. Pat.* p. 104.

[9] *Flores Historiarum* (R.S.), ed. H. R. Luard, ii. 98 ; *Rot. Chart.* p. 208*b*.

[10] *D.N.B.* ; Lambeth palace MS. 1212, fo. 75, a witness *c.* 1215.

[11] *Chronica Johannis de Oxenedes* (R.S.), ed. H. Ellis, p. 121 ; *Ann. Monast.* iii. 51 (Dunstable) ; *Flores Historiarum*, ii. 153, 156.

[12] *Flores Hist.* ii. 153.

obtain the favour of Pope Innocent III. He secured a royal letter of protection on 1 June.[1] With certain canons of the cathedral he went to Rome, apparently being there on 13 September.[2] At the instance of King John the election was quashed, the pope fearing the prospect of two brothers as enemies of his vassal, the king of England.[3] Simon's truculent nature [4] led him, upon his return to England, into the camp of Prince Louis of France and even to become his chancellor, encouraging him to disregard the legate, Gualo.[5] For this he incurred the legate's excommunication by name on 29 May 1216.[6] He was excepted from the general absolution in 1217 and apparently forced to go to Rome.[7] On 31 May 1218, now a papal subdeacon, he received permission to hold a prebend or other benefice in France ' if such is offered him.' [8] Possibly at this time the canonry at Paris was bestowed upon him. We should expect Louis to care for him. Although restored to papal favour he was not allowed to return to England.[9] For some years he ceased to be prominent ; [10] possibly he was ' custos ' of St. Quintin.[11] In 1227 he was at the papal curia, but he had lived for a long time in France.[12]

In 1227 his exile was terminated in time for him to join his brother before his death. A royal patent of 10 January granted him protection as long as he remained faithful ; [13] papal permission to return came on 19 May; [14]

[1] *Rot. Litt. Pat.* p. 142*b*.

[2] *Flores Hist.* ii. 153.

[3] *Ibid.* ; *Rot. Litt. Claus.* p. 269.

[4] The phrase is Lacombe's (*loc. cit.*).

[5] *Flores Hist.* ii. 181. [6] *Ibid.* p. 182.

[7] *Ibid.* p. 225 ; *Ann. Monast.* iii. 51 (Dunstable).

[8] *C.E.P.R.* i. 55 ; Pressutti, i. 231–2.

[9] Pressutti, i. 228, 234.

[10] He was mentioned as being in France in a letter of August 1225 (*ibid.* i. 265).

[11] C. Hemeraeus, *De scholis publicis sancti Quintini* (Paris, 1633), p. 62.

[12] Annals of Dover, B.M. MS. Cotton, Julius D. v, fo. 27.

[13] *C.P.R.*, 1225–32, p. 106 ; *cf. Rot. Litt. Claus.* i. 603*b*.

[14] *C.E.P.R.* i. 118.

royal permission to enter England to talk with the archbishop was issued on 18 June.[1] He entered Dover on 25 July.[2] By 28 July the king could say that all his hard feeling for Simon had gone.[3] Simon apparently returned to France for a time.[4] Before the end of the year he was among the royal 'familiares,'[5] and, what was probably more important, with his brother,[6] who had made him archdeacon of Canterbury.[7] He was an executor of his brother's will.[8]

On 24 Sept. 1229 Simon secured permission to go to Rome again, probably staying there the better part of three years,[9] apparently securing the rejection of Ralph Neville as archbishop-elect in 1231[10] and of John Blund [q.v.] in 1232.[11] With Edmund, however, he seems to have worked in harmony, but Edmund was a saint. Simon's former connexion with French royalty was probably Henry III's reason for appointing him as his representative in France, granting him power to swear by the king's soul to the truce.[12] Many items in the rolls refer to his share in these negotiations in 1234

[1] *C.P.R.*, 1225–32, p. 129.

[2] 'die sancti Jacobi' (Annals of Dover, B.M. MS. Cotton, Julius D. v, fo. 27).

[3] *C.P.R.*, 1225–32, p. 136.

[4] The king ordered a boat for him on 17 August (*C.L.R.*, 1226–40, p. 47).

[5] *Ann. Monast.* iii. 107.

[6] *C.P.R.*, 1225–32, p. 183; London, Lambeth palace MS. 1212, fos. 79, 102*b*, 204; Guild Hall MS. 136, p. 27; B.M. Add. MS. 33354, fo. 67*b*; P.R.O., ancient deed, L.S. 4; Camb. Univ. Lib. MS. Ee. v. 31, fo. 154*b*; Bodl. Lib. MS. Tanner 223, fos. 45*b*, 47.

[7] Probably before the end of 1227 (H.M.C., 5th Rep., App. p. 430); the chronicler says that Simon was made archdeacon 'die tertia ante intronatione Henrici Rofen' epi,' which took place 'xviikal. Jun.' (Annals of Dover, B.M. MS. Julius D. v, fo. 27).

[8] *C.Cl.R.*, 1227–32, p. 110.

[9] *C.P.R.*, 1225–32, p. 268.

[10] *Flores Hist.* iii. 16.

[11] *Cf.* Heironimus and Russell, *Shorter Latin Poems of Henry of Avranches* (Mediaeval Acad. of America), pp. 127-9.

[12] *C.P.R.*, 1232–47, pp. 82, 85, 90, 108, 116; P.R.O., Chancery, C. 76/1, several letters from king in treaty rolls telling of the progress of the project.

and 1235.[1] The pope gave him a task in 1236 at Paris.[2] By 1237 he was again in England. At the council of St. Paul's on 20 November of that year he requested the legate Otto to read his commission.[3] He was named by the pope to assist in the installation of Roger de Wendene as bishop of Rochester.[4]

A quarrel with St. Augustine's of Canterbury broke out the same year.[5] A confirmation of a composition of 1237 was made the following year at Rome.[6] As procurator for the archbishop Simon went to Rome again,[7] this time opposing the monks of Christchurch. Their chronicler says that he accused them of forgery,[8] and in 1240 he is alleged to have usurped certain of their privileges.[9] In 1241 he threatened to carry his case to Rome. The king interfered, making dire threats, and the archdeacon yielded, according to the chronicler, because of age and infirmity.[10] Documents remain showing his activity in 1241,[11] 1243,[12] and even as late as 1247.[13] His death in 1248 ended the career, according to Matthew Paris, of a great disturber of church and realm.[14]

[1] *C.P.R.*, 1232–47, *passim.*

[2] *Registres de Grégoire IX*, ed. L. Auvray, p. 236 (23 January).

[3] *Chr. Maj.* iii. 417.

[4] H. Wharton, *Anglia Sacra*, i. 349.

[5] B.M. MS. Cotton, Claudius D. x, fo. 271*b*; Julius D. ii, fo. 81.

[6] *C.E.P.R.* i. 171. For other relations with St. Augustine's see William Thorn's chronicle in Twysden, *Historie Anglicane Scriptores* (1652), cols. 1891–2, and B.M. MS. Faustina A. i, fo. 332.

[7] *Flores Hist.* ii. 226.

[8] *Hist. Works of Gervase of Canterbury* (R.S.), ed. W. Stubbs, ii. 132.

[9] *Ibid.* pp. 180–2; this chronicler says of him, 'cuius memoria in maledictione est' (*ibid.* ii. 131).

[10] *Chr. Maj.* iv. 103.

[11] B.M. MS. Cotton, Julius D. ii, fo. 111.

[12] *Ibid.* Claudius D. x, fos. 275, 276; Faustina A. i, fo. 335.

[13] Lambeth palace MS. 241, fo. 118.

[14] *Chr. Maj.* v. 41; documents of uncertain date are in B.M. MS. Faustina A. i, fos. 234*b*, 273*b*; Lambeth palace MS. 1212, fo. 77; Bodl. Lib. MS. Tanner 223, fo. 46*b*. He apparently held at some

Simon Stock, O.C., was an alleged author of several pieces (T. p. 673) :—' De Scelerum Penitentia ' or ' De Christiana Penitentia ' : *inc.* ' Amos vero super tribus sceleribus Iuda, et super ' (Bale, *Index*, p. 414, as ' ex Ramesiensi monasterio ' ; T. p. 674). ' Super Tribus Sceleribus ' : *inc.* ' Super tribus sceleribus et super quarto ' (Bale, *Index*, p. 414, as ' ex collegio regine, Oxon,' but apparently not there now). ' Flos Carmeli Vitis Florigera ' : *inc.* ' Ave, stella matutina ' (T. p. 674). Tanner gives several other titles, but they may be merely suggested by his career.

The life of St. Simon Stock was apparently not written until long after his death, and therefore is open to question in view of the considerable body of myths which had grown up about him.[1] He was alleged to have been a centenarian and to have lived for a long time in a tree trunk. He was apparently general of the carmelites from 1245 to 1258 and spent the last seven years of his life at Mount Carmel.[2] His death occurred at Bordeaux on 16 May 1265.

Simon, monk of Walden, was a legal commentator.

> Simon Monachus coenobii Waldensis, juris utriusque peritissimus. Jus pontificium Cantabrigiae publice praelegit A. MCCXCVII. Scripsisse putatur *Comm. super majorem partem juris*. Claruit A. MCCXCVII. Pits, *Append*. p. 909 (T. p. 673).

Simon of Walsingham, monk of Bury St. Edmunds, was an Anglo-Norman poet. ' La Vie Seinte Fey, Virgine et Martire.' (a) Welbeck, library of the duke of Portland MS. I, C. i, fos. 147–56*b* (13th–14th cent.). Lines 50–1 give the author's name :

> Symon de Walsingham ai nun
> serf Marie a seinte ad nun.

time the prebend of Holywell of Finsbury (Le Neve, *Fasti*, ii. 394). He added endowment to the Priests' Hospice of the Grey Friars at Canterbury (C. Colton, *Grey Friars of Canterbury*, p. 7 ; Tanner, *Notitia Monastica*, Kent, xii. 10).

[1] For the traditional life see *Monumenta historie Carmelitarum*, pp. 313–22.

[2] Bale in MS. Harley 3838, fo. 21*b* ; T. p. 673.

Extracts are published by Louis Karl in ' Notice sur l'unique manuscrit français de la Bibliothèque du Duc de Portland a Welbeck ' (*Revue des Langues Romanes*, liv, 1911. 219–21). Karl says that Simon was a monk of Bury St. Edmund, but he does not cite the source of his information. Other items are only conjectural.[1]

Simon of Warwick was abbot of St. Mary's, York.[2] Bodl. Lib. MS. Bodley 39 contains ' records relating to the benedictine abbey of St. Mary, York, collected by or in memory of Simon de Warwik and continues to 1333 ' (Madan and Craster, *Summary Cat. of Western MSS*. ii. pt. 1, p. 102). On fo. 92 begins the ' De fundatione abbatie,' the work of the first abbot, Stephen of Whitby, and continued to 1267 as a list of abbots and brief annals. The detailed annals are from 1258 to 1326. A list of monks is given on fo. 116 as of 1258. The collection would seem to have been begun by Abbot Simon.

Simon of Warwick had become a monk of St. Mary, York, on 11 July 1244.[3] On 4 Oct. 1255 the king appointed him, with John de Ocketon, knight, and Adam de Fraxino, to keep his house from falling into debt.[4] He was elected abbot of the monastery on 24 June 1258 [5] and saw the temporalities restored on 25 July. In 1263 he was out of York on account of trouble with its citizens ; he visited the abbey's cells in 1266, and probably attended the council of

[1] A Reginald de Walsingham, also a monk of this house, assisted Roger Compotista (Infans [q.v.]) in a work (*cf. Isis*, xviii, 1932. 16). A charter of the house is attested by a ' Mr. —— de Walsingham,' but the name is missing (Camb. Univ. Lib. MS. Ff. ii, 33, fo. 69*b*). A Simon of Walsingham was a burgess of Lynn *c.* 1283 (*Cat. Ancient Deeds*, ii. 141, A. 2979 ; P.R.O., Chancery, C. 85/4). He was excommunicated, according to the latter document.

[2] T. p. 673 ; frequently called Simeon of Warwick.

[3] *Chronicon de Lanercost* (Bannatyne Club), ed. J. Stevenson, p. 66 ; Bodl. Lib. MS. Bodley 39, fo. 117.

[4] *C.P.R.*, 1247–58, p. 428.

[5] *Chronicon*, p. 66.

London in 1268.[1] In 1269 he obtained from Henry III the forest rights of the whole forest of Farindale, except hunting privileges.[2] The next year he commenced work upon a new choir in his church.[3] Probably soon after this (1273) he bought the township of Dicton from Hugh de Neville.[4] Items of 1276, 1279, and 1280 refer to his activity.[5] In 1284 he attended the council of Lyons from May to September.[6] He died on 6 July 1296 and was buried before the great altar of his abbey church.[7]

Simon, monk of Waverley, wrote in French a request to have his name inscribed in the chapter book of Winteney abbey, which remains in the Winteney obituary, B.M. MS. Cotton, Claudius D. iii, fo. 1*b* (13th cent.), edited by P. Meyer in 'Jahrbuch für romanischen und englischen Literatur,' vii (1866), 47. Simon is probably the monk who wrote Latin verses upon the character of Abbot John, who died in 1201, incorporated in the 'Annals of Waverley' (*Ann. Monast.* ii. 253).

If the Latin and Anglo-Norman Simons are identical, Simon must have lived at Waverley in the first half of the 13th century. In 1214 a monk Simon tapped a new spring for the abbey at Ledwell and wrote verse commemorating the achievement.[8] He is also possibly author of some of the verse in the chronicle under the years 1226–40.[9] His Anglo-Norman request to Winteney states that he was an old man.

Stephen Langton was archbishop of Canterbury and a famous theologian.[10] For an authoritative statement of the research completed and in progress upon the life and work of Langton see F. M. Powicke in '*E.H.R.*' xlviii (1933). 554–7.

1 Bodl. Lib. MS. Bodley 39, fos. 122, 122*b*, 124*b*.
2 Leland, *Collect.* i. 23 ; MS. *cit.* fo. 126*b*.
3 *Ibid.* fo. 127*b*.
4 *Ibid.* fo. 128*b*.
5 *C.Cl.R.*, 1272–9, pp. 263, 360 ; *Ibid.* 1279–88, pp. 33, 194, 372, 413.
6 MS. *cit.* fo. 129, a long account.
7 Leland, *Collect.* i. 24 ; MS. *cit.* fo. 163.
8 *Ann. Monast.* ii. 284–5.
9 *Ibid.* pp. 304–27.
10 T. p. 466 ; *D.N.B.* under Langton.

Stephen of Exeter, O.F.M., was the alleged author of the 'Annales Domus Montis Fernandi (45–1274),'[1] Armagh, Archiepiscopal Lib., Dublin, Trinity Coll. MS. 347 (?), edited in 'Tracts relating to Ireland,' Irish Archaeol. Soc. (1843). ii.

Stephen of Exeter 'was apparently born in 1246 and entered the franciscan order at Multyfarnham, Westmeath, in 1263.'[2] The family was already connected with that order through the gift, in 1252, of a house to the order at Strade in Mayo by his father Jordan of Exeter, lord of Athlethan,[3] or by his son, Stephen.[4] The chronicle is carried to 1274. However, in 1286 the king ordered that certain officials be reimbursed forty shillings which they had paid out for the expenses of Fr. Stephen of Exeter, O.F.M., for going to see the king upon Irish affairs.[5]

Stephen of Easton, abbot of Sawley, wrote books of devotion. The better known is the 'Meditations upon the Joys of the Virgin': (various *incipits*). (a) Glasgow, Hunterian Museum MS. 231, pp. 62–75 (14th cent.) ; (b) B.M. MS. Harley 3766, fos. 38*b*–48 (14th cent.) ; (c) B.M. MS. Harley 5234, fos. 111–3 (14th cent.) ; (d) London, Lambeth palace MS. 151, fos. 316–25 (late 13th cent.) ; (e) Paris, Arsenal MS. 412, fos. 45–61 (14th cent.) ; (f) B.N. MS. lat. 1201, fos. 24*b*–38 (late 14th–early 15th cent.) ; (g) B.N. MS. lat. 10358, fos. 193–201*b* (13th cent.), with a rubric 'Hic incipiunt meditationes de gaudiis beate et gloriose semper uirginis Marie edite a dompno Stephano uenerabili abbate de Salleya ad petitionem claustralis.' The treatise is edited

1 T. p. 692 ; *D.N.B.* under Stephen.
2 *D.N.B.*
3 Archdale, *Monasticon Hibernicum*, p. 509.
4 Possibly not the same as the alleged chronicler.
5 *Cal. of Documents pertaining to Ireland*, 1285–92, nos. 171, 217.

by A. Wilmart, ' Les méditations d'Etienne de Sallai sur les joies de la Sainte-Vierge ' (*Revue d'Ascétique et de Mystique*, x, 1929. 368–89). The lesser known is the ' De Modo Oracionis et Meditationis ' : *inc.* ' Igitur, quacumque hora diei.' (a) London, Lambeth palace MS. 151, fos. 311*b*–5 (13th–14th cent.) ; (b) B.N. MS. lat. 1201, fos. 17–24 (14th–15th cent.). This has no colophon, but precedes the ' Meditations ' in both MSS. This is edited by A. Wilmart, ' Le Triple Exercice d'Etienne de Sallai ' (*Revue d'Ascétique et de Mystique*, xi, 1930. 355–74).

An early biography of Stephen, abbot of Sawley, probably this author, reads as follows :

> Anno Domini 1252, viii. Idus Septembris, obiit Stephanus de Eston xi^us, abbas de Fontibus, completis abbaciatu suo quinque annis, mens. 10. diebus quinque ; sed in fundacione Foncium habetur quod vi. annis ecclesiam Fontanensem gubernavit. Verumtamen annus Christi non est in datis mortis ejus. Iste Stephanus primo Cellararius de Fontibus factus ; postea Abbas de Sallay per x. annos constitutus ; inde de Sallay ad Novum Monasterium translatus ; novissime ad primam matrem reassumitur in patrem. Abbatizavit tempore Henrici terrii. Sepultus est coram sede Presidentis, in Capitulo monasterii Vallis-dei, ubi miraculis choruscat.[1]

Stephen was apparently first a monk of Fountains and became its cellarer.[2] From this office he was elected abbot of Sawley, in which capacity he appears in 1226 and 1230 :[3] thus his ten year period of rule falls within the limits of 1220–36.[4] The dated documents of his term as abbot of Newminster belong to 1240,[1] 1241,[2] and to the time of Bishop Nicholas Farnham [q.v.], 1240–8. A document said to be of 1243 shows a Simon as abbot.[3] If this information is correct, Stephen must have retired from this office before he was elected abbot of Fountains in 1246. The date of his consecration was probably 1 Nov. 1246, that is, nearly six years before his death on 6 Sept. 1252.[4] Miracles were reported at his tomb in the monastery of Vallis-Dei.[5]

Stephen, the Subdeacon, was author of part of a ' Vita Sancti Edmundi.' See above under Eustace, monk of Christchurch.

Thomas of Boarstall was an augustinian friar [6] and author of a ' Dictionarium Theologie ' : *inc.* ' Abiicere debemus divitias temporales ' (Bale, MS. Glynn ; T. p. 113). The other items given by bibliographical tradition, ' Lecture Sententiarum,' ' Ordinarie Disceptationes,' and ' Quodlibeta Scholastica,' look like conjectures.

This Thomas of Boarstall is supposed to have lived about 1290, to have been a doctor of theology at Paris, and to have been buried in the house of his order at Norwich.[7] A curious item upon a volume of distinctions

[1] *Memorials of Fountains* (Surtees Soc.), ed. J. R. Walbran, i. 137–8.

[2] ' Primam matrem ' of the account above suggests this.

[3] York, chapter library, Magnum Registrum Album, fo. 87*b* ; Wilmart, *op. cit.* p. 368 ; *Chartulary of Sallay* (Yorks. Arch. Soc.), ed. J. McNulty, p. 184, from B.M. MS. Harley 112, fo. 84*b*, crastino St. Andrew at York (29 November) ; *Feet of Fines, Yorkshire*, 1218–1231, ed. J. Parker, pp. 83, 159 ; Wilmart, *op. cit.* p. 369, *n.* 5.

[4] Undated documents bearing his name as abbot of Sawley are : *Chartulary of Sallay*, pp. 8, 108, 153, from B.M. MS. Harley 112, fos. 4, 46*b*, 69 (Ralph of Maidstone [q.v.], archdeacon of Chester, among witnesses), 138*b* (Ralph, abbot of Kirkstall, among witnesses), 150*b*, 153 ; B.M. MS. Egerton 3053, fo. 15 ; Bodl. Lib. MS. Rawlinson B. 455, fo. 221*b* ; *Abstracts of the Cistercian Abbey of Fountains*, ed. W. T. Lancaster, ii. 696 ; *Docs. Illustrative*, ed. H. Cole, p. 197.

[1] *Newminster Cartulary* (Surtees Soc.), ed. J. T. Fowler, pp. 67, 201.

[2] *Feet of Fines, Northumberland and Durham*, nos. 157, 171, 172 ; *Newminster Cartulary*, pp. 54, 80. A predecessor, Robert, appeared in 1220 (*ibid.* pp. 179, 215 ; B.M. MS. Harley 112, fo. 8*b*).

[3] *Newminster Cartulary*, p. 68.

[4] ' Successit Joanni Stephanus de Eston, abbas Novi Monasterii ' (Leland, *Collect.* iv. 109). For official activity *cf. Feet of Fines, Yorkshire*, 1246–72, ed. J. Parker, *passim*.

[5] As in biography above.

[6] T. p. 113 ; *D.N.B.* under Borstall.

[7] T. p. 113 ; Bale gives as sources ' Chronicles of the Augustinians ' (*Scriptorum Illustrium*, p. 345).

of about 1200 states that the MS. was first given away by a Thomas of Boarstall, chaplain.[1] The patron of the Oxford house of the Austin friars was John Handlo of Borstall (Bucks.), whose charter was confirmed by Henry III in 1269 ; [2] the friar may well be of this family.

Thomas of Bungay, O.F.M., was a theologian and scientist.[3] Like many others, he wrote a ' Commentary on the Sentences ' : *inc.* ' Fidem vestram clypeis munire, queritur an fides qua creditur articulus.' (a) MS. described as ' Ex domo magistri Grey, Burie ' (Bale, *Index*, p. 433) ; (b) MS. mentioned in the ' Catalogue of Illustrious Franciscans ' (Leland, *De Script. Brit.* p. 302) ; (c) MS. formerly in St. Augustine's, Canterbury, ' Literales dubitaciones T. de Bungey super primum et 2m sent. ' (James, *A.L.C.D.* p. 262) ; (d) MS. in the same library, ' Questiones Thome de Bunge super 4m Sentenc.' (*ibid.*).

Reference to some work, probably a commentary upon ' Romans,' remains in Cambridge, Pembroke Coll. MS. 87, fo. 143*b* (13th–14th cent.), in a note on Augustine's ' De Cognitione Vere Vite ' :

> Frater T. de Bungeye sic tetigit hanc questionem super hunc locum apostoli. Rom. 14 Omne autem quod non est ex fide.

His ' Questiones super Libros de Celo et Mundo ' : *inc.* ' Summa cognitionis nature,' remain in Cambridge, Gonville and Caius Coll. MS. 509, fos. 208–52*b*, with the colophon ' Hic terminantur questiones super 3 celi et mundi a mag. T. de Bungeya.'

[1] Oxford, Merton Coll. MS. 200 ; Powicke, p. 192 :

' Orate pro anima Thome Burstal capellani qui dedit istum librum Johanni Brokholes, capellano, qui Johannes dedit Henrico Gairstang, et idem Henricus dedit collegio Marton in Oxonia ad orandum pro anima magistri Ric. de Scrop, nuper Ebor. archiepiscopi et pro animabus supradictorum ' (T. Hardy, *Descriptive Catalogue*, iii. p. lxvii).

[2] Dugdale, *Monasticon*, vi. 1596.

[3] T. p. 140 ; *D.N.B.* under Bungay. Best life in Little, *F.S.O.* pp. 851–2.

Possibly other treatises in the same MS. are his. Some academic exercises also remain in Assisi MS. 158, nos. 37, 41, 47 (Little, *F.S.O.* p. 852).

Thomas of Bungay acquired the character of a magician with Roger Bacon in the course of the centuries : it is possible that he may have been associated with him at Oxford.[1] His questions upon ' De Celo et Mundo ' have his name as master instead of frater ; possibly this means that he entered the franciscan order after he became an M.A. He was tenth regent master in theology for the Oxford franciscans about 1270,[2] and eighth provincial minister between 1270 and 1275.[3] He was probably fifteenth master at Cambridge about 1275.[4] He was buried at Northampton.[5]

Thomas of Chobham, subdean of Salisbury, was the author of a famous ' Summa de Penitentia ' [6] : *inc.* ' Cum miserationes,' *expl.* ' de penitentia dicta sufficiant.' MSS. give as author Master Thomas de Chabeham, Cabaham (or some similar form), subdean of Salisbury. There are very many MSS. extant.

[1] Bale says that Thomas wrote *In Necromanticis*, but this may be a conjecture based upon his reputation (*Index*, p. 433).

[2] *Cf.* Little's discussion of dates for William of Hedley, Thomas, and John Peckham (*F.S.O.* pp. 851–853) ; also App. A.

[3] Little, *op. cit.* p. 851.

[4] *Mon. Fr.* i. 555 ; *Eccleston*, p. 72 ; App. A.

[5] *Mon. Fr.* i. 537, 560. A Thomas Bunghay was a priest and monk of Christchurch (?), Canterbury, dying upon 31 October (Lambeth palace MS. 20, fo. 236). A Thomas de Bungeye le coureyur, a citizen of London, made a grant about 1271 (*Cat. Ancient Deeds*, i. 196). If he was of this family he might be the Master Thomas of London, subdean, who was instituted as rector of Mistreton in 1258–9 (*Rot. R. de Gravesend*, p. 138).

[6] T. p. 172 ; *D.N.B.* under Chabham. He has been confused with the better known Thomas Cobham of the following century. He may also be identical with Thomas of Salisbury [q.v.]. In any case the glossator's identification of the Thomas of Salisbury who taught at Paris with Chobham would seem to show that Chobham also taught there.

He is said to have written a 'Speculum Ecclesie': *inc.* 'Penitentiam agite, appropinquabit,' said to be 'ex officina Gerbrandi bibliopole' (Bale, *Index*, p. 434).

Thomas of Chobham appears as a frequent witness of the charters of Bishop Richard of London[1] in the latter part of his episcopate while Alard was archdeacon of London.[2] Shortly after the death of this bishop on 10 Sept. 1198 Thomas probably began his long association with Salisbury. He appears as a witness of charters dated 18 Apr. 1202, 5 July 1202,[3] 19 Sept. 1203,[4] 8 Oct. 1203,[5] 1206–7,[6] and 1207,[7] as a clerk of the bishop of Salisbury, Herbert Poore.[8] Probably he went into exile with him during the interdict. He acted as official for the bishop, probably just after the interdict.[9] In 1213 he received a gift of twenty marks for serving as the king's messenger 'in partibus transmarinis,' and also the privilege of 'assartandi et excolendi' three acres in the forest of the abbot of Chertsey.[10]

[1] P.R.O., ancient deeds, L. 220; 35th Rep. D.K., App. p. 29; Norman Moore, *History of St. Bartholomew's Hospital*, pp. 163–4, 231; Westminster abbey, Domesday, fos. 474, 627; B.M. MS. Harley 3697, fo. 49.

[2] MS. Domesday, fo. 474; Norman Moore, *op. cit.* p. 230; H.M.C., 9th Rep., App. p. 27*b*; Dean and Chapter of St. Paul's, A, box 11, no. 243; B.M. MS. Harley 3739, fo. 121*b*.

[3] B.M. MS. Egerton 3031, fo. 97*b*; *Charters and Records of Hereford Cathedral*, ed. W. W. Capes, p. 126.

[4] *Newington Longeville Charters*, ed. H. E. Salter, pp. 59–60.

[5] *Cal. of Docs. preserved in France*, ed. J. H. Round, p. 344.

[6] Archives of Queen's College, Sherborn Priory (Typescript, Bodl. Lib.), p. 12.

[7] H.M.C., 4th Rep., App. p. 453*b*.

[8] Undated instances appear in: B.M. MS. Egerton 2104a, fos. 96*b*, 97*b*; F. T. Wethered, *St. Mary's, Henley, in the Middle Ages*, p. 101; *Sarum Chs. and Docs.* p. 64; H.M.C., *Wells MSS.* i. 526.

[9] While Richard [Grosseteste] was archdeacon of Wilts.; B.M. MS. Stowe 925, fo. 68; MS. Cotton, Vitellius A. xi, fo. 81 (two documents); *Sarum Chs. and Docs.* p. 79

[10] *Docs. Illustrative of Eng. History*, ed. Henry Cole, p. 260; *Rot. Litt. Claus.* i. 159.

According to Le Neve's 'Fasti' Thomas was subdean in 1214 and 1230,[1] and these dates seem to cover the time in which he served in that capacity fairly accurately.[2] As such he appears in a document of about 1218.[3] He held the prebend of Cherminster, valued at eighty marks, in 1226.[4] As subdean he gave his consent to the election of Robert Bingham as bishop in 1228.[5] Earlier in the year he had secured a special papal writ giving him the privilege of not being a bishop.[6] By 1236 a Master Adam was subdean of Salisbury.[7] This may not mean that Thomas was dead, however. He held in 1220 a pension of two marks a year from the chapel of Chidingford.[8] He may have resigned his subdeanship, for one who would avoid being made a bishop might well resign a lesser office. In 1249 a Master Thomas of Chabham seems to have acted as proctor for a royal relative.[9]

Thomas of Docking, O.F.M., was a theologian.[10] Of his education in arts only a 'Tabula super Grammaticam' is said to have existed in Lincoln Cathedral MS. F. 18, but it is apparently no longer there (T. p. 230). He wrote a 'Commentary

[1] 'Ex cartis in baga de diversis in offic. Augment' (ii. 619).

[2] Undated charters appear in: B.M. MS. Stowe 925, fo. 143; MS. Cotton, Vespasian F. xv, fo. 169 (3), 170; Add. Ch. 26619.

[3] *Register of St. Osmund* (R.S.), ed. W. H. Rich Jones, ii. 33.

[4] *Ibid.* p. 70.

[5] *Ibid.* p. 108.

[6] *Ibid.* pp. 104–5.

[7] R. C. Hoare, *Hist. of Modern Wiltshire*, vi. 731; *C.Cl.R.*, 1234–7, p. 515.

[8] *Register of St. Osmund*, i. 297.

[9] *C.Cl.R.*, 1247–51, p. 195. A 'capa' called 'Chabeham' in the inventory of 1222 is surmised to have had some connexion with Chabham (*Register of St. Osmund*, ii. 130). A Thomas, subdean probably de Eblesburne [q.v.], witnesses a charter of Bishop Robert on 17 Aug. 1239 (B.M. MS. Egerton 3013, fo. 111).

[10] T. p. 229; *D.N.B.* under Docking. Little gives most of the items about Docking's bibliography and biography (*G.F.* p. 151; *F.S.O.* p. 846).

upon the Sentences.' (a) MS. possibly in Oxford, Merton Coll. MS. 134 (*cf.* Powicke, p. 148, *n.*); (b) MS. formerly in the library of the austin friars, York (James, *Fasciculus J. W. Clark dicatus*, no 243), entitled 'Dokhyng super sentencias' ('20 fo est tandem'); (c) MS. mentioned in the 'Catalogue of Illustrious Franciscans' (Leland, *Cat. de Scriptoribus*, p. 315).

His longest works were apparently biblical commentaries. 'Expositio super Librum Deuteronomii': *inc.* 'Legitur Exodo 16. g. quod Dominus iussit.' (a) Dublin, Trinity Coll. MS. 204 (15th cent.); (b) Lincoln Cathedral library MS. 5, fos. 141 *et seq.* (15th cent.), entitled 'Postille mag. Thome [ ]ynges super Deu[ ]'; (c) B.M. MS. Reg. 3, B. xii (15th cent.), on which a 16th century hand has written:

> Liber magistri Thome Gude (i. bonus) doctoris sacre theologie Oxonie et ordinis minorum, vocati docking de quo natus fuit in villa vocata Docking;

(d) Oxford, Balliol Coll. MS. 28 (A.D. 1442). His 'Expositio Decalogi' seems to come from this (Little, *F.S.O.* p. 847). (a) Cambridge, Gonville and Caius Coll. MS. 270 (15th cent.); (b) Lincoln Cathedral Lib. MS. 229, fos. 164 *et seq.* (14th–15th cent.); (c) Bodl. Lib. MS. Bodley 453, fos. 57–91*b* (15th cent.), with a colophon 'Explicit expositio fratris Thome Dockyng super preceptis de catalogi secundum formam textus Deuteronomii quinto.'

Commentary on Isaiah: *inc.* 'Habemus firmiorem sermonem propheticum.' (a) Cambridge, Gonville and Caius Coll. MS. 270, fos. 1–178 (15th cent.); (b) Oxford, Balliol Coll. MS. 29 (15th cent.).

Commentary upon the Epistles of St. Paul: (a) Oxford, Balliol Coll. MS. 30 (15th cent.); (b) Oxford, Magdalen Coll. MS. 154 (15th cent.), entitled 'Expositio doctoris Thome Dockyng fratris minor. super prolegom. apostoli ad Galathas.' The *incipits* of the several pieces are:—

Galatians: 'Epistole Pauli ad Galathas premittitur,' (a) fos. 1–48.

Ephesians: 'Ephesii sunt Asiani,' with the colophon 'Explicit lectura secundum v.d. Dockyng,' (a) fos. 48–114*b*.

Philippians: 'Philippenses sunt Macedones, aliqui,' (a) fos. 114*b*–46.

Colossians: 'Collocenses et hii sunt Laodicenses,' (a) fos. 146*b*–77*b*.

Thessalonians, I: 'Thessalonicenses sunt Macedones,' (a) fos. 177*b*–207, with the colophon 'finitur explanatio epistole prime ad Thessalonicenses secundum venerabilem doctorem Thomam Dockyng.'

Thessalonians, II: 'Ad Thessalonicenses secundam scribit apostolus,' (a) fos. 207*b*–18.

Timothy: 'Timotheum instruit et docet,' (a) fos. 218–98*b*.

Titus: 'Titum commonefacit et instruit,' (a) fos. 298*b*–321*b*.

Philemon: 'Philemoni familiares literas,' (a) fos. 321*b*–29.

Hebrews: 'Incipit epistola ad Hebreos, circa cuius,' (a) fos. 329–409*b*.

He seems to have written some 'Questiones' upon St. Luke. (a) B.N. MS. 3183, fos. 169–73 (14th cent.); (b) MS. mentioned by Bale: *inc.* 'Non misit me baptizare, sed.' 'Ex bibliothecis Oxoniensibus' (*Index*, p. 437). This work is probably different from a Commentary on Luke: *inc.* 'Fluuius egrediebatur de loco.' (a) 'Ex bibliothecis Oxoniensibus' (Bale, *Index*, p. 436; Leland, *Collect.* iv. 61); (b) MS. formerly at Cambridge, Queen's Coll.: 'Dokking super Lucam' (Leland, *Collect.* iv. 18). Upon Job, 'Questio Utrum Job in Prosperis fuerit Altior coram Deo quam in Adversis' exists in B.N. MS. 3183, fos. 178–82, and is probably the same as the MS. described by Bale (*Index*, p. 437). He also wrote a work formerly at Syon, MS. N. 27, fo. 107, described as 'Dokkyng ordinis minorum in suis correctionibus super sacram scripturam abbreviatus' (*Cat. of the Library of Syon Monastery*, ed. M. Bateson, p. 221).

Thomas of Docking may have borne the

surname 'Good.'[1] In a letter of 1253 Adam Marsh [q.v.] requested for Thomas the Bible belonging to the recently deceased 'P. de Worcester.'[2] Docking 'was distinguished by good morals, pleasant manners, a clear head, great learning and ready eloquence.' He was a student of Roger Bacon or so closely associated with him that he was under his influence.[3] He was the seventh regent master of the franciscans at Oxford, probably about 1264–6.[4] He was still at Oxford and took a part in a great controversy with the dominicans in 1269.[5] For some curious reason most of his writings have come down in 15th century manuscripts.

Thomas of Eblesburne, canon of Salisbury, was probably the author of a 'Medical Recipe': *inc.* 'Sirupus . . .,' *expl.* 'et reubarb in bona quantitate,' with a marginal note 'Secundum magistrum Th. de Ebl.'[6] B.M. MS. Reg. 12, B. xii, fo. 170*b*.

Although the author's name is abbreviated it is still quite distinctive,[7] and probably refers to a man who appeared at Salisbury from 1222 to about 1246.[8] As early as 1207 he paid £33 to the bishop of Winchester for the farm of the manor of Fontel.[1] He attested an undated charter of Peter des Roches, bishop of Winchester, probably before 1222.[2] He was present in chapter at Salisbury in 1222 and again in 1224,[3] attended the first service in the new cathedral in 1225,[4] and was again in chapter on 15 Aug. 1226.[5] In this year he held the prebend of 'Rotefen,' valued at eight marks.[6] He was in chapter in 1227[7] and witnessed a charter of Bishop Richard Poore on 3 Oct. 1227. He was given a portion in the church of Grantham by Bishop Richard.[8] He consented to the election of Robert Bingham [q.v.] in the following year.[9]

Thomas attested charters in the first[10] and second years of Bingham's episcopate.[11] At about the same time he witnessed a charter of Master Elias of Dereham[12] and on 20 Apr. 1229 a charter of confirmation.[13] He was in chapter at Salisbury on 13 Feb. 1230 (or 1231)[14] and again on 19 Oct. 1233.[15] In 1234 he appeared as patron of two churches, Grantham 'Australis' and Harlaxton.[16] He attested charters of 17 Feb. 1236, 12 Jan. 1240, and 11 Nov. 1243.[17] In this period he probably witnessed a document for Ela,

[1] B.M. MS. Reg. 3 B. xii. A clerk, Thomas of Docking, attested a quitclaim of 'Wm. Bechylde' to Stephen Alderman and the burgesses of Bury St. Edmund (Camb. Univ. Lib. MS. Gg. 4/4, fo. 250*b*).

[2] *Mon. Fr.* i. 359–60; for the date see Little, *F.S.O.* p. 846; *G.F.* p. 151.

[3] 'Thomas Docking and his relations to Roger Bacon' (given by Little in *Essays presented to Reginald Lane Poole*, pp. 301–31).

[4] *Mon. Fr.* i. 550, 552; see App. A.

[5] Little, *G.F.* pp. 324–6, 335.

[6] *Annals of Medical History*, N.S. vii (1935). 328.

[7] Note a 'Physionomia' by a Thomas Anglicus: *inc.* 'Diverse membrorum dispositiones' (B.M. Add. MS. 15107, fos. 43*b*–4*b*). A 'Mr. Thomas Medicus' attested a charter of 'J. prior of Spalding' (B.M. Add. MS. 5844, fo. 219). A 'Mr. Thomas Physicus' received a gift of cloth from the king in 22 Hen. III (1237–8) (P.R.O., Chancery, issue roll, chanc. misc. 3/43, no. 3).

[8] Not designated as 'medicus': this also applies to such men as Roger of Lacock, Nicholas of Farnham, Gilbert de Aquila.

[1] *Pipe Roll of the Bishopric of Winchester*, ed. Hubert Hall, p. 80.

[2] B.M. MS. Cotton, Vespasian F. xv, fo. 189*b*, Alan of Stoke, official, with Robert Basset and Humphrey. About the same group appears between 1205–22 (*Chartulary of Winchester Cathedral*, ed. A. W. Goodman, p. 199).

[3] *Register of St. Osmund* (R.S.), ed. W. H. R. Jones, i. 339; ii. 22.

[4] *Ibid.* ii. 38, 60.

[5] *Ibid.* p. 60.

[6] *Ibid.* p. 73.

[7] *Ibid.* i. 3, 319.

[8] *Sarum Chs. and Docs.* p. 189; *Rot. H. de Welles*, iii. 152.

[9] *Register of St. Osmund*, ii. 109.

[10] '12 Kal. May' (Dugdale, *Monasticon*, vi. 503).

[11] 'Vii ides Aug.' (B.M. MS. Cotton, Claudius C ix, fo. 184*b*).

[12] *Sarum Chs. and Docs.* p. 205.

[13] J. Stevens, *History of the Antient Abbeys* (1722–1723), ii. 356.

[14] *Register of St. Osmund*, i. 388.

[15] *Sarum Chs. and Docs.* p. 229.

[16] *Rot. H. de Welles*, iii. 216.

[17] *Sarum Chs. and Docs.* pp. 237, 238, 254, 289; R. C. Hoare, *Hist. of Modern Wiltshire*, vi. 731.

countess of Salisbury.[1] Probably he became subdean of Salisbury by 1239–40,[2] but he had resigned by 1240.[3] He presented the church of Graham in that year.[4] In 1241–2 he presented Adam de Percy to Colsterworth rectory,[5] in 1245–6 he promoted William from Graham to Welby,[6] and filled the vacancy at the former place.[7] Obviously a man of wealth and influence, he died before 6 Nov. 1246.[8]

Thomas of Eccleston, O.F.M., was author of a unique treatise 'De Adventu Minorum in Angliam'[9]: *inc.* 'A.D. 1224 tempore domini Honorii.' (a) Cheltenham MS. 3119 (13th cent.), containing the whole chronicle minus certain stories; (b) Lamport House, a fragment possibly of the following; (c) B.M. MS. Cotton, Nero A. ix, imperfect; (d) York Cathedral lib. MS. xvi, K. 4, a transcript of which is in B.M. Add. 35260; (e) MS. formerly at Oxford, Queens Coll. (Bale, *Index*, p. 437).

This work has been edited by Brewer (*Mon. Fr.* i. 3–72), by the Quaracchi franciscans (*Fratris Thomae de Eccleston liber de adventu Fratrum Minorum in Angliam*), and by A. G. Little (*Tractatus Fr. Thome vulgo dicti de Eccleston de adventu fratrum minorum in Angliam*). See also Father Cuthbert's 'The Friars and how they came to England' and E. Gurney Salter's 'The Coming of the Friars Minor to England and Germany.'

Thomas of Eccleston is known only from remarks in his work,[10] which he wrote about 1258–9[1] after he had spent twenty-six years in the order.[2] Thus he entered the franciscan group about 1232–3. It was probably before this that he had the training in the 'ars dictaminis' which enabled him, as Little notes, to use the 'cursus velox.'[3] He was a student at Oxford, possibly at the time that Grosseteste was master of the franciscans, about 1232–5.[4] In the time of the provincial Prior William of Nottingham (1240–54) he was at the London house of his order.[5] He dedicated his work 'predilecto patri suo, fratri Simoni de Esseby.'[6]

Thomas of Hales, O.F.M.,[7] wrote in English 'A Luve Run,' Oxford, Jesus Coll. MS. 29, fos. 187–9 (13th cent.), with the rubric:

> Incipit quidam cantus quem composuit frater Thomas de Hales de ordine fratrum minorum ad instanciam cuiusdam puelle deo dicate.

It is edited by Richard Morris in *An Old English Miscellany* (E.E.T.S.), pp. 93–9. Line 82 mentions the time of Henry III as of the present. Thomas apparently wrote one sermon in Anglo-Norman, Oxford, St. John's Coll. MS. 190, fos. 179 *et seq.* (13th cent.) entitled 'Secundum fratrem Thomam de Hales' which has been edited by M. D. Legge, *Mod. Lang. Review*, xxx (1935). 212–8. Some Latin sermons in the same MS. are probably his.

A friar Thomas wrote a 'Life of the Virgin,' a 'Life of St. Francis,' and a 'Life of St. Helena.' (a) Paris, Dominican Lib. Rue St. Honoré; (b) Paris, Abbey of St. Victor, MS. 690, in which the prologue has the following:

> Vitam Virginis gloriose matris Jesu Christi Marie cum eiusdem omnipotentis Jesu Christi opitulatione secundum seriem sancti Evangelii cupiens, ad similitudinem vite beati patris nostri Francisci necnon et

1 Stevens, *op. cit.* p. 355.
2 See Thomas of Chabham above; a Thomas, subdean, appears in a charter of 17 Aug. 1239 (B.M. MS. Egerton 3013, fo. 111); called 'Eblesburne' (*Rot. R. Grosseteste*, p. 43).
3 *Reg. of St. Osmund*, p. 254; Hoare, *op. cit.* p. 732 (Nicholas now subdean, Thomas a witness).
4 Grantham 'Australis' (?) (*ibid.*).
5 *Rot. R. Grosseteste*, p. 64.
6 *Ibid.* p. 83.
7 *Ibid.* p. 89.
8 *C.P.R.*, 1232–47, pp. 492, 494.
9 T. p. 249; *D.N.B.* under Eccleston. Best life appears in Little, *op. cit.* p. xx.
10 Ecclestons appear in the *Coucher Book of Whalley Abbey* (Chetham Soc.), ed. Hulton, *passim.*

1 *Mon. Fr.* i. 3.
2 *Op. cit.*
3 'Ut diceret dominus Lincolniensis quod . . .'; possibly Eccleston entered at Oxford (*Mon. Fr.* p. 39).
4 *Ibid.* p. 9.
5 *Ibid.* pp. 9, 17.
6 *Ibid.* p. 3.
7 T. p. 369; *D.N.B.* under Hales.

vite sancte Helene, breviter ordinare per capitula queque distinguere (Quétif-Echard, i. 490).

The franciscan Thomas of Hales who lived and wrote in the reign of Henry III is probably the one mentioned by Adam Marsh as a friend.[1] He apparently joined with the guardian and prior of his house in London in a letter to Fulk Basset, bishop of London, 1244–58.[2]

Thomas Jorz, O.P., was a theologian.[3] His only certain extant piece, and it may be only a report, is a sermon preached at Oxford about 1290, in Worcester Cathedral Library MS. Q. 46 (Little-Pelster, p. 181; Little, *F.S.O.* p. 868).

Quétif-Echard, on the authority of Ludovicus Valeoletanus, gives the following attributions to Thomas: 'Commentary upon the Four Books of the Sentences,' 'Quodlibeta,' 'Liber de Beata Visione,' 'De Paupertate Christi,' 'Commentarii Super Logicam Aristotelis,' 'Super Philosophiam Naturalem et Moralem,' 'Questiones cum Tractatibus Multis,' and 'Super Psalterium.' No trace of evidence remains apparently of these either in extant books or in the very full lists of published dominican works in 'Archiv für Litteratur- und Kirchengeschichte,' ii. 226–40.

Thomas is said to have had six brothers, all dominicans.[4] However, a brother, Robert de Jorz,[5] appears frequently as verderer, coroner, and in other capacities in Sherwood forest and in Nottingham.[6] In view of the hereditary nature of offices we may well believe that Robert and consequently Thomas were the sons of Richard de Jorz, verderer of Sherwood forest, who died in 1288 or earlier.[1] Robert and probably Richard held a knight's fee in Birton Jorz, whence the family apparently drew its name.[2] Thomas had a brother William who was a dominican[3] and two others, Walter and Roland, who were in turn archbishops of Armagh.[4]

The bibliographical tradition that Thomas studied and taught at Paris and Oxford and taught at London is apparently conjectural.[5] He was among the rather outstanding men who preached at Oxford about 1290. He was regent master in 1292–3 and possibly later.[6] In 1295 he was prior of the dominicans at Oxford and secured a safe-conduct to accompany Hugh of Manchester [q.v.] to the general chapter of the order at Argentyne.[7] He was elected provincial prior of the English province at Oxford in 1297.[8] As such he probably attended the yearly general chapters: there is evidence that he went to the meeting at Marseilles in 1300[9] and to Besançon in 1303 when he was absolved from this office.[10] Not much evidence of his priorate remains. He debated five days in February 1302 in the chapter house of the cathedral at Exeter before finally coming to an agreement.[11] In March 1303 he informed the king of two renegade friars who were to be arrested.[12]

On 1 Jan. 1304 Thomas was issued a

[1] *Mon. Fr.* i. 181, 395.
[2] C. L. Kingsford, *Grey Friars of London*, p. 54.
[3] T. p. 749; *D.N.B.* under Jorz; Little-Pelster, pp. 187–8.
[4] *D.N.B.*
[5] Robert is called brother of Thomas and connected with Sherwood Forest (*C.Cl.R.*, 1302–7, p. 481).
[6] *Ibid.*, 1296–1302, p. 273; *ibid.*, 1307–13, pp. 88, 108, 109; *C.Ch.R.*, 1257–1300, p. 468; *C.Cl.R.*, 1296–1302, p. 401.

[1] *C.Cl.R.*, 1279–88, p. 516.
[2] *Feudal Aids*, iv. 96, 105, 113.
[3] He was at a baptism at Nottingham on the day of Holy Trinity, 10 Edw. I; not called a brother of Thomas (*Inquisitions, Edward I*, iv. no. 165).
[4] *D.N.B.*
[5] *D.N.B.*; T. p. 749 under Walleys, Thomas.
[6] Little-Pelster, p. 181.
[7] *C.Cl.R.*, 1288–96, p. 440; *C.P.R.*, 1292–1301, pp. 130, 131.
[8] *E.H.R.* viii (1893). 522.
[9] *C.P.R.*, 1292–1301, p. 497; London, Society of Antiquaries MS. 119, fo. 35; royal oblates, the prior received his 40 marks expenses from the king.
[10] *E.H.R.*, viii. 522; *Thes. Nov. Anecd.* iv. 1888–9.
[11] A. G. Little and R. E. Easterling, *Franciscans and Dominicans of Exeter*, pp. 41–3, 67 *et seq.*
[12] *C.P.R.*, 1301–7, p. 123.

safe-conduct to go to Rome for two years,[1] apparently on the king's business.[2] A master of theology, he was made cardinal priest of St. Sabina before Christmas 1305.[3] On 13 Jan. 1304 he wrote from Lyons thanking the king for his aid in his promotion.[4] In April 1306 the king made a series of requests of the new cardinal [5] and in September begged to be kept informed about affairs at the curia.[6] In May 1307 the king was ordered to hold a living worth three hundred marks for the cardinal,[7] probably for his brother Walter, who was made archbishop of Armagh in the same year.[8] Twice Edward I wrote him, once about his affairs with France [9] and earlier about the canonization of Robert Grosseteste.[10]

Under Edward II Thomas remained in both papal and royal favour. In 1308 the king registered a complaint with him about papal action and urged the canonization of Thomas of Cantelupe.[11] By this time the cardinal seems to have had a large entourage : in 1308 permission was given for his chaplain, Mr. Adam de Cirencester, and two yeomen conducting his horses and harness to go beyond seas.[12] On 4 March 1309 the king granted a yearly pension of one hundred marks to Thomas, with lesser amounts to other cardinals.[13] The instalment for the first six months is recorded ; [14] possibly the prebend of Graham South may have been substituted for this.[15] In 1310 he was one of the group chosen to consider the doctrine of the franciscan Peter Johannis Olivi.[1] Later in the year he started upon a papal mission to the Emperor Henry VII, but died at Geneva on 13 December.[2] His body was returned to England and buried among the dominicans of Oxford.[3]

[1] *C.P.R.*, 1301–7, p. 206.

[2] *C.Cl.R.*, 1302–7, pp. 212, 351.

[3] *Rishanger, Chronica* (R.S.), ed. H. T. Riley, p. 227.

[4] P.R.O., 7th Rep. D.K., App. II, p. 270.

[5] *C.Cl.R.*, 1302–7, pp. 431, 436, 439.

[6] *Foedera*, ii. 1024.

[7] *C.Cl.R.*, 1302–7, p. 534.

[8] *Foedera*, iii. 4.

[9] *Ibid.* ii. 1058.

[10] *Ibid.* p. 1054.

[11] *Ibid.* iii. 56, 77.

[12] *C.P.R.*, 1307–13, p. 64.

[13] *Ibid.* p. 105.

[14] *Foedera*, iii. 181.

[15] He held at death this prebend (T. p. 749, citing 'Reg. Jo. Dalderby'). For other instances of his desire for revenue see *C.E.P.R.* ii. *passim.*

Thomas of Kent was probably the author of an Anglo-Norman 'Roman d'Alexandre' or 'De Toute Chevalerie' (Vising, p. 47). (a) Cambridge, Trinity Coll. MS. 1446 (O. 9, 34) (13th cent.), 46 fos. ; (b) Durham Cathedral Lib. MS. C. iv, fo. 27*b* (14th cent.) ; (c) Oxford, Robartes MS. (mid 13th cent.), fragment of 32 lines ; (d) B.N. MS. fond fr. 24364 (*c.* 1300).

There are several instances of 13th century Thomases of Kent, but the Anglo-Norman writer cannot be definitely identified with any of them.[4]

Thomas of Kidderminster, monk of Tewkesbury, was probably the author of part of the 'Annals' of that house, B.M. MS. Cleopatra A. vii, edited by H. R. Luard (*Ann. Monast.* i. 108–24, 154–65).

At the bottom of fo. 31*b* in red ink is the note 'Isto anno [1236] factus est Thom. Kyderminster monachus a sancto Roberto abbate circa fest. sce. Katerine.' This sort of note is frequently added by monastic writers. (*Cf.* Arnald Fitzthedmar, Gregory of Kaerwent, John of Everisden, John Taxter, and others.) The main part of the chronicle, 1063–1238 and 1252–3, on

[1] *Annales Ordinis Minorum*, ed. Wadding, under 1310. On 15 Mar. 1310 the king granted a safe-conduct to his chaplain, Robert de Giseburne.

[2] *D.N.B.*

[3] Leland, *Collect.* iv. 59.

[4] At Bath a vicar and canon (H.M.C., Wells MSS. pp. 82, 98 ; *Archaeologia*, li. 345) ; a clerk of the name (*Register of St. Osmund*, R.S., ed. W. H. R. Jones, ii. 43) ; in 1266–7 a subdeacon was presented to the church of Bokeby (*Rot. R. Gravesend*, p. 108) ; another witnessed a charter, following knights and a chaplain, and called dominus (*Coucher Book of Whalley Abbey*, Chetham Soc., ed. W. A. Hulton, p. 341).

fos. 7–34*b*, 41–52*b* is clearly in another hand. Thomas's share apparently covers the years 1238–52 and 1254–8 on fos. 34*b*–40*b*, 52*b*–8. He is also probably responsible for many notes in the margin of the earlier scribe's work. He had a rather untidy hand and a marked preference for red ink.

Thomas of Kidderminster thus entered Tewkesbury about 25 Nov. 1236. Possibly he was made secretary, an office which was endowed at Tewkesbury.[1] A reference in 1260 speaks of him as almoner.[2]

Thomas Lemman, see under **Richard of Thetford.**

Thomas of Lichfield was dean of Chichester.[3] In a MS. (now Oxford, University Coll. MS. 148) Thomas of Lichfield included much that interested him. Thus he included the statutes of his church:

> Statuta ecclesie cathedralis Cicestrensis et pertinet liber idem ad decanatum eiusdem et sic ad eandem ecclesiam.

See 'Archaeologia,' xlv (1877). 160, where the volume is described. The beginning of the statutes gives Thomas as dean, and the date, which shows that this was Thomas of Lichfield rather than Thomas Bergstede at the end of the century. Among the pieces is a Meditation: *inc.* 'Cum ad iuventutis immo,' with the note 'Meditatio Thome decani Cycestrens' (fos. 55–6*b*). There is also an 'Oratio': *inc.* 'Deus in misericordia dives,' entitled 'Oratio eiusdem Thome decani' (fo. 56*b*). A note says 'Iste liber totus pertinet ad decanum Cicester' (fo. 56*b*).

Master Thomas of Lichfield had letters of presentation to the church at 'Huntenton' of 18 Aug. 1212.[4] At Durham on 31 Aug. 1213 he was paid thirty marks as a royal

[1] MS. cit. fo. 94*b*; 'ad secretarium pertinet,' an endowment for parchment (*ibid.* fo. 95*b*).

[2] 'Fr. Tho. Kidder. tunc temporis elemos. Tewk' (*ibid.* fo. 60*b*).

[3] T. p. 481.

[4] *Rot. Litt. Pat.* p. 94.

gift when leaving for the papal curia.[1] In May 1214 he was paid fifteen marks by the king.[2] He seems to have been in the family of Bishop Richard Marsh of Durham in the autumn of 1218.[3] Bishop Pandulf appointed him proctor in a case at the royal court in 1219.[4] 'H. canon Lond.' and he were appointed royal proctors at Rome on 6 Nov. 1221.[5] In the summer of 1222 he and 'H. chancellor of London' were to receive three hundred marks for expenses in going to Rome as messengers for the king.[6] On 5 June 1223 he witnessed another charter of Bishop Richard as chancellor, probably of Lichfield.[7] He was apparently in this office in 1226.[8] By 1225 he witnessed a charter at York;[9] in the next year he was a canon there.[10] Probably he held the two prebends simultaneously. He was canon still in 1228.[11] By Wednesday after Easter

[1] *Documents Illustrative of Eng. Hist.*, ed. H. Cole, p. 240.

[2] *Ibid.* p. 264.

[3] 22 September, Durham cathedral muniment room, cart. 1, fo. 73; *Foederatum Prioratus Dunelmensis* (Surtees Soc.), pp. lxxxviii, 3, 4; *C.E.P.R.* i. 135, 241; *Registres de Grégoire IX*, ed. L. Auvray, p. 756; B.M. Add. MS. 15351, fo. 268.

[4] *C.P.R.*, 1216–25, p. 197.

[5] *Ibid.* p. 319.

[6] 'Liberate de thr'o H. London eccle. cancellar. et magro Thom' de Lichefeld [blank] versis a cur' Rom' ubi profecti sunt in nuntium nrm per preceptum nrm trigint' m. de exp. suas acquietandos' (P.R.O., Exchequer of receipt, receipt roll 6 Hen. III, E. 401/5).

[7] *Reg. Walter Gray*, p. 148; given as Lichfield in P.R.O., ancient correspondence, S.C. vi. 120.

[8] *Archaeologia*, xlv. 207. His statutes as chancellor apparently appear also in B.M. MS. Harley 6973, fo. 28, a late transcript.

[9] Recites letter of Honorius III, dated '13 Kal. Jan. pont. nost. ix' (B.M. MS. Cotton, Nero D. iii, fo. 55).

[10] 8 January (Pressutti, ii. 394); 4 May (B.M. MS. Cotton, Nero D. iii, fo. 52); first Wednesday after the Annunciation (*ibid.* fo. 53); 4 September (B.M. MS. Cotton, Claudius B. iii, fo. 66*b*; *Rot. Litt. Claus.* ii. 153).

[11] *Reg. Walter Gray*, p. 232*n*; undated attestations as canon of York include ones in *ibid.* p. 139*n*; B.M. MS. Cotton, Claudius B. iii, fos. 23, 39*b*, 101*b*; York cathedral muniments, Magnum registrum album, fo. 46*b*.

1230 he was dean of Chichester.[1] In 1232 he had the statutes of the cathedral drawn up. The next year he made arrangements for the founding of a chantry for his soul.[2] Other business left extant documents.[3] He had died by 1241, when his successor appears.[4]

Thomas of Malmesbury, O.P., was a disputant at Oxford *c.* 1289 (Little-Pelster, p. 93).

Thomas of Marlborough, abbot of Evesham,[5] was a man of many interests of which some were literary. He wrote a 'Vite et Gesta Patronorum et Abbatum Eveshamie (714–1214)': *inc.* 'De constitutione Eveshamensis cenobii et benefactoribus et malefactoribus et abbatibus eiusdem ecclesie, et operibus eorum bonis et malis, collectus a Thoma priore Eweshamie ex variis cartis et scriptis et factis manifestis.'

(a) Bodl. Lib. MS. Rawlinson A. 287, fos. 117 *et seq.*, probably in Thomas's own hand, in which the continuator writes 'Post prioratum fecit . . . Haymonem super Apocalypsim et vitas et gesta patronorum et abbatum Eveshamie in uno volumine'[6] (*Chronicon de Evesham*, pp. xxxiv, 268); (b) possibly Thomas wrote out another copy as the continuator adds 'Et iterum easdem vitas et eadem gesta seorsum in alio volumine' (*ibid.* p. 268).

This chronicle has been edited by W. D. Macray, 'Chronicon de Evesham' (R.S.). It is translated in part by G. G. Coulton, 'Five Centuries of Religion,' pp. 347–378.

Thomas also abridged a 'Life of St. Egwin.' It appears in the same MS. and is edited by Macray (*Chronicon*, pp. 39–67). It begins:

> Incipit Prologus Libri Secundi de Miraculis Sancti Egwini quæ Deus per illum operatus est postquam ab hac mutabili luce decessit; editus a Dominico Priore Eweshamiæ.

He also wrote a 'Life of St. Wistan,' which appears in the same MS. and is edited by Macray (*Chronicon*, pp. 325–37) with the note:

> Rogatus fui aliquando a fratribus ut vitam eximii martyris Wistani advocati nostri sine solœcismo et alio vitio, quod nondum factum fuit, stilo commendarem prolixiori; necnon et vitam sanctissimi patroni nostri beati Ecgwini episcopi, quæ prolixius tractabatur, solvo per omnia historiæ tenore, in tantum abbreviarem ut fastidiosi auditores tædio non afficerentur, ita videlicet stilum temperans . . . qualitate natalitiorum eorundem in eisdem festivitatibus ad legendam in nocturnis vigiliis sufficeret (*ibid.* pp. 27–8).

Thomas of Marlborough had studied at Paris with Richard Poore under Stephen Langton (*Chronicon*, p. 232). Subsequently he taught law at Oxford and Exeter (p. 267): probably he had also studied there under three clerks of the archbishop of Canterbury, John of Tynemouth, Simon of Sewell, and Honorius (p. 126). Although Thomas became a monk of Evesham in 1199 or 1200 (p. 264), he had probably been connected with the abbey as novice or legal advisor even in the time of Abbot Adam (1160–91) (p. 102). One may suspect from the number of his books (p. 267) that he either had a private fortune or had succeeded well as a canon lawyer. Since these books possibly represent his interests early in life the list is inserted here. He possessed:

> . . . libros utriusque juris, canonici scilicet et civilis, . . . et libros physicæ, scilicet librum Democriti et librum Antiparalenionis et librum Graduum secundum Constantinum, et Isidorum de Officiis, et Quadrivium Isidori, Tullium de Amicitia et alterum librum Tullii, et Tullium de Senectute et Tullium de Paradoxis, Lucanum et Juvenalem, et multos alios auctores, et multos sermones et notas et quæstiones theologiæ et multas notas artis grammaticæ cum verbis præceptivis et libro accentuum.

[1] *Abstract of Feet of Fines relating to Sussex*, ed. L. F. Salzmann, p. 70; *C.Cl.R.*, 1227–31, p. 576.

[2] *Archaeologia*, xlv. 172; *cf. ibid.* 168 for a second chantry; British Archaeol. Assoc. *Journal*, xxii. 116.

[3] *Chartulary of the Priory of St. Peter at Sele*, ed. L. F. Salzmann, p. 44; *Sussex Archaeol. Collections*, li. 45, 48, 51, 54, 56, 60, 64.

[4] *Sussex Archaeol. Collect.* li. 49, 60.

[5] *D.N.B.* under Marleberghe.

[6] Haymo precedes the 'Vite' in this MS.

On 15 Aug. 1202 Thomas was summoned to advise the abbot, Roger Norreys, in regard to a proposed episcopal visitation of the bishop of Worcester (p. 109). He advised resisting the visitation, and the convent agreed with him, refusing to admit the bishop when he appeared on 23 August (p. 117). Excommunicated by the bishop, Thomas sought the archbishop of Canterbury three miles from London on 27 August (p. 119). On 3 September the case was heard at Worcester, but adjourned to Lincoln (p. 121). Thomas first sought the abbot at Newbury near the sea (p. 121), then went to Lincoln and thence to London by 19 October. For his services Thomas probably was made dean of Christianity in the Vale of Evesham (pp. 196, 264).

Thomas seems to have led a revolt in 1203 against the abbot, who harvested some land farmed out by the monks (p. 125). Before the archbishop and his clerks, Thomas's former masters, he spoke to good effect, threatening a renunciation of the habit by the monks and convincing the judges (p. 127). However, he was captured by the abbot's men, but was rescued by friends from death (as it seemed to him) (p. 127). The archbishop came to Evesham and caused both parties to select arbitrators, at Thomas's suggestion (pp. 129–30). Marlborough and three others were banished for a time (p. 130).

Faced with episcopal visitation the abbot and his monks laid aside their hostility. The abbot, Thomas of Warwick, and Thomas of Marlborough proceeded to Rome. Thomas of Marlborough left on 29 Sept. 1204 and reached Rome on 7 November (p. 142). Upon the pope's promising to reopen the case, Thomas gave a gift of a silver cup. Meanwhile the abbot had been imprisoned at Chalons : to seek him Thomas went on 20 Jan. 1205 to Piacenza and then to Pavia (p. 143). Even after the abbot's arrival in March Thomas avoided him for a time, but finally agreed to stay at his lodgings (pp. 144–5). Thomas was somewhat afraid of his superior (p. 145) and took the precaution of leaving money with a third party to pay for his release in case the abbot should imprison him (p. 144). Upon the advice of the abbey's patron, Cardinal Hugolino, and with the bènediction of pope and abbot, Thomas left Rome on 18 Apr. 1205 and studied at Bologna for six months (p. 147). Returning to Rome in October he took up the prosecution of the case at the hearing in December (pp. 149–51). Selecting as his advocates two very distinguished Bolognese lawyers, a papal chaplain, and a clerk of the papal chancellor, he conducted the case with obvious pride (p. 153). He entitles one section of the narrative 'De subtilissima responsione Thome et advocatorum eius circa interpretationem privilegiorum' (p. 165). The fifth hearing took place on 22 December (p. 164) and two days later sentence was pronounced in his favour (p. 169). Thomas fainted for joy. The judicial decree is dated 18 Jan. 1206 (p. 179).

The case of the Vale of Evesham's jurisdiction came up next (pp. 184 *et seq.*). Too poor to pay for lawyers, he undertook to defend the cause himself, and on 3 February the case was referred to judges in England (p. 191). Being without means to pay the usual gifts to pope and cardinals Thomas slipped away from Rome without bidding them adieu (p. 200).[1]

Upon Marlborough's return, doubtless with increased prestige, the quarrel with the abbot was renewed (p. 200). After a council at Reading on 19 Oct. 1206 (p. 202) Thomas of Norwich and Thomas of Marlborough were expelled by the abbot, but they were accompanied on 25 November by thirty other monks (p. 203). After a vain attempt to use force, the abbot secured their return by making promises. For some years conditions were better. However, in 1213 at Wallingford on 31 October Marlborough made arrangements for the

[1] Macray publishes one of the bonds held by a Roman merchant (*Chronicon*, p. xxvi).

payment of debts to Roman creditors (p. 230). The abbot refused to pay and in general acted tyrannically. Marlborough took the matter to the archbishop and then to the papal legate (pp. 232–3). The legate came to Evesham and there commanded Thomas to repeat his previous charges: negligence, criminal activities, illegal election, and unchastity on the part of the abbot (pp. 236 *et seq.*). Sentence of deposition was passed upon the abbot on 22 Nov. 1213 (p. 250). Marlborough ends his chronicle with advice to the brethren (pp. 257–60).

With the cessation of Thomas's account the information about his activity is naturally less detailed. He seems to have restored or repaired, acting probably as architect, some of the damaged parts of the buildings (p. 265). In 1215 he accompanied Abbot Ralph to the fourth Lateran council and seems to have improved his stay there by increasing the privileges of Evesham (p. 266).

In the 'second year of his return' he was elected sacristan (p. 266). In a year, 1217–8, he made a long series of notable improvements and additions, including an augmentation of the revenues of the sacristy (p. 267). Largely as a result of his activity he was elected prior. In this office (1218–29) he continued his varied and energetic activity (pp. 267–72). He helped to make, bought, or wrote quite a notable series of books for Evesham (pp. 268–9), added to the equipment of his church, augmented the revenues of the monastery, and built monuments for his predecessors. In 1229 the brothers elected Thomas abbot by acclamation, for which the pope annulled the election (pp. 272-3). In 1230 he was re-elected properly (p. 273), consecrated on 12 July and installed on 29 September. His immediate problem was the abbey's debt, which he succeeded in reducing rapidly. He prepared his own monument magnificently besides erecting episcopal insignia upon the monuments of his two predecessors (p. 275). He continued his benefactions and energetic care of his abbey until death,[1] on 12 Sept. 1236 (p. 278). The 13th century saw few like him.

Thomas of Muskham was a monk of Dale or Stanley Park and author of a 'History of Dale or Stanley Park.' (a) B.M. MS. Cotton, Vespasian E. xxvi, fos. 180–7*b*; (b) *ibid.*, Julius C. vii, p. 265 (a late transcript). The work is edited by W. H. S. Hope in the Derbyshire Archaeological and Natural History Society's *Journal*, v. 1–19, in Latin with an English translation, and appears also in Dugdale's 'Monasticon,' vi. 892–7. The author's name comes from the letters beginning each section:

> Ego tum invocatus Spiritus Sancti gratiam talium oblatratus non verens serenarij vices [2] olixis exemplo: aure surda pertransibo nomen meum meritis legencium conscribi faciat altissimus in libro vivencium volenti tamen illud scire de faceli constare poterit per litteras capitulares (*Journal*, v. 3–4).

The letters read 'Thomas de Musca.' Among the books given by Humphrey, duke of Gloucester, to Oxford in 1439 was a 'Musca super "Cantica Canticorum"' (*Munimenta Acad.*, R.S., ed. H. Anstey, ii. 759).

From his chronicle it appears that Thomas entered the abbey as a boy in the time of John Grauncorth (1233–53),[3] and had outlived him. In the cartularies of Dale there is a reference to a Thomas de Muskham, canon, probably the author.[4] Possibly he is the Thomas, canon, who attests a charter of a Hugh de Muskham, among charters of this family.[5] From the documents the

[1] Some documents of his administration survive: a confirmation of a gift by a predecessor to the church of Bretford (B.M. MS. Harley 3763, fo. 154); an acknowledgement of the right of visitation of the archbishop of Canterbury (B.M. MS. Cotton, Titus C. ix, fo. 22*b*); Lambeth palace MS. 1212, fo. 92*b*; Bodl. Lib. MS. Tanner 223, fo. 53*b*; *Chronicon*, p. xxxii; possibly P.R.O., ancient deeds, D. 2050.

[2] Voces?

[3] Hope, *op. cit.* pp. 16–7; for Graunforth see *ibid.* pp. 82, 84.

[4] *Ibid.* p. 2; B.M. MS. Cotton, Vespasian E. xxvi, fo. 79.

[5] B.M. MS. Harley 1063, fos. 97, 101*b*.

following genealogy of the Muskhams is drawn [1] :

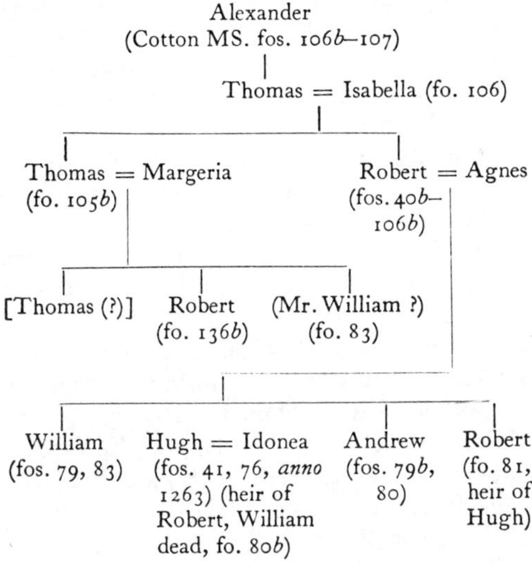

The author of the chronicle is possibly the son of Thomas, son of Thomas. The one clear date, that of Hugh's charter, 1263, suggests that the author is of that generation.[2]

Thomas of Quappelod (Cappelad), O.F.M., preached a sermon at Oxford, 1292 (Little-Pelster, p. 184).

Thomas Rondel or **Rundel, O.F.M.,** was the author of a 'Commentary upon the Sentences,' [3] cited by William of Ware (Florence, Bibl. Laur. MS. plut. 33 dext. cod. I, fo. 23*b*), 'Pro ista opinione sunt auctoritates Anselmi De Concordia . . . vide apud Rundell.' His response at a disputation is in Assisi MS. 158, quest. 119, 'Respondit Rundel minor.'

Thomas lectured at Paris upon the Sentences, probably composing his treatise there.[1] He became, about 1296–8, the twenty-seventh regent master of the franciscans at Oxford.[2] In 1309, a master of theology, he was one of the inquisitors appointed to hear the accusations against the knights templars.[3] He was buried at London.[4] His family is unknown.[5]

Thomas of Salisbury [6] was the author of a 'Treatise on Preaching' : *inc.* 'Humane nature condicio secundum,' Cambridge, Corpus Christi Coll. MS. 455, fos. 1–96 (13th cent.), *expl.* 'Explicit summa de arte predicandi quam fecit mag. Thomas de Salesbiriensi.'

A Master Thomas of Salisbury witnessed a charter of Hugh de Templo,[7] who was a clerk in 1208, a canon of Salisbury in 1214, and probably dead by 1226.[8] John of Garland [q.v.], who was at Paris before 1220, speaks of a famous master named Thomas who came from Salisbury,[9] and the glossator identifies him with Chobham, but that may be merely a guess.[10] On the other hand, if it is accurate, then this treatise on preaching must be added to Chobham's works.

Thomas Sperman, O.P., was a theologian.[11] An ancient catalogue of dominican writers gives 'Fr. Thomas Anglicus scripsit postillas super Apostolum [Paulum in one MS.],' who is identified as Sperman in *Archiv für Litteratur- und Kirchengeschichte*, ii (1886). 231.

1 From the Cotton MS.

2 There are references to Thomas, son of Thomas of Muskham, in the Harley MS. fos. 102*b*, 104*b*, 155*b*–157, and to 'Mr. William,' brother of Robert de Muskham, in time of Abbot John in P.R.O., Exchequer, Augmentation office, Misc. Books, E. 315/47, no. 217.

3 Little, *G.F.* p. 162 ; *F.S.O.* p. 862.

1 *Eccleston*, p. 68, *n.* 10 ; 'qui legerat sentencias Parisius' (Phillipps MS. 3119, fo. 76).

2 Little, *F.S.O.* p. 862 ; *cf.* App. A.

3 Wilkins, *Concilia*, ii. 336, 337.

4 *Eccleston*, p. 68.

5 In Kirkstead charters a 'Mr. Gilbert Rundel' is mentioned (B.M. MS. Cotton, Vespasian E. xviii, fos. 3*b*, 33*b*) ; and at Stoke near Clare, Norfolk, there was a William Rundel and his wife Agnes (B.M. MS. Cotton, App. 21, fos. 88*b*, 92*b*).

6 T. p. 711.

7 Gift of Andrew Giffard to St. Mary of Stanley in Sutton (*Cat. Ancient Deeds*, iv. 322, A. 8529).

8 *Register of St. Osmund* (R.S.), ed. W. H. R. Jones, i. 190, 259, 292, 380 ; ii. 49.

9 B.M. MS. Cotton, Claudius A. x, fo. 64.

10 *Ibid.* fo. 64*b*.

11 T. p. 684.

Tanner, quoting Bale and Pits, gives: 'Comm. in Genesis,' 'In Paulum ad Hebraeos,' 'In Canonicam Jacobi,' and 'Questiones Disputatas' (T. p. 684).

Thomas Sperman is included in an untrustworthy list of dominicans associated with the university of Paris (*Archiv*, ii. 191). Even his dates are uncertain.

Thomas Sprot was a monk of St. Augustine's, Canterbury, and chronicler.[1] His work apparently remains in B.M. MS. Tiberius A. ix, fos. 102 *et seq.* (burned badly at end): *inc.* 'Lux vera que illuminat omnem hominem.' This MS. is identified by M. R. James (*A.L.C.D.* p. 519) as no. 931 in the ancient catalogue of St. Augustine's library. This work, broken off sharply in 1221 (corresponding to fo. 168 of the preceding MS.) remains in (a) B.M. MS. Vitellius E. xiv, fos. 237–52*b*; (b) B.M. MS. Vitellius D. xi, fos. 39–69*b*; (c) B.M. MS. Harley 692, fos. 75*b*–193*b*.

Sprot's chronicle was used by Thorne and Elmham (C. Hardwicke, *Historia Monasterii S. Augustini, Cant.*, R.S., p. 77). Thorne, just before writing of the year 1232, remarked:

> Hucusq; Cronica sua partim perduxit *T. Sprot*; abhinc idem frater *Willelmus* sui temporis digessit historiam (Twysden, *Historiae Anglicanae Scriptores* x, col. 1881).

But in the preface he said:

> Et quia quidam laborarunt, utputa *Thomas Sprot* & alii, quos desiderium hortabatur proficiendi, . . . Intendens a fine dicti *Thomæ*, scilicet anno incarnationis Dominicæ M.CC.lxxij. abbate *Rogero* de *Cicestria* debitum suæ carnis tunc exsolvente (*ibid.* col. 1757–8).

The suggestion that MCCLXXII can be explained away as a corruption of MCCXXXII, advanced by Hardwicke (*Historia Monast. S. Augustini*, p. xv), is invalidated because Abbot Roger died in 1272. Another explanation is possible. Thorne, upon commencing, intended to incorporate Thomas's work and to continue it from 1272. However, he found that Thomas had ceased to be thorough after 1228 and the rest was only a miscellaneous set of notes. Thus when he finished the earlier portion, to 1228, he decided to add additional material. Leland states that the chronicle ended in 1272 (*Collect.* iii. 51).

[1] T. p. 685; *D.N.B.* under Sprott.

The chronicle edited by T. Hearne in 'Thome Sprotti Chronica,' pp. 3–164, is in its present form obviously a St. Augustine's chronicle of a much later date, and its 13th century chronology is so preposterous that it can hardly have been based upon work of that time. W. Bell edited a curious roll under the title 'Thomas Sprott's Chronicle of Profane and Sacred History.' The chronicle goes into the reign of Edward I, but the editor failed to notice that the genealogical charts go to Henry IV through St. Thomas of Lancaster.

Thomas may have been a member of the Sprot families who figure prominently in St. Augustine's register.[1] From the books given by him to his house it is clear that he lived into the third quarter of the 13th century. They also show that he had probably studied grammar, rhetoric, natural science, and law.[2]

Thomas of Sturey,[3] monk of Christchurch, Canterbury, gave his house a very large number of books (James, *A.L.C.D.* pp. 89–

[1] *Register of St. Augustine's, Canterbury*, ed. Turner and Salter, *passim*.

[2] Under numbers in the ancient catalogue of St. Augustine's library: 718 'Sermones T. Sport in quaterno'. 859 'Ordinarium vite religiose, . . . et collac[c]iones Wallensis ad omne genus hominum T. Sport'. 1043 'Liber de vegetalibus et in eodem Methephisica, de celo et mundo, de sompno et vigilia, de longitudine et breuitate vite, de differencia spc̄ et anime et, liber de causis cum commento T. Sport. 2º fo. *sunt quidem*.' 1094 'Questiones super iiijor libros Ethicorum T. Sport'. 1300 'Lib' Elenchorum thome sprot 2º fo. *quiahec*.' 1334 'Tabula super sentenciarum fratris thome sprot in quaterno et in eodem Sententie versificate. Item versus de concordia veteris et noui testamenti'. 1657 'Item decretales T. sprote sine glo' (James, *A.L.C.D.* pp. 271, 288, 309, 316, 351, 354, 391).

[3] T. p. 697.

94, nos. 907–65). It is probable that the evidence of his ownership has been mistaken for evidence of authorship of the following works:

'Commentarius in Canonem Misse': *inc.* 'Vere dignum et justum est. Gratias agamus.' Bodl. Lib. MS. Digby 4, fos. 1–30 (13th cent.), with a title in different hand, 'Tractatus super canonem misse Thome de Stureya' (James, *A.L.C.D.* no. 954). See also MSS. Laud Misc. 160 and 161, where also another writer adds the name of Thomas Sturey after the original title.

'De Sacramentis': *inc.* 'Inter opera nostre salutis,' 'ex officina Reineri Wolff,' and (with *incipit*) 'Nicolaus Brigan in collectionibus' (Bale, *Index*, p. 455).

'Moralitates in Apocalipsin': *inc.* 'Vidi angelum Dei per medium celi' (Bale, *loc. cit.*).

'Exceptiones Philosophorum' and 'Prognosticon de Utroque Seculo': no *incipit* (*ibid.*).

Thomas Sturey entered Christchurch about 1249.[1] He was one of two monks deputed to install the new prior, Adam, on 16 Apr. 1264,[2] and he was sub-prior in 1270.[3] If his books reflect his interests, he enjoyed a variety of subjects. In the catalogues he is called 'senior' to distinguish him from Thomas Sturey, junior, who entered about 1275 and died in 1298.[4]

Thomas Sutton, O.P., was a theologian.[5] The starting point for his bibliography is the ancient list of dominican writings:

> Fr. Thomas de Sutona natione anglicus mag. in theologia, scripsit super predicamenta, super sex principia. Item complevit scriptum super periermenias. Item super priora. Item de unitate formarum. Item duo quolibet. Item de relatione. Item summam Thome. Item super Psalterium (*Archiv für Litteratur- und Kirchengeschichte*, ii. 239).

Of these the logical works were formerly at the Austin Canons, St. Mary de Pré, Leicester. In its ancient catalogue under 'Logica' appears the title 'Sutton' (John Nichols, *History and Antiquities of Leicestershire*, i. 104). At Bruges, MS. 491, is a 'Tractatus fratris Thome Anglici de productione formarum substantialium': *inc.* 'De productione forme substancialis in esse.' The 'Quodlibeta' and 'Questiones,' now extant, have been edited by Ehrle (*op. cit.*; *cf.* P. Glorieux, *Bibliothèque Thomiste*, v. 291–6). Grabmann and Pelster were the editors of 'Thomae de Sutton, O.P., Questiones de reali distinctione inter essentiam et esse.' Possibly the 'summa Thome' is the same as the 'Fr. Thomas de Sutone librum de concordia librorum Thome' (*Archiv für Litteratur*, ii. 233).

Besides those mentioned in the lists other works remain. 'Contra Emulos et Detractores Fratrum Predicatorum': *inc.* 'Quia quidam emuli fratrum ordinis predicatorum.' (a) Oxford, Lincoln Coll. MS. 81, fos. 32–3 (14th cent.); (b) MS. formerly at Syon monastery, entitled 'Determinatio fratris Thome de Sutton contra emulos et detractores fratrum predicatorum' (Bateson, *Catalogue*, p. 148).

'Commentary on the Generation and Corruption of Aristotle.' Oxford, Merton Coll. MS. 274, fos. 92–107, with a note 'Hic terminatur expositio fratris Thome et incipit expositio fratris de Sutthona' (Ehrle, *op. cit.* p. 431; T. p. 700). He seems to have written some poetry, with a note on

[1] *Cf.* App. C. Searle, *op. cit.* p. 174: his name is the 18th after that of Roger de Sco Elphege.

[2] *Hist. Works of Gervase of Canterbury* (R.S.), ed. W. Stubbs, ii. 229.

[3] *Ibid.* p. 252.

[4] *Cf.* App. C. See also Searle, *op. cit.* p. 176: his name is 5th after 'John de Well.' Probably it is the latter who figures prominently in Christchurch accounts from 1280–95 (Lambeth MS. 242, fos. 61*b*, 70*b*, 110, 113, 153, 161, 163*b*, 167, 169*b*, 174, 175, 179, 184*b*. This Thomas was custodian of the seal from 1290.

[5] T. p. 700; Fr. Ehrle, 'Thomas de Sutton, sein Leben, sein Quolibet, et seine Questiones disputatae' in *Festschrift Georg von Hertling*, pp. 426–50; F. Pelster, 'Thomas von Sutton, O.P. ein Oxforder Verteidiger der thomistischen Lehre' in *Zeitschrift für katholische Theologie*, xlvi (1922). 212–54, 361–402; Little-Pelster, p. 282.

Arnald of Villa Nova. 'Isti versus compositi a m. Thoma Sutton.' Cambridge, Peterhouse MS. 139, flyleaf. Reports of his sermons possibly remain in Worcester Cathedral library MS. Q. 46, 'Sutton, predicator,' and in Oxford, New Coll. MS. 92, fo. 73 (14th cent.) (Little-Pelster, p. 282).

Sutton is said to have been a fellow of Merton before becoming a dominican.[1] By 1274 he was a member of the order and a deacon.[2] He may easily be confused with both a contemporary Master Thomas of Sutton [3] and another Sutton, O.P.[4] He was a master of theology, probably at Oxford, where he was disputing about 1282–90.[5] He was preaching there in 1292–3.[6] He may also have studied at Paris; [7] his 'quodlibets' are of the years 1284–7. He was licensed to hear confessions in 1300 and disputed at Oxford in the years following.[8]

Thomas de Wick was a poet and possibly chronicler.[9] He wrote a poem 'In Praise of Edward I': *inc.* 'Eadwardi regis Anglorum me pepulere.' B.M. MS. Cotton, Vespasian B. xiii, fo. 130*b* (13th cent.), with the colophon 'Expliciunt versus secundum Thomam de Wyta [probably Wyca] compositi de domino Eadwardo Anglie rege illustrissimo.' This has been edited by T. Wright in 'The Political Songs of England' (Camden Soc.), pp. 128–32. Bale records two other compositions, both 'ex camera Nicolai Grimoaldi':

Thomas Wycke, canonicus regularis, tribus modis vinum carmine laudauit, incipit 'Syncerum mihi dede merum si vis mea dicta.'

Scripsit commendationem vini et increpationem gule, incipit 'Prandens in mensa, ventris deponere pensa' (*Index*, p. 460).

A treatise 'De Fallaciis' is attributed to a man of this name: *inc.* 'De sophisticis autem elenchiis.' Oxford, Bodl. Lib. MS. Digby 204, fos. 81*b*–7*b* (early 14th cent.), entitled 'Tractatus de fallaciis [secunda manu] Thome de Wyk.' This may belong to the later Thomas de Wick. The most important work, a 'Chronicle,' is attributed to him by Bale: *inc.* 'Anno incarnat. Dom. nostri J. Chr. 1066 Willelmus dictus le Bastard' (ii. pp. iv, 72). B.M. MS. Cotton, Titus A. xiv. It has been edited by H. R. Luard in 'Annales Monastici,' iv. 6–319. Luard believes him to have been responsible for portions of the contemporary 'Oseney Chronicle' (*Ann. Monast.*), B.M. MS. Cotton, Tiberius A. ix, fos. 52–98, edited parallel to the other chronicle. Luard's belief that Thomas de Wick is the chronicler is based upon several references to members of the Wick family, and upon identity of political feeling. There is little poetry in the chronicle: see, however, under 1277. Excerpts have been edited from both chronicles in *M.G.H.SS.* xxviii. 484–503.

Of Thomas de Wick, the poet, it is only known that he wrote the 'Praise of Edward I' probably about 1275. If he was the chronicler more items may be added. His memory probably went back as far as 1258, and he was associated with Oxford. In 1282 he became a monk of Oseney.[1] In 1285 he became chronicler of the monastery, writing both his own and the Oseney chronicle until 1289 and continuing the Oseney until 1293.[2] He mentions the death of Robert de Wyka in 1246, of Edith de Wyka in 1269, and the vow of John de Wyka in 1283.[3] Possibly he was the son of Thomas de Wyke who made a fine with Oseney for a messuage in Oxford: the

[1] Ehrle, *op. cit.* p. 434; 'Quodlibetum magistri Thome Sutton, socii domus de Merton, postmodum ordinis predicatorum' (Merton Coll. MS. 138).

[2] *Reg. Walter Giffard*, p. 196.

[3] Probably a relative of Bishop Oliver Sutton, of Lincoln, and canon there from 1270 (*Rot. R. Gravesend*, pp. 43, 70, 158, 161). He became archdeacon of Nottingham *c.* 1291 (Ehrle, *op. cit.* p. 429).

[4] *Collectanea*, 2nd Series (Oxford Hist. Soc.), p. 219.

[5] Little-Pelster, p. 282.

[6] The dates of his sermon.

[7] *Archiv für Litteratur*, ii. 191, an unreliable list, however.

[8] Little-Pelster, p. 282.

[9] T. p. 773; *D.N.B.* under Wykes.

[1] *Ann. Monast.* iv. 292.

[2] *Ibid.* p. xv.

[3] *Ibid.* pp. 96, 230, 295.

latter had a widow Clementia and a son John.[1] A Thomas de Wyke, clerk and rector of Edmundsbury (' Castro Sancti Edmundi,' Caistner, Norfolk), gave Oseney in 1269–71 Elm Hall in Oxford.[2] He had a brother, Robert.[3] There are other references to an earlier parson [4] and a later monk of Worcester [5] as well as a notice of excommunication in 1275 of two ' religiosi,' John and Thomas de Wichio, possibly of Hales.[6]

Thomas de Ylleya, O.C. The works attributed to this man seem conjectures except ' Commentaria in Apocalypsim S. Johannis ' : *inc.* ' Apocalypsis, revelatio dicitur ' (Bale, *Scriptorum Illustrium Catalogus*, p. 351).

Thomas de Ylleya was born about 1254 ; he testified in 1307 that he was 53 years of age.[7] He was at Oxford during the riots in which Thomas Cantilupe was injured.[8] A ' Thomas de Illeghe Monachorum ' took the holy orders of acolyte in 1284, of subdeacon in 1287, and of deacon and priest in 1288.[9] He was said to have been in the Ipswich house of his order.[10] In 1303 he opposed the division of the carmelite province of England at the general chapter. For punishment he was sent with John of Chelveston to Bruges.[1] However, he was back in England, testifying to the sanctity of Thomas of Cantelupe, on 13 July 1307,[2] being a master of theology.

[1] *Feet of Fines for Oxfordshire* (Oxford Hist. Soc.), ed. H. E. Salter, pp. 198, 221 ; *C.Cl.R.* under 25 July 1266.

[2] *Cartulary of Oseney Abbey* (Oxford Hist. Soc.), ed. H. E. Salter, i. 97–101 ; ii. 98 ; iii. 34–5.

[3] *Ibid.* iii. 34.

[4] *Rot. R. Grosseteste*, p. 356 ; Waddesden, 1240–1 ; Bodl. Lib. MS. Dodsworth 144, fos. 48, 139 ; *Mon. Fr.* i. 350.

[5] *Documents illustrating early education in Worcester*, ed. A. F. Leach, p. 27 ; see also flyleaf of Worcester Cathedral Lib. MS. Q. 42. A ' Mr. Thomas Wykis ' once possessed Oriel Coll. MS. 31, supposedly of the next century. The Worcester chronicle (*Ann. Monast.* iv. 495–550) contains a good deal of poetry of precisely this period. Was the Worcester monk the poet ?

[6] P.R.O., C. 85/2 (8 id. July).

[7] *Acta Sanctorum*, Oct., i. 546–7, 558.

[8] *Ibid.*

[9] *Reg. Peckham* (R.S.), iii. 1035, 1044, 1047, 1048.

[10] B.M. MS. Harley 3838, fo. 23*b*.

Thomas of York, O.F.M., was a metaphysician.[3] His great work was a ' Sapientale,' ' die einzige grosse Darstellung des Systems der Metaphysick aus der Ära der Hochscholastik ' (Martin Grabmann, ' Die Metaphysik des Thomas von York,' *Festgabe zum* 60 *Geburtstag Clemens Baeumker*, p. 191). (a) Florence, Bibl. Naz. Conv. Sopp. A. 6/437 (13th cent.) ; (b) Rome, Vatican Lib. MS. Lat. 4301 (13th cent.) ; (c) Rome, Vatican Lib. MS. Lat. 6771 (13th cent.). See P. Ephrem Longpré's ' Fr. Thomas de York, O.F.M. Le première Somme metaphysique du XIII siècle ' (*A.F.H.* xix, 1926. 875–930), and Grabmann's ' Die Metaphysik,' pp. 181–93. Thomas also preached a ' Sermon ' : *inc.* ' Aspicientes in autorem fidei. In singnum huius numeri 21,' etc. (Cambridge, Trinity Coll. MS. 373, fo. 201, entitled ' Sermo fr. Thome Ebor. de passione d. n. Jhesu Christi '). According to the ' Catalogus Illustrium Franciscanorum ' he also wrote a ' Commentary on Ecclesiastes ' (Leland, *Commentarii de Scriptoribus Britannicis*, p. 272). To him has also been attributed a treatise in defence of the friars against William of St. Amour : *inc.* ' Manus que contra Omnipotentem tenditur,' edited by Max Bierbaum (*Bettelorden und Weltgeistlichkeit* a.d. *Univ. Paris*). For authorship see the ' Bettelorden,' pp. 273–342 ; Pelster in *A.F.H.* xv. 3–22 ; xix. 875 *et seq.*

The franciscan was possibly the Thomas of York, deacon, presented to the church of Garthorpe in 1238–9.[4] By 1245 he was a

[1] B.M. MS. Harley 3838, fo. 27*b*.

[2] *Loc. cit. n.* 1.

[3] T. p. 709 ; Little, *F.S.O.* p. 839.

[4] *Rot. R. Grosseteste*, pp. 403, 404. Another ' Mr. Thomas ' of York, subdeacon, and therefore to be distinguished from the other, was given a living in 1239–40 and died in 1268–9 (*ibid.* pp. 43, 151 ; *Rot. R. Gravesend*, p. 35).

franciscan and possessed a book which Adam Marsh wanted.[1] Most of the information about Thomas comes from Adam's letters. Adam mentions, in a letter to the newly elected bishop of Roskild, John Erlandi, that he had consulted Thomas upon the question of sending English franciscans to Denmark.[2] About 1250 Thomas had written to Adam upon the failure of Louis IX's crusade.[3] Adam wrote to Thomas, who was probably at London then,[4] requesting him to send the work, probably 'De duce dubiorum' of Maimonides.[5] In a letter addressed to the prior provincial about 1251 Adam pictures a brilliant future for Thomas if he is assigned to Oxford.[6] Thomas incepted at Oxford on 14 Mar. 1253, although he had never been master of arts.[7] From this date until probably 1256 he remained regent master of the franciscans at Oxford.[8] In 1256 William de Meliton [q.v.] was ordered to finish the 'Summa' of Alexander of Hales [q.v.]. Thomas of York succeeded him probably at this time. If he is the author of the defence of the friars it may mean that he went to Paris not many years after this.

W. de Bradewas, monk of Worcester, was probably the author of a short chronicle later copied into the 'Annals of Worcester.' B.M. MS. Cotton, Caligula A. ix. (early 14th cent.), edited by H. R. Luard (*Ann. Monast.* iv. 356–560). Under 1219 appears the statement :

Terra matris meæ traditur H. fratri meo libere tenenda pro xx. solidis annuis ; et homagium ejus receptum fuit a Simone priore, præsentibus W[illemo] de Bradewas sacrista, Rogero de Bathonia celerario, Ernaldo de Beverburne, monachis, Radulfo de Knichetone milite, Gervasio de Waltone, Johanne Senati persona de Bradewas, Ricardo de Grimele janitore, Roberto de Waltone chamberlango, qui habuit cappam pro homagio, Johanne Paschali et aliis (*ibid.* p. 411).

Presumably the author's mother had died that year. In the obituary of that year before the bishop of Hereford, the regent of England, an outstanding baron, and a monk, is the name, Albreda de Bradewas. The chronicle may well be a list of gifts to the sacrists by prelates consecrated there to which additional items, chiefly of local interest, have been added (see pp. 380, 384, 385, 389 *et passim*). There was also a 'Gesta Sacristarum' of Bury St. Edmunds. In the circumstances it seems probable that the author was the sacrist, W. de Bradewas. His brother H. may be the 'Helias de Bradewas' to whom the priory gave the church of Sedgeberrow in 1226 (p. 419). The 'W' may stand for either Walter or William.

In 1202 a group of Worcester monks returned from Rome, having procured the canonization of St. Wulstan : Walter of Bradewas was apparently their leader, probably already a monk of long experience and much wisdom, to be entrusted with such a mission (p. 391). In 1216 William de Bradewas refused to consent to be the abbot of Alcester (p. 407). In the same year he resigned as sub-prior at the wish of the bishop in order that he might join him, but he was taken ill and could not fulfil his plan (p. 407). In 1218 'W. [Walter or William] de Bradewas' became sacristan (p. 410). On 14 July 1218 the king granted Walter de Bradewas and another monk licence for their house to elect a bishop of Worcester.[1] In 1220 under the sacristan's superintendence the great bells were cast (p. 412), but in the next year he was deposed (p. 414). He may have continued the chronicle, if he was the author, until 1228, when the annual entries become very meagre (p. 420).

W. de Cornwall preached a sermon reported in Bodl. Lib. MS. Laud Misc. 171,

[1] *Mon. Fr.* i. 378.
[2] *Ibid.* pp. 90–1.
[3] *Ibid.* pp. 114–5, 176.
[4] Adam sends greetings to the guardian of London (*ibid.* p. 396).
[5] *Ibid.* p. 395. For identification of treatise see Little, *F.S.O.* p. 839.
[6] *Mon. Fr.* i. 357.
[7] Little, *F.S.O.* p. 823 ; *Mon. Fr.* i. 338, 346–9.
[8] Little, *F.S.O.* p. 840 ; see also App. A below.

[1] *C.P.R.*, 1216–25, p. 163.

fo. 148 : *inc.* ' Cum ignoremus quid agere debeamus.' A second hand has written in the margin ' Sermo fratris W. Cornubiensis in cathedra S. Petri.'

This friar who preached in a church of St. Peter (or on the feast ' Cathedra St. Peter ') is possibly to be identified with the franciscan William of Cornwall who represented his group in a curious controversy with the dominicans in 1269.[1]

Walter Anglicus was author of a group of ' Versified Fables.' (a) Madrid, Bibl. Nat. MS. M. 110 (new no. M. 4220) ; (b) Oxford, Bodl. Lib. MS. Add. A. 170 (Madan, *Summary Cat. of Western MSS.* v. 47–8) ; (c) Paris, B.N. MS. lat. petit format 1084 (14th cent.) ; (d) *ibid.* MS. lat. 14381, fos. 27–35. The work has been edited by L. Hervieux in ' Les fabulistes Latins,' ii. 316–31 (*cf.* also *ibid.* pp. 352–91).

Walter, a poet and called ' Anglicus,' therefore presumably living outside England, is possibly to be identified with a poet who lived at Paris, teaching on the Petit-Pont in the first half of the 13th century.[2] John of Garland [q.v.] wrote of him :

> Gautier, inspired by Homer with golden song, with his fine taste enriches the University of Paris, as the petasus of Mercury eclipsed the stars, an athlete of Pallas Athena, in name and in deed a poet, for his highest aim is the joyous triumph of Phoebus.

Walter of Bibbesworth, knight, was an Anglo-Norman poet.[3] His most famous work was a ' Treatise on the French Language.' (a) Camb. Univ. Lib. MS. Gg. i. 1, fos. 279*b et seq.* (early 14th cent.) ; (b) Cambridge, Corpus Christi Coll. MS. 450, fos. 241–51 (14th cent.) ; (c) Cambridge, Trinity Coll. MS. 1125 (O. 2/21), fos. 120 *et seq.* (14th cent.) ; (d) MS. formerly at Cheltenham, Phillipps Lib. MS. 8188, now at Paris, B.N. nouv. acq. 699, fo. 134 ; (e) Phillipps MS. 8336, fos. 2–14 (early 14th cent.) ; (f) B.M. MS. Cotton, Vespasian A. vi, fos. 60*b et seq.* (14th cent.) ; (g) *ibid.* MS. Reg. 13, A. iv (early 14th cent.), giving only the beginning ; (h) *ibid.* MS. Harley 490, fos. 5–31 (14th cent.) ; (i) *ibid.* MS. Harley 740, fos. 4 *et seq.* (14th cent.) ; (j) *ibid.* MS. Arundel 220, fos. 297–305*b* (early 14th cent.) ; (k) *ibid.* MS. Sloane 513, fos. 139 *et seq.* (14th cent.) ; (l) *ibid.* MS. Sloane 809 (parchment roll) ; (m) Oxford, Bodl. Lib. MS. Selden supra 74, fos. 1 *et seq.*, fragment (14th cent.); (n) *ibid.* All Souls Coll. MS. 182, fos. 331–40 (14th cent.) ; (o) MS. formerly at Tichfield, MS. 2/1, entitled ' Tractatio Walteri de Bybbesworde de doctrine sciendi Gallicum ' (B.M. MS. Harley 6603, fo. 39*b*). A note in (m) runs :

> Coe est le tretyz ke moun syre Gautier de Biblesworth fist a ma dame Dionyse de Mountchensy, ke vous aprendra le fraunceys de plusour choses de ce mound pur fyz de gentyls home enfourner la langage, dount tut dys troverez le fraunceys et puis le engleys par desus (*Romania*, xiii, 1884. 502).

This was published by T. Wright, ' A Volume of Vocabularies,' p. 142, from MSS. (j) and (l) ; and by Wright and Halliwell (*Reliquiae Antiquae*, ii. 78) from MS. (a) (see Vising, p. 76). The work has been edited from all MSS. by Annie Owen (*Le traite de Walter de Bibbesworth sur la langue française.* For MSS. see pp. 30–2).

He wrote two shorter pieces which have survived. ' Dialogue with Henry de Lacy.' Bodl. Lib. MS. Fairfax 24 (early 14th cent.), published by F. Madden (*Rel. Ant.* i. 134). ' Dytees.' Cheltenham, Phillipps Library MS. 8336, fos. 92–3 (early 14th cent.), with a note ' Cy comencent les dytees moun syre Gauter de Bybeswurthe.' Extracts have been edited by P. Meyer in ' Notice et Extraits du MS 8336 de la Bibliothèque de Sir Thomas Phillipps à Cheltenham ' (*Romania*, xiii. 532).

[1] Little, *G.F.* p. 320. A William of Cornwall was a student at Bologna in 1283 (M. Sarti et M. Fattorini, *De Claris Archigymnasii Bononiensis Professoribus*, i. 322). A Master William of Cornwall was parson of Towcester on 6 Oct. 1305 (*C.P.R.*, 1301–7, p. 382).

[2] *Morale Scolarium of John of Garland*, ed. L. J. Paetow, p. 167. Two glosses call him an Englishman. Paetow refers to him in his edition of *The Battle of the Seven Arts*, p. 58, line 402.

[3] T. p. 100 ; *D.N.B.* under Bibelesworth.

This poet, Walter de Bibbesworth, had as patrons Henry de Lacy and Dionisia de Munchensi. With at least two Walters and two Dionisias in the century there is room for confusion. The 'Treatise' contains a section upon the education of children : since the younger Dionisia had none, the patron has been assumed to be the elder, whose life extended over nearly the whole of the 13th century. Thus the author would have to be the Walter of Bibbesworth who appears so frequently about 1250–70 in various documents.[1] However, an attestation of a document of Henry de Lacy by a Walter de Bybbesworth on 1 Oct. 1302 [2] would indicate that the author was a later Walter and his patron, Dionisia the granddaughter, who married Hugh de Vere in 1296 and died in 1314. His poem to her was probably before her marriage, since it gives her maiden name.[3] The dates of the many surviving MSS. favour a late date also. The author probably held a knight's fee of Henry de Pynkenye at Bibbesworth and another at Shenfield, Hertfordshire.[4] He was to be distrained, presumably for knighthood, in 1304.[5] He was not heir to the earlier Walter,[6] but may have been to a Walter of 1280–3.[7]

Walter of Coventry was supposed to be the author of a 'Chronicle' at Cambridge,

[1] *Cf. D.N.B.* and my article in *Modern Philology*, xxviii (1931). 265–6.

[2] P.R.O., D.L. 42/1, fos. 30*b*–1.

[3] Miss Owen suggests that the poem was written for the elder Dionisia to aid in the education of her granddaughter (*op. cit.* p. 23). The introduction leaves the impression that the patron was to be the student, however.

[4] *C.Cl.R.*, 1296–1302, p. 504.

[5] *Ibid.*, 1302–7, p. 197 ; *cf. Cat. Ancient Deeds*, vi. 336 (C. 6381).

[6] *C.Ch.R.*, 1257–1300, p. 202.

[7] *C.Cl.R.*, 1279–88, p. 19 ; *Receuil de lettres anglo-françaises*, 1265–1399, ed. F. J. Tanquerey, p. 40 ; *C.P.R.*, 1281–92, p. 64. The coats of arms of the various Walters, not probably identified, are given in *Knights of Edward I* (Harleian Soc.), i. 92 ; *Archaeologia*, xxxix (1863). 407, 427; and in the collections in B.M. MSS. Harley 6137, 6589 ; Cotton, Tiberius E. viii, fos. 104–10 ; and London, Society of Antiquaries MS. 17.

Corpus Christi Coll. MS. 175. This was edited by W. Stubbs (R.S.), who believed that Walter of Coventry was the author, because of the notation of the MS. flyleaf 'Memoriale fratris Walteri de Coventria' in another hand probably contemporary with that of the text. Tanner suggests that the word 'Memoriale' means a gift (T. p. 353). In view of the impressive list of instances denoting gifts, given by M. R. James in his catalogue of the MSS. of Corpus Christi College, and in the absence of evidence in favour of use to designate authorship, it seems best to regard the chronicle as anonymous. For other uses of 'memoriale' see Powicke (pp. 123*n*, 133). The 'Annales Walteri Coventrensis' of Gale were probably by Richard de Durham [q.v.].

The author was probably a monk of St. Mary's, York, who wrote soon after 1293. (See *D.N.B.* under Coventry).

Walter of Hemingburgh was canon of Guisborough and author of a Chronicle.[1] (a) Cambridge, Corpus Christi Coll. MS. 100 (late transcript) ; (b) *ibid.* MS. 250 ; (c) Cambridge, Trinity Coll. MS. R. 7/9 (fragment ending 1297) ; (d) Edinburgh, National Lib. MS. 33/5/3, all 169 fos. (14th cent.) ; (e) B.M. MS. Cotton, Tiberius B. iv (14th cent., ends in 1297) ; (f) *ibid.* MS. Cotton Vespasian A. ix (fragment) ; (g) *ibid.* MS. Harley 691, a transcript of MS. (i) ; (h) *ibid.* MS. Lansdowne 239, fos. 1–120 (14th cent., ends in 1307) ; (i) London, College of Arms MS. 13 (14th cent., ends in 1297) ; (j) Bodl. Lib. MS. Digby 170 ; (k) Oxford, Magdalen Coll. MS. 53, p. 253 ; (l) MS. formerly at Ashburnham Place, MS. S. 859; (m) MS. formerly at Wells, 'Chronica Walteri de Gisburn a Gulielmo ad Edwardum primum' (Leland, *Collect.* iv. 155). A colophon *c.* 1350 in MS. (h) runs :

> Expliciunt tres libri compilati a domino Waltero Hemingburght canonico de Gyseburn, de gestis Anglorum ab adventu Willelmi Bastardi Conquestoris usque ad mortem strenuissimi regis Edwardi primi post conquestum.

[1] T. p. 390 ; *D.N.B.* under Hemingburgh.

The chronicle is edited by H. C. Hamilton, 'Chronicon dom. Walteri de Hemingburgh' (Eng. Hist. Soc.), and excerpts appear in *M.G.H.SS.* xxviii. 627–46.

A chaplain, Walter of Hemingburgh, appears in a Yorkshire hundred roll of 1275–6,[1] and is possibly the author. His chronicle indicates that he was probably writing from personal knowledge in the reign of Edward I. He was a canon of Guisborough by 1297.[2] By 1302 he was subprior, designated by his house to represent it before the archbishop of York.[3] Some versions of his work end in 1304 and 1307, indicating that he had written part of his chronicle by that time. In 1307 he made a gift of a volume of sermons to his house.[4] He apparently survived the death of Archbishop Winchelsey in 1313,[5] but, since he was probably already an old man, it is doubtful whether he lived much longer.[6]

Walter of Henley was the author of a well-known Anglo-Norman Husbandry.[7] (a) Camb. Univ. Lib. MS. Dd. vii. 6; (b) *ibid.* MS. Dd. vii. 14; (c) *ibid.* MS. Ee. i. 1 (late 13th cent.); (d) *ibid.* MS. Hh. iii. 11; (e) Canterbury, Cathedral Libr. Registers J. and P.; (f) B.M. MS. Add. 6159; (g) London, College of Arms MS. H. xiv, fos. 222–30; (h) Bodl. Lib. MS. Ashmole 1524, fos. 28*b*–9*b*; (i) *ibid.* MS. Digby 147, fos. 1–9 (14th cent.); (j) Oxford, Merton Coll. MS. 321, fos. 152–60 (14th cent.); (k) B.N. MS. fonds fr. 7011 (14th cent.). For other MSS. see introduction to Miss Lamond's edition and Eileen Power's 'On the Need for a New Edition of Walter of Henley' (Royal Hist. Soc. *Trans.*, 4th Series, xvii, 1934. 101–16). A note occurs in MS. (a):

> Ceste ditee si fesoyt sir Waltier de hengleye qui primes fu chivalier e puis se rendesist frere precheur e le fist de housebonderie e de gaygnerie e de isane de estor.

MS. (g) bears the information 'Cette dictee fist Water de Henleye,' and (i) the statement that 'Carmen domini Walteri de Henleye quod vocatur Yconomia sive Housebundria.' The work is edited from MS. (k) by Lacour in 'Bibl. de l'Ecole de Chartres,' 1856; and from MS. (c) by Elizabeth Lamond in 'Walter of Henley's Husbandry' (see also Vising, p. 69). Probably the great variations represent different redactions. One variant from MSS. (d), (e), (f), (j), and (k) is edited by Miss Lamond. Parts of the treatise in translation appear in F. H. Cripps-Day's 'The Manor Farm.' The 'Art of Love' in MS. (g), attributed to Walter by Vising (p. 63), is actually anonymous in the MS.

From Walter's treatise it is certain that he served for a time as a bailiff.[1] One note on a MS. says that he was a knight,[2] and a colophon given above states that he was first a knight and then a dominican friar. If the last is true he must have lived between the time that the dominicans arrived, about 1220, and the date of the earliest surviving MSS. about 1280,[3] one of which is said to have been written in the hand of John de Gare, clerk of the prior of Canterbury in the early years of Edward I.[4] There were Canterbury farms near Henley.[5]

1 Hamilton, *op. cit.* p. viii.

2 Under this year the phrase occurs 'Quorum unus mansit apud nos per tempus aliquod.'

3 *Reg. Corbridge* (Surtees Soc.), p. 134; *Cartularium de Gyseburne* (Surtees Soc.), ii. 367; *Hist. Papers and Letters from the Northern Registers* (R.S.), ed. J. Raine, p. 160.

4 B.M. MS. Reg. 3, A. xiii; *Chronicon W. de Hemingburgh*, p. vi:

> 'Liber sancte Marie de Gyseburn assignatus armariolo claustri, ex dono fratris Walteri de Hemyngburch quondam canonici eiusdem domus anno scilicet Domini M CCC septimo.'

Inscription in later hand.

5 *Chronicon*, ii. 148.

6 *Cf.* T. F. Tout in *Political History of England*, iii. 456.

7 T. p. 353; *D.N.B.* under Henley; *Modern Philology*, xxviii (1931). 260.

1 *Walter of Henley's Husbandry*, ed. Lamond, p. 33.

2 *Ibid.* p. 2.

3 *Ibid.* p. xxi.

4 *Ibid.* p. xxi.

5 *Ibid.* p. xxii.

A Walter (or Walters) of Henley appears frequently as a witness of charters in the cartulary of Messenden, co. Bucks.[1] One document gives a date, 1220,[2] and in several he is called a knight.[3] He is probably the same as the Walter of Henley to whom King John, on 2 Nov. 1215, gave lands formerly belonging to William Fitzreynar, valued at forty pounds, and to Nicholas of Kennett, valued at forty-one pounds.[4] Two days later the order was sent to the sheriff of Kent.[5] There are a number of other references to Walter of Henley.[6]

Walter of Hyde was probably the author of a poem, 'On the Death of Simon de Montfort': *inc.* 'Ubi fuit mons est vallis.' Cambridge, Gonville and Caius Coll. MS. 85, flyleaf. This was edited by F. W. Maitland (*E.H.R.* xi, 1896. 314–8). The MS. was the property of Walter of Hyde, who seems to have used it for canon law collections and for documents of his own composition which seem, as far as they can be controlled, to be accurate. The information below is from Maitland's article.

Walter, according to an item in the MS., 'tam in artibus quam in decretis laudabiliter rexit Parisius.' The poem may be a product of his arts training. If he wrote the poem, which Maitland does not suggest, he might be the Walter Anglicus mentioned above: both taught at Paris and both were interested in the classics. The poem mentions Hector, Ulysses, and Achilles.

The contents of the MS. show Walter's interest in canon law. It includes the

[1] B.M. MS. Harley 3688, fos. 19*b*, 26*b*, 62, 95*b*, 96*b*, 97 (3), 98, 99 (4), 100 (3), 102*b* (3), 104*b*, 105, 108, 109*b*, 110*b*, 118.

[2] B.M. MS. Harley 3688, fo. 98.

[3] *Ibid.* fos. 33, 102*b*.

[4] *Rot. Litt. Claus.* i. 234.

[5] *Ibid.* i. 234*b*, 235*b*, 323.

[6] B.M. MS. Cotton, Otho A. ii, fo. 10*b*, Bayham; B.M. MS. Stowe 924, fo. 49*b*; *Two Chartularies of the Priory of St. Peter at Bath* (Somerset Record Soc.), ed. William Hunt, ii. 55, 84, 87; *Abstracts of the Inquisitions P.M. relating to Wilts.* (British Rec. Soc.), ed. E. A. Fry, p. 29; F. Palgrave, *Parliamentary Writs*, i, pt. i, p. 254.

'Ordo Iudicarius,' the 'Summa de Matrimonio' (1234–45) of Raymond de Pennefort, and the 'Summa Aurea' (about 1239) of William de Drogheda [q.v.]. A. Master Walter of Hyde was presented by Merton Priory to the church of Clive in 1236.[1] On presentation of a certain 'M. de B.,' knight, the bishop of Chichester instituted him in the church of 'N.' In 1272 Walter gave a bond to a lady, A. Savage, widow of R. Savage. On Monday before Easter 1274 Adelynya la Savage, lady of 'Brawater' (Broadwater), presented him to S., bishop of Chichester, for institution as rector of Broadwater. This document can be checked: Stephen was bishop of Chichester then, and a family named Savage held the designated church. Walter was of gentle but illegitimate birth, receiving a dispensation from this handicap from the pope. Possibly then he was the Master William [*sic*] de Hyde, an acolyte of the diocese of London and a proctor of certain English prelates who received such a dispensation on 10 May 1278.[2]

Walter de Knolle, O.F.M., was a disputant at Oxford *c.* 1282–90 (Little-Pelster, p. 76).

Walter of Maddeley, O.F.M.,[3] it was of whom Adam Marsh wrote 'In scriptis et eloquiis tam fratribus quam secularibus utilis et acceptus' (*Mon. Fr.* i. 355). None of his writings are known now.

While studying at Oxford Walter of Maddeley had ventured to wear shoes one day, contrary to the custom of the friars. That night he dreamed that robbers had attacked him, refusing to believe that he was a franciscan since he was wearing shoes (*ibid.* p. 28). The incident of the dream took place in a dangerous pass between Oxford and Gloucester; Walter may have come from that part of England or from Wales beyond. Walter was 'socius' of the provincial minister, Agnellus of Pisa, and

[1] *Rot. R. Grosseteste*, p. 164.

[2] *Registres de Nicholas III*, ed. M. J. Gay, p. 19. But possibly this man was Walter's brother.

[3] Little, *G.F.* p. 188.

at Oxford at the time of his death in 1235 (*ibid.* p. 53). He was in Germany with the minister, Peter of Tewksbury, probably at Cologne (*ibid.* p. 308), but returned to England in 1249. He lectured in theology at an undesignated franciscan house and was well thought of as a theologian, especially by Adam Marsh (*ibid.* pp. 353–5). Adam conferred with him upon a theological question and recommended to the minister provincial that Walter should be given the clerical assistance which, though given to Walter's predecessors, had been denied him. In writing of him Eccleston says 'bone memorie Walterus de Madele' (*ibid.* p. 28), suggesting that he had died by 1260.

Walter Map was a humorist whose life and literary efforts belong largely to the 12th century.[1] Here his career will be considered only from 1197,[2] when he resigned the precentorship of Lincoln to become archdeacon of Oxford.[3] At this time he shared with his friend, Gerald of Wales, a pride in Welsh extraction, a contempt for the cistercians, and a liking for Lincoln and Hereford. Gerald suggested his friend as a candidate for the bishopric of St. David's in 1203.

While archdeacon, Walter witnessed a charter of Bishop William de Vere of Hereford,[4] went with a Hereford delegation to see the king in 1199 at Angers after the bishop's death,[5] and gave a grant of twenty

[1] T. p. 507 ; *D.N.B.* under Map.

[2] For earlier references see B.M. MSS. Harley 3586 and 6726, relating to the Map family at Wormsley ; *Charters and Records of Hereford Cathedral*, ed. Capes, p. 31 ; Bodl. Lib. MS. Rawlinson B. 329, fo. 14 ; *Historia et Cartularium Mon. S. Petri Glouc.* (R.S.), ed. W. H. Hart, ii. 156 ; B.M. Cotton Ch. xvi. 40 ; Oxford, Balliol Coll. MS. 271, fo. 66*b* ; B.M. MS. Harley 236, fo. 49*b* ; *Reg. of Richard Swinfield* (C.Y.S.), ed. W. W. Capes, p. 56 ; Madox, *Hist. of Exchequer*, i. 701 ; *Cartulary of Flaxley Abbey*, ed. A. W. Crawley-Boevey, pp. 20, 21*n*, 79, 135, 163 ; *Liber Vitae Ecclesiae Dunelmensis* (Surtees Soc. fo. 23*b*.

[3] *Hist. Works of Ralph de Diceto* (R.S.), ed. W. Stubbs, ii. 150.

[4] P.R.O., ancient deed, B. 10846.

[5] *Magna Vita S. Hugonis* (R.S.), ed. Dimock, p. 281.

shillings by charter to the priory of Hereford.[1] The proceedings of an inquisition in his presence remain.[2] As archdeacon he was ordered to seize Gerald's property in his jurisdiction.[3] His seal remains.[4] Letters close of 15 Mar. 1208 are addressed to him.[5] He died on 1 April (the proper day for a humorist),[6] probably in 1209 or 1210.[7]

Walter, Abbot of Margam, was a poet.[8] Leland says that he saw in the 'Granarium' of John Whethamstede that 'Gualterus, abbas Morganensis, scripsit librum de avibus et animalibus carmine': *inc.* 'Dicitur accipiter' (*Collect.* iv. 58). This item does not seem to be in portions of the 'Granarium' in B.M. MSS. Nero C. vi, Tiberius D. v, or in Add. MS. 26764.

Bale placed this writer on the same page as Maurice [q.v.] because both were connected with Margam.[9] Bibliographical tradition has assigned Walter's death to the year 1219, but it is a wild conjecture. The list of abbots of Margam is fragmentary even to the end of the Annals of Margam in 1232. The annalist quotes poetry under the years 1225, 1226, and 1228.[10] It should also be noticed that Leland mentions Walter with Geoffrey de Vinsauf, Walter de Chatillon, and John de Hauteville, all belonging to the end of the 12th century.

Walter Reclusus was an austin friar,[11] said by Bale to have written 'De Mundi

[1] Oxford, Balliol Coll. MS. 271, fo. 55*b*.

[2] *Cartulary of the Monastery of St. Frideswide at Oxford* (Oxford Hist. Soc.), ed. S. R. Wigram, ii. 247.

[3] *Giraldi Cambrensis Opera* (R.S.), ed. Brewer, Dimock and Warner, iii. 20.

[4] *Collectanea* (B.S.F.S.), i. 120. Catalogue of Hereford Cathedral Library, under MS. O. 3, viii.

[5] *Rot. Litt. Claus.* i. 106.

[6] Gough, *History and Antiquities of Hereford*, p. (10).

[7] *Giraldi Cambrensis Opera*, v. 410 ; *Curia Regis Rolls*, vi. 93.

[8] T. p. 353.

[9] Bale, *Scriptorum Illustrium Catalogus*, p. 257 ; Clark (*Cartae et Alia Munimenta de Glamorgancia*) mentions no Abbot Walter at all.

[10] *Ann. Monast.* i. 35, 36.

[11] T. p. 619.

Contemptu,' 'De Vita Solitaria,' and 'Meditationes' (*Scriptorum Illustrium Catalogus*, p. 338). Probably Bale's information about this austin friar came in the same indirect way as his information about William of Sengham [q.v.]. The titles may have been suggested by the 'Reclusus' of his name: the lack of 'incipits' is ominous. Bale associates Walter with Paris about 1287. Walter has been suggested as the author of a rule for anchorites, edited by L. Oliger in 'Antonianum (1933).' Miss Dorothy M. B. Ellis kindly wrote me that she knows of no recluse who might be identical with this friar.

Walter of Richmond was author of a book of religious exhortations entitled 'Ypotecha': *inc.* 'Pauci admodum dies sunt quod.' Bodl. Lib. MS. Arch. Selden B. 36, fos. 71 *et seq.* (Madan and Craster, *Summary Cat. of Western MSS.* i. 612–3), with a rubric 'Liber magistri Walteri de Richemund qui appelatur Ypotecha.'

The book is dedicated, in part, to R. de Thalewrthe,[1] probably Robert de Taleworth who succeeded his father, Adam, in the possession of the manor of Wratting, Suffolk, in the honour of Clare, probably about 1210.[2] Robert, or a namesake, held one and a half knight's fees there in 1242–3.[3] One reference is to Walter Map (*d. c.* 1208): 'Et noster comicus fortunatum putat qui uxorem numquam duxerit.'[4] The author may be the Walter of Richmond who was proctor for the priory of Durham in 1254.[5]

Warin of Newport was a disputant at Cambridge (*c.* 1282 according to Little-Pelster, p. 98, but *c.* 1275 according to App. A below).

[1] Fo. 109.

[2] *Curia Regis Rolls*, vi. 2–3.

[3] *Book of Fees*, ii. 918. About 1200 there was a Master Ralph of Tamworth who might possibly be the patron (Camb. Univ. Lib. Add. MS. 4220, fo. 362*b*; *Cal. of Docs. preserved in France*, ed. J. H. Round, pp. 161, 271, 349, 466).

[4] Fo. 73.

[5] *C.E.P.R.* i. 297; *Registres d'Innocent IV*, ed. E. Berger, no. 7306.

'Watecumbe,' O.P., preached a sermon at Oxford in 1293 (Little-Pelster, p. 190).

William of Abingdon, O.P., was probably author of a 'Tractatus de vii Vitiis' (a) MS. which was at Glastonbury by 1274, entitled 'Quidam tractatus de vii viciis secundum Willelmum de Abundone' (T. Hearne, *Johannis Glastoniensis Historia de rebus Glastoniensibus*, p. 443); (b) MS. formerly at Thornton,[1] entitled 'Tractatus Willelmi de Abyndon de septem viciis' (B.M. MS. Reg. App. 69, p. 4).

The treatise was written too early to have been the work of the secular William of Abingdon [2] or of the franciscan.[3] It was probably written by a dominican. In 1238 the writer protested against a dispensation for marriage given to Simon de Montfort by the pope.[4] About 1244 he was engaged in securing money for the dominican house at Gloucester.[5] Eccleston repeats a story that, previous to this time, Abingdon had been a famous preacher, but that now he could only say 'Give, give, give.'[6] He died in 1247.[7]

William of Altona, O.P., was a theologian.[8] The old statement of his writings gives:

Fr. Willelmus de Altona, nat. anglicus, mag. in theologia, scripsit postillas super Mattheum, de decem virginibus. Item super Ecclesiasten (*Archiv für Litteratur- und Kirchengesch. des Mittelalters*, ii. 238).

[1] Tanner gives Thorney (T. p. 354). Abingdon, Berkshire.

[2] Tanner identifies the writer with this man (T. p. 354), who was at Cambridge in 1289, archdeacon of Wiltshire in 1291, precentor of Salisbury in 1297, and admitted to Horton in 1298 (*Vetus Liber Archidiaconi Eliensis*, ed. C. L. Feltre and E. H. Minns, p. 24; Prynne, *Hist. of King John, King Henry III*, etc. (1670), iii. 445; *Reg. Godfrey Giffard* (Worc. Hist. Soc.), ed. J. W. W. Bund, ii. 495).

[3] *Collectanea* (B.S.F.S.), i. 148; *Mon. Fr.* i. 549.

[4] *Chr. Maj.* iii. 487.

[5] *Archaeological Journal*, xxxix (1882). 297; *C.L.R.*, 1240–5, *passim*; *Eccleston*, p. 58.

[6] *Eccleston, loc. cit.*; *Mon. Fr.* i. 36.

[7] T. p. 354, quoting '*Cronica Cestr.* in MS. Cotton, Otho. B. 3.'

[8] T. p. 37; Glorieux, pp. 113–6.

(a) The 'Postille super Mattheum' remained at Paris, Univ. Lib. Liber rectoris, 'Item postille fratris de Alton super Mattheum' (Quétif-Echard, p. 244); (b) a copy was sold by the executors of Richard of Gravesend, bishop of London, about 1307, 'Et de iv s de Lectura fratris Willielmi de Alton super Matheum vendita' (*Account of the Executors of Richard, Bishop of London* (Camden Soc. N.S. x.), ed. W. H. Hale and H. T. Ellacombe, p. 51; Denifle-Chatelain, *Cartularium Univ. Paris*, i. 646). The 'Postille super Ecclesiasten' remains at Paris, B.N. MS. fond S. Victor 976, fos. 119–54, with the colophon 'Postilla super Ecclesiasten. Explicit supra Ecclesiasten secundum fratrem Guillelmum de Altona.' William also wrote 'Postille super Sapientiam Solomonis.' *Ibid.* fos. 155–206, with the note 'Super sapientiam secundum fratrem Guillelmum de Altona ordinis fratrum predicatorum': *inc.* 'Fons sapientie verbum Dei.' His 'Postille super Isaiam' were also at Paris in the Liber rectoris (*loc. cit.*). A series of his Commentaries upon Old Testament books remain in MSS. 3637 and 2628, in Bibl. Colbert. On Genesis: *inc.* 'Transite ad me omnes'; On Exodus: *inc.* 'Hec sunt nomina filiorum Israel'; On Leviticus: *inc.* 'Vocavit autem Moyses'; On Numbers: *inc.* 'Locutus est Dominus ad Moysem'; On Joshua: *inc.* 'Fortis in ullo'; 'On Judges': *inc.* 'Iudicabit Dominus populum suum'; On Ruth: *inc.* 'Brevis in volatilibus apis'; *ibid.* MS. 3638, On Isaiah: *inc.* 'Venio cum propheta. Hieronymus' (Denifle-Chatelain, *Cartularium Univ. Paris*, i. 646); On Jeremiah: *inc.* 'Direxit opera eorum'; On Lamentations: *inc.* 'Quis dabit capiti meo aquam' (Quétif-Echard, p. 245).

William of Alton [1] was master of theology at Paris, succeeding Thomas Aquinas in the chair for foreigners in 1259–60.[2] He preached sermons on 24 June, 9 and 23 Oct. 1261, on 4 and 12 August, 16 and 30 Sept. 1263, and 10 Feb. 1264, which remain.' He is said to have died in 1265.[1]

William Anglicus [2] was a citizen of Marseilles and an astrologer. His work has been discussed in the following books: P. Duhem, 'Le système du monde,' iii. 287–91; Lynn Thorndike, 'A History of Magic and Experimental Science,' ii. 477–87; Steinschneider, 'Etudes sur Zarkeli,' in the *Bolletino da B. Boncompagni*, xvii (1884). 771–5; xx (1887). 576–9, 596–7. His works now known are:

'De Urina non Visa': *inc.* 'Ne ignorantie vel potius invidie redarguar, mi Germane, qui quandoque apud Massiliam aliquando mecum studuisti.' Cambridge, Trin. Coll. MS. 1406, fo. 173, has the following rubric: 'Inc. liber urinarum Mag. Guilelmi astronomici Anglici, civis Massiliensis medicine professoris.' There are many MSS. of this treatise.

'Astrologia,' probably the same as the following MS. at Seville, Colombina Lib. MS. 5/1/25, with the colophon:

> Explicit astrologia magistri Werbillini, civis Massiliensis, qui Anglicus est natione, professione medicus, astronomus appelatus, compilata per ipsum anno domini 1220 (S. D. Wingate, *Mediaeval Latin Versions*, p. 38).

'Abridgement of Almagest': *inc.* 'Quoniam astrologie speculatio.' (a) Erfurt, see MS. catalogue, 'Explicit astr. mag. Willel. civis Massil.'; (b) B.N. MS. 7298, fos. 11–124, 'Incipit astrologia W. Massiliensis'; (c) MS. formerly at Norwich (Bale, *Index*, p. 114), entitled 'Speculum astrologie.'

'Tractatus de Metheoris.' B.N. MS. fonds lat. 6552, fos. 39*b*–41*b*, with a colophon 'Completus est tractatus de metheoris a magistro W. anglico mathematico, anno domini MCCXXX.'

[1] Probably near Southampton (T. p. 37).

[2] Glorieux, p. 115; Denifle, in *Archiv für Litteratur*, ii (1886). 206, says 1256.

[1] Glorieux, *loc. cit.*

[2] T. p. 262.

Abridgment of Al Zarkali's 'Opus Astrolabii.' (a) B.N. MS. fonds lat. 7195; (b) *ibid.* 16652.

'Tabula de Stellis Fixis secundum azarchelem.' (a) Erfurt, see MS. catalogue; (b) B.N. MS. fonds lat. 7195; (c) *ibid.* 16652; (d) Vienna MS. 5311 (Philos. 225), fos. 42–52*b*, entitled 'Scripta Marsiliensis super Canones Archazelis.'

'Secretissimum Regis Cateni Persarum de Virtute Aquile': *inc.* 'Est autem aquila rex omnium avium.' Oxford, Merton Coll. MS. 324, fos. 142 *et seq.* (15th cent.), with the colophon 'Explicit iste tractatus a magistro Willelmo Anglico de lingua Arabica in Latinum translatus.'

In addition to these Bale gives the following: '*Ex bibliotheca Nordouicensi*': 'De quadratura circuli' (*inc.* 'Aristoteles in eo qui de categoriis'); 'De motu capitis' (*inc.* 'Motum accessionis et recessionis'); and 'De magnitudine solis' (*inc.* 'Dico quod sol apparet mag.') (*Index*, p. 114). 'Ex officina Hugonis Shyngleton,' he gives 'De qualitatibus et proprietatibus astrorum' (*inc.* 'Cum humana corpora sint omnia') (*ibid.* p. 115).

The colophons of the MSS. are the sources of information about William Anglicus. He studied with a cousin (germane)[1] at Marseilles probably in medicine before 1219, when he dedicated his 'De Urina non Visa' to this relative. His interests at this time seem primarily astrological. In the following year he abridged the 'Almagest.' In a statement of 1231[2] he says that he had been busy for six years upon Al Zarkali's 'Canons.' Probably his interests had then become more purely astronomical. By 1230 he had written his treatise 'De Metheoris.' His translation from the Arabic is undated, but since his interest in Al Zarkali probably implies a knowledge of that language it may have been written in the interval from 1220 to 1230. Identifications of this man with William of Aragon[1] and William Grisaunt[2] are not very convincing.

[1] Duhem conjectures that this cousin may have been Gilbertus Anglicus (*op. cit.* iii. 291).

[2] Translated by Duhem (*op. cit.* p. 288).

[1] Thorndike suggests the possibility of identification, since both had medical experience and a tendency to give an astrological interpretation of everything, but doubts the identity (*op. cit.* ii. 301). It is not so unlikely as he thinks, though, that Aragonia should be confused with Anglia, especially if one scribe was reading to the other.

[2] T. p. 262.

William of Arundel was archdeacon of Huntingdon and a Hebrew translator.[3] No certain work of his remains, but there is some evidence concerning its nature. Adam Marsh wrote to John of Basingstoke [q.v.] telling him that the 'Interpretatio Biblie,' corrected by William of Arundel, was not at Oxford (*Mon. Fr.* i. 204). This title usually designates a Hebrew-Latin glossary of biblical words. Then the king ordered the sheriff of Huntingdon to permit William to keep a Jew with him to assist in translating a tract for the conversion of the Jews (*C.Cl.R.*, 1237–42, p. 238). Finally, a statement of Matthew Paris (*Chr. Maj.* iv. 553) about a 'Robert' de Arundel probably refers to this man:

> Et circa idem tempus [March–April 1246] magister Robertus de Harundel, qui in Hebræo idiomate fuerat peritissimus et multa de Hebræo in Latinum fideliter transtulerat, humanis rebus exemptus, mundum salutavit.

This translator's connexions may have been with Exeter before Lincoln: a 'Mr. W. de Arundel' was a canon there in 1236,[4] and is said to have been precentor of that place in 1242.[5] If this was the translator he was a pluralist, because by 1239–40,[6] and possibly earlier,[7] he was archdeacon of Huntingdon. As such he was engaged in the usual official work; his activity appears in the 5th, 6th, 7th, 11th, and 12th years of

[3] *Harvard Theological Review*, xxvi (1933). 170–1. Arundel, Sussex.

[4] B.M. Add. ch. 13970, dated Exeter, kal. April.

[5] Le Neve, *Fasti*, ed. Hardy, i. 409.

[6] *Rot. R. Grosseteste*, p. 269.

[7] A predecessor, Gilbert, acted in the first three years of the bishop (*ibid.* pp. 250–6, 389, 391).

Bishop Grosseteste.[1] In 1240 he was working upon the tract mentioned above. In the following year he acted with John of Basingstoke as representative of the bishop in a dispute with John Mansel before the king.[2] His successor appears in the 12th year of the bishop (Feb. 1246–7).[3] William was buried in the monastery of Wymondesley, Hertfordshire, to which he gave one and possibly more books.[4] He was doubtless one of the scholars who assisted Grosseteste when he 'multa de glossis Hebreorum extraxit.'

William Banastre was an English writer.[5] The Anglo-Norman version of the romance of 'Blancheflour and Florence' has the following lines :

Banastre en englois le fist
E Brykhulle cest ecrit
En franceois translata.
(*Romania*, xxxvii, 1908. 224.)

The piece is given by J. E. Wells (*Manual of the Writings in Middle English*, i. 5), who thinks that it belongs to the east midland dialect of about 1250. The MSS. are : (a) Auchinleck (1330–40) ; (b) Camb. Univ. Lib. MS. Gg. iv. 27/2 (1250–1300) ; (c) B.M. MS. Cotton, Vitell D. iii (1250–1300) ; and (d) *ibid.* Egerton 2862 (end 14th cent.). It is edited by Hausknecht in 'Sammlung Englische Denkmäler,' and in the 'Minor Poems of the Vernon MS.' (E.E.T.S.), ed. F. J. Furnival, ii.

The 'Scalacronica,' written in 1355, speaks of a William Banastre with an English writer, Thomas of Erceldoune, which suggests that Banastre might have been a writer in English also and therefore probably identical with the romancer. His words are given thus by W. W. Skeat, tracing a note in Leland (*Collect.* ii. 510) :

It is a long paragraph, in which the name of 'Merlyns' occurs repeatedly ; some remarks at the end imply that he spoke much 'en figure' as to render the interpretation of his meaning very doubtful. It is remarked that much is said about boars, dragons, bears, eagles, lions, asses, moles, trees, and brooks ; and that the object seems to have been to make the prophecies obscure—'ne purra estre determyne en certayne, si fussent, en le hour de lescriuer de cest cronicle, passe ou auenir. pusq*ue* tau*n*tes des Roys sount passez. tanco*m* durerent les Regnes des. vij reaulmes Saxsouns. en queux la gr*an*t bretaigne estoit deuise. et dez autres puscedy Engles & Norma*n*des. pur quoy ne agreast a le deuisour de cest cronicle plus dez p*ar*olis de Merlyne de soy entremettre. ne dez autres queux hom disoit en le houre p*re*destinou*rs*. co*m* de Willam Banastre. ou de Tho*mas* de Erceldoun. les parolis de queux furount ditz en fig*ure*. od diuers entendeme*n*tz aptez a lestimaciou*n* de les comentou*rs*. que en cas *pur*roint desacorder' (*Romance and Prophecies of Thomas of Erceldoune*, E.E.T.S., ed. J. A. H. Murray, p. xviii, *n.* 1).

His 'Prophetia' were said to be in possession of H. Worsely, and his 'Vaticinalia Carmina' with H. Mason (T. p. 72). The 'Pars Visionis domini Willelmi Banistre milytis' in Bodl. Lib. MS. Rawlinson C. 813, fos. 142*b*–4*b* is an English prose prophecy of about 1333, but rewritten in later English, probably not by Banastre. It shows, however, that he had a reputation as a writer of English prophecy.

The date of 'Blancheflour' and its relation to the Anglo-Norman version suggest that Banastre belonged to the 13th century. While there are several contemporaries of the name[1] the most probable is a knight, son of John Banastre, who lived near Silhamstead by Reading. He was a benefactor of both Reading abbey and Winteney priory.[2] A contemporary Richard Banastre was abbot of the former, 1262–8,[3] and a

[1] *Rot. R. Grosseteste*, pp. 270-89 *passim*.

[2] *Chr. Maj.* iv. 152. The controversy was over the prebend of Thame. The index attributes a speech to William, but the text gives only 'unus archidiaconorum.'

[3] *Rot. R. Grosseteste*, pp. 290, 291.

[4] *Mon. Fr.* i. 204.

[5] T. p. 72.

[1] *C.P.R.*, 1247–58, p. 64 ; *ibid.*, 1266–72, p. 146 ; *C.Cl.R.*, 1231–4, p. 382 ; P.R.O., C. 85/1.

[2] Reading (B.M. MS. Cotton, Vesp. E. xx, fo. 34). His name is also in B.M. MS. Add. 28870, fo. 21*b* ; *C.Ch.R.*, 1257–1300, p. 257 ; in Winteney obituary under '11 kal. Feb.' (*Johannis de Trokelowe Annales Edwardi II*, ed. T. Hearne, pp. 384–93).

[3] *C.P.R.*, 1258–66, pp. 207–8 ; Dugdale, *Monasticon*, iv. 31. His name is in the Winteney obituary under '9 kal. April.'

Cecilia Banastre was prioress of the latter, resigning in 1294.[1]

William of Barnwell or **Berneville,** see App. B.

William of Boderisham, O.P., it was of whom Tanner, quoting Pits (p. 344), says :

Scripsit *In Cantica Salomonis,* lib. i. *In threnos Hieremiae,* lib. i. *In epistolam ad Romanos,* lib. i. Claruit A.C. MCCLXII (T. p. 109).

William of Bonkes was the author of a series of commentaries and questions upon the works of Aristotle,[2] and of one of Priscian :—

'Questiones super Priscianum' : *inc.* imperfect. Cambridge, Gonville and Caius Coll. MS. 344, fos. 1–27*b*, with a colophon 'Expl. questiones primi libri et secundi Prisciani date a mag. Willelmo Bonkys.'

'Questiones super Librum Peryermenias.' *Ibid.* fos. 173–198, with a colophon 'Questiones super librum Peryermenias dicte sec. mag. Will. Bonkys.'

'Questiones Totius Metaphisice.' (a) *Ibid.* fos. 29–88*b*, with a colophon 'Expl. quest. tocius metaphisice dicte a mag. Will. Bonkys a. d. M CC ducentesimo nonag. secundo' ; (b) MS. formerly at Austian Friars, York MS. Q. 328, 'Questiones xii librorum methaphisice arist. secundum eundem (bonnkus)' (M. R. James, *Fasciculus Ioanni Willis Clark dicatus*, p. 51).

'Questiones super Phisica.' (a) Cambridge, Gonville and Caius Coll. MS. 344, fos. 106–72*b* ; (b) MS. formerly at Austin Friars, York MS. Q. 328, 'Questiones vi librorum phisicorum secundum bonnkus' (M. R. James, *op. cit.* p. 51).

'Questiones super Librum de Celo et Mundo' : *inc.* 'Queritur utrum celum sit alterabile.' (a) Cambridge, Gonville and Caius Coll. MS. 344, fos. 104–5*b*, with a colophon 'Finiunt questiones super librum de celo et mundo dicte a mag. Will. Bonkis cuius curam habeat Deus' ; (b) Bodl. Lib. MS. Digby 204, fos. 151*b*–4 (early 14th cent.), with a colophon 'Questiones libri celi et mundi, date a magistro Willelmo Bonkys.'

'Questiones super Librum de Generatione et Corruptione.' Cambridge, Gonville and Caius Coll. MS. 344, fos. 93–103, with a colophon 'Questio ultima dicta per mag. W. bonkis cui sit honor et gloria.'

'Questiones Metheororum' : *inc.* 'Queritur de subiecto quid sit.' Bodl. Lib. MS. Digby 204, fos. 126–51, entitled 'Questiones metheororum a magistro Willelmo Bonkis.'

Master William of Bonkis was possibly a fellow of Balliol : he appears in a deed of theirs in 1291–2.[1] He wrote his treatise on the 'Metaphysics' in 1292 and probably was engaged upon the others at the same time. On 22 Feb. 1293 he was granted the custody of Henry le Waleys, who was not yet ready to take charge of his prebend of Dufton.[2] In 1298 he was put in charge of the rectory of Long Marton as coadjutor for a blind rector.[3] Apparently this half prebend of ten marks a year was expected to support him in the schools in 1299.[4] He appears also in an undated document.[5] His connexions were mostly with the diocese of Carlisle.

William of Bougevilla, monk of Bec, was the author of an historical compilation called 'Unus Omnium.'[6] (a) Formerly in Cambridge, King's Coll. Lib. (Bale, *Index*, p. 117) ; (b) B.M. MS. Harley 692 has

[1] *Reg. Johannis de Pontissara* (C.Y.S.), ed. C. Deedes, pp. 67, 509. Her name is in the Winteney obituary under '4 id. Sept.'

[2] T. p. 112.

[1] *Oxford Deeds of Balliol Coll.* (Oxford Hist. Soc.), ed. H. E. Salter, p. 17. He shared another undated transaction, also with 'Mr. Walter de Forderingeye' (*ibid.* p. 18).

[2] *Register of John of Halton* (C.Y.S.), ed. W. N. Thompson, i. 6.

[3] *Ibid.* p. 113.

[4] *Ibid.* pp. 135–6.

[5] H.M.C., 4th Rep., App. p. 446.

[6] T. p. 116.

extracts of this on fos. 228–9*b*. The copyist wrote :

> Liber cronicarum fratris Willelmi de Bougevilla cui nomen imposuit unus omnium, cuius libri primi prologus incipit, 'Quotienscunque divinarum scripturarum,' et liber sic incipit, 'In nomine Jesu Christi.' Incipit cronica in librario collegii Cant.

The author wrote :

> Vidi (inquit) et legi in regno Anglie, in excellenti ecclesia martyris Eadmundi, historias et chronicas quamplures, vbi multa notabilia vidi et inserui. In ecclesijs Albani, in Westmonasterio, et in regno Francie ad sanctum Dionysium, ac Parisijs . . . (Bale, *Index*, p. 117).

An item among the Harleian excerpts copied from a lesser Bury chronicle confirms this statement.[1] These excerpts are of the years 1165–1242. Bale gives 1288 as a date in his life. This seems probable : the author is probably to be identified with a prior of St. Neot's, a cell of Bec. He was holder of that office after 2 Dec. 1276 [2] and probably after the death of Bishop Richard Gravesend of Lincoln in 1279.[3] By 1281 he had left his post without permission and had returned to Bec, where his actions were condoned.[4] He is to be distinguished from a prior of Bec of the same name who died in 1275.[5]

William of Cirencester, sacristan and prior of Worcester, was possibly author of a part of the 'Annals of Worcester' to be found in B.M. MS. Cotton, Caligula A. x, edited by H. R. Luard in 'Annales Monastici' (R.S.), iv. 421(?)–49(?). See the articles on W. de Bradewas and Nicholas of Norton above for evidence of the sacristan's writing.

[1] *Cf.* a statement beginning 'Tempore Johannis tota Anglia' (fo. 228) with one set out in *Memorials of St. Edmund's* (R.S.), ed. T. Arnold, ii. 16.

[2] *Rot. R. Gravesend*, p. 182.

[3] In the full list of nominations to the office William is not mentioned.

[4] *Tempore bone memorie domini Petri quondam abbatis Becci fr Wills de Bugevilla tunc prior sci Neoti recessit a dicto prioratu et apud Beccum venit non mandatus nec licentiatus et expositis domino abbati causis adventus sui absolutus fuit a dicto prioratu* . . . (B.M. MS. Cotton, Dom. A. xi, fo. 114).

[5] Migne, *Patrologia Latina*, cl. 150, 662 ; Porée, *Chronique de Bec*, pp. 40, 44, 216.

Possibly this author may have written the full portions from 1229 on until 1263 and the meagre pieces later. He was admitted as a monk in 1235 ;[1] how much earlier he may have been a novice is uncertain. After 1242, when Sacristan Richard became prior (*Ann. Monast.* iv. 434), he attained the office, though not necessarily at once. In 1272 William succeeded Richard de Dumbleton as prior (*ibid.* p. 462)[2] and had died by 1274.[3]

William the Clerk, see App. B.

William, Cantor of Combe, was author of some hymns to St. Thomas Becket. (1) *Inc.* 'Frangit inclementiam rigor hiemalis,' Bodl. Lib. MS. Bodl. 509, fo. 12, entitled 'Willielmi Cantoris de Cumba Hymnus.' (2) *Inc.* 'Ara fit a Thoma Thome, Thomas quia Thome,' *ibid.* fo. 14, with a rubric 'Versus eiusdem.' (3) *Inc.* 'Virginis ingenite de virgine prolis honorem,' *ibid.* fo. 14*b*. All three are edited by J. A. Giles in 'Anecdota Bedæ, Lanfranci' (Caxton Soc.), pp. 191–6. The dates of the poems and of their author are uncertain. Combe was a cistercian house in Warwickshire.

William, probably a monk of Croyland abbey, wrote an 'Epitaph on Waltheof,'[4] seen by John Leland (*Itinerary*, ed. 1907, ii. 130–2). The last lines read :

> Clare comes, praecharæ Deo, Gualdeve beate
> Wilhelmi sint quæso tui laudes tibi gratæ.

The translation of Waltheof took place at Croyland in 1219. The abbot, Henry Longchamp, was a notable patron of literature.[5] Both the time and the circumstances

[1] *Ann. Monast.* iv. 426.

[2] *Reg. of Godfrey Giffard* (Worc. Hist. Soc.), ed. J. W. W. Bund, pp. 50–1.

[3] *Ibid.* p. 61.

[4] T. p. 363 ; *D.N.B.* under William of Ramsey. This literary character is apparently an invention of John Leland (*cf. Bulletin of the Institute of Historical Research*, viii, 1930. 109).

[5] For his patronage see Heironimus and Russell, *Shorter Latin Poems of Master Henry of Avranches* (Mediaeval Acad. of America), pp. 105-8.

favour the suggestion that this piece was written at about this time. There is a possibility that other works about Waltheof and St. Neot may have been written by this William.

William of Dallyng was the author of some 'Questions' upon Aristotelian works,[1] collected by John Rudham, in Cambridge, Gonville and Caius Coll. MS. 512 (late 13th cent.) :—'Questiones super librum peryarmenias mag. Willelmi Dallyng,' fos. vi–13 ; 'Questiones super librum posteriorum mag. Willelmi Dallyng,' fos. 57–80*b* ; 'Questiones super librum de generatione et corruptione date a mag. Will. Dallyng,' fos. 183–192 (M. R. James, *Cat.* p. 582).

In this same MS. are questions by Peter de Insula [q.v.], John of Felmingham, Walter Burley, and de Lyde. They come from the turn of the century. A Master William Dallyng was presented to Surlingham St. Mary by the prioress of Carrow in 1304 and held it until 1324.[2]

William of Dover was possibly the author of the 'Annals of St. Martin's, Dover, 1–1234' : *inc.* 'Annis quingentis decies iterumque ducentis.' B.M. MS. Cotton, Julius D. v, fos. 14–30*b*. The Annals are very meagre to the year 1226 and were evidently put together at that time at Dover. The years of the Creation are inserted at the left-hand bottom corner of each folio to that year. The hand remains the same until 1234, the date of the death of William of Dover, who is the only Dover person mentioned prominently. This would tend to show that he was the direct or indirect author. Excerpts of the chronicle appear in Dugdale's 'Monasticon' (iv. 534). The 'Annals' have been described by William Stubbs in the 'Historical Works of Gervase of Canterbury' (R.S.), ii. pp. xxii–xxv.

1 T. p. 216.

2 Blomefield, v. 464 ; B.M. MS. Cotton, Nero E. vii, fos. 78, 97*b*, showing attestations by William, rector of Dalling and a 'dom. Will. de Dallinghe, capellanus.'

William of Dover was a monk of Christchurch, Canterbury. If he was the author of the chronicle he was almost certainly at Dover in 1226, possibly as sub-prior.[1] He was penitentiary of the archbishop of Canterbury in 1228, the authority for a miracle to a woman in that year (fo. 27*b*). On 26 June 1229 he was made prior of Dover and by mandate of the archbishop was installed on 1 July (fo. 29). Some of his documents remain.[2] In 1234 he attempted to share in the election of the archbishop, Edmund of Abingdon, but was repulsed and appealed to Rome. There, at the instance of Simon Langton, he withdrew his appeal. He secured various privileges for his priory and evidently impressed the pope so favourably (or Simon Langton did) that he was given the extraordinary privilege of visiting the exempt monasteries of the English black friars. Upon returning to England the archbishop refused to sustain the prior's privileges and left him to the mercy of the Canterbury monks, who promptly forced him to give up his privileges and even to resign (fos. 29*b*–30*b*). He did not survive his year of humiliation and doubtless remained at Canterbury until his death. Another Canterbury monk of the same name was alive in 1238 :[3] either he or the prior made a gift of certain vessels to the house.[4] The prior possibly left many books on law to Canterbury.[5]

William of Drogheda[6] was the author of a treatise on canon law entitled 'Summa

1 *Literae Cantuarienses* (R.S.), ed. J. B. Sheppard iii. 377 : William of Dover is given in list of subpriors of Dover.

2 Lambeth Palace MS. 241, fos. 41, 161*b*, 184*b*, 225*b*.

3 Searle in Cambridge Antiq. Soc., octavo publ. xxxiv (1902). 173. Two men of the name entered : the first probably about 1218 and the second about 1233. See App. C for method of calculation.

4 James, *A.L.C.D.* pp. 113, 117.

5 John Dart, *Hist. and Antiquities of the Cathedral Church of Canterbury*, p. xxi.

6 Wahrmund, *Die Summa*, introd., and De Zulueta, *William of Drogheda*, pp. 655–7.

Aurea,' edited by Ludwig Wahrmund in 'Die Summa Aurea des Wilhelmus de Drokeda' (Quellen zur Gesch. des römisch-kanonischen Processes in Mittelalter, Band 2, Heft 2).

Incipit summa aurea continens modum advocandi, opponendi, responendi, consulendi, distinguendi verum a falso a magistro W de Drocheda apud Oxoniam.

The author gives his name, 'Ego magister W. de Drokeda opus instans composui' (*op. cit.* p. 3). The treatise has been discussed by F. de Zulueta ('William of Drogheda' in *Mélanges de droit Romain dédiès a Georges Cornil*, pp. 641–57); F. W. Maitland (*Roman Canon Law*, pp. 107 *et seq.*); Bethmann-Hollweg (*Der Civil-Process des gemeinen Rechts*, iv. 123–4); and by A. Gentilis (*Landes Acad.*, 1605, p. 54).

The family of William of Drogheda came from Limerick, Ireland.[1] His parents had apparently come to England, probably with William, since they were buried at Monks Sherborne, Hampshire.[2] A professor of law at Oxford,[3] he went security for a student there accused of participation in the riot of 1238.[4] In the 'Summa Aurea' he gives instances of cases in which he figured: as an alternate in a case in 1239 before the precentor of Hereford at Oxford,[5] as a delegate in a case, appointed by Archbishop Edmund,[6] and possibly as an advocate for Oliver Deincourt[7] against the bishop of Lincoln. He apparently wrote his treatise about 1239.[8] In the years 1241–5 he was the principal advocate for William de Montpellier in litigation over his election as bishop of Coventry.[9] He was probably rector of Petham in Kent,[10] and was instituted into the church of Grafton Underwood in 1242–3, a living in the patronage of the monastery of St. Fromund.[1] A papal indult of 6 Mar. 1245 authorized him to hold an additional benefice.[2] He probably never enjoyed this privilege, since he was killed by his valet in his Oxford home in the same year.[3] This house, known as Drawda Hall, was sold a few years later.[4] He had willed it to the monastery of Sherborne, where he expected to be buried next to his parents. He held land elsewhere.[5]

[1] De Zulueta, *op. cit.* p. 657, citing inquest.

[2] *Ibid.*

[3] *Ibid.* p. 650.

[4] *C.Cl.R.*, 1237–42, p. 135.

[5] Wahrmund, *Die Summa*, p. 190.

[6] *Ibid.* p. 253.

[7] *Ibid.* p. 24. For the Deincourt family see B.M. MS. Lansdowne 207E, especially the genealogical chart on fo. 41.

[8] *Die Summa*, pp. xvi–xvii.

[9] *Chr. Maj.* iv. 423.

[10] *Die Summa*, p. 647.

William of Durham was a master at Paris and theologian.[6] He wrote a 'Summa' which is now at Douai.

William of Durham is said to have been at Paris in the years 1226–9.[7] He certainly left there in 1229,[8] and may have gone to Oxford, as did some of those mentioned with him. Upon the resignation of Adam Marsh [q.v.] from Wearmouth, probably in 1232, Bishop Richard Poore probably gave the living to William. At least he was parson there at his death,[9] and Richard gave him the income from the manors of Wearmouth and Ryhope.[10] When the bishop died the king raised the question of William's holding, but finally confirmed

[1] *Rot. R. Grosseteste*, p. 213.

[2] *C.E.P.R.* i. 214.

[3] *Chr. Maj.* iv. 423; *Eynsham Cartulary* (Oxford Hist. Soc.), ed. H. E. Salter, ii. 174.

[4] *Cartulary of the Monastery of St. Frideswide of Oxford* (Oxford Hist. Soc.), ed. S. R. Wigram, i. 329.

[5] *Eynsham Cartulary*, ii. 174. Probably he is the Master William 'de Roked' who witnessed a Sherborne priory document (Archives of Queen's College, Oxford, typescript cat., p. 44).

[6] T. p. 356; *D.N.B.* under William. The best life is in Glorieux.

[7] Glorieux, *loc. cit.*

[8] *Chr. Maj.* iii. 168. Ralph of Maidstone [q.v.] and John Blund [q.v.] are known to have gone to Oxford.

[9] *C.E.P.R.* i. 251; *Chr. Maj.* v. 91. He is not called parson of Wearmouth in the documents of 1237 and 1238.

[10] *C.Cl.R.*, 1234–7, p. 447. On 30 July 1237 the king ordered that 309 cattle should be returned to him (*ibid.* p. 477).

it.[1] The king made him gifts in 1237 and 1238.[2] Probably William was in England then. However, he was granted letters of protection for two years on 10 Sept. 1244.[3] Upon the resignation of Bishop Nicholas Farnham the question of his holding was apparently raised again: the pope, calling him a papal chaplain, ordered that he should not be molested in his rights.[4] He was said to have been archbishop-elect of Rouen, possibly about 1237 or 1245.[5] He has been confused with William of Sherwood[6] and William de Monte, and has been called archdeacon of Durham without sufficient evidence.[7] At his death in 1249 he left a sum of 310 marks to the university chest at Oxford[8] for the support of several masters.[9] About 1280 a group was organized supported by this fund, which became first Durham Hall and then University College.[10] Nevertheless his earlier relations with Oxford are very uncertain. He is said to have held wealthy livings and to have been desirous of more, but none besides those mentioned above are known.[11]

William of Erpingham was a disputant at Cambridge (*c.* 1282, according to Little-Pelster, p. 79, but *c.* 1275 according to App. A).

William of Exeter was the author of a 'Sermones super viii Beatitudinibus': [1] *inc.* 'In illo tempore. Videns turbas Jhesus ascendat in montem, etc. Sermonem istum quem.' Bodl. Lib. MS. Laud 368, fos. 106–64, with the rubric 'Incipit tractatus Willelmi Exoniensis de vii beatitudinibus.'

Dr. Little has suggested that this is possibly the franciscan of the name,[2] summoned in 1289 from Oxford by Deodatus, warden of the friars minors of Exeter, to assist him in choosing a new site for the convent.[3]

William of Ferrieres[4] was the author of an Anglo-Norman poem 'Eustaces,' or 'Placidas': *inc.* 'Un riches hom esteit en Rome jadis.' York, Chapter Lib. MS. 16, K. 13, fo. 104, with a rubric 'Guilaume de Fereres.' This has been published in part in *N.E.M.S.* xxxiv. 2, 225.

William Frazer, bishop of St. Andrews, was the author, according to Tanner, of treatises entitled[5] 'De iure successionis regni Scotiæ' and 'Concordantias in evangelia.'

A Master William Fraser witnessed a charter of William of Scremerston and Elizabeth, his wife, date unknown. He was dean of Glasgow and chancellor of Alexander, king of Scotland, in 1277.[6] He became bishop of St. Andrews in 1280 and died in 1297.

[1] Accepted on 6 May 1238 (*ibid.*); *C.P.R.*, 1232–47, p. 218.

[2] 20 oaks 'ad hospitandum' on 26 Nov. 1237, from forest of Haya near Durham (*C.Cl.R.*, 1237–42, p. 8); 40 'fustra ad cheverones' in the forest of 'Middewud' on 28 Apr. 1238 (*ibid.* p. 47).

[3] *C.P.R.*, 1232–47, p. 435.

[4] *C.E.P.R.* i. 251.

[5] *M. Parisiensis Hist. Angl.* (R.S.), ed. F. Madden, iii. 67, 311.

[6] *Hist. litt. de la France*, xviii. 391–3.

[7] Le Neve, *Fasti*, ed. Hardy, under Durham.

[8] *Chr. Maj.* v. 91; *Munimenta Academica* (R.S.), ed. H. Anstey, ii. 780–3. Apparently all that William requested was that:

'emerentur redditus annui ad opus decem vel undecim vel duodecim vel plurium Magistrorum, qui essent de redditibus illius pecuniæ sustentati.'

[9] To judge from a letter from Adam Marsh concerning this fund it apparently was intended for a loan fund (*Mon. Fr.* i. 251).

[10] *Mun. Acad.* i. 56, 87; ii. 490, 586–8, 780.

[11] *Chr. Maj.* v. 91.

[1] T. p. 357.

[2] *G.F.* p. 217; *Mon. Fr.* ii. 289.

[3] Oliver, *Monasticon Diocesis Exoniensis*, p. 331.

[4] Vising, p. 55; *cf.* also *Hist. litt. de la France*, xxxiii. 347. There is some uncertainty about him being Anglo-Norman.

[5] T. p. 297.

[6] On 23 Mar. 1277 Pope John XXI permitted him to hold an additional benefice; William held then the church of Ar besides his deanery (*Les Registres de Jean XXI*, ed. E. Cadier, p. 39).

William de Frumentaria.[1] In B.M. MS. Reg. 8, C. xvi is a treatise entitled 'Pharetra' commonly attributed to St. Bonaventura, but rejected by the Quaracchi editors (viii. p. cxv), according to the *B.M. Cat. of Western MSS. in the Old Royal and King's Coll.*, ed. Warner and Gilson, i. 239. A MS. note states :

> Liber que vocatur Pharetra, opus fratris Gwillelmi de la Furmentarie Anglici quondam de ordine fratrum minorum, cuius anima requiescat in pace.

The abbey of St. Mary of Leicester possessed a volume described as 'Historiale Scolasticum W. Frumentyn per se cum albo.' This probably denotes that he made a gift of the volume to the abbey.[2] The 'Pharetra' MS. was a gift of '—— de St. Neot' to Ramsey abbey. Possibly William was a relative of the abbot of Leicester, Robert Furmentyn (1244–7).[3]

William of Gainsborough[4] preached a sermon at Oxford in 1291 (Little-Pelster, pp. 185–6).

William Giffard was the author of an Anglo-Norman 'Apocalypse,' of which a 14th century MS. is in the possession of J. C. Fox, who gives extracts from it in the 'Modern Language Review,' viii (1913). 338–51. The author gives his name :

> Cest livere treita willame giffard
> Chapelein del iglise seint edward.

Mr. Fox believes it to belong to the second half of the 13th century.

St. Edward was the patron saint of Shaftsbury abbey, a house close to the king, for which Walter and Geoffrey Giffard secured a favour in 1266[5] and of which Mabel Giffard was abbess from 1291 to 1302.

[1] T. p. 303.

[2] John Nichols, *Hist. and Antiquities of the County of Leicester*, i. 102.

[3] Dugdale, *Monasticon*, vi. 462.

[4] T. p. 357.

[5] B.M. MS. Harley 61, fo. 31*b*.

One would expect this author to be of the same family :

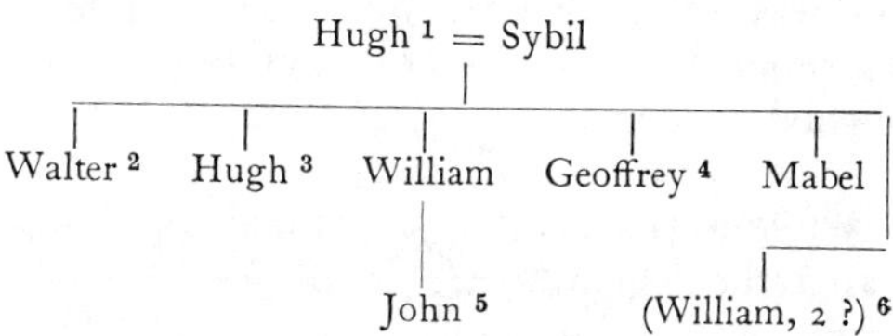

In 1242 William Giffard, son of Hugh Giffard, was to have conferred upon him a church of from twenty to fifty marks a year value, a very wealthy church.[7] In 1251 the king ordered that the two sons of Sybil Giffard be given three 'damos' for their inception 'de artibus dialectice' at Oxford.[8] One of these was probably Walter, the other possibly William.[9] If this William wrote the Anglo-Norman piece it must have been a product of the next few years.[10] By 1256 he seems to have been acting as a county

[1] In charge of Edward I as a prince : died in 1246 (*Chr. Maj.* v. 553). His heir was Walter (*C.Ch.R.*, 1257–1300, p. 67).

[2] Walter Giffard, a master by 1256, archbishop of York, died 1279. He and his mother were given the castle of Oxford in which to live (*C.P.R.*, 1247–58, p. 479). His heir was Geoffrey, see below.

[3] Hugh was presented to a church in 1242, which he resigned in favour of Walter in 1247 (*C.P.R.*, 1232–47, pp. 303, 510). He probably entered a militant order. In 1248 the king gave 'fr. H. Giffard' 'quandam loricam et unum par caligarum ferrearum' (*C.Cl.R.* 1247–51, p. 48).

[4] Born *c.* 1235, heir of Walter (*Cal. Gen.* i. 281). His heir was John, son of William.

[5] J. C. Fox suggests two Williams in the same family (*op. cit.*).

[6] Born 1270 or 1272 (*Cal. Gen.* ii. 625). His mother may have been a Katherine (*C.Ch.R.*, 1257–1300, p. 382). Probably he was the John Giffard who helped William Twiti to compose his treatise on hunting.

[7] *C.P.R.*, 1232–47, p. 283.

[8] Hugh as a fighting friar had probably ceased his schooling ; Geoffrey was about 17, possibly too young to be incepting.

[9] *C.Cl.R.*, 1247–51, p. 459.

[10] A William was a chaplain of Shaftsbury in the time of Abbess Maria, but the date of her rule is uncertain (B.M. MS. Harley 61, fos. 91, 92, 93*b*). Dugdale says about 1247 (*Monasticon*, ii. 473). An abbess, Agnes Ferrars, was elected in that year.

knight,[1] and in 1272 as a sheriff.[2] He was still alive in 1279 upon the death of Walter,[3] but was probably dead by 1302.[4] There are other William Giffards, but none with so good a claim.[5]

William (Paganerus) de Hanaberg, O.C., was a theologian.[6] He is alleged to have written 'Questiones Ordinarie': *inc.* 'Utrum actus virtutis moralis' (Bale in B.M. MS. Harley 3838, fo. 57). The other pieces attributed to him appear to be guesses based upon his career.

William de Hanaberg, possibly a doctor of Oxford, from the carmelite house at London, was made fourth provincial minister of the order at Norwich in 1278.[7] He is said to have held councils twice at Lincoln and Oxford, and once at Lynn. He possibly held office until 1281, when he was succeeded by Henry of Hanna [q.v.]. In 31 Edw. I (1302–3) he was sent to England to inspect the carmelite houses there: he

1 *Cat. Ancient Deeds*, iii. A. 4211, A. 4484; v. A. 11344, A. 11345, A. 11353, all of 42 Hen. III.

2 Fox, *op. cit.*; *Ancient Deeds*, iii. D. 221.

3 *Reg. Godfrey Giffard* (Worc. Hist. Soc.), ed. J. W. W. Bund, pp. 116, 406.

4 His will in William Thomas's *Survey of the Cathedral Church of Worcester*, App. p. 79, names William Giffard to receive certain properties, but Geoffrey's heir was William's son, John.

5 A Master William Giffard appears in the 14th century (*C.Ch.R.*, 1257–1300, p. 382; *C.E.P.R.* ii. 207; *C.P.R.*, 1324–7, p. 341; *ibid.*, 1327–30, p. 1; *ibid.*, 1330–4, p. 407). A Mr. William Giffard was a benefactor of Luffield Priory (Westminster Abbey, Luffield cartulary, fo. 245*b*); a friar William Giffard witnessed a charter of King David of Scotland (B.M. MS. Egerton 3031, fo. 36).

6 T. p. 376.

7 Bale says that at the chapter at Norwich, Henry of Hanna presiding:

'omni applausu receptus est in quartum Anglicane congregationis monarcham Guilhelmus Hanabergh, doctor Oxoniensis ex Londonensi cenobio literatissimus. Constat hunc virum fuisse omni laude dignum prudentem in agendis et solertem fama et opinione preclarum magne memorie et tenacitatis. Consilia celebravit Lincolnie semel atque Lynnee, bis autem Oxonie et plusquam viginti annis ac tandem extremum diem obiit anno domini MCCCXI (ut fertur) Londini' (B.M. MS. Harley 3838, fo. 57).

was then called William Paganus de Hanaberg.[1] According to Bale,[2] William Paganerus was among those who opposed the division of the English province at the council of Narbonne in 1303. In spite of his opposition he was permitted to remain in England by the council of London in 1305.[3] He seems to have been re-elected provincial minister in 1310, but died the following year and was buried at London.[4]

William de Hecham, O.P., preached a sermon at Oxford, 1292 (Little-Pelster, p. 186).

William of Hedon was the author of a commentary upon the Latin translation of Aristotle's 'De Anima.' (a) Cambridge, Gonville and Caius Coll. MS. 342; (b) Oxford, Corpus Christi Coll. MS. 107, fos. 148 *et seq.* (early 14th cent.). At the end appear these words:

Auctoris nomen quisquis cognoscere queris
Signat eum signis distinctio tertia veris
Nam primos apices si iungas particularum
Et genus et nomen auctoris erit tibi clarum.

The initials stand for 'Guillelmus Hedonensis.' The following is Father Pelster's note in the Gonville and Caius College copy of the library catalogue:

No doubt, the autograph of William of Hedon. It is the first detailed treatise of *De Anima* of the English School, date, ca. 1250–1260. It is particularly interesting because it shows clearly the coming in of the Aristotelian philosophy and its conflict with the older school. This treatise leans pretty closely on Aristotle.

Two possible Williams of Hedon may be traced in the Lincoln documents. In 1250–1 a chaplain was presented by the prior and convent of Durham to the church of Biscaythorp.[5] Upon the death of a William, probably the same, the patrons presented another candidate to the church in 1269–70.[6] In 1276–7 a Master William of Hedon was

1 T. p. 376.

2 Bale, *op. cit.* fo. 27.

3 *Ibid.* fo. 28.

4 T. p. 376.

5 *Rot. R. Grosseteste*, p. 119.

6 *Rot. R. Gravesend*, p. 38.

presented to the church of Beningfeld upon 31 October by the king's mother, Eleanor.[1] He had died or resigned this church by 1297.[2] He presided over one of the exercises in which Richard of Cnapwell [q.v.] shared.[3]

William of Hothum, O.P., was a theologian.[4] The early list of dominican writers gives as his literary output :

Fr Wilhelmus (de Hotun) nat. anglicus, mag. in theologia et archiepiscopus Dublinensis scripsit super primum librum sentent. Item lecturam supe romnes. Item de unitate formarum. Item de immediata visione divine essentie (*Archiv für Litteratur- und Kirchengeschichte*, ii, 1886. 238).

Some of his questions ' de quolibet ' remain in B.N. MS. Lat. 15805, fos. 17–9, with the colophon :

Expliciunt questiones de quolibet disputate a fratre Guillelmo de Hozum die lune proxima post festum beati Nicholai videlicet in crastino conceptionis beate Marie virginis anno gracie MCCLXXX [8 Dec.] (P. Glorieux, *La littérature quodlibetique de* 1260 *à* 1320, Bibliothèque Thomiste, pp. 175–6).

A sermon of his is given in Worcester Cathedral Lib. MS. Q. 46. Other sermons are attributed to him by A. Lecoy de la Marche (*La Chaire française*, p. 510).

William of Hothum was described by a dominican who may have seen him as follows :

Hic frater Willelmus, postquam ordinem ingressus est, cum esset vir acutissimi ingenii, doctor in theologia Parisiis factus est. Erat autem jocundus in verbis, in affatu placidus, religionis honestæ, in omnium oculis gratiosus.[5]

His brother, John, became bishop of Ely and willed property to Welbeck abbey for the sake of William's soul.[6] A nephew, Geoffrey, was collated in 1289 to the rectory of South Waltham.[1] A namesake, very probably a relative, was a fellow of Merton college in 1286 and a prebendary of St. Patrick's, Dublin.[2] Some of the letters sent to William were carried by a ' garcio,' Robert de Hothum,[3] while Peter de ' Othum ' was one of the procurators who brought him his pallium in 1297.[4]

William of Hothum, who entered the dominican order as a youth,[5] was reading the Sentences at Oxford in 1269 and shared in the controversy over the question of mendicancy between the dominican and franciscan orders.[6] He seems to have been a good friend of Walter Giffard, archbishop of York, and received presents from him in 1270 and 1271.[7] Probably he was the dominican William who received a gift of a bible from the king about 1276,[8] and the William who received expenses for going on the royal business in 1278.[9] He apparently incepted as master of theology at Paris in 1280 [10] and probably taught there for the next two years.[11] In the provincial chapter of the dominicans at Vienne he was named prior provincial for

[1] *Rot. R. Gravesend*, p. 133.

[2] *C.P.R.*, 1292–1301, p. 228.

[3] Fr. Pelster in *Zeit. für Kath. Theol.* lii (1928). 479 ; Little-Pelster, p. 82.

[4] T. p. 414 ; *D.N.B.* under Hothum ; Glorieux, p. 145. *Cf.* also *Archaeol. Journal*, xxxv (1878). 140–2.

[5] *Triveti Annales* (Eng. Hist. Soc.), ed. T. Hog, p. 364.

[6] B.M. Harley ch. 45, A. 31.

[1] *Registrum Johannis de Pontissara* (C.Y.S.), ed. C. Deedes, p. 31.

[2] *Memorials of Merton* (Oxford Hist. Soc.), ed. Brodrick, p. 178 ; H. Cotton, *Fasti Ecclesiae Hibernicae*, ii. 135.

[3] P.R.O., Exchequer, K.R., various accounts, E. 101/308/10 ; treasury of receipt, Misc. Books, E. 36/201, fo. 28*b*.

[4] *Registres de Boniface VIII*, ed. A. Thomas, i. 726, no. 1904.

[5] E. Langlois, *Registres de Nicolas IV*, p. 698, no. 4959.

[6] ' Cum socio Willelmo de Hodum, eorume cursor de sententiis ' (Little, *G.F.* p. 334).

[7] *Reg. Walter Giffard*, pp. 123, 116.

[8] P.R.O., Exchequer, K.R., various accounts, E. 101/350/24 : ' xv s fri Willo predicatori ad unam Bibliam emendam de dono regis lxvi s, viii d,' 5–6 Edw. I.

[9] P.R.O., Chancery Misc. 4/1, fo. 36*b* : ' pro expensis fris Willi et socii sui frm predicatorum existen' et eunti in negotio suo.'

[10] *Cf.* his ' de quolibet ' given above.

[11] He preached sermons at Paris, 16 Nov., 25 Dec. 1281 (Glorieux, p. 145). For the two year custom see App. A.

England and retained this office until 1287.[1] In 1282 he went to north Wales with Edward I. 'On October 28 the king paid him and his confrere 20s. for some private expenses, and 24s. 6d. for the expenses of themselves and their grooms and horses in going from Bath to Blaina to the lady of the latter vill, as royal messengers, and in returning to St. Sena, their absence at the court extending to eleven days.'[2] In 1283 he witnessed the will of the Queen Mother.[3] The following year he received exemption from duties at Dover for his order.[4] He probably went to the general chapter at Montpellier in June.[5] At the end of 1284 he entered into a dispute with Archbishop Peckham over the archbishop's rights with respect to the dominicans, especially about Richard Cnapwell and over the question 'de pluralitate formarum' at Oxford.[6] During his provincialate he was in touch with the king and pope.[7]

In the general chapter at Bordeaux, in 1289, Hothum was absolved and appointed to read at Paris.[8] He evidently did not obey: the general chapter at Lucca in the next year censured him for upsetting the school at Paris by his absence.[9] Probably he yielded and taught at Paris for the next two years; at this time he may have become known to the French king, Philip IV.[1] About Easter 1289 King Edward had a horse purchased for William.[2] In May 1289 he left with Otho de Grandisson on an embassy to the papal curia. He left Rome, apparently on 7 November, and reached London on 31 December.[3] In 1290 he was in England and in touch with the king. At michaelmas he received money willed by Queen Eleanor to dominicans of Derby. On 14 October the king at Clipstone in his presence agreed to go on crusade. He was elected prior provincial again on 8 Sept. 1290,[4] and two days earlier was offered the bishopric of Llandaff.[5] The pope ordered him to accept it again on 26 Apr. 1291, even requesting that his books be returned to the dominican order.[6]

William of Hothum preached a sermon at Oxford in 1291. Apparently on his advice Edward I opened the question of Scottish succession by demanding that each of the candidates should acknowledge his suzerainty. He was at the parliament in May 1291.[7] On 15 Feb. 1292 the king ordered certain letters sealed with the great seal of England for the pope to be turned over to William.[8] Later in the year William attended the parliament at Berwick, where he thought that

[1] *Acta Capitulorum Generalium ord. praed.*, ed. B.M. Reichert, i. 220, 242.

[2] *Archaeol. Journal*, xxxv. 140.

[3] *C.P.R.*, 1281–92, p. 218.

[4] *Ibid.* p. 124.

[5] *Archaeol. Journal*, xxxv. 140, documents not cited.

[6] *Reg. Peckham*, pp. 541, 865, 909; *Reg. Pontissara*, pp. 301, 307.

[7] Exchequer, K.R., various accounts (nuncii), E. 101/308/7, 12–3 Edw. I:

'die. dom. 14 Feb.' 'Arn. Bon. nuncio defer. lras regis Willo de Hothom, priori provinciali ordinis frm prdi in Anglia pro suis expensis ad xii dies iii s; *ibid.* 'die veneris,' 25 Feb. at Donington, letters to same; *ibid.* 'die dom.' 12 March. See also Exchequer, K.R., E. 101/308/10; Treas. of Receipt, Misc. Books, E. 36/201, fos. 23, 28*b*, 32*b*, 33; *C.P.R.*, 1281–92, p. 124; P.R.O. Ancient Deed, L.S. 62; *Registres d'Honorius IV*, ed. M. Prou, nos. 539 and 1287.

[8] *Acta Capitulorum*, i. 242.

[9] *Ibid.* p. 246.

[1] *D.N.B.*; and *Chronicon Walteri de Hemingburgh* (Eng. Hist. Soc.), ed. H. C. Hamilton, ii. 160.

[2] Exchequer, K.R., E. 101/352/18.

[3] The king on 2 May paid Robert de Hothum for carrying letters to preachers in Guienne (Exchequer, K.R., E. 101/308/10, 17–8 Edw. I). See also *ibid.* E. 101/352/18; Stevenson, *Hist. Doc. Scot.*, 1286–1306, i. 134, 136; *Foedera*, i. 714, 719; *Registres de Nicholas IV*, ed. E. Langlois, p. 397.

[4] Exchequer, K.R., E. 101/352/27. In June the arrears of his expenses to Rome were ordered to be paid (Chancery misc., c. 47/5). In October the king sent Robert 'garcio' of Walter of Winterburn for going from Clipstone to seek William with three horses and three 'garciones' (Chancery misc., c. 47/4; *Foedera*, i. 741).

[5] *Acta Capitulorum*, i. 519, 520; *Registres de Nicholas IV*, pp. 532, 534.

[6] *Registres*, pp. 698, 699.

[7] *Chronicon*, Hemingburgh, ii. 33.

[8] *Cal. Chancery Warrants*, i. 31.

Edward should decide the succession by English rather than written (Roman) law, and said that Balliol had a better claim than Bruce.[1] In 1293 Hothum had a dispute with Archbishop John of York in consequence of his insistence that penitents who had confessed to friars had no need of confessing to their parish priests.[2] On 4 Aug. 1294 he preached a Latin sermon before the king and two cardinals sent by Boniface VIII.[3] On 16 Jan. 1296 his prayers were asked for peace.[4] On 24 Apr. 1296 the pope ordered his election, and on 16 June the king acceded and supported him as archbishop of Dublin.[5] He died in 1298.

William of Hotot, Hotoft. Tanner has the following account :

Hotot [Gulielmus de] natus apud Carltonam juxta Cottingham in comitatu Northampton. monachus abbatiae Burgi S. Petri ; dein A. MCCXLVI abbas electus, quo munere ultro cessit A. MCCXLIX. Scripsit *Collationes super Gul. Antissiodorensem abbreviatum.* Obitus ejus celebratur Januar. vi. *Histor. Petroburg.* 33. 210. 307. 308. Quidam Gul. Hotoft frater praedicator, alius ab abbate Petroburgensi scripsit *Sermones plures*, etc. ex quibus excerpsit plurima Joh. de Schepeia. MS Merton Oxon. P. iii. 15. fol. i. et 218 (T. p. 414).

The 'Collationes' are more probably a gift (*cf.* James, *Peterborough*, pp. 23, 66). A biography of the abbot is in the 'Walteri de Whitlesey Historia Coenobii Burgensis,' ed. J. Sparke, *Historiae Anglicanae Scriptores Varii*, pp. 125–8.

William Jaclyn, O.P., preached a sermon at Oxford, 1292 (Little-Pelster, p. 187).

William of Lafford was the author of an 'Omelia de Muliere Cananæa'[6]: *inc.* 'Egressus Ihesus secessit in partes Tyri et Sidones.' London, Lambeth palace MS. 488, fos. 101–6, with a colophon 'Explicit omelia Willelmi de Lafford de muliere cananea.'

The author speaks of Alexander Neckam in the present tense.[1] The treatise has as patron a newly elected abbot,[2] whose surname was probably Black.[3] Probably the author was a monk of the early years of the 13th century. There are several persons of the name.[4]

William de la Lee[5] was probably the author of one or more of the Battle abbey chronicles such as that in B.M. MS. Cotton, Nero D. ii, which has been edited by F. Liebermann in 'Ungedruckte Anglo-Normanische Geschichtsquellen,' p. 35, to 1207. Leland saw at Battle abbey, Sussex, 'Liber Chronicorum fratris Wilhelmi de la Lee' (*Collect.* iv. 68). Sermons of a Master William de la Lee, preached at Oxford in 1291 and 1292, remain (Little-Pelster, p. 188). Probably he disputed at Oxford some years earlier (*ibid.* p. 91).

William of Leicester, see **William de Monte.**

1 *Rishanger, Chronica* (R.S.), ed. H. T. Riley, ii. 255, 260.

2 *Letters from Northern Registers* (R.S.), ed. J. Raine, pp. 102–3 ; *Reg. of John le Romeyn* (Surtees Soc.), i. 40, 313.

3 *Chronicon, Hemingburgh*, ii. 66.

4 *C.Cl.R.*, 1288–96, p. 507.

5 *Registres de Boniface VIII*, ed. A. Thomas, i. 398 ; ii. 145. For the rest of his career see *D.N.B.*

6 T. p. 462.

1 'Nam sicut venerabilis Nequam solet dicere,' 'ex operibus misericordie rexitur lorica iusticie' (fo. 103) ; 'Et pleniter venerabilis Nequam docet cum dicit, "furibus et viciis vigil obluctretur honestas."' Possibly he had been Neckam's student (fo. 105*b*).

2 'Promotus estis in abbatem' (fo. 101).

3 'Sic sane vos decet gloriosi paterni vestri verum esse filiolum . . . sic et Nigra' (fo. 101). The Catalogue suggests 'Fitz-Nigel.'

4 A Master William of Lafford is mentioned in charters of 1182 (*Transcript of Charters relating to the Gilbertine Houses*, Lincoln Rec. Soc., ed. F. M. Stenton, pp. 82–3) ; he was among the representatives of the 'Boriales' named in the terms of a treaty of peace at Oxford on 27 Mar. 1274 (*Mediaeval Archives of the University of Oxford*, Oxf. Hist. Soc., ed. H. E. Salter, i. 31). Other references appear in *Abstracts of Final Concords*, ed. W. Boyd, pp. 90, 140, 213 ; B.M. MS. Lansdowne 402, fo. 26.

5 T. p. 474.

William of Leominster,[1] **O.P.,** preached sermons at Oxford in 1292 and 1293 (Little-Pelster, pp. 180–1, 260–70). Bale attributes to him 'Questiones theologie' and 'Collationes in sententias' 'Ex officina Ioannis Cocke' (*Index*, p. 130).

William of Lidlington, O.C.,[2] is said to have written a treatise 'In Evangelium Matthei': *inc.* 'Anima mea conturbavit me.' Possibly this exists in Oxford, New Coll. MS. 47 (T. p. 358). Bale says, 'Interim Parisiis splendide se gerebat Ludlingtonus et varia scripta opuscula' (B.M. MS. Harley 3838, fo. 58*b*). Probably this is a conjecture.

Lidlington was possibly a M.A. of Oxford and from the diocese of Lincoln. In 1299 he was made provincial prior in succession to Henry of Hanna [q.v.] and ruled for four years. In 1303 he objected to the division of the English province and in 1305 he was sent to Paris as a punishment. Later, in 1309, he was promoted to be prior provincial of the province of the Holy Land, returning to England to die at Stanford.[3] The later dates are not known.

William of London was a grammarian, an excerpt from whose work is in B.M. MS. Harley 325, fo. 148, with a marginal note 'Ex magistro W. de Lond.' He is also quoted by Gervase of Melcheley [q.v.]: 'Cum tamen nusquam esset revera aliquis talis ignis, unde ait Willelmus Londoniensis' (Oxford, Balliol Coll. MS. 276, fo. 148).

William of London was probably the most common name in 13th century England. We have to discover a grammarian who lived before about 1216. In 1212 the pope, Innocent III, sent a Master William de London to preach the crusade in England.[4] A master of this name witnessed charters of Bishop Geoffrey de Muscham of Coventry

1 T. p. 477.

2 T. p. 357; *D.N.B.* under William.

3 Bale in B.M. MS. Harley 3838, fo. 58*b*.

4 *Ann. Monast.* iii. 40 (Dunstable under 1212).

(1198–1216).[1] Another witnessed a charter of Henry, archbishop of Dublin, about 1219.[2]

William of Macclesfield, O.P., was a theologian.[3] The early list of dominican writers gives:

> Fr Wilhelmus de Masfelt (Machelefield) anglicus, mag. in theol., scripsit contra Hinricum de Gande, quibus impugnat Thomam. Item contra corrupt. Thome. Item de unitate formarum. Item de immediata visione dei (*Archiv für Litteratur- und Kirchengeschichte*, ii., 1886, 239).

These have not been identified. Another list is given in Bale, 'Ex Ioanne Pullano Oxoniensi.'

> Guilhelmus Maunsfelde, Dominicanus quidam scripsit, Obiectiones contra Gandauum, li. i. De comparatione statuum prelatorum ac religiosorum contra eundem, li. i. Defensorium Thome contra corruptorium illius, li. i. In questiones de anima, li. i. Processus bonus domini Lincolniensis, li. i. (*Index*, p. 137).

The early life of William of Macclesfield is unknown.[4] In 1308 a subdeacon, John de Macclesfield, received papal dispensation from his duties as rector of Mattram in Coventry to spend three more years without taking orders to study canon and civil law. He had already had one dispensation for seven years.[5] Probably he was a relative, possibly a cousin. From the titles of his treatises it would seem that William had written against both Henry de Gandavo and William de Mara [q.v.] at Paris, probably about 1285. However, he does not seem

1 'In the presence of E, bishop of Ely and of the abbots of St Edmundsbury and Ramsey' (Bodl. Lib. MS. Ashmole 1527, fo. 94*b*); P.R.O., Exchequer, Augmentation Office, Misc. Books, E. 315/51, no. 58; Derbysh. Archaeol. Soc. *Journal*, xiii (1891). 56.

2 20th *Rep.*, D.K.P.R., Ireland, App. vii. p. 41.

3 T. p. 358; *D.N.B.* under Mykelfeld; Little-Pelster, pp. 270–2.

4 Early in the century a 'Wm fil. Galfr. de Mykelfeld' appears in charters (B.M. MS. Cotton, Claudius B. iii, fo. 35; *Reg. Walter Gray*, Surtees Soc. p. 186 *n.*); B.M. Add. ch. 37349 gives a will of Thos. of Macclesfield of 1303, but does not mention William.

5 *C.E.P.R.* ii. 39.

to have taken his degree in theology there.[1] He represented his order at the synod of Besançon of 1303 and was nominated by Pope Benedict XI cardinal priest of St. Sabina on 18 Dec. 1303.[2] He died at Canterbury early in 1304.

William de Mara, O.F.M., was a famous linguist and theologian.[3] His writings and their MSS. are listed by Longpré. They included the usual scholastic 'Questiones' and commentaries, a commentary on the 'Sentences' of St. Bonaventura and a 'Correctorium Fratris Thome [Aquinas],' of which article XXVIII is edited by B. Geyer in 'Florilegium Patristicum,' xiv. 63–6. He also wrote upon the Greek and Hebrew texts of the bible.

De Mara's knowledge of Greek and Hebrew was about the best of his age. An English franciscan of such attainments was obviously a product of the school of Oxford and of Grosseteste. Roger Bacon, writing in 1267,[4] tells of a scholar who had devoted nearly forty years to the study of Hebrew, Greek, and Latin, and was therefore probably the only man really qualified to correct the text of the scriptures. This is probably de Mara, whom Bacon could hardly have not known. Thus he was probably studying these languages since about 1227. A William de la Mare, deacon, was presented by Henry de la Mare to the chapel of Alvescot in 1229.[5] In 1250–1 a Master William de Mara, also a deacon, was presented by Bicester priory to the rectory of Oddington.[6] William de Mara seems to have preached a sermon at Lincoln in the decade 1260–70.[1] It is possible that he did not enter the franciscan order until late in life. His 'Questiones' and 'Commentary' upon St. Bonaventura seem to have been written before the controversies of 1270 and 1277 : he was regent while writing.[2] After 1277 he devoted himself to his 'Correctorium Fratris Thome,' which the franciscan general chapter of 1282 at Strasburg adopted as a necessary commentary upon St. Thomas.[3] He then dropped out of sight.

[1] *Archiv*, ii. 206.

[2] *Triveti Annales* (Eng. Hist. Soc.), ed. T. Hog, p. 400 ; *Rishanger, Chronica* (R.S.), ed. H. T. Riley, p. 221.

[3] T. p. 223 ; *D.N.B.* under Mara ; E. Longpré in *Dictionnaire de théologie Catholique*, viii. 2467.

[4] *Opera Inedita* (R.S.), ed. J. S. Brewer, p. 94.

[5] *Rot. H. de Welles*, ii. 31. The next notice of a vacancy is in 1276 (*Rot. R. de Gravesend*, p. 231).

[6] *Rot. R. Grosseteste*, p. 497 : the official who instituted him was also named W. de Mara (*ibid.* pp. 495, 499, 501). There was a subdeacon of a little later date named Master William de Mara (*Rot. R. de Gravesend*, pp. 198, 199, 236 ; *Ann. Monast.* iii. 256, 283 ; *C.Cl.R.*, 1272–9, p. 44). In Erfurt MS. Qu. 182, flyleaf, are references to a Mara family connected with Paris about 1271. Notes on Hebrew names occur on fo. 296.

[1] Longpré, *loc. cit.*

[2] *Ibid.*

[3] Longpré in *Analecta Bollandiana*, xviii (1899). 292.

William of Milton, O.F.M., was a theologian.[4] He was apparently a prolific writer whose works remain mostly on the continent. The following is but a preliminary checklist. 'Postille' of his were being sold at Paris upon the Psalter, Twelve Prophets, Mark, Ecclesiasticus, and Job for three or four shillings apiece in the 13th century (Denifle-Chatelain, *Cartularium Universitatis Parisiensis*, i. 647). The second of these, the postils upon the Twelve Prophets, were in the dominican library at Piacenza (Sisto da Siena, *Bibliotheca Sancta*, Paris, 1610, p. 238). In the same library were 'Postille in Ep. Hebreorum' : *inc.* 'Ad Aquilone pandetur malum.' The postille upon Job are possibly the same as a long commentary upon that book discussed by B. Haureau, *Notices et extraits de quelques manuscrits*, iii. 2. He was apparently the author of a work upon the Song of Songs (*ibid.* v. 1). His sermons 'de tempore et de sanctis' remain in Munich, Cod. Mon. 14812, with the colophon 'Explicit opus magistri Wilhelmi de Militona.' His most popular work was probably a long treatise 'Super Apocalypsin' : *inc* 'Spiritu

[4] T. p. 521 ; *D.N.B.* under Meliton.

magno vidit. Premissis causis principalibus.' It is found at Assisi; Berlin, MS. 412; Prague, MSS. 550, 760, 1052; Vienna, MS. 4211. He also probably shared in the completion of the 'Summa' of Alexander of Hales.

According to an 'exemplum' William of Milton related to John de Rupella at Paris in 1245 a prophetic dream about the death of Alexander of Hales and Guerricus de St. Quintin.[1] He probably became regent master of the franciscans at Paris in 1248, succeeding Eudes Rigaud.[2] He shared in the condemnation of the 'Talmud' in that year.[3] He was regent master of franciscans at Cambridge, probably about 1255.[4] He was appointed in 1256 to finish the 'Summa' of Alexander of Hales, a task which probably took him back to Paris.[5] He ended his life there in 1261,[6] dying a serene death, which the friars liked to recall.[7]

William de Monte, chancellor of Lincoln, was a theologian.[8] A critical study of his many writings is much needed. Probably it will be provided by the research of Miss E. Rathbone and Mr. R. W. Hunt. One question of interest is that of the many books

[1] *Fratris Gerardi de Fracheto Vite Fratrum*, ed. B. M. Reichert, p. 274.

[2] *Bibl. thomiste*, xiv. (1930) 225; Denifle, *Cartularium Univ. Paris.* i. 210, 328.

[3] William is lauded in legate's pronunciamento (Quétif-Echard, p. 488).

[4] See App. A.

[5] *Cart. Univ. Paris.* i. 328.

[6] Little, *Bibl. thomiste, loc. cit.*; *Chronicon de Lanercost* (Bannatyne Club), ed. J. Stevenson, p. 71.

[7] For examples see *L'Exemplum dans la littérature religieuse et didactique du moyen age*, ed. J. Th. Welter, p. 248; *Cat. of Romances*, ed. J. A. Herbert, iii. 648. Fr. William had received a golden seal from a franciscan novice who had received it from the Virgin Mary in a dream. Quétif-Echard (p. 488) gives from Thomas Cantimpré, li. 2, cap. 1 (B.M. MS. Harley 3832, fo. 32):

'Vir eminens de ordine fratrum minorum et magister theologie qui vitam duxit sanctissimam, cum Parisius predicaret obmutuit per horam, moxque verbum vite resumens omnibus valedixit serenissimo vultu sicque in pace quievit.'

[8] T. p. 361; *D.N.B.* under William of Leicester.

under his name in the old Peterborough catalogue. Were they writings or gifts or both?

Bibliographical tradition has also called William de Monte William of Leicester,[1] but there seems no direct evidence for this. His family is unknown.[2] He had become, probably by 1180,[3] a well-known professor at the Mont St. Geneviève in Paris, where he numbered Gerald of Wales and Alexander Neckam among his students.[4] His name 'de Monte' may have come from this circumstance,[5] although the alternate name 'de Montibus' is not favourable to this. The ancient list of canons of Lincoln of about 1184 does not contain his name.[6] Brought to Lincoln by Bishop Hugh (1186–1200),[7] before 1189 he became a canon there.[8] About 1191 he became chancellor, and from this time until his death shortly after Easter (14 April) 1213 his name appears constantly in the Lincoln charters.[9] He was

[1] Probably the Leicester is due to confusion with Richard de Wetheringsett, who is sometimes called 'de Leicester.' From the confusion caused by the 'reportatio' of William's 'Summa' by Richard, the latter is called 'de Montibus' by Pits (*Relationum Historicarum*, p. 895). The matter is still somewhat uncertain.

[2] B.M. MS. Cotton, Faustina B. i, fo. 57*b*. William de Montibus quitclaims to St. Mary of Barlings an annual return of some houses in Lincoln. His father is Richard de Myreford, but he is not called master.

[3] F. M. Powicke, *Stephen Langton*, p. 10.

[4] *De Naturis Rerum of Neckam* (R.S.), ed. T. Wright, p. 460.

[5] *Cf.* the case of John of Garland [q.v.].

[6] *Statutes of Lincoln Cathedral*, ed. H. Bradshaw and C. Wordsworth, ii. 793.

[7] *Giraldi Cambrensis Opera* (R.S.), ed. J. F. Dimock, vii. 107.

[8] B.M. MS. Reg. 11, B. ix, fo. 27*b*, witnessed by Hamo, archdeacon of Leicester: he became dean in 1189 apparently.

[9] The charters need such careful study as Canon Foster was giving them. Those containing the name of William may be divided according to time. A (from accession of Hamo as dean to the substitution of William for Stephen as chancellor about 1191); B (from 1191 to the election of Roger de Rolveston as dean in 1195); C (from 1195 to the murder of the sub-dean, William de Bramfeld, on 25 Sept.

buried the next year in the cathedral.[1] He was a very famous authority and gave immense prestige to the cathedral school of Lincoln in his time.[2]

William of Nottingham, O.F.M.,[3] was the author of a compendious work entitled 'Unum ex Quatuor,' a commentary upon the 'Concordance of the Gospels' by Clement of Lanthony : *inc.* 'Da mihi intellectum.' (a) Cambridge, Corpus Christi Coll. MS. 305, extracts ; (b) B.M. MS. Reg. 4, E. ii (1381) ; (c) Oxford, Balliol Coll. MS. 33 (14th cent.) ; (d) Bodl. Lib. MS. Laud Misc. 165 (early 14th cent.) ; (e) Oxford, Magdalen Coll. MS. 160 (15th cent.) ; (f) *ibid.* Merton Coll. MS. 156 (14th cent.) ; (g) *ibid.* Merton Coll. MS. 157 (14th cent.) ; (h) *ibid.* St. John's Coll. MS. 2 (15th cent.) ; (i) 'Notyngham superevangelia, willed to Durham cathedral by Thomas Langley in 1436 (*Catalogue of the Library of Durham Cathedral*, Surtees Soc., p. 120). That this was written by the earlier franciscan of the name is made clear by Thomas of Eccleston [q.v.] :

> Verba Sancti Evangelii devotissime recolebat ; unde et super unum ex quatuor Clementinis (Phillips MS. fo. 80 reads Clementis) canones perutiles compilavit, et expositionem quam idem Clemens fecit complete scribi in ordine procuravit (Little, *G.F.* p. 185).

He may also be the author of the work 'De Obedientia' : *inc.* 'Quia peregrini et advene sumus.' (a) Cambridge, Pembroke Coll. MS. 265, fo. 195, with title 'Sermo bonus de obedientia fratris Willelmi de Notyngham' ; (b) MS. formerly in the library of the franciscans of Cambridge, possibly the same as (a), entitled 'Epistola fratris Gulielmi Notingham de obedientia' (Leland, *Collect.* iv. 16).

William of Nottingham had heard Robert Grosseteste [q.v.] when he was teaching the franciscans at Oxford about 1232–5 : he was probably studying there under him.[1] He completed and probably started his great work 'Unum ex Quatuor' after Grosseteste became bishop.[2] He was vicar for Haymo of Faversham as prior provincial of England in 1239–40 without holding any previous executive office.[3] When Haymo became general of the order in 1240 William was elected provincial minister in his place [4] and retained the office until 1254.[5] As minister he was well liked. From youth he had high regard for the virtues of the franciscans, and for poverty,[6] and a disregard or even dislike

1205) ; and D (to the death of William de Monte in 1213). A : P.R.O., ancient deeds, B. 11398 ; B.M. MS. Reg. 11, B. ix, fo. 27*b* ; *ibid.* MS. Harley 2110, fo. 122*b* ; *Documents illustrative of the Social and Economic Hist. of the Danelaw*, ed. F. M. Stenton, p. 69 ; Bodl. Lib. MS. Top. Northants C. 5, p. 415 ; B.M. MS. Reg. 11, B. ix, fo. 25 ; *ibid.* Harley ch. 54, A. 45 ; *ibid.* Cotton ch. xxvii. 196. B : H.M.C., *Rutland MSS.* iv. 114 ; B.M. MS. Cotton, Vesp. E. xx, fos. 33–4 (3). B or C : B.M. MS. Reg. 11, B. ix, fo. 97*b* ; *ibid.* Harley ch. 48, C. 11 ; *ibid.* 48, C 12 ; Assoc. Architectural Soc. *Rep.* xxvi. 357, 359 ; xxvii. 45 ; xxvi. 59, 60, 355. B, C, or D : *ibid.* xxvi. 24. C : *Rot. R. Grosseteste*, p. 516 ; Assoc. Archit. Soc. *Rep.* xxvii. 52, 72 ; B.M. Harley ch. 45, E. 43 ; and E. 45 ; *ibid.* MS. Cotton, Claudius D. xi, fo. 58*b* ; and Vesp. E. xx, fo. 35*b* ; *ibid.* Harley ch. 44, E. 18 ; Assoc. Archit. Soc. *Rep.* xxvi. 29, 38, 51, 60, 336 ; B.M. Harley ch. 56, i. 37 ; Assoc. Archit. Soc. *Rep.* xxvi. 65, 358 ; xxvii. 80. C or D : B.M. MS. Cotton, Vespasian E. xx, fos. 92*b*, 240, 241. D. Assoc. Archit. Soc. *Rep.* xxvi. 330 ; xxvii. 79 ; B.M. Harley ch. 44, A. 29 ; *ibid.* Cotton ch. V. 72.

1 *Chronicon de Lanercost* (Bannatyne Club), ed. J. Stevenson, p. 10 ; *Chronica de Mailros* (Bannatyne Club), ed. J. Stevenson, sub anno 1213 ; a poem upon his death is in B.N. MS. Lat. 15157, fo. 52 : *inc.* 'Filius in matris utero merito sepelitur.' *Cf.* **Nicholas,** monk **of Rivaulx,** above.

2 Gerald of Wales thought it worth while to study under him there (*Opera*, i. 93). Gerald relates a story by William who was 'familiaris eius [of St. Hugh of Lincoln] et delectus' of how Hugh kissed a leper (*ibid.* vii. 107, 175 ; also in *Flores Historiarum* (R.S.), ed. H. G. Hewlett, i. 304.

3 T. p. 362 ; *D.N.B.* under Nottingham. The best biography is by Little, *G.F.* p. 185.

1 *Mon. Fr.* i. 69.

2 'Secundum translationem Lincoln' (B.M. MS. Reg. 4, E. ii, fo. 2).

3 *Mon. Fr.* i. 59, 551.

4 *Ibid.* p. 59.

5 *Cf.* the story given in Little, *G.F.* p. 185 ; *Mon. Fr.* i. 72.

6 *A.F.H.* iv. 428–30.

of women and magnates.[1] He was a sturdy defender of the rights of his order against the dominicans,[2] and of his own ideas within his own order. With two helpers he pushed through one plan of his in the general chapter of Genoa.[3] Possibly at the time of his struggle with the dominicans he stayed several months in the franciscans' house at Rome and got fat on chestnuts, to his embarrassment.[4] This was probably in the time of Innocent IV, of whose household William's brother Augustine was a member before going with the patriarch of Antioch, the pope's nephew, to Syria, and becoming bishop of Laodicea.[5] William was an enthusiastic educator, largely responsible for the franciscan educational system in England.[6] He was upheld in the general chapter of Oxford by the brethren,[7] but deposed at Metz in 1254.[8] The English franciscans re-elected him,[9] and Adam Marsh congratulated him and asked him not to refuse.[10] On a trip to Rome he stayed at Genoa to care for his associate, Richard, and was stricken also with the plague and died.[11] He may have been taken to Marseilles.[12]

William of Peterborough (de Burgo) was the author and owner of several books formerly at Ramsey abbey.[13] His ' Eufrastica ' (*inc.* ' Cum intuitum oculatum quoad ducit') survives in Bodl. Lib. MS. Bodley 833, fos. 1 *et seq.* (13th cent.). Contemporary titles are ' Eufrastica inter libros magistri Willelmi de Burgo,' and ' Incipit prologus in eufrastica Willelmi.' ' Distinctiones Theologie ' : *inc.* ' Alpha prima Græcorum litera.' ' Sermones in Cantica ' : *inc.* ' Dilectus meus candidus et rub. ' Other ' Sermons ' : *inc.* ' Aspiciens a longe vidi,' and ' Reverenter docet experiri ea' (T. p. 355). Camb. Univ. Lib. MS. Add. 3470, a transcript of the catalogue of Boston of Bury, mentions these on p. 143.

Bibliographical tradition from the time of Boston of Bury has made William a monk of Ramsey and from the time of John Leland has placed him about 1188. The former is probably a deduction from the fact that his books were in the Ramsey library and the latter is probably a conjecture. The record of his gift is not in the library's catalogue.[1] Possibly he is the Master William de Burgo of the time of Robert Grosseteste, whose interest in languages was much like his own. This William witnessed a charter at Lincoln in the bishop's first year,[2] and other documents of Thorney and Ramsey about 1247–8.[3] His interest in Hebrew is much like that of Robert Dodford [q.v.]. Another William de Burgo was bishop of Llandaff, 1244–53.[4]

William of Ramsey[5] was a ' literary ghost ' created by John Leland. For a summary statement of the evidence see *Bulletin of the Institute of Historical Research*, viii (1930), 109. Most of the work attributed to him is actually by Henry of Avranches. On the curious history of the latter's reputation see Heironimus and Russell's ' Shorter

[1] *Mon. Fr.* i. 70.
[2] *Ibid.* p. 56.
[3] *Ibid.* p. 32.
[4] *Ibid.* p. 72.
[5] *Ibid.* pp. 62, 551.
[6] *Ibid.* pp. 38, 69.
[7] Probably *c.* 1248 (*ibid.* p. 68).
[8] *A.F.H.* iv. 428–30.
[9] *Mon. Fr.* i. 70, 303.
[10] *Ibid.* p. 373.
[11] *Ibid.* p. 70.
[12] ' Iacet Marsilie ' (*ibid.* p. 559). A royal letter to him not long before his death is recorded in a payment to a messenger going to him : ' D'nica proxima ante festum St. Gregorii,' between St. John Baptist 36 and 37 Hen. III, about 12 Mar. 1253 (P.R.O., Exchequer, K.R., various accounts, nuncii, E. 101/308/1).
[13] T. p. 355 ; *D.N.B.* under William.

[1] In *Chronicon Abbatiae Rameseiensis* (R.S.), ed. W. D. Macray, pp. 356–67.
[2] Camb. Univ. Lib. MS. Add. 3020, fos. 220*b*, 432.
[3] P.R.O., Duchy of Lancaster, D.L. 42/2, fo. 9*b* : Dugdale, *Monasticon*, iii. 315 ; iv. 549 ; P.R.O., Exchequer, Augmentation office, Misc. Books, E. 315/48, nos. 153, 154 : ' Mr. Willelmus de Burgo, rector ecclesie de Bernak, Thomas Wallensis, archdeacon of Lincoln ' ; *Registres d'Innocent IV*, ed. Berger, no. 1336 ; *Chr. Maj.* iv. 616 ; *C.E.P.R.* i. 217.
[4] *Chr. Maj.* iv. 379, 413, 647 ; v. 322, 382 ; *Ann. Monast.* 136, 156.
[5] T. p. 363 ; *D.N.B.* under William.

Latin Poems of Master Henry of Avranches' (Mediaeval Acad. of America), pp. 13–7.

William Rufus, author of a 'Treatise on Preaching': *inc.* 'In omni scriptura et sermone.' Oxford, Magdalen Coll. MS. 168, fos. 128*b*–49 (13th–14th cent.), with the title 'Willelmus Rufus de modo predicandi.'

The date of the treatise shows the author to have been probably as early as the 13th century. A note on the margin says 'De doctrina bone memorie fratris Ricardi de Thetford' [q.v.]. This is not conclusive evidence that Richard preceded William, however. A Master William Rufus attested a charter of 1221 with Gervase of Melcheley [q.v.].[1] More probably the author was a canon of Hereford about 1265–70 [2] and treasurer of Hereford by 1272.[3]

William de Sanvico, O.C., was a chronicler.[4] His great work was the 'Chronica de Multiplicatione sui Ordinis per Provincias Syrie et Europe et de Perditione Monasteriorum Terre Sancte': *inc.* 'Religiosi Carmelite sicut in terra.' This has been published in the 'Acta Sanctorum,' May, iii. prologue pp. lx-lxiv, in 'Speculum Carmelitarum' (Ant. 1650), and by G. Wessels in 'Annales Ordinis Carmelitanorum,' ii. 302–15.

What does the 'Sanvico' represent: the Holy Land or Sandwich? Carmelite tradition,[5] including John Bale,[6] asserts that the name was probably due to his association with the Holy Land. However, the Sanvico may have stood for Sandwich.[1] There was a later man of probably the same name famous among the carmelites.[2] William as diffinitor of the province of the Holy Land attended the general chapter at Montpellier on 22 July 1287.[3] He was the last inhabitant of the house on Mount Carmel when the friars were driven thence by the mohammedans. He was in Acre when it was taken in 1291.[4] His 'Chronica' is very impersonal and fails to give biographical information.

[1] B.M. MS. Otho D. iii, fo. 78. There is reference to a William Rufus, status unknown, in some entries (1284–9) of a chaplain or steward on Bodl. Lib. MS. Bodley 35, fo. 97*b* (Madan and Craster, *Summary Cat. of Western MSS.* ii. pt. 1, p. 97).

[2] *C.P.R.*, 1258–66, pp. 426, 427, 442, 443; *ibid.*, 1266–72, pp. 115, 415 (?); P.R.O., ancient deeds B. 3366; *Reg. R. de Swinfield* (C.Y.S.), ed. W. W. Capes, ii. 57.

[3] *Reg. Swinfield*, ii. 163, 164.

[4] T. p. 654.

[5] B.M. MS. Harley 1819, fo. 13*b*, gives two short poems by Burellus (Saltet in *Etudes carmélitaines*, i. 42).

[6] 'Guilhelmus de Samuco, natione sirus vel Palestinus.' 'Ex reg. ordinis' (Bale in MS. Harley 3838, fo. 161*b*).

William of Scarborough was the author of a work entitled 'Sophestria': *inc.* 'Amatus sum vel fui. Circa nunc sermonem.' Worcester, Cathedral Lib. MS. Q. 13, fos. 37–42.

Possibly this was the Oxford student mainprised by Roger Niger, bishop of London, and Robert Grosseteste in 1238.[5]

William of Sengham was an austin friar.[6] John Bale, bishop of Ossory, Ireland, found items about William in the collections of Thomas Colby, bishop of Waterford *c.* 1400 (*Scriptorum Illustrium*, pp. 302–3). Colby had been a carmelite of Norwich and seems to have found his information about the austin friars there. He states that William had written 'De Fide et Legibus,' 'De Claustro Anime,' 'De Professione Novitiorum,' and 'De Tentationum Remediis.' A table upon the 'De Fide et Legibus' of William de Perault was formerly at Lincoln,

[1] A Ralph de Sandwyco was custodian of the carmelite house in London, 18 Edw. I (P.R.O., Chancery misc., C. 47/4/4, fo. 45); William of Lidlington was a successor of William de Sanvico as diffinitor of the province of the Holy Land, and Englishmen were prominent among the carmelites.

[2] *Speculum Ordinis Fratrum Carmelitarum noviter impressum* (1507), p. 104.

[3] Bale, MS. Harley 3838, fo. 26*b*; *Acta Capitulorum Generalium*, ed. G. Wessels, p. 10.

[4] *Acta Sanctorum*, May, iii. A William of Sandwich, priest, was deprived of Stanes by a papal sentence of 1264 (*C.E.P.R.* i. 406).

[5] Wood, *History of Oxford* (1792), p. 225.

[6] T. p. 662; *D.N.B.* under Sengham.

entitled 'Ista tabula prescripta facta est super librum "De fide de Legibus" a fratre Gul. Sengham.'

Apparently Colby had also said that William was among the first augustinians sent to England. Henry III gave the initial group a patent of welcome in 1249.[1] Later bibliographical and austinian tradition seems merely to improve upon these simple facts, except perhaps in one point, the association of William with B. Albertinus of Verona in the establishment of houses of his order in England.[2] A William of Sengham of Kent was connected with Merton College.[3]

William of Sherwood was a treasurer of Lincoln and a scholar.[4] He wrote a treatise on logic, 'Syncategoreumata': *inc.* 'Quoniam ad cognitionem,' Bodl. Lib. MS. Digby 55, fos. 205–24*b* (13th cent.), with a colophon 'Expliciunt sincategreumata magistri Willelmi de Sirewode.' 'Introductiones in Logicam': 'Cum duo sunt tantum rerum principia,' B.N. MS. lat. 16617, entitled 'G. de Lincoln.' Extracts of this are given by Carl Prantl (*Gesch. der Logik*, iii. 11–24). William's authorship of the 'Introductiones' is very doubtful. He is said to have written 'Distinctiones Theologice,' formerly at Cambridge (T. p. 669). A treatise 'Super Sententias,' entitled 'Sherwood super sententias,' was formerly in the library of the dominicans of Exeter (Leland, *Collect.* iv. 151), but it may have been written by another Sherwood. An 'Insolubilia': *inc.* 'S . . . pratum quorundam est solucio,' Cambridge, St. John's Coll. MS. 100, is attributed by a colophon to 'm. Richardi de Schirwode.'

William of Sherwood probably spent his life teaching at Paris. He was the master of Petrus Hispanus (born *c.* 1210–20),[5] and was regarded by Roger Bacon in 1267 as the wisest of Christians, even greater than Albertus Magnus.[1] His 'Syncategoreumata' shows him at Paris.[2] Sherwood became treasurer of Lincoln about 1254,[3] before 2 Jan. 1258,[4] when he received papal permission to hold an additional benefice.[5] Probably he then received the Little Rectory manor of Atleburgh (Aylesbury),[6] which he held in 1266.[7] He held this on his death in 1279 or earlier.[8] He may have been at Oxford in 1252, but this is doubtful.[9]

William of Shoreham, vicar of Chart near Leeds, was the author of some English

[1] *C.P.R.*, 1247–58, p. 49.

[2] This might come from a biography of Albertin, but I have not been able to trace its source.

[3] P.R.O., Exchequer of pleas, plea roll E. 13/21, *m.* 53*b*. He was a person of some importance *c.* 1297.

[4] T. p. 668; *D.N.B.* under Shirwood.

[5] S. D. Wingate, *Mediaeval Latin Versions*, p. 79.

[1] *Opera Inedita* (R.S.), ed. J. S. Brewer, p. 14; 'magister Gulielmus de Shyrwode, Thesaurarius Lincolniensis ecclesie in Anglia' (T. p. 668). What was in England, the church or William? *Cf.* also *ibid.* p. 428.

[2] 'Nullus homo legit Parisius nisi asinus' (Bodl. Lib. MS. Digby 55, fo. 220).

[3] After the death of Peter Chaceporc, on 24 Dec. 1254 or 1255 (*D.N.B.*).

[4] *Cf. C.P.R.*, 1247–58, p. 651: 'Mr. R the Treasurer' should probably read 'Mr. R. the dean, Mr. W. the treasurer' (*C.E.P.R.* i. 355).

[5] *Ibid.*; *Registres d'Alexandre IV*, ed. J. de Loye, ii. 756.

[6] Blomefield, i. 523, says that the following list of rectors, *temp.* Hen. III, came from a MS. of about the 14th century:

'*Godfrey Giffard.* HUGH DE ALBANY [patron, died 1243].

'*Peter Giffard*, clerk. HUGH DE ALBANY [patron].

'Master *William de Shirewood.* ISABEL, widow of *Hugh de Albany*, in rights of *Plasset's* manor, which she holds in dower [patron].

'*Haman de Warren*, on *Shirewode's* death. The same ISABELL, who holds it in dower, remainder to Sir *Robert de Tateshale*.' Haman was rector when Norwich Domesday was compiled.

Peter Giffard secured exemption from assizes at the instance of Robert of Tateshale in 1257 (*C.P.R.*, 1247–58, p. 579).

[7] Inspeximus of an inspeximus, 29 June, 1274, of the original dated 7 Oct., 1266 (*C.P.R.*, 1313–7, p. 304).

[8] P.R.O., Exchequer, 7 Edw. I, E. 13/7; *cf.* also E. 13/8, *mm.* 4, 12*b*, 15; Le Neve gives notice of another treasurer in 1275 (*Fasti*, ed. Hardy, ii. 88).

[9] A Master William de Skirwodde was one of those who swore 'ex parte Borealium' (*Munimenta Academica*, R.S., ed. H. Anstey, i. 22).

poems :—' Seven Sacraments.' B.M. Add. MS. 17357, fos. 150–82 (14th cent.), with a note :

Oretis pro anima domini Willelmi de Schorham, quondam vicarii de Chart iuxta Ledes. Qui composuit istam compilationem de septem sacramentis.

' Pater Noster.' *Ibid.* fos. 182–5, no colophon.

' Ten Commandments.' *Ibid.* fos. 185–192, no colophon.

' Seven Deadly Sins.' *Ibid.* fos. 192–8, with the prayer :

Oretis pro anima domini Willelmi de Schorham quondam vicarii de Chart iusta Ledes qui composuit istam compilationem de septem mortalibus peccatis. Et omnibus dicentibus orationem dominicam cum salutatione angelica xl^ta dies venie a domino Symone Archiepiscopo Cantuarie conceduntur.

' Five Joys of the Virgin Mary.' *Ibid.* fos. 198–204, with the prayer,

Oretis pro anima Willelmi de Schorham quondam vicarii de Chart iuxta Ledes.

' On the Virgin Mary.' *Ibid.* fos. 204–205*b*, with the colophon ' Oretis pro anima domini Roberti Grosseteyte quondam episcopi Lincolnie.'

' On the Trinity.' *Ibid.* fos. 206–20*b*, no colophon.

These poems have been edited by T. Wright, *Religious Poems of William de Shoreham* (Percy Soc.), and by M. Konrath, ' Poems of William of Shoreham ' (E.E.T.S., extra series no. 86). The authorship of the last two pieces is based on the assumption that Robert Grosseteste was author of the piece from which William translated his work.[1]

The MS. was evidently written by a person who had copied writing by a scribe who had probably written in the time of Archbishop Simon (1327–33). William was evidently dead at the time. It has been further assumed that William was vicar after the church of Chart had been appropriated to the priory of Leeds in 1320, and that therefore William was a member of that house.[1]

Neither statement is necessary. Even had the church a rector he might have appointed a vicar in his place : thus the time is not limited to the period after 1320. Furthermore, ' dominus,' together with the title ' vicar,' almost of necessity assumes a secular rather than a regular. Three persons, at least, seem to have borne this name near the end of the 13th century. One, status undesignated, was made vicar of Harnhulle in Bocton, presented by Nicholas de Knoville, in 1282–3.[2] In 1287 a William of Shoreham was ordained acolyte, probably the same man.[3] On 3 May 1299 another was collated to the benefice attached to the celebration of the high mass in the abbey church of the nuns of Malling.[4] He seems to have taken the orders of acolyte in 1301, of subdean in 1303, and of priest in 1304.[5] A friar William of Shoreham, monk of Boxgrove, was deacon in 1304 and priest in 1305.[6]

William of Southampton, O.P., was a theologian.[7] Of his writings apparently only the following remain :—

' Tabula super Tres Libros Sententiarum.' Cambridge, Peterhouse MS. 262, fos. 68–79, described as ' Tabula Suhampton super 3 libros sententiarum et super Ieronimum contra Iovinianum in duabus peciis.' ' Tabula ' is apparently a student summary. He is said to have written the following :—

' Super Sententias.' MS. formerly at St. Paul's, London. ' Guilhelmus de Southampton, Dominicanus . . . , scripsit, Super sententias, li. iiij ' : *inc.* ' De vti, primo queritur, cum sit actio ' (Bale, *Index*, p. 149).

' Commentary upon the Librum Summarum.' MS. formerly at St. Paul's, London, ' Frater Willelmus de Southampton

[1] *Cf.* Wells, *Manual of the Writings in Middle English*, vi. 1 [10], for writings about William of Shoreham's poems.

[1] Konrath, *op. cit.* p. xiv ; *C.P.R.*, 1317–21, p. 433.
[2] *Reg. Peckham*, p. 1018.
[3] *Ibid.* p. 1046.
[4] *Reg. Winchelsey*, p. 346.
[5] *Ibid.* fos. 109*b*, 113*b*, 115,
[6] *Ibid.* fo. 115.
[7] T. p. 364.

super totum librum Summarum, 2nd fo. "quod in aspectu non est in virtus"' (W. Dugdale, *Hist. of St. Paul's Cathedral*, App. p. 66). Possibly this is the same as the previous item.

'Directorium in Moralia Gregorii': *inc.* 'Abstinentia. Solus in illicitis non cadit, qui se a licitis caute' (Bale, *Index*, p. 149). MS. formerly at St. Paul's, London, described as above.

'Sermones in Sanctis': *inc.* 'Sapientiam sanctorum narrant po.' MS. formerly 'ex collegio academie, Oxon.' (Bale, *Index*, p. 149).

'Postille in Isaiam': *inc.* 'Esaias propheta magnus in' (T. p. 364).

On 10 Mar. 1273 a friar William of Southampton was sent by the king to the convent of Canterbury to inquire into the expulsion of a monk.[1] In 1276 a Canterbury account book contains an item of sixteen pence for spices 'ad opus fratris W. de Suthampton.'[2] Possibly William was the theologian, a doctor at Cambridge *c.* 1275, referred to as of 'So.'[3]

All the information about William of Southampton as prior provincial of the dominicans comes from 1278. On 9 January he was an associate of R., bishop of Bath and Wells, in a suit between Anthony Bek and Master Roger de Seiton.[4] At his instance on 14 June the king pardoned John, son of Master Robert de Abbinton, for the death of Gilbert le Pestur.[5] He is mentioned again a few days later.[6] He also witnessed a charter of King Edward I[7] and served in another suit.[1] He died at the end of the same year.[2] One rather surmises that he was elected prior provincial only in 1277.

[1] *Hist. Works of Gervase of Canterbury* (R.S.), ed. W. Stubbs, ii. 276.

[2] Lambeth Palace MS. 242, fo. 32*b*. Possibly he is not the dominican; however, his name does not appear in the profession list of Christchurch.

[3] Little-Pelster, pp. 100, 108, 112. One would expect a dominican. However, for Southampton we should expect 'Su' rather than 'So.'

[4] *C.P.R.*, 1272–81, p. 254; *cf.* P.R.O., Exchequer, K.R., various accounts (nuncii), E. 101/308/3 and 4.

[5] *C.P.R.*, 1272–81, p. 269.

[6] *Reg. Johannis de Pontissara* (C.Y.S.), ed. C. Deedes, pp. 647, 649.

[7] B.M. Add. ch. 8853 (1), confirmed by Henry IV.

William of Sumery[3] was the author of medical 'Experimenta': *inc.* 'Huius opuscula series circa.' 'Incipit experimenta mag. Will de Sumere.' Cambridge, Corpus Christi Coll. MS. A. xii (279), fos. 127*b et seq.* (late 13th cent.), with the colophon at the end 'Expl. parvus viaticus mag. W. de Sumereie.' The preceding document in the MS. belongs to 1235: it gives the only hint about the time of the author.

William of Sutton was abbot of Oseney. Tanner wrote:

> Gul. Button [rectius Sutton] abbatis Osneiensis, de fundatione et dotatione dicti coenobii et rebus gestis abbatum historiam, sive chartarum registrum ms. olim in bibl. cl. Walteri Copi, postea in Cottoniana, nunc in thesaurario eccl. Christi Oxon. fol. pergam (*Notitia Monastica*, ed. 1744, p. 420*b*).

Probably this is the Oseney cartulary at Christ Church, Oxford, edited as volume iv. of the 'Cartulary of Oseney Abbey' by H. E. Salter (Oxf. Hist. Soc.; *cf. ibid.* i. p. x).

William of Thornay, dean of Lincoln, was the author of some 'Questiones.' (a) MS. formerly at Ramsey, entitled 'Libri Roberti de Glintone. Principium Marci Evangeliste glosati, ligatum cum questionibus magistri Willelmi de Thornay' (*Chronicon Abbatiæ Rameseiensis*, R.S., ed. W. D. Macray, p. 361); (b) MS. also formerly at Ramsey, 'Libri Roberti de Daventre. Questiones magistri Willelmi de Tornay' (*ibid.* p. 359). Possibly he also wrote some 'Vite Sanctorum' (C. Visch, *Bibliotheca Scriptorum Sacri Ordinis Cisterciensis*, Douai, 1649, p. 126).

[1] P.R.O., Anc. ch. A. s. 483.

[2] C. F. R. Palmer in *Archaeol. Journal*, xxxv (1878). 139.

[3] T. p. 700; B.M. MS. Harley 3697, fo. 132, has two charters which refer to a William of Sumery and certain of his relatives.

This is probably the William of Thornay who had a notable career at Lincoln and ended his days at Louth Park. His name appears in many Lincoln cathedral documents from 1215 to 1220.[1] He was possibly there as early as 19 Aug. 1213.[2] At first probably a canon,[3] he was archdeacon of Stowe by 30 Dec. 1217.[4] Between 10 April[5] and 22 May 1219[6] he became archdeacon of Lincoln.[7] He was chosen dean of Lincoln before 1 Apr. 1223[8] and held the office until 1239. He went to Rome in 1228 as dean and was in difficulties with Dunstable priory in 1234.[9] He had a large 'familia' as dean, several of whom later testified concerning the dean's property.[10] He became a monk of Louth Park abbey, a cistercian house, in 1239.[11] There he left a reputation not only for generosity but also for the example which he set before the brothers. He died on 25 June 1258 and was buried in the Lady Chapel where he had often prayed and which he had helped build.[12]

William de Torto Collo, O.P., was probably the author of a second edition of the 'Correctorium Corruptorii' (P. Glorieux, *Premières Polémiques Thomistes*, p. liv). Madrid MS. vii, H. 5 (early 14th cent.), gives the colophon 'Explicit (correctorium) corruptorii fratris Guillermi de Torto Collo Anglici, magistri in theologia, ordinis fratris predicatorum.' There is great controversy about this character. Dr. Little and Fr. Pelster suggest that he is a corruption of Robert of Orford (p. 98). Possibly 'Torto Collo' is a mistake for some other English name: the William is somewhat difficult to explain away.

William of Waddington was the author of an Anglo-Norman poem, or possibly an interpolation, in the 'Manuel des Pechiez.' For MSS. see Ward, *Cat. of Romances*, iii. 272, and Hope E. Allen, 'The Manuel des Pechiez and the Scholastic prologue,' *Romanic Review*, viii (1817). 442. Certain lines give the authorship:

De Deu seit beneit chescun humme
se prie pur Willam de Wedindone
Kar ky pur autre prie e hure
pur sey memes dithun labure
En deu finisse cest escrit en pere
e fiz e seint espirit. Amen.

(See also Allen, *op. cit.* pp. 435, 450–1.) It has been edited from two MSS. by Furnivall, 'Robert of Brunne's Handlyng Synne' (Roxburghe Club).

The piece was probably written during the years 1275–9.[1] The author is probably the priest in the deanery of Rydal of the archdeaconry of Cleveland who gave 5 shillings as a 'crucesignatus' in 1275.[2]

William of Wanda, dean of Salisbury, was probably the author of portions of the 'Vetus Registrum Sarisburiense,' containing an account of the events in the cathedral chapter of Salisbury from about 1217 to 1229 (*Register of S. Osmund*, R.S., ed. W. H. Rich Jones). In telling of the papal confirmation of the election of Robert Bingham the author writes 'Littere iste venerunt mihi in conversione S. Pauli per Willelmum, nepotem electi.' As dean, William de Wanda would be the person to receive such letters. (*Cf. ibid.* p. x for references showing the author as an eyewitness.)

Already a master, Mr. William de Wanda

1 *Liber Antiquus de Ordinationibus Hugonis de Welles*, ed. A. Gibbon, pp. 74–100, 105.
2 *Ibid.* p. 79, but the year number 'IV' may be a mistake for 'VI.'
3 *Ibid.* pp. 74, 77, 79, 80, 81, 88.
4 *Ibid.* pp. 83, 87, 88, 89, 90, 91, 92, 93, 94.
5 *Ibid.* p. 94.
6 *Ibid.*
7 *Ibid.* pp. 94, 95, 97, 100, 105.
8 *Rot. H. de Welles*, iii. 97–124.
9 *Ann. Monast.* iii. 109, 141.
10 Derbysh. Archaeol. and Nat. Hist. Soc. *Journal*, xiii (1891). 77–8.
11 *Chronicle of Louth Park Abbey* (Lincoln Record Soc.), ed. E. Venables, p. 12.
12 *Ibid.* pp. 16–7.

1 Allen, *op. cit.*
2 *Reg. Walter Giffard*, p. 282; *Historical Papers and Letters from Northern Registers* (R.S.), ed. James Raine, p. 53.

was made precentor of Salisbury by Bishop Richard Poore in advent (*c.* 16 December) 1218,[1] with the prebend which Thomas de Disci had previously held. Evidence of his activity as precentor remains.[2] He went into the bishopric of London in 1219 to secure funds for the new cathedral.[3] He was elected dean on 20 Sept. 1220 [4] and remained in this office until some time in the period 18 Feb. 1236–24 Feb. 1237.[5] He carried on the tasks of his office apparently with diligence, but made singularly little impression on the records of his time outside Salisbury.

[1] *Reg. S. Osmund*, ii. 9. A document of 28 June 1218 has as a witness Master William, precentor of Salisbury (*Sarum Chs. and Docs.* p. 84). Possibly he appears earlier (*Cat. Ancient Deeds*, iv. 234, A. 7896).

[2] *Sarum Chs. and Docs.* pp. 91, 92, 96, 100, 101.

[3] *Reg. S. Osmund*, ii. 12.

[4] *Ibid.* p. 15.

[5] *Sarum Chs. and Docs.* pp. 238, 240.

William of Ware, O.F.M., was the author of a famous ‘ Commentary upon the Sentences.’ [1] The MSS. of this are given by Longpré in ‘ La France Franciscaine,’ v. 71–82. Little has added notices of two former MSS. (*F.S.O.* p. 867) ; see also Leland, *Collect.* iv. 51, 54). The following studies are to be mentioned : M. Schmaus in ‘ Aurelius Augustinus,’ A. Ledoux's ‘ Antonianum,’ v. 137–56, and Lechner in ‘ Franziskanische Studien,’ xix (1932). 99–127.

Not much is known about this friar except that he was teaching at Paris a little while before his famous student, Duns Scotus.[2] He was probably at Oxford about 1290, possibly studying under John of Berwick.[3]

[1] T. p. 755 ; *D.N.B.* under William ; Little, *F.S.O.* p. 867.

[2] ‘ Claruit autem Parisius paulo ante discipulum suus, doctorem subtilem,’ quoted by Little (*F.S.O.* p. 867).

[3] Lechner, *op. cit.* pp. 102–7.

APPENDIX A

THE FRANCISCAN LECTORS AT OXFORD AND CAMBRIDGE

THE apparently complete lists of franciscan lectors at Oxford and Cambridge contain the names of a number of writers. For the 13th century list of Oxford Dr. Little has already fixed approximate dates for all,[1] and for one group very accurate dates.[2] Practically nothing has been done toward defining dates for the Cambridge list.[3] Of course, to go beyond Dr. Little's work is apt to be hazardous, and at best the following list must be labelled conjectural. It is based upon a few definite dates plus the following hypotheses :—(1) That the university arrangements were inclined to be regular ; (2) that the Cambridge franciscans had had a regular two-year term for their lectors ; (3) that it was the custom for Oxford lectors assigned to Cambridge to proceed directly from one university to the other.

By their very nature school arrangements tended to be regular. A year's work was a unit, and appointments tended to conform to this unity. In order to attain the status of doctor of theology the candidate must have studied a required number of years, the last of which had to be at the institution conferring the honour. Then after inception the candidate was required to serve as regent master for two years. Possibly residence for two years was not entailed : the duties connected with regency are none too clear. After completing these requirements a master might move elsewhere and ' resume ' his teaching. Parisian masters might ' resume ' without going through the preliminary academic exercises again, but no English institution had this much-valued privilege. Thus, if an Oxford franciscan master was transferred to Paris he had to ' incept ' again.

[1] Little, *F.S.O.* pp. 31–63.

[2] Little-Pelster, pp. 68–70.

[3] *Cf.* A. G. Little in *Mélanges Mandonnet, bibliothèque thomiste*, xiv (1930). 389–402.

Among the mendicant orders the yearly chapter usually held in the summer provided a further element of regularity : probably the assignments to teach were made at this time.[1]

The Cambridge list consists not only of the candidates who incepted there, but it also contains the names of several who incepted first at Oxford or, in the case of William of Milton, at Paris. It would seem that, if no candidate was available, one was transferred to Cambridge. This at once suggests that a term system existed. If there were no system one scholar, we should expect, would have remained until another qualified, no matter what time elapsed. This hypothesis is strengthened, at least for the period 1259–1303, by the little evidence available. Humphrey de Hautboys was lector probably in 1259, and Adam de Hoveden clearly held this office in 1303. For the period of 44 years there were 22 lectors. At once the assumption of the two-year period of necessary regency seems plausible. We do not know of any breaks in the academic schedule which would have interfered with the regularity of the scheme. Upon this basis the list of Cambridge lectors for the period 1259–1303 is drawn up. Furthermore, this scheme tends to be corroborated by the next evidence.

Among the lectors transferred from Oxford to Cambridge it will be noticed that the eighth, tenth, and twelfth lectors at Oxford were respectively the thirteenth, fifteenth, and seventeenth masters at Cambridge. The easiest explanation for this would be that they went directly from one institution to the other : that is, that they were transferred directly after the period of necessary regency at Oxford and incepted again at Cambridge.

[1] For conditions of academic procedure see Little-Pelster, pp. 25–64.

It will be noticed further that this hypothesis not only seems to hold for three men mentioned above, but also for Walter of Knolle and Adam Hoveden later in the century. All appear as lectors at Cambridge, according to the earlier hypothesis, about five years after they seem to have incepted at Oxford. In our present knowledge an attempt to fix the two-year period more accurately seems inadvisable. However, since the Oxford system after 1270 was probably based upon changing the lectors on the even-numbered years, it may be surmised that the same system prevailed at Cambridge.

As mentioned above, Dr. Little and Fr. Pelster have verified the Oxford list for the years 1286–94. There a system of annual inception seems to have been introduced in order that all the qualified candidates might incept. From 1270, probable date of Bungay's inception, to 1286 eight masters ruled: thus probably each had two years apiece. There was apparently a shortage of candidates: Peckham was brought from Paris and Marston from Cambridge. Likewise two-year terms seem probable for the men from 1294 to 1300. How far back did this system go? Back, we may assume, as far as the end of the previous system.

The earlier system had apparently been based upon indefinite terms, first of secular masters, and then of distinguished pioneers of the order. The last of these pioneers was Richard Rufus. His death may have ended the old system.

For the franciscan masters before 1259 the dates supplied by Dr. Little (*F.S.O.*) are our best evidence. In the Cambridge list some conjectures may be made. Eustace de Normanville probably spent the year 1252–1253 at Cambridge under the previous regent, W. Pictavensis. The three masters following him were probably at Cambridge before 1257, when William of Milton is supposed to have returned to Paris. Since Humphrey was probably lector in 1258–9 Thomas of York was there in the previous year, probably 1257–8.

CONJECTURAL LISTS

		Oxford	*Cambridge*
1.	1248–50.	Adam Marsh (1247–50)[1]	
2.	1250–2.	Ralph de Colebruge (1249–52)	1. Vincent of Coventry (by 1252)
3.		Eustace de Normanvile	2. W. Pictavensis (by 1253)
	1252–3.	Adam Marsh (1252–3)	
4.	1253–6.	Thomas of York (1253–6)	3. Eustace de Normanvile
			4. J. de Westone, *c.* 1253–7
5.	1256–62.	Richard Rufus of Cornwall (1256–1259)	5. William de Milton
			6. Thomas of York, *c.* 1257–8
			7. Humphrey de Hautboys, *c.* 1258–1259
			8. W. de Winbourne, *c.* 1261
6.	1262–4.	John of Wales (1259–62)	9. Robert de Roiston, *c.* 1263
7.	1264–6.	Thomas of Docking (1262–5)	10. Walter of Ravigham, *c.* 1265
8.	1266–8.	Hugh of Brisingham (1265–7)	11. W. de Assewelle, *c.* 1267
9.	1268–70.	William Heddele (1267–70)	12. Roger de Merston, *c.* 1269
10.	1270–2.	Thomas Bungay (1270–2)	13. Hugh of Brisingham, *c.* 1271
11.	1272–4.	John Peckham (1272–4)	14. J. Letheringfot, *c.* 1273
12.	1274–6.	Henry de Apeltre (1274–6)	15. Thomas Bungay, *c.* 1275

[1] Dates in Little, *F.S.O.*

WRITERS OF THIRTEENTH CENTURY ENGLAND

		Oxford	*Cambridge*
13.	1276–8.	Robert de Cruce (1276–8)	16. Robert de Worstede, *c.* 1277
14.	1278–80.	Radulfus de Toftis (1278–80)	17. Henry de Apeltre, *c.* 1279
15.	1280–2.	Alan de Rodano (1280–)	18. Bartholomew de Stalam, *c.* 1281
16.	1282–4.	Roger Marston ( )	19. Richard de Soutwerk, *c.* 1283
17.	1284–6.	Alan de Wakerfield (1284–)	20. Richard Burton, *c.* 1285
18.	1286–7.	Nicholas of Ocham (12 –86)	21. Geoffrey de Tudington, *c.* 1287
19.	1287–8.	Walter de Knolle (1286–7)	
20.	1288–9.	Hugh of Hartlepool (1287–9)	22. John Russell, *c.* 1289
21.	1289–90.	John de Pershore (1288–)	
22.	1290–1.	John de Berwick (1289–90)	23. Walter Knolle, *c.* 1291
23.	1291–2.	Thomas de Barneby (1290–)	
24.	1292–3.	Adam of Lincoln (1292–)	24. I. de Kimberley, *c.* 1293
25.	1293–4.	Wm. of Gainsborough (1292–4)	
26.	1294–6.	J. Bassett (1295–6)	25. W. de Fingrinho, *c.* 1295
27.	1296–8.	Thomas Rondel (1297–)	26. J. de Linpenho, *c.* 1297
28.	1298–1300.	Adam Hoveden (–1300)	27. Richard de Templo, *c.* 1299
29.	1300–	Philip de Bridlington	28. Geoffrey de Heyroun, *c.* 1301
			29. Adam de Hoveden, 1303

APPENDIX B

ANGLO-NORMAN WRITERS NAMED WILLIAM

THE name William appears as that of the author of several pieces usually with the information that he is a clerk (or 'Le Clerc'), a Norman, or a chaplain. This information is not very definitive. It is possible that the bulk of the work was done by a William the Clerk of Normandy, or that there were several writers. The problem, if it must be considered with present evidence alone, is rather a matter for the philologists. The pieces by a William, Clerk, Norman, or both, are given below chronologically [1] :—

'Bestiary.' (a) Cambridge, Trinity Coll. MS. 1118, fos. 32*b*–67 ; (b) B.M. MS. Reg. 16, E. viii. See the lines :

Li cler fu nés de Normandie
Qui auctor est de cest romans ;
Or oijez que dist li Normans.

It was written in the time of the interdict in England for 'sire Raol sun seignor.'

Guillame qui cest liure fist
En la definaille tant dist
de sire Raol sun seignor.

For bibliography see Gröber, *Grundriss*, ii. 710.

'Contes et Fables.' In his 'Besant de Dieu' he says that he has previously written 'Contes et Fables,' some of which may be included below.

Guillaume, un clers qui fu Normans
Qui versifia en romans,
Fables et contes soleit dire
En fole et en vaine matire,
Pecha sovent, Dieu li pardont.

'La Male Honte.' St. Germain MS. 1830. For bibliography see Gröber, *op. cit.* p. 836. This has been edited by Barbazon, *Fabliaux et Contes*, iii. 210. Line 150 runs :

Ce dit Guillaum en son conte.

It was written against an English king.

[1] Tanner mentions a William the Clerk, astronomer of 1186 (p. 184). A Master William the Norman attests a charter of Geoffrey, bishop-elect of York, 1189 (*Cal. of Documents, France*, 918–1206, p. 13).

'Prestre et Alison.' St. Germain MS. 1830. For a bibliography see Gröber, ii. *op. cit.* p. 904. This has been edited by Barbazon, *op. cit* iv. For lines see :

Savoir poez par ceste fable
Qui fist Guillaume li Normanz
Qui dist que cil ni est pas sachanz.

'Fregus et Galienne, Le Roman du Chevalier au bel escu.' For a bibliography see Gröber, *op. cit.* p. 515. It was dedicated to Alan of Galloway, who died in 1233. It was edited by Martin in 1872. The author is given as William the Clerk.

'Tobias' : *inc.* 'Cil ke sente bone sentence.' For a bibliography see Gröber, *op. cit.* p. 656. This work is dedicated to William, prior of Kenilworth, probably W., sub-prior of Oseney, elected prior of Kenilworth in 1214 (*Rot. litt. claus.* i. 207) and dead by 1227 (*C.P.R.*, 1225–32, p. 141, when Henry was elected). The author's name was William the Clerk.

Le priors Guillaume me prie
De leglise seinte Marie
De Kenilworthe en Arderne.

'Besant de Dieu' was edited by E. Martin in 'Le Besant de Dieu von Guillaume le Clerc de Normandie.' It was written about 1226–7 (line 160), and was based upon the 'De miseria humane conditionis' of Innocent III. The author states that he was married (lines 96 *et seq.*). For bibliography see Gröber, *op. cit.* pp. 693, 704.

'Les Treis Moz,' B.N. MS. fr. 19525, fos. 125–9, has been edited by R. Reinsch in 'Les Joies Nostre Dame des Guillaume le Clerc de Normandie' (*Zeitschrift für Romanische Philologie*, iii, 1879. 200–31). This work mentions the 'Besant' (lines 185–7) and is thus of a later date. For bibliography see Gröber, *op. cit.* p. 694. It was dedicated to Alexander of Stavensby [q.v.], bishop of Coventry (*d.* 1238).

'La Vie de Madelein,' B.N. MS. fr. 19525, edited by Reinsch in 'Archiv für das Studium der neuern Sprachen und Literaturen,' lxiv (1880). 85–94. A bibliography appears in Gröber, *op. cit.* ii. 643. This work is undated.

'Les Joies Nostre Dame.' B.N. MS. fr. 19525, fos. 86–95*b*, entitled 'De Nostre Dame par Willaume.' The work was edited by R. Reinsch in 'Zeitschrift für Romanische Philologie,' iii (1879). 211–25.

A Master William the Poet, a chaplain, was given the church of St. Giles of Northampton by the prior and convent of St. Andrew of that place in 1230 and had been replaced by 1240 (*Rot. Hugonis de Welles*, i. 152, 236 ; *Rot. R. Grosseteste*, *passim*). He might possibly have been William Banastre or a Latin or Anglo-Norman versifier. In view of his connexion with the monastery of St. Andrew and his status as chaplain it is interesting to note that a contemporary Anglo-Norman 'Passion of St. Andrew' was written by a chaplain. (a) Bodl. Lib. MS. Canonici 74 ; (b) Paris, Arsenal MS. 3516. This work was edited by A. T. Baker ('The Passion of St. Andrew,' *Modern Language Review*, xi, 1916. 420–49). E. Levi would identify the author with William de Berneville because St. Andrew was a patron saint of Barnwell (*Archivio storico Italiano*, vii série, iv. 647). William wrote a 'Vie de Saint Gilles,' the other saint of Barnwell. (a) Florence, Laurentian Lib. Conventi Soppressi MS. 99 (early 13th cent.), edited by G. Paris, and A. Bos, 'Vie de Saint Gilles' (Soc. des anciens textes Fr.). The author was probably a canon of Barnwell :

> al chanoine sace gré
> ki s'est pené e travaillé
> de ceste vie translater.
> Il ne queit pas sun nun celer
> Gwillames ad nun de Bernevile
> ke par amur Deu e seint Gile
> enprist cest labur e cest fés.

A William Adgar translated a series of 'Miracles of the Virgin' for a patron Gregory which he said that he discovered in a bookcase at St. Paul's, London. For a bibliography see Gröber, *op. cit.* p. 650. Probably he belongs to the late 12th century. A William de Ferrieres was also a contemporary [q.v.].

APPENDIX C

THE PROFESSION LIST OF CHRISTCHURCH, CANTERBURY

THE profession list of Christchurch, Canterbury, is apparently arranged according to date of entry.[1] After the return from exile in 1214 no date is given until 1285, although eleven groups are separated before then. Since several of the monks are writers, it seems advisable to try to secure some chronological information, if possible, from the list. The following theory is based upon the presumption that there was a fairly regular admission of monks. Its conjectural basis is acknowledged by stating each time that the time of profession is of about a certain year. In the years 1285–98 46 monks entered, an average of 3·3 a year. For the eleven undated groups 54 names are given, so many that it would seem more than eleven years are represented. For the 71 years between 1214 and 1284 279 names appear, an average of 3·85 a year. Thus we assume that the following table is approximately correct.

Years	*Names of monks in list*	*Pages*
1214–23.	Ralph of Westgate to Phil. de Cantuaria	172–3
1224–33.	Jeremias to Joh. Pittenote	173
1234–43.	Galf. sacerdos to Joh. de Clyve	173–4
1244–53.	Rog. de Sco. Elphego to Rodlandus	174–5
1254–63.	Stephen of Wodechurch to Wm of Clynstede	175
1264–73.	Tho. de Ryngmere to Hen. de Bene	175–6
1274–84.	John de Well to Joh. de Ringmere	176–7

[1] Published by Searle in Cambridge Antiquarian Soc., octavo publications, xxxiv (1902). 172–96.